Europea: Ethnomusicologies and Modernities

Series Editors: Philip V. Bohlman and Martin Stokes

1. *Celtic Modern: Music at the Global Fringe*, edited by Martin Stokes and Philip V. Bohlman, 2003.
2. *Albanian Urban Lyric Song in the 1930s*, by Eno Koço, 2004.
3. *The Mediterranean in Music: Critical Perspectives, Common Concerns, Cultural Differences*, edited by David Cooper and Kevin Dawe, 2005.
4. *On a Rock in the Middle of the Ocean: Songs and Singers in Tory Island, Ireland*, by Lillis Ó Laoire, 2005.
5. *Transported by Song: Corsican Voices from Oral Tradition to World Stage*, by Caroline Bithell, 2007.
6. *Balkan Popular Culture and the Ottoman Ecumene: Music, Image, and Regional Political Discourse*, edited by Donna A. Buchanan, 2007

Europea: Ethnomusicologies and Modernities

Series Editors: Philip V. Bohlman and Martin Stokes

The new millennium challenges ethnomusicologists, dedicated to studying the music of the world, to examine anew the Western musics they have treated as "traditional," and to forge new approaches to world musics that are often overlooked because of their deceptive familiarity. As the modern discipline of ethnomusicology expanded during the second half of the twentieth century, influenced significantly by ethnographic methods in the social sciences, ethnomusicology's "field" increasingly shifted to the exoticized Other. The comparative methodologies previously generated by Europeanist scholars to study and privilege Western musics were deliberately discarded. Europe as a cultural area was banished to historical musicology, and European vernacular musics became the spoils left to folk-music and, later, popular-music studies.

Europea challenges ethnomusicology to return to Europe and to encounter its disciplinary past afresh, and the present is a timely moment to do so. European unity nervously but insistently asserts itself through the political and cultural agendas of the European Union, causing Europeans to reflect on a bitterly and violently fragmented past and its ongoing repercussions in the present, and to confront new challenges and opportunities for integration. There is also an intellectual moment to be seized as Europeans reformulate the history of the present, an opportunity to move beyond the fragmentation and atomism the later twentieth century has bequeathed and to enter into broader social, cultural, and political relationships.

Europea is not simply a reflection of and on the current state of research. Rather, the volumes in this series move in new directions and experiment with diverse approaches. The series establishes a forum that can engage scholars, musicians, and other interlocutors in debates and discussions crucial to understanding the present historical juncture. This dialogue, grounded in ethnomusicology's interdisciplinarity, will be animated by reflexive attention to the specific social configurations of knowledge of and scholarship on the musics of Europe. Such knowledge and its circulation as ethnomusicological scholarship are by no means dependent on professional academics, but rather are conditioned, as elsewhere, by complex interactions between universities, museums, amateur organizations, state agencies, and markets. Both the broader view to which ethnomusicology aspires and the critical edge necessary to understanding the present moment are served by broadening the base on which "academic" discussion proceeds.

"Europe" will emerge from the volumes as a space for critical dialogue, embracing competing and often antagonistic voices from across the continent, across the Atlantic, across the Mediterranean and the Black Sea, and across a world altered ineluctably by European colonialism and globalization. The diverse subjects and interdisciplinary approaches in individual volumes capture something of—and, in a small way, become part of—the jangling polyphony through which the "New Europe" has explosively taken musical shape in public discourse, in expressive culture, and, increasingly, in political form. Europea: Ethnomusicologies and Modernities aims to provide a critical framework necessary to capture something of the turbulent dynamics of music performance, engaging the forces that inform and deform, contest and mediate the senses of identity, selfhood, belonging, and progress that shape "European" musical experience in Europe and across the world.

Balkan Popular Culture and the Ottoman Ecumene

Music, Image, and Regional Political Discourse

Edited by
Donna A. Buchanan

Europea: Ethnomusicologies and Modernities, No. 6

The Scarecrow Press, Inc.
Lanham, Maryland • Toronto • Plymouth, UK
2007

SCARECROW PRESS, INC.

Published in the United States of America
by Scarecrow Press, Inc.
A wholly owned subsidary of
The Rowman & Littlefield Publishing Group, Inc.
4501 Forbes Boulevard, Suite 200, Lanham, Maryland 20706
www.scarecrowpress.com

Estover Road
Plymouth PL6 7PY
United Kingdom

British Library Cataloguing in Publication Information Available

Library of Congress Cataloging-in-Publication Data

Balkan popular culture and the Ottoman ecumene : music, image, and regional political
discourse / edited by Donna A. Buchanan.
    p. cm. — (Europea: ethnomusicologies and modernites ; No. 6)
  Includes bibliographical references (p.), discography (p.), filmography (p.), and
index.
  ISBN-13: 978-0-8108-6021-6 (hardcover : alk. paper)
  ISBN-10: 0-8108-6021-X (hardcover : alk. paper)
  1. Popular music—Social aspects—Balkan Peninsula. 2. Popular music—Political
aspects—Balkan Peninsula. 3. Popular music—Balkan Peninsula—Turkish influences. 4.
Popular culture—Balkan Peninsula. I. Buchanan, Donna Anne.

ML3917.B35B35 2008
781.6309496—dc22   2007026089

In memoriam

Mirjana Laušević
(1966–2007)

Contents

Illustrations

Figures

x   Contents

Tables

Contents of CD-ROM

Plates

Sound Recordings

Contents

Video Recordings

Series Foreword

By inhabiting the world of the Ottoman ecumene popular music invests its soundscapes with universality. Contradiction, complementarity, conjunction, contestation. The very doubleness of the Greek *οἰκουμένη* conflates knowing and inhabiting the world, localizing the place in which one lives and expanding its boundaries by encountering and understanding that which lies beyond it. Already in the classical world, the ecumene stretched from the physical world that converged along the boundaries of Europe and Asia to the very limits of the known universe. The classical ecumene was a world to which many levels accrued through the accumulation of experience and the expanded knowledge of the world beyond the known world. Already in the classical sense, there was a necessary flow between the centripetal forces of knowing the local and the centrifugal pull to encounter the global. Such ebb and flow, the tension between inhabiting a world only to push at its boundaries, the sounding of places known and unknown—these are the historical movements that music sounds and resounds on the geography formed at the meeting of Europe and Asia, stretching along the Mediterranean and into Africa's littoral, resonating as one of the richest spaces for the popular music that inhabited the Ottoman world.

The essays in *Balkan Popular Culture and the Ottoman Ecumene* draw us into the worlds of some of Europe's most contested regions and fraught histories, and they do so by allowing music to resonate in new, even unexpected ways. More traditionally, the Ottoman ecumene is conjured from the traces of a past that lingers at the margins or exposes the traces that expose a receding pastness. The very notion of the Ottoman, of a Turkey that once claimed empire but was reduced by modernity to inhabit a mere nation, may be redolent with nostalgia but it is also resistant to the choral sound arising from cohabiting the present. Even the contemporary literature that chronicles the Ottoman ecumene—no less than the fiction and memorywork of Nobel Prizewinner Orhan Pamuk—encounters that world in the sepia-toned melancholy, the *hüzün,* of the past. We are left wondering why, even, anyone could continue to inhabit such a world.

And then we meet the musicians and music-making that inhabit the worlds that so resonantly open through the chapters of this book. Rather than the ennui of the past, music in these chapters calls forth dynamism. Musicians move across borders, political, ethnic, and religious. Music resists stasis, instead inhabiting new genres, passing from venue to venue, language to language, wantonly opening its boundaries to variants and covers. The popular asserts itself through the people empowered by the power and potential of musical ecumenism. The musical sense of place resists reduction to a single place, southeastern Europe or Turkey, abandoned by the retreat of the Ottoman Empire. Instead, the musical sense of space opens outward through the movement of musicians and the media upon which they produce music for diasporas that at once expand and fold back in on themselves. The sound of Balkan popular music acquires its power precisely because it restlessly redefines the Ottoman ecumene, rather than being defined by it. The geographic space seemingly signified by the "and" separating the two parts in the title of this book collapses, but what might become a singularly inhabited world actually undergoes a expansive movement that pushes the boundaries of the *οἰκουμένη* toward the most capacious meanings of its evocation of universal understanding.

What makes the book particularly compelling and such a critical contribution to the "Ethnomusicologies and Modernities" that concern all works in the "Europea" series is that the authors of the following essays never lose sight of the ways in which agents—musicians, audiences, human communities, and collectivities—live the lives that truly invest the Ottoman ecumene with meaning. Crucial to the commitment to the popular that fills the essays is that the Ottoman ecumene continues to be inhabited, no less by traditional communities than by those whose voices reconfigure the future with new musical sounds and styles. The local community of the Balkans—the lived-in worlds of Roma, Albanians, Bosnians, Bulgarians, or of Muslims, Christians, Jews, and heterodox believers—has never been wanting for global dimensions. Popular music and popular culture afford the connections necessary for maintaining those dimensions. Popular music is the language of translation and communication, of the vernacular and the lingua franca, of the nostalgia echoing from the Ottoman past and the hopefulness resonant for a European future. Eloquently and presciently, popular music emerges from the voices of those inhabiting the collective world of the essays filling this book as the very language of the Ottoman ecumene itself.

Philip V. Bohlman

Preface and Acknowledgments

Donna A. Buchanan

ecumene *n*. Geog. 1. An inhabited area. 2. The inhabited areas of the world . . . . The ecumene of a nation is its more densely inhabited core.

ecumenism *n*. A movement seeking to achieve worldwide unity among religions through greater cooperation and improved understanding.

The initial impetus for this project was a 1998 newsletter article published by Slavicist Andrew Wachtel that debated various strategies for organizing college courses devoted to South Slavic literatures. One proposed constructing such courses around the Balkans because it could be presumed that those countries "whose historical experience combined a connection to orthodoxy and vassalage to the Ottoman empire share core cultural experiences that are reflected in cultural practice" (1998:7). However, for Wachtel a disadvantage of this approach was that "despite some significant historical similarities," he did not discern "a deep Balkan cultural identity shared by the cultures of these highly disparate nations" or "a burning desire among writers and intellectuals to see themselves as part of a larger Balkan culture sphere," currently or in years past (1998:7).

Wachtel's observations reveal the tension between similarity and difference, commonality and diversity, cohesion and discord that have characterized both external and internal typifications of the Balkans as concept, metaphor, and place for at least the past 150 years (Fleming 2000:1219). On the one hand, Western scholars, journalists, travel writers, and politicians have burdened *Balkan* with a host of negative, conflict-ridden associations: backward, primitive, uncivilized, savage, irrational, lazy, superstitious (Todorova 1997). Thus *balkanization,* another Western construct employed extensively during the 1990s in discussions about the wars in the former Yugoslavia, signifies the militant, brutal fracturing of nation-states along ethnic, religious, and linguistic divides (cf. Bjelić 2002:10). On the other, such pejorative associations derive from the territory's interstitial and often uncertain position, historically, politically, and geographically, between continents (Europe/Asia), empires (Austro-Hungarian/Ottoman; Soviet-Communist/West-capitalist), and belief systems (Christianity/Islam) (2002:7). In this view, the Balkans are Europe's periphery—in it, but not really of it. They are Europe's dark shadow, its inherent Other, and possibly, its very own internal Orient (cf. Razsa and Lindstrom 2004:633).

This discourse, termed *balkanism* by Bulgarian historian Maria Todorova (1997), is dichotomous and polarizing, pitting center against periphery, West against East, North against South, and civilized against barbaric. In this sense, and to the extent that it always places Westerners in a relationship of "positional superiority," balkanism strongly resembles another polarizing discourse, *orientalism*, as elucidated by Edward Said (1979:7). However, recent scholarship, much of it by experts born in the region, reveals fundamental differences between these two epistemologies.[1] While orientalism is rooted in "imputed opposition" between a Western Self and Eastern Other, balkanism is a relational discourse—within Europe—that thrives upon the "imputed ambiguity" of the Balkan region's "symbolic geography" (Todorova 1997:17; Bakić-Hayden and Hayden 1992). Both discourses are the result of colonization, but where the exoticized East was dominated by the European West, giving rise to orientalism, Europe's Balkans were colonized by the very Other targeted by orientalist stereotypes. Balkanism, then, "meanders between Orientalism and Occidentalism" in accordance with the speaker's agenda (Bjelić 2002:5), a phenomenon whose successively Eastern gaze Milica Bakić-Hayden (1995) has termed *"nesting orientalisms."* Just where the Balkans are and who lives there shifts with context. Orientalism preys upon the Other without; balkanism plays up (and sometimes with) the Other within.

Wachtel's commentary caught my eye because his emphasis on intercultural disparity implicitly challenged the viability of the Balkans-as-region at a time when my own field research in Bulgaria, and that of my colleagues across the southeast European tier, was revealing remarkable, intraregional confluences of style in the instrumental music, song, and dance of local ethnopop artists. These similarities, whose eclectic interweaving suggests an emergent world music circuit extending from southeastern Europe through Greece and Turkey, are attributable to at least four factors: 1) a shared history of membership and intercultural exchange within the Ottoman Empire; 2) the longtime presence of locally distinct but often similar customs, instruments, musical genres, choreography, and other cultural practices; 3) the prolonged and dexterous contribution of Romani musicians to musical life, especially in the urban environments that are typically the locus of popular culture production; and 4) the impact of recent political transition away from Soviet-style state socialism, a move that has inspired the development of new market economies and a concomitant explosion of popular culture industries across the region.

Some of the intercultural musical endeavors that I have encountered just in my own recent field research seem indicative not only of emerging intraregional relationships, but of a growing, broader desire among musicians to look beyond the nation and in a variety of novel directions for artistic engagement and inspiration, with the potential for transnational impact. The following brief illustrations are cases in point.

❖ In August 2002 the Turkish vocalist Sezen Aksu, who is the subject of chapter nine, launched a concert series under the banner "Let Us Sing Together," during which she sang Turkish, Armenian, Kurdish, and Jewish songs. A performance at Istanbul's Summer Theater also enlisted the participation of an Armenian and Kurdish choir. Although this concert met with harsh criticism in some corners, Aksu sang publicly in Armenian at the event for the first time, together with the Armenian ensemble. Significantly, information about this concert appeared in a weekly newspaper published in Bulgaria for Armenian Bulgarians (Anonymous 2002a; see also Stokes, this volume).

❖ The 2004 recording and music video *Bezumna lyubov* [Reckless love], released by Payner Music,[2] features a collaboration between the Bulgarian ethnopop artist Emiliya and Arab vocalist Nidal Kaisar. The lyrics of their tormented love duet are rendered in two languages—his in Arabic, hers in Bulgarian.

❖In a second 2004 release from Payner Music, *Imam nuzhda ot teb* [I need you], the late Romani vocalist Reihan, singing in Turkish and with Turkish styling, is joined by a male Bulgarian hip hop artist who raps his desire for her in Bulgarian.[3] Throughout the video, which is replete with orientalisms, her lyrics are subtitled in Bulgarian, his in Turkish.

❖In spring 2004 the internationally celebrated Philip Kutev Ensemble for Bulgarian Folk Song and Dance launched a new program on the stages of London, Paris, and Tokyo. Called "Wild Strawberries," its music, composed by Georgi Andreev, showcases the music of the country's minority and border populations.

These illustrations are not isolated instances; similar developments are occurring all over the region. This volume is therefore devoted to teasing out what these and other musical crosscurrents might mean for various communities in the Balkans, and how they are intersecting with at least three prevalent and interrelated regional political discourses: balkanism, postsocialism, and for want of a better term, EU-topianism. These discourses embed other issues and phenomena addressed by the authors: the revision of history; a reevaluation of the Ottoman legacy and its pertinence to contemporary identity construction and state-building; nostalgia for the communist and pre-communist past; shifting gender codes; privatization of media and industry; continuing debates over cultural and ethnic purity played out, to great extent, in the public sphere of popular culture; aspirations to new lifestyles—in short, new and refashioned modes of thinking and being in the nation-state, the Balkans, Europe, and the world.

The approach taken is one that shifts the analytical gaze from the disjuncture and dissension of balkanization to the dialogue and interchange of a potential Balkan cosmopolitanism, while at the same time attending carefully to the local distinctiveness and significance of musical phenomena in specific moments and places. In its use of the term *ecumene,* the book's title reflects this shift; it signals a deliberate reconsideration of the Balkans as a geopolitical construct whose inhabitants were once linked, for hundreds of years, by a sprawling, multicultural, cosmopolitan Ottoman theocracy. Across the Balkan peninsula, the Empire's official presence was strongest in its "more densely inhabited core"—its urban centers—where it prompted the development of new musical genres, ensembles, and classes of musicians whose legacy continues to inform musical practices today. As implied in the notion of ecumenism, an ecumene is a space evidencing an intentional sharing, interchange, collaboration, or dialogue across boundaries of some sort, here of nation as well as faith.

It is in this sense of trafficking and exchange across vast distances or other barriers that the term has been employed in studies of globalization, public culture, and world systems. For scholars such as Robert Foster (1991) and Ulf Hannerz (1989a, 1989b), "global ecumene" provides a means of describing the cultural interconnectedness wrought by the transnational flow and interface of "images, objects, and people" (Foster

1991:236). Hannerz here follows Igor Kopytoff (1987:10), who defines an ecumene as a "region of persistent cultural interaction and exchange" (quoted in Hannerz 1989a:215n2). Similarly, Arjun Appadurai (1996:28) identifies ecumenes as large-scale social formations, "whether religious, commercial, or political," in which "congeries of money, commerce, conquest, and migration" created "durable cross-societal bonds" that served as the basis for "a permanent traffic in ideas of peoplehood and selfhood," which in turn informed the "imagined communities (Anderson 1983) of recent nationalisms throughout the world." In the past few decades, the explosion in communications and computer technology has greatly facilitated and accelerated the creation of overlapping ecumenes, of which the trans-peninsular flows of music, imagery, and choreography in the Balkans, predicated on the older Ottoman ecumene and inflected by that of Soviet socialism, are just one result.

Synopsis of the Volume

Each contribution to this volume thus provides an ethnographic perspective on the commonalities and differences given shape, historically, by the Ottoman presence and at play in the territory once spanned by the Ottoman ecumene. So as to juxtapose vantage points both internal and external to the region, the volume's contributor list is intentionally international, including ten scholarly experts native to seven different countries whose studies supply geographic coverage of Albania, Bosnia-Hercegovina, Bulgaria, Croatia, Greece, the Republic of Macedonia, Romania, Serbia (including Kosova), and Turkey. Three studies (chapters one, six, and eleven) additionally concern either large sweeps of Balkan territory or the region as a whole, and three (chapters one, eight, and ten) extend their analyses into diasporic communities.

The articles are organized in two sections. Those in Part I, "Post-1989 Culture Industries and Their Nationalist Icons," focus on specific post-socialist ethnopop genres—their history, production, key performers, and significance—largely within the framework of the nation-state. Ljerka Rasmussen considers two related trends, Bosnian Muslim *sevdah*-rock and Serbian *turbo folk*, both of which developed in relation and reaction to socialist-era Yugoslav "newly composed folk music." Her comparative analysis highlights continuities, fractures, and developments within and between the Sarajevo and Belgrade music scenes, situated in the careers and repertories of leading artists such as Rambo Amadeus and Dino Merlin, and the politics of the Bosnian war and its aftermath.

Margaret Beissinger's investigation of Romanian *muzică orientală,* an urban dance-song genre performed almost exclusively by Romani musicians, highlights paradoxes inherent in Romanian identity construction in the post-Ceauşescu era. The genre's hybridic style, which incorporates Bulgarian, Romani, Serbian, Turkish, and Romanian elements, is embraced by rural and "rurban" populations for its participatory and celebratory qualities, but dismissed as kitsch by well-educated urban elites, for whom this styling destabilizes Romania's position *vis-à-vis* Europe. These opposing responses, which hinge upon older, power-laden debates concerning ethnic and cultural purity, place confrontations of class, ethnicity, nationalism, gender, and generation in sharp relief.

In its ethnic eclecticism, strong Romani associations, controversial social position, and musical substance, *muzică orientală* bears close resemblance to Bulgarian *pop-folk* or *chalga,* a genre of dance music that developed during the mid-1990s and whose MTV-style video culture is the subject of Vesa Kurkela's chapter. Following a brief discussion of *chalga*'s history and the political debates that continue to swirl around its production, Kurkela presents a classification of *chalga* videos and an analysis of their musical, textual, and visual attributes. Although the oriental signifiers identified by Kurkela's analysis have helped make *chalga* the subject of political debate, his investigation also reveals that these same stereotypes can be deliberately employed by *chalga* performers as a means of self-irony and social commentary.

Kevin Dawe contemplates the popular music scene in 1990s Greece from two complementary angles. On the one hand, a diverse constellation of regional musical styles, genres, ensembles, and practices remain essential to the construction of Greek identity in the new millennium; this musical periphery is kept at the center of national consciousness through the activities of state-supported folkloric institutions. On the other, artists and ensembles such as Mode Plagal, Kristi Stassinopoulou, and the Irish Ottoman music revivalist Ross Daly are looking beyond the temporal and physical borders of the modern Greek state to craft a new genre of Greek world music, *ethniki mousike,* whose creative stylistic fusion invites the Balkan and Mediterranean milieus in which Greece is situated into the national soundscape.

The second half of Dawe's article hints at the broadening geographic and conceptual stance exhibited by the studies in Part II, "Beyond Nation: Regionalisms in a Cosmopolitan Frame." Based on musicological and field research in the churches of several postsocialist Balkan states, Gabriela Ilnitchi provides an iconographic analysis of frescoes whose musical and theological scenarios reveal a "dialectical relationship between inherited Byzantine representational practices and contemporaneous Ottoman social and cultural demands." Accompanied by a series of plates, her article presents evidence, gleaned from the frescoes, regarding the dissemination of Ottoman instruments, especially the *davul* and *zurna,* across the region during the sixteenth and seventeenth centuries, the stratification of musical practices into rural and urban traditions, and the rise of new rural and urban classes of professional Romani musicians. Like the volume's first chapter, this historical portrait of Ottoman-era Balkan popular culture supplies data on socio-musical practices critical to understanding current developments across the region. It also stands out as among the only English-language studies to address Balkan instrumental music prior to the nineteenth century.

The consideration of local musical developments in a regional context continues in the seventh chapter, on Bulgarian ethnopop. Like Kurkela, I assess the significance of 1990s musical trends as emblems of postsocialist life, particularly in regard to political change, the privatization of music industry, the growth in organized crime, and changing gender codes. However, my article highlights *pop-folk*'s historical and stylistic junctions with Romani musicianship, Yugoslav newly composed folk music, and Turkish *arabesk,* while also situating the genre in the environment of two other postsocialist productions, the recordings of *Le mystère des voix bulgares* and the television show *Xena: Warrior Princess,* which engage similarly in the commoditization of gendered orientalist stereotypes.

I conclude that *pop-folk* may represent a Bulgarian expression of orientalism as a central Balkan sensibility—a means of enacting, musically, the tension between European integration and regional distinction, and where Bulgaria fits along this continuum. A similar tension emerges in Jane Sugarman's research on commercial music production in Albania and among Albanians in diaspora since 1990, but with a different connotation. Sugarman's focus is a style of "amplified folk-pop music" called *muzika popullore* that, like the other musics treated in this volume, blends musical characteristics of formerly Ottoman areas with the studio apparatus and electronic instruments of high technology. The result is a contested genre presenting "a specific vision of an Albanian countermodernity that challenges many of the modernist aesthetic principles long championed by the Albanian elite." However, while the obvious commonalities between *muzika popullore* and the other genres under discussion might signal a degree of intercultural kinship, Sugarman cautions that stylistic affinities do not necessarily signify the affirmation of a shared Balkan identity by all national groups. She argues, rather, that these musics retain an ethnic specificity in language if not musical idiom, and in this respect they perhaps comment most significantly on "emerging geopolitical realignments within the region," as each group reevaluates its relationship to Europe in the face of a globalizing West.

The Middle Eastern inflections pervading every musical tradition surveyed by the authors raises the question of Turkey as a locus of regional musical power—a sort of fuse box from which the widening grid of regional musical circuits and crosscurrents draws its creative energy. But Martin Stokes's study of the eclectic Turkish songstress Sezen Aksu suggests that, for those artists wishing to reconfigure Turkish national idioms into a world music offering, the Balkan states to the north and east have equally served as a sonic sandbox. To decipher Turkey's Balkan imaginary and its significance, Stokes examines two CDs released by Aksu in the mid-1990s: *Ex Oriente Lux* [Light from the East], which engages "the regional diversity of Anatolian music," and *Düğün ve Cenaze* [Wedding and Funeral], a collaboration with the Bosnian Serb composer Goran Bregović that incorporates a panorama of Balkan musical styles. The Aksu-Bregović comparison is particularly instructive, leading Stokes to surmise, much like Sugarman, that such cross-Balkan collaborations might best be interpreted as "local responses to a shared predicament, whose insistence on the possibility of conversations flowing across national boundaries may yet lead to a broader and more dialogical sense of national self."

In her multipronged analysis of the 1999 Gypsy Caravan Tour, Carol Silverman takes the Balkans out of their borders and onto the world stage, appraising critically many of the book's most persistent issues (orientalist stereotypes, exoticism, authenticity, cosmopolitanism, modernity) in a diasporic context and expanded, global forum. Her article examines the marketing and consumption of "Gypsy" music as they chart a nexus of relationships between international festival producers, managers of Romani musical acts, audience members, the press, and Romani musicians themselves. Although these musicians belong to an ethnic group that has been subjected to intense and prolonged persecution throughout Europe, Silverman explores how they actively construct, negotiate, and then market their own images and representations to outsiders and elites, sometimes capitalizing on the latter's stereotypes of Romani culture, while in other instances counteracting and overcoming these expectations to find employment and serenity.

The book's nine central chapters are framed by an introductory case study and reflective epilogue. Chapter one charts the unprecedented trek of an Ottoman Turkish song called *Üsküdara gider iken* [On the way to Üsküdar] across the entire Balkan region and into manifold diasporic communities from the late nineteenth century to the present day. Embedded in the song's genealogy is a primer of Balkan music-making, a chronicle of Ottoman interculturality, and a history of modern regional politics. By considering this song's metamorphosis, at every stop along its route, into a range of national styles, this well-traveled ballad about travel furnishes an illustrative introduction to the cultural background and stylistic development of many of the trends, genres, instruments, and ensembles that appear in subsequent chapters.

As an American-trained Croatian ethnomusicologist who resides in Slovenia and works with Romani musicians who have migrated from Kosova to many other parts of Europe during the last decade, Svanibor Pettan is in a unique position to reflect on the Balkans from multiple angles. Using Croatia, the region's northwestern boundary, as a springboard, the first portion of his postlude considers how the Balkans have been defined by geographers, historians, politicians, and most significantly, musicologists, and illustrates how balkanism threads through regional musicological scholarship as well as music productions. The final pages of his essay suggest ways that ethnomusicology can help us better understand and transcend precisely those borders that discourses such as balkanism perpetuate.

What emerges collectively from these studies can be summarized as follows. Whether we consider new stylistic mergers, covers of one artist's work by another across state bounds, or collaborative projects, trans-Balkan musical conversations mushroomed during the 1990s and remain a major feature of the soundscape in the first decade of the new millennium. The evidence for this is pervasive and overwhelming. This interchange has been greatly facilitated by Romani musicians now as in the past, but non-Roma are also currently contributing to this phenomenon in significant ways. Importantly, while these local artists are engaging with a barrage of new recording firms, media franchises, and concertizing networks indicative of the postsocialist era, their increasingly sophisticated musical productions are being marketed chiefly for domestic, regional consumption rather than distribution by powerful international media giants. These regional markets, however, are also expanding into burgeoning diasporic communities (themselves sometimes the source of new means of production), whether through the internet, international festivals, or personal contact, as for the first time in decades, southeast Europeans from formerly socialist Balkan states are emigrating in large numbers around the world.

In their insightful analysis of 1990s Croatian political rhetoric, Maple Razsa and Nicole Lindstrom convincingly demonstrate how balkanist essentialisms have been wielded not just by Western politicians in defiance of Croatia's European identity, but by Croatian leaders themselves on two fronts: against other Balkan states in defense of Croatia's European heritage, and against their own citizens to incite change away from attitudes and situations perceived as stereotypical of the region. This purposeful absorption of stereotypes as a platform for revitalization leads Razsa and Lindstrom (2004:649–50) to conclude that "it is always possible for those objectified by categories to reappropriate them, make them one's own, give them new meaning, and thereby redirect them as forms of political engagement and critique." While the redeployment of essentialisms in this manner is also constrained, at some level, by an acknowledgment of the very social hierarchy that is impeding acceptance by the mainstream (in this case, Croatia's accession to the EU), it also signals a crucial power shift, in which control over the redirection of stereotypes has been seized by their subjects, thereby creating an opening through which these typifications can be transformed, inverted, and invested with new local meanings.

That the majority of genres explored in this volume creatively manipulate the musical legacy of the Ottoman past or that of the Middle East more broadly provides a comparative basis for similarly exploring how and why artists may be exploiting regional stereotypes through expressive culture. The sociologist Janet Abu-Lughod has recently observed that, in trying to understand transnational global flows, our "own not fully-globalized perspective makes us blind to how the cultures of rising cores . . . are diffusing within their own circuits" (1997:131–32). Perhaps, then, the celebratory cultivation of "orientalisms" or "turkisms" in the peninsula's music productions portends a blossoming recognition of the Balkan as an exclusive representation of the European—one of potentially several new cores springing up in Europe's former periphery.[4]

Indeed, in the enduring debates concerning the consolidation of the European Union, there is no question that economic and political forces outside the Balkans are formally dictating Europe's future boundaries (cf. Razsa and Lindstrom 2004:634; Todorova 1997:139). However, the studies presented here reveal that the region's musicians are not waiting upon these events to determine who they are and where they fit. Rather, they are wresting the definition of place out of the hands of local and international politicians and are remaking it, literally, through music, song, dance, and visual imagery. In this process, the Balkan, Ottoman, and oriental seem to be mapping onto each other in ways that suggest a fount of aesthetic sensibilities to react against, but also to call upon, conjure up, or employ as the stuff of creativity in the continuing construction of identities and modernities. Thus while the interstitial geographic and historical qualities assigned to the Balkans have prompted scholars such as Kristen Fleming (2000:1232) and Dušan Bjelić (2002:6–7) to describe the region and its affiliated discourse as inherently liminal, it is this very liminality—characterized in the Turnerian sense by the "subjunctive mood," the condition of being poised on the threshold of possibility, of being or emerging anew—that is also driving the transformative power evidenced by contemporary cultural performances.[5] The undeniable commercial appeal of the resulting artistic productions speaks to a lively, ongoing reinterpretation of the Balkans' significance among the region's citizens, as geopolity, discursive subject, aesthetic awareness, and most importantly, home.

Acknowledgments

I am deeply grateful to all of those individuals and institutions who contributed to this project in one way or another over the many years demanded for its completion. Gage Averill enthusiastically encouraged the volume in its earliest stages; my research assistants, James Randall, Andrew Granade, Ioannis Tsekouras, and Maria Radeva, cheerfully and obligingly pursued various proofreading, fact checking, and other editorial tasks; Ryan Haynes enthusiastically and skillfully compiled the index; Phil Bohlman, Martin Stokes, Renée Camus, and others associated with the editorial staff at Scarecrow Press provided valuable answers to a multitude of questions, displaying infinite patience with the volume's progress; and Brad Decker expertly and efficiently designed the accompanying CD-ROM. To each, my most heartfelt thanks. I also wish to express my sincere appreciation to the University of Illinois Campus Research Board, for supplying the assistantships awarded to Randall and Granade, and to the staff of the Russian, East European, and Eurasian Center for the gift of their friendship and moral and logistical support. Finally, I am most profoundly indebted to the volume's contributors for never losing faith in this project, and for years of intellectual inspiration, debate, and camaraderie.

Notes

1. See, especially, Bakić-Hayden 1995; Bakić-Hayden and Hayden 1992; Todorova 1997; and the essays in Bjelić and Savić 2002.

2. See *Hitovete na Planeta Payner,* 2004.

3. *Hitovete na Planeta Payner,* 2004.

4. One could look, for example, to the Baltics, the Mediterranean, and Russia for other emergent cores.

5. See Turner 1988, especially 25, 41, and 101–02.

PRELUDE

❖ 1 ❖

"Oh, Those Turks!"
Music, Politics, and Interculturality
in the
Balkans and Beyond

Donna A. Buchanan

In 1973, the late Bulgarian ethnographer Raina Katsarova published an exhaustive article documenting the extraordinary circulation of an Ottoman Turkish song entitled *Üsküdara gider iken* [On the way to Üsküdar] through many Balkan locales during the late nineteenth and early twentieth century.[1] In each place musicians refashioned the song to suit local aesthetic sensibilities, substituting a new vernacular text for the Turkish lyrics. Although Katsarova details *Üsküdara*'s migration, she does not consider why this particular song gained such popularity with diverse audiences, what the stylistic changes visited upon it by various communities might signify, or the larger implications of its circulation for local, regional, national, or transnational senses of identity.

Through a comparative analysis of numerous recordings, transcriptions, and film clips, I wish to re-examine and extend Katsarova's investigation into the present to explore these and other questions. My findings demonstrate two broad hypotheses. First, while most of the renditions have resulted from intercultural contact, their significance lies elsewhere, in their stylistic content, which documents the changing social, political, and economic circumstances of one or another Balkan people

3

over the past century. Put differently, specific features of text and tune mark each variant as associated with a particular community, time, and place to such an extent that in recent years these markers have sometimes symbolized powerful ethno-nationalist sentiments. Second, in contrast to this strongly asserted diversity, the popularization of a single song in so many venues also reveals circuits of Balkan interchange well-established prior to those of contemporary global media. Conversely, similar circuits are also informing the mass-mediated, stylistic interculturality permeating today's Balkan ethnopop genres, whose significance is linked in part to the re-positioning and re-defining of the Balkans, as region and states, within the New Europe.

On the Way to Üsküdar

Turkey

Our journey begins with a common Turkish version of *Üsküdara*, transcribed here as performed by Ümit Takcan, a contemporary folk singer. Takcan renders the melody as a *türkü*, or Turkish folk song, with accompaniment provided by the *saz*, a long-necked strummed lute, in a style related to that of the once itinerant Sufi (predominantly Bektaşi or Alevi) minstrels called *aşık*-s (Fig. 1.1; CD 1.1).

While such a performance might suggest a rural provenance for the song, *Üsküdara*, whose title refers to the city of Üsküdar, located directly across the Bosporus Strait from Istanbul, may have originated or at least spent its early life in an urban venue. Üsküdar was called Scutari during the Byzantine period; the Ottoman Turks dubbed it Üsküdar, meaning "Courier," because Asiatic couriers used it as a post station. Ottoman Üsküdar was thus a town of some importance, serving also as the seat of military operations and the final destination of caravans en route from Syria and Asia.[2] One theory holds that *Üsküdara* served as an Ottoman Janissary march song commemorating either the Turkish sacking of Constantinople in 1453 or the 1877 Russian seige of Pleven, a Bulgarian city held by the Turks during the Russo-Turkish war that resulted in Bulgaria's emancipation from Ottoman rule. In both contexts the song's first line, "On the way to Üsküdar," is thought to have symbolized the soldiers' homeward trek to the Ottoman capital.[3]

Makam Nihavent

Üsküdara gider iken aldı da bir yağmur.	On the way to Üsküdar it began to rain hard.
Kâtibimin setiresi uzun, eteği çamur.	The clerk I love wears a long frock coat; its long skirt is muddied.
Kâtip uykudan uyanmiş, gözleri mahmur.	My clerk just awoke; his eyes are still languid.
Kâtip benim ben Kâtibin, el ne karışır.	That clerk is mine—I am his— that's no one else's business.
Kâtibime kolalı da gömlek ne güzel yaraşir.	That starched shirt looks so lovely on my clerk.
Üsküdara gider iken bir mendil buldum,	Going to Üsküdar I found a handkerchief,

Mendilimin içine lokum doldurdum.	And filled it up with Turkish delight.
Ben Kâtibi arar iken yanımda buldum.	I went in search of my clerk, and found him right beside me.
Kâtip benim ben Kâtibin, el ne karışır.	That clerk is mine—I am his—that's no one else's business.
Kâtibime kolalı da gömlek ne güzel yaraşir.	That starched shirt looks so good on him!

Figure 1.1: *Üsküdara gider iken,* transcribed as recorded on 16 September 1980 by Ümit Takcan for the King Records CD *Turkish Folk Songs and Instrumental Music.*

A second theory postulates that *Üsküdara* originated as an Ottoman-era *şarkı.* A Bulgarian-Armenian friend living in Sofia told me that her elderly mother, who was born in Istanbul in the early 1900s, categorized the song, which she remembered from her youth, in this manner. The *şarkı* (Bulg. *shargiya*) was a popular, semi-classical, strophic, *makam*-based Ottoman song genre of urban derivation that was embraced by the elite and performed at the court and royal palaces by the mid-1600s to the accompaniment of long-necked lutes like the *bozuk* and *tanbura*, which provided instrumental introductions and interludes (Erguner 1991:5; Feldman 2002:115; cf. Katsarova 1973:121). Most were love songs whose sentimental, nostalgic texts expressed yearning for one's beloved, the pain of unrequited love, or helplessness in the face of fate (Erguner 1991:5). For aristocrats, the genre's melancholic character reflected the Empire's impending decline, as Western European influences mitigated the Sultan's power. The song's wide range, conjunct pitch movement, four-line verse structure (if repeats are taken into account), and modal construction in *makam Nihavent* mark it as potentially associated with the Ottoman courtly tradition, while its narrative, which describes the singer's love for a *"kâtip,"* the bureaucratic title for a scribe or clerk, points to the Ottoman system of occupational guilds.[4] Importantly, as we will see below, some of these same features, especially the song's duple meter and modal construction, which does not employ any microtones, eventually facilitated its performance by a wide range of ensembles and across myriad traditions.

Further evidence that *Üsküdara* circulated as a *şarkı* comes from Russia, where it appears in the compendium *Opyty Hudozhestvennoi Obrabotki Narodnykh' Piesen', Tom 1* [Experiments in artistic arrangements of folk songs, Volume 1], published in Moscow in 1913 under the

Üsküdara gider iken bir mendil buldum,	Going to Üsküdar I found a handkerchief,
Mendilin içine şeker doldurdum.	And filled it up with Turkish delight.
Ben yarımı arar iken koynumda buldum.	While I was looking for my lover I found him in my arms.

Nakarat

Refrain

Kâtib benim, ben Kâtibin, el ne karışır?	That clerk is mine—I am his— whose business is that?
Kâtibime elmas yüzük, ne güzel yaraşir.	On my clerk a diamond ring would look so nice!

Figure 1.2: *Sharky Negavend: Lyubovnaya.* Muzykal'no-Etnograficheskaya Komissiya 1913:51–52. Translated from the Turkish by Derviş Vural.

direction of composer Aleksandr Grechaninov by the Musical-
Ethnographic Commission of the Ethnography Department of the Imperial
Society of Amateur Naturalists, Anthropologists, and Ethnographers at
Moscow's Imperial University.[5] Throughout the first decade of the 1900s
the Commission gathered and arranged Russian and other folksongs,
which they then published in volumes directed at school classrooms and
choirs. The present collection features 133 songs representing 32 peoples
(including several indigenous groups) ranging from the Russian empire to
New Zealand, set to simple piano accompaniments by 16 different Russian
composers. Although their arrangements are not attributed by name, the
contributors include well-known figures such as Reinhold Glière,
Grechaninov, Mikhail Ippolitov-Ivanov, Aleksandr Kastal'sky, and Sergey
Taneyev (Yanchuk 1913:iv). One of two Turkish selections incorporated
into the volume is *Üsküdara*, which is presented under the title *Sharky
Negavend: Lyubovnaya* [*Şarkı* Nihavent: Love song], together with a
variant of its Turkish text transliterated into Cyrillic and translated into
Russian (Fig. 1.2). A spare harmonization preserves *Üsküdara*'s rhythmic
character by reiterating and developing, throughout, the dotted motive that
opens each of the song's phrases. Drone and open intervals (especially
fifths and octaves, rendered both in sequence and simultaneously)
accentuate the melody's modality and represent a bow toward Middle
Eastern performance practice. That these same characteristics are also germane to the indigenous vocal polyphony of Russian villagers with which
members of the Ethnographic Commission were working as well is
probably significant; the resulting arrangement is not unlike the sentimental urban romances and salon pieces popular in Russian towns and cities
in the late nineteenth century, many of which were themselves stylized
settings of Russian folk songs for voice and piano.

    With the decline of court patronage for Ottoman art music in the late
1800s, *şarkı* performance moved into the Turkish-owned urban coffee-
house (*kafehane*) and emerging European-style Greek-owned *gazino*
(nightclub, casino), where the genre flourished as the basis of a new song
cycle that eventually eclipsed the earlier courtly suite, or *fasıl,* in
popularity. The *şarkı* thus served as a musical bridge between the larger
populace of major urban centers and the Ottoman court (Feldman
2002:114–16). Such establishments were also the scene of professional
female oriental dancers called *çengiler* (sing. *çengi*), often Jews, Roma, or
other minorites, who worked as entertainers and sometimes, prostitutes.
Such entertainers were employed by the Ottoman nobility until ca. 1840,
when new laws prohibiting their presence at the court encouraged them to
seek employment in commercial establishments (2002:116).[6]

Urbanized renditions of *türkü*-s, which were performed alongside *şarkı*-s in these entertainment venues, played a similar role, appealing to broad sectors of the population (Feldman 2002:116), and Turkish scholarship suggests that *Üsküdara* perhaps better typifies this category. First, *şarkı* texts were usually penned by major poets according to specific Persian-Arabic poetic conventions and set by named composers who strived to conjure melodies that would enhance each line (Erguner 1991:4–5; Feldman 2002:115; Reinhard 2002:773). By contrast, *Üsküdara*'s author and composer are unknown, and its melodic structure less elaborate. Second, according to the ethnomusicologist and Turkish music specialist Sonia Seeman, Turkish musicologists identify *Üsküdara* as an urban song and associate it with the nineteenth-century Tanzimat reforms that looked ahead to the Ottoman Empire's modernization, rather than to nostalgia associated with its decline (p.c., 4 November 2004). Thus the song lyrics portray a debonair scribe sporting a Western-style business suit—a "long frock coat" and "starched [white] shirt."

This Clark Gable-esque vision of the clerk caught the public's imagination, perhaps representing, metaphorically, Turkey's continuing transformation as a secular state and the changing gender norms that accompanied it. A reflective essay by Ali Rıza Alp (1951) suggests that, for the elite woman of the late Ottoman period, who viewed the world through shuttered windows, shielded from the public eye, the clerk was a striking figure whose romantic appeal caused them to profess their attraction or liaison publicly, contrary to social norms ("That clerk is mine—I am his—that's no one else's business"). She fills up a handkerchief, whose gift signifies romantic interest or courtship, sometimes from an otherwise unapproachable admirer, with Turkish delight, a sweet metaphor of their abundant love. A 1962 Turkish film starring Zeki Müren and called simply *Kâtip (Üsküdara Gider Iken)*, which extends the song's plot into a longer romantic narrative, depicts the clerk similarly.[7] In an interview with Bulgarian filmmaker Adela Peeva, whose own 2003 documentary about *Üsküdara* was released as I finished researching this study, *Kâtip*'s director explained that for Turkish audiences, the clerk was a generic figure, beloved of women. He was "handsome and respected," "well-mannered," with "a walking stick and manicure."[8]

After the founding of the Republic of Turkey in 1923, in conjunction with his own reformist modernization campaign, Kemal Atatürk prohibited the formal teaching of Ottoman classical repertory, a sonic symbol of the former regime. But small ensembles of mixed Turkish and Western European instruments, manifestations of the earlier Ottoman *ince saz*, or "fine orchestra," continued to play this music as well as other popular

repertory in the nightclubs and cafés.[9] For example, a historical recording
of *Üsküdara* (here titled *Kâtibim*) sung by vocalist Safiye Ayla (b. 1907)
and released by Columbia Records in 1949 features accompaniment by a
typical *ince saz* of violin, *kanun, ud,* and clarinet.[10]

Greece

A fourth theory suggests that *Üsküdara* originated or was widely
disseminated through performances of Western opera in the late Ottoman
period. The song's melody figures in the operetta *Leblébidji Hor-hor
Agha,* composed ca. 1880 by Dikhran Chukadzhian[11] (1837–1898), one
of several Armenian composers active during the waning years of the
Ottoman Empire.[12] One of the work's first performances was given by the
Beglian Theater Company at the Kordelion Theater in Smyrna (Turk.
Izmir) ca. 1882 (Solomonides 1954).[13] In summer 1883 the same troupe
brought the operetta to the Phaleron Theater (est. 1871) in Athens,[14] after
which it continued to be staged periodically in both cities by the Beglian
and other companies, spreading quickly throughout Asia Minor, including
to islands such as Mytilene (Lesbos) (Dionysopoulos 2002:72, 74).[15]

The Athens performance of *Hor-Hor Agha* marked a watershed in
Greek musical theater, providing a prototype for a new form of Greek
musical comedy combining the Western European sensibilities of French
operetta (harmonization, orchestration, genres) with so-called "oriental"
subject matter (i.e., Ottoman Turkish language, melodies, costumes, and
settings). The plot follows the exploits of a Turkish villager who travels
to Istanbul in search of his daughter, only to be teased by the city's
residents for his old-fashioned, peasant ways ((Dionysopoulos 2002:
74n.1). Although the production was originally condemned as immoral
and backward by the Athenian upper class, it met with such success that
its detractors were soon won over, prompting the composition of other
"oriental" operettas performed especially by the Beglian troupe. In 1886
the music of *Hor-Hor Agha* also served as the immediate basis for an
amateur production by Dimitrios Kokkos that represents the first example
of *Komeidyllion*, a new genre of Greek romantic comedy whose characters
are caricatures of social stereotypes (Hatzipantazis 1986:54; Sitheris
2000). Like *Üsküdara* itself, then, *Hor-Hor Agha*, in style and substance,
reflects the growing tension between rural and urban lifestyles as increased
urbanization and migration altered the demographic face of the region.

Although it is unlikely that Chukadzhian wrote the *Üsküdara* tune, which was probably in circulation prior to 1880,[16] the operetta boosted its popularity up and down the Asia Minor coast, entering the vernacular tradition in a number of variants. The contemporaneous Greek antiquarian and musician Nikolaou Fardys, whose unpublished writings, which include song lyrics and their variants from the Aegean, Thrace, and Constantinople with accompanying melodies transcribed in Byzantine notation, became the basis of a compilation published by the musicologist Markos Dragoumis in 1991, presents a Greek text, *Apo kseno topo ki ap alaryino* [From a faraway foreign land], to which the *Üsküdara* tune became attached. Fardys speculates that this text was probably originally fixed to a different melody in *makam Hicaz* (Fig. 1.3). He surmises that the song originated in Smyrna, where he collected it during 1877–78, and was performed as a quick-tempo dance.

In 1888, while Fardys was living on his native island of Samothrace, he collected a variant of the same text, but this time set to our favorite melody. As illustrated in Figure 1.4, this version uses but two verses of the *Apo kseno* text—those comprising an interchange between the male and female protagonists. Katsarova (1973:124–25) likewise cites two close variants of the same lyrics, also set to the *Üsküdara* tune, from the islands of Rhodes (in the Dodecanese), published by the Swiss ethnomusicologist Samuel Baud-Bovy in 1935 (Fig. 1.5) and Skiathos (in the Sporades), published by Georgios Rigas in 1958 (p. 98), illustrating that the song was known throughout the Aegean basin. Yet another close textual variant circulated in Epirus, but to a second tune in *makam Hicaz* unrelated to either *Üsküdara* or that in Fig. 1.3 (see Vrelis 1985, No. 6).

Several elements of the *Apo kseno* version are also central features of other *Üsküdara* variants found in Greece, Bulgaria, Serbia, and Macedonia. The lyrics are structured in couplets that contain an internal dialogue—a teasing exchange of courtship between a young man and woman or girl, in which the man tries to persuade the young woman to sell, lend, or give him any of several specific physical attributes. She generally refuses, sometimes because of her age, but then suggests that the young man return at a later date, when she will be old enough to comply.

By contrast, a second popular Greek text commonly sung to our melody, *Ehasa mantili* [I lost a handkerchief], shares some features of both the Turkish and *Apo kseno* narratives (Fig. 1.6). In both Greek variants the narrator is usually male rather than female (as in the Turkish). In *Ehasa mantili* he loses (rather than finds) a handkerchief usually given to him (and sometimes lovingly embroidered) by his sweetheart as a token of her devotion; it is usually filled with gold coins which, like the *lokum*

Apo kseno topo ki ap alaryino	From a faraway foreign land
irthe ena koritsi dodeka hrono.	came a twelve-year-old girl.
Oute sti porta vyeni oute sto steno	She doesn't appear at the door, on the road,
mite sto parathiri mia ora na ti do.	or in the window so I can see her for a moment.
Me tis margiolies mou tin eplanepsa	With my sly tricks I seduced her
ki is ta wonata mou tin ekathisa.	and made her sit on my lap.
Piano ksekoubon t'aryira koubia	I undo her silver buttons
vlepo tis elitses pou he sta vizia.	to see the freckles on her breasts.
Kan' saranda iton, kan' saranda dio	There were forty or forty-two,
horia ti megali pou xe sto lemo.	not counting the big one on her neck.
"Des mas tes danizis de mas tes poulis	"Why don't you sell or lend me
tis elitses pou 'his kai mas tiranis?"	the little freckles with which you torment me?"
"De sas tes danizo, de sas tes poulo	"I will not lend or sell them to you,

tis elitses pou ho ke sas tirano.	the little freckles that are your torment.
Ante ksene sire, sire sto kalo, ki is to yirismo sou peras' apo do.	Go away, guest, farewell, and on your way back home, stop by again.
Tote stes danizo, tote stes poulo, tes elitses pou ho ke sas tirano. "	Then I will lend or sell them to you, these little freckles that are your torment."

Figure 1.3: *Apo kseno topo ki ap alaryino.* Dragoumis 1991:392, No. 33. Translated from the Greek by Ioannis Tsekouras.

of the Turkish song, are a metaphor of the couple's romantic wealth. The handkerchief is found by another eligible maiden, often the daughter of a local priest, with whom he flirts and to whom he offers the gold in return for the handkerchief.

| *"De mas tes danizis de mas tis poulis, Panayia mou, tes elites po his, fos mou, ke mas tiranis?"* | "Why don't you lend or sell them to us, my Virgin Mary, those freckles of yours, my light, with which you are tormenting us?" |
| *"De sas tes danizo de sas tes poulo, Panayia mou, mono sas tes dihno, fou mou, na sas tirano."* | "I won't lend or sell them to you, my Virgin Mary, I'll only show them to you, my light, to torment you." |

Figure 1.4: *De mas tes danizis.* Dragoumis 1991:282, No. 34. Translated from the Greek by Ioannis Tsekouras.

Moderato

A - po kse - no   to   -   po   ki_a - po ma - kri -

no,_____   Irthe e - na ko - ri - tsi, fos_mou,

1.   2.

do - de-ka hro - no.   do - de-ka hro - no.

Apo kseno topo ki apo   From a faraway foreign land
    makrino
Irthe ena koritsi, fos mou,   came, my light, a twelve-year old
    dodeka hrono . . .   girl . . .

Figure 1.5: *Apo kseno topo ki apo alaryino.* Baud-Bovy 1935:114–15, No. 45.

E - ha - sa man - ti - li   m'e - ka - to   flou -

-ria a - man, a - man.   Ki e ma-tha pos   to__ vre,_ fos_mou,

1.   2.

mia ap- ta Pli - tha - ria   mia ap-ta Pli - tha - ria

Ehasa mantili m' ekato   I lost a handkerchief filled with a
    flouria, aman, aman,   hundred golden coins, *aman,*
                                   aman,
ki ematha pos to vre, fos mou, and I heard that a maiden from
    mia ap' ta Plitharia.   Plitharia found it.

Dos mou to mantili krata ta flouria	"Give me the handkerchief but keep the coins,
ki' im' aravoniasmenos sta Dabakaria.	for I am engaged [to a girl] in Dabakaria.
Sa de mou to doseis the na rtho mia vradia	If you don't give it to me I will come at night
tha se filo sto stoma ki apano stin elia.	to kiss your mouth and beauty spot."

Figure 1.6: *Ehasa mantili. Archives musicales de folklore,* Athens, Aivali, Volume II, No. 4, cited in Katsarova 1973:125–6. Translated from the Greek by Ioannis Tsekouras.

The home town of the priest's daughter (or girl who finds the handkerchief) varies with the song's location. In the example that follows, (Fig. 1.7; CD 1.2), a variant from Smryna, the narrator claims that the handkerchief, which is found by a young woman from Bournova (Smyrna's Greek quarter), belongs to his sister, who is to be married on the coming Sunday. There are several ways that this situation might be interpreted. If literally true, it helps make sense of his romantic interest in the Bournova girl, whom he calls "my light." On the other hand, the handkerchief might belong to his beloved, whose identity and sentiments he hides because he wants to flirt with the Bournova maiden, or because their relationship is secret, whether because she is about to be married to a rival suitor on the weekend, or conversely, because he himself is to be wedded on the weekend to a woman whom he doesn't love. At one time Greek custom mandated that a man not marry until his sisters had all been wed; thus it is also plausible that his sweetheart is the Kouklutza girl—his sister's friend or bridesmaid—who ostensibly embroidered the handkerchief on behalf of his sister for her dowry, but gave it to him (perhaps even through his sister) as a sign of her love, and that he will propose to her following his sister's nuptials.

Ehasa mantili m' ekato flouria,	I lost a handkerchief filled with a hundred golden coins,
ki imatha pos to vre mia Bournovalia,	and I learned that a young woman from Bournova found it,
ki imatha pos to vre, fos mou, mia Bournovalia.	and I learned that a girl, my light, from Bournova found it.
"Dos mou to mantili, krata ta flouria,	"Give me the handkerchief, but keep the golden coins,

emorfi, tsahpina, glikia	pretty, pert and saucy, sweet
Bournovalia,	Bournova girl,
emorfi, tsahpina, fos mou,	pretty, pert and saucy, my light,
kori tou papa.	daughter of a priest.
Ine ts' adelfis mou pou to he	It is my sister's, for her dowry;
sta proukia;	
tsi to he kendimeno mia	a girl from Kouklutza embroidered
Koukloutzalia,	it for her,
emorfi, tsahpina, fos mou,	pretty, pert and saucy, my light,
kori tou papa.	daughter of a priest.
Tin Keriaki pantrevete, to xer'	This Sunday she will marry, and the
i gitonia	neighborhood knows that,
emorfi, tsahpina, glikia	Pretty, pert and saucy, sweet
Bournovalia,	Bournova girl
emorfi, tsahpina, fos mou,	pretty, pert and saucy, my light,
kori tou papa. "	daughter of a priest."

Figure 1.7: *Ehasa mantili.* As performed by a group of Erythraean women on *Songs and Dances of Smyrna and Erythraea,* 1994. Transl. by Ioannis Tsekouras.

Sometimes the handkerchief-finding maiden engages in a teasing dialogue with the narrator similar to that in the *Apo kseno* version, refusing to give or sell him back his prize. Such is the case in the example below from Mytilene (Fig. 1.8, CD 1.3).

Ehasa mantili m'ekato	I lost a handkerchief filled with a
flouria.	hundred golden coins.
Mou pan pos to vrike mia	They told me that a maid from
Bournovalia.	Bournova found it.
"Dos mou to mantili krata ta	"Give me the handkerchief but keep
flouria.	the coins.
Mou to hi kentisi mia	It was embroidered for me by a
Mitilinia.	maid from Mytilene.
Den mou to harizis de mou to	Why don't you give or sell it to me,
poulas,	
to morfo mantili pou heis kai	the beautiful handkerchief with
me tiranas? "	which you torment me instead?"
Oute to harizo oute to poulo.	"I'll neither give it nor sell it to
	you.
Mono tha to eho na se tirano.	I'll just keep it to torment you."

Amanes

Amanes

Aman, orea pou ne tin avgi,
otan glikoharazi,
Aman, otan glikoharazi,
hara s' ekini th kardia pou den
anastenazi.

Aman, how beautiful is the dawn,
when the sun rises sweetly,
Aman, when the sun rises sweetly,
joyful is the heart that doesn't sigh.

Figure 1.8: *Ehasa mantili.* As sung by Stratis Rallis. *The Guardians of Hellenism, Volume 1: Chios, Mytilene, Samos, Ikaria.* Translated from the Greek by Ioannis Tsekouras.

Throughout Greece, both *Apo kseno* and *Ehasa mantili* are rendered as dance songs. *Ehasa mantili* is usually set to the lilting, syncopated, 8/8 meter (divided 3–3–2) of the *syrtós,* which characterizes many Greek tunes. The *Ehasa mantili* variant seems to have been most widespread in Athens, Smryna, and the Aegean, especially the islands of Mytilene, Aivali, and Erythraea; consequently, its performance style often takes on the Ottoman-inflected character typical of these locales.[17]

Although Aegean music had long exhibited a mixture of Ottoman and Venetian characteristics, during the late nineteenth century Ottoman influence became particularly evident in the entertainment provided at musical cafés called *café-amans.* These were taverns and coffee houses—similar to the *gazino* and *kafehane* of contemporaneous Istanbul—established in Greek seaports, trade centers, and towns where the Ottoman military was garrisoned. In these new urban commercial venues, first street musicians, and later professionally hired Greek, Romani, Armenian, and Jewish musicians performed local folk tunes, dervish melodies, and Ottoman classical repertory in an *alaturka* style that came to be known as Smyrnaica and which represents an early form of rebetica.[18] In Athens the first *café-amans* were established by 1874; although initially situated in poor, suburan areas and associated with the working class, the celebration of orientalism prompted by *Hor-Hor Agha* facilitated their proliferation and embrace by the bourgeoisie throughout the city during the 1880s and 1890s (Hatzipantazis 1986). They flourished in Aegean ports after 1900 and prospered among refugee communities in Athens and Piraeus after the population exchanges of 1922, when all Christians living in Asia Minor were forcibly relocated to Greece, and Greek Muslims to Turkey. A result of the Greco-Turkish war and tragic

Syrtos/Ballos

Apo tin Athina os ston Peria,	Between Athens and Piraeus,
Ehasa mantili m'ekato flouria.	I lost a handkerchief with a hundred golden coins.
Moupan pos to vrike mia niko-kira,	They told me a housewife found it,
Emorfi kiria, kori tou papa.	a beautiful lady, the priest's daughter.
"Dos mou to mantili, krata ta flouria,	"Return the handkerchief, but keep the coins,
Emorfi kiria, Athnniotissa."	beautiful lady of Athens."

Amanes

Aman, omorfa pou ine tin
*   avgi,*
otan glikoharazi,
pou isixazi to kormi,
kai den anastenazi.

Amanes

Aman, how beautiful is the
    dawn,
when the sun sweetly rises,
when the body calms,
and doesn't sigh.

Figure 1.9: *Apo tin Athina/Azizie,* as perfomed by Sophia Bilides on her CD *Greek Legacy.* Translated from the Greek by Ioannis Tsekouras.

fire that burned the city of Smyrna, these exchanges brought an influx of professional musicians formerly associated with Istanbul's *gazino* nightlife into the Greek capital. At this time it became common for *café-amans* to hire small orchestras of mixed Turkish or Greek (*kanun, ud, sandouri, laouto, defi, zilia*) and Western European instruments (violin, clarinet) called *kompanies* (similar to the Turkish *gazino* ensembles), whose performances were situated in a designated space at one end of the café. The *kompania* included both men and women, the latter playing finger cymbals (*zilia*), spoons (*koutalia*), or Arabo-Turkish tambourine (*defi*) and serving as featured vocalists and oriental dancers (Morris 1981:85).[19]

The regional orientation of *café-aman* entertainment distinguished it from the contemporaneous *café-chantant,* which supported *à la franka* (aka. *alafranga*) performances by mostly female singers from France and western Europe. The designation *"café-aman"* derives from a plaintive, nostalgic, highly expressive genre of solo vocal improvisation, the *amanes* (pl. *amanedhes*) or *mane*s, which developed from the Turkish *ghazal.* The vocal equivalent of the instrumental *taxim,* these slow-tempo, richly ornamented, modal extemporizations on formulaic textual couplets were marked by repetitions of the Turkish word *aman,* a deeply emotional exclamation of sorrow or passion.[20] The fact that, when repeated without pause (*amanamana . . .*), one common Greek word for mother, *"mana,"* is heard probably further boosted the genre's popularity (Tsekouras, p.c., May 2006). In the Aegean islands the *amanes* became an essential component of the *ballos,* a dance whose underlying rhythmic character is similar to that of the *syrtós* (Dionysopoulos 2002:111–13). Thus, the Smrynaica-style performances of *Ehasa mantili* typical of the Aegean generally conclude with a *ballos amanes,* as illustrated in Figures 1.8 and 1.9.[21]

Even before World War I, British and German recording firms traveled to Smyrna to document local musicians. By the late 1920s, Smyrnaica had been disseminated throughout Greece, Turkey, and major

U.S. cities by the growing recording industry, as waves of emigration brought professional Greek musicians to New York and Chicago. Yet another example of *Ehasa mantili*, performed by the Greek-Italian-American singer Sophia Bilides, represents the legacy of these developments (Fig. 1.9; CD 1.4). Entitled *Apo tin Athina* [From Athens], its by now familiar romantic text adds an additional line indicating that the handkerchief is lost as our suitor journeys from Athens to Piraeus—two cities that, as we have seen, became home to thousands of Asia Minor refugees after 1922. At that time Piraeus was an industrial center and many refugees commuted there daily from Athens along specific routes still identified as such today (the "Piraeus Road," for example), to work in the factories, so dropping or losing something along the way was probably a scenario with which local citizens could identify (Tsekouras, p.c., May 2006). Bilides performs "From Athens" in the Aegean style with an appended *ballos amane* that she learned from the repertory of Mytilene vocalist Nikos Kalaitzis (Bilides 1991:5). A Greek island ensemble of *sandouri* (hammered dulcimer) and violin provides accompaniment, but Bilides's vocal style, like that of the violin, reflects the Ottoman-inflected timbre and melismatic ornamentation indicative of Smyrnaica performance practice. Although Bilides is a second-generation American, she has a personal connection with this music; her grandparents, Mihalis and Domna Potioglou Bilides, grew up in Asia Minor, in the Greek village of Permata, and their families were relocated to Thessaloniki and Piraeus during the population exchanges (Bilides 1991:3).

One final version from Greece, a unique text collected by Rigas (1958:100) on Skiathos and set to the *Üsküdara* tune, draws together qualities of all the Greek and Turkish variants examined thus far (Fig. 1.10).

Mia kali kontoula do sti yitonia	A nice, cute girl here in the neighborhood
ihe sta malia tis armatha ta flouria.	has bunches of gold coins in her hair.
Mana tis ti derni ke ti tirani.	Her mother beats and punishes her.
"Pes mas, more kori, pios se filise?"	"Tell us, my girl, who kissed you."
"Mi me dernis, mana, mi me tiranis,	"Don't beat me, Mother, don't punish me,
ki ego tha martiriso poios me filise.	and I'll tell you who kissed me.

Out' ap' ta ksena ksenos, out'
    alaryinos,
 mone o gramatikos sima sti
    yitonia."
 "Pes mas, mori kori, pou se
    filise."
	He is not a stranger, he's not from a
	    faraway land;
	 he is the clerk from the neighbor-
	    hood nearby."
	 "Tell us, my girl, where he kissed
	    you."

"Mia for a st' abeli, dio sto
    mayerio,
 teseris ke pente mess ton
    argalio."
	"Once in the wine yard, twice in the
	    kitchen,
	 four and five times in the weaving
	    room."

Figure 1.10: *Mia kali kontoula.* Rigas 1958:100.

In this text the girl's hair is adorned, in traditional fashion, with gold coins given to her by a suitor, implying engagement. When her mother encounters her and sees the coins, she begins beating her for being involved in a romantic relationship. However, the daughter protests, exclaiming that her beau is not a stranger from a faraway land—a probable reference to the *Apo kseno* texts above—but that he is the village "clerk" or "secretary." In rural Greece, where most community members were illiterate prior to the twentieth century, this individual maintained the village records (births, deaths, marriages, and other statistics) and mediated between villagers and public services (Tsekouras, p.c., June 2006). Along with the local priest, teacher, village head, and policeman, he was a figure of authority; his educated status and clerical occupation relate him, of course, to the Ottoman *kâtip* of the Turkish song. When her mother asks her where the clerk has kissed her we expect to hear about her forty freckles. But the girl outwits her mother, pointing instead to various places around the homestead where their tryst has taken place.

Both *Apo kseno* and *Ehasa mantili* remain well-known today. During the summer of 2003, while teaching a Balkan music seminar in Olympia, three of the Greek undergraduate women in attendance treated me to the *Apo kseno* variant, which they had learned in grade school, where it is taught as a common children's song, and then encountered again in college, as part of their pedagogical training in music.[22] On the other hand, Ioannis Tsekouras, a graduate student in ethnomusicology at the University of Illinois, told me that he learned the *Ehasa mantili* version in school and that in Athens, where he grew up, the song is strongly associated with Mytilene.

The Jewish Diaspora

At about the same time that Smyrnaica was thriving in Greece, *Üsküdara* made its way across the Atlantic and into the Jewish klezmer repertory of Polish-born clarinet virtuoso Naftule Brandwein, who recorded it under the title *Terk in Amerika* with his orchestra in 1924 (Fig. 1.11).[23] Brandwein's rendition varies the tune's original rhythm fairly dramatically, interpolating numerous "filler" melismas at cadences and between phrases. He also tacks on an entirely new section, which is borrowed from a different tune that exists in other klezmer variants and which accentuates the modulation to *makam* Hicaz alluded to in the Turkish melody.[24]

Ethnomusicologist Joel Rubin, whose doctoral dissertation (2003) focuses on Brandwein, believes that the clarinetist encountered *Üsküdara* through New York City's Greek community, which exploded between 1890 and 1915 as many Greek citizens sought relief from the military and economic problems then facing their homeland. The Greek connection also helps make sense of the tune's new name. Greek musicians clearly knew and performed the melody at this time; they may also have communicated its Turkish origins to their new Jewish-American colleagues, with whom they likely peformed in ensembles of mixed ethnicity in the context of New York City's entertainment scene. Rubin writes that while klezmer artists, who were largely Ashkenazi Jews, generally only played klezmer repertory for in-group audiences and functions, musicians such as Brandwein also occasionally performed for the city's "Ukrainian, Polish, Russian, Hungarian, Rom, Greek, Sephardic Jewish, Turkish, German and Italian communities"(2003:136–37). When doing so, they performed the preferred style of the ethnic group that hired them. Such musicians were sought out "not only because of their flexibility and virtuosity, but also because many of these ethnic groups, such as the Russians, Rom[a] and Greeks, often did not have enough of their own music professionals to provide for the entertainment needs of their communities"(2003:137). In addition, by 1920 New York City had become a center for the production of Greek Smyrnaica recordings, and it is quite possible that the *klezmorim* discovered the melody in this fashion (Morris 1981:87). Jewish musicians may also have associated the immigrant Greeks, especially those from Asia Minor or whose musical style and repertory inclined toward the older tavern or *café-aman* tradition, with the Ottoman Empire, hence conceiving of them as Turkish and dubbing the tune *Terk in Amerika*.

Figure 1.11: *Terk in Amerika*, as performed by Naftule Brandwein, transcribed by Pete Sokolow, and published in Sapoznik 1987:56–57. Used by permission.

It is also possible, however, that *klezmer* musicians learned the tune through their Turkish brethren. As noted above, Jews were deeply involved with the performance of Ottoman Turkish music. Some Turkish Jews apparently found the melody so appealing that they set to it the

Hebrew poem *Yodukha Rayonai*, written by Rabbi Israel ben Moses
Najara (1555–1625), to create a *pizmon*, or devotional song. A version of
this *pizmon* was recorded in 2002 by a contemporary and eclectic Mizrahi
and Sephardic Jewish quartet, "Divahn," based in Austin, Texas (CD
1.5).[25] The name of the group signifies a style of poetry embraced by
Najara, whose manuscripts also provide melodies to which his *divan*-s
should be sung. According to Walter Feldman (2001:5), Najara resided in
the Arab Middle East—in Damascus, Safed, and Gaza—and most of the
featured melodies are of Turkish, Arab, or Greek origin. The high number
and style of the Turkish melodies leads Feldman to believe that Najara
might have heard them in Damascus coffee houses patronized by Janissary
soldiers (2001:5). If our melody is found in Najara's writings this would
date it to ca. 1600 and possibly place its origin once again in the hands of
the Janissaries, but it is just as possible that it became fixed to Najara's
divan centuries later.

Whatever the case, the tune was or became well known in other
Jewish communities, particularly amongst Sephardic and Oriental Jews of
the Balkans and Middle East, in both sacred and secular contexts.
Katsarova reports that in 1963 she encountered a variant in Tel Aviv,
where it was sung by seventy-year old Bracha Menachim, who was born
in Aden, South Yemen, with a religious text as part of a Shabbat celebration (1973:127). In 1968 Leo Levi recorded yet another sacred variant in
Djerba, Tunisia, which he identifies as a "Turkish melody." Held in the
National Sound Archives of the Jewish National and University Library,
this is a Jewish hymn with Hebrew lyrics called *Eftah pi berrina* [I will
open my mouth in song], sung in unison by a male chorus and accompanied by hand drums (CD 1.6).[26] The hymn was performed for the early
summer Lag ba-'omer festival, which typically entails "two days of
spectacle and processions accompanied by music making" (Davis
2002:523). Ethnomusicologist Ruth Davis has found that, even in the early
twentieth century, the Djerba Jewish community frequently set sacred texts
to secular melodies, some taken from external sources to which they were
exposed especially through the Lag ba-'omer celebration (2002: 529–31).
Eftah pi berrina seems an excellent illustration of this phenomenon.

In 1958 a secular Jewish rendition was recorded by the American-
born Sephardic singer Gloria Levy, who learned it from her mother, a
native of Alexandria, Egypt, who learned it in turn from *her* mother, a
native of Asia Minor (Fig. 1.12; CD 1.7). This version retains certain
images of the original song text: romance, walking down the street, and by
implication, rain. But here, as in the Greek version, the song is narrated
from a male perspective, and the handkerchief becomes an umbrella used

to strike the unfortunate speaker. The text sets lyrics in five different languages (French, Spanish, Italian, Arabic, and English) to the Turkish melody, thereby reflecting the historical and geographic trajectory of the Sephardim, as well as the singer's own multi-lingual upbringing (Ladino, French, English).[27]

Fel sharah canet betet masha	Walking down the street was
la signorina aux beaux yeux noirs	the girl with the beautiful dark eyes,
come la luna etait la sua facha,	her face was like the moon,
qui eclairait le boulevard.	which illumined the boulevard.
Velevo parlar shata metni	I wanted to speak to her, but she insulted me,
Because her father was a la gare	because her father was nearby, at the station.
E con su umbrella darabetni	So she struck me with her umbrella
En rosponse a mon bonsoir.	in response to my "good evening."
"Perque my dear tedrabini,	"Why, my dear, do you hit me,
quando yo to amo kitir?	when I love you so much?
And if you want tehebini	And if you want to show me your love,
Il n'ya pas lieu de nous conquerir.	No cause will stand in our way.
Tout a la notte ahlanbiki,	All night I'll wait for you,
et meme jusqu'au lever du jour,	even until the sunrise,
and every morning astankai	and every morning after,
pour le voeu de notre amour."	for the sake of our love."

Figure 1.12: *Fel sharah canet betet masha,* as recorded by Gloria Levy on the 1958 Folkways LP, *Sephardic Folk Songs.*

The Arab Middle East and Arab-American Diaspora

The Jewish performances establish that *Üsküdara* disseminated into the Arab Middle East at some point and indeed, the melody is also well-known among musicians of the Arab diaspora in the United States. The ethnomusicologist Ali Jihad Racy (b. 1943), an outstanding performer of

Arab music, told me that he first learned the tune during his youth in his native Lebanon (p.c., 2003). Although he believes it probably traveled to the Arab countries with the Ottomans, again perhaps as a Janissary march, it was adapted there to new lyrics both sacred and secular. He explained that during the early twentieth century Protestant missionaries working in the Levant began setting Christian devotional texts to local melodies to attract a larger following. Such was the case with *Üsküdara,* whose melody became the basis both for a Lebanese hymn and a secular Arab song called *Yia banat Iskandaria* (or *Benat Eskandaria*) [The girls of Alexandria].

In 1957, the Egyptian immigrant composer and vocalist Muhammad al-Bakkar (also transliterated Mohammed El-Bakkar) recorded a well-known version of *Yia banat Iskandaria* with his "Oriental Ensemble" on the LP *Port Said: Music of the Middle East* (Rasmussen 1992:76, 79, see also 1997:16), which further popularized the tune among Arab, Turkish, Armenian, and Greek communities in the United States. Since at least the 1980s, however, it has also circulated within and through Middle Eastern and Near Eastern music ensembles at American universities, where it attests to Racy's teaching legacy. As a professor and ensemble director at UCLA Racy transmitted the song to his students, such as ethnomusicologists Scott Marcus (University of California at Santa Barbara) and Anne Rasmussen (College of William & Mary), who in turn have passed it on to their own students and colleagues. My own first encounter with the song came in this form, when Rasmussen taught it to the Middle Eastern music ensemble at the University of Texas at Austin, where we were both visiting professors in 1991–92. The Arab version usually adopted by such ensembles, which typically emulate the mixed indigenous and Western European instrumentation of an early twentieth-century Arab orchestra, or *firqah* (*ud, nai, kanun, riqq, darabuka, def,* violin, violoncello, accordion), is often instrumental, features a lively introduction that constitutes a variation of the song, and is rendered over the Arab rhythmic mode *maqsūm* (Turk. *düyek;* Fig. 1.13, CD 1.8).[28]

The Urban Balkans: Sacred and Secular Variants

In Macedonia, Bulgaria, Bosnia, and Serbia *Üsküdara* flourished as an urban song with various romantic texts, most related to each other but unconnected to the Turkish original. During the early 1900s it circulated in Serbia, Bosnia, and Macedonia as a Europeanized *sevdalinka* entitled

Maqsum

Figure 1.13: An Arab rendition of the *Üsküdara* tune often performed by Middle and Near Eastern music ensembles at U.S. colleges and universities.

Ruse kose, curo, imaš [What fair hair you have, girl], or some variant thereof. This bears some explanation.

According to Katsarova (1973:126–27), in Albania the tune was known in at least three contexts. In Korçe it circulated as a lyrical, homophonic love song whose words incorporate typical, gendered metaphorical imagery (nightingales, roses), as well as the Turkish expression *"aman,"* a legacy of the Ottoman presence (Fig. 1.14). In northern Albania it was sung in the Geg dialect as a school song about fishing (Fig. 1.15). The musicologist Ramadan Sokoli supplied Katsarova with this variant, which he remembered from his school days in Shkodër, where the Bune river referred to in the song is located. Curiously, Shkodër (or Skadar) was once, like Üsküdar, called Scutari, although "going to Üs-

Mu në bashtën tënde	In your yard a nightingale sings,
të kendon bilbili, aman,	aman, aman,
aman,	
na sevdaja jote çupe e vogël,	for your love, young woman, a rose
çeli trandafili.	blooms.

Figure 1.14: *Mu në bashtën.* Katsarova 1973:126; originally published in D. Pjeter's *Lyra Shiptare* (Tirana, 1940). Translated from the Albanian by Irena Kola.

küdar" or Scutari does not seem to be a theme in the Albanian variants. Rather, in Shkodër the melody was also popularized as a Muslim devotional song or hymn called an *ilahi*. Such devotional songs, originally with Arabic texts, were brought to Albania by the Ottomans and sung by Muslim dervishes, prompting Katsarova to ask if *Üsküdara* did not perhaps originate within an Ottoman dervish order.

   In nearby Bosnia such *ilahije* (sing. *ilahija*) played an important role in the musical life of both Bosnian Muslims and Jews. Ethnomusicologist Ankica Petrović asserts that *ilahija* melodies were often adopted into the religious musical practices of Sarajevo's Sephardim (2000:968). Bosnian Muslim mothers sang such *ilahije* as lullabies, thereby also instilling the moral and ethical values of Islam in their children (Laušević 1996:124). At

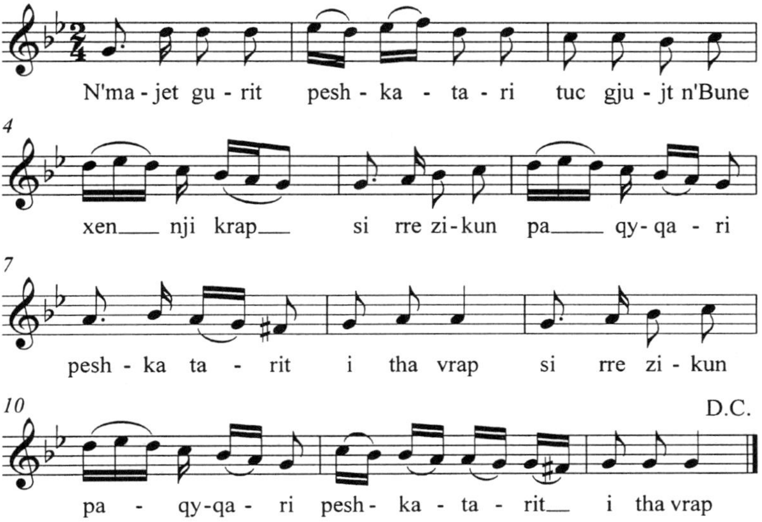

N'maje t'gurit peshkatari tuc,

gjujt n'Bune xen nji krap,

si rrezikun pa qyqari
peshkatarit i tha vrap,
si rrezikun pa qyqari
peshkatarit i tha vrap.

On the top of a rock sits a
    fisherman,
his feet in the river Bune, he catch-
    es a krap,
when the poor fish saw the danger,
"Run," it said to the fisherman,
when the poor fish saw the danger,
"Run," it said to the fisherman.

Figure 1.15: Albanian school song recorded by Katsarova (1973:127) from the Albanian musicologist Ramadan Sokoli. Translated from the Albanian by Irena Kola.

the same time, it was not uncommon for Muslim villagers to set secular lyrics to *ilahija* tunes (A. Petrovic 1988). The *sevdalinka,* an urban, melancholic love song genre, arose in this manner; many *sevdalinka* melodies originated as *ilahije.* The very designation *"sevdalinka"* derives from the Turkish *"sevda,"* denoting love, amorous yearning, passion, and even depression. In their sentiments and aesthetic, then, *sevdalinka* texts strongly resembled the Ottoman *şarkı.* In fact, they were called *turčija*-s (Turkish-style songs; 'singing in the Turkish manner') until the turn of the century (Petrovic 1993:3).

The *sevdalinka*'s expressive, melismatic vocal melodies were sung by professional musicians at Bosnia's aristocratic Muslim courts and urban *kafana*-s well into the twentieth century (Petrovic 1993:3). The songs were rendered as solos, or with solo *saz* accompaniment—a further link to the Turkish minstrelsy tradition surrounding our first example. With time the genre became Europeanized. Non-tempered intervals associated with Turkish modality became tempered, and the formerly heterophonic texture replaced by precise playing techniques and four-part polyphony, as melodies were harmonized with chords. In addition, the *saz* was supplanted by small ensembles of accordion, clarinet, violin, *tambura*, and bass, and then during the socialist era, by *tamburitza* orchestras. The genre thus never disappeared from the Bosnian soundscape; in fact, during the recent war it experienced a new upsurge in popularity as a symbol of Bosnian and especially, Bosnian Muslim identity (see Laušević 1996). "*Ruse kose*" is somewhat of a *sevdalinka* standard, appearing in many *sevdalinka* songbooks and at *sevdalinka* websites.[29] The version presented

"Ruse kose, curo, imaš, žališ li   "Oh, what fair hair you have, girl,
  ih ti?"   do you regret it?"
"Aman, da ih žalim ne bi ti ih   *"Aman,* if I regretted it, I wouldn't
  dala, da ih mrsiš ti!"   have given it to you, to
                                             entangle you in it."

"Crne oči, curo, imaš, žališ li   "Oh, what black eyes you have, girl,
  gi ti?"   do you regret them?"
"Aman, da gi žalim, ne bi ti gi   *"Aman,* if I regretted them, I
  dala, da gi piješ ti."   wouldn't have given them to
                                             you, for you to drink in."

"Medna usta, curo, imaš, žališ   "Oh, what a honey-sweet mouth
  li gi ti?"   you have, girl, do you regret
                                             it?'

"Aman, da gi žalim, ne bi ti gi   *"Aman,* if I regretted it, I wouldn't
  dala, da gi ljubiš ti."   have given it to you, for you to
                                             love."

Figure 1.16: *Ruse kose, curo, imaš. Sevdalinka* popular in Bosnia, Serbia, and Croatia, published in a *sevdalinka* songbook.[30]

in Figure 1.16, provided to me by Marija Marković, a student from the former Yugoslavia, was taken from one such songbook. Its text is a romantic repartee between a young man and woman, much like that found in some variants of the Greek *Ehasa mantili* and *Apo kseno* songs.

In Macedonia *Üsküdara* circulated with a similar text in an essentially identical style. Katsarova notes that the actress and vocalist Zorka (aka. Zora) Drempetić recorded the *sevdalinka* under the title *Ala, tsuro, kose imash* [Oh, girl, what hair you have] and offers the illustration you see in Figure 1.17, transcribed by the Bulgarian ethnographer and choreologist Anna Ilieva. A related performance by the same singer (misidentified in the liner notes as Zorka Drebetic), dating from 1924, appears on a recent compilation of historical recordings from Macedonia re-released by the Greek firm FM Records (CD 1.10).[31] Here Drempetić is accompanied by the M. Karnevac folk ensemble featuring accordion, bass, and clarinet.[32] While the vocal style is lyrical and bel canto, the marked change in tempo evident between the orchestral introduction and verse recalls the older, Sarajevo style of *sevdalinka* performance, in which the *saz* provided a pulsed, rhythmic introduction and interlude, but the song verses them-selves were rendered in a rhythmically elastic or unpulsed fashion. The

"*Ala, tsuro, kose imash,*   "Oh, what hair you have, do you
   zhalish li gi ti?"   regret it?
"*Aman, da gi zhalim, ne bi ti*   "*Aman,* if I regretted it, I wouldn't
   gi dala, da gi roshish ti."   have given it to you, to
                                       tousle."

"*Ala, tsŭrni ochi imash,*   "Oh, what black eyes you have, do
   zhalish li gi ti?"   you regret them?"
"*Aman, da gi zhalim, ne bi ti*   "*Aman,* if I regretted them, I
   gi dala, da gi piyesh ti."   wouldn't have given them to
                                       you, to drink in."

"*Ala, medna usta imash,*   "Oh, what a honeyed mouth you
   zhalish li gi ti?"   have, do you regret it?
"*Aman, da gi zhalim, ne bi ti*   "*Aman,* if I regretted it, I wouldn't
   gi dala, da gi lyubish ti."   have given it to you, to love."

Figure 1.17: *Ala, tsuro, kose imash.* As sung by Zorka Drempetić. Transcribed by
Anna Ilieva. Originally published in Katsarova 1973:128–29.

sentimental, rubato, and lavishly ornamented accordion style resembles
that sometimes associated with the accompaniment of Italian love songs,

and the overall aesthetic is one of nostalgia and schmaltz frequently characterizing urban songs of this era.

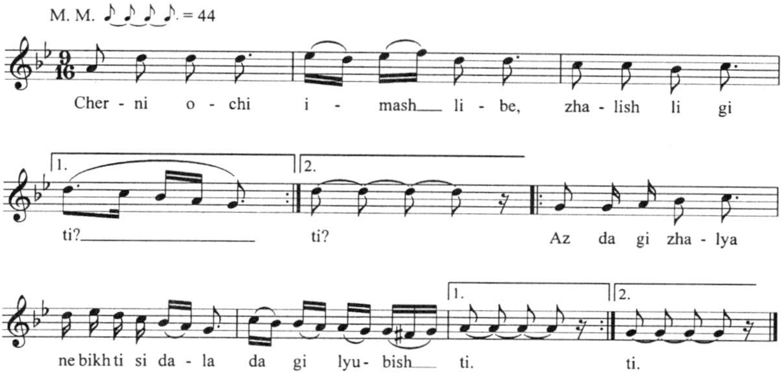

"Cherni ochi imash, libe,
    zhalish li gi ti?"
"Az da gi zhalya ne bikh ti
    dala, da gi lyubish ti."

"Tŭnka snaga imash, libe,
    zhalish li ya ti?"
"Az da ya zhala, ne bi ti ya
    dala, da ya kŭrshish ti."

"Usta cheresha imash, libe,
    zhalish li ya ti?"
"Az da ya zhala, ne bi ya dala,
    da ya tseluvash ti."

"You have dark eyes, love, do you
    regret them?"
"If I regretted them I wouldn't give
    them to you, for you to love."

"You have a slender waist, love,
    do you regret it?"
"If I regretted it I wouldn't give it
    to you, for you to bend."

"You have a mouth like a cherry,
    love, do you regret it?"
"If I regretted it I wouldn't give it
    to you, for you to kiss."

Figure 1.18: *Cherni ochi imash, libe.* As published in Katsarova 1973:129.

Bulgaria's relationship with the song was particularly longstanding. Katsarova writes that, according to testimony supplied by elderly townspeople in several major urban centers, by the 1870s, every town and city in the country was "drowning in this melody"; it sounded, she says, from "every corner, from every window." By 1912 it was regularly heard in the northern Bulgarian cities of Pleven and Vratsa at evening women's work bees and outdoor celebrations in a lively 9/16 dance song variant that was also preferred by Vratsa's Romani musicians, who apparently per-formed it to accompany a particular *horo* called "forward-backward" in

Chapter 1

which the dancers alternated a step in one direction with two in the other (Katsarova 1973:129–30; Fig. 1.18).[33]

M. M. ♩ = 110

Ah, Ma - ri - ke pi - len - tse, ot ka - de si ti,

ti? Az sam ot Pa - na - gyu - ri - shte, lyu - bish li me

ti, az sam ot Pa - na - gyu - ri - shte, lyu - bish li me ti?

"*Ah, Marike, pilentse ot kade si ti?*" "Ah, little Mariya, little chicken, where are you from?"

"*Az sam ot Panagyurishte, lyubish li me ti?*" "I'm from Panagyurishte, do you love me?"

"*Imash, mome, cherni ochi, davish li gi men?*" "You have, girl, dark eyes, are you giving them to me?"

"*I da imam i da nemam, ne ti gi davam, ne gi davam, ne gi davam, da gi lyubish ti.*" "Whether I have them or whether I don't, I'm not giving them not giving them, not giving them, to you to love."

"*Imash, mome, ravna snaga, davash li ya men?*" "You have, girl, a slender figure, are you giving it to me?"

"*I da imam, ne ya davam da ya lyubish ti.*" "Even if I've got one, I'm not giving it to you to love."

Figure 1.19: *Ah, Marike, pilentse.* Sung by thirty-five-year-old Stiliyan Dimitrunkov, Samokov, May 1935. Published in Katsarova 1973:128 and Stoin 1975:454, No. 877.

Likewise, in 1935 folklorist Vasil Stoin encountered and transcribed the song in the southwest Bulgarian town of Samokov (in the Pirin-Macedonia region), where it circulated as a duple-meter dance song entitled *Ah, Marike, pilentse* [Ah, little Mariya, little chicken] (Katsarova 1973:128; Fig. 1.19).

Such "foreign" songs were the popular music of their day, gaining and losing currency rapidly. In this case, however, two events kept *Üsküdara* alive for Bulgarian audiences. In 1945 it was performed by a visiting mixed choir from Radio Belgrade (Katsarova 1973:124). Shortly there-after, it was also popularized in the sound track to a black and white Yugoslav film, *Ciganka* (Gypsy Girl; 1953), directed by Vojislav Nanović and adapted by Aleksandar Vuco from the well-known play *Koštana* by Serbian author Borisav (Bora) Stanković (1876–1927). First published in Belgrade in 1902, the play recounts how a turn-of-the-century gentleman from the south Serbian town of Vranje—Stanković's birthplace—loses his heart and fortune to a Romani *çengi* (cf. Sugarman 2003:101).[34] Stanković subtitles his stage work a "play from the life of Vranje with songs" (*komad iz vranjskog zhivota s pesmama*), and indeed, Koštana, a "Gypsy singer and dancer," and her father Grkljan, a "Gypsy instrumentalist," perform several well-known songs throughout the script. Koštana sings a textual variant of *Ruse kose* in the second scene (Fig. 1.20).[35]

Mirjano, oj Mirjano,	"Mirjana, oh Mirjana,
imaš ruse kose, Mirjano!	what fair hair you have, Mirjana!
Daj da gi mrsim ja,	Give it to me so I can tousle it,
daj, Mirjano, daj, daj!	give it here, Mirjana, give it, give it to me!
Mirjano, oj Mirjano,	Mirjana, oh, Mirjana,
imaš čarne oči, Mirjano!	what dark eyes you have, Mirjana!
Daj da gi pejem ja,	Give them to me so I can drink them in, Mirjana,
daj, Mirjano, daj, daj!	give them here, Mirjana, give them, give them to me!"

Figure 1.20: *Mirjano, oj, Mirjano.* As published in Borisav Stanković's *Koštana* (Stanković 1966:41).

Karen Peters has traced this variant to the fourth *Rukovet* (1890) of the Serbian composer and musicologist Stevan Mokranjac, which is subtitled *Iz Moje Domovine: "Mirjana"* (2002:351–52).[36] She provides the complete text used by Mokranjac (excerpted here in Fig. 1.21), which closely resembles the Bulgarian, Macedonian, and Serbian variants provided above with three exceptions: the young woman whom the

narrator addresses is given a name, Mirjana; a new refrain is appended to
the usual lyrics; and this refrain replaces the young woman's anticipated
response. Thus the song is transformed from a dialogue to a monologue.
Citing the work of Serbian musicologist Milenko Živković, Peters
indicates that the poet Dragutin J. Ilić created the refrain at Mokranjac's
request (Peters 2002:351n28). Because a variant of this refrain also
appears in *Koštana,* Peters suggests that Stanković's source for this
material was Mokranjac's *Rukovet.* She further notes that although
Živković was able to place *Mirjano, oj Mirjano* in Prizren (in Kosovo) as
early as 1882, where it was known as a *čoček avasi* [*čoček* melody] and
from where it supposedly traveled to Vranje, its melody, at least as the
song appears in Mokranjac's *Rukovet,* is not that of *Üsküdara.* It is
therefore difficult to know exactly what melody Stanković had in mind
when he cited *Mirjano,* but at some point, perhaps with the release of
Ciganka, the play was performed with the *Ruse kose* lyrics and the Turkish
melody.[37]

Mirjano, oj Mirjano,	Mirjana, oh Mirjana,
imaš ruse kose, Mirjano.	what fair hair you have, Mirjana.
Daj da gi mrsim ja, oj!	Give it to me so I can tousle it, oh!
Refrain	**Refrain**
Daj, Mirjano, ruse kose,	Give me, Mirjana, your fair hair,
daj, daj, daj,	give it here, give it, give it to me,
daj da gi mrsim ja,	give it to me so I can tousle it,
izgoro', Mirjano, za tebe!	I'm burning, Mirjana, for you!

Figure 1.21: *Mirjano, oj Mirjano* (excerpt). Peters 2002:352, after Mokranjac
1957:39–41.

In 1931, Serbian composer Petar Konjović (1883–1970) created an
opera called *Koštana,* based on Stanković's play, which is considered one
of the country's best (Djurić-Klajn 2006).[38] The play was later also the
source for two Yugoslav television movies by the same name, released in
1962 (directed by Jovan Konjović) and 1976 (directed by Slavoljub
Stefanović-Ravasi).[39] In the 1953 film the part of Koštana is played by
Elma Karlowa, but her singing voice is provided by Drempetić.[40]
Katsarova believes that it was this film which probably inspired my next
example.[41]

American Orientalism

During the early 1950s, *Üsküdara* was recorded by the black American vocalist and dancer Eartha Kitt, who toured Greece, Turkey, and Egypt with great success at that time. Like the *çengi*-s, Kitt was celebrated for her "sultry, exotic" appeal; the jacket notes to an RCA Victor LP featuring her work suggest that "her engimatic face, haunting voice and tantalizing dances made her the most popular entertainer in the Near East," and her rendition of our song on this album, dubbed *Uska Dara,* plays up its orientalist associations.[42] Kitt sings the song in Turkish, with its original text, but in between verses narrates her own interpretation of its tale: an unnamed woman, flirting coquettishly from behind her veil, erotically feeds her male secretary candy from the handkerchief that she finds on their way to Üsküdar and fills with Turkish delight (Fig. 1.22). The accompanying orchestra contributes to the caricature by deliberately playing slightly out of tune, thus conveying their misguided perception of a Turkish ensemble's heterophonic texture and use of untempered intervals. Certain features of rhythmic and clarinet styling refer to klezmer, thereby conflating the Jewish and Turkish traditions in a single orientalist package.

First Section

Üsküdara is a little town in Turkey.
And in the old days, many women had male secretaries.
Oh well, that's Turkey.

Second Section

They take a trip from Üsküdara in the rain, and on the way they fall in love. He's wearing a stiff collar and full dress suit. She looks at him longingly through her veil, and casually feeds him candy.

Ooooh, those Turks!

Figure 1.22: Eartha Kitt's spoken narrative between verses of her *Uska Dara,* as performed on *RCA Victor Presents Eartha Kitt,* ca. 1953.

From the 1950s through the 1970s, a flourishing multiethnic Greek and Near Eastern nightclub scene in major American cities on the East Coast prompted numerous Greek instrumentalists and singers to emigrate to the United States, where they pursued careers as performers and recording artists. As Anne Rasmussen (1992:65–70) has convincingly demonstrated, such clubs appropriated visual, choreographic, culinary, and musical stereotypes of the Orient to create a commercial venue that targeted a cosmopolitan American and even international clientele. Ensembles dominated by Western European instrumentation but employing traditional instruments selectively to give the music a Near Eastern tinge performed popular melodies with simple harmonizations in a style that two of Rasmussen's interlocutors, Eddie Kochak and Hakki Obadia, described as "Ameraba," or, "music with that Oriental flavor, geared to the American ear" (1992:70). Bellydancers became an essential entertainment highlight, prompting an amateur fitness fad among American women and a spate of bellydance recordings whose jacket notes and cover imagery abound in exotic symbolism (1992:67–69, 76–80). The musicians and dancers themselves hailed from various ethnic backgrounds, whether Arab, Greek, Armenian, Turkish, or even Anglo-American, as the emigré professionals took on local pupils.

Kitt's *Uska Dara* is an early illustration of what later became a major trend, as American immigrant communities were increasingly inspired to take pride in their ethnic heritage during the 1960s (Rasmussen 1992:79). Nor was it the only recording of the song to emerge from the nightclub context. An instrumental version by the Greek-American clarinetist Gus Vali with his Casbah Ensemble appears on the 1963 LP *Dance Bellyrina, Dance!,* and a version with new Greek lyrics, *Mi mou ksanapis yia agapi* [Don't speak to me again of love], was recorded by Greek vocalist Betty Daskalaki on *Boujouki ke Kaymi No. 5,* one of several bouzouki-style rebetica recordings produced on the Standard Colonial label during this period.[43] Muhammad al-Bakkar's *Yia banat Iskandaria,* on the *Port Said* album mentioned above, is particularly noteworthy as its jacket cover pictures a (decidedly Anglo-American-looking) bellydancer wearing a veiled headdress, pasties, and a diaphanous, hip-hugging, chiffon split skirt, set against a curtained backdrop whose tent-like interior is strewn with pillows and a prominently displayed hookah. In Rasmussen's words, "The allure, the titillating exoticism, and the carnal pleasures that accompanied a distant imagination of the Middle East were a brilliant advertising strategy for the music, the dance, and the environment of the nightclub" (1992:81). In the United States, recordings of *Üsküdara* clearly contributed to the oriental imaginary of a growing popular culture industry with transnational implications, as illustrated by the next several examples.

Transnational Ethnopop

More recently, *Üsküdara* achieved new popularity as an ethnopop hit entitled *Raspiči-opiči* (Fig. 1.23; CD 1.11) by the Croatian band Vatrogasci, or Firemen, which has recorded numerous parodies of Serbian and Bosnian *novokomponovana narodna muzika* [newly composed folk music; hereafter NCFM].[44] This genre, which combines the electronic instrumentation of European and American pop music with Balkan dance meters, Serbo-Croatian texts, and Turkish modes, ornamentation, vocal timbre, and rhythms, arose in Yugoslavia during the 1950s and '60s, dominating the popular music scene by the 1980s. Most of the parodies set new postsocialist lyrics to internationally recognized pop songs performed with NCFM styling. A broad spectrum of substyles falls under the NCFM rubric; Vatrogasci's Croatian parody, however, targets the so-called "oriental" subgenre that developed among Bosnian performers in the 1980s, identified by its "Turkish" qualities: in this case, a modal melody, melismatic vocal ornamentation, and a pronounced, tremolo-like vocal vibrato (see Rasmussen 2002:123–38 and this volume).[45]

Verses 1 & 2

Četvrt kruha, jogurat, pašteta,

tezhak zhivot zhivim ja.
Do čim ja sam uzeo Mercedes,
Pa da gonim ja.

Svakog prvog operem se fino,

pa na cagu krenem ja.

Puscam business kad mi djecki dodju,
odlazim u grad.

Refrain

Rah! Rah! Raspiči! Samo dobro opiči,
i tadi ono što radim ja.
Rah! Rah! Raspiči! Samo dobro opiči,
i čagaj ludo sa nogama.

Verses 1 & 2

A quarter loaf of bread, yogurt, paté—
it's a difficult life I'm living.
So I took a Mercedes,
in order to drive it.

Every first of the month I bathe well,
to take off down the highway.

I'm talking business when my friends arrive—I'm going into the city (i.e., downtown).

Refrain

Rah! Rah! Raspiči! Getting only good projects going,
and I do what I'm doing.
Rah! Rah! Raspiči! Only good knocks,
and dance wildly with your legs.

Verse 3   **Verse 3**

Ima jedna čagerica ljuta,   There is one hot girl—
pleše nogama k'o ja: she dances with her legs as I do:
masna kosa, majica bez leda,   greasy hair, a backless shirt, sweaty
kozha znojava.   skin.

Refrain   **Refrain**

Figure 1.23: *Raspići-opići.* Performed by Vatrogasci on their album *Vatrogasno Zabava Vol. 3: Hit-Parada,* ca. 2001.

Raspići's male protagonist lives humbly, but aspires to the playboy lifestyle associated with the urban, postsocialist noveau riche businessman, showing off his Mercedes and zooming downtown in pursuit of hot girls and a wild dance. This figure signifies both the stereotypical image of a male NCFM superstar and the former communist bigwig who frequented the bars and nightclubs in which NCFM was listened and danced to, and whose wealth often derived from underworld activity. No good English translation exists for *opići,* which is a crude Croatian slang term for hitting, banging, or knocking.[46] In this context, the "wild leg dance" might refer to sex, or to the shimmying movements of *čoček,* a Yugoslav Romani women's solo dance whose choreography, descended from the art of the *çengi*-s, figured prominently in NCFM dancing.[47]

In text and style, then, *"Raspići"* parodies the "oriental" and erotic character of many NCFM songs. It is also an assertion of difference that, in the context of the Bosnian and Kosovo wars, and subsequent EU aspirations, distances an increasingly west European-oriented Croatia from the Balkan and Turkish associations evident in NCFM.[48]

But *Raspići* holds an additional level of significance; its title is a pun, and the piece a remake of *Rasputin,* a Euro-disco song by Boney M., a Caribbean disco-reggae band that toured Moscow in 1978 and, in the words of the British historian and journalist Stephen Ashley (1994:158), which was marketed throughout Eastern Europe as "the voice of the Third World" and a "genuine collective enterprise" during the early 1980s (Troitsky 1987:46). Like the contemporaneous Swedish quartet ABBA, Boney M.'s members did not so much cultivate fame as individual superstar rock idols but as a group. Although they worked in Germany and other western European locations and were created and produced by the German pop vocalist Frank Farian, of key importance is that the band's four members (three female, 1 male) were black, born in the West Indies and thus outside the bourgeois West, and released some songs, such as *No more chain gang,* calling for black civil rights. From the Soviet perspective they therefore represented and were giving voice to the downtrodden masses that socialism would liberate and uplift.

Rasputin originally appeared on Boney M.'s 1978 album *Nightflight to Venus;* it is currently available on any of several Boney M. "best of" or "greatest hits" compact discs. On the original LP the band segues into *Rasputin* from the album's first, title track, resulting in an unusual disco medley over ten minutes in length. Although one might tentatively venture that *Rasputin* was inspired by the 1913 harmonization of *Üsküdara* published in Moscow (Fig. 1.2 above), Boney M. may actually have learned the tune from the Yugoslav wife of band member Bobby Farrell.[49] Employing a fake Russian accent, *Rasputin*'s gravelly-voiced narrator relates a mythologized biography of Grigory Yefimovich Rasputin (1869–1917), a Siberian peasant mystic and healer who served as spiritual advisor to the Empress Alexandra, wife of Tsar Nicholas II.[50] Desperate to cure her youngest child and only son, Alexei, from hemophilia, Alexandra believed that Rasputin had been sent to her by God, and that he would guide the royal family in their reign (Riasanovsky 1977:466–67). Rumors surrounding Rasputin's purported psychic powers, miraculous healing capabilities, and sexual prowess sprang up both during his lifetime and after his assassination at the hands of Russian artistocrats in December 1916. He was vilified as a power-hungry womanizer, an unseemly influence on the crown, and the Tsarina's paramour. "Rah! Rah! Rasputin! Lover of the Russian queen" and "Rah! Rah! Rasputin! Russia's greatest love machine," the ballad's refrain declares. In a clear link with Kitt's *Uska Dara* (yet another possible source of inspiration), the song concludes, in the narrator's growling, accented, spoken baritone, "Oooooh, those Russians!"

According to Timothy W. Ryback, author of *Rock around the Bloc,* the Soviet government embraced disco in the late 1970s as a means of drawing the attention of young people away from rock music (1990:159–61). In contrast to rock musicians, disco stars sported a more elegant image; male artists dressed in leisure suits and were relatively clean shaven, with shorter haircuts. In addition, their song lyrics were rarely as politically explosive. Consequently, Melodiya began to press Western disco albums and hundreds of discotheques were established throughout Russia. Domestic disco music, too, received unprecedented support. The Latvian studio band Zodiak released an album of "synthesized electronic disco music" called *Disko Alliance* immediately prior to Boney M.'s visit. While working on my Master's thesis concerning Soviet popular music in 1984–85, I was surprised to find *Rasputin,* together with Boney M.'s

Nightflight to Venus, on the flip side of what was surely a pirated Zodiak cassette that I ordered from the Evgeniya Koneva "Russian and International Songs Co., Inc." in Jersey City.[51] In the 1960s and 1970s, it was common for Soviet pop and rock recordings to circulate through *magnitizdat,* a kind of cassette culture indicative of the second economy. That *Rasputin* appears "hidden" on the Zodiak cassette speaks to the band's great popularity among Soviet audiences and their limited access to recordings produced on Western labels (or relicensed by Melodiya), whether for reasons of expense or availability. However, it also signifies the relatively ambivalent position occupied by Western pop artists in Soviet politics, even when the band concerned had been more or less sanctioned by cultural administrators. Thus, Gosconcert (the Soviet state concert agency), probably fearing unruly fan behavior, asked Boney M. not to perform *Rasputin* at their Moscow concert. The group complied, playing only the song's refrain (Ryback 1990:161).[52] Yet there is no question that the band was viewed favorably within the Soviet bloc. Even in 1990, the Bulgarian Socialist Party, then newly re-formed from the remnants of the Bulgarian Communist Party, contracted Boney M. to perform in Sofia at the gala rock concert that concluded its political campaign, shortly following the transition (Ashley 1994).

Just as Boney M.'s rendition mocks the mystical, politically influential Rasputin and by extension, the imperialist regime that favored him, using the Turkish melody as a signifier of his orientalist, mysterious powers, so too the Croatian parody comments on the corrupt power of the socialist legacy. And just as Boney M. transforms Kitt's exoticized "Oh, those Turks" into an equally exoticized "Oh, those Russians," so too does the Croatian parody translate the disco dance beat of the Boney M. song into the ethnopop dance beat of NCFM, but with contrasting political agendas. Both versions represent exoticizing gestures. But whereas the Boney M. version eschews the orientalism of Rasputin's Russian imperium in favor of Soviet socialism, the Croatian version, through parody, holds socialism responsible for the emergence of a Yugoslav, and by extension, Balkan Orient predicated on the region's Ottoman heritage and signified by NCFM's Turkish and Romani musical qualities— qualities derided by the Balkans' urban intellectuals for decades as kitsch or worse. The shortages and poor quality of material goods, the restrictions and isolationist policies characterizing late socialism further positioned the Balkans on Europe's periphery. The reckless consumer consumption, brutal materialism, crime, corruption, and licentiousness indicative of the transition toward democracy and capitalism, this song suggests, are the legacy of socialist politics. Such excesses, personnified and stereotyped in the figure of the song's protagonist, have only strengthened the prevailing view that the Balkans are *in* Europe but not *of* it. The Croatian song distances itself from the orientalist scenario developed under socialism's auspices in favor of a more Western European orientation, while at the same time acknowledging (for this is the power of the parody) that all that is signified by NCFM is embedded in Croatian identity of the Yugoslav past. Thus the song acknowledges Croatia's participation in a Yugoslav Orient, while simultaneously representing a decided disassociation from it.

Orbiting the Ottoman Ecumene

So what can this comparative exercise tell us about music and interculturality in the Balkans and beyond? Following *Üsküdara*'s trail maps the movement of populations and cultural influences both within the Balkans and transnational contexts. It also highlights the role of minority groups—especially Roma and Jews—in disseminating and reinterpreting Ottoman Turkish repertory and musical styles in new, syncretic local forms. In contrast to socialist scholarship on Balkan culture, which frequently depicts the Ottoman period as an era of cultural stagnation, this study reveals it as one of intense creativity and interchange resulting in numerous new genres wherever Turkish music-making touched local performance practice. Socialist cultural policy may have denied the Ottoman legacy in the national musical heritage of some Balkan countries, but the fact that *Üsküdara* has circulated through so many Balkan and Near Eastern communities, at home and in diaspora, is evidence of the cultural eclecticism and musical wealth that this influence fostered. The Balkans have always been a cosmopolitan place, with well-established avenues of cultural interplay bearing transnational implications. As Katsarova (1973:129) observes in regard to the relationship between Serbian and Bulgarian variants of *Ruse kose*:

> Where did the text performed by Bulgarians and Serbs arise? Who took it from whom? Did we take it from the Serbs or did they from us? An exchange of songs has existed between the two countries for ages, [one] made easier in the past by the free mingling resulting from the absence of borders—visits, weddings, fairs, the interchange of Gypsy orches-tras.[53]

Thus what were once Ottoman orbits of trade, commerce, transhumant herding, military conquest, demographic shift, and political authority have been transmuted today into Balkan cultural circuits, facilitated literally by the electronic circuits of mass mediated technology. Finally, whereas *Üsküdara's* oldest renditions appear in genres aimed at carving out regional musical emblems *vis à vis* Ottoman Turkey, today's Balkan ethnopop, which draws on similar sources, seems to signify a similar emergent regionalism within the context of an impending new dominion: that of the EU.

This, at least, was my original thesis. But Adela Peeva's recent film documentary, *Whose Song is This?*, which was released in Europe as I finished researching this study, tells a parallel but much more harrowing tale.[54] Tracing *Üsküdara's* steps through the Balkans at the turn of the millennium, Peeva finds that while all nations call the song their own, within certain communities these claims embed virulent ethnonationalist sentiments rooted especially in the local texts that the tune conjures up. On the one hand, for Sarajevo Bosnians, it remains a beloved *sevdalinka* whose poetic text, suffused with evocative metaphors of love and Islam, remain a point of national pride (Fig. 1.24):

| "Look at me, Anatolian girl, in the name of the Prophet Mohammed! And I will sing love songs to you. | I will give you a drink of rose syrup, to wash your sighs away. I'll wash you in dew, my flower, and cover you with silk, my love." |

Figure 1.24: Bosnian *sevdalinka* text sung to the *Üsküdara* melody in Adela Peeva's film documentary *Whose Song is This?*

"It is a true Sarajevo song. No one else sings these lyrics," remarks the celebrated *sevdalinka* vocalist Emina Zečaj, in an interview with Peeva. A Bosnian accordionist friend of Peeva's further observes that the song signifies the ecumenical and multicultural atmosphere so indicative of Yugoslav Bosnia: "This is a Bosnian song. It is so beautiful, I have no words. Everyone—Catholic, Orthodox, Muslim—we all have loved and protected it because it is a nice Bosnian song. It brings East and West together." Indeed, when his band performs the song for Peeva, it does so in a style that reflects such a merger: Turkish and Islamic references appear in the text and urban instrumentation (accordion, violin, clarinet) is employed, but the performance exhibits the rubato styling characteristic of the Sarajevo *sevdalinka* model described earlier.

On the other hand, for a Bosnian Muslim choir rehearsing in a Sarajevo *medresa*, or religious school, the song functions as a powerful symbol of post-Yugoslav religious freedom and the extent to which religion has become a nationalistic marker for some in the Bosniak community. The melody now sets a *kasida* (a devotional hymn of Arab heritage, like an *ilahija*) praising Allah, the lyrics for which were written, according to the choir director, by "a religious woman from Sarajevo some thirty to forty years ago." He explains that during the socialist era, people were thrown in jail for singing such songs. The choir performs it in the style of a Sufi *zikr*: in unison and with great passion, accompanied only by hand drums, heads nodding lightly in time with the music. Later, in conversation with Peeva about the recent war, the choir director observes that should someone threaten him, his faith, his family, or its honor, then he would find it possible to kill him. That religion, kinship, honor, and nation have traditionally been inextricably bound up with one another throughout much of the Balkans in ways that have sometimes prompted conflict is only underscored by the next scene.

In Skopje, Peeva plays the *kasida* version for a Sufi dervish named Baba Erol, who immediately recognizes the song's source as the Turkish *Üsküdara* (he sings her the Turkish words), but identifies this particular version of it as one of several "jihad songs" sung by Bosnian Muslims during times of war as an aid in Islamization. He singles out Srebrenica and Banja Luka as sites during the Bosnian war when this occurred, locales that in reality witnessed death camps and the massacre of Muslims. From his perspective Bosnian Muslims brought this fate upon themselves. In a racist remark rooted in the primordialist sentiments of ethnic purity, in turn stemming from religious purity, he observes: "In Bosnia there were 750,000 mixed marriages: Catholics, Orthodox, Muslims—in one tribe, in one house. How would you know if a child is Orthodox, Catholic or Muslim? The same mistake could have happened in Macedonia, too." And when Peeva airs the *kasida* for Serbian men relaxing in a tavern in Vranje, where she has gone in search of Koštana, they term it "theft," an "abuse," a "provocation," a "war appeal," and threaten to beat her until she is "flat on the floor."

Peeva's experience in her native Bulgaria is no better. Although I learned that during the socialist period, "You have black eyes, girl" (in duple meter) was taught throughout the country in the elementary school,[55] and while Karen Peters has documented its postsocialist performance by the amateur choir Grupa Ju in the southwest Bulgarian city of Blagoevgrad (2002),[56] Peeva finds that in the southeastern region of Strandzha, the song is a nationalistic anthem commemorating insurgents who rose against

Ottoman forces (Fig. 1.25). At an annual festival celebrating this rebellion, when she suggests that the song's origin is Turkish, local men tell her she risks being stoned or hung on a nearby oak tree until her "bones dry out." Later that evening a vicious grass fire erupts, engulfing the festival grounds in flames. As the film draws to a close the conflagration rages out of control, leaving the viewer with the chilling impression that the incendiary commentary interpolated into the film's narrative is similarly raging just below the surface of everyday life, masked merely by a thin veneer of musical artistry that is only seemingly shared. As the credits roll, the German *klezmer* band Di Grine Kuzine launches into a contemporary version of *Der Terk in Amerika*, a Jewish musical reference that subtly asks the viewer to contemplate how the sort of chauvinistic nationalism experienced and observed by Peeva also incited the Holocaust (which, notably, originated in Western Europe).[57] Thus a film that Peeva says she created to illustrate intercultural commonalities and to enable audiences to see the ridiculousness of nationalistic claims concludes on a serious and somewhat balkanizing note, for it presents the region as still potentially mired in the ethnonationalist views that helped inspire the wars in the former Yugoslavia during the 1990s (Wood 2004).

Yasen mesets vech izgryava nad balkanskata (zelenata) gora,	A clear moon is already rising above the Balkan (green) forest,
v tsyala Strandzha rob zapyava pesen nova yunashka.	throughout all of Strandzha slaves begin singing a new heroic song.
Bŭrzat, bŭrzat da pristignat predi petli sŭrmashi.	They hurry, hurry to arrive before the morning roosters crow.

Figure 1.25: *Yasen mesets vech izgryava.* As sung in Peeva's *Whose Song is This?*

One final point concerning *Üsküdara*'s ethnic derivation should throw the entire controversy into perspective. At least one Turkish scholar, Reşat Ekrem Koçu (1997), believes that the melody originated as a soldier's march popularized by a Scottish military regiment stationed in the so-called Selimiye or Üsküdar Barracks during the Crimean War (1853–56). In fact, the 8,000 British soldiers who died while fighting that war are buried in Üsküdar's cemetery.[58] Again, the song's first line might thus resonate with the unit's homeward trek to their Ottoman post. But Koçu proposes an alternative interpretation born of Sultan Mahmud's mid-nineteenth-century clothing reforms, which demanded that all soldiers and military officials adopt western European pants. The larger populace rejected this notion, but during the Crimean War, Padishah Abdülmecit demanded that all civilian men, too, take up the new pant style, starting with the government clerks. For Koçu, then, *Üsküdara* is not a "melody of love from a girl's mouth written for a young and beautiful *kâtip*," but "from the mouth of a trickster" poking fun at a clerk wearing the then unpopular pants (1997:446). One common variant of the last line, *"Kâtibime kolalı da gömlek ne güzel yaraşir"* [That starched shirt looks so good on my clerk], reads, *"Kâtibime setre de pantolon ne güzel yaraşir"* [Those trousers look so good on my clerk]. By extension, the song's opening phrase, "On the way to Üsküdar," might be interpreted as "pointing at the foreigners-with-pants living in the barracks there" (1997:46). This mocking text became grafted onto the Scottish march, resulting in the *türkü,* which was then disseminated throughout Istanbul as the hour-chiming theme in a wildly popular newly designed series of Swiss-model cuckoo clocks. Koçu explains:

> In those days clocks came to us from Europe . . . . Back then Swiss clocks were not common in Istanbul . . . .When the representative of a clock factory in Istanbul realized the popularity of this *türkü,* they decided to make an alarm clock—*türkü* clocks . . . . People responded to this as a craze. Even I remember from my childhood that whenever I went to smaller neighborhoods in Istanbul, there was not a chiming clock without the *Kâtibim türkü.* You could hear . . . the melody of the *Kâtibim türkü* [even] from behind the balconies of houses with peeling wooden coverings (1997:46).

That as a member of the honorable Buchanan clan, albeit an Irish branch, your American-born author could claim the "Scottish" *türkü* tune on behalf of her kinsmen across the waters, reveals, on the one hand, the absurd desperation and hyperinflated bombast behind such factional claims, and on the other, how the symbolic properties of an otherwise innocuous tune can be dangerously cultivated to suit a range of political agendas, such as those evident in the Serbian and Bulgarian commentaries. The disturbing persistence of such sentiments, even in the aftermath of the recent Yugoslav wars, warns of both centripetal and centrifugal tendencies at play in the Balkans, and that apparent transregional commonalities may conceal antithetical, and even contradictory or ironic local interpretations, trajectories, and realities.

Üsküdara's journey does not end here. Anne Rasmussen (p.c., 16
November 2004) has told me that she has heard versions of the song
performed in Indonesia, and that an Islamic singer named Hadad Alwi
recently recorded it, accompanied by an orchestra from Australia in an
arrangement by Dwiki Dharmawan, keyboard player for the Indonesian
fusion group Krakatau, using a thirteenth-century Arabic devotional text.
The tune also seems to be experiencing a renaissance in the Balkans themselves. Tom Solomon (p.c., 16 November 2004) has collected no less than
nine recent Turkish recordings (other than those cited above) in various
genres and styles, two of which are informally distributed "underground"
rap releases (one by a Turkish rap group in Munich).

Some of these ventures appear intentionally cosmopolitan and
multiethnic—perhaps politically so. An introductory instrumental passage
in the song *Reise nach Jerusalem* (*Journey to Jerusalem/Kudüs'e
Seyahat*), written by the German composers Ralph Siegel and Bernd
Meinunger and performed by the German-Turkish group Sürpriz for the
1999 Eurovision contest, at which it secured third place, echoes *Üsküdara*'s concluding phrase, whether coincidentally or purposefully.[59]
Jerusalem hosted the contest that year and the song's title, possibly a play
on "As I was going to Üsküdar," signifies the band's—and Germany's—journey to the event. According to Solomon (p.c., 9 May 2005),
the title is also that of a German children's game similar to the American
"musical chairs" (which the lyrics both make reference to and enact),
leading him to surmise that the song was meant to "invoke the innocence
of the children's game while making a plea for peace in the Middle
East."[60] Sung in German, Turkish, English, and Hebrew, and incorporating, from time to time, Turkish styling, in text and tune the song brokers
a musical rapprochement directed at Germany's relationship with Israel
and growing Turkish immigrant community.

A second illustration comes from Thessaloniki, Greece, which hosted
a collaborative concert called "The Sound of the Balkans" in early
November 2004.[61] This event showcased four bands, each of which
performed selections from their native Bulgaria, Greece, Serbia, or
Turkey. Perhaps inspired by Peeva's film, for the finale the bands
participated in a joint version of *Üsküdara,* each supplying a variant from
their homeland.

Arjun Appadurai suggests that, "If the genealogy of cultural forms is
about their circulation across regions, the history of these forms is about
their ongoing domestication into local practice" (1996:17). In this essay
I have tried to show how a song such as *Üsküdara* can be, as Appadurai
has shown for Indian cricket, a "site for the examination of how locality

emerges in a globalizing world, of how colonial processes underwrite contemporary politics, of how history and genealogy inflect one another, and of how global facts take local form" (1996:18). Therefore, as the song has disseminated throughout the Balkan peninsula and beyond, it has been transformed by local sensibilities and local performance practices indicative of specific historicities that are themselves in a certain tension with larger concerns holding sway in the world. The human capacity for creative agency is infinite, while always also dialectically engaged with a host of environmental considerations. Much of the material in the last third of this chapter suggests that nationalism remains a powerful and potentially destructive force for some regional populations. However, the last few examples, like so many others in this volume, demonstrate that, in the midst of the intensive sociopolitical changes accompanying EU formation and integration, there are those musicians who are actively chal-lenging their audiences to rethink "Balkan" as a place, subjectivity, and aesthetic sensibility that can and should be celebrated for both its many remarkable inherent commonalities and its equally abundant, intriguing, and captivating differences. My hope is that such efforts represent a new Balkan future.

Notes

1. Earlier versions of this article were delivered as papers for a conference on "Music and Cultural Identity" sponsored by the Institute for Art Studies at the Bulgarian Academy of Sciences in Sofia, Bulgaria in October 2002; a conference on "Interculturality in a Globalizing World" at the University of Illinois, Urbana-Champaign during November 2003; the University of Illinois Russian, East European, and Eurasian Center Noontime Scholars lecture series (February 2004); the 49th Annual Meeting of the Society for Ethnomusicology (November 2004); and the Northwestern University Musicology Colloquium series (May 2005). My sincere thanks to all those who offered further illustrations for and helpful commentary on this study, but especially Ivan Elezovic, Martha Mavroidi, Ali Jihad Racy, Joel Rubin, Sonia Seeman, Tom Solomon, Richard Tempest, and Ioannis Tsekouras.
2. Encyclopædia Britannica Online 2004.
3. This theory was suggested to me by Richard Tempest and Maria Todorova and is also alluded to in Peeva's 2003 film, *Chiya e taya Pesen* [Whose song is this] (see below).
4. Reinhard (2002:773) maintains that the preferred verse structure of the most important Ottoman song forms, including the *şarkı,* was four lines. In this context the third line was particularly important, serving as a link to the song's

climax and second half. As such this line bore its own name, *meyan*, and was highlighted by new melodic material, a modulation, a change in register, or other differentiating techniques. *Üsküdara*'s melodic structure seems to hint at this practice; the raised seventh scale degree (G♯), which is found in the third line (mm. 18–19), comprises part of a typical cadential passage in *makam Nihavent*, whose tonic is typically approached by the leading tone, but also marks a fleeting modulation to the lower tetrachord of *makam Hicaz* on scale degree 5 (E), and the lowest point in the vocal melody.

5. The word *obrabotki* (sing. *obrabotka*) in the title of this collection is significant, because it implies not just an arrangement, but a reworking or development of the musical material in order to improve it.

6. For more on the *çengiler* see And 1976; Feldman 2002; Seeman 2002; Sugarman 2003; and chapter seven in this volume.

7. See Stokes 2003 for an insightful study of Zeki Müren's role in Turkish popular culture.

8. One Turkish essay about *Üsküdara* that Seeman shared with me is accompanied by a pen and ink illustration depicting the scribe in exactly this fashion. Although he wears a fez on his head, the rest of his attire is Western European: a white shirt, black tie, and vest paired with tailored suit pants, a cutaway suitcoat with a boutonniere on the lapel, and black dress shoes. From the overturned umbrella that he wields as a walking stick, to the waxed and gently curled black mustache adorning his upper lip, to the pince-nez sitting astride his nose, he is the perfect image of the Turkish *alafranga* gentleman of the early twentieth century.

9. The *ince saz*, which was frequently associated with indoor performance of classical or semi-classical repertory, was distinguished from the *kaba saz*, or thick, loud, outdoor ensemble comprising *zurna* and *davul* (Brandl 1996:15–16; Morris 1981:83).

10. *Masters of Turkish Music, Volume 2*, Track 1.

11. Aka. Dikran Tchouhadjian, Tigran Ch'ukhajyan, Dichran Tchochadjian, Dihran Dzochatzian, Dihran Tsohatzian.

12. A selection from the operetta, although not that based on the *Üsküdara* melody, can be heard on *Lesbos Aiolis: Songs and Dances of Lesbos*, CD 1, Track 3. See Feldman 2001 for information about other prominent Armenian composers active in Ottoman musical life from the late 1600s until the Republican period.

13. Kordelion is a seaside suburb of Smyrna that was populated mostly by Greeks.

The Beglian Theater Company was probably also of Armenian origin and quite possibly based in Smyrna; Arsak Beglian, who died in Smyrna in 1923, was the most popular singer cast in the role of Leblébidji Hor-hor Agha (Solomonides 1954).

14. Phaleron (now old Phaleron) is a seaside suburb on the southern edge of Athens near the Illisos River delta. By the late nineteenth century it had developed into a bourgeois district in which wealthy Athenians resided during the summer. The Phaleron was an outdoor theater that catered to the cosmopolitan tastes of this

population, which began to embrace French operetta and other Western European music during the 1870s. The Athens Conservatory, like the Phaleron, was founded in 1871.

I thank my research assistant, Ioannis Tsekouras, for this and so much other helpful information from Greek-language sources for this section. See also Hatzipantazis 1986 and Sitheris 2000 for a more in-depth discussion.

15. In Athens it was performed through the 1880s, in Smyrna through the 1920s, and in Mytilene as late as 1934 (Dionysopoulos 2002:75n2; Sitheris 2000; Solomonides 1954).

16. See below: Katsarova suggests that it was well-established in Bulgaria in the years surrounding the country's liberation in 1878.

17. Rigas (1958:99) features a version of *Ehasa mantili* with the usual text but set to a third melody in *makam Hicaz* that differs both from that in Fig. 1.3 and that published by Vrelis (1985, No. 6). However, the rhythmic structure is that of an island *syrtós*. This was the only instance I encountered of the *Ehasa mantili* text set to a tune other than that of *Üsküdara*.

18. On Smyrnaica see Cowan 2000:1018–20 and Morris 1981.

19. For example, Morris (1981:89) writes that Roza Eskanazi (b. Kavala, ca. 1908), one of the most preeminent and widely recorded Smyrnaica vocalists, got her start as a dancing girl in a *café-aman*.

20. The *amane* was rejected both by the Greek upper class and Turkish leader Kemal Ataturk for its "oriental" properties, which in each case were viewed pejoratively as associated with provincial, lower-class, inter-ethnic sensibilities that were an obstacle to modernization and, in the case of Greece, a "pure" national heritage (Dionysopoulos 2002:112–13).

21. A marvelous field recording of *Apo tin Athina* made in Mytilene by the Greek Society for the Dissemination of National Music (SDNM) during the 1970s appears on the LP *Songs of Mytilene and Chios*. This recording, which features sandouri, violin, and solo male vocalist in the island tradition, closes with an instrumental *ballos* during which the violin emulates a brief vocal *amanes*.

22. The Greek-born ethnomusicologist Martha Mavroidi also indicates that she learned the *Apo kseno* variant at the music high school from which she graduated (p.c., 11 November 2004).

23. *Naftule Brandwein: King of the Klezmer Clarinet*. Rounder Records 1127, 1997, Track 8.

24. I thank Joel Rubin for this information.

25. The group's leader and vocalist, Galeet Dardashti, is an anthropologist who is writing a dissertation on contemporary Mizrahi and Arab music in Israel at the University of Texas at Austin. She is also the granddaughter of Yona Dardashti, a celebrated singer of Iranian classical music.

26. I was directed to this variant by a posting on the East European Folklife Center discussion list. For further information, see the website of the National Sound Archives: <http://jnul.huji.ac.il/dl/music/lagbaomer/index.html>

27. A more recent rendition of this variant has been recorded by KlezRoym, Italy's most acclaimed Jewish music ensemble, on their 1997 debut album of the same name.

28. This livelier instrumental version is also in circulation among contemporary Turkish performers. On his ca. 1999 compact disc *Göc Yollari (1): Instrumental Folk Music from Anatolia, bağlama* virtuoso Erol Parlak (b. 1964), a graduate of the Turkish Music Department of the State Conservatory at Istanbul Technical University, performs a similar variant, *Istanbul türküsü,* using a plectrum-less playing technique called *şelpe* executed, in this case, on the neck of the instrument (CD 1.9).

29. This and other *sevdalinke* can be found at the following two sites: http://members.tripod.com/SredanovicB/sevdah.html and http://www.angelfire. com/ab/Beograd/sevdah.html (both accessed 5 September 2001).

30. The use of the pronoun *"ih"* in this example is quite unusual; similar texts use *"gi"*.

31. *Music of the Balkans: Songs and Dances, Volume 1: Albania, Central Balkans, 1920–1940,* Track 18.

32. Importantly, such small ensembles, which in Macedonia typically included both Slavic and Romani musicians, were predicated upon the Romani *čalgija* groups active all over Macedonia, Kosovo, and Albania from the late 1800s through World War II, and which in turn, like the Turkish *gazino* ensembles and Greek *kompanies,* grew out of the Ottoman *ince saz.*

33. A brief Romani performance of an *Üsküdara* variant can be heard on Jeremy Marre's 1992 video *The Romany Trail: Part Two: Gypsy Music into Europe.* In this documentary, a Romani ensemble of Yugoslav guestworkers living in Germany dances to an instrumental tune based in part on the second half of the *Üsküdara* melody. The setting is a town hall in Dusseldorf, where the ensemble performs a concert of their own folklore. The dancing is gender-segregated. As the scene opens the camera focuses on the women executing a line dance; after a few phrases they step to the back and the men step forward to perform in their own line, only to be moved to the back in favor of the women in the same fashion after the requisite number of phrases. My thanks to Lynn Hooker for reminding me of the Marre video clip.

34. Brief excerpts from this film can be viewed in Peeva's documentary, *Whose Song is This?*

35. For a complementary discussion of songs from this play see Peters 2002:339–58 and 2003.

36. The *rukovet* [bouquet] is a secular choral rhapsody. Mokranjac's fifteen *rukoveti* incorporate more than 90 folk songs, many collected by the composer himself as part of his musicological activities (O'Loughlin 2006).

37. Serbian composer Petar Krstić (1877–1957) composed incidental music for the play in 1907 (Pejović 2006). Examination of his score would likely help solve this puzzle.

38. Konjović revised his opera in 1940 and 1948 (Djurić-Klajn 2006).

39. Gordana Lazarević sings selections from one of the two *Koštana* films, including *Ruse kose, curo, imaš,* on Jugoton LSY 61369; a second recording of selections from one of the films, sung by Divna Radić Djoković but minus *Ruse kose* or any variant thereof, appears on RTB LP-1180. My thanks to Jane Sugarman and Karen Peters for calling these recordings to my attention.

40. See "Zora Drempetic" and related links. The Internet Movie Database (IMDb): http://www.us.imdb.com/title/tt0179721/. Accessed 17 May 2006.

41. Others believe that Kitt was inspired by the 1949 Columbia 78 RPM recording of *Kâtibim* sung by Safiye Ayla and rereleased on *Masters of Turkish Music, Volume 2.* See Beken 1996:5.

42. *RCA Victor Presents Eartha Kitt.* RCA Victor LPM 3062.

43. These discographic citations were provided by Joe Kaloyanides Graziosi, a highly respected independent scholar and teacher of Greek music and dance, in a lengthy and informative posting to the Rembetiko Forum website (http://www.rembetiko.gr). As of this writing, the cover of the *Dance Bellyrina, Dance!* LP may be viewed at http://www.radiobastet.com/covgal/covgal30.html (retrieved 5 November 2006).

44. For more on this genre see L. Rasmussen 1995, 1996b, 2002, and this volume.

45. A Serbian colleague, Ivana Perković, who heard an earlier presentation of this article at an international conference in Sofia in October 2002, told me that the pronunciation of *Raspiči*'s lyrics is Bosnian in inflection, another possible parodic element.

46. My thanks to Ivana Perković for this clarification.

47. On *čoček* see Buchanan, this volume; Dunin 1971, 1973; Kurkela, this volume; Silverman 2003; and Sugarman 2003.

48. The same may also be true of the Slovenian perspective. During summer 2002 I spent about two weeks in Ljubljana as a guest of ethnomusicologist Svanibor Pettan. It was Pettan who brought the Vatrogasci version of *Üsküdara* to my attention; the band and its parody were also popular in Slovenia. While I worked with Pettan's students at the University of Ljubljana. In conversations I was surprised to hear them speak about the Balkans and Balkan musics as existing elsewhere—as divorced from Slovenia itself. Rather, they positioned their country north and west of things Balkan, on the periphery of the EU.

49. This theory was proposed to me both by Richard Tempest, who followed the band during his years in Moscow and who teaches a course on Soviet popular culture, and by the Bulgarian ethnomusicologists Lozanka Peicheva and Ventsislav Dimov, whose work focuses on Balkan ethnopop. However, one Boney M. website indicates that Farrell did not marry the Yugoslav model Jasmina until 1981, three years after *Nightflight to Venus* was released (see Diezi and O'Shea 2000–05), although she may have been in contact with Farrell and other band members prior to that time.

50. It is not impossible that the notion to create this ballad was inspired by Robert K. Massie's highly popular *Nicholas and Alexandra,* originally published in 1967, or even by Robert and Suzanne Massie's *Journey* (1975), as Rasputin is

an important figure in both.

51. The cassette's title, "*Rok-Grupa 'Zodiak,'*" appears in typescript on the generic liner, its contents are unidentified, and the extremely poor sound quality is that of a tape that has been rerecorded hundreds of times.

52. I thank my colleague Richard Tempest, who was living in Moscow when this concert was held, for confirming this information.

53. See also Peters 2002:355.

54. For a review of this film see Sugarman in press b.

55. I am grateful to my Bulgarian colleague Gencho Gaitandzhiev for this information. Gaitandzhiev further indicated that the 9/16 version was not taught because of that meter's association with *kyuchek,* a dance associated with Turkish and Romani ethnicity (see chapter 7).

56. Grupa Ju's version, *Tsŭrni ochi imash libe* [You have dark eyes, love], is a textual variant of Fig. 1.18. See Peters 2002:249, Ex. 8-5A for a complete transcription of the melody and lyrics. I am also very grateful to her for sharing her field recording of this selection with me.

57. Di Grine Kuzine performs a version of *Üsküdar* on their 1999 CD *Klezmer's Paradise.*

58. Encyclopædia Brittanica Online 2004.

59. The passage in question occurs between 11 and 21 seconds into the piece.

60. I am deeply indebted to Tom Solomon for bringing this song to my attention and for his informative commentary on its signficance. For further information about this song and its lyrics go to "The Diggiloo Thrush": <http://www.diggiloo.net/?1999>.

61. I am very grateful to Martha Mavroidi for notifying me about this concert (p.c., 11 November 2004).

Part I

POST-1989 CULTURE
INDUSTRIES
AND THEIR
NATIONALIST ICONS

❖ 2 ❖

Bosnian and Serbian Popular Music in the 1990s: Divergent Paths, Conflicting Meanings, and Shared Sentiments

Ljerka Vidić Rasmussen

Toward the mid-1990s, with images of Bosnian-Hercegovinian battlefields still dominating media coverage of the Balkans, hearing about *turbo folk* felt like a glimmer of life. From a distance, the term kept seeping in like a vision of new music, compelling thoughts of creativity amid devastation. My initial return to this region, where "life" was still a precarious commodity, brought no quick answers as to what *turbo folk* represents musically, beyond a few musicians' sparse definitions foregrounding its rhythmic dance element—an obvious sign of the turn toward modernity that music in Yugoslavia, as elsewhere, had taken in the 1990s.[1] The label, however, proved to have considerable analytical potency in the politically charged musical debates of the later 1990s. "Turbo discourse" emerged, its various dimensions springing up like semantic flotsam—drifting from one place to another, from one time period to another, from signification of war to signification of a particular lifestyle.

Although it technically arose first in Serbia, *turbo folk* eludes a single point of origin. Its musico-symbolic reach is wide, mapping across the Balkans and their East–West surroundings. Near Eastern influences are readily recognized in this genre, as is its regional *istočni* [eastern] locus: Serbia's north–south route leading to Macedonia, with occasional excur-

sions into Greek territory. *Turbo folk* reproduces itself in locally "dis-
guised" forms: as commercial newly composed folk music in Bosnia, and
as an "Eastern" idiosyncrasy in Croatian music. It has also traveled to the
West, stripped, for the most part, of the discursive significance it enjoys
at home. There, this music literally enjoys a micro-cultural life, typically
in rented clubs, among hundreds of immigrants and new refugees—a
reminder of home and displacement, and a non-event for the world outside
the south Slav diaspora.

That *turbo folk* represents kitsch of the first order is one point of
consensus among its large and varied group of detractors. This view
echoes a familiar charge by the critics of newly composed folk music, a
neo-folk genre which dominated Yugoslav popular music throughout the
1980s until its semantic takeover by *turbo folk* toward the end of the
decade. The aesthetic condescension toward a "folk" style in the 1990s,
however, had political weight; *turbo folk* signified a particular outlook on
the Yugoslav wars. Moreover, many saw in it the chief (anti-) cultural
product of the Greater Serbia project. The artifice implicit in the descript-
or "newly composed" now revealed an added dimension—power—in its
incarnation as "turbo."

The final, militant chapter of the second Yugoslavia continues to
inform our discussions of musical changes in its successor states.
Surveying dominant, and apparent, patterns of musical change we often
draw on structuralist terms such as divisions, breaks, or fractures. In this
chapter I use *turbo folk* as a springboard for addressing conspicuous and
persistent threads of continuity in locally produced forms of popular music
in Serbia and Bosnia-Hercegovina. Rather than discussing the fate of
"Yugoslav" music in the successor states, I examine new and re-emerging
facets of music in the more evocative context of borders, exchange, and
cultural space.

This is necessarily a partial account of the intersections of politics and
music. As the literature on (post-)Yugoslav culture(s) proliferates, a
growing cloud of "inevitability" has gathered, forcing the imaginary into
the ethnographic. Although many political analyses aim for even-handed
treatments of the "warring parties" (Serbs, Croats, and Bosniaks, or
Bosnian Muslims), or purport to be unbiased portrayals of war behavior,
they often intertwine causes and accounts of the war.[2] Historical griev-
ances are used to explain the conflict, implying a symmetry of guilt, and
hence shades of apology for the crimes committed.

My own engagement with the Yugoslav Imaginary owes, in part, to
the general proclivity of outside observers to view Bosnia's dismantling,

specifically, as a "series of black-and-white slides" (Laušević 2000:289). Two slides in particular inform my colorless vision: the siege of Sarajevo (1992–1995), and the Srebrenica massacre (1995), in which thousands of Muslim men and boys perished. Not to acknowledge my own partiality in the clearly complex *political* story of the Yugoslav collapse presents the appearance of acquiescence, for one, to a grotesque view perpetuated by Serbian media throughout the 1990s: that the citizens of Sarajevo were responsible, if not for the siege itself, then for "some" of the massacres in that city. By extension, an "ethnically disengaged" scholarly objectivity circumvents moral issues (Muršič 2000:57), diminishing the significance of voices such as those clamoring within "Druga Srbija" [Another Serbia], a broad-based oppositional group comprising citizens who actively opposed the nationalist regime from its very inception to its end.

Finally, maintenance of impartiality for the sake of interpretive balance seems particularly "off balance," now that the issue of account-ability has been raised in Serbia, and possibilities of communication across the Serbian and Bosnian borders have opened up. Both issues, as discussed later, are deeply implicated in musicians' outlooks on their professional work and dealings across the Drina river.

The Better Past?

By the mid-1980s the Yugoslav music market experienced a sharp decline in record sales, in both the rock/pop and folk fields, the latter chiefly represented by the genre of newly composed folk music. Within a year or so (1983–1984), sales of releases by leading musicians, which had formerly neared a million copies per recorded unit, plunged to 100,000–200,000 copies. (The latter figures appear to be the highest recently achieved in the new states.) These tangible indicators of market decline had little effect on the cultural impact of *estrada* [lit., music for the stage, for popular entertainment; also the industry supporting such performances], or the standing of its star personnel.[3] The title of a then popular folk song, "From Vardar to Triglav," which refers, respectively, to the lowland Macedonian river region and the Alpine heights of Slovenia, quite accurately reflected the regional pattern of touring itineraries by most leading artists. While musicians gravitated toward recording in their home republics, the overriding factor determining their loyalty in the 1980s appears to have been the relative profit associated with a recording contract, whether proffered by firms in Zagreb, Belgrade, Sarajevo, or Ljubljana, the four principal centers of music production.

Though located at opposite ends of the popular music spectrum, commercial folk and rock music tended to converge around mainstream pop, that is, Yugoslav *zabavna* [lit., entertainment] music. This is important, because *zabavna* music was the backbone of the Yugoslav music industry, inspiring its growth, especially, in its early "festival phase" of development (Vrdoljak 1984:25). Folk musicians followed in the footsteps of their *zabavna* counterparts. With the guiding involvement of broadcasters, both as program adjudicators and promoters, two major festivals, Belgrade "Sabor" and Sarajevo "Ilida," propelled the commercial rise of "new folk" music in the early 1970s. As the 1980s began, the culturally privileged pop market increasingly shaped and assimilated this folk field.

At this point Yugoslavia experienced an unprecedented influx of recorded music from Western pop markets. The licensing of such recordings accelerated to the point where they were issued in both locales nearly simultaneously; a case in point is Pink Floyd's album *The Wall,* which Jugoton licensed and issued only a few weeks after it hit Western markets. However, during this time the Yugoslav rock scene, on the whole, hardly fit the subcultural stereotype of an underground youth culture associated with resistance politics, the basic frame of reference for rock in old Eastern Europe. The modus (or necessity) of working within, rather than against the political order, is perhaps best illustrated by Sarajevo's Bijelo Dugme [White Button], the most commercially successful rock group bearing both a lasting musical and institutional impact on Yugoslav popular culture. The group's philosophical stance remained firmly rooted in that rock music ideology which emphasizes individual freedom and the quest to be "different," rather than challenges to the political system. In brief, Yugo-rock's "soft" articulation of resistance, combined with excellent record sales, has always made its political relevance a matter of debate.

In his star-centered historiography about the rise of popular music since its early post-1945 years, Belgrade music critic Petar Luković takes the political high road when explaining the social significance of *estrada*. Written in 1989, a time of heightened political alertness in the country, the book reflects on the "better past" as it anticipates a bad future. Luković dwells on the enthusiasm of *estrada*'s pioneering actors; broadcasters, festivals, record companies, musician associations, and friendships were permeated with the process of socialist nation building. Yet he deliberately taunts the coherence of this narrative by linking the creation of an authentic Yugoslav pop culture with market growth and political liberalization. In the final analysis, Luković suggests, this was achieved despite a counteractive environment of communism and balkanism. If the crumbling structure of the socialist past allowed him to interpret entertainers' popularity as a political virtue, some musicians, consumed by the impending political turmoil, had a great deal to say about the social changes taking place, literally, before their eyes: first, divisions among *estrada* singers along nationality lines, then the withdrawal of the entertainment business into the republican borders, and, finally, the severing of those ties between local audiences upon which the very definition of popularity in Yugoslavia's multinational context depended.

Drawing Borders: Songs of War

The growing political fragmentation evident at the start of the 1990s was paralleled by an equally conspicuous musical trend: the artistic malleability that characterized genres and issues throughout the 1980s was reversed. Diverse intraregional aesthetic alliances seemed all at once to be replaced by a single form of solidarity—songs supporting battles for independence and/or defense. In regard to the Serb-Croat conflict in particular, graphically clear lines of separation were drawn between the genres of pop and newly composed folk music. Croatia eliminated the latter from public circulation, while Serbia propelled it forward in the form of *turbo folk*. Engulfed in protracted war, Bosnian Serbs, Croats, and Bosniaks emulated the official, three-way territorial division of their country by each (re-) creating highly selective and homogenized bodies of national music.

The conflicts generated a new genre—"war songs"—a new frame of reference—"war production"—and a new kind of illegal activity that would undermine an already weakened regional music industry in the years to come—piracy. It is often noted that war songs proliferated on all sides of the front lines during the 1991–1995 wars. Until a few years ago, it was not difficult to find such topical songs, many simply extolling a nation's virtuous traits and aspirations to independence while drawing on the familiar stock of Serbo-Croatian folk poetry in a contemporary, colloquial form. Serbian and Croatian "paramilitaries" particularly excelled in producing hastily and cheaply recorded cassette repertoires, characterized by hateful, obscenity-filled portrayals of adversaries, including those international mediators involved in the conflict (Longino-vić 2000:637–39; Pettan 1998:17–18).

One may be hard pressed to find the Bosniak equivalent to such productions in regard to their scope or use of foul language. But radical foreign nationals who aided their Muslim brethren infused their visions of pure Islam into Bosnia's cassette battlefield. The ideological utility of a chanting voice emoting lyrics calling for *jihad* poignantly illustrated how a religious style can exacerbate negative perceptions of Muslim national-ism. Such songs, which in Bosnia became associated with images of *mujahideen* fighter squads, were heard and seen against the background of another image: a historically naturalized South Slav (Christian) warrior, personified musically by an epic singer. Importantly, these projections of Bosnia's statehood might have been as unacceptable to Bosniaks committed to Islamic piety and the democratic ideals of European Bosnia as they were to Croat and Serb listeners.

A particular kind of contradiction typifies the reconfiguration of musical meanings in such recordings: messages of ethnic purity, often with racial overtones, were set to familiar tunes of enemy origin or of "multieth-nic" character (Pettan 1998:22; L. Rasmussen 1996b:115). Musical archeology, historical memory, and piracy built off each other, producing, at times, truly bizarre results. On the lighter side of these conceptual tensions, Bosniak musicians/soldiers often addressed their everyday concerns with a mixture of social criticism and humor. One example is the cassette *My Bosnia, My Apple: HELP,* recorded in the northern Bosnian city of Tuzla, "in the war year of 1992." It includes songs with titles such as "Black marketeers, war profiteers" (*Šverceri ratni profiteri*), performed in an appropriate hard-rock manner, and "Artillery, Bosnian the reveler" (*Artiljerija, bosanac bekrija*), which opens momentously with drums in military cadence, then promptly transforms itself, ironically, into the rhythmically bursting section of a Serbian *kolo* dance tune, only to end in an energetic synthesizer rendition of the same idiom in the "turbo" manner.

While it is clear that the majority of musicians of all stylistic stripes—folk, pop, rock, village music—supported, either overtly or tacitly, the official positions of nationalist governments, it is essential to see war songs in their many contexts, including the specific stages of the conflicts, the circumstances of their production, and the personnel involved. In the course of the wars many popular singers refrained from overt nationalist engagement; some, for reasons of professional repute, publicly refused to join the fray of banal patriotic sing-alongs, while others simply withdrew from public view.

One anecdote will serve to illustrate the transiency of political contexts as well as the perhaps foolish tenacity of a fieldworker looking for evidence of musical offenses on all sides. It involves the *Song of the SDA*, or of the Bosniak Party for Democratic Action led by the one-time President of Bosnia-Hercegovina, Alija Izetbegović. The song's nationalist pitch is rather benign; beyond, for example, references to the "Muslim" color green, the refrain accommodates the democratic rhetoric characterizing Bosnia's first free elections, which took place in 1990: "SDA, democracy; SDA, human rights, let's all sing in one voice; nobody will win over us." Musically, the recording is notable for its poor production and mediocre performance by a local singer in the highly commercialized "Eastern" cast of newly composed folk music. Several years after this Party jingle was made, it was difficult to find the recording in Sarajevo's music shops. At last, a street vendor selling religious materials reluctantly produced the cassette from where he had tucked it into a drawer, citing complaints by passersby at seeing such items on display. He suggested that its exclusion from view was a good thing in these changing times and praised the ongoing modernization of Bosniak music, for "one people (*narod*) cannot live alone."[4]

The era in which music and musicians served nationalist causes and at times, murder, was short-lived, which explains in part my cursory treatment of the topic.[5] The musical legacy of the 1990s fully revealed not only the potency of institutionalized entertainment as an instrument of political propaganda, but also that music and musicians played precarious roles in a society that unquestioningly presumed their loyalty to the nation. This co-agency of political and popular acceptance continues to define new forms of cultural capital within and across the successor states. The case of *turbo folk* provides a vivid illustration.

Serbia: *Turbo Folk*

In 1999, two months after NATO's air strikes in Serbia ended, the intensity of anti-Western sentiments was fully displayed on the streets of Belgrade. Bookstores competed in their offerings of titles pronouncing the end of Western civilization and its betrayal of liberal ideals, and the creation of a New World Order. As part of a poster exhibit entitled "Windows 99," an elite downtown gallery proffered buyers elegantly packaged images of Serbia's destruction in the form of advertisements for Western brand names. A colorful collage of shattered windows on a Novi Sad building represented the "Windows 99" theme; meanwhile, Peugeot, advertising the "Ride of Your Life," featured a van dangling toward the Danube river from the end of the collapsed half of a bridge, while a "Good Year" advertisement depicted a pile of tire rubble. Says the creative director of the advertising firm that supported the project: "We used communication symbols to tell our story more clearly and palatably to people who don't comprehend what's happening here."[6] On city streets, the ethnography of national pain was inscribed in graffiti—mostly curses directed at NATO—and on postcards. Some mapped out the imperialist reach of the US toward a tiny target in the heart of the Balkans, others showed children in candle-lit basements, and yet others documented the destruction of particular buildings. One, bearing the inscription "The Freedom of Information," depicted the burning of the Radio Television Serbia building, a pillar of the regime that would be dethroned within the year. Beneath a picture of the shattered Chinese embassy, a single-word caption asked the viewer, "Why?"

The subversive urban guerilla actions of "Otpor," the student "Resistance" movement, quickly resumed after the cessation of air strikes, as did protest concerts organized by independent Radio B-92 as part of the station's campaign to reclaim its frequency and its property, seized by the government a few days into the bombing. "Free B-92," a concert of support held in late August, mobilized the "best Yugoslav rock bands," as the organizer put it (see Plate 2.1). The lineup during the several hours of continuous performances reflected the station's broadcast policy: a ferocious commitment to the core of Belgrade alternative rock, and a consummate indifference to mainstream acts, many with the "state band" reputation. As has happened often before, solidarity with the station's plight was demonstrated by veteran bands—Električni Orgazam [Electric Orgasm], Rambo Amadeus, and Partibrejkers [Party Breakers]—the leading bands of the 1990s—Kanda, Kodža and Nebojša, and Darkwood Dub—and members of the evolving alternative scene, including Obojeni Program [Colored Program], Eyesburn, and Veliki Prezir [Great Disdain].

Live concerts were an integral element of political protests on Belgrade streets throughout the 1990s, including the spectacular mass demonstrations of 1996–1997 that helped install the winning oppositional candidates at the local level of governance. Unlike these rock-oriented events, concerts organized during the early stages of the NATO intervention reflected a musical consensus across the socially and musically fractured field of popular music. For example, the documentary compact disc compilation entitled *Pjesma Nas je Održala* (The song sustained us; a familiar phrase from the revolutionary song repertoire of the Second World War) featured Serbian folk and pop-rock standards from the 1980s (a few in "war versions"), and newly produced songs in the Band-Aid mold of pop patriotism. This was, arguably, the only time when a key political concept of post-Yugoslav Serbia—unity—found contextual momentum in the defiant solidarity of the nation. This sentiment is captured in the song "Only unity saves the Serbs," by Serbia's most enduring rock singer-songwriter, Bora Đorđević (Fig. 2.1). The closing verses read:

Nema gore tragedije nego biti iz Srbije.	There is no worst tragedy than to be from Serbia.
Danas ceo svet navija da se razbije Jugoslavija.	Today the whole world is cheering the breakup of Yugoslavia.
Ali ne može tako.	But it can't be so.
Neka se spuste na zemlju; onda ću umesto pevanja pogledati u oči i pucati bez oklevanja.	Let them descend on [our] soil; then, instead of singing, I'll look in their eyes and shoot without hesitating.
E, tako već može.	Ah, it can be so.
Pomozi nam Bože.	Help us God.
Refrain	**Refrain**
Sad' kad' nas bombama gađaju Srbi se više ne svađaju, Jer naše geslo saopštava da samo sloga Srbina spašava da samo sloga Srbina spašava.	Now that they are hitting us with bombs, Serbs quarrel no more, Because our slogan says, only unity saves the Serbs, only unity saves the Serbs.

Figure 2.1: "Only unity saves the Serbs." Music and text by Bora Đorđević.

But while Belgraders were eager to say that everybody of note in *estrada* participated in these concerts, the musicians' apparently spontaneous responses seem to have resulted from a balancing act between moral obligation and official invitation. As one influential and non-participating folk musician intimated, for him, "waving" from concert stages and bridges to the dishonorable forces of NATO, while those who invited these forces were somewhere else, represented an act of utter foolishness.

In a specific sense, the war on Serbian soil culminated the liminal state of a nation under a decade-long media siege. Many observers have pointed out the key role of the mass media in igniting Serbia's military crusades in the early 1990s. The populace's steady subjection to the discourse of victimization diminished after the war in Bosnia subsided, only to explode again with the arrival of Western forces. A troubling testimony to the effects of the government's isolationist grip on the public word was the fact that Serbian military intervention in Kosovo, which precipitated Western involvement, was, at best, buried in newspaper articles pondering the question, "Why us?" voiced in relation to NATO intervention.

To date, perhaps the most compelling analyses of Serbia's withdrawal into a mythically reconstituted reality are those produced by the members of a think tank called the Belgrade Circle. In the postscript to a Serbian translation of Jean Baudrillard's book *The Perfect Crime*, Obrad Savić (1998:198–233), a Circle member, notes that sudden Serbian interest in this author coincided with the breakdown of society's normative process of rationalization at the onset of Yugoslavia's disintegration. But, Savić argues, Baudrillard arrived in Serbia by way of a shortcut, the wrong way, because his "images of a hyper-real world ha[d] nothing to do with the exotic construction of nationalist reality in Serbia" (1998:202). Savić examines the political background behind the government's perverted appropriation of the social function of signs, pointing out "the systematic fabrication of hybrid links between causes and effects, and a continual intersecting of good and evil, the victim and the hangman"—in brief, an amnesty on facts (1998:201). He also raises a broader issue: "The intensive use of simulation tricks, shams, and witticisms, in Serbia and in the Balkans, points to the mimetic diligence of the 'periphery' which reveals concealed messages of the 'center!'"(1998:201). But these simulation strategies, he suggests, are unstructured emanations of a cosmetically retouched society, lacking the historical trajectory of simulacra. Probing into the forced reconciliation of tensions between the real and symbolic, the actual and imaginary, within a logic whose very values and symbolic laws have been usurped, Savić is led to conclude that "the brutal reality of the Balkans and Serbia is increasingly becoming subreal" (1998:205).

No form of expressive culture has added more to the chaos of signs in Serbia's media space, while at the same time articulating the historically hypertrophied image of the Nation, than *turbo folk* music. Its very label is the product of a particular form of cultural conflict ignited by the nationalist takeover of popular culture production in Serbia. It was pop artist Rambo Amadeus (a.k.a. Antonije Pušić), well-known for his musical experiments and oratorical theatrics, who apparently, during a concert in 1989, uttered the term *turbo folk* within a barrage of parodic references to neo-folk culture. In this context, the distinction between his parodic references to "folk" and his own self-identification with it through his authorial claim to *turbo folk* seem blurred; or rather, this seems a deliberate creative ploy. In a recently published Yugo-rock encyclopedia, a Belgrade critic (Janjatović 1998:146) puts it this way: "He called his music *turbo folk,* before the meaning of this rubric would be filled with frightening contents in the first half of the 1990s." What is clear, however, is that Rambo's popularity among a broad cross-section of the audience may owe more to the material he parodically exploits—newly composed culture—than to the critical distance he projects by such an approach.[7]

Rambo excels in bricolage methods, bringing into his pop mix common (and banal) terms of politics, high culture, low life, and above all, Balkan characterology. Politically unconscious and charmingly backward, the idealized Balkan man personified through Rambo's performances appears to be the measure of cultural types inhabiting the self-proclaimed geocultural center of the Balkans in the 1990s—Serbia—and its environs, where Rambo's works held great appeal. In reality a mix of *gastarbeiter* [guest worker], folk singer, and neighbor, the "Balkan man" provides authentically primitive artistic material, for Rambo wants "to break into his consciousness and create a civic culture out of it" (quoted in Gordy 1999:119).

Correspondingly, Rambo's music is an eclectic aggregate of pop, rock, jazz, rap, and the expressive riches of neo-folk. An early example, the 1989 song "America and England," based on a rap-style delivery of lyrics and a repetitive bass line, is a vivid sample of domestic pop culture. The motives of one-string, bowed *gusle* (old peasantry), newly composed folk music (urban peasantry), *Schlager*-pop (bourgeois class), and partisan marches and cartoon characters (revolutionary class), are all juxtaposed to create a highly readable critique-parody of the communist rhetoric lingering over Yugoslavia's disintegration and socialist/capitalist relations at the end of the decade. "The sworn enemy, out of fear and sadism, persistently ruins the basis of communism; Step on the tail of imperialism, revive the prestige of socialism," read the closing lines of the song, accompanied by the dull *gusle* ostinato rendering a well-known revolutionary chorus line, "America and England will be proletarian lands." In "Balkan boy" Rambo narrates a story about becoming a folk star. A young lad waiting for a ride in front of the PGP building (State Record Production of Radio Television Serbia) is approached by a producer who offers to conduct an "economic experiment" with him. After the deal is made, he quickly enters the folk *estrada* industry and attains the stature of Elvis Presley, proudly declaring in a refrain (which musically breaks into the Rolling Stones' "I can't get no satisfaction"): "I'm a Balkan boy, because I smell of sweat; sooner or later I'll be yours." In Rambo's cover performance of *Hey Joe,* his emulation of a Bosnian folk singer heralds the Balkans' fate in one small detail: his delivery of the word *aman.* Here full-fledged Hendrix-like guitar riffs meet the depth of Bosnian *dert* [pain, wretchedness], from which the voice rises in a *glissando,* taking repose in a gutturally vibrating trill on the last syllable, *aman.* This oriental "twang" is a cliché; it caricatures the café (*kafana*) manner of singing associated with the earlier *orijental* style of newly composed folk music.

But for Miodrag Ilić, one producer who "orientalized" Serbian folk music in the 1980s, *turbo folk* represents yet another unseemly attempt at the denunciation of everything that was "original, functioning, and profitable" in Serbia's society, past and present.[8] The charismatic leader of the Južni Vetar [Southern Wind] band, Ilić is credited with propelling the *orijental* from an ephemeral trend to an influential style which, in the later 1980s, served as a catalyst for increasingly divisive musical projections of a Yugoslav east and west, with attendant Islamic contro-versy. While I have litanically noted the musical significance of this style and discussed, in greater detail, its political implications in the wake of Yugoslavia's disintegration (Rasmussen 1996b:99–116), I could least foresee, in the rapidly changing political "field" of the time, the lasting impact this style would exert on music in both Serbia and post-war Bosnia in the 1990s.

A semantically overloaded term, *orijental* clearly suggests that historic point where numerous stylistically cognate musical practices in the larger region of the Balkans originated—the Ottoman past. While Yugoslav *orijental* does exhibit stylistic affinities with contemporary Turkish music, among others, it is a label that came into use out of necessity, and by professionals, not by audiences. Though similarly generic, the alternate label, "Eastern" (*istočna*) music, widely used in Bosnia, is locally more idiomatic, as is the colloquialism "*turcism,*" borrowed from linguistics. Yet to interpret this Eastern-*orijental* amalgam of local styles as a modern incarnation of Ottoman antiquity would obscure the dynamics of new sources, changing musical sensibilities, and larger market forces.

The nature of *orijental* is extremely diffuse, ranging from reworkings of the newly composed folk music model to its more highly stylized forms, often hardly distinguishable from traditional types of ensemble music such as the brass band and *čoček* dance-based repertoires widely performed in south Serbia and Macedonia, particularly by Roma. Many of these "Eastern" or, more accurately, southern emanations of the Balkan Orient can be found in the repertoires of leading *turbo folk* singers such as Mira Škorić, Svetlana Ražnatović-Ceca, and especially of Dragana Mirković, one of five Serbian and Bosnian singers who worked with the Southern Wind group in the 1980s. Asked to evaluate the current musical scene in Belgrade and the legacy of *orijental*, Miodrag Ilić characteristically brings into the unregulated *estrada* picture the symbiotic linkage between creative plunder and institutionalized piracy.

> So much is mixed now. It is no longer "turkism": What does turkism mean? It means a Serbian song with a Turkish sound, with a Turkish arrangement. It has come to this, now, that the greatest Turkish hits are just re-recorded. Piracy has ruined everything. And just because of the existing sea of degraded [*orijental*] sound, I have moved it back a bit, more toward that continental, central part of our country.[9]

The stylistic distinction of *orijental*, in fact, lies in its "turkisms"; it is precisely these features, once considered religiously and intrusively Middle Eastern, that survive in the present production of *turbo folk*. First, ornamentation practices have changed. Singers favor extensive, elaborate trills over measured appoggiaturas, the latter representing the more "disciplined" approach to ornamenting characteristic of the *sevdalinka* singing style. This profuse ornamentation tends to fragment the main melody rather than accentuate its linear shape; this is expressed, most formulaically, by elaborating a short melodic phrase with a trill or two, and then repeating it at different pitch levels. Typically, instrumental openings and interludes by synthesizer as well as accordion and lead guitar trade off with or echo a singer's phrases.

A second novel feature involves male back-up voices singing, characteristically, in unison. This manner of singing, in which a male chorus responds to and alternates with a soloist, contrasts strikingly with the usual musical texture and format of the performance, traditionally based on doubling a singer's line in thirds (typically in refrains), and straightforward solo singer–instrumental interlude alternation. The use of this device in Serbian *turbo folk* at present is perhaps the most effective way to construct an orientalist affect without evoking the religious setting of Muslim male chant.

Beyond oriental junctures, what distinguishes *turbo folk* is a straightforward adoption of the rock idiom and new dance music, building on the latter's disco legacy. The music's "turbo" quality is apparent in its "techno" production techniques: ubiquitous drum machines, sampling, new leading roles for electric guitars, and a hard-driving rhythm section. The high level of creative investment in studio production is also reflected in a newly defined relationship between the singer and instrumentalists, who are now promoted together, on almost equal footing, as project "teams."

A striking example is the 1997 song *Neka hvala* [No thanks] by Mira Škorić and the Futa Band. The band, which features bass guitar, drum set, and roaring guitar solos, performs in a classic hard rock manner. To the old critics' complaint that female NCFM vocalists sing aggressively, Mira here responds with a masculine cliché; in the dramatic solo introduction she sings in a strong, sultry alto voice that retains a few familiar elements of folk styling, including off-beat entrances, appoggiaturas, and vibrato. At one point within the extended chorus, her female back-up voices introduce a novel stylistic gem by profiling the tune with upward glissandi that turn into the "cutting" shouts of village singing practice; a third layer emerges as male back-up voices begin to add high-pitched "female" trills to Mira's line. These (trans-) gendered sparks of authenticity complement the musical projection of female power expressed in the song lyrics: the singer asserts her independence in a romantic relationship, seemingly going against the patriarchal grain of much *turbo folk* imagery which, nevertheless, accommodates the role of woman as warrior.

The ability of folk musicians to absorb elements of contemporary musical trends while in the process setting a standard for the mainstream is not just a phenomenon of the 1990s, as political analyses of *turbo folk*'s success story suggest. As early as the 1970s, folk producers eagerly tapped into domestic popular (*zabavna*) music, unfettered by the cultural inhibitions maintained by the pop establishment, which rejected newly composed folk music in favor of all varieties of Western popular music. Eric Gordy (1999:140) provides a fresh illustration of this deepening schism: the extraordinary territorial breach exemplified by a Serbian folk singer's appropriation of the Rolling Stones song, *Paint it black.* Calling it "a historic document epitomizing the new dominance of turbofolk," Gordy captures the sentiment shared by many anti-folk Belgraders.

The singer, Dragan Kojić-Keba, a leading male *turbaš* ["turbo man"], explains his motivation to recreate the rock song: "That song has a lot of elements of our folklore, although maybe that might sound astonishing. Its harmonic resolutions are very close to ours. So, you could say that the Stones ripped us off. Why not?" (Gordy 1999:140). It is difficult not to sympathize with the singer when he points out that while no one complained about his performance, many questioned his "right" to do it: "It simply bothers them that a folkie (*narodnjak*) did the cover" (1999:140). Indeed, the reverse has not been the case. The reception of pop singers who turned to *Yugo-folk* [i.e., newly composed folk music] for inspiration has been, for the most part, lukewarm; a few critics dismissed these *Schlager*-folk fusions as succumbing to the majority's culturally encoded preference for folk.

That the folk industry co-opts the terms of popular culture for its own purposes is vividly documented by a compact disc compilation titled *Turbo Folk 2000,* a veritable "user's manual" for discovering the genre's riches. The stylistic range represented is as wide as any modest anthology of the genre should be, rendering the *turbo* label graphically misleading. It includes a song in the Serbian *dvojka* [duple] idiom (2/4 meter), characterized by moderately florid singing and the use of accordion (and no synthesizer); an *orijental* item with a highly embellished vocal line that alternates with male chorus; and a standard *čoček* tune in a characteristically fast-paced 2/4 by an ensemble that incorporates *darabuka,* accordion, and trumpets. In a number of pop, techno/dance, and disco renditions, a few genre-specific details place these songs into the folk category of listening experience: vocal timbre, melismatic interludes and cadences, male back-ups, augmented seconds and, of course, the topical motifs of *kafana* and loneliness. Configured within high-tech arrangements and enlivened by fast-paced rhythms, these turbo-energized songs invite proactive reception, rather than old-time passive indulgence in the call of destiny.

The ascent of *turbo folk* as the "national" musical idiom in the 1990s has had a twofold effect on popular music. It has undermined the pop mainstream, and eclipsed its rock wing in all but a few alternative media outlets. In the process, it has helped create an officially sanctioned pirate market, a development which in Serbia, as in other new states where it now flourishes, had no precedent in the former Yugoslavia. Further, *turbo folk*'s commercial viability has pressed the once malleable demarcation between folk and pop-rock to the level of an internal culture war. Much Belgrade rock, marginalized by the state media and with no access to major production and promotion outlets, became deeply political and indeed, oppositional, evoking earlier Western portrayals of rock "behind the Iron curtain." This is an extraordinary development—perhaps the most dramatic change in the geoculturally remapped constellation of musical genres inherited from the former system (Rasmussen 2001:70–71).

Antagonism toward the folk establishment in Belgrade was most intensely felt by the young, who organized around Radio B-92, the fledgling dance club scene, and the polit-pop core of the city's alternative rock. Once thriving, Belgrade's rock culture became the minority voice of Another Serbia, a term eventually synonymous with the work of those anti-war and human rights activists who struggled to preserve the idea of European Serbia and keep the spirit of cosmopolitan Belgrade alive (Prošić-Dvornić 1994:179–99). Finally, the unprecedented high political standing achieved by some folk singers marked the definitive collapse of the local value system, effectively nullifying the longstanding issue of newly composed folk music's cultural legitimacy. At issue, on the most basic level, were resources and the visibility of *turbo folk* culture.

The downfall of the Serbian economy and ongoing privatization allowed a few entrepreneurs to create a small music industry parallel to the old state structure. In Belgrade, in addition to the PGP of Radio Television Serbia, the folk music business became highly concentrated around a few privately owned production venues, notably, the influential City Records and Grand Production firms, and the television stations Palma and Pink. These outlets, reportedly, were directly linked to the political power structure, revealing the spectrum of ideological loyalties evident among the main protagonists of folk *estrada*: the Socialist and Yugoslav Left, closely related through the ideologies and marriage of their respective party leaders, Slobodan Milošević and Mirjana Marković. Two notorious cases, with melodramatic twists, illustrate this merger of interests: journalistic reports of the nomination, in 1999, of Zorica Brunclik, a leading singer of the 1980s and a prominent member of the Yugoslav Left, for the post of Minister of Culture; and the fact that a *turbo folk* star of the 1990s, Svetlana Ražnatović-Ceca, was the wife of Željko Ražnatović-Arkan, hero of the Serbian wars, respected businessman, and alleged war criminal indicted by the Hague Tribunal for the Former Yugoslavia (assassinated in Belgrade in 2000).

Brunclik's ministerial episode generated considerable outrage, expressed in newspaper commentaries with disbelief, disdain, and outright ridicule. In contrast, the symbiotic relationship of crime and glamour evident in the Ceca-Arkan partnership was veiled by perceptions that are the stuff of national soap opera and mythology—popular acceptance and quiet revulsion. But the reach of Ceca's popularity beyond Serbia's borders—including Bosnia—suggests that in the politically insular world of local music consumption, the feminine projection of soft-nationalism, assisted by the genre's oriental appeal, helped *turbo folk* to transcend critical judgement. Ceca's eroticized nationalism effectively canceled out the threat of the East upon which her music heavily depends. And this calls into question any clear-cut correlation between style and ideology implied in monolithic portrayals of *turbo folk* as the political regime's construction of Serbian culture.

Part of Ceca's song repertoire is easily categorized as local pop of the *zabavna* lineage. Her other songs fall into the Balkan bin of commercial "world music"; they descend from earlier works that commercially appropriate Serbia's own orient—its south. An example is the song *Vreteno* [Spindle], produced in 1997. The insistent rhythmic motion, enfolded by a spiraling melody that recalls the routine of wool-spinning, at first strikes the listener as affirming the perpetual motion associated with problematic Ottoman imagery in Serbia's music. The performance does not conjure up the soulful "mystic[ism] and beauty" of Eastern music, of which Miodrag Ilić enthusiastically spoke years ago, as he tried to explain his attraction to it. Ceca's team recreates a complementary bodily image by allowing the infectious dance-melodic movement to drive the studio performance. Trumpets, percussion, electric bass, and synthesized strings dominate the texture. The lead vocal line evolves with the continuous bass line, in interplay with "flashy" strings echoing the short vocal cadences, and choppy, conversational trumpet phrases throughout. In the refrain proper, the voice is joined in unison by the low strings, adding timbral depth akin to the male back-up grounding of *orijental* texture. The band's spinning energy is controlled by the steady percussion section, which issues the idiomatic, duple-meter "world beat" of Serbian vintage.

To use Obrad Savić's (1998:205) analytical terms, by maximizing dependence on "attractive codes of occidentalism and obsessive icons of orientalism," *turbo folk* enhances the visibility and import of all such codes on the field of the Serbian imaginary. He argues: "The wholesale flirting with East[ern] and West[ern] heritage fashionably seeks some theatrical sociability which pleases only itself" (1998:205). But herein, of course, lies the musical appeal and social power of *turbo folk*. Similarly, the complementary images of glamour and wealth have defined the iconography of folk *estrada* since its early days. But in a society stricken by poverty and social despair, the mimetic qualities of *turbo folk* are potent political signs of confused images of both West and East.

In the fall 1999 issue of the entertainment magazine *Pink Revija* [Pink Review] an editorial contained a "Happy birthday, masters" note, congratulating Pink Television on the fifth anniversary of its founding.[10] This is the most watched 24-hour television program in Serbia, featuring folk videos, talk shows, and foreign (mostly American) films. In an interview with a currently popular singer, Goca Božinovska, readers were to absorb, within a paragraph or two, all that a good, fast-paced life has to offer: her performance at a Gypsy wedding in France, shopping for her kids in Frankfurt, and an upcoming concert on the Montenegrin coast. A brief note on another page informed readers that Ceca had begun studying English, "which [would] help her in conquering world music scenes." With its announcements of new releases, promotional parties, gossip columns, lavish weddings, and the like, the magazine was a glossy version of its socialist predecessor, *Sabor*. Singing stars from the previous era appeared regularly in its pages; a leading folk star of socialist Yugoslavia, Lepa Brena, was now a prominent businesswoman with wide-ranging investments in Belgrade *estrada*.

Indeed, in the *turbo folk* establishment's vocabulary, epithets of sophistication and power abound: productions are "grand," song-writers/producers are "dream teams," the colors are elegant white and black, or poetic pink. Writings by Mirjana Marković document some of the most extravagant, benevolently phantasmagoric, Yugo-nostalgic projections of Serbia's socialist utopia. Marković is the author of a series of volumes written in the eclectic form of highly personal political diaries featuring poetically idiosyncratic analyses of world affairs and Yugosla-via's place in them. In Belgrade's select bookstores, her publications were easily recognized by their distinctly colored packaging; one book in the series, entitled *Between the East and the South*, presented the author's full image against the background of a globe and a tapestry of purple, pink, and white hues (see Marković 1998). In an isolated and impoverished society subsidizing the state's protracted war engagements, it is easy to see how the aloofness of Marković's prose and the *turbo folk* imagery of prosperity coalesced to create escapist routes for the masses.

Importantly, the volume of this music in national media vacillated synchronously with the curve of political crises and Serbia's openings toward the West. The rhetoric of peace, on the rise in the later part of 1994 and paving the way for the signing of the Dayton Peace Accord a year later, proved that the *turbo folk* establishment was as much a politically expendable commodity as any other component of the political-economic oligarchy. The music's promotion, especially its more explicitly nationalist stream, was reduced, and a media campaign, captured in the slogan "It's nicer with culture," was launched by the Ministry of Culture. In the commanding, re-educational style of this advertising action, the Ministry aimed at greater institutional support for, and media exposure of the masses to, high-culture forms. One image still on display in 1999 on a few billboards showed a sheep asking the viewer: "What are you staring at? Engage in Culture."

A few individuals from the Belgrade art community had worked independently toward the same goal, but with a clearer sense of the magnitude of the problem and with a policy solution: they founded the "Center for Cultural Decontamination." Predictably, these highly centralized attempts at curbing the dominance of neo-folk genres had little effect on changing citizens' musical needs. They did, however, encourage critical responses to an increasingly indiscriminate contempt for *turbo folk*. Along with a greater awareness of the commercial rise of ethnopop in Western markets, some receptive commentators called for the re-evaluation of turbo-phobic rhetoric. As one critic pointedly asked: "Are Rednex, Ofra Haza, and Youssou N'Dour *turbo folk* in their own countries? And if not, why not?" (quoted in Gordy 1999:161).

The cover page of a recent issue of the major political weekly NIN shows a concert stage with the inscription "New Culture in Novi Sad" (see Otašević 2001). The lead article, "Theirs has passed," opens: "A decade of *turbo folk* is behind us; in Serbia a new cultural model is being born." This symbolic birth took the form of a week-long "Exit Noise Summer Festival," which featured electronika, ethno, techno, and drum'n'bass musical variety. Political decree and the will of young people seemed to have happily coalesced, as thousands of teenagers from Serbia and neighboring areas descended on Petrovaradinska Fortress, marking the grand return of urban youth to the Serbian cultural stage. The line-up of organizers and sponsors reveals the unique nature of the Serbian musical transition: the chief organizer, a powerful group of Serbian economic reformers called G17 Plus, was followed by the Federal Ministries of Internal and Foreign Affairs, the European Union, McDonald's, Radio B-92, and TV Pink.

The writer does not fail to note the duplicitous reorientation of TV Pink, that bastion of *turbo folk* "primitivism," towards a new "urban and global culture of youth." Yet the station's ability to win, together with B-92, the rights to promote this event might in the long run be less a case of ideological shift—participation in the "new government concept"—than of a solid entrepreneurial instinct to tap into a re-emerging Western pop niche so prominently endorsed by the central powers in Belgrade and Europe. Indeed, the pendulum swing of politico-musical alliances reached the far left when the young Governor of the National Bank of Yugoslavia also became a member of the rock group "Monetary Attack."

The case of *turbo folk* illustrates a larger process of musical national-ization experienced in all the Yugoslav successor states. Serbia's "choice" of the folk idiom, however, is hardly the single factor defining the conservative ideological outlook of this music and its practitioners. In neighboring states, notably Croatia, Western-style pop music met similar demands for political mobilization in the early 1990s. As suggested earlier, not all causes of Yugo-rock's demise can be attributed to the *turbo folk* political takeover of *estrada*. Undeniably appealing and imaginative musical arrangements and music videos were contributed by a number of top-notch rock musicians and television producers, who chose to enter the lucrative folk market as opportunities in the pop field rapidly diminished. Critics should perhaps take note of the fact that Belgrade music production commands respect among music professionals in neighboring countries. In Bosnia-Hercegovina, to which I turn below, the tripartite territorial division of the country into ethnic entities has seemingly sealed local cultural exchanges; but it has also encouraged new musical overtures to the outside world and, in the process, careful renewals of familiar pathways within "Yugoslav cultural space."

Bosnia: *Sevdah*-Rock

The new Bosnian governments have invested much effort in nationalizing music through the selective promotion of particular styles, traditions, and even individual performers. This process, manifested outwardly as homogenization, internally displays dynamic diversification—that is, greater assertion of local identities. These new identity configurations seem to indicate two modeling principles at work: replication of the former Yugoslav dynamic between the local and the national, and the idea of multiculturalism, recast in Western rhetoric as democratic transitions and human rights. Post-war Bosnia-Hercegovina provides a particularly poignant example of the imposition of prescriptive multiculturalism: it is a place that rightly claims this philosophy as a fact of its history, but it was also a targeted casualty of war, and is now the major obstacle to the creation of a functioning post-war state (see Plates 2.2 and 2.3).[11]

The most salient new facet of expressive culture at present is the new authority of religious institutions within the process variously described as a religious awakening or turn to spirituality (*duhovnost*). Along with the initially explosive, public profusion of religious ideas and rituals, numerous forms of religious music for secular consumption have been created. An often cited Bosnian example is the *ilahija*. Unlike its highly cultivated secular model, the *sevdalinka* (a yearning love song steeped in Bosnia's urban culture), the *ilahija* is a form of Muslim worship that has become a "popular" song promoted both by performers from institutional religious ranks and neo-folk singers of socialist pedigree.

The *sevdalinka* itself has been undergoing a process of cultural authentication through wholesale nationalization, characterized on the one hand by revivalist interest in its historical performance (*saz* or small ensemble accompaniment), and on the other by artistic aggrandizement in the form of symphony orchestra accompaniment. It is not a coincidence that the first performance of *sevdalinke* with massive accompaniment—provided by the Sarajevo Philharmonic Orchestra, two folk ensembles, and a chorus—took place in 1998 on a concert stage at "Baščaršija Nights." This major summer festival in Sarajevo strives to showcase Bosnia's musical heritage and emerging affinities with Muslim cultures while maintaining links with Europe. Efforts to make the *sevdalinka* more palatable to international audiences were clearly inspired by the recognition of its representational value. Since European classical music remains a favored choice for official events, the organizers were led to "elevate" the *sevdalinka* to the highest level of state pageantry.

Many musicians, critical of religious promotion through music and the nationalization of styles, speak in terms of cultural ghettoization and musical autism. Within the normatively nationalized framework of Bosnian expressive culture, for example, music commentators now write of "Bosnian" newly composed folk music, thus extricating it from the larger regional and historical context of its development. This genre's ethnographic past is, for the moment, frozen in the present of the new statehood. Importantly, neither form of this music, oriental or pop, is typically referred to in Bosnia as *turbo folk*. Musicians readily recognize musical links and stylistic similarities, but do not think the Serbian term replicable for music produced in Bosnia. As a potent political metaphor, it is clear why arguing for *turbo folk*'s coexistence with other local forms may suggest cultural subjugation.[12] Yet there is a countervailing sense of renewed Bosnian diversity. This can be seen in the parallel eastward and westward directions of both the current folk music scene and the re-emerging pop mainstream, best represented by the work of Hanka Paldum and Dino Merlin, respectively, and dubbed, under the new rubric of local authenticity, *sevdah*-rock. The term *sevdah*, which also comprises the etymological root of *"sevdalinka,"* derives from the Turkish *sevda,* meaning love, desire, and melancholy.

A striking illustration of the wholesale adoption of a highly commer-cialized, "orthodox," version of the *orijental* is the degree to which it has permeated local performance. In 1999, a major festival of folk music named after the Bosnian town Bihać showcased a dozen singers who hardly diverged from a stereotypical performance by Southern Wind. Although such performances are now widely accepted and even broadcast on major television outlets in Sarajevo, many commentators and musicians alike consider them an aesthetically lowly kind of newly composed folk music. At the same time, some experienced musicians hail Miodrag Ilić as a musical innovator who succeeded in recreating authentically Eastern music, but interpret *orijental* as in direct opposition to *turbo folk*. A partial answer to these apparent contradictions lies in a changed perspective of Muslim ethnicity and the rise of a distinctly Bosniak identity in popular music. If in the 1980s *orijental* dramatized tension between the Yugo-folk mainstream and the trend-setting periphery as a reflection of waning Yugoslavism and the perception of an Islamic threat, the turbo-cycle of controversy recast the meaning of "East" in terms of Serbian-Bosnian political dis-association.

Tomislav Longinović (2000:640–41) traces the origin of *turbo folk* to Halid Bešlić, Halid Muslimović, and Lepa Brena, the three stars of 1980s newly composed folk music, all originally from Bosnia. This stylistic linkage is very well taken. In the final analysis, however, it becomes reduced to the very orientalist predicament around *turbo folk* that Longinović critically examines—the Muslim identity of these singers. In the early 1980s the "two Halids" became a nickname for a "new wave" that combined Bosnian singers' propensity for vocal ornamentation with pop arrangements and a rhythmic drive derived, for the most part, from Macedonian music. The style left its mark on the national market as a distinctly Bosnian contribution. But it was the extraordinary success of

Lepa Brena that showed the power of Belgrade *estrada* to absorb both locality and ethnicity into the ultimate national garb of stardom. Brena's Muslim ethnicity was played down from the very beginning of her career, and instead, her inclusive, pan-Yugoslav orientation was cultivated in both her eclectic repertoire and professed Yugoslavism.

The trajectory of *turbo folk* can be followed in the musically even more compelling career of Hanka Paldum, one of the finest performers of traditional *sevdalinke*, and a commercially successful singer who was the first to propel the "fusion" of newly composed folk music with Yugoslav rock in the early 1980s. Her album *Čežnja* [Longing], which featured several leading rock musicians, was hailed at the time as a collaborative effort at "reconciling" domestic folk and pop (*zabavna*) music. According to the producers, this forward-looking experiment was not about deconstructing the folk idiom, but rather creating an original form of popular music out of local music sources.

Paldum's most recent album exhibits lavish pop production with an extravagant array of diverse musical idioms. Along with a moving performance of "Mother gave her sons away," which draws on a dramatic and texturally rich arrangement akin to a film soundtrack, the album includes a generic "old-town song" with classic Croatian *tamburitza* accompaniment. Turkish sources figure prominently on this album, from borrowed tunes to samples of "oriental" percussion. One recording, *Gazi, gazi,* characterized by fractured melody and a jumble of percussion and wind instruments, leaves the listener wondering if this is how janissary music sounded centuries ago. Even Paldum finds the song uncharacteristic of her style, explaining that it fit the producer's conception of the overall "ethnic" sound he sought to achieve on this album. On the other hand, a song featuring tambourine and brass ensemble strongly recalls the familiar terrain of south Serbian music. Paldum disputes this characterization, suggesting that the song's rhythmic elements and instrumental timbres must not be isolated from its melodic character and her "Bosnian voice."[13]

In 1999, a rising star of Bosnian pop, Dino Merlin (a.k.a. Dino Dervišhalidović), intimated his need to depart from the local musical habitat and explore different creative paths.[14] He had already begun this trek with the French singer Beatrice in a duet performance of the song, *Putnici* [Voyagers] which in 1999 represented the Bosnia-Hercegovinian entry in the Eurovision Song Contest in Jerusalem (Fig. 2.2; CD 2.1). At the start of his career in the mid-1980s, Merlin was one of many Sarajevo musicians working in the shadow of Goran Bregović, the leader of Bijelo Dugme. Today, Merlin's work epitomizes the revival of Sarajevo's pop

scene and the individual artist's pursuit of a place in the international
arena. With an eye on the Arabic-Francophone niche of European
ethnopop, Merlin aims at affirming locally a "new way of communicat-
ing." Until the release of "Voyagers," rarely could one find religiously
inspired spirituality in Bosnian pop music. Individual "choice" emerges
here as fateful commitment.

Ja vjerujem u Boga i Božje odredenje,	I believe in God and God's determi- nation,
i vjerujem da ništa nije priviđenje.	and I believe that nothing is illu- sion.
Sve je tako stvarno, sve tako realno.	Everything is actual, everything is real.
Ja vjerujem u to, ja vjerujem u to.	This I believe; this I believe.
Ne, ništa nije bilo a da nije moralo;	No, nothing ever happened that didn't have to be so;
nema toga lica što se nije boralo,	Never was a face that didn't have to wither;
nema kamena što neće jednom postat' prah,	there is not a stone that will not some day be powder;
i ni ramena što neće osjetiti strah.	and not a shoulder that will never have to tremble.

Refrain   **Refrain**

Qu'est ce que tu veux,	What do you want?
Tu es le voyageur.	You are the voyager.
Nous sommes, vous êtes, ils sont, elles sont,	We are, you are, they [men] are, they [women] are,
nous sommes, vous êtes	we are, you are
les voyageurs.	the voyagers.
Nous avons, vous avez, ils ont, elles ont,	We have, you have, they [men] have, they [women] have,
nous avons, vous avez,	we have, you have
la maison.	a home.
Dolazak je samo jedne knjige korica,	Arrival is only the jacket of a book,
a odlazak njena sestra parica.	and departure is just its sister copy.
Šta smo ti i ja, do putnici bez mjesta,	What are you and I but travelers without a place?

nikad saznat' nećemo kud nas vodi ova cesta.	We shall never know where this road will lead us.
Reci da li žališ, reci dal' se kaješ,	Say whether you are sorry, say if you have regrets.
ako kažeš "da," ti ustvari sebe daješ.	If you say, "Yes," you give yourself away.
Reci da li žališ, reci dal' se kaješ,	Say whether you are sorry, say if you have regrets.
ako kažeš "da," to je dokaz izbora.	If you say, "Yes," you prove you've made a choice.
Refrain	**Refrain**

Figure 2.2: *Putnici.* Music and text by Dino Merlin. *Putnici/Voyagers/Les voyagers*, Menart MCD 092, 1999.

The presence of violin and *saz* points to the cultural loci of Bosnia, where any further sense of place stops. (Instrumental tracks were recorded in an Istanbul studio, utilizing Turkish violin and *saz.*) The Slovenian producer, working in London, devised a fluid texture for the arrangement; the *saz* and violin tracks are featured as brief interludes or melodic interplay with the vocal line(s) against the percussion-driven background, which blends *darabuka,* tambourine, and acoustic guitar. Ambiguity of cultural locale is most effectively achieved by the song's bilingual performance; verses in Bosnian are sung by Merlin and the refrain by both singers in French. Apparently the cultural mix was not expected among the contest participants. After the first rehearsal Dino noted, "it was no longer the image of Bosnia from 1993; people began asking . . . 'what is this?'"

Two years later, Merlin's new album *Sredinom* [Through the middle] broke down many musical and ideological barriers, reportedly becoming the best selling record of the decade across the new states (Fig. 2.3; CD 2.2). When a journalist suggested that with this album, Merlin had reunited the formerly Yugoslav market, he retorted that he intended to "unite himself," not the markets, and least of all the new states.[15] He maintained that the calculated strategy of ethnic appeal—this bit for Croatian ears, this bit for Serbian consumption, this bit for Bosnian taste—was doomed to failure. In other words, original ideas come from within an artist, not the environment. Though "Through the middle" perhaps avoids the "socialist brand of hybridity," similar interactive strategies pertaining to production and world music excursions figure prominently.

Sarajevo has always figured as a cultural force in Merlin's songs, nurturing but unforgiving of those who betray its spirit—a blend of provincial attitudes and cosmopolitan outlooks. In the title song Merlin suggests a middle road for Bosnia, literally between the (Near) East and (Central European) West, urging a neighborhood kid to recognize that his home is where it has always been: between Istanbul and Vienna. But apart from physical distance, perceptions of cultural proximity between Sarajevo and these imperial sites have changed, pitting the Euro-American protectorial authority in Bosnia against Bosnia's new eastward alliances, with Iran, Turkey, and Saudi Arabia most recently in the lead. Forming the backdrop to Merlin's call for self-reliance are competing and conflicting visions of Bosnia's future voiced by local nationalist ideologues and the "international community," namely a 30,000-strong contingent of administrators, policy makers, and cultural mediators found only in Sarajevo.

[*Do you love me? Reach higher. Higher consciousness.*]

Ovo je vrijeme kad se uči,	This is the time of learning,
slovo po slovo, riječ po riječ.	letter by letter, word by word.
Sjedi mali, tu je tvoj dom,	Sit down, little one, there is your home,
daleko su Istambul i Beč.	Istanbul and Vienna are far away.
Sad si, mali, tu na raskršću,	You, little one, are at the cross-roads now,
svi su pametni svi šapuću.	all are clever, all whisper.
Ti ne vjeruj nikome na riječ,	Trust no one's word,
svaki korak sam moraš preć.	every step you must take alone.
Furaj, mali, sam sredinom	Push on through the middle, little one,
furaj, mali, tom dolinom.	push on [through] that valley, little one.
Bog te čuva, ti pazi ljude,	God takes care of you, you take care of people,
pa šta bude neka bude.	what's to be, let it be.

Figure 2.3: *Sredinom.* Title track from the album by the same name. Music and lyrics by Dino Merlin. In Takt Records CD-060, 2000.

Some novel stylistic elements in Merlin's music might be interpreted as the aesthetically rationalized effects of his religious upbringing, but the album as a whole supports the notion of cultural empowerment that global pop provides for its local articulation. Merlin is particularly attracted to what he sees as culturally contiguous areas on the world music map: France and the cultures of the Maghreb, including *rai* music, which has led to his own exploration of "sources." Thus the song *Halima* features Tunisian singer Lotfi Bouchnak and the *ney* player Matri Mohsan, whose tracks were recorded in Bouchnak's studio in Tunis during a session with Merlin. The "Tunisian voice" opens with an expressive soloistic improvisation, accentuating the basic *flamenco*/eastern Mediterranean feel of the performance. The recording's use of sampling technology, on the other hand, makes possible a specter of the world as contextless fragments of identification; here Arab *darabuka* easily coexists with Persian *tar*, Turkish *saz* with Indian *sitar*. Within the cultural distance conveyed by the sparse *sitar* introduction, the appeal of oriental color in its many geocultural and marketing hues is graphically revealed. Overall, the album's coherence is provided by conventions of local pop, here strongly influenced by that old internationalist favorite, Spanish-Gypsy guitar, plus a new layer—percussion-driven Latin pop rendered faithfully by Merlin's band.

The commercial success of this album beyond Bosnia, however, resulted from the Eurovision-styled song *Godinama* [Through the years], sung by Merlin and Croatian pop singer Ivana Banfić. The song derives its broad appeal from a polished "Cro-pop" production characterized by the ample use of technology to create wide textural spaces for the vocals, string section, and synthesized rhythmic background. Banfić's refrain, conjuring the Italianate/Mediterranean lineage of Croatian music, contrasts with Merlin's dynamically understated authorial voice. Bosnian input is suggested by occasional entrances of a *ney*-like instrument and the folk-ish refrain motif: "you cheated on me." In 2001, the song won a "Porin," a major Croatian music industry award.

Yet love for this "federal" hit seems to have arisen primarily among its audiences, especially forward-looking professionals. Some Croatian industry insiders questioned whether a Bosnian singer was qualified to compete for the highest Croatian national music award. Nor was international recognition enough to mute political scrutiny in Sarajevo. In an at times excruciating interview for the *BH Dani* weekly, a journalist pressed anew the issue of Merlin's writing a song "about Alija" (Izetbegović), which came out in the darkest hours of the Sarajevo siege.[16] Distancing himself from this association, Merlin reminded all interested parties that he had filled Sarajevo concert halls long before the likes of Izetbegović was able to do so in the early 1990s. In our recent interview he passionately discussed the issue of "party affiliation." He said he was weary of ideological insinuations, suggesting that he has no control over the reception of his songs either by his audience or by the politicians who capitalize on the eloquent statements about Bosnian belonging in his lyrics.[17] Another song involving a key Serbian exponent of *turbo folk*, Svetlana Ražnatović-Ceca, raised a similar issue of accountability dramatized in newspaper headlines by the question, "Did Dino write a song for Ceca?" Merlin had, admittedly, contributed to the public furor by issuing conflicting statements about a potential Belgrade concert, his determination vacillating between pro and con with the dramatic turns of Serbian politics.

Returns and Exchanges

Deep resentment and a desire for return often overshadow musicians' responses to the war. A poignant illustration, appearing after the Bosnian conflict erupted, is the dualistic career of one of the most popular Sarajevo bands, Zabranjeno Pušenje [Smoking Forbidden; i.e., No Smoking], the self-proclaimed originator of the new primitives movement that captured national attention in the latter 1980s.[18] During the early stages of the Sarajevo siege, two bands emerged bearing this same name: one in Belgrade, led by the original lead singer, and another in Zagreb, led by the original guitar player. Each group made headway in their new environ-ment: the Zagreb recordings of Zabranjeno Pušenje received considerable attention and airplay in Sarajevo; the success of the Serbian wing of the group has been equally remarkable, if only in Belgrade. A recent declaration by the latter's vocalist not to return to the city that nurtured his primitive poetics was spoken, uncharacteristically, without any introspec-tive satire: "I am a man who cares about his own dignity and feelings. Sarajevo and Bosnia have chosen the path that doesn't interest me. I don't believe that they will fail without me, and I think that I'll be better off by not being with them" (Mitrinović 1999).

Another Bosnian expatriate in the Belgrade pop scene, a concert promoter from Banja Luka, offered a different perspective on return and exchange. As weary of local politicians as of the politics of international mediation, he suggested a third way of cultivating business ties through independence.

> Why would politicians establish ties with my friends ahead of me: like they created something, and we are fools. I was normal before, and

according to them, I became a fool. This is why I won't have concerts in Sarajevo done for me by SFOR [Special Forces] or OSCE [Office for Security and Cooperation in Europe], instead I'll do them with my friends, with whom I grew up (Mitrinović 1999).

Being "normal" during the Sarajevo siege became symbolic of resistance to the chaos of war, a tool to negotiate reality (Maček 1997:25–58). Normalcy provided that bit of distance from the incomprehensible and absurd conflict and, as the above quote suggests, the divisiveness that was the making of politicians, and not the people. In the post-war period, a new phrase cropped up: "the time is not yet" ("the time is not ripe"). This phrase, which commented on the much debated, potential re-establishment of diplomatic relations between Serbia and Bosnia, also captured a personal dilemma faced by musicians: whether to return to concert stages in neighboring countries.

The moral dimensions of this issue were brought to the forefront with the highly publicized first post-war concert of the legendary Sarajevo pop-rock group Indexi in Belgrade in 1998. For leading commentators in both Belgrade and Sarajevo, the enthusiasm with which the group was greeted in Belgrade provoked the illusion that nothing had happened. Even Belgrade's alternative rock insiders were somewhat at a loss to explain the attendance of some members of Serbia's political establishment. Critical reviews of this successful revival of cultural ties only raised the stakes for musicians in their collective quest to face what happened, and only then, perhaps, to move forward.

Appraisal of Indexi's concert by Sarajevo commentators appears particularly harsh since its members have remained loyal to Sarajevo and the "idea" of Bosnia.[19] But at issue was not, as one commentator clarified, that the group was expected to open their shows by reading UN Security Council resolutions on the aggression against Bosnia-Hercegovina. Rather, it was the ability of the band's new cultural managers to co-opt the revivalist urges in *estrada*, and by this nostalgic gloss over reality, aid in collective forgetting. In the wake of both Indexi's concert in Belgrade and that of Goran Bregović in Sarajevo, the commentator pointed to a key issue:

Thawing of relations between the lands of the former Yugoslavia, almost by consensus is even here [Sarajevo] accepted as inevitable. Even if artists make mistakes in building the new bridges of cooperation, it is even more dangerous to give away their cooperations to the governments that destroyed the previous ones (Pečanin 1998).

Outside the official realm of cultural politics and the press, the respect that musicians in Serbia and Bosnia express toward each other shows a great deal of professional solidarity. Commenting on Serbian music in terms of a new generation of singers, one Sarajevo vocalist singles out Mira Škorić, a "great Serb, but a great singer too, pushing the boundaries of the genre." On a number of occasions in Belgrade I have heard nostalgic references to Sarajevo, its casual attitude, and its good singers, and once, a self-effacing complaint by a folk producer that Sarajevo musicians "can't seem to be able to do business without us." In the politically unfavorable climate of the mid-1990s, a number of musicians, folk and pop, visited Belgrade, seeking projects. These were private visits, typically not reported in local newspapers. On the whole, the private and later public reception of such visits by Sarajevo and Belgrade commentators fluctuated between cautionary applause to disapproval of a "business as usual" approach, depending on the artist in question and organizational details of the visit.

In the Bosnian court of public opinion, one artist who most infamously "crossed over" both the border and moral lines is the Sarajevo-born film director Emir Kusturica, who distanced himself from this city, accusing it, in the phantasmagoric style of his film poetics, of a murder plot if he returns.[20] Although more tactful in his public statements during the Sarajevo siege, another noted Sarajevan, Goran Bregović, was faulted for his non-partisan "UN attitude." During the 1990s, both artists' appropriation of Romani culture became increasingly controversial. The interesting trajectory of the pair's Gypsy carnivalesque on the European stage was initiated in 1989 by Kusturica's Palm d'Or film *The Time of the Gypsies*, whose soundtrack, supplied by Goran Bregović in collaboration with Macedonian Romani musicians, was integral to the film's success. Here performance is for the most part entrusted to the Romani musicians, and Bregović's light production treatment of their local repertoire became a hallmark of his future collaborative projects.

In the 1990s, however, Bregović's connection with "folklore" entered a new level of both authorial intimacy and Balkan exotica. As a meeting place of Islam, Eastern Orthodoxy, and Roman Christianity, he seemed to imagine the Balkans as a frontier musical heaven, stating that he was interested in the region as a cultural, not political concept. Having transformed himself into an internationally successful film music composer, he boosted his performance career by concertizing with a number of band/ensemble formations rooted in Balkan and Slavic traditions, most notably, the "Orchestra for Weddings and Funerals." On stage his music was a spectacle of drama, poetics, roots music, oriental soulfulness, and energy. A reviewer in Madrid wrote enthusiastically about Bregović's concert in 2001: "The mysterious and sublime echo of the three Bulgarian voices, the opaqueness and density of the powerful male choir from Belgrade and a large array of string instruments are overshadowed by what Bregović calls his Wedding and Funeral Orchestra, seven Gypsies who blow their brass instruments with an irresistible drive."[21]

Is this the postmodern condition or "stealing" around? Bregović himself is not sure. He is keen to indulge interviewers with his mischievous evasion of questions about appropriating sources from the Balkan storehouse, or lending his work to political causes, or expressing loyalty to any border. If he has lost some former supporters in the process of extricating himself from the Yugoslav conundrum toward the larger Balkan home, a new generation of fans has already secured his place on the map of global pop, in Italy, France, Greece, Argentina, Russia, Spain, and the former Yugoslavia. The collaborative lineup of this "master of recycling," as one Sarajevo critic put it, includes Iggy Pop and the late Ofra Haza, as well as Turkish singer Sezen Aksu, Polish singer Kaya, and Greek vocalist George Dalaras, most of whom have sung covers of his old Yugoslav hits in their respective languages.

The enduring appeal of Bregović's work and personality is undeniable. Although he chose Paris and Belgade as his new residences, audience reception at his recent concert in Sarajevo—his first post-war visit—was favorable. For local observers of Bregović's generation, this native son of Sarajevo, who once reportedly spoke of the city's undeserved world fame, the blur of nostalgia and resignation lingers on. The pioneering dimension of his work is readily apparent and recognized by musicians, particularly those within the growing ethno-circles of post-Yugoslav pop; this is a significant achievement that speaks to the consistency of his refined populist aesthetics and his ability to meaningfully articulate the local within the exponentially larger geocultural circles of belonging afforded by global pop. Even if this perspective is politically naive, as some commentators argue, there is a larger pattern of border crossovers which demonstrates that listening habits die hard.

Conclusions

Today, the flow of music across the new borders takes many forms: increased availability of music produced in neighboring states, re-licensing of records produced in Croatia by Belgrade producers and distributors, recordings of Sarajevo musicians in Zagreb and Ljubljana, and concert appearances of selected Serbian pop singers in Zagreb, to name a few. Although relations between Zagreb and Belgrade remain profoundly strained, it is worth noting that for both Serbian and Bosnian musicians, long isolated by economic sanctions and war, Croatia served as the western music frontier. One possible source of *turbo folk*'s techno inspiration might be Croatian dance music, which reached Belgrade in the early 1990s, facilitating the creation of the local dance-club scene.[22] Today, Croatian pop seems everywhere; it dominates trendy cafés in Sarajevo and competes with local pop and rock fare in Belgrade's abundant market of legitimate and pirated recordings. Examples of individual musicians' collaborations are too numerous to be discussed as special cases. A few Croatian musicians are defiantly involved in Balkan musical affairs by promoting the controversial "Eastern" music in Croatia, most notably the neo-folk *enfant terrible* Siniša Vuco, and the Balkan girl of Croatia's popular music scene, Alka Vuica. The swapping of song tunes, with or without copyright acknowledgment, may connect performers who are musically as far afield as Croatian pop diva Doris Dragović and *turbo folk* star Mira Škorić, a case in point being their individual releases of the songs *Maria Magdalen* and *Maria the Maiden,* in Croatian and Serbian, respectively. More than a coincidence of titles, Škorić's folk-styled but interpretatively powerful rendition of the song is answered by Dragović's exceedingly dramatic performance based on a similar tune.

These examples, among many others, run counter to the litany of cultural incompatibility between the central European locus of Croatian culture, and the Balkan/Ottoman core of Serbian and Bosnian culture. At issue here is not that these larger patterns of identification and self-identification are not valid; it is that they are politically activated and ideologically constructed to become normative frameworks within which musical convergences and sentiments of shared cultural experiences are deemed irrelevant. But they are there—and recognized by audiences.

The recent rise in popularity of Bosnian music in Slovenia, for example, strikingly illustrates a shift in local perceptions of the Yugoslav southeast, which Slovenians now refer to in generalized Western terms as "the Balkans." The warm reception of *sevdalinke* by Slovenian audiences indicates a larger process in which cultural symbols are being recontextualized, but also the combination of new incentives—revivalist, educational, and commercial. At the center of these efforts has been singer/songwriter Vlado Kreslin, the key exponent of Slovenian pop with ethnic leanings, who, in collaboration with the "cultural wing" of the Bosnian refugee population, helped showcase Bosnia as a distinctive culture—and not just distinct to refugees. A Bosnian music critic involved in the project explained succinctly that the receptivity of Slovenian audiences to artists from the successor states was an expression of Yugo-nostalgia (Andreé-Zaimović 1998:191–92). Neither an anachronism of a discredited political system nor a political dream of reunification, Yugo-nostalgia, at least in this context, recognizes the achievements of the past.

A question posed by the editors of *Music and the Racial Imagination* (Radano and Bohlman 2000:36) helps illuminate the complex issue of identity as represented by both *turbo folk*'s and *sevdah*-rock's East–West intersections.

> The breaking down of racial boundaries and differences has been one result of postcolonial histories. It is the question of realignment and, more to the point, of affiliation that gives us pause. Moreover, whereas the recourse to a rhetoric of hybridity is indeed attractive, it becomes more fragile—and not less fully convincing—through its globalization. Is all hybridity the same?

Turbo folk is clearly not a "global" style, if only because it lacks that distribution niche in Western transnational markets which would translate localness into worldly relevance. But even as a singularly Balkan style, it operates on already tested precepts of ethnopop globalization: manipulat-ing myriad local sources and those of a few selected Mediterranean locales, appealing to a larger Balkan home, and rejuvenating its modernity by co-opting the latest from the West. And yet, against the backdrop of ethnic cleansing in Bosnia and elsewhere, *turbo folk*'s "schizophonic" insistence on Orient-ornament hybridity—indeed fetish—gives us pause, because it reveals Muslim ethnicity as a function of stylistic decorum devoid of compassion for the centuries-old other—in other words, more of the same, as Tomislav Longinović's (2000:641) reading might suggest:

> *Turbo folk* is the sound of an unacknowledged postcolonial culture that had been dormant under the communist veil of forgetfulness until the latest war. The techno rhythms are embraced from the colonial cultures to the North and West (Europe proper) as markers of racial/cultural superiority, while the wailing voice of the singer articulates a sup-pressed, shameful legacy of one's slavery to the Turks who are regarded as a part of inferior cultures and races of the East and South. At the same time, this music reveals the emptiness of myths of racial and ethnic authenticity.

The cultural opposition's critique of *turbo folk* culture is simultaneously a critique of the "position" (*pozicija*)—the regime—which empowered politically various uncultured types: the old rural migrants and the new entrepreneurial upper class. More nuanced analysis points to the complicity of folk entertainment in what Eric Gordy (1999), in his engaged and insightful analysis, terms the "destruction of alternatives" within Serbia's society of the 1990s. But both approaches, though eloquent statements of cultural resistance to the patriotic kitsch decorum of criminal wars, convey a sense of intolerance towards cultural others, thus partaking of that very exclusionary thrust of the nationalist discourse.

Beneath the assumption of ideologically disinterested knowledge is the never ending quest for legitimacy. Can one take "scholarly" interest in *turbo folk*, when it is so obviously allied with a corrupted system? It is a question tacitly raised by indiscriminate criticism and a skeptical attitude even toward researchers, which fails to acknowledge that it was Serbia's intellectual elite who provided the blueprint for the country's political orientation in the 1990s. The music's guilt by regime-association affords *turbo folk* a political power that, in reality, it never had.

I have argued that Bosnian and Serbian eastern junctures, variously aided by the sway of Turkish music, seem stronger than ever. Both *turbo folk* and *sevdah*-rock show that this Orient has never been the site of cultural imagination constructed by the West. Few Serbian musicians would be inclined to invoke an Ottoman heritage to account for the deeply-rooted syncretism they skillfully interpret and manipulate in their present music-making. While one may easily argue here for a case of short memory, in sharp contrast to the total collapse of historical time evident in contemporary invocations of the Kosovo myth, the ahistorical perspectives of musicians must be taken into account when mapping out the new musical Balkans and Orients within. Similarly, the ideological orientation of Bosniaks toward the Muslim world speaks more to the agony of the recent past than the centrality of Islam in the ongoing and arduous process of rebuilding the nation. Both Bosnia and Serbia are at a crossroads, Bosnia searching for both its place and identity, and Serbia beginning the process of re-discovering itself.

Notes

1. This essay draws on my research in Yugoslavia throughout the 1980s, in 1991 (Bosnia-Hercegovina and Serbia), 1997 (Bosnia-Hercegovina), and 1999 (Sarajevo and Belgrade). A portion of the present essay is based on the paper "Belgrade, Spring 1999: Songs That Sustained the Nation," delivered at the Annual Meeting of the Society for Ethnomusicology, Toronto, Canada, 2000.

2. In 1994, at the first Parliament meeting of the newly formed Federation of Bosnia-Hercegovina, a constitutional amendment was introduced replacing the religious denomination "Musliman" with the ethnonym "Bošnjak," thereby recognizing the Muslim community of Bosnia as a national one, on a par with its Croat and Serb counterparts. Originally, Bošnjak (pronounced Boshniak) was an inclusive identity referent used by peoples from Bosnia irrespective of their religious affiliations. It is an archaic, slightly turkicized equivalent of "Bosnian." The noted writer Ivan Lovrenović commented approvingly and yet regretfully on this further revision of Bosnian historical experience: "It was clear to me that something rare was happening [at the meeting] . . . something that will shake up many relations: some will be clarified, some complicated for years to come (*BH Dani*, 21 December 1998).

3. A few names that typically make lists of leading singers/groups, many of whom are still active, include the rock groups Indexi and Bijelo Dugme (Sarajevo); Azra, Film, and Parni Valjak (Zagreb); Riblja Čorba, Idoli, and Električni Orgazam (Beograd); Leb i Sol (Skopje); and Lačni Franz and Laibach (Ljubljana); folk singers from Serbia and Bosnia such as Miroslav Ilić, Lepa Brena, Šaban Šaulić, Zorica Brunclik, Halid Bešlić, and Hanka Paldum, as well as Romani representatives of the genre such as Esma Redžepova, Šaban Bajramović, and Muharem Serbezovski. Still ranking high among equally numerous pop singers are Zdravko Čolić, Oliver Dragojević, Kemal Monteno, and Josipa Lisac; though fewer in number, singer-songwriters such as Ibrica Jusić, Đorđe Balašević, and Arsen Dedić have received acclaim from critics and discriminating audiences alike.

4. In 2001, the Bosnian Muslim party, along with the Croat national party, lost their governing stranglehold to a broad anti-nationalist coalition, the democratic Alliance for Change, led by the charismatic leader of the Social Democratic Party, Zlatko Lagumdija.

5. Forcing prisoners to sing nationalist songs for the purpose of humiliation and torture was a practice in POW camps reported by a number of journalists and human rights groups (for a rare witness account in the ethnomusicological literature see Pettan 1998:17–18).

6. *Reporter*, 1 September 1999.

7. Without going further into the ideological implications of Rambo's brand of eclecticism, two details in his prolific career show that, in fact, there may be nothing contradictory about an artist working for the folk business and serving as the key oppositional voice of Belgrade *estrada*. For example, he wrote songs for

the leading folk singers Lepa Brena and Vesna Zmijanac. More memorable is his behavior at a 1992 concert, when he interrupted the performance of another singer and began to castigate the audience for entertaining itself while someplace else bombs were falling, all in the face of television audiences tuned into the live broadcast.

8. Interview with Miodrag Ilić, Belgrade, September 1999.

9. Interview with Ilić, September 1999. Ilić echoes the view shared by many in the former Yugoslavia: "Powerful people, in fact, have moved [into] piracy in 1992–93. So, Serbs produced pirates for Croatia, Croatian pirates came here, then Bulgaria took over all this by CDs."

10. *Pink Revija,* 8 September 1999.

11. The Dayton Accord, signed in 1995 in Dayton, Ohio, brought peace to Bosnia-Hercegovina and solidified the country's division into three peoples (nationalities) and two political entities, the Bosniak/Croat Federation and Serbian Republic (Republika Srpska).

12. One anecdote illustrates the official dimension of the issue. I visited a small recording firm in Sarajevo, founded in the early 1980s, to inquire about the availability of a song by a Bosnian singer for inclusion in a potential compilation of "newly composed folk music." After learning that singers from Serbia would, of course, be included, and that a Belgrade producer had expressed support for the idea, the official retorted that such a decision had to be made at higher levels. First, approval by the Bosnian Ministry of Culture was needed, followed up by direct communication between Sarajevo and Belgrade producers. Otherwise, we would all have to wait for the official re-establishment of diplomatic relations between Belgrade and Sarajevo. Extraordinarily new here was the notion that the Ministry of Culture now patronizes a style that it formerly proclaimed anti-cultural, and now potentially considers a part of Bosnia's musical heritage.

13. Interview with Hanka Paldum, 18 August 1999, Sarajevo.

14. Interview with Dino Merlin, 26 August 1999, Sarajevo.

15. See *BH Dani,* 11 May 2001.

16. *BH Dani,* 11 May 2001.

17. Interview with Dino Merlin, 27 May 2001, Atlanta, Georgia.

18. The term "new primitives" is most closely associated with the activities of the rock bands Zabranjeno Pušenje, Elvis J. Kurtovich, and the weekly Radio Sarajevo show, "Top List of Super-Realists." In a distinctly Sarajevo response to the polished new wave imagery of rock bands and alternative art groups emerging in Belgrade, Zagreb and Ljubljana in the early 1980s, the new primitives used street jargon and self-effacing satire to develop an ironic parody of a stereotypical-ly uncouth Bosnian (Rasmussen 2002:191–94).

19. Bosnian Serbs, too, have claimed Indexi as part of their popular culture. The group's members tell the story of a song they recorded years ago, containing an excerpt played on *gusle,* the only song that the Serb radio station at Pale headquarters chose to broadcast during the Sarajevo siege. Musicians speak of this exercise in musical archeology with amusement, and few among the group's fans

are aware of its existence (Interview with Bodo Kovačević and Đorđe Kisić, August 1999, Sarajevo).

20. *Slobodna Bosna*, 19 September 1998.

21. See http://www.goranbregovic.com@co.yu. For more on Bregović's collaborations see Stokes, this volume.

22. Interview with Dragan Ambrozić, promotion manager of B-92, September 1999, Belgrade.

❖ 3 ❖

Muzică Orientală:
Identity and Popular Culture
in Postcommunist Romania

Margaret H. Beissinger

Muzică orientală [oriental music] is a Romanian, urban-based song and dance style that combines traditional and popular music with various Romani, Turkish, Serbian, and Bulgarian elements, particularly in rhythm, melody, and instrumentation.[1] It is performed in public—especially at weddings, baptisms, and other family celebrations—almost exclusively by professional male Romani musicians. Its audience is primarily Romanian, though also Romani.[2]

Formerly shunned and even banned by the communist government, *muzică orientală* is now performed widely throughout the country. As a cultural phenomenon, it both expresses and challenges problematic aspects of identity in contemporary Romanian society. The music is at once championed by rural and "rurban" working-class populations, while simultaneously reviled by many from among the urban elite—typically educated office and service employees, professionals, and intellectuals. For the public which revels in it, *muzică orientală* provides an exhilarating form of popular participatory entertainment that exemplifies postcommunist cultural expression permitted without formal censure. By contrast, for its critics, this music implicitly juxtaposes kitsch with good taste, urban with rural or rurban lifestyles, Balkan with Romanian, East with West, "Gypsy" subculture with ethnic mainstream, tradition with modernity, and young with old. In the divergent responses that it evokes, *muzică orientală* generates complex convictions about power, identity, aesthetics, and culture. It brings into sharp focus questions of class, ethnicity, and nation, as well as gender and generational tensions.

Orientalism as a cultural phenomenon assumes implicit contrasts. Edward Said's well-known work on this topic (1978) provides a useful model for understanding how and why *muzică orientală* is perceived in various ways by Romanian society today. Said argues that for those with a European mind set, who view themselves as superior, oriental culture has long been viewed as the subordinate, uncivilized, less advanced, and less cultured Other against which it—the superior West—gains its own integrity. Moreover, the binary opposition deriving from the East vs. West dichotomy in the sorting out of identity centers on the control and superiority of the West (or the Western-oriented) over the lesser, inferior East. As Said notes, "the relationship between Occident and Orient is a relationship of power, of domination, of varying degrees of complex hegemony" (1978:5). Along similar lines, Larry Wolff maintains that Eastern Europe evolved during the eighteenth century as a "paradox of simultaneous inclusion and exclusion" that contrasted with Western Europe and was "made to mediate between Europe and the Orient" (1994:7). He proposes that "the invention of Eastern Europe" was "an intellectual project of demi-Orientalization" (1994:7).

In the Balkans, the proverbial "crossroads between East and West," oriental and occidental cultures coexist, or at least exist concurrently, but are constantly in conflict with each other in struggles over identity and power. In "demi-orientalized" societies such as the Romanian (and other Balkan), affinities with the West are seen by the elite as affording privilege and prestige, while associations with the East (equated with Turkey and the Middle East—the "Orient") are viewed as degrading and undermining culture. Furthermore, internal nationalist tendencies espoused by the ethnic majority perpetually clash with non-native—especially Romani—culture in yet other manifestations of tensions between East and West. How "oriental" is conceptualized and coded locally—both historically and in the postcommunist world—informs the uneasy relationships between the Romanian "native" and non-western "foreign," elements perceived as existing both outside of and within society. In this article, I demonstrate how *muzică orientală* is a cultural phenomenon that mirrors these identities and indexes a variety of divergent responses. Throughout the Balkans, comparable contemporary oriental trends in music also generate forms of social, cultural, and generational discord.

I argue here that *muzică orientală*, as an expressive form that simultaneously attracts and repulses segments of the public, challenges deeply held assumptions about culture and aesthetics. *Muzică orientală*, which appeals to the young non-elite in society, represents a form of counterculture. It is a formerly forbidden music that is now experienced as exotic, seductive, "Gypsy," Balkan, oriental, and even Western, as well as contemporary and relevant. Yet it is an anathema to those who form the reasonably educated, ethnically dominant elite because it subverts their attempts to emulate Western European culture as well as to promote Romanian native culture from within. Moreover, embedded in the associations between foreign culture from abroad and non-native culture from within is the tendency to submerge oriental with Romani culture—a conflation, as I will show, that is vividly present in today's *muzică orientală*. Finally, I explore how the music creates and perpetuates tensions and divisions within the Romani community, especially as nuanced distinctions among Romani musicians—based on generational dynamics and urban vs. rural disparities—are considered. *Muzică orientală* threatens beliefs not only about where Romania lies in relation to Europe and the "Orient," but also about where Romanian national and ethnic minority cultures find their places within a complex, evolving, and ever more global contemporary society.

My examination begins with a brief cultural-historical portrait of Romania in the context of Eastern and Western Europe, followed by a consideration of the Turkish musical culture, interpreted locally as oriental, that figured in the Ottoman-dominated Romanian principalities (now contemporary Romania). As part of this discussion, I chart the development of the *manea,* a Romani genre that has circulated since the Ottoman period and now refers, in colloquial usage, to the markedly evolved ethnopop[3] fusion song and dance form also called *muzică orientală*. I explore how *muzică orientală* as a style emerged in the twentieth century and how it figures in the postcommunist period, examining in particular its relationships to class, ethnicity, nation, gender, and generational divisions. My ethnographic findings for this study are based on yearly periods of fieldwork in southern Romania from 1998 through 2003. I attended weddings and baptisms and frequented restaurants where *muzică orientală* was performed in cities and villages. I also spoke at length with many musicians (most of them Roma) who perform *muzică orientală*, as well as with the ethnic Romanians and Roma who form its audiences.[4] My observations throughout are augmented by relevant commentary on other Balkan societies where comparable oriental musical cultures are also manifest and conflict in various ways with the music and culture of urban elites and intellectuals.

Historical and Cultural Considerations

Romanians have long had an anxious, even vexed, sense of who they are and how they fit into Europe—both Eastern and Western. Maria Todorova describes this as "the self-conscious and troublesome feeling of being trapped in an ambiguous status, the in-betweenness of East and West" (1997:48). Romania's identity embraces several important "Eastern" historical and cultural conditions that find parallels elsewhere in the Balkans. First, significant portions of Romania (mainly in the south and northeast, historically the Romanian principalities) formed part of the Ottoman Empire from the early 1500s to 1878, at which time Romania became a kingdom. Second, after roughly six decades as a monarchy, including the ultra-nationalist inter-war period, Romania was incorporated into the Soviet bloc in 1944. Romania's brand of communism was particularly repressive, epitomized by the dictatorial rule of the late Nicolae Ceauşescu, in power from 1965 until his assassination during the Romanian Revolution in December 1989. Third, until the mass industrialization that began during the mid-twentieth century, the majority of Romanians, like so many others in the Balkans, lived in rural communities (many, in fact, still do). Fourth, the predominant religion among Romanians is Eastern Orthodoxy.[5] Finally, despite its Romance roots, Romanian forms part of a Balkan linguistic nexus: along with Bulgarian, Macedonian, and Albanian, it forms part of a regional group of similar languages termed the Balkan *sprachbund*.[6]

Notions about language also characterize much of Romania's "Western" European cultural identity. Romanians cling to the conviction—realized by the late eighteenth century—that Romanian is Romance in origin and derives from the Latin language that was brought to the ancient territory of Dacia (present-day Romania) by Roman soldiers who occupied the region for 150 years almost two thousand years ago. Ever since this "Latinism" took root among the learned in society, Romanians have never ceased proclaiming the Romance nature of the language they speak. By extension, they self-identify as Latin. Regarding the sanctity of this ancient legacy, Walker Connor remarks that Romanians ardently believe that they "are the otherwise unadulterated product of the fusion of

Latins with the Dacians (a Thracian people) during the days of the Roman Empire." He goes on to point out that the

> "Latinist" movement, with its stress on Roman heritage, the Latin alphabet, and purity of blood had been promoted by intellectuals . . . beginning in the late eighteenth century [such that] an image of the Romanian nation as a Latin isolate surrounded by Slavs to the north and south and Magyars to the west has by now deeply penetrated the popular psyche (1994:216).

Beginning in the nineteenth century, ties between Romania and France in particular developed and were bolstered as young Romanian intellectuals, many of whom subsequently became influential political and cultural figures in Romania, pursued their studies in Paris. A significant aspect of Romanian national identity, then, lies in the conviction that Romanians find themselves surrounded by dissimilar Slavs and Hungarians and thus constitute an enclave of Latin, Western-oriented culture in an Eastern world.

Within Romania, as well, the sense of "us" (Romanians) and "them" (the ethnic Others) plays a significant role, particularly when the Hungarians (who live mostly in Transylvania) and Roma (who live everywhere) are considered.[7] The Romani community presently totals about two million in a country of twenty-three million inhabitants (Fraser 1992). Despite the fact that Roma began settling in the Romanian principalities already in the fourteenth century, they are still viewed by many among the dominant population as outsiders. The Romani experience in Romania is one marked by marginality, poverty, injustice, and hardship. Not only were Roma enslaved for approximately five hundred years, but during the communist period, a policy of "social homogeneity" was pursued internally by the State, including repressive measures to assimilate Roma (Verdery 1996:92–93). Postcommunist Romania continues to incorporate various complex relationships: one finds anti-orientalism and an obsession with the West simultaneously with the ever more explicit expressions of internal xenophobia—articulated in the most extreme nationalist terms from the radical right.[8]

"Oriental" or Turkish Music from the Sixteenth Century to 1989

The written history of music in Romania includes many gaps. In the narrative that follows, I have pieced together a brief account of oriental musical culture and how it evolved from the Ottoman period to the present. The story that emerges is at times very sketchy and leaves many questions unanswered. It will be evident that the designation "oriental" is employed locally to indicate not only Ottoman Turkish and Turkish art music, but that by the late twentieth century it also references a fusion of diverse musical effects and influences that form a distinct Turkish (Middle Eastern) ethnopop style—also coded as Romani.

The Ottoman Period

The historic Romanian principalities (Wallachia in the south and Moldavia in the northeast) came under Ottoman suzerainty in the early sixteenth century. Two hundred years later, starting in 1711, power was reinforced through Ottoman-appointed Greek rulers who governed until 1821 during what was called the Phanariot period.[9] Romania was declared independent from Ottoman domination at the Congress of Berlin in 1878 (Michelson 2000:676).

From the sixteenth to the nineteenth centuries Ottoman Turkish art music was cultivated in upper-class society in the Romanian principalities. It was during the early years of Ottoman influence that Turkish art culture became favored among the Romanian urban elite. Turks, Greeks, and Armenians settled in large numbers in the urban areas of the Romanian principalities, bringing with them culture and music from their respective homelands. Throughout the second half of the sixteenth century, many Romanian boyars from rural areas moved into the cities, where they embraced Turkish culture, notably music (Ciobanu 1974a:93). Ottoman Turkish art music culture was wholeheartedly adopted—first by the nobility in the courts and later by the bourgeoisie (Alexandru 1980b:266, 268). Among the early performers of this music were Turkish entertainers from Istanbul.[10] These included Ottoman Turkish Janissaries (elite military units) who played in the *mehterhanea*, a "Turkish ceremonial and quasi-military ensemble" (Garfias 1981:97) that was sent as an emblem of the sultan and his nobility to the Romanian aristocracy. The music of the *mehterhanea* "combined courtly and popular forms" (Feldman 2002:114) and in the Romanian principalities "was included in official events and played at meal time and at the princes' celebrations" (Ciobanu 1974b:108).[11] Gheorghe Ciobanu describes the repertoire of the *mehterhanea* as comprising "military songs of the Janissaries but also lyric pieces known as *manele* [sg. *manea*]" (1974b:108), an Ottoman Turkish form that I will return to shortly. First let us turn our attention to the Romani musicians in the Romanian principalities at that time.

Lăutari (sg. *lăutar*)[12] are male Romani professional musicians who, as slaves, performed on the estates of the Romanian nobility and in monasteries from at least the late fifteenth century in Wallachia and by 1570 in Moldavia (Cosma 1996:10, 22–24; Iorga 1925:27).[13] Their occupation was and still is hereditary, passed along the male kinship line within families. During the Ottoman period, the local urban *lăutari* eventually assimilated the styles and genres of the visiting Turkish musicians; by the eighteenth century, Ottoman Turkish art music had become their domain (Cosma 1996:18). The luxurious boyar lifestyle during this time included such frequent merry-making that nearly every boyar had his own household ensemble, or *taraf* (pl. *tarafuri*),[14] of *lăutari* (Cosma 1996:18; Ciobanu 1974a:92–93). Indeed, *lăutari* were so much a part of upper-class life that the boyars "couldn't even imagine celebrations without them" (Cosma 1996:18). The appropriation of Ottoman culture and music, and with it the role of *lăutari,* intensified among the upper classes during Phanariot rule. *Lăutari* frequently traveled to Turkey and played music there, acquiring repertoire that they then brought back home.[15] Tiberiu Alexandru notes that "circa 1800, the best violinists in Constantinople were Gypsy Romanians" (1980b:267).

Returning now to the *manea* (pl. *manele),* we are speaking of a genre that is rooted in Romania's Ottoman-dominated past and was adopted by *lăutari,* later becoming an urban Romani song and dance and eventually evolving into today's *muzică orientală*.[16] Overall, there is little written on the *manea*. As a social dance form, it was not documented until the twentieth century; the history of the *manea* as song, however, is somewhat fuller. The early *manea* circulated and became known in the Romanian principalities as a non-metrical, partly improvised Ottoman Turkish art song form performed, along with other urban Turkish genres, in the *mehterhanea*. The genre spread among *lăutari* during the Phanariot period (Ciobanu 1974a:93). Robert Garfias provides the most complete picture of the historic *manea,* writing that it was "of distinctly Turkish origin, arising from Turkish street vendors' cries (Turkish *mani*)" (1984:91): "[It] subsequently became an Anatolian folksong which was later adopted as a light classical form in Turkish music, beginning with an elaborate text, no longer related to the vendor's text, sung in free rhythm, and followed by a continuation of the song in *Duyek* rhythm" (Garfias 1981:99).[17]

Garfias notes that the *manea* "was always primarily a vocal form of a somewhat improvizatory [sic] nature" (1984:92). We also learn that it was "popular in the rich Greek/Turkish climate of the big cities and particularly in the *mahalale*" [sing. *mahala;* outlying, ghetto-like neighborhoods] around Bucharest (1984:91). Alexandru claims that *manele* at that time were "melancholy love songs" (1980b:256). We find glimpses of the *manea* in various other sources as well. A publication that was issued in Istanbul in 1830 titled *Euterpi* included thirty songs with Romanian texts and a variety of traditional dances, among them "songs called Manele, Turkish, Persian, and Greek songs" (Alexandru 1980b:264–65). I will revisit the *manea* as a form that evolved in post-Ottoman Romania shortly, but let us turn briefly to the Western musical influence developing among *lăutari* in the nineteenth century.

By the mid-1800s, European trends, including Western music, had permeated urban culture. Supplementing their oriental repertoires, urban *lăutari* adapted and learned the fashionable European dance and "salon" music, much of it German and Polish, to accommodate the new tastes of their audiences (Garfias 1981:98; 1984:86–87). These genres included waltzes, quadrilles, polkas, and mazurkas (Cosma 1996:29). Indeed, *lăutari* exploited both Turkish and European styles, reflected in the hybrid music emergent at that time (Alexandru 1980b:270). Between 1830 and 1852, Anton Pann published the influential *Cîntece de Lume* (Songs by the people; see Ciobanu 1955), an anthology that epitomized the variety of music then popular, including what Alexandru dubs "Oriental," "Western," and "ambiguous Oriental-Occidental" styles (1980b:256, 270). "Oriental" refers to Pann's collected "songs of the *mahala*" performed by Roma: "very richly ornamented, with fluctuating intervals and abundant chromaticisms, with a large range and a complex formal structure, yet fluid and with a free rhythm" (Alexandru 1980b:273). Regarding how deeply embedded "oriental" (Turkish) music was in Romanian culture then and how closely oriental musical style was associated with Romani style, Ciobanu argues that "the Occidental influence on *lăutari* and their creations was fully felt only after 1860. In other words, we need to emphasize that the vast majority of urban popular creations that were circulated, if not also created, by *lăutari* continued to remain still for a long time primarily under the influence of Oriental music" (1974b:114).

Viorel Cosma points out that by the nineteenth century, *lăutar* as a designation had come to represent not only a musician who played popular music but also a musician who could not read music, fostering a negative association that still holds true to some extent today (1996:10). At the same time, *lăutar* also exemplified the popularly romanticized image of the innately endowed musician (who indeed does not *need* to read music). It was during the nineteenth century that the highly idealized image of the "Gypsy" took root in European culture, including stereotypical "Gypsy" qualities such as passion, beauty, artistic sensitivity, freedom, free will, wandering, marginality, exotic "Otherness," and the unwillingness to play by mainstream society's rules.[18] *Lăutari* relate well to this cluster of sentimentalized traits since they frequently are attributed—and attribute to themselves—romantic identities that embrace a deep, soulful, and inborn sense of music-making. Along with this identity, however, is another image, also well-established in the European mind set—one that represents the negative "Gypsy" persona—likewise marginal and Other but in a deviant and even criminal sense. This image emanates from the long history of poverty, injustice, rootlessness, and unmitigated racism that has been part of the Romani experience ever since the fourteenth century; in Romania, 500 years of slavery is also part of Romani collective memory. The paradoxical image of the gifted Romani musician who is, at the same time, the socially despised Rom, is germane to understanding much of the fascination as well as contempt for the "Gypsy" music that has flourished in postcommunist Romania, topics that will be explored ahead.[19]

The Emancipation and Kingdom of Romania

The Emancipation of Roma took place in 1864 (Crowe 1996:120). Fourteen years later, Ottoman rule ended and was followed by the establishment of the Kingdom of Romania in 1881 (Michelson 2000:675). As a result of these transitions, where and what *lăutari* performed evolved significantly. While a considerable number of *lăutari* continued to reside in urban areas, numerous others, who no longer served as slaves, relocated in villages and towns where they assumed the performance of traditional music for Romanian audiences. Moreover, the demands of their profession were changing in those years as the Ottoman Turkish repertoire was by and large replaced by European and native Romanian traditional regional songs and dances (Garfias 1981:100). With the demise of the Ottoman

Empire in the late nineteenth century, Romania and the other newly independent Balkan nations sought to move beyond their Ottoman past, forging ahead with new identities and musical forms based on native culture and associations with Western Europe (Pennanen 1995:95). The music scholar Nicolae Filimon remarked in 1862 that the "musical anatomy" of the urban compositions played by *lăutari* was a "mixture of Oriental and Western music, interwoven at every turn with native [Romanian] music" (quoted in Alexandru 1980b:270).

Lăutari were masters, by the late nineteenth century, of professional traditional music-making at weddings, family celebrations, and venues such as marketplaces and inns in both rural and urban locales. They typically played the *vioară* [violin], *cobză* [short-necked strummed instrument with between eight and twelve strings], and *nai* [panpipes]. As time passed, the combination of *taraf* instruments expanded. By the early twentieth century, the *ţambal* [cimbalom] had joined the classic ensemble—both the large concert-style instrument and a smaller portable hammered dulcimer that could be easily played at rural weddings. By the mid-twentieth century, the *acordeon* [accordion] and *bas* [string bass] had also become indispensable to the *taraf;* meanwhile, the *cobză* and *nai* were in decline (Garfias 1981:101).

While *lăutari* played primarily for Romanians, they also performed at Romani weddings and festivities where in-group songs and dances were cultivated. The *manea*, though of Ottoman Turkish derivation, was, by the post-Ottoman period, part of the urban Romani repertoire (Garfias 1984:92). *Muzică lăutărească* [*lăutar* music] also was and is an urban style of both song and dance that evolved in southern Romania for Romani in-group events. It developed through a synthesis of regional Romanian traditional music, Ottoman Turkish art music, and the Western European music that circulated during the nineteenth century in the Romanian principalities (Garfias 1981). As song, *muzică lăutărească* is a style noted for a "personally expressive melismatic character, microtonal pitch modifications and frequently an intense sense of drive" (Garfias 1981:99). As dance, the music includes the *horă lăutărească* [*lăutar* hora], also called *horă ţigănească* [Gypsy hora], a traditional social dance in duple meter. The *horă lăutărească* is performed individually (solo) with a slightly inclined upper body; it is marked by improvisation, sudden changes in direction, active arm movements and finger-snapping, rhythmic foot-stamping, and in general an engaged, energetic style.[20] The *horă românească* [Romanian hora], also in duple meter, is the Romanian national dance and is performed in a circle with hands held—a style that contrasts significantly with the *horă lăutărească*.[21] The musical styles of the Romani and Romanian horas differ as well.[22]

The Communist Years

Romanian and Romani Repertoire

The communist period in Romania lasted from 1944 to 1989. By the mid-twentieth century, the music that *lăutari* performed in public was dictated not only by the preferences of their primarily Romanian audiences but also by the agendas and policies of the communist government. In larger cities, folk orchestras were established by the state. The performers in these state ensembles, as well as in many state-sponsored recordings, were by and large urban *lăutari*. They performed exclusively Romanian genres, conforming with the government's attempts to monitor cultural expression by permitting only "pure, traditional" Romanian music in public. During Ceauşescu's rule (1965–1989), the restrictions placed on music played by *lăutari* became progressively more severe. Romani music (such as the *manea*) was not included in the repertoire of state-sponsored ensembles since it was viewed as representing cultural influences that undermined Romania's purported social homogeneity (Rădulescu 1994:28).

Oriental and Romani musical styles have long been perceived in Romania as overlapping. Commentary during the communist period includes Ciobanu's assertion that "the taste for Oriental music did not stop with the boyars but eventually turned up . . . in the world of today's *mahalale* where it lives on in the so-called 'Gypsy' songs or songs of the *mahala*" (1974b:111). Alexandru also points out that the genres circulating among *lăutari* in Romani neighborhoods in the late 1960s were still called, "just like in Anton Pann's day [almost 100 years earlier], songs of the *mahala*, drinking songs, table songs, listening songs, . . . and *lăutar* or Gypsy songs" (1980b:273). Moreover, he tells us, older *lăutari* from the southern regions of Romania "still performed" the *manea* now and then, noting that "the melody unfolds freely, without restraint, sustained, however, by a giusto accompaniment formed by an ostinato rhythmic formula frequently met in the music of the Middle East" (1980b:273). Garfias also mentions that the *manea* as song "retains the romantic, yet sensuous quality of old Turkish and Greek popular song" (1984:91). The *manea* was still to be found in those years only in in-group settings frequented by Roma, to which Romanians rarely ventured.[23]

Because of the dearth of scholarship on the early *manea*, it is not clear when the *manea* song form developed dance associations. In his fieldwork in 1977, Garfias found the *manea* "in strong evidence" (1984:91) as a Romani female song and dance drawn "from Gypsy or Turkish sources" (1984:88) and performed during in-group events such as weddings (1981:99). Based on comparative findings in southern Romania and Dobrogea, he suggests that "more than likely the *manea* was always a vocal dance form" (Garfias 1984: 92).[24] Garfias describes the *manea* that he witnessed:

> [T]he beginning of a *manea* is announced by sounding the characteristic beat. Immediately, one notices that more women are dancing than before, and that often the women may dominate the dance area . . . . The pulse of the *manea* is slow, requiring as it does, four beats to complete the cycle . . . . In the *manea*, the arms are raised slightly and to the sides, the body pivots a little with the feet stationary, and there is just a slight suggestion of undulation (1984:91).

The Emergence of Muzică Orientală

By the 1970s, various types of eclectic pop musics combining traditional, popular, and rock elements often with a Middle Eastern sound were rapidly becoming extremely popular in the Balkans. The Serbian *novokomponovana narodna muzika* [newly-composed folk music or NCFM], played frequently—though not exclusively—by Romani musicians in Yugoslavia (Rasmussen 1991), began to sneak into Romania at this time primarily through Banat (a region in the southwest of Romania which borders on Serbia), as Serbian musicians traveled there to perform at weddings.[25] It circulated in Romania mainly through such live performance channels and audio cassettes from Yugoslavia. At that time, there were no recordings of the music officially sold in Romania; nor, of course, was it aired on the media (Rădulescu 1998:1–2). In Bulgaria, a communist neighbor directly to the south (to which Romanians could travel relatively easily at that time), *svatbarska muzika* [wedding music], performed mainly by Roma, was likewise immensely popular starting in the late 1970s.[26] It too made its way unofficially into southern Romania.

By the 1980s, the musical style that in the 1990s would come to be called *muzică orientală* had become an underground phenomenon and was genuinely popular, especially among youth in Banat and southern

Romania. In Timişoara (the provincial center of Banat), unauthorized studios emerged where *lăutari* recorded and sold the music on the black market. At that time, the most prominent and creative figure to circumvent prohibitions and forge ahead with a fusion style was Dan Armeanca, a Romani guitarist (b. 1961) whose grandfather, Alecu Vasile, was a *lăutar* (accordionist) who had taught him music (Lupaşcu 1994:103). Armeanca popularized an NCFM-derived ethnopop with a Romanian and Romani imprint that originally circulated mainly among Roma, then termed *muzică sîrbească* [Serbian music]—a fitting term since it was effectively a remake of Serbian NCFM. Now viewed as a *muzică orientală* guru by enthusiasts throughout the country, Armeanca was relatively little known during the communist period since both the new style and Romani music in general were rarely heard.

The Romanian communist government initiated a series of measures during the 1980s to eradicate what was then called *muzică sîrbească* which, from their point of view, was problematic (Rădulescu 1994:27). For one thing, it was illegally recorded, produced, and sold—something that the government could not tolerate. Second, the musical content was "foreign": after all, it was dubbed "Serbian." As such, it violated the official sense of a homogeneous Romanian national culture. Third, the musicians who performed it were by and large *lăutari* who, despite being musicians, were still from the much maligned Romani minority, then enduring harsh assimilationist measures at the hands of the state (Crowe 1991:72–74). The fact that the music was customarily performed by Roma contributed both to its "alien" as well as "contaminated" status in the eyes of the government. Speranţa Rădulescu notes that during the last ten years of communist rule, *lăutari* "were not allowed to sing or play 'polluted folklore,'" which meant *muzică sîrbească* and Romani songs of the *mahala* (1994:27, 28). The official repudiation of *muzică sîrbească* then circulating in Romania closely paralleled the phenomenon of wedding music in Bulgaria, which was also banned by the communist government there.[27]

The predominant music played at Romanian weddings during Ceauşescu's last decade in power was traditional Romanian song and dance. Yet numerous *lăutari* with whom I spoke about the earlier taboos placed on "Gypsy" and "foreign" music recalled that though banned in public, these genres were still performed at occasions where there was little threat of disclosure, such as at Romani weddings. Rădulescu observes that the musicians frequently ignored the official interdictions though they were also on guard to not be caught "in the act"; although punishments for

ignoring these ordinances officially included a fine and revocation of the
right to perform, apparently they were rarely enforced (1994:28). A village
lăutar reminisced to me about playing in a *taraf* at a wedding in April
1989 in which the musicians briefly performed *muzică sîrbească:* "After
we finished, we were warned by a security policeman that we better not
sing any more of this music during the wedding," he told me. "Later in the
wedding, again we played [*muzică sîrbească*]. Then the policeman jumped
out of his seat, ran over, and told us to stop immediately, and that if he
heard it one more time, we would be in big trouble."[28]

Muzică Orientală in Postcommunist Romania

Many changes have taken place in the world of traditional culture since the
1989 Revolution. Prohibitions on freedom of speech and cultural
expression in general no longer exist and previously outlawed musical
genres performed by *lăutari* are now freely permitted in public. Moreover,
given the open borders and communication channels, cultural information—especially Western media—flows freely into Romania and is
accessible everywhere. This has all radically altered the present status of
traditional music, musicians, and the repertoires they play. *Muzică
orientală,* currently performed primarily in two arenas, is a case in point.
The first venue is live performances—mainly weddings and baptisms, as
well as restaurant gigs. The second is recordings; the music circulates
through an extensive audio-cassette business that is commodified mostly
through private sellers on a small-scale market that was formerly
unauthorized.

What the Music is Called

As the NCFM-derived ethnopop style in Romania developed during
the late 1980s and 1990s, it underwent a series of name changes reflecting
popular usage.[29] Early on, as noted, the style was termed *muzică sîrbească*
[Serbian music], used more or less until the early 1990s and reflecting its
initial Serbian NCFM impetus. It was called *muzică turcească* [Turkish
music] during the early to mid-1990s, as recognition of the music's
apparent Turkish qualities was articulated. The style was also dubbed
muzică țigănească [Gypsy music] during the mid-1990s, reflecting how
Turkish and Gypsy musical traits were perceived to overlap. By the mid-

to late 1990s, the term *muzică orientală* was coined. "Oriental," earlier denoting Ottoman Turkish and/or Turkish style, became at that time a term that served in a looser but distinctly nuanced way to cover the three influences (Serbian, Turkish, and Gypsy) that earlier had been employed individually to characterize the music. "Oriental" served in this way to embrace a broad Balkan–Middle Eastern identity. It is telling that all of these adjectives highlight how the music was consistently regarded as something "other" than native Romanian, as well as "other" in a non-Western sense.

Meanwhile, the term *manea* was also creeping into usage to denote *muzică orientală*. In other words, the older in-group song and dance form *manea*—played by Romani musicians and danced by Romani women—was evolving, by the 1990s, into a flashier, more amplified, more visible, and less exclusively female genre. By the early 2000s, the appellation *manea* had been adopted wholesale for *muzică orientală*. Indeed this musical style had itself become more complex by then than during the communist years since it had been influenced in the meantime by an assortment of styles that had permeated popular culture in Romania since the Revolution, including many from the West (such as rock, blues, jazz, disco, rap, hip-hop, and salsa). By summer 2003, the term *muzică orientală* was rarely used in the colloquial language, having been replaced virtually everywhere by *manea*. The current term *manea*, like its predecessors, also conveys a sense of otherness since in Romanian, it is coded both as Turkish and Gypsy. There is admittedly a disconnection (in part due to the lack of literature on the *manea*) between the earlier *manea* and the *manea* of the postcommunist period, yet there is also a continuity of stylistic features that have endured as the music has evolved, a topic to which I now turn.

Stylistic Content: "Oriental" Music

Ask any *lăutar* and you will be told that *muzică orientală* is an amalgam. As an elderly *lăutar* in Bucharest once told me, "*Muzică orientală* is a mixture—not a horse nor a donkey, but a mule."[30] In addition to the local, Balkan, and Western influence in the music, the orientalism that characterizes the style is an assortment of effects from different traditions that blend to form a distinct Middle Eastern sound, coded as oriental as well as Romani. These stylistic effects are primarily rhythmic, melodic, and instrumental.

Figure 3.1: *Învață, nevastă, să mă prețuiești* [Learn, wife, to value me], mm. 1–5, as sung by Ştefan de la Bărbuleşti on *Mi-e Dor de Tine*, Amma, 2000.

Muzică orientală's conspicuously Turkish/Middle Eastern flavor is due in large part to its characteristic syncopated Arab rhythms. As I interviewed *lăutari*, I frequently asked them, "what specifically makes *muzică orientală* 'oriental'?" Interestingly, virtually every musician responded that it was the rhythm in the music that comprised the chief defining "oriental" feature.[31] Indeed, in performance, the intensity and power of the rhythm of *muzică orientală* is striking and lends itself extremely well to dancing—as demonstrated by the scores of guests who jump to their feet to dance whenever *lăutari* strike up this music at weddings. Middle Eastern patterns in duple meter are ubiquitous in *muzică orientală*, especially the rhythmic modes called *ayyūb* and *maqsūm* by Arab musicians, or *düyek* as the latter is known in Turkey. In Figure 3.1 (CD 3.1), the percussion and bass double the *maqsūm/düyek* pattern in 4/4. This example also illustrates the use of polymeter in that the melody proceeds in 12/8, while the accompanying parts are in duple meter. This causes a rhythmic tension as the constant triplets in the melody are heard above the duple harmonic and rhythmic background. Its complexity figures in the textured "oriental" sound of the music.

The syncopated Middle Eastern rhythms of the *manea* style by *lăutari* in both pre- and post-1989 music are clearly part of its oriental/Romani musical lexicon. Alexandru (1980b:273) identifies *düyek* in the *manea* forms that he found in the 1960s. The *çiftetelli* rhythmic pattern has also been intrinsic to the music coded as oriental and Romani for decades. Commenting on the Romani music that he encountered in the 1970s, Garfias observes that

> [t]he distinctive element and distinguishing characteristic of the *manea*—that which sets it apart from all other forms found in Romania—is the use of the *chiftitelli* rhythm, that pattern so frequently associated with the stereotypical image of the Middle Eastern and Balkan belly dance. The appearance of this rhythm in Romania is unique to the urban Gypsies (1984:91).

Figure 3.2 illustrates the *ayyūb* rhythmic pattern in 4/4 (dotted quarter, eighth, quarter, quarter) in the percussion; in this excerpt, the final beat of each measure is divided into two eighth notes, a typical variation on the mode. Moreover, the rhythm of the bass line echoes, with some amount of variation, the rhythm in the percussion. This passage also illustrates the metrically compound melodic line over the duple harmonic and rhythmic lines, as in measures 3, 4, and 8.

Orientalism in *muzică orientală* is also reflected in Turkish scale types and melodic motifs. Historically the Turkish *makam* system was prominent in the urban Romani music of southern Romania.[32] Garfias and A. L. Lloyd both found scales related to the *makam* system in the Romani music that they explored in the 1960s and 1970s (Garfias 1981:100; Lloyd 1963:19).[33] Garfias cites the *Hijaz* (Arabic; Turk. *Hicaz*) mode as most typical to the music he encountered (1981:103), noting that "[i]t is noteworthy that among Turkish musicians *hijaz* is often referred to as the Gypsy *makam*" (1981:103). The melodic modes of *muzică orientală* include the conspicuous augmented seconds (the signature "oriental" interval) and chromatic passages that generate a distinctly Middle Eastern aura (Ciobanu 1974c:57). Figure 3.2 illustrates the pronounced role of the augmented second in this particular piece, labeled (a) in the excerpt. Indeed, the sequence in the first measure is composed entirely of this interval. Chromaticisms in *muzică orientală* are also significant. Figure 3.2 (CD 3.2) includes such passages, labeled (b), such as in measure 3, where

Figure 3.2: *Nu ştiu dacă m-ai iubit* [I don't know if you loved me], mm. 1–9. Composed by Sile Dorel; sung by Mihăiţă Nămol. *Romanian Gypsy "Manele" 2004: Sile Dorel Păun and Guests*, Sile Dorel, 2004.

a sequence of five chromatic steps is characteristic. Furthermore, the ascending passage in measure 8 is dense with chromaticisms. Figure 3.3 (CD 3.3), consisting of eight measures of a vocal melody, illustrates a passage that, except for the initial leap of an octave in measures 1 and 5, is entirely composed of augmented and minor seconds, often in alternation. The effect of these melodic intervals produces a rich Middle Eastern texture.

Though often associated with the so-called "Gypsy scale,"[34] the modes exploited by *lăutari* are not indigenous to them (or to Romani music but were adopted over time. Refuting the notion of a "Gypsy scale"

Verse 1

Ce fată frumoasă-am întîlnit,   What a beautiful girl I've met,
și de ea eu m-am îndrăgostit,   and I fell in love with her,
și vreau să mă-însor cu ea   and I want to marry her
să-i fac de plăcut măicuța   to make my little mama happy.
mea.

Figure 3.3: Ce fată frumoasă am întîlnit [What a beautiful girl I've met], mm. 13–20. As sung by Adrian Copilul Minune, *Băiefii de Aur, Vol. 5,* Amma, 2000.

possibly originating in India, the early homeland of Romani populations, Ciobanu argues that

> because Greek-Turkish-Persian-Arabic music in which this scale is found circulated intensely and for a long time among Romanians, it is not a question of a Gypsy scale but rather of a typical Oriental scale which came to us—as it did in other countries where it still is found—with a certain repertoire of Oriental origins (1974a:97).

Muzică orientală is also characterized by melodic passages that are elaborately ornamented, virtuostic, and often improvisational. Both improvisation and bravura in performance are associated with Romani musicianship in the Balkans.[35] Figure 3.4 reveals a striking density of ornamentation in the solo accordion line (doubled by the clarinet), such as in measure 1 on beats 3 and 4, labeled (a). Some of the ornaments include chromatic steps that do not conform to the mode employed, such as in measures 5, 6, 9, and 10, labeled (b). This in turn at times generates yet other augmented seconds. Such is the case in measures 1 and 11, labeled (a), and in the measures designated as (a) in Figure 3.3—the vocal melody of the same song. The conflation of rhythm, melodic mode, ornamentation, virtuosity, and improvisation associated with *muzică orientală* and its practice by Romani musicians affirms both Romani and oriental identities in the mélange of attributes that *muzică orientală* embraces.

Figure 3.4: *Ce fată frumoasă am întîlnit* [What a beautiful girl I've met], mm. 1–12, as sung by Adrian Copilul Minune on *Băieţii de Aur, Vol. 5,* Amma, 2000.

Distinctive instrumentation also elicits oriental effects in *muzică orientală*. The most common instruments employed are the accordion, *orgă* [synthesizer or other keyboard], *tobe* [small drums or other drum sets],[36] *clarinet*, and *chitara electrică* [electric guitar].[37] Other less common instruments include the *saxofon* [saxophone] and string bass. The instruments are always amplified with an electric sound system. Much of the music's Middle Eastern acoustic quality is cultivated by the synthesizer, which can produce diverse timbres, some of them distinctly Turkish and even Indian[38]—yet another influence that informs the eclectic oriental sound that is generated in this music. In some ensembles, the synthesizer has replaced individual instruments since it can produce virtually any sound consistent with *muzică orientală*. During fieldwork in the early 2000s, I observed that urban ensembles were sometimes composed of just a synthesizer (or two) and an additional melody instrument such as accordion or clarinet (Plate 3.1).

Conspicuously absent from urban *muzică orientală* ensembles is the cimbalom, one of the long-time staples of the classic *taraf* that in many ways defines the traditional southern Romanian urban Romani sound; it simply is not compatible with *muzică orientală*. Conversely, several of the most popular and characteristic instruments for *muzică orientală* were never part of conventional traditional ensembles (synthesizer, drums, electric guitar, and saxophone).

Instrumentation directly determines the repertoire played. An accordionist from Bucharest explained that when customers hire *lăutari* for a wedding, they frequently specify which instruments they wish to hear, thus denoting the style of music they are requesting. He pointed out that if patrons wish to hear the older, traditional style of music, they request that violin, string bass, accordion, and cimbalom be played. By contrast, since *muzică orientală* necessitates the synthesizer, keyboard, drums, and so on, patrons specify that those instruments be performed. At some weddings two ensembles are hired—one for the traditional repertoire and one for *muzică orientală*. Village *tarafuri*, by contrast, sometimes lack the flashy sound of city-based ensembles since they still employ mostly traditional instruments (such as the cimbalom), producing combinations that do not correspond to the urban style of *muzică orientală* (Plate 3.2).

How the Ottoman Turkish music that played such a significant role in the culture of the Romanian principalities relates to the music performed by *lăutari* throughout the twentieth century and into the present is a question that local scholars have not entirely resolved, irrespective of the commentary offered by foreign specialists. Garfias suggests that the twentieth-century *manea* represents a remnant of Turkish musical influence; he finds evidence for this particularly in the use by *lăutari* of the *makam* system (1981:100). Moreover, he argues that musically speaking, while

> Turkish influence dates back to the period of Ottoman influence in
> Romania . . . there is little to preclude the possibility of sporadic but
> continued contact and influence. The tendency to use *makams* now
> associated in Turkey with later light classical forms and such forms as
> the *manea* suggest that contact may have, in fact, continued after the
> Ottoman rule (1981:106).

Lloyd also maintains that what he came upon as "the Turkish *manea*" in
the early 1960s contains traces of Ottoman Turkish influence from the
Phanariot period (1963:17). "Indeed," he asserts, referring to the
prominence of rhythm, the Arabic *makams*, and the chromaticisms in the
music played by *lăutari* at that time, "there is much that is Oriental in the
musical thinking of the *lăutari*" (1963:16). In reference to *lăutari* from
southern Romania who also still occasionally played a "Turkish *manea*"
in the 1960s, Alexandru describes such performances as evoking "the
Oriental music of yesteryear" as well as the *lăutar*'s "personal creativity
in an Oriental spirit" (1980b:273). Ciobanu likewise argues for a
recognition of oriental influence in the urban music of *lăutari* well into the
twentieth century (1974b).

Not all contemporary Romanian scholars, however, are content with
such historical connections. One camp considers a "continuous story"
from the Ottoman period up to the late twentieth century untenable; the
oriental craze in today's Romania is viewed instead as a means for Roma
to assert their own identity.[39] Another repudiates any connection between
the Ottoman Turkish art music of the past and the "sounds coming from
today's Gypsies."[40] Though the expression of Romani identity is admittedly an important aspect of *muzică orientală,* and though no one blindly
subscribes to an unbroken continuum of orientalism from the sixteenth to
the twenty-first centuries, one cannot hastily dismiss hundreds of years of
Turkish influence from southern Romania's cultural past. As Garfias
remarks, clearly referring to nationalist inclinations among Romanian
scholars at the time he wrote (the communist period), "the Turkish origins
of many of the elements in Romanian music have been too long overlooked" (1981:100). Ottoman Turkish art music was critical in the
development of Romanian traditional and popular music, as both local and
foreign scholars recognize. To deny this too forcefully is problematic,
especially in the context of the ultra-nationalist ideologies that now
circulate in Romania. Whatever else one may have to say about *lăutari*, it
is clear that through their long-time role as professional urban musicians

who unremittingly learned and performed what their audiences requested, and as members of society who still are by and large viewed as "foreigners," they were and still are ideal mediators for oriental genres and styles.

Finally, though it is not my intention to pursue Western musical trends here, it must be noted that they, too, have profoundly affected *muzică orientală*. Rock and disco have long been exploited in this style and there has been experimentation with rap as well. In the early 2000s, a local rap style—in which the vocalists spoke in a heavy, rhythmic diction against the music—was introduced in *muzică orientală*. Soon rap was intermittently part of *muzică orientală* performance on recordings.[41] Rap has not permeated the world of live *muzică orientală* performance, however; as one village *lăutar* told me, "It will never become wedding music."[42] Other recent trends include "blues *țigănesc*"[Gypsy blues] and samba *țigănească* [Gypsy samba], both of them innovative styles performed within the broader *muzică orientală* repertoire.

Gender, Power, and Ethnicity

The Lyrics

Muzică orientală as song consists of stanzas with regular refrains. This poetry in song is a conspicuously male form—from the musicians who perform it to the topics they sing about and the perspectives they adopt. The subjects expressed in the songs are essentially about love, power, and status and are conveyed in verse that has been called hackneyed, inane, and at times vulgar by its critics. The lyrics speak above all about love and sex, typically from a male heterosexual point of view. The most common themes are sexual attraction and desire. Song texts are comprised of couplets that rhyme, though verses are not necessarily isometric. The ubiquitous hit of summer 2000, heard repeatedly at weddings, was *Sexi, sexi* [Sexy, sexy] (Fig. 3.5). The poetic meter is uneven in stanza 2, where the verses have ten, eleven, nine, and twelve syllables respectively, preventing a metrical agreement between text and music. Indeed, a common criticism of *muzică orientală* is that "the words and music don't connect." The excerpt begins with a refrain that is repeated intermittently throughout the song, followed by the first and second stanzas, which express sheer lust in undeniably prosaic terms.

Refrain	Refrain
Sexi, sexi, ştiu că mă vrei,	Sexy, sexy, I know that you want me,
toată noaptea mă gîndesc la femei.	all night long I think about women.
Sexi, sexi, nu mai visa,	Sexy, sexy, don't dream any longer,
hai la mine la o cafea.	Come with me for a coffee.

1.	1.
Trupul tău e atît de fin.	Your body is so fine.
Eşti cea mai senzuală, ai un chip divin.	You're the most sensuous; you have a lovely face.
Mă atragi, sincer tu îmi placi.	You attract me; really, I like you.
Eşti foarte sexi, îmi place cum te îmbraci.	You're very sexy; I like how you dress.

2.	2.
Vreau să te sărut de sus pînă jos.	I want to kiss you from head to toe.
Pentru mine e lucrul cel mai frumos.	For me it's the most wonderful thing.
Privirea ta provocatoare te face fiinţa cea mai fermecătoare.	Your alluring look makes you the most bewitching beauty.

Figure 3.5: *Sexi, sexi.* As sung by Marian Zaharia (with an ensemble from Mârşaa) at a wedding in Cartojani, 3 June 2000.

Innumerable erotic songs in *muzică orientală* style have delighted audiences over the past decade, from *Haide, fată, cu mine* [Come on with me, girl] and *Sunt îndrăgostit* [I'm in love] to *Eşti femeia visurilor mele* [You are the woman of my dreams] and *Salomeea* [Salome] which, with its echoes of the treacherous Biblical Salome, expressly articulates an oriental connection.[43] The lyrics of *muzică orientală* overtly celebrate masculinity and virility, as in *Sînt bărbat adevărat* [I'm a real man], *Sînt sigur pe mîna mea* [I'm sure of myself], and *Sînt un bărbat cel mai frumos* [I'm the most handsome man]. Songs such as *Eu sunt mare gagicar* [I'm a big girl-chaser], *Am succes mare la femei* [I have great success with women], and *E greu, Doamne, să iubeşti două femei* [Oh God, it's hard to love two women] articulate male potency with women—a prime concern of *muzică orientală*. Some songs are outrightly pornographic, such as *Scoica* [Seashell], the title of which refers in slang terms to female genitalia and whose lyrics explore the singer's repeated acts of sexual prowess on the beach, complete with the sound of water splashing and a woman's cries of physical pleasure in the background (Plate 3.3). *Pe la spate* [From the back] graphically depicts "how girls want to be made love to all night," as one musician at a wedding explained it to me and as its recurrent refrain expresses in Figure 3.6:

Pe la spate, pe la spate,	From the back, from the back,
c-aşa vor fetele toate.	because that's how all girls like it.

Figure 3.6: *Pe la spate,* as sung by Bobi (with an ensemble from Bucharest), at a wedding in Piteşti, 25 August 2002.

Infidelity, usually marital, and betrayal are also familiar topics in the songs of *muzică orientală*. Songs such as *Şi-a aflat, Doamne, nevasta mea* [Oh God, my wife has found out] and *M-a prins nevasta* [My wife caught me] represent a common theme of the unfaithful husband who sings of his adventures—another version of the empowered male. The male vocalist in Figure 3.7 juxtaposes his wife and home with his mistress in the first two stanzas of *Prinţesa mea* [My princess]:

Am copii şi am nevastă,	I have kids and I have a wife,
şi am tot ce-mi doresc acasă.	and I have everything I could wish for at home.
Dar am o inimă lovită	But I have a heart that's been smitten
de o prinţesă denumită.	by someone I call princess.
Mă ceartă nevasta mea	My wife reproaches me
că nu mai mă tem de ea.	since I no longer fear what she thinks.
Eu nu ştiu ce să-i mai zic ei, of.	I don't know what to tell her any longer, oh.
Îi spun că-s obosit, mă.	Hey, I just tell her that I'm tired.

Figure 3.7: *Prinţesa mea,* as performed by Adrian Copilul Minune on *Prinţesa Mea*, S.C. Studio Recording S.R.L., Timişoara, 1998.

Related to songs of masculine potency are songs that assert male power through imagery focusing on money, such as in *Sînt şmecher şi fac mulţi bani* [I'm sly and make a lot of money] and *Sînt un bărbat luxos* [I'm a rich man]. Sex and money also come together, such as in *Bani şi fetele* [Money and girls] and *Dragostea şi banii* [Love and money]. Money is also associated with envy, rivalry, and gaining enemies; *Am duşmani că am bani* [I have enemies because I have money] and *Banii-ţi fac duşmani* [Money gives you enemies] include these themes.

Possessions as symbols of status and prosperity are expressed in songs such as *Am o casă aşa mare şi maşina cea mai tare* [I have such a big house and the fastest car]. *Mi-am cumpărat un celular* [I bought myself a cell phone] combines the image of the carefree drifter, his newly purchased cell phone, car, and even swooning women, all in the first few verses (Fig.3.8):

Mi-am cumpărat celular.	I bought myself a cell phone.
Sînt un vagabond hoinar.	I'm a wandering vagabond.
Din maşină eu vorbesc,	I talk [on my phone] from my car,
pă femei le zăpăcesc.	I drive women crazy.

Figure 3.8: *Mi-am cumpărat un celular,* performed by Nelu Petrache on *Muzică Orientală: Mi-am Cumpărat Celular,* Amma, Bucharest, 1999.

Money, cars, big houses, and cell phones are all emblems of power and status that resonate in today's Romania, where poverty is widespread and memories of the communist period—when most people in Romania lived far more modestly and few owned or drove cars—still linger (Plate 3.4).

Maternal love is also a theme earnestly expressed by singers who, in an inversion of power, are also dedicated sons, such as in *Doamne, te-aş ruga ceva, ai grijă de mama mea* [Oh God, I ask you one thing: take care of my mama] and *Am o mama credincioasă* [I have a devoted mama]. The same men who brazenly announce their virility, complete with car, girl, and cell phone, also kneel humbly before their beloved mothers in this music, providing a fitting illustration of what Andrei Simić calls the "seemingly paradoxical relationship between the subordination of men to their mothers and the machistic role assigned to them" in Balkan society (Simić 1999:27).

Despite the fact that the lyrics are all in Romanian, songs are also at times framed by expressions and imagery that evoke Romani culture.[44] Themes of longing and melancholy, for example, are often enhanced by

"Gypsy" nuances. *Of, viaţa mea* [Oh, my life] expresses the despair of an embittered man who wails: "M-ai amăgit, m-ai chinuit, şi tot te-am iubit" [You deceived me, you tormented me, and still I loved you]. The exclamation *of* [oh] in the title, which recurs throughout the refrain, is coded as a Romani interjection with a plaintive resonance, thus intensifying the "Gypsy" flavor of the performance; *of* has long been a stylistic device associated with traditional Romani songs (Ciobanu 1974b:120).

Of, viaţa mea,	Oh, my life,
of, inima mea,	oh, my heart,
of, degeaba plîng,	oh, I cry in vain,
tare necăjit mai sunt!	I'm still so miserable!

Figure 3.9: *Of, viaţa mea* [Oh, my life], performed by Adrian Copilul Minune on *Of, Viaţa Mea,* Cristian's Studio, Craiova, 2001.

Some songs not only invoke *of* but also depict the life of Roma, such as *Ţigani din ţigănie* [Gypsies from the Gypsy ghetto] and *Of, of, of, mor toţi ţiganii că eu mă distrez cu bani* [Oh, oh, oh, all the Gypsies are dying (of jealousy) while I enjoy my money], in a union of Gypsy and money themes. The choice of ethnonyms to self-identify in the lyrics of *muzică orientală* (as well as most other Romani songs) reflects complex levels of meaning since *lăutari* typically refer to themselves as *ţigani* (Gypsies, sg. *ţigan*), not *romi* (Roma, sg. *rom*). The term *ţigan* is considered derogatory when Romanians use it (which is virtually always), while within in-group colloquial usage, it conveys a sense of intimacy, informality, and affection. Moreover, the use of *ţigan* permits *lăutari*—who consider themselves elite within the larger Romani community, with affinities to Romanians that other Roma lack—to appropriate the vocabulary of the dominant in society as a means of asserting their proximity to them; in so doing, they also distance themselves from other Roma.[45] Employing *ţigan,* then, is a means by which *lăutari* express a variety of insider-outsider dynamics that inform modes of self-identity.

Ciobanu remarks that "the poetic form of the urban song is most frequently inferior to its music form" (1974b:134). Indeed, while the music of *muzică orientală* is actually quite complex in terms of rhythm, melody, and ornamentation, the words sung and topics treated are remarkably ordinary and mundane. The song lyrics are pedestrian; the sentiments and predicaments they describe are commonplace—at least from a male perspective. Virtually anyone can compose these hackneyed verses, something that I observed during a recording session that I recently attended among urban *lăutari*. The vocalist, dissatisfied with the lyrics that had already been composed by one of the instrumentalists, stopped the session and hastily jotted down new verses to replace them. Their only requirements: that they be rhyming couplets and express platitudes on love and longing, something he instantly succeeded in producing. From the point of view of devotees, many of whom are youthful and concerned with love, power, and status, these songs provide accessible ideas that they can easily relate to; the words are relevant and instantly understandable. From the point of view of the Romanian intellectual and professional elite, however, these same lyrics are alienating. They are aesthetically vapid and represent crude and banal perspectives (Rădulescu 1998:5).

Dance

Although the *manea* as dance was originally bounded by gender and ethnic lines, these divisions have broken down in Romania and throughout the Balkans during the postcommunist period due to a general loosening of traditional social conventions and the increased influence of Western media. While the pre-1990 *manea* was a female genre, this gender boundary collapsed during the 1990s; although women still dance the *manea* more frequently than men, it is now a mixed gender form. Moreover, while the *manea* was formerly performed solely at Romani events, in the years following 1989 it was also adopted by ethnic Romanians so that in today's world, both Roma and Romanians include the genre at their weddings and festivities. Paradoxically, the *manea*, which was suppressed during the communist period because of its Romani associations, has by now become standard in the dance repertoire of Romanians. One village *lăutar* recalled that after years of restrictions, it took only several days after the Revolution in 1989 for the genre to enter the routine village wedding repertoire. Already by early January 1990 (i.e., less than two weeks after the execution of Ceauşescu), he told me, the *manea* was freely danced in public in his village.[46] The *manea* finds an analogue in the *čoček,* a Macedonian solo female Romani dance, termed *kyuchek* in Bulgarian.[47] Silverman writes that the contemporary *čoček* "is a widely popular dance form all over the Balkans and is related to folk-pop fusions such as *čalga* in Bulgaria and *muzică orientală* in Romania" (2003:129). Whereas the *čoček*, like the *manea*, was formerly a female Romanian-group solo dance form, now in the post-1989 Balkans, it too is danced by both men and women as well as by Roma and the ethnically dominant (non-Romani) members of society (Plate 3.5).

Decades ago Garfias characterized the *manea* as subtle but expressive; the effect of the dancing, he noted, was "one of a powerful yet demure sensuousness" (1984:91). The postcommunist *manea* is, like the earlier *manea*, a solo (individual) improvisatory dance typified by subtle, sensual movements enacted by the outstretched hands and arms and small steps in which the feet alternately step forward and back. The effect is suggestively sexual but not exaggeratedly so, at least depending on who is dancing. Dancing the *manea* is an expressive public event that incorporates "oriental" and "Gypsy" cultural meanings. Citing the current popularity of "the Turkish *manea*," Anca Giurchescu argues that "there is a basic affinity between the Gypsy and 'oriental' music and dance styles" (2000:328) in contemporary Romania. She points out that the *manea* serves as a visible and legitimate means for Roma within postcommunist Romanian society to assert their own cultural identity. But it also serves as a means for many non-Roma to articulate an inverted identity through empathy and mimicry of what is perceived as "Gypsy" culture through the lens of orientalism. In dancing the *manea* to *muzică orientală*, Romanians are enabled, albeit fleetingly, to assume an exotic, expressive "Gypsy" persona (Plate 3.6).

Performers of *Muzică Orientală*

Romani Bands

Most of the musicians who play *muzică orientală* in Romania today are Roma and many are from *lăutar* families. The young and middle-aged *lăutari* who performed primarily Romanian repertoire in small ensembles at weddings in the 1970s and 1980s are many of the same musicians who play *muzică orientală* at weddings today. Many musicians who came of age in the 1990s now play exclusively *muzică orientală*, never having performed either during the communist period or in traditional ensembles. One such group, which played at a wedding that I attended in Bucharest in 2000, was composed of five teenage male musicians who called themselves Copiii Orientului [The Children of the Orient], a name that ironically places them squarely in the postcommunist era. Ensembles that play *muzică orientală* generally consist of between three and six musicians with an additional vocalist, usually male, although at times female singers also perform.[48] As a rural *lăutar* pointed out, "Mainly men sing *muzică orientală* since the timbre goes better with the male voice."[49] He did not point out that virtually all of the song texts also speak from a male perspective—another incentive for men to sing. In urban ensembles, the vocalists do not ordinarily play an instrument, while among rural musicians, vocalists—with the exception of females—are also usually instrumentalists (Plates 3.7–3.8).

Muzică orientală has created a star-driven market originating in Bucharest that is disseminated throughout the country. Its biggest stars are young male vocalists who rose to fame after the Revolution, particularly in the mid-1990s and later. Many of them have nicknames that serve as their public monikers, much as traditional *lăutari* also use nicknames professionally.[50] The most acclaimed vocalist, who virtually controls the music in terms of setting trends, is Adrian Simionescu, a Rom from a *lăutar* family. He is known as Adrian Copilul Minune [Adrian the Child Wonder] because his talent was discovered when he was still a child (though he is now in his twenties; see Plate 3.3 for an album cover photograph). In addition, even as an adult, he is very short, ostensibly as short as a child. Adrian originally made a name for himself as a young boy singing *muzică lăutărească* in the early 1990s. His first recording of *muzică orientală* came out in 1997, which established his fame in that style.[51] The vocalist Vali Vijelie [Vali the Whirlwind], in his early thirties and also from a *lăutar* family, is also among the most renowned *muzică orientală* vocalists.[52] Others—virtually all male Roma—include Ştefan de la Bărbuleşti [Ştefan from Bărbuleşti], Guţă, Liviu Puştiu [Liviu the Kid], Florin Salam Fermecătoru [Florin Salami the Charming], and many more. Some—such as Adrian Copilul Minune, Guţă, and Vali Vijelie—are so popular that they must be booked months in advance for wedding engagements; they also charge rates far higher than the normal market price. Vali told me that he is so booked that clients wait up to six and eight months for him to sing at their weddings.[53]

Non-Romani Bands

Muzică orientală became so popular during the 1990s that it also began to attract ethnic Romanian musicians. Such musicians also perform at weddings and restaurants, either in all-Romanian ensembles (of which there are relatively few) or in ensembles of *lăutari,* with whom they mostly play synthesizer. This is becoming progressively more common. In fact, it is a source of concern for *lăutari* since, as they see it, "better-off" Romanians—who can afford to buy good quality synthesizers—are moving into this corner of the market, thus making jobs for *lăutari* scarcer.

Interestingly, an ethnic Romanian urban musician whose instrument is the synthesizer, recently conveyed the opposite impression to me, noting that "the really good synthesizers are those bought and played by the rich Gypsies."[54] Clearly these mutual suspicions are informed by ethnic tensions.[55] Indeed, most *lăutari* hold that playing the synthesizer is neither difficult nor demands great artistry. It is, as they view it, something that Romanians—whom they generally see as less "gifted" than themselves in music-making—can "get away with," even without much talent. One *lăutar* told me, as he decried the rise of Romanians playing synthesizers, that the better the instrument is, the less adept the musician needs to be.[56] After all, *lăutari* by and large believe that they are inherently better musicians than Romanians, part of the romanticized image that they project. *Lăutari* regard Romanians who play the synthesizer—or any other instrument in their domain—as impinging upon their occupational niche (Plate 3.9).

As a matter of fact, ethnic Romanians have generally not competed with Romani instrumentalists, who play the more demanding (and proverbially "Gypsy") accordion, clarinet, or violin. In urban areas, a few entirely ethnic Romanian ensembles exist; such groups are far outnumbered by Romani groups. An all-Romanian ensemble that I recently heard perform at a restaurant was comprised of two men who played synthesizers and an electric guitarist, who was also the vocalist. In general Romanians do not rival Romani vocalists either, although there are a few exceptions. The most celebrated ethnic Romanian vocalist of *muzică orientală* is Costi Ioniță, a young male singer from Constanța. Costi was born in 1978 and entered the *muzică orientală* scene with his first recording during the fall of 1999.[57] By spring 2000, he had produced a joint recording with Adrian Copilul Minune. Costi is an artist who has managed to break into a more or less closed world. He represents the appropriation by an ethnic Romanian of a style that is perceived as Romani. Significantly, he was even awarded the title "King of *Manele*" on a recent CD, a designation that Adrian Copilul Minune and Vali Vijelie frequently boast. Interestingly, however, unlike his Romani counterparts, Costi does not sport a nickname. He is also careful not to identify himself entirely with any single musical style, including *muzică orientală*, thus avoiding being viewed as too closely associated with the Romani world. In a published interview (Popescu 2001), a question posed to him was: "On the album 'Best of Costi,' there are a multitude of musical genres. Why have you changed your tune? Don't you believe in the *manea* anymore?" To this,

Costi responded: "I wanted to show the world that I'm not a person with a narrow perspective. I can sing in any style: rock, opera, dance, *manea*."

Performance Contexts

Wedding Banquets

Muzică orientală is performed first and foremost by hired ensembles at long, festive wedding parties in both cities and villages. After various ritual events at the bride's and groom's homes (which are typically accompanied by several *lăutari* playing traditional repertoire) and the wedding ceremony at the church, the feast-celebration take place—a lengthy, elaborate, all- or late-night banquet. In cities it usually occurs at a restaurant or large dining area such as a school or dormitory. In villages it is set up in the courtyards belonging to the bride's and/or groom's families. The festivities normally begin during the early evening and continue on through the night, often breaking up anytime between 2:00 a.m. and 7:00 a.m. The wedding feast is customarily an extended four-course meal which is served in a leisurely manner over a stretch of up to eight hours. Formalized ritual gift-giving (usually sums of money called the *dar*) and other marriage customs also take place near the end of the banquet. Music plays a central role in the celebration; the events of the evening (and entire day) are circumscribed by the *lăutari*, who play almost non-stop, with short breaks to rest and eat. The music prompts virtually uninterrupted dancing, which most wedding guests engage in when they are not eating or drinking.

I have attended numerous Romanian and Romani weddings at which *lăutari* perform in postcommunist southern Romania. My fieldwork reveals a clear picture in terms of preferred genres: it is the *manea* that is by far the most popular dance among both Romanians and Roma. The hora, which as discussed earlier, is danced in either Romanian or Gypsy style, follows the *manea* in popularity. And of these two styles, the Gypsy or *lăutar* hora is increasingly favored at Romanian weddings, something I have noticed even during the past several years. At weddings I now regularly see ethnic Romanians (usually men) who are seemingly Gypsy hora fanatics, as they dance with extraordinary energy and passion. This is, no doubt, representative of a larger phenomenon akin to the appeal of *muzică orientală*—namely a fascination with "Gypsy" culture and expression. Clearly, one of the trends in postcommunist Romania is the appropriation of "Gypsy" traditional culture—especially music and dance—by Romanians. Just as the *manea*, coded as Gypsy, has been adopted by Romanians especially since 1989, so the Gypsy hora is also superseding the Romanian hora among Romanians. Through dancing "like a Gypsy" (be it the *manea* or the Gypsy hora) to "Gypsy music," Romanians can briefly effect a romanticized Gypsy identity, momentarily becoming like idealized images of Gypsies—passionate, intense, and free-spirited. For many young Romanians, selectively adopting the romance of Gypsy culture, especially music and dance, is a part of their post-1989 experience (Plate 3.10).[58]

The Media

Muzică orientală originates chiefly in Bucharest and is disseminated to other urban and village musicians and locales largely by way of audio cassettes.[59] As in other postcommunist Balkan countries, there has been a massive increase in the number of private recording companies in Romania since 1990 (Kurkela 1995). A thriving cassette (and to a lesser extent, CD) industry circulates and popularizes the songs, stars, and style of *muzică orientală*, with hopes that increased publicity will bring more jobs, especially at weddings (Kurkela 1995:133). In the struggle to be recognized through recordings, most younger and middle-aged urban and even rural *lăutari* aspire to making cassettes if they have not already broken into the industry. The "stars" maintain their standing by regularly producing cassettes; Vali Vijelie told me that he must put out a cassette every three months.[60] Vali's reputation, however, like that of Adrian Copilul Minune, is so established that he often sings only one or several songs on a given album, while other musicians are featured in the remaining songs.[61] The cassette industry also serves as a prime source for musicians to pick up new songs. The rapid spread of *muzică orientală* throughout the country in the decade after the Revolution is, in fact, largely due to the myriad of cassette recordings; they are the key to the dissemination of the music.[62]

Some cassettes and CDs, especially those recorded by well-established musicians on reputable labels, are sold in state and private music stores (such as *"Muzica"* in Bucharest). During the 1990s, however, the majority of *muzică orientală* recordings were pirated and sold through small, private dealers in cities and towns throughout the country. Typically, male peddlers would advertise their wares by blasting cassette music from boomboxes in kiosks on the street or at the open market (*piață*), where produce and a myriad of "things" (jewelry, underwear, gadgets, and so on) are also hawked. Vesa Kurkela points out that the "production of unauthorized cassettes" became "an established part of the south-east European phonogram market," including the sale of contemporary "dance music containing ethnic and Pan-Balkan features" (1995:113). In 1995, over 90% of the audio cassettes produced in Romania were pirated (Kurkela 1997:181).

While the unauthorized marketing of cassettes was rampant throughout the 1990s, several ordinances were later imposed in an attempt to control sales. First, starting in 2000, every cassette and CD sold, regardless of where, had to have a silver seal on its cover with the words *produs original* [original product] to indicate that it was authentic and had not been pirated. Second, a ruling was enacted in 2001 that forbade peddlers to set up kiosks on public ground (mainly sidewalks) as they had done for years. Vendors could still sell cassettes, CDs, and other goods from kiosks in designated market areas; in fact, this remains the most significant venue for the hawking of cassettes in much the same way as before the ordinance. But the difference now is that cassettes are sold only in authorized areas and must, by law, have the official seal proving their authenticity. The executive director of a large *muzică orientală* record company in Bucharest, who distributes cassettes to individual sellers throughout the city, admitted that their best outlet for the vending of cassettes was still the kiosks and open markets, since they sell many more cassettes there than in stores.[63] While the new ordinances have resulted in a decrease in the marketing of pirated cassettes, the music is still distributed for the most part from individual sellers in kiosks at marketplaces.

Despite its indisputable role in contemporary Romanian culture, *muzică orientală* is not well represented in the local media. Although it has been performed freely in public since 1990, it has rarely been transmitted on radio or television. For years the music was considered simply too problematic to be aired. The widespread anti-Romani bias of those who control the media also have prevented all but a few television programs to be broadcast on an infrequent basis.[64] Over the past few years I have been informed of, though have not located, isolated programs, all of them in Bucharest. For example, a radio statio that was founded in 2000 which plays *muzică orientală* supports itself through greetings for which listeners pay a fee. Several television programs (on Saturdays and Sundays) featuring Romani culture, including *muzică orientală*, are now shown on cable. Despite these openings, *muzică orientală* still exists somewhat in the shadows of the Romanian media.

Muzică Orientală and Identity

Muzică orientală dramatically polarizes segments of Romanian society: it is reviled by some people, while championed by others. Recognizing both its fans and its foes is crucial to understanding its role in postcommunist Romanian identity construction. As we have seen, *muzică orientală* became firmly incorporated in the wedding repertory during the 1990s and its audiences have included rural, rurban, urbanite, working-class, young Romanians, and Roma.[65] Young people are among its biggest devotees (after all, the principal participants of weddings and baptisms are either young couples or young parents). As a seasoned *lăutar* in Bucharest remarked, "After '90, there was a new generation; now oriental dance music is what is played."[66] Some fans form part of a nouveau-riche class that has emerged during the postcommunist period, while others have belonged to the urban working class for generations.[67] Yet others are formerly rural families who may still maintain village homes but who are now working-class inhabitants in cities and towns. Many university students also revel in the music. At the Politechnical Institute in Bucharest, the largest single campus in Romania, there are four discothèques for students. In 2001, one played *muzică orientală* all of the time, while the remaining three played it part of the time in addition to other popular music.[68] In other words, university students in large numbers also appreciate *muzică orientală*, even in dance situations outside of weddings and celebrations.

But it is not only the youth that relishes the music. There are also many people who are by no means young who enthusiastically dance the *manea* at weddings. Guests of all ages—except the very young and very old—dance *manea* after *manea* for hours on end, which sometimes means all night long. Both urban and rural *lăutari* in southern Romania consistently estimate that *muzică orientală* comprises between 80 and 95% of the music they perform at weddings. Vali Vijelie explained the music's appeal as follows: "Before they begin to drink," he told me, "the wedding guests want to listen to romances or tangos. But after two *sprițuri* [sing. *spriț*, white wine with carbonated water], they want to hear *muzică orientală*."[69] In other words, context frequently determines whether one is in the "mood" to appreciate *muzică orientală*. In a related comment, the director of a record company (which markets *muzică orientală*) remarked that he would not choose to listen to *muzică orientală* at home when he is relaxing. But at a wedding or party, after a glass of wine, it is just fine; he likes it there because it fits the context.[70] In discussions that I have had with ethnic Romanians about *muzică orientală*, many of them admitted that they themselves "put up with" and in fact "almost enjoy" such music at weddings or celebrations. Some intellectuals even confessed that while most of *muzică orientală* is "rubbish," there are a few musicians who do have talent, such as Adrian Copilul Minune.

A consideration of the appeal of *muzică orientală* during wedding festivities is only part of the story. Given that the cassette industry is so critical to the music, questions about customers and sales are also important. At one record company in Bucharest that specializes in a variety of music styles, 80 to 90% of their sales in 2001 were of *muzică orientală*. People who bought these cassettes were of all ages; most were of the working class.[71] Another major record company sells twice as many recordings of *muzică orientală* as they do of all their other recordings combined. Moreover, fans of *muzică orientală* buy far more cassettes per person than do fans of other music, a point that underscores the "cassette culture" nature of this music and perhaps all current Balkan ethnopop (Kurkela 1997). Twenty-five thousand copies of a much anticipated album of *muzică orientală* were completely sold out within three days of being issued while I was in Romania in the summer of 2001, at which point 30,000 more were produced to meet the demand.[72]

Why are so many Romanians such *muzică orientală* enthusiasts? First, *muzică orientală* is intensely pleasing to many people; it is powerful, seductive music in which they delight. Its vigorous rhythms, exotic melodies, and modern sounds are appreciated as both oriental and Gypsy, creating a strongly contrasting Other as compared to the familiar style of traditional Romanian music. Second, the fans of *muzică orientală* worship the style as dance; the *manea* is expressive, sensual, and differs considerably from the more modest steps of the standard Romanian traditional dances. And because the music and dance were, during the communist years, part of a counterculture, they still have a slightly subversive aura. To engage in a formerly taboo, erotic Romani dance is exhilarating and liberating for many Romanians; it combines the allure of the sexy and forbidden with the romance of an imagined "Gypsy" culture. Contemplating the current craze, an older *lăutar* in Bucharest told me with much amusement that "the Romanians have become more 'Gypsyized' than the Gypsies!"[73] The *manea* as dance is also emblematic of the cultural freedoms and sexual imagery now heavily promoted throughout the Balkans through Western media. It permits what Jane Sugarman calls (in reference to the *çoçek* among Prespa Albanians) a "new sense of a more 'sexualized' gendered identity" (2003:106), thanks to Western mass culture. Third, the lyrics, while at times sexually suggestive and risqué, are in any case very ordinary and accessible, especially to young people. And fourth, the performers of *muzică orientală* are "Gypsies" who, despite their long and ubiquitous presence in Romania, are really very little understood by the ethnically dominant population. Roma are still effectively perceived as exotic outsiders who inherently possess, in their role as marginalized musicians, the key to truly soulful music-making.[74] In short, *muzică orientală* creates an opportunity for wedding guests to break out of their mundane existence and step into a heightened atmosphere of music and dance as they implicitly challenge the social and cultural mainstream and engage in exotic, liberating, and "sexualized" behavior. Many of those who champion the music experience this enthusiasm chiefly in specific, circumscribed contexts that depart from the normal routine of everyday existence: at all-night weddings where everyone is eating, drinking, and celebrating. It is through *muzică orientală* and the *manea* as dance that Romanians can lose themselves, embracing, in a sense, an alternative identity that empowers them for an evening.[75]

Clearly not all Romanians, nor all Roma, are fans of *muzică orientală*, however; nor do all weddings include the music of *lăutari*. Those who despise the music are, by and large, the urban elite—the ethnic Romanians who are relatively or very well-educated: office- and service-employees, professionals, and intellectuals. Some have traveled in the West. I have many Romanian friends and colleagues from this broad social category and have discussed *muzică orientală* extensively with them; most of them dislike it profoundly (or at least objectively say they do). Instead, they listen to art music and traditional Romanian music; the younger among them listen to rock, pop, rap, and hip-hop. Paradoxically, some of the most outspoken criticism of the "foreign" nature of *muzică orientală* comes from those who relish Western European and American popular music without seeing the irony within their own perceptions of what "foreign" means. Foes of *muzică orientală* hear its "alien" sounds, "contaminated" culture, and "banal" lyrics; some also hear the death throes of the traditional genres with which they identify.[76] Many view "Gypsy" musicians as altering the direction of Romanian popular culture, a trend they loathe. This phenomenon, of course, is not unique to Romania. It was and is happening elsewhere in eastern Europe, as this volume demonstrates.[77]

Why *muzică orientală* is so objectionable can be illuminated by juxtaposing postcommunist Romania with both East and West and by examining Romania internally. First, *muzică orientală* subverts Romania's professed cultural comradeship with the West by articulating connections with the East—conceived of as a foreign, exotic, and undifferentiated "place" that resonates locally in diverse and powerful ways. The very term that designates the style, *muzică orientală*, denotes the East; significantly, the term "Turkish music" is sometimes employed as an alternative. Such attributes conjure up images of the centuries-long Ottoman presence in the Romanian principalities, a time which for most represents a past that forcibly placed a civilized (Christian, Western) Latin people in the hands of uncivilized (Muslim, Eastern) infidels. Romanians repeatedly blame negative features of their society—particularly in the south of the country, where the Ottomans dominated and Phanariots ruled—on "the Turks." An educated Bucharest woman (who grew up in rural Transylvania) recently lamented the corruption and lack of integrity among inhabitants of southern Romania; she was quick to point out that these qualities are due to "the Turks who were here in the past."[78] Despite the important role that Ottoman Turkish musical culture historically played among urban elites, there is deep resentment to a cultural phenomenon—such as *muzică orientală*—that would reinstate references to that uncomfortable past. The music challenges the Western-looking perspective of a post-Ottoman and now post-Soviet Romania.[79] Speaking of comparable tensions created by NCFM and other Middle Eastern musics in Serbia, Ljerka Rasmussen points out that a "modern orientalism" confronts a "negatively stereotyped Ottoman legacy in the region," underscoring the "regression of national culture" (Rasmussen 1996a:248).

Second, *muzică orientală* threatens the sacrosanct and inviolate notions of the Romanian nation as expressed in native cultural terms, that is, in the realm of folklore. Katherine Verdery points out that due to their own high stakes in culture and knowledge, intellectuals in Romania often engage in a "defense of culture, of 'authentic' values"; this is frequently "wrapped around definitions of national identity and national values" (1991:94). At the very heart of "nation" in Romania is the venerable notion of folklore, including traditional music. Practically speaking, oriental rhythms, melodies, and instrumentation threaten the classic sounds of traditional Romanian music, including the older acoustic instruments of the conventional *lăutar* ensembles (such as cimbalom). The notion that "pure" Romanian folklore represents the "soul" of the nation has circulated for 200 years, having taken root during the early nineteenth century as romantic nationalism swept through Europe. Verdery aptly notes that the "national idea" includes, among other things, an obsession with an historical, "unbroken Romanian peasant tradition" (1996:69). This conviction is still fervently felt among Romanians who reject cultural forms such as *muzică orientală*, which they see as interfering with Romanian folklore. In defending "pure" folklore against "intruders" such as *muzică orientală*, intellectuals assume a "cultural authority" over aesthetics and cultural virtues in society. They see the music and its mass appeal as eliminating the very core of what "Romanian" means.

Third, the urban elite's disdain must also be understood as antagonism toward those who perform *muzică orientală*, namely Roma, who continue to endure widespread discrimination and prejudice in the Balkans. While *lăutari* are routinely hired and valued as performers, "when the music stops and they put their instruments down," as a Romani musician once told me, they are "just Gypsies all over again." Despite their indispensable music-making, Roma are symbolically regarded as non-native members of society whose presence and achievements contest Romania's desired cultural homogeneity. Many also view *muzică orientală*'s fans with contempt, perceiving a clash between urban and rural/rurban lifestyles, equated as a cultured vs. uncultured conflict.

But it is not only Romanians who are conflicted about *muzică orientală*. Its remarkable popularity has created tensions within the *lăutar* community as well. In an ironic twist, both traditional *lăutari* and elite Romanians find themselves united in their opposition to *muzică orientală*. Though their motives differ and they represent contrasting cultural perspectives, they both treasure the classic Romanian genres and lament their demise at the hands of the practitioners of *muzică orientală*. Many older *lăutari* who established their professions during the communist period feel antagonism toward *muzică orientală* since for them it represents an intrusion into their professional world and excludes the genres they know best. Traditional Romanian repertoire, which they excel in, is in far less demand now than formerly. An elderly *lăutar* (violinist) in Bucharest remarked that he does not perform *muzică orientală* at all since in his day, it was not performed; as he told me, "I'm not good at it."[80] A violinist who performs traditional Romanian repertoire in a Bucharest restaurant relayed that he feels both good and bad about the fact that *muzică orientală* can now be performed in public. He is glad since it signifies more cultural freedom (especially for Roma) but also dismayed since it "is pushing out the pure Romanian folklore."[81] There is considerable nostalgia expressed by most older *lăutari* for the communist, and particularly Ceaușescu, era, which represents to them years of regularly occurring performances (at weddings) and thus reasonable prosperity. The economic plight of *lăutari* continues to worsen due to widespread unemployment and poverty; there are correspondingly fewer engagements at which they are hired to perform. If there is one complaint that virtually all *lăutari* voice about the postcommunist period, it is that the general population is now so impoverished that they can hardly afford to hire live musicians for weddings. The result is, of course, fewer engagements for *lăutari* and less income all around. Most middle-aged and older *lăutari* remember the 1970s and 1980s fondly, recalling it as a time when they performed frequently at weddings. The performance of the older genres ensured these musicians, who are now scrambling to find job opportunities, a relatively steady income. Indeed, they feel loyalty to that music and a certain commitment to "preserving" it as Romanian folklore.

Tensions generated by *muzică orientală* also exist between urban and rural *lăutari*. There is no question that urban *lăutari* who excel in *muzică orientală* make more money than rural ones, much of it simply in tips from clients. Urban musicians also have more expensive, up-to-date instruments—especially synthesizers—than do their rural counterparts, translating into more requests for jobs. This is directly relevant to the *muzică orientală* craze since the synthesizer is now indispensable to its performance. A *lăutar* (accordionist) who lived temporarily in Bucharest during the Ceauşescu years but was unable to obtain permission to reside there for good is still embittered that he was not able to make Bucharest his permanent home.[82] He knows very well that had he been able to establish himself as a accordionist in the city, he would have had a more successful career, both making more money and—at least he imagines—establishing his reputation more widely. Instead, he plays in a village *taraf*, struggling to make ends meet with traditional instruments (including a poor quality synthesizer). Indeed, the role of musical instruments plays a significant part in the generation gap between older and younger *lăutari*. Older musicians cannot afford to purchase expensive new synthesizers or drum sets, let alone learn to play them. There is a lamentable feeling among many *lăutari* that instruments such as the beloved cimbalom (an instrument that effectively epitomizes urban lăutar music) are in decline. Many of the older *lăutari* whom I know are heavy-hearted; they are stuck in impossible dilemmas, having been robbed in a sense of their professions through the mass cultural changes that occurred in postcommunist Romania. Yet some have adapted. An established vocalist in Bucharest in his early sixties, who resisted learning *muzică orientală* for years, has, as I found out in 2003, finally mastered the style—purely out of necessity in order to earn a living. No doubt it is easier for vocalists than violinists or cimbalom players to pick up *muzică orientală* since they are not required to purchase and learn new instruments.[83]

Thus, generational schisms related to music and instruments, as well as rivalries based on city versus village venues have permeated the *lăutar* community in southern Romania, creating tensions and feelings of competition and envy. *Lăutari* are both insiders and outsiders with regard to *muzică orientală*. Artistically, they are insiders insofar as they, not Romanians, dominate the style of the music. In popular thinking, it is they as "Gypsies" who innately hold the key to this music-making, while Romanians just aspire to it.[84] As a *lăutar* recently commented, "Romanians really like the *manea* but they sure don't know how to dance it right!"[85] At the same time, socially, *lăutari* are outsiders; they stand on the margins of mainstream Romanian society. Within the larger community of Roma, yet other insider/outsider tensions emerge. Here *lăutari* behave as an artistic elite, maintaining an exclusive, insider identity and even confidently calling themselves, in contrast to other Roma, *țigani de mătase* [silk Gypsies]. And finally, in an even more nuanced sense, through the fateful generational shifting of music and instruments since 1989, *lăutari* who have not adequately adapted to the newer styles and genres have become outsiders—left behind by the younger, usually urban insider musicians.[86] These multivalent tensions underscore the complex web of social dynamics that *muzică orientală* articulates in contemporary Romania.

Muzică orientală powerfully challenges urban, elite constructions of identity. Yet its appeal among Romanian youth, rurbanites, and the working class, as well as most Roma, is unmistakable. The music represents a fusion of identities that reside in a broad Balkan regional framework and that are informed by cultural, social, and historical conditions. What *muzică orientală* effectively evokes is linked to the larger social conflicts that Romanians face as they continue to make the painful transition from communism to postcommunism and find their place in the Balkans, in Europe, and in the world.

Notes

1. I wish to extend a special word of thanks to Donna Buchanan for her invaluable questions, comments, and suggestions in the writing of this article. I am also grateful to Michael Zocchi for his superb musical transcriptions and for bringing to my attention a number of observations regarding the music.

2. When I employ the terms Rom (noun, pl. Roma) or Romani (adjective or language), I am adopting designations that refer to individuals or collectives. I use the English word Gypsy (without quotation marks) when I translate directly from the Romanian noun *ţigan* or adjective *ţigănesc*. My use of the term "Gypsy" in quotation marks denotes a culturally-constructed, "imagined" identity (perpetuated by both non-Roma and Roma) consisting of romanticized, idealized traits and/or negative, deviant attributes. In this way, I attempt to reflect the various contextual nuances of these ethnonyms.

3. I use "ethnopop" advisedly here since the Romanian term *etnopop* now has a local meaning: it refers to a new style of music that is performed exclusively by ethnic Romanians and is based on traditional Romanian genres that are arranged in a pop style with a rock beat and played on amplified instruments. This music has no relation to *muzică orientală*; instead, it more readily has right-wing nationalist overtones.

4. The sites for my fieldwork included Bucharest, Craiova, Piteşti, and Târgovişte (cities), as well as Blejeşti, Cartojani, Celei, Icoană, Mârşa, Milcovăţu, Palancă, and Preajbă (villages), all in south-central Romania.

5. This is true especially in the areas that formed the Romanian principalities.

6. As Donald Dyer notes, "a number of grammatical features have led linguists to characterize Romanian, together with Bulgarian, Macedonian, and Albanian as a *sprachbund*—a group of languages displaying typological similarities, ostensibly owing to their geographic contiguity" (Dyer 2000:696). Among the most salient of their shared grammatical features are the post-positional definite article, the "loss of the infinitive and its replacement with a subordinate clause," future-tense formation with the auxiliary verb "want," the use of the dative possessive, and the "reduplication of object pronouns" (Dyer 2002:119).

7. Historically, Romanian Jews also constituted a significant Other but now comprise only a tiny minority.

8. The most visible nationalist organization is the "Greater Romania" Party, led by Corneliu Vadim Tudor who, along with other like-minded Romanians, has "not hesitated to use xenophobic, anti-Semitic, anti-Gypsy, and anti-Hungarian rhetoric, inflaming public opinion" (Verdery 1996:89).

9. Phanariot rule was imposed in 1711 in Moldavia when the Ottomans replaced the prince of Moldavia—Dimitrie Cantemir (1673–1723)—with a Greek prince from the Phanar district of Istanbul, and in 1716 in Wallachia when a Phanariot prince was installed (Michelson 2000:668–69).

10. These included, as Alexandru notes, "singers and instrumentalists, dancers and jugglers, in order to make the celebrations as magnificent as could be" (1980b:266). He points out that Greek, Armenian, and Jewish musicians from Turkey were also probably among the early performers in the Romanian principalities (1980b:264).

11. Ciobanu goes on to note that "toward evening, every day, as the sun was setting, it was also played for the urban populace in the surroundings of the princes' courts" (1974b:108). Elsewhere we learn that the *mehterhanea*

"accompanied royal processions and was performed . . . during the donning of the caftan by prominent boyars " (Alexandru 1980b:256).

12. *Lăutar* is a Turkish word from the stringed instrument *alăută* or *lăută* (Alexandru 1980b:271). Early *lăutari* played stringed instruments—viols—such as the *scripcă, diblă,* and *ceteră,* as well as the *keman,* a Turkish bowed instrument (Alexandru 1980b:255); see also Beissinger 1991and 2001.

13. *Lăutari* were household slaves; on the enslavement of Roma in the Romanian principalities, see Crowe 1991and 1996.

14. *Taraf,* also from the Turkish, denotes a small traditional musical ensemble (Alexandru 1980b:255).

15. Dimitrie Cantemir, who wrote a well-known treatise on Turkish art music (ca. 1700), epitomized the Ottoman Turkish cultural contacts during the seventeenth and eighteenth centuries. He was an eminent composer and musical pedagogue who formulated a system of musical notation based on the letters of the Arabic alphabet. He was also a talented musician who studied in Istanbul intermittently between 1688 and 1710 and a virtuoso performer of the Ottoman *tanbur* and *ney.* See Feldman 1996, 2002; see also Alexandru 1980a.

16. I will treat the *manea* as a dance form in my discussion ahead of *muzică orientală* in the postcommunist period.

17. Garfias associates the *Duyek* rhythm with the *"Chifti-telli"* rhythm (1981:99), a topic I treat ahead.

18. Literary works such as Aleksandr Pushkin's *Tsygany* [*The Gypsies*] (1824) and Prosper Mérimée's *Carmen* (1845) were instrumental in this process of creating and fostering the romanticized "Gypsy" of the popular imagination.

19. This "paradox" with regard to musicians has been written about at length; see Silverman 1996a; van de Port 1999; and Beissinger 1991, 2001.

20. On the Gypsy or *lăutar* hora, see Giurchescu 2000:325–26.

21. The generic Romanian hora performed at weddings is called the *horă mare* [great hora] (Niculescu-Varone, et al.1979:72, 92). The other most common southern Romanian dance, rarely performed at Romani weddings, is the *sârbă,* a circle (or semi-circle) dance in duple meter with a shoulder hold (1979:155). As if to underscore the boundaries drawn between Romanian and Romani social dance repertoire, the young Romani wife of an urban *lăutar* recently told me that she had no idea how to dance the traditional (and very simple) Romanian *sârbă* (p.c., 28 July 2003, Bucharest).

22. This is a topic beyond the scope of this article (and about which little has been written).

23. The most prominent *manea* soloist at that time was the female Romani vocalist Romica Puceanu.

24. Garfias argues that "available evidence suggests . . . [that] not only is the *manea* . . . found in this form throughout the Cîmpia Dunării [Danube plain], it is also an improvised song and dance form found among the Tatar ethnic minority community living in the Black Sea coast region of Dobrogea" (1984: 92).

25. *Lăutari* seldom traveled to Yugoslavia to bring back Serbian music since it was almost impossible for Romanians to travel there during the Ceauşescu years.

26. See Buchanan 1996b and Rice 1994:240–50.

27. For a discussion of the production of unauthorized music cassettes and piracy in the 1980s in Bulgaria, see Buchanan 1996b:206–12 and Kurkela 1997:191–93.

28. *Lăutar* (accordionist), p.c., 5 July 1998, Celei.

29. Colleagues and friends in Romania (especially Speranţa Rădulescu) have generally guided me in the chronology that I present here since there is no written account yet of *muzică orientală* (and I was not in Romania to observe it myself after 1987 and before 1995).

30. *Lăutar* (violinist), p.c., 26 June 1998, Bucharest.

31. Underscoring this idea, A.L. Lloyd remarks that "one still finds [Romani] musicians who cling to the oriental notion that the rhythm instrument is more important than the instrument carrying the tune" (1963:16).

32. On *makam,* see Feldman 1996.

33. Lloyd comments that "the Arabic *makams* . . . have long exerted their special influence on the repertory of occupational popular musicians in the Balkans" (1963:19).

34. The "Gypsy scale" that Ciobanu discusses comprises g–b♭–c♯–d–e♭–f♯–g (1974a:84).

35. Referring to Bulgarian Romani music, Timothy Rice notes that "improvisation as valued musical practice seems to have been mainly the province of Gypsy musicians, who borrowed the improvised, non-metrical *mane* from Turkish tradition." "Oriental" qualities in Bulgarian Romani music, he continues, include "the augmented second, glissandi, melodic sequences, and timbral manipulation" (1994:109). These observations resonate with Romani musicianship north of the Danube River, as well.

36. Other percussion in *muzică orientală* ensembles sometimes include bongos or conga drums.

37. Urban ensembles that play exclusively *muzică orientală* are now often called *trupe* (troupes; sg. *trupă*) instead of the traditional *taraf.*

38. From the late 1960s until the mid-1970s, Indian culture was popularized in Romania; a substantial number of Indian films were shown in Bucharest and gained a following, especially among Roma. Later in the 1970s, a Romanian female singer named Narghita sang in an Indian style which also attracted Romanifans (Marin Marian-Bălaşa, p.c., 25 May 2000, Bucharest).

39. Ethnomusicologist, p.c., 25 May 2000, Bucharest.

40. Folklorist, p.c., 25 July 2003, Bucharest.

41. Rap music was also embraced by Bulgarian wedding music artists in the 1990s and was very popular but has since lost some of its favor (Carol Silverman, p.c., 20 June 2001).

42. *Lăutar* (accordionist), p.c., 2 June 2000, Mârşa. In fact, I have never heard anything even faintly resembling rap performed live at weddings by *lăutari.*

43. Countless other erotic songs characterize *muzică orientală: Vino cu mine* [Come with me], *Doar pe tine te iubesc* [I love only you], *Fata din vis* [Dream girl], *Eşti frumoasă foc* [You're super beautiful], *Te iubesc* [I love you], and

Strînge-mă, sărută-mă [Hold me, kiss me].

44. Few Romani musicians in southern Romania actually speak or even sing in Romani; on the use of Romani among *lăutari*, see Beissinger 2001:43–45.

45. On the use of *ţigan* vs. *rom* among *lăutari*, see Beissinger 2001:45– 47.

46. *Lăutar* (accordionist), p.c., 5 July 1998, Celei. This is a striking reminder of the significance of music as an indicator of political change. On musical change in other formerly communist East European countries after 1989, see Slobin 1996.

47. See Garfias 1984:91–92; see also Silverman 2000b:278. On the *čoček* and *kyuchek*, see Silverman 2003.

48. Female vocalists do not typically perform *muzică orientală* but rather Romanian and other Romani lyric songs and song-dances (such as the hora or *sârbă*). Some of the currently best-known female vocalists in Bucharest are Carmen Şerban, Mirela Mihalache, and Cristina. The late Romica Puceanu, though not associated with *muzică orientală*, was a legendary female Romani singer celebrated for her singing of earlier *manele* during the communist period, as was Gabi Lunca.

49. *Lăutar* (accordionist), p.c., 2 June 2000, Mârşa.

50. Such nicknames include Pelcaru [The Furrier], Băieţică [Little Boy], Bebe [Baby], Ursuleţ [Little Bear], and so on.

51. Costin Popovici (Director, L'Esperance Music Production), p.c., 5 June 2001, Bucharest. Vali Vijelie told me that he heard Adrian in the early 1990s when Adrian was fourteen, and, recognizing his talent, began singing with him then (p.c., 31 May 2000, Bucharest). Adrian Copilul Minune was featured in the French film *Gadjo Dilo* (1997), directed by Tony Gatliff, about a Romani village and its musicians in southern Romania. Adrian appears several times in the film, playing the accordion and singing. Other *muzică orientală* stars, such as Jean de la Craiova, launched their careers in similar fashion, originally singing *lăutar* music and then turning by the late 1990s to the popular new style.

52. Vali was born in Bucharest in 1969; his father was a *lăutar* who played the cimbalom. Vali began to study music at age eleven and played *lăutar* music in an ensemble between 1984 and 1990, at which time he turned to *muzică orientală* (p.c., 31 May 2000, Bucharest).

53. P.c., 31 May 2000, Bucharest.

54. Romanian musician (synthesizer), p.c., 22 July 2003, Bucharest.

55. For a discussion of impressions that *lăutari* and other Roma have of Romanians and vice versa, see Beissinger 2001:32–36.

56. *Lăutar* (accordionist), p.c., 4 June 2001, Mârşa.

57. *Revista Ioana* (2001:9); Anca Lupeş (Executive Director, Nova Music Entertainment), p.c., 6 June 2001, Bucharest.

58. The fascination with Romani culture, especially among young Romanians, also extends to the increasing use of sub-standard Romani lexicon as Romanian slang, creating a counterculture stratum of linguistic usage; see Marian-Bălaşa 2003.

59. Bucharest has long been the center for the various styles of Romani music that spread throughout Romania (Garfias 1984:85).

60. P.c., 31 May 2000, Bucharest. According to another urban vocalist, it is relatively easy to break into the cassette world and get a first cassette produced, but much more difficult to continue to sell them with regularity (*lăutar*, p.c., 29 May 2000, Bucharest).

61. On a cassette from 2001, for instance, titled *Adrian şi Invitaţii săi* [Adrian and his guests], out of eleven songs, only one includes Adrian Copilul Minune as soloist.

62. A rural accordionist explained to me how he learns songs from newly released cassettes. He selects songs from recordings that he likes and then picks up the music simply by listening to them, a process that for him is almost immediate and is, as he pointed out, the earmark of an accomplished *lăutar*—something that "Romanian musicians can't do," in another expression of how ethnicity and superior musicianship are linked in the minds of many *lăutari*.

63. Anca Lupeş (Executive Director, Nova Music Entertainment), p.c., 6 June 2001, Bucharest.

64. For example, on Saturday nights *lăutari* played traditional music on television, a program I saw for the first time in Craiova in July 1998. Otherwise, however, as Kurkela noted when he visited the Romanian Radio in Bucharest in 1994, the "Head of Light Music absolutely refused to speak about pirated oriental music cassettes. In his opinion, this music is so terrible and of poor quality that it was better to forget the whole thing completely" (1995:113).

65. On how musical taste conforms to the deep conflicts within the Belgrade population, and is related, in large measure, to urban-rural divisions, see Gordy 1999:105–108 and Rasmussen, this volume.

66. *Lăutar* (vocalist), p.c., 31 May 2000, Bucharest.

67. Among them are formerly working-class Romanians who have managed to amass a significant amount of wealth since the Revolution and now boast ostentatious signs of affluence such as hosting lavish weddings at costly venues and driving SUVs.

68. Young male employee (university student) at L'Esperance Music Production, p.c., 5 June 2001, Bucharest.

69. Vali Vijelie, p.c., 31 May 2000, Bucharest.

70. Costin Popovici (Director, L'Esperance Music Production), p.c., 5 June 2001, Bucharest.

71. Costin Popovici (Director, L'Esperance Music Production), p.c., 5 June 2001, Bucharest.

72. It featured Costi Ioniţă and Adrian Copilul Minune (Anca Lupeş, Executive Director, Nova Music Entertainment, p.c., 6 June 2001, Bucharest).

73. *Lăutar* (violinist), p.c., 26 June 1998, Bucharest.

74. See van de Port's analogous account of "Gypsies as musical specialists" in Vojvodina (1999:295–96).

75. See van de Port (1999) for a view of this phenomenon among Serbs and Romani musicians in Novi Sad.

76. Gordy comments on similar reactions by Belgrade "intellectuals" to "the erotic display and simply written texts of the songs" of *turbo folk* (1999:151).

77. See also Buchanan 1996b; Gordy 1999:151; Lange 1996:76.

78. P.c., 24 May 2001, Bucharest.

79. As Todorova so aptly notes, "Romanians have usually insisted on their direct connections to the Western world (not even via Central Europe) and on their missionary role as outposts of Latinism and civilization among a sea of (Slavic and Turkic) barbarians" (1997:46).

80. *Lăutar* (violinist), p.c., 26 June 1998, Bucharest.

81. *Lăutar* (violinist), p.c., 3 July 1998, Bucharest.

82. During the communist period, one needed special permission to move to and settle in Bucharest.

83. Whether audiences want to hear a sixty-something *lăutar* as opposed to a slick, young vocalist sing *muzică orientală* while they dance is perhaps another question.

84. See van de Port's discussion of the purported in-born "secrets" of Gypsy musicianship and artistry in Vojvodina (1999).

85. Quoted by Speranţa Rădulescu, p.c., 26 July 2003, Bucharest.

86. They are not all older, however. I know a good number of younger urban *lăutari* who love the traditional repertoire and play it with great mastery but who must play *muzică orientală* most of the time in order to put bread on the table.

❖ 4 ❖

Bulgarian *Chalga* on Video: Oriental Stereotypes, Mafia Exoticism, and Politics

Vesa Kurkela

Since the mid-1990s, music video has been an essential part of the Bulgarian mediascape.[1] Local video production was born as an outgrowth of the expanding music cassette business and even today most music videos are released for purposes of promotion. However, during the last three years Bulgarian video production has been so prolific that it is not difficult to see it developing and advancing the local popular music scene in the near future. The increased availability of music video has been facilitated considerably by a commercial cable television net that has spread to all the bigger towns. By spring 2001 at least one Sofia-based cable TV channel, ONIX, broadcasted predominantly domestic video clips nonstop to private homes, and music bars and other public places (Dimov, p.c., 2 April 2001).

Compared to other Western countries, the era of Bulgarian music video is just beginning. Nevertheless, the style of production has changed remarkably during its short history, from amateur one-camera shots to sophisticated professionalism. Still, the Bulgarian music market is small and the country is relatively poor. This means that local music video is typically based on low-budget production. Accordingly, the first topic of this chapter is to demonstrate how, if at all, Bulgarian music video differs from the global Music Television format. My research materials comprise commercial videocassettes released for the Bulgarian market from 1995 to 2000.[2] While Bulgarian video production encompasses various kinds of

143

popular music, in the pages that follow I concentrate on the most popular genre, *chalga*.

In today's Bulgaria *chalga* is the general name for a new dance music that is a complex mixture of various musical styles and traditions. Quite often modern *chalga* is also called *pop-folk* or *etno-pop*. The components of this fusion include Serbian, Macedonian, Greek, and Turkish popular music; older Bulgarian pop songs; various styles of Balkan Romani music; Western pop, rock, techno, and rap; as well as the global currents of Afro-Cuban music, among others. *Chalga* is stylistically such a hybrid that defining it is not an easy task. However, at its stylistic core *chalga* features very distinguishable rhythmic patterns also associated with "oriental" or bellydance. These and other characteristics refer directly to an imagined "East" and specifically, to dance music styles found throughout the eastern Mediterranean.

To a Westerner's ears, *chalga* no doubt sounds quite oriental. However, what makes this problematic is the fact that Bulgarian culture as a whole is in several respects the opposite of the West. In Bulgaria the borderline between East and West is unclear and vacillating. Nevertheless, the oriental flavor of *chalga* is undisputed even among Bulgarians themselves, and accordingly, the *chalga* style is easily discerned from Bulgarian folk music and older popular styles by anyone who understands music in general. The central topic of this article is to determine what kind of meanings the oriental aspect of *chalga* constructs among Bulgarian audiences. An important point of departure is Edward Said's concept of orientalism (1995[1978]), which has been widely utilized in various studies connected with postcolonial criticism. However, while the peculiar oriental world presented by *chalga* videos may have some roots in the history of colonialism, I very much doubt the suitability of the Saidian interpretation for the analysis of Bulgarian culture and music in general. Nevertheless, I shall try to find an alternative explanation, one more relevant to the Bulgarian situation.

Before presenting these more theoretical arguments I shall analyze the content of *chalga* videos from various perspectives. Of particular concern is how "the oriental" in *chalga* has been produced. What are the main methods and models employed by musicians, actors and video directors in creating the oriental aura of these videos? My analysis deals with music, dance, and lyrics, but also with visual narration and set decoration. All of these elements are essential when producing the oriental or otherwise exotic and fairy-tale-like sentiments of *chalga* videos.

The politics of *chalga* is also one of my central topics. Contrary to Bulgarian popular music in general, many *chalga* songs and videos are full of social criticism. They comment on social problems, often in ways that may confuse serious students of culture. Sexist soft porn seems to be a widely used method for ensuring the commercial success of *chalga* songs. The videos also contain aggressive jokes that display little respect for anyone or anything. The objects of mockery are various—politicians, the state administration, the *nouveaux riches,* the Bulgarian mafia, policemen, macho culture, the sex business, Arab sheiks, superficial lovers of fashion, Russian folklore troupes, and various Western fashion phenomena. Ironic criticism is often so well hidden that the outsider cannot understand it without the guidance and explanation of local cultural experts. Nothing in *chalga* is serious and its contents stray very far from Western political correctness.

Background on *Chalga*

In the 1990s, in the wake of general political and cultural breakthroughs, most European postcommunist countries experienced great changes in the music media. Two central features of this development were rapidly increasing local cassette production and music piracy, especially of Western hit music. In the beginning piracy also plagued music cassettes, but quite soon focused more exclusively on CDs. Centers for eastern European pirate production have moved from one country to another; the first were Poland and Bulgaria, followed by Estonia and Romania, and most recently, Ukraine. Over the last decade Russia has also acquired a notorious reputation in this field of black marketing.[3] Changes in production sites have followed the anti-piracy campaigns by the US and EU governments and the International Federation of Phonogram Industries (IFPI), which have targeted the most blatant cases of international copyright law violations. Governments have been urged and pressed to intensify anti-piracy monitoring and to tighten copyright legislation.[4]

In many former Eastern bloc countries the consumption of Western popular music has increased markedly. Cheap pirated phonogram copies have effectively circulated hits, and local recording industries have suffered from lack of demand and capital. Bulgaria, however, seems to be a different case. Especially since the mid-1990s, a real boom in domestic dance music has dominated the music media, and at the center of this trend is oriental *chalga*. *Chalga*'s popularity can be interpreted as a kind of protest and reaction against the communist regime's mono-ethnic cultural policy of the 1980s, according to which all people living in Bulgaria were accounted for as ethnic Bulgarians, and the existence of any minorities was officially denied. Muslim minorities, which include

Pomaks, Turks, and some Roma, were persecuted. In the 1980s, the Turkish minority especially fell victim to severe and aggressive discrimination. These measures consisted of compulsory Bulgarianization of Turkish names, forced resettling, and deportation (Poulton 1991:129–51).

All kinds of cultural idiosyncrasies and symbols of the respective minorities were also suppressed. Accordingly, all kinds of oriental dance music referring to Turkish or Romani culture were practically banned (Buchanan 1996b:207–212; Pennanen 2001). The collapse of the Communist regime at the turn of the 1990s also meant a great change in Bulgarian cultural policy. One of the most noticeable and far reaching expressions of this change was *chalga* and its enormous popularity.

The Balkans abound in paradoxes, and even in this case the models for oriental pop did not come first from the east, but from the west and south—namely, from Serbia and Greece. Before its dissolution Yugoslavia pioneered a new kind of popular music based on local traditions (NCFM), which also became well-known and popular in communist Bulgaria, mainly with the aid of pirated cassettes. Just as Yugoslavia was an ethnic patchwork quilt, so also were there a great many different local musical styles under the title NCFM; the most popular in Bulgaria was Serbian folk pop. In addition, the Greek pop song style called *laika* was very much liked by Bulgarians. (Dimov 1996b:31–33).

Only at the beginning of the 1990s did the term *chalga* come to refer mainly to dance music performed by Roma. Similarly, in the European part of Turkey, Rumelia, professional Romani bands are still called *çalgıcı* today, and in Macedonia the analogous term is *čalgija* (Seeman 2000:7–11; Silverman 1996b:71–72). All of these terms derive from Turkish, where *çalgı* means "musical instrument." The history of these orchestras goes back to the Ottoman era, when their repertoire mainly consisted of Turkish classical and light music. Their historical roots in the Middle Eastern *makam* system can also be seen in recent times. Accordingly, the repertoire of modern electronic *čalgija* is full of bellydance pieces (*cacique*), with typically long improvised solo passages in *tempo rubato* that follow the changing modalities of the dance tune.

In Bulgaria *chalga* also first became well known in association with similar *cacique* songs, which are typified by a bellydance rhythm in 4/4 or 9/8, long clarinet solos, and often, Romani lyrics.[5] However, many *kyuchetsi* are instrumentals, where a short theme is followed by almost endless improvisatory passages, often played in a very virtuosic manner. The cassettes containing *kyuchek* music from the early 1990s are technically of the poorest quality with severe distortion. Heavily distorted sound was no doubt one reason why Romani music was anything but highly valued among average Bulgarians.

During these years Romani *kyuchek* was shadowed by another *chalga* style. The orchestras playing Thracian wedding music (*svatbarska muzika*) enjoyed top popularity at this time. The best known soloist, clarinetist Ivo Papazov, was nearly a national hero.[6] Although *svatbarski* musicians were also often ethnic Roma and/or Turks, their music was in all respects better and more respectable than *kyuchek;* it was professionally performed, technically well recorded, extremely virtuosic, breathtakingly swinging, colorfully oriental and even the symbol of political resistance during the old regime (Buchanan 1995:387; 1996b:204–206). Nevertheless, wedding music had one big drawback. By stressing its virtuosity wedding music became very complex and fast, which made it unsuitable for dancing. During the 1990s, due to the lack of commercial success, many Thracian wedding musicians also started to play mainstream *chalga* with more danceable—and simple—rhythms.

By the mid-1990s a very interesting development had occurred. Bulgarian musicians mixed Romani *kyuchek* with Serbian- and Greek-influenced folk pop and adopted various new models from suitable international styles and artists, like the Gypsy Kings. This new combination started to be called *chalga*, a previously derisive word for anything of poor quality with a strong association to Romani culture. The development of *chalga* thus resembles the change in Yugoslav NCFM some ten years earlier. In Yugoslavia the Romani oriental sound, which incorporated several international hit tunes originating in Indian film music, also gave birth to a new music style that utilized Eastern musical stereotypes and was widely popular. As mentioned already, all this also influenced new Bulgarian popular music (Rasmussen 1991:128–32).

At the end of the 1990s the new style became an undisputed success on the Bulgarian popular music scene. The most popular *chalga* hits sold more than 100,000 copies, whereas domestic rock records could at best reach sales of 10–15,000 copies (Ivo Dochovski and Ventsislav Dimov, Interviews, 1999).

Commercial success considerably increased the cultural value of *chalga* with the Bulgarian public. Many Bulgarians often consider *chalga* the music of the new economic elite—the *nouveaux riches*. However, I have never understood the basis of this argument. One possible explanation is that *chalga* songs quite often portray a jet-set life and dreams of Western prosperity. On the grounds of audience consistency one could argue that the most eager *chalga* fans are to be found in certain youth groups and—somewhat surprisingly—among children. Strange or not, even some members of the intellectual elite have shown interest in *chalga*. However, based on interviews with local experts such as Ventsislav Dimov (1999) and Rozmari Statelova (1999), and my own observation of *chalga* audiences (1997–2000), my sense is that intellectuals' interest mainly focuses on attempting to understand how on earth this sort of music—from their perspective, such "bad music"—could achieve such enormous popularity.

Nevertheless, a more typical academic attitude seems to follow the earlier line of the communist cultural elite. This attitude is nicely mirrored in literary historian Julia Stefanova's (n.d.) comment that Bulgarian culture "is being *chalga*gized"; here the term refers to "the general decline of culture—and the all-pervasive feeling that it is being submerged in subculture and surrogates." *Chalga* is also seen as evidence of how the new economic elite is totally unable to create convincing cultural legitimacy (Kessi 2001:5). On the other hand, the typical American feminist interpretation of *chalga* argues that the soft porn eroticism of many songs "glorifies the short-skirted, gold-digging *mutressa* as the ultimate expression of successful femininity" (Ghodsee 2000:10). According to this argument, *chalga* presents Bulgarian women as "ambitious bimbos" and thus strengthens the inequality between the sexes, which according to recent studies, has heavily increased in the era of transition economy (Ghodsee 2000:10).

The Style of *Chalga* Videos

In regard to content, roughly three basic types of *chalga* videos can be found: *concert videos, narrative videos* and *music-based videos*. These types came to mind quite spontaneously during preliminary analysis. However, they are similar to the classification schemes of early Western video producers. According to Simon Frith (1988:217), in the 1980s record companies divided "pop videos" into three broad categories: performance, narrative, and conceptual. Several different classifications can also be found, but usually they have been made by visual media scholars, for whom music is mainly seen as subordinate and thus having a minor role in visual and artistic design. However, my point of departure is quite the opposite. Due to my musicological background I tend also to interpret the visual content of the video with reference to music.

Concert Documentations

Many *chalga* videos can be called *concert documentations*. Stylistically this is the oldest type and clearly old-fashioned from the perspective of modern video language. Such videos stress the musicians' role in performance and are documentary in many respects. Their content consists mainly of concrete descriptions of musical performance, which may then be diversified by inserts illustrating contextual landscapes and audience reactions.

Concert documentation is the dominant production model in the videos of Thracian wedding orchestras and some (other) Romani bands (e.g., Kristal, Kristali, Kitka). However, the spatial contexts employed are quite diverse; music is not only performed on a nightclub stage, in a concert hall, or a discothèque, but in strange and even absurd performance locales. Accordingly, the video clip *Sexy* by the group Kitka was shot on a Black Sea beach, where the musicians stand up to their knees in water and desperately try to appear to be playing. Not even the player of the electronic drums seems to be afraid of a short circuit, but allows the rhythmic accompaniment to continue between wet waves.

A subcategory of this type is the various festival videos produced every year at local folk pop mass events, such as the Trakiya Folk and Pirin Folk fests. Due to the technological advances of the late 1990s, *chalga* singers began performing live without orchestra—with the aid of a playback tape. However, this change did not cause the production of concert videos to cease. Several *chalga* artists continuously favor playback in their music videos. Dance groups performing pseudo bellydance or other choreography compensate for the absence of live instrumentalists. Interaction between singers and audiences is also illustrated in a more versatile way than was the case in older videos of dance band performances.

Narrative Videos

The other two types of *chalga* videos more closely resemble the so-called MTV format, which seems to have become the primary model for video production all over the globe. In the following analysis they will be called *narrative videos* and *music-based videos.* The narrative type consists of two or three separate visual plots. The first is more or less (often less) related to the song lyrics. Its main protagonist may be the singer herself, but this role may also be filled by an actor. The second is the singer's performance of the song, which she renders without any dramatic connection to the first plot. The third concerns dancers or landscapes that are also quite separate from the narrative of the lyrics.

Danŭtsi [Taxes], by Petra, the hit singer of the Payner company (1999) is a prime example of a narrative video whose primary plot is only tenuously connected to the lyrics (Video 4.1). The song text is mildly populist and consists of a long list detailing various taxed objects, as well as some exploiters of collected taxes. Its main theme is based on humorous juxtapositions (Fig. 4.1):

Taxes on *rakiya,*	Taxes for Reds,
taxes on the neighbor's wife,	taxes for Greens,
taxes on cars,	taxes for Blues,
taxes on women,	taxes for penguins,
taxes on trash,	taxes on olives,
taxes on ash,	taxes on bikinis,
taxes on *mezze,*	taxes on begging,
taxes on beach life	taxes for nothing.

Figure 4.1: *Danŭtsi.* Music by Stefan Tsirkov, lyrics by Pavel Fotev, performed by Petra. Payner Music, 1999.

The song's message is crystallized by its refrain:

Taxes, taxes,	you burn me,
you fatty cheese pastries,	you ruin me.

The song's melody is in the Phrygian mode and its harmonization is based on only a B minor chord. The refrain is quite contrastive; its accompaniment comprises a descending chord progression beginning in the subdominant: Em–D–C–Bm. In accordance with the general style of *chalga,* in the middle of the song there is a richly embellished trumpet-like solo with twisting melodic line, played on the synthesizer with the harmonic accompaniment based again on a B minor triad.

The visual narration is based on parody. Tax collection has been delegated to two lively militiamen with uniform caps. At the very beginning the hero of the story loses his temper because his car has broken down, and kicks it hard. The militiamen appear on the scene and fine the driver; then they walk away and tap an extra large pocket calculator. In the second episode the hero is sitting at a restaurant table with his girlfriend. He chats her up, clinks glasses with her and munches some *mezze* [snacks; appetizers]. Every action is suddenly disturbed by the militiamen, who demand payment with the huge pocket calculator. The same scenario is repeated in a hotel room, where the hero intends to make love to his girlfriend. The girl is supposedly involved in the taxation intrigue, and the funny militiamen appear again, this time from behind a wardrobe door.

Again it is time to pay taxes. Very soon the hero is totally without means and uses his last pennies for a cheese pastry. The militiamen pass by and snatch the pastry out of his hand: taxes, taxes. In the final episode the poor hero sits on the street begging and the merry tax authorities come once again and confiscate the beggar's pennies. Thereafter the militiamen throw their military caps to the ground and walk away tapping their large calculator while commenting: "super, super!"

The second level of visual composition consists of the vocalist, whose performance is inserted frequently between takes of the main plot, from which she is totally absent. She sings standing up, without moving, and her position is clearly that of an outside commentator, like a bard or a griot. These inserts follow the musical periods and are well synchronized with the visual narration.

Music-Based Videos

The *music-based* or *non-narrative chalga* video normally consists of countless segments of very short duration. The primary function of its visual components is to reinforce the musical structure and message. At its best this MTV-style format becomes a kind of music of pictures. Very often the visual rhythm can be even more complex than the musical rhythm. Among the videos in my collection only a few attained this postmodern version of the Wagnerian *Gesamtkunstwerk*. The reason is obvious. Video production is normally based on a very low budget that favors documentary but also narrative videos (cf. Fenster 1993:119–20). Producing a music-based video, with its innumerable visual fragments and many technical tricks is simply too expensive for Bulgarian producers.

Many non-narrative *chalga* videos are hybrids between the MTV format and old-fashioned stage style. Production development, however, is moving in a more international direction. In many of the most recent *chalga* videos the effects of new digital technology have been successfully utilized, resulting in various unrealistic but attractive special effects like partially invisible bodies or flying human figures.

A good example of a music-based *chalga* video is the 1997 hit song by Sashka Vaseva, *Levovete v marki* [*Leva* into marks] (Video 4.2). The work is similar to disco in style; the tempo is faster than in normal bellydance (M.M. 117) and the rhythmic accompaniment is a skillful mixture of monotonous techno pounding and some elements of *kyuchek* rhythm (see Fig. 4.2). It is in just this mixture that techno-*chalga* seems to deviate from global techno models, since the rhythmic accompaniment is stuffed with various percussion sounds. The result is a playful game between the often contradictory connotations of disco dance and belly-dance.

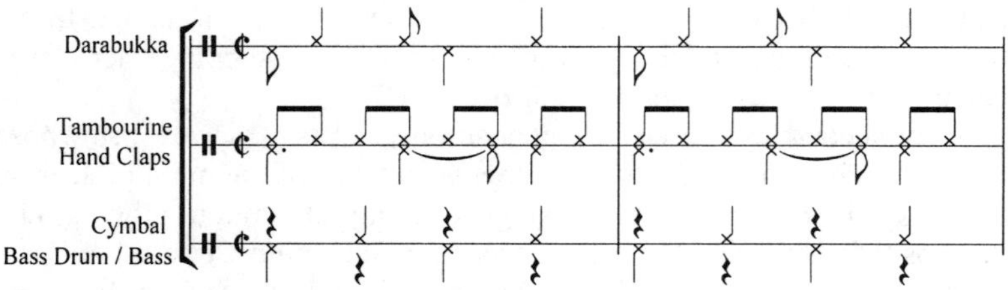

Figure 4.2: *Levovete v marki,* rhythmic accompaniment. Music by Sashka Vaseva. Payner Music, 2000.

The visual tempo, with its few constantly recurring inserts, is very fast when compared with other *chalga* videos. *"Levovete"* has no visual plot; the visual content comprises a semi-picture of the singer moving from right to left and vice versa, whereas the fast visual rhythm is constructed from rapid flashes of half-naked male and female dancers. A shot of a young man dancing is also digitally manipulated—only his torso is visible.

Nevertheless, this video is typical of the *chalga* genre. The verse melody emphasizes the *Hicaz* tetrachord C–D♭–E–F, while the harmonic accompaniment consists of the chord cycle C–D♭–C–B♭m, which stresses the semitone C–D♭. However, in the refrain the tonal center moves to F with the aid of the descending chord progression Fm–E♭–D♭–C. The lyrics are also quite political when related to the problems of today's Bulgarian society (see Fig. 4.3).

The Politics of *Chalga*

When compared to Western pop videos Bulgarian *chalga* is quite political music. Nevertheless, this does not mean that Bulgarian videos do not follow the conventions of international media entertainment. Most *chalga* videos deal with the traditional topics of pop songs: human relations, romantic love, passion, eroticism, and other daydreams. However, many artists' repertories also consist of songs that comment on everyday life and problems, even very bluntly.

At first glance the politics of Sashka's song seem quite farfetched, since the singer only wants to have fun:

> Listen to me my darling,
> listen to my request,
> that I could get drunk tonight.
>
> I'll exchange my *leva* for marks,
> that I can drink wine at the moment.
> Dollars are OK, *leva* are not;
> if I get drunk,
> let it at least happen in dollars.
> You ain't got, you ain't got money, my love.
> You ain't got any marks, dollars.
> Nowadays it is dreadful and gloomy
> if you have no money.
> But if I should sing and drink all day long
> it can't go on.

Figure 4.3: *Levovete v marki.* Music and lyrics by Sashka Vaseva.

A closer study, however, reveals that the lyrics also criticize the country's economic situation. Without dollars or (German) marks nobody in Bulgaria is anybody. A penniless boy cannot have a girlfriend as girls give their love to rich businessmen who have foreign currency. Importantly, this video was released in 1997, when the Bulgarian economy almost totally collapsed. Nearly all the banks went bankrupt and the value of the *lev* sank by tens of percents in one week (Kessi 2001).

The social and political problems that *chalga* videos target are usually connected to corruption, economic insecurity, and civil rights. The very same topics are frequently commented upon in the Bulgarian media. The term "political" refers here to all kinds of expressions and phenomena that are connected to cultural oppression and power relations. Thus the videos deal with questions of Bulgarian domestic policy, but also very typically refer to the more private sphere of society (family life, sexual relations, paternalism, women's liberation, the generation gap).

I shall now analyze another *chalga* video that comments on and challenges political questions widely discussed by the Bulgarian public. *Zhega* [Heat] was released by Valentin Valdes in 1997 (Fig. 4.4; Video 4.3). Valdes, in addition to Petra, is the most specialized artist critiquing and parodying political issues. His critical style is often very straightforward, but also ambivalent. From the Western feminist perspective Valdes's songs probably sound like nothing else but swinish chauvinism.

They are by no means politically correct, but quite brutal and insulting. As one of my friends in Sofia remarked, "Why should we be politically correct, since our everyday life is far from correct?"

Even the singer's own image is ambivalent. He looks like a senior mafia boss—slightly balding, with a stockily built body—and enjoys acting mafioso roles in his own videos. In addition, Valdes is famous for the flashy covers of his music cassettes, which display naked girls posing in various seductive positions reminiscent of Playboy pin-ups.

Zhega's Mixolydian melody is not typical of *chalga*. Still, as in several other songs, a Middle Eastern tone is created through a long improvised passage in the middle of the song, where the synthesizer, a sound well known in almost all *chalga* hits, plays a lengthy wailing melody with lavish embellishment.

The visual plot imitates the road movie typical of many Hollywood films and TV series. The artist is both singer and main actor. The plot consists of fast driving, car chases featuring Western luxury cars (a BMW and an Alfa Romeo), shooting, shady business, and bribing of customs officers and policemen who, of course, drive Russian Ladas. In his solo segments Valdes dances *kyuchek* with pretty young girls. He batters his girlfriend and his hobby seems to be serial polygamy (having several girlfriends one after another). To sum up, the hero of the song is a big bully and a frightening man whose orders will be obeyed.

The repeated references to "holding" in the refrain require explanation. "Holding" comes from the term "holding company" and refers to the private banks and insurance companies owned by the Bulgarian mafia, which were quite a common and hot topic in the Bulgarian press in the mid-1990s. The biggest insurance companies were VIS-2 and SIC, and their businesses were based on high profile advertising and even more aggressive marketing. The victims of these businesses were anyone who possessed any visible property—a car, *objets d'art*, an office, or detached house. The companies' method was simple and effective. A salesman approached a potential client to persuade her to take out an insurance policy. If the client refused, the companies' henchmen, the *bortsi* [wrestlers], were later sent to steal her car or ransack her office. Immediately thereafter the victim understood the benefits of an insurance contract (see, e.g., Nikolov 1997).

Such businesses were one of many money laundering schemes adopted by Bulgarian crime syndicates. During the socialist regime of 1994–1997, the government was unable to close down these businesses, in spite of ever increasing criticism in the Bulgarian press. In spring 1997 the new right-wing liberal government of Ivan Kostov came to power and was more effective in its anti-mafia policy. Very soon such insurance businesses were declared illegal and the companies disappeared. Some politicians and officials with governmental ties allegedly were involved in these activities. This is probably the background against which the singer-mafioso's boasts about his future career as Sofia's mayor are set (Anonymous 1997).

I bought a BMW, yes I did.
I am sitting in a bar;
if someone touches my car
he will see bad visions every
    day.

Heat, heat in the center of
    Sofia. Oh-oh.

Take out an insurance policy
    with us.
"Holding" is a symbol of
    power.
"Holding" is a good thing.
Congratulations, Sofia!
Oh, oh, oh-hoo!

A ship landed at the port of
    Burgas,
with goods for me from
    Honduras.
Bravo, bravo, customs
    officers,
Bravo, bravo, policemen.
A frog is singing "Daddy,"
and I bought a Caddy.
Oh, oh, oh-hoo.

Heat, heat in the center of Sofia.
Oh-oh.

Do not ask me who I am,
but ask how much power I have.
Three years in succession
I shall be the mayor of the capital.
Oh, oh, oh-hoo!

They are speaking of me:
"he is competent but unfit."
I know it.
I won't even twiddle my thumbs.
Be aware, if you don't pay in cash.

"Holding" is a good thing.
Congratulations, Sofia!
Oh, oh, oh-hoo!
Are you ready?

"Holding" is a good thing.
Congratulations, Sofia!
Take out an insurance policy with
    us.
"Holding" is a symbol of power.

Figure 4.4: *Zhega.* Music and lyrics by Valentin Valdes. Payner Music, 2000.

Producing the Oriental: Dance and Music

Connecting *chalga* to orientalism requires the presence of "Eastern" features in the music, lyrics, or visual language of the videos under study. One must, however, point out that "Easternness" in orientalist art is a very elusive and relative quality. According to the often cited definition, orientalism refers to an imagined "Easternness" and the representation of the East in Western culture; in the words of Derek Scott (1997:9), "Orientalist music is not a poor imitation of another cultural practice: its purpose is not to imitate but to represent." Consequently, oriental features of orientalist art can be either fully invented or based at least partly on a certain cultural model from the East. Audiences need only recognize the oriental signifier, which is often stereotyped as a shared experience of the East. For instance, according to British cultural historian John MacKenzie (1995:142), in the eighteenth century Turkishness or Turkish flavor was signified by Western composers with the aid of the C major scale, but also with fast shifts between major and minor keys, sudden chromaticism, and especially through various percussion effects like loud drumstrokes and gong noise.

Pinpointing *chalga*'s oriental stereotypes is complicated by the fact that, for some Westerners, Bulgarian music in general already sounds oriental. One possible solution can be found in *chalga*'s Romani associations. Accordingly, it is likely that even today *chalga*'s "Easternness" is mainly constructed by Bulgarian audiences in reference to stereotypical, shared images of Romani music. Furthermore, the oriental tinge of ·*chalga*'s overall sound is typical of and attributed to Romani musicians. For many decades, if not centuries, in all the Balkan countries Romani musicians have been the messengers of popular music from the eastern Mediterranean and even from India (cf. Pettan 1996b:37–41). This is important to keep in mind when analyzing the oriental features of *chalga* in terms of musical, visual, and mental imagery.

In *chalga* videos fewer references to the Middle East can be found in the song texts. In fact, only when the video plot is geographically located in "Eastern" surroundings does this occur. In such cases the oriental context generally also appears in the name of the song, as in *Kapali charshiya* [The biggest bazaar in Istanbul], *Mechtata na sheiha* [The dream of the sheik], and *Harema* [The harem]. However, these are rare among the great majority of *chalga* songs. This observation reveals something very essential about *chalga*'s "Easternness." Usually *chalga* videos do not directly refer to the Eastern world; rather, such references are almost always more indirect.

The videos' choreographic content favors Eastern references considerably more. Most striking is the role of "Eastern" dance. Here and elsewhere the use of "Eastern" in quotes indicates that we should speak of dance orientalism, where "Easternness" is represented by both imagined and real references to the East. One such fictional East is that presented by the dance troupes that have evidently been recruited for video clips from top tourist restaurants in Bulgaria and elsewhere. Their performance style is often a pastiche of Western revue tradition and socialist staged folklore, and their "Easternness" has more to do with decorative costumes and props than choreography. For instance, the dancers do not concentrate on hip and stomach movement, but on limb movement; such performances may even involve raising the legs *à la* the can-can.

Since the early 1990s Bulgarian videos have featured a dance style that resembles Turko-Arabian bellydance, and gradually this style has taken an "authentic" turn. The oldest *chalga* video of my corpus, Knezha's *Mechtata na sheiha* [The dream of the sheik], consists of a veiled dance that fits the sheik theme well. During the performance two relatively tall female dancers shake themselves to a *çiftetelli* rhythm. The only hint of a more conventional harem bellydance is the hand movements. The dancer's torsos are quite stiff, their hips move very moderately, and their high-heeled shoes make clear that this performance is but an adaptation of more traditional Ottoman Turkish dance.

During the years 1995–1996 several videos with more typical Turkish bellydance were released. Stiletto heels gave way to slippers or bare feet. Dancers' bellies were typically well structured and their hip movements so intensive that they had clearly undergone lengthy training. Such performances can be seen on video clips by the groups Kozari, Kristal, and Yuzhen Polah, although there are also artists performing more imagined oriental dance in the very same videos. In *chalga,* both real and imagined orientalism interact to form a very exciting texture and very often it seems quite pointless to try to define its authenticity.

The same exciting fabric appears in the music itself. In Bulgarian music it is not easy to define "Easternness" on the grounds of musical sound and tone, which is a relatively appropriate method for the analysis of Western musical orientalism. The reason is, of course, the already mentioned "Eastern" flavor of all Bulgarian vernacular music, which can be heard among other things in the sound of traditional folk instruments. The sound of lutes, flutes or clarinets used in Bulgarian folk and popular music does not particularly differ from that of their more eastern and southern counterparts. Even the accordion, which is usually associated with Western music, has adopted quite unique ways of embellishment and phrasing from Bulgarian vernacular instruments like the *gaida* [bagpipe] and the clarinet. This all makes Bulgarian accordion playing very original in comparison with Central European or Russian accordion styles.

Nevertheless, the musical signs of *chalga* orientalism can be found and analyzed, and the best way is to start with the striking stereotypes that seem to come into nearly every *chalga* song, but are totally absent from other kinds of Bulgarian vernacular music. The first and most striking feature is no doubt the bellydance rhythm, which in the Balkans is usually known as *çiftetelli*. Bulgarian *kyuchek* consists of various rhythmic patterns (2/4, 4/4, 9/8), but modern *chalga* seems to favor the duple-meter patterns resembling *çiftetelli* rhythm. The same 4/4 rhythmic pattern is to be found in most of my research material (Fig. 4.5). Typical of this pattern are the main beats on the first and third and counter beats on the second and fourth quaver and on the fourth quarter. The most central syncopation beat is the quaver. The bellydance rhythm cannot be identified without it, and I have never observed the quaver to be absent even in the most reduced versions of *chalga* accompaniment. On the other hand, emphasizing the quaver is essential for the process of *chalga* modernization. This is an important point of departure when mixing this rhythmic pattern with Latin-influenced global dance rhythms.

Figure 4.5: The *kyuchek* rhythm in 4/4 time.

Chalga songs are usually rendered at a relatively slow tempo (M.M. 80–85), which makes their rhythmic syncopation clear and effective. A steadily rolling accompaniment with thrilling syncopation also makes hip swinging easy, and this very fact has probably been one of the main reasons for the long-lasting popularity of *çiftetelli* in the eastern Mediterranean cultural sphere.

Simple bellydance rhythms have contributed to *chalga*'s development in two ways. Firstly, *çiftetelli* differs decisively from the additive rhythms typical of Bulgarian music, which have become a kind of trademark of traditional *hora* [line dance tunes], folk songs, as well as academic *narodna muzika.* In the case of *chalga* rhythmic simplicity guarantees stylistic distinction. It differentiates the genre from older dance tunes. Secondly, the bellydance rhythm is easily modified. It fits well with various models of international popular music and thus facilitates musical fusion.

The second stereotypical sign of orientalism is the melodic structure of *chalga* songs. Actually there are only two types of melodies that directly refer to the "East." Most *chalga* songs follow these types. The melodies in question contain the minor second, which occurs in both the Phrygian minor form and in a major form that recalls *makam Hicaz,* and the augmented second, which occurs in the latter mode. These modes are also well known in traditional Bulgarian music, but their use has occasionally proven problematic for aesthetic and political reasons. According to Donna Buchanan (1995:402), *Hicaz* was sometimes coded

by the professional folk musicians as inauthentic and a symbol of
Turkishness and Gypsiness, especially when the melodic line of a song
persistently emphasized the mode's lower tetrachord. Notably, this very
feature seems to typify *chalga* melodies. In addition, some professional
folk musicians disdained compositions in which different regional
traditions were mixed together. Yet exactly this kind of fusion seems
fundamental to *chalga* aesthetics.

  Chalga songs usually exhibit a verse-refrain structure. The harmonic
background of the verse usually consists of just one chord, while the
melody emphasizes the intervals of the lower tetrachord of *makam Hicaz*
(for example, C–Db–E–F). Another typical harmonic formula utilizes
three chords surrounding the finalis and emphasizing the minor second:
C–Db–Bbm–C (see Fig. 4.6). The same chord progression is typical of
Phrygian melodies (for example, Cm–Db–Bbm–Cm). The harmonies of
the refrain, however, typically begin on the fourth tone of *Hicaz* and form
a descending harmonic line (Fm–E–Db–C). This ambivalent feeling of
tonality is characteristic of many *chalga* songs. A similar accompaniment
pattern occurs in the standards of international Romani music; in Spanish
flamenco it is called *cadencia andaluza* (Huotari 1999:105). This
similarity is persuasive evidence of *chalga*'s background as a musical
fusion between domestic Bulgarian, Romani, and international repertoire.

Figure 4.6: *Levovete v marki.* Melody and harmonic accompaniment. Music by
Sashka Vaseva.

Accordingly, the refrain's mode utilizes F as its tonic and the *Hicaz* tetrachord as the upper four tones of the harmonic minor. The move of the tonic from C to F also makes it possible to interpret a *chalga* song according to Western music theory. This connection enables many *chalga* composers to create a new harmonic line for the refrain according to the so-called circle of fifths, a standard technique widely used in Western art and popular music since the Baroque era.

The next example is the *chalga* hit *Menteta, menteta* [Fake, fake] by Kiril Lambov (CD 4.1; Fig. 4.7).[7] The song shows that not even modern pop-*chalga* can always resist the powerful local tradition of additive rhythms. Instead of a simple 4/4 bellydance rhythm the song is played in 9/8, which is a very typical meter in various styles of traditional dance music—not only in Bulgaria, but all over the Balkans. The arranger has used the circle of fifths in such a way that the tonic becomes the fourth tone of the *Hicaz* tetrachord. Simultaneously, when the sequence moves on, the chord cycle temporarily takes the melody out of the *Hicaz* mode. The refrain structure is typical of many other *chalga* songs.

Refrain (follows each verse):

The fake, the fake,
it brings thick coins,
foreign and our own.
It goes straight to the
    businessman's heart.

1.Today, every second drink
    on the marketplace,
my brother, is a fake.
Original labels and caps,
and the bundles of banknotes
    will increase.

2. The fake is in fashion.
Though the distilleries were
    closed,
in garages, cellars, and base-
    ments
a nice substitute will be made.

3. The day before yesterday,
    my neighbor Iliya

bought a bottle of *rakiya*.
Though he drank it with *mezze* and
    salad,
he still landed in the Orlandovtsi
    graveyard.

4. There is fake whiskey and fake
    gin.
First your purse is lightened
and then, if you sip it enough,
in the morning you may find your-
    self in a hospital.

5. Now you can also find policemen
one hundred percent fake.
They stop tourists on the highway
and pick up foreign currencies.

6. All of life, brother, is a fake.
If you look at those in the Parlia-
    ment,
they are disputing, quarreling, de-
    bating,
and still the laws are failing.

Figure 4.7: *Menteta, menteta.* Composed and arranged by Kiril Lambov; lyrics by Mimi Taralkova; performed by Georgi Sergiev & Orchestra Diamant; transcription by Jarkko Niemi.

A third musical signifier of the "East" is the synthesizer timbre in *chalga* songs. It can be easily recognized due to the fact that nearly all the *chalga* bands use the same sound palette resembling a nasal wind instrument (oboe, clarinet, *zurla*). A synthesizer sound akin to the Balkan folksy trumpet is also often used—the trumpet solo is an important part of Serbian folk pop (*turbo folk*), which also makes it useful in *chalga*. The main function of the synthesizer is to play an "Eastern" wind solo (i.e., a *taksim*) in the middle of the song. This instrumental passage is a regular element of every *chalga* song, almost without exception. The nasal and harsh synthesizer sound makes *chalga* different from the other types of Bulgarian national songs that can also be found in the video hit collections released by the Payner company. Most non-*chalga* hits typically speak about romantic love and longing and are strongly influenced by an older type of local popular music called *starogradski pesni* [old urban songs]. The synthesizer is also used in those recordings, but the overall sound is very different—the synthesizer typically imitates a violin section, the flute, or other instruments close to the European salon orchestra tradition.

Producing the Oriental: Visual Content

My next topic of analysis is the various visual symbols and images referring to the Orient in *chalga* videos. A firm point of departure is an argument according to which the narration and myths behind today's popular culture are fragmentary (cf. Barthes 1985:110–15). They are places to visit, to fall into short-term ecstasy and then return to everyday life. In global entertainment, orientalism and oriental culture are likewise not real, but mythical fragments marked by exotic moments and excitement. Oriental styling is thus akin to a remote corner of the world, where well-to-do tourists travel, usually not to become acquainted with local habits and conditions but, above all, to take a rest, experience oblivion, adventure, or ecstasy.

Table 4.1: Oriental Myths and Stereotypes in *Chalga*

Classic Oriental Images	Modern Exoticism
1. Erotic bellydance; harem women	1. Sexist soft porn
2. Sheiks, sultans, and eunuchs	2. Mafia, machismo, *mente*
3. Arabian and Indian wonderlands	3. Western opportunities, money-making
4. Palmreaders, miracle workers, snake charmers	4. Atavism, the sovereign Big Brother
5. Nomadic Gypsies	5. Sailing, wind surfing, costly hobbies
6. Old cabaret props	6. Western fashions
7. Horse and camel riding	7. Expensive German cars
8. Old Bulgarian townscapes	8. Seascapes; waterfalls
9. Wine drinking and conviviality	9. Whiskey drinking
10. Orient as fairytale	10. Orient as political satire

Chalga hits consist of at least two kinds of mythical images, continuously intermingling, which I call classic oriental images and modern exoticism. The former derive from older stereotypes of orientalist entertainment. They form an interesting mixture of images recalling Romani culture, the Middle East, the Far East, and the miraculous Shangri-La, the Never-Never-Land of the Orient. The second group reflects the political and cultural situation of today and the recent past; they are thus more topical, local, and often full of references to political blunders and economic decay. Nevertheless, the two sorts of imagery are connected to each other; as I show below, it is not difficult to find a modern equivalent for each classic oriental stereotype (see Table 4.1).

Furthermore, there is a third, potential group of orientalist stereotypes that are conspicuous by their absence. I call these sanitized oriental images. Their absence is best explained by Bulgarian cultural history and especially by the nation's problematic relation to the Ottoman past (see Table 4.2).

Table 4.2: Sanitized Oriental (Ottoman) Images

Landscapes with mosques and minarets
Praying Muslims and veiled pilgrims
Ottoman culture; the fez
Modern Turkey; the crescent flag

In *chalga* videos, mythical references to the Ottoman past seem quite exceptional. This music is mainly for entertainment, and references to Ottoman culture, Islam, or even to modern Turkey are probably too sensitive for Bulgarian show business. However, this does not mean that orientalism connected to the Ottomans is unknown in Bulgarian culture. According to Maria Todorova (cited in Buchanan 1996b:216–17), during the communist regime, the Ottoman past was a very common way of explaining the backwardness of Bulgarian culture. Even today, I suppose, Ottomanism is used to explain many cultural and economic characteristics, which could be much better understood as a result of the communist system: ineffectiveness, regionalism, parochialism, mental apathy, resistance to economic change, and lack of Western rationalism, among others. Therefore, if some sensitive topics seem to have been omitted in *chalga* videos, other highly political topics appear instead. Some of the most popular images of the modern exoticism are directly connected to the politics of *chalga* and reflect the main problems of postcommunist Bulgarian society: organized crime, corruption, and poverty.

1. From Erotic Belly Dance and Harem Women to Sexist Soft Porn

The first topic on the list, dance and eroticism, is one of the most popular and, likewise, most natural types of oriental imagery. As noted above, a common denominator of oriental hits is the *kyuchek* rhythm, which is closely related to oriental bellydance. Thus it is not surprising that a female dancer can be seen in almost every *chalga* video. Thanks to scanty costumes and seductive choreography, bellydance nearly always has an erotic undertone, which may also be the secret of its success, at least in the Balkans. Nevertheless, it seems quite typical of the recent cultural climate that *chalga* producers would replace politically correct eroticism with sexist soft porn.[8] The trend is pronounced on cassette covers. A typical cover consists of a photo of a singer or an orchestra. From time to time, however, musicians are replaced with an almost naked girl, dressed in a traditional courtesan costume or otherwise seductively. Mitko Dimitrov, the director of the Payner company, Bulgaria's biggest video publisher, explained this convention as follows: "The question of what the musicians look like is no problem to us. If an artist is not good-looking enough, we use these pin-up girls for our cassette covers" (Interview 9 October 1996).

2. From Sheiks and Sultans to the Mafia and *Mente*

Mighty sheiks and sultans as well as cruel and bestial eunuchs are an obligatory aspect of classic orientalism; nor does it take long to find them in Bulgarian *chalga*. In popular narratives, however, these mythical personalities are usually set in the present time. So, for instance, the sultan in Valentin Valdes's hit song *Harema* is by no means an Ottoman sultan, but a modern sultan of Brunei, who tries to seduce a pretty Macedonian girl called "Sexy Madonna." After the girl turns him down, explaining that she is too young and already has a boyfriend, the sultan promises to pay millions of dollars and a huge amount of oil, if only this "most beautiful lady of Macedonia" will consent to his proposal.

Such classic heroes of orientalism also have their modern equivalents, and in Bulgarian *chalga* they are the mafia, the macho personality, and the *mente*. Though most Bulgarians obviously dislike mafia culture and the ever-blossoming underground economy, the logic of popular culture very easily makes these criminal anti-heroes into famous heroes. Accordingly, there are several new pop songs that speak in flattering terms about macho-type businessmen, for whom everything in the world is possible. For instance, the 1996 hit song *Tigre, tigre* [Tiger, tiger] by the group Belite Shisharki is a story of illegal business and the generosity of a mafia boss. In 1997 the song was allegedly popular especially among the young macho gentlemen with sun glasses and well-tailored suits hanging around in the bars of Sofia's nuclear center.

The *mente* motif is also associated with criminality, but in a more ambiguous way. The word *mente* means a fake, substitute, or fraud. In Bulgaria and elsewhere in postcommunist European countries, one side effect of the economic crisis has been moneymaking with the aid of inferior and counterfeit goods. In marketplaces and kiosks, homemade spirits with original-looking labels are sold; the worst of these brews may cause sudden death or destroy the drinker's sight. Such fabricated goods can also be found when buying canned food, clothes, watches, or recorded music. The *mente* motif is presented from many angles in Kiril Lambov's 1995 *chalga* song *Menteta, menteta* above (Fig. 4.7), where the problem of compromised goods moves from street vendor level to political satire. In this song "the fake" refers not only to *rakiya* (clear grape brandy), but also to policemen and politicians. By the song's conclusion the entire political system is explained as belonging to the same *mente* category.

3. Eastern Wonderlands and Western Business Opportunities

As already mentioned, the orientalism of *chalga* seems to neglect images connected to Ottoman culture and modern Turkey. Instead, Eastern exoticism in general, from Arabia to India and even to the Far East, is abundantly presented. Alongside these classic images *chalga* favors several modern symbols, especially any reference to Western wealth, such as luxury cars and foreign currency. American banknotes are a popular motif on cassette covers. A very nice example is a 1996 cassette cover by the band Melodiya, whose central theme is an American hundred-dollar bill. However, it has been manipulated so that its right half is that of a one hundred *leva* note. Could the Bulgarian dream of wealth and prosperity be better represented?

Aspirations to a wealthy Western lifestyle have been ironically interpreted in the song *Zavrŭstane v Berlin* [Return to Berlin] by Valentin Valdes (1996). The singer is totally fed up with poor economic conditions in Bulgaria and plans to travel to Berlin as a gigolo. He knows some elderly ladies there with whom he will be able to live a jetset life. At the end of the song our hero concludes his playboy career by marrying an aged *Berliner Frau*—for money.

4. Miracle Workers and Big Brother

The fourth oriental image on the list, various fortune tellers, recalls the strong position of Romani exoticism in Bulgarian *chalga*. Accordingly, a very typical personality in oriental videos is a female Romani palmreader. Snake charmers can also be found, as can miracle-mongers, whose abilities include healing a sick woman with the aid of a melancholy oriental tune, played with the clarinet directly into the patient's ear. All these examples prove that ancient magic rites remain powerful, even in modern video culture.

The modern form of miracle working is the myth of the Big Brother or Robin Hood who helps weaker citizens with their everyday problems. The Big Brother may be a mafia boss, as was the case in *Tigre, tigre,* but he may also be a Party leader, as in the song *Dyado Mraz* [Santa Claus] by the same orchestra (1995). The song tells of a benefactor who arrives on Christmas Eve with his black Mercedes from the well-known residence of the Bulgarian government on Vitosha Mountain. The singer is sitting at home and eagerly waits for this political Santa Claus, hoping to get roasted ham, lots of wine, and a new car for Christmas. The message of the song is clear: one has only to sit and wait; Big Brother will certainly help. My critical friends in Sofia pointed out that this kind of paternalist mentality was very typical of communist times. The citizens were somewhat apathetically used to waiting for Party decisions. As Katherine Verdery (1996:25) put it, the Communist Party "acted like a father who gives handouts to the children as he sees fit. The Benevolent Father Party educated people to express needs it would then fill, and discouraged them from taking the initiative that would enable them to fill these needs on their own." Similarly, the Bulgarian state had its Big Brother or Father in Moscow, who in the name of socialist fraternity, helped its smaller and weaker vassal.

5. – 7. Romani Exoticism, Fashion, and Travel

The abundant Romani exoticism of *chalga* videos is mirrored by the abundant utilization of the Eastern European cabaret tradition. When a recording stage is needed, the video producers seem to favor the night-clubs of huge tourist hotels; dancing girls and "variety ballet" corps working in the hotels are hired to play belly dancers, nomadic Gypsies, or dancing courtesans, as needed. The results are often tragi-comic, as young girls with little aerobic training attempt to perform bellydance, or classically trained ballet dancers romp about in a staged Romani camp.

As a modern equivalent to cabaret scenes, various images of modern jetset and tourist life are also favored by the videos. Expensive hobbies, like sailing and windsurfing, are presented on several clips. Fashionable clothes seem to be an extraordinarily important aspect of these modern images. Actually, it is not easy to find a video where the lead singer could not simultaneously work as a fashion model. The general rule is that an artist dresses in at least three different costumes for each song, and these clips are frequently mixed with each other.

Horse and camel riding, so typical of classic oriental stories, are almost completely absent in *chalga* videos. These images have been replaced by Western luxury cars, usually German cars made by BMW and Daimler-Benz. During the communist regime, a Western car was an indisputable symbol of power. Only diplomats, Politburo members, and top officials had Western cars, usually a black Mercedes. The general public could not buy any Western cars; if lucky enough, they purchased Russian Ladas or East German Trabants. A Western luxury car continued to be a power symbol in the 1990s, when Bulgarian mafiosi and more reputable *nouveaux riches* started displaying their prosperity with the aid of big foreign limousines. Now common citizens can afford Western cars, but usually only in theory, due to the poor economic situation. So far a luxury car continues to be a popular image, not only of power but of daydreams of Western living standards.

8. Townscapes and Water

Beyond nightclubs and restaurants, *chalga* videos use only two other basic backdrops: old picturesque townscapes and touristic scenes of the Black Sea coast. These scenes are often used one after another several times during a video clip; the former strengthens classic oriental images, while the latter symbolizes a desired modernity and wealth. Nevertheless, old town scenes, usually from Plovdiv or Veliko Tŭrnovo, undoubtedly also have strong national symbolic value. Old buildings are important evidence of Bulgaria's long history and its unique civilization before the Ottoman period; Veliko Tŭrnovo was the country's capital in the Middle Ages.

Furthermore, nearly all Bulgarian music videos—not just *chalga* —continually use one and the same symbol: flowing water. It is very likely that water means happiness in two different ways. Flowing water is a symbol of mountainous Bulgaria, a guarantee of life and continuity. On the other hand, water has a very positive meaning in oriental mythology. The Arabian nomads and other heroes of mythology found water in the oases, the paradise-like places in the middle of arid deserts. Accordingly, water is a fundamental part of the oriental paradise.

9. Wine to Whiskey

The fact that delicious and spicy food can be found everywhere in the country demonstrates that Bulgaria belongs to the Orient. Although the Ottoman past is commonly rejected, the tradition of the Turkish kitchen has not disappeared. Bulgarians are also proud of their marvelous wines; these are the subject of several hit songs stressing national and regional spirit. No wonder the actors drink and feast on all kinds of delicacies in every second *chalga* video. Delicious food and wine are an indispensable part of Bulgarian happiness, a foundation of social life.

Whiskey drinking, so typical of many oriental videos, is more difficult to explain. However, the suffering and absent-minded singer-heroes very often drink whiskey—not *rakiya, mastika,* or other Balkan spirits—but Scotch whiskey. Perhaps whiskey refers simply to one of the global luxury symbols exoticized by the videos. On the other hand, I have realized that whiskey drinking is also a fundamental part of night life in Athens and Istanbul. It is possible that whiskey is one of the most important traces that the British Empire left behind in the Balkans—and in the Orient—as a remembrance of its previous influence.

10. From Fairytale to Political Satire

At the most general level, *chalga* videos usually present two moods in association with their main messages. The first is the Orient as fairytale and the second is the Orient as political satire. The first type is used far more often, since a fairytale mood is closer to the romantic and harmless character of popular songs and videos. However, political satire is also quite often present to some extent, as has been shown in the previous examples of political *chalga*.

Conclusions:
Chalga and the Discourse of Orientalism

Chalga production can be perceived as entailing the revival of strong oriental features in Bulgarian popular music. Those features refer directly to Turkish and Greek dance music, although formerly they were usually adopted through a circuitous route, via Serbia and Macedonia. *Chalga*'s popularity seems to be based on these features. It makes one wonder if *chalga*'s reception can be explained in terms of the orientalism that for centuries has been influential in Western art and entertainment. However, linking Bulgarian music to orientalist discourse is not a simple matter.

At first sight the discourse of orientalism seems irrelevant, when the meaning of the term, Bulgaria's geographic position, and its cultural history are considered. Orientalist discourse stresses at least three factors that do not suit the Bulgarian situation well. Firstly, orientalism usually derives from Western attitudes toward the East, or conversely, to the representation of an Eastern cultural heritage in the Western world. Accordingly, orientalism tells us more about Westerners than about Eastern cultures (Said 1995:21; Scott 1997:9). Secondly, orientalism is based on the peculiarities of Eastern culture. For the peoples and states of western Europe and North America, the East has really meant the "foreign Other," ideas about which have been based more on imagination than reality, fact, or cultural contact. Thirdly, in its truest essence, orientalism reveals the history of Western man's feelings of cultural superiority. It firmly views the East as a land of insecurity, chaos, violence, and corruption. For centuries orientalist images remained quite unchanged with the aid of the stereotypes created by belles lettres, visual arts, and travel reports (Said 1995: 6–7, 300–301).

According to Said, orientalism is directly connected to the history of colonialism as well as to postcolonialist media criticism. Orientalism is seen as an effective tool for harnessing nonwestern cultures to the maintenance of Western political and cultural hegemony. Orientalism has guaranteed that the East has remained of lower value when compared to the West. Orientalism also means that the Orient can only be understood and interpreted by relating it to the Western worldview. In a way, Western orientalism does not accord the East the right to an independent existence.

It seems obvious that Saidian theory does not fit well with Bulgarian *chalga*. All the essential attributes and connections between orientalist discourse and *chalga* seem upside down.

Can Western orientalism appear in Bulgaria, although the country and its culture belong to the East? Theoretically speaking this is possible, since one of the core areas of classic orientalism in the last century was colonial India. However, Bulgaria's case is still different; it was never colonized by the West. From Bulgaria's eastern border it is slightly more than 200 kilometers to Istanbul, maybe the most important center of oriental myth, and the metropolis where most of the images and stories of the Ottoman Empire are located. Just behind Bulgaria's eastern border is Edirne, formerly Adrianople, where the winter camp of the Ottoman army was regularly situated for centuries and from which the military expeditions to Europe usually started (Wheatcroft 1995:52).

A second reason for Bulgaria's "Easternness" can be found in more recent history. In the period 1945–1989 the country was a loyal member of the Soviet bloc. During the Cold War years the Soviet Union was not only politically the opposite of the West, but a real objective of neo-orientalism. In Western publicity and in the Westerner's imagination the Soviet Union was connected to stereotypes similar to those of earlier, colonialist orientalism: inefficiency, cruelty, irrationalism, wickedness, secrecy. In recent Bulgarian publicity, classic orientalism, Soviet orientalism—and the newest type, mafia orientalism—as well as their related images and explanations seem to be merging in an interesting fashion.

Bulgaria was a possession at the heart of the Ottoman Empire and later on, the Soviet Union's most obedient vassal. Except for the relatively short era of the Bulgarian kingdom in modern times (1879–1944), the orientation of the country was more to the East than to the West. Superficially, the recent political trend favors an eastern orientation since in the complex political scene in the Balkans, Bulgaria and Turkey seem to have found each other. The old political struggle of ethnic minorities seems to belong to the past, and bilateral trade has increased greatly. The trade boom also concerns the music business: raw material for domestic music and videotapes, for example, is mainly imported from Turkey. Istanbul, the largest metropolis in the Balkans, is again becoming the Bulgarian Tsarigrad, the Emperor's town. (Suvilehto 1999:153–56; Ivo Dochovski, Interview, 1999).

Rapprochement with Turkey, however, is basically a result of regional power politics; culturally speaking the eastern cardinal point does not necessarily mean anything. Actually, even the Eastern connection possesses a predominantly Western-oriented objective. Like all the Balkan countries—including Turkey—Bulgaria's greatest political goal is integration with western Europe in the European Union. Especially during the recent liberal right regime Bulgaria has officially been strikingly Western-minded and Western-oriented. The same holds true for public opinion, where freedom of travel without the so-called Schengen visa has been a subject of much discussion and even public demonstrations. Nevertheless, the recent desire for European integration and Western living standards together with the Eastern-oriented past form the ultimate reason why orientalism seems to be a valid point of departure for the analysis of modern Bulgarian culture. However, postcolonial criticism is not necessarily the best perspective on Bulgarian orientalism.

Orientalism still contains one feature that explains its popularity in the Balkans as well as in other cultural areas between East and West (e.g., Russia, Ukraine, Romania, and no doubt also in Finland). Orientalism is a means of withdrawal, of cultural distinction. Although "Eastern" culture is very close, orientalism helps maintain a distance from it. Orientalism does not usually represent "Eastern" culture as serious and real. On the contrary, the East of orientalism is fabled, playful, and mythical. Since the Orient is unreal, the eastern engagement is also unreal. Paradoxically, an orientalist attitude to the East means rejecting the East. Finally, orientalism furthers the process of westernization.

Rejecting the Orient is also the result of the carnivalist tone often related to cultural products utilizing the oriental myth. It may not be coincidental that in the Balkans as well as in Russia and eastern Central Europe Roma have been important producers of orientalism as well as typical representatives of the "East" in music, literature, and the visual arts. Roma are an ethnic group that cannot be easily located or assimilated. In the modern nation-state Roma have no easily defined space or cultural locus, and therefore they make an excellent symbol of imagined "Easternness." For centuries, especially in Russian tradition, Roma have been a mythical cultural niche associated with various carnivalesque activities. Accordingly, in Russian literature and folklore Roma are always present when local heroes want to forget everyday life by feasting and boozing, gambling and dissipating, or in a word, when they want to turn cultural values upside down (Broms 1985:159; Crowe 1996:164–69). It is not unlikely that a similar stereotype would function in the Balkans. As a matter of fact, I argue that the popularity of modern Bulgarian *chalga* is rooted in this very stereotype.

In general, a carnivalist attitude surrounds the style and production of new *chalga* songs. Performing serious matters as jokes or ambiguous hints suits texts dealing with politically sensitive topics well. In the modern media political parody is very often the more effective way of communication than political seriousness and propagation. In light music, actually, there is no other way of performing sensitive matters. At the very moment when a performance takes a propagandist turn, the music's lightness disappears. Political songs like the *Marseillaise,* the *Internationale,* or *Horst Wessel* are no doubt popular music—music for the masses—but it is absolutely wrong to connect them to the terms pop, light music, or entertainment.

In conclusion, the meaning of orientalism is for Bulgarians very different from what it means for western Europeans or Americans. Bulgaria's orientalism is not based on a Western-dominated, colonialist past. On the contrary, there the colonialist past has involved subordination to eastern empires: the Byzantine, Ottoman, and finally, Soviet. The Ottoman legacy makes the meanings of oriental popular music positive— the negative connotations typical of the Saidian idea of orientalism disappear. *Chalga* is a music of freedom and distinction that neither mocks nor devalues "Eastern" culture. For Bulgarians, the Orient of *chalga* is also a source of self-irony. It helps them to find and comprehend their identity. Furthermore, the orientalism of *chalga* helps its fans to break free from the hegemony of the cultural elite that was formed by the Bulgarian nation-state. At least they can take a more critical and liberal attitude to highly praised national culture. In the final analysis *chalga* orientalism paradoxically mirrors and emphasizes its apparent antithesis, the westernization of culture. After the sultans and fairytale figures with "Eastern" treasuries have been transformed into mafia businessmen and Western luxury goods, the target of irony is no longer the East but Western life and the dreams connected to it.

Notes

1. This article is a result of several field trips to Bulgaria during 1995–2001, and the final part of my research project "Cassette Culture in the Post-Communist Balkans" funded by the Alexander von Humboldt Foundation (Bonn), the Academy of Finland, and the Bulgarian Academy of Sciences. I wish to thank the following colleagues for their abundant advice and help in completing the article: Lozanka Peicheva, Rozmari Statelova, Ventsi Dimov, Ralf Petrov, Ivo Dochovski, Risto Pennanen, Risto Blomster, Antti-Ville Kärjä, Jarkko Niem, and, of course, Donna Buchanan. Special thanks to Ilkko Suvilehto, who translated the Bulgarian song texts to Finnish.

2. This collection comprises 40 videos, 150 cassettes, and 15 CDs of *chalga.* However, the in-depth analysis presented here focuses mainly on those hit videos released by the Payner company and some LPs (see Discography).

3. See Anonymous 1999; IFPI 2000; and Kurkela 1997:183–84.

4. The IFPI anti-piracy campaign has only been partly successful. The situation is worst in those countries where the so-called second economy (black market) is extensive. Accordingly, in all of the above-mentioned states the domestic piracy production rate still exceeds 50 percent. In Russia the piracy rate is estimated at 75 percent of all phonogram production (IFPI 2000).

5. The terms *cacique* and *kyuchek* derive from the Turkish *köçek*, which originally referred to young boy dancers at the Ottoman court, and now refers to bellydance in general (see Feldman 2000:4–11).

6. Papazov's given name is Ibrahim Hapasov; this was changed to the more Slavic Ivo Papazov in accordance with the former Bulgarian premier Todor Zhivkov's ideological campaign against Turkish and Muslim minorities. Papazov has has been marketed in the West as Ivo Papasov. For the sake of consistency, he is referred to as Ivo Papazov throughout this volume (Ed.).

7. The song's text is explained below.

8. This phenomenon is also common in Romania, where concerts of Romani oriental music are usually combined with beauty contests, cabaret evenings, or strip-tease presentations. Peter Manuel (1993:215–21) has also found in North Indian popular music a commercial *rasiya* genre that is full of oozing eroticism. However, the *rasiya* cassette covers introduced by Manuel (1993:231–33) seem to be more tame than my own Bulgarian examples.

❖ 5 ❖

Regional Voices in a National Soundscape: Balkan Music and Dance in Greece

Kevin Dawe

Scene-Setting

Italian chic and oriental-mystique meet with unequal force in the department stores of Athens.[1] Designer clothes, jewelry and cosmetics provide the necessary ingredients for "the look." Italian designs but a Hollywood look, that is. Chinese and Turkish rugs, mock military arms, Egyptian hookah (smoking pipes), and the Greek equivalent of British Habitat home furnishings (from shelving units to throws) provide for the shabby chic interiors of homes owned by the more prosperous inhabitants of the city. Perhaps too, pop, ambient, and world music CDs will be purchased to set the mood and add sonic tones to the overall effect. Usually there are mementos brought from the home village, too—even a cassette recording of one or two musicians from the home area (who may also reside in Athens), for many Athenians were born in the country or have family homes or land there. More than just allegiance to trends and fads in the marketplace, the high street shopping of modern Greeks casts more than a casual glance in several directions. New items are taken into the home, but older sensibilities remain. More than retail therapy, a study of the exteriors and interiors of the socially mobile reveal a common concern with much deeper issues and problems.

Family in the home village *may* have running water and electricity; they may even live in contested homelands where the threat of ethnic cleansing and border flare-ups is constant. Such is the legacy of Greece as a place, the Greeks as a people, and the potential of the expressive arts in this land as an outpouring of struggle and strife. Cosmopolitanism can be deceiving in this context. Hookah, *sazi*, and the music of the Balkans might be expected to have special resonance in Greece, a country at the crossroads where music, musicians, song and dance function as icons of ethnicity, are historically (re)placed and (re)peopled, nostalgic, conjurers of bittersweet memories (of domination, liberation, tragedy and personal loss).[2] Such sites of negotiation and contest are hyperactive in the construction of self and others, local and non-local, "outsiders" and "insiders."

Regional Music and Dance

Within this context, a constellation of regional musical styles, genres, and instrumentation continue to be important in the formation and expression of national cultural identity in early twenty-first-century Greece, for young and old people alike. The musical periphery is kept at the center of the musical life of many Greeks—in the national consciousness, if you will—through a tight network of government-sponsored Folklore Associations and other musical networks. These networks are part of the national musical grid, a social, cultural, political, and economic generator whose current is strong but prone to fluctuation. In addition and more than an add-on is the highly developed and well-established Greek music industry, a veritable powerhouse that attracts a national, international, and diasporic audience (see Dawe 2002). Its importance for maintaining an interest in regional musics cannot be understated; neither must the role of the television and radio, local/national press and advertising/promotional culture be forgotten. Thus a mediated reconfiguration of local musical sounds and dances provides a sense of cultural orientation for many Greeks at the time of writing. This may be seen, for example, in the appearance of regional sounds in many new popular musical productions and the ways in which Dance Associations continue to grow as part of youth culture (even if they struggle to survive outside of urban centers).

Regional sounds, images, and choreographies provide yet another important means by which a vision of a shared but varied cultural heritage can be maintained, disseminated, and appreciated—a means by which "connections" are made. The stamp of an all-inclusive and common cultural identity is put upon a rich and diverse range of music and dance. Regional musical and dance scenes, cultural events, festivals, and celebrations are part of a national musical infrastructure. Musical genres and styles, musical instruments, dances, and costumes are emblematic of towns and villages, symbols of local and community pride, history, and nostalgia; they provide a multifaceted civic function while also contributing to the marking and marketing of regional identity. There are *aficionados* and "experts," authorities and cultural crusaders whose notions of "authenticity" in music and dance are waxed lyrical even if contested. Regional musics are also recorded commercially by a well-established set of producers, sometimes working through local labels and usually subsidized by major recording and distribution companies based in Athens, but with international links. This adds a further layer of debate about representation and ownership, especially when "traditional" regional sounds are fused with the latest trends in pop. One might, for example, hear a Thracian bagpipe foregrounded as part of a techno dance mix.[3] I proceed with caution, therefore, in my examination of the Greek music industry; its infrastructure, circuits, products, and patterns of consumption; and its role in the construction of a Balkan music scene. The aim here is to provide a critically alert but neutral overview of the ways in which the "local" and the "global" meet in Greek popular music. Perhaps models presented here may flow across national borders as indicative of the ways in which Balkan popular music culture as a whole is now constituted. However, at the time of writing, the "healing sounds" of a Balkan musical landscape as some world music producers, pop musicians, and folklorists would have it, continue to have little effect on the deeply problematic and complex politics of the region.[4]

Interest in regional music seems to have been given renewed profile as the legacy of a conscious and serious exploration of roots by younger musicians and scholars in Greece during the 1980s. The sounds of the periphery have stuck in the popular imagination possibly as a consequence of neo-nationalism, nostalgia, novelty-seeking and exoticism. But the folk revival of the 1980s was part of a genuine attempt to preserve and inject new life into old music and dance, and even reach out to Balkan neighbors at the same time. Certainly, the rediscovery of regional music and dance has drawn attention to the affinity of much Greek music and dance with the music of other Balkan nations (including that of the Roma who also live in Greece).[5] The younger generations in Greece—many of whom are now growing up in a cosmopolitan urban-based culture—are much more accepting of the cultural affinities that connect the Balkan nations and are rather tired of the politicking that divides the region. This has given renewed and greater scope to the careers of local virtuosi (musicians and dancers of all ages) and folklorists who are now culturally, if not economically, mobile. It has also affected the musical direction of the younger generations of pop, rock, and jazz musicians.

Clearly, the habit of musicians looking further afield for inspiration has been spurred on by the growth of *ethniki mousike* or world music in Greece, but here, as elsewhere, there has always been an exchange of ideas in places where the frontiers of the nation-state now stand. In this context, music, like everything else, may be talked about in *guarded* terms. But times are changing. For many young Greeks, performances of traditional music and dance still epitomize simultaneously the spirit and character of the nation, the region, and the community, but these constructs are now subsumed within a further regional grouping—the Balkans—pulling Greece further into "Europe." Regional music and dance forms therefore enable several layers of identification: a means of placing people, marking if not contesting official boundaries, channeling creative ideas if not filtering the soundscape, and invoking what Doreen Massey has called elsewhere "power-geometry."[6] This might be seen as an attempt to reconfigure the Old World in new or revived Greek music while shaping and angling Greek music in response to the world at large.

Regions are known by their musics and these also form convenient marketing labels: music from Epirus is promoted as *Epirotika*, from Greek Macedonia, *Makedonitika*, from Thrace, *Thrakiotika*, from the Islands, *Nisiotika*, from Crete, *Kritika*, and so on. Indeed, this regionalism in music has been consciously explored and exploited by musicians and producers. As Jane Cowan notes:

> The increase in commercial folk-music recordings and of folklore programmes on radio and television has accelerated the movement of songs across regions as folk musicians borrow—or, as they say, "steal"—and rework new tunes, as they always have, to expand their repertory. This tendency has diluted the purity of regional and local musics while leading musicians to exaggerate unique regional features. Even with newly borrowed elements and the addition of new instruments (like the ubiquitous electronic synthesizer), regional musics remain recognizable (Cowan 2000:1009).

Such developments as these are also mirrored in dance. Irene Loutzaki (1999:193-247) acknowledges the role that Dance Associations have played in shaping the dance culture of Thrace, from their instigation of dance lessons in the 1950s to their current role as cultural heritage centers. Loutzaki notes that the Associations have tended to propagate a homogenous dance culture in the region but, in fact, that there has in recent years been a move by them to address the gradual disappearance of dances distinct in their form and even unique to one village. She also notes how the particular ideologies that drive and maintain the Associations are played out, from the selection of repertoire to the empowering potential of costume. She notes, too, how the activities of the Associations intersect with television productions on local dance culture. Loutzaki draws our attention to the complexity of this situation:

> Whether filmed live or in a studio, a number of presentations of local dances and customs of the villages of the Evros region have been televised. Through television, every community, protagonist or viewer, critic or critically viewed, comes into contact with the repertoires from other regions, thus being given the opportunity as well as being obliged to make comparisons with their own material. The initiative for participation in these programs comes from those responsible for them or from the community council. The television producer sets his own rules, by which every village has to abide. As to appearance, the wearing of local costume is an essential condition. As far as the execution is concerned, what carries most weight is the authenticity, liveliness, brio and spontaneity of dancing. A wedding is an unfailing subject of interest for both producers and viewers, ensuring good ratings every time . . . . Nevertheless, in television productions there are interventions, additions, corrections, adulterations, "for it to look better". So the director's aesthetic opinion overrides that of the members of the community who know how things should be, but who, in this case, *must* conform . . . . Very few programs underline continuity and change, or attempt to portray the image of the community as it is today (Loutzaki 1999:231).

Preferring not to work against the producers, the women in these ensembles work with them, using the apparatus of television to get noticed and promote their village in order to "preserve" their culture through its increased exposure. The problems, tensions, and conflicts inherent in such activity are brought to light by Loutzaki's probing and skillful analysis, as she provides an important insight into the ways in which dance culture is contested and negotiated in the region.

Greek musical culture, as evidenced in the structure and repertoire of regional forms in particular, has affinities with and incorporates influences from a variety of musical worlds that border the nation (i.e., Albania, Macedonia, Bulgaria, and Turkey). A few examples will suffice here: a form of polyphonic singing found in Epirus is also found in Albania. The Pontic Greeks of Greek Macedonia retain music and dance traditions also found in their original homeland—the Black Sea area of Turkey. Greek Macedonian brass bands mirror those found elsewhere in the Balkans as does the *zurna* and *daouli* ensemble of the Roma. The Thracian *lyra* is similar in morphology and playing technique to the Bulgarian *gŭdulka*,[7] while the *gaida* or "bagpipe" of northern Greece is found in Bulgaria with the same name. The additive/asymmetrical rhythms of Thracian dance are also found in Bulgaria.

Not surprisingly, then, questions about musical origins have serious political consequence in a region of contested homelands. Indeed, the replies of several Greek informants to my questioning of such matters still ring in my ears. These may be reduced to one response: "But who was influenced by whom?" I will not try to deal with this conundrum here except to say that in the Balkans, the political stakes remain high even in an investigation of musical origins.

Ethniki Mousike: Greek "World Music"

The Greek soundscape derives from musics found throughout the Balkan peninsula and extending eastward far into the Mediterranean Sea: often to Turkey but usually beyond to Armenia, Turkmenistan and northern India (see Dawe 2002). These orientalizing sounds spice up Greek popular music and have helped to erode the *bouzouki*-based musical monoculture that has dominated the airwaves (that is, strangely, a *bouzouki*-dominated monoculture that probably owed much to the Ottomans at root).[8] Although this culture still predominates, at present one also hears a rich tapestry of regional sounds variously fused with pop, rock, jazz and dance (club) music. Sometimes (as in Crete), one also hears regional traditional music unmixed on disc, radio, and TV. That is, the music is not combined with jazz or other pop musics, but is performed live in regional and local contexts for pleasure, ritual, and celebration as it probably has been for many generations. But one also hears clarinet and *sitar* with Latin percussion and *toumbeleki*, and Trio Bŭlgarka polyphonic voices with electronica, or *Epirotika* with *rebetiko* on an essentially *laiko*-based album. Some regional songs are known throughout Greece and are now part of the standard repertoire of most singers wherever they are based, but local singers specializing in songs distinct to their native areas also exist (for example, Manolis Mitsias).

Several experiments with the fusion of popular and regional traditional musical forms in Greece have found success internationally. Mode Plagal and Kristi Stassinopoulou and her band are just two acts who have achieved (variously) international acclaim. Mode Plagal plays to an international jazz audience as much as a world music one. Kristi Stassinopoulou and her band with their mix of Greek traditional, punk, and electronica also play a range of venues.

Ross Daly, an Irishman born in England who plays Ottoman-influenced music in Athens and Crete, is also increasingly acclaimed by a world music audience. There is hope that he might achieve some commercial success with his highly elaborate and subtle arrangements of traditional melodies in an ensemble that crosses cultural boundaries sensitively. As someone who has injected new life into Greek musical culture at the hub of the folk revival, he surely deserves financial as well as musical rewards. His recognition of the richness, diversity, and potential of Greek traditional music (at a time when it was in its death throes)—as well as his insistence on its affinity with those musical cultures beyond national boundaries—has had a lasting influence on how Greeks view their musical world.

What follows is a series of brief vignettes illustrating first, how musicians in Greece such as Daly, Stassinopoulou, and Mode Plagal perceive and incorporate varied Balkan traditions into their compositions to produce an eclectic regional sound oriented toward an international audience, and second, in the subsequent section, how other Greek musicians, dancers, and scholars, many of them of the younger generation, perceive a general Balkan regional sensibility as intrinsic to and a reaffirmation of their national heritage.

Ross Daly and Crete

Daly is perhaps one of the most important figures in Greek music of the late twentieth and early twenty-first century. He has studied and played with a number of master musicians from Crete, the Balkans, the Middle East and northern India and, in turn, has influenced their work. Moving between Athens, Thessaloniki and Crete, he performs and teaches music from and across many cultures and traditions. In particular, he has constantly drawn attention to the similarity of musical traditions from the Balkans, into West Asia and beyond. His vision of a broadly based Greek musical culture has influenced generations of young Greek musicians and scholars (including the direction of a number of doctoral theses-in-progress as I write). His work has also affected many virtuosi in Greece and beyond.[9] These musicians acknowledge the complexity of Greek musical traditions and their affinity with non-Greek musics and display a willingness to collaborate and explore links with musical cultures both near and far.

If there was dust on the Rosetta stone of Greek music Daly has blown this away and provided translations. His arrangements and compositions highlight the deeper layers and influences in Greek music, many of which are historically or stylistically related to the Ottoman and post-Ottoman repertories of the Middle East, if not further afield. Thus he will play traditional Cretan melodies in the style of the great Turkish and Greek composers of the Bosporus, or refer to north Indian classical traditions or those of Central Asia in an attempt to set the melodies he has collected within a broader cultural framework. His works also frequently feature extended melodic improvisations using the sophisticated modal systems of the Middle East and South/Central Asia, as well as the musical instruments found there.

In a version of his composition *Black Sea,* recorded in 1992 on the album *Mitos,* Daly plays an opening improvisation on the Afghani lute, the *rababa,* "in the style and technique of an Arab *outi* and an Indian *sarod* (fretless plucked lute), combined with Greek and Turkish phrasing" (*Mitos* liner notes; see also Dawe 1999). The Turkish *fasil kemence,* goblet-shaped Iranian *zarb* drum, and Indian *tampura* drone also appear. Daly rarely uses electronic instruments such as the synthesizer in his work; he is committed to using a range of acoustic instruments whether in the studio or in live performance. His attention to detail is legendary, not only in his insistence on accurate tuning and suitable acoustics in live venues but also in the time he takes to make a record. He told me that it took him eleven months to record the track *Elefthero simio* [Free point] on the album of the same name (1996). This extraordinary composition, over twenty-one minutes in length, takes the listener through a range of sections or movements and "scenes" using multi-tracked bowed and plucked acoustic instruments, including the *yayli tambur* [bowed, upright lute] and Cretan *lyra. Ney* and *kanonaki* are also featured, as is the clarinet playing of the late Vasilis Soukas. If listeners envision a musical map of Greece, they are immediately pulled in two or three directions at the same time—to Epirus in northwestern Greece (the home of Soukas), to Crete, the southernmost outpost of Greece, and eastward to Turkey (the nearest home of the *ney* and *kanonaki*). A regional sound cannot readily be discerned on these tracks. This is the Daly norm.

By contrast, the basis for traditional instrumental music in Crete is largely the *lyra-laouto* ensemble. The *lyra* (pl. *lyres*) is a three-stringed, short-necked, pear-shaped bowed upright lute, while the *laouto* (pl. *laouta*) is a long-necked plucked lute with eight strings arranged in double courses. This ensemble is often augmented by a second *laouto* or mandolin. The *lyra* player is usually but not always the lead singer within the group. Both of these instruments are found elsewhere in Greece (such as the Thracian version referred to above). Musicians in Crete look north to the mainland and the Balkans in terms of their musical orientation and inspiration, however much they may spice up their work with instruments and melodic inflections more clearly derived from the Middle East.[10]

Although my music teachers in Crete could play unmetered improvisations (*taximi*) in various *makamlar* (although they did not know their specific names) in a *fasil* [classical] style, most played them to me as an example of what *not* to do when playing their Cretan music. "Turkish improvisations" were seen as complete *"fantasia."* Nonetheless, like Daly, some Cretan musicians with whom I worked, such as the late, great *lyra* virtuoso Thanasis Skordalos, judged their music by the standards of some other place, pointing to Istanbul and Bulgaria as definitive centers of musical excellence. They had played in festivals in Greece and further afield at which various musicians from the other Balkan countries had also performed. When I first expressed to Skordalos my interest in his music, he could not understand why I did not want to study with musicians elsewhere in the region. "Why study *lyra* with me when you can study *gŭdulka* with one of the great virtuosi in Bulgaria?" he said. Similarly, Nikiforos Aerakis, one of my *lyra* teachers, from Anoyia village, Crete, used to teach me *amanes* phrasing from Turkey (*"anatolikos*, from Turchia," he said) when showing me how to improvise *taximi*. Sensitivity to these and other issues is required, therefore, when approaching the musics of Greece, an attention to detail sometimes lacking in the world of pop mixes, world music productions, and their reportage.

Kristi Stassinopoulou and the Balkans

Ross Daly's compositions and arrangements present not so much a musical map of the traditional musics of the Eastern Mediterranean area as a highly imaginative landscape full of possibilities and potential. Daly has no aspirations to enter the Greek musical mainstream, but there are those pop musicians who have felt his influence. While he told me that he has not been tempted to put a dance beat underneath his arrangements just yet, Kristi Stassinopoulou, whose *Trigona* features on the *Rough Guide to the Music of the Balkans* (2003), has done just this. On the liner notes to her album *Echotropia* (1999) she observes that, "As the heliotrope turns its face towards the sun, so does echotropia follow the orbit of a wide landscape of sounds deriving from Greek traditional music, psychedelic rock and electronica." Working with multi-instrumentalist and composer Stathis Kalyviotis, Stassinopoulou has developed an intriguing blend of traditional and contemporary sounds. The traditional acoustic instrumentation features *zurna* (shawm), clarinet, violin, accordion and Turkish *saz* (*baǧlama*). These instruments are used within a rock-electronica band setting where shimmering guitar chords but also slowly picked out arpeggios provide a spacious accompaniment to the vocals, while a heavy (drum and bass) beat may feature underneath with *zurnades* or synthesized bagpipes (imitating the *gaida*) on top. Throughout, Kristi's plaintive voice is heard, often processed, with its intriguing melismas and multi-tracked Trio Bŭlgarka-style choral effects. An ethereal yet earthy sound is produced, somehow giving the feeling of being rooted in folk tradition (with traditional songs taken from places as far apart as Epirus and Iran), while using the very latest technology in terms of synthesizers, electric guitars, and effects. The sense of space created in these recordings captures the feeling of a mountain landscape (a comment from a Greek friend), as if the sound of celebrations from numerous villages are echoing through the valleys and merging into one. This is also the way in which Ross Daly described a section of *Eleflhero simio* to me.

There is certainly a sense of Kristi looking northwards on *Echotropia*; indeed, her attempts to convey a journey in music are confirmed by the lyrics to the track *Aeolos*. The lyrics refer to a night-time train journey through snowy landscapes, from Athens to Thessaloniki: "blurred images passing by, Balcans [sic] in the wagons, celebrating all together."

Mode Plagal: Jazz and the Balkans

Mode Plagal is one of the better known Greek jazz groups, combining virtuosic and Greek traditional music-influenced alto saxophone playing with blues-grunge-electronica-influenced guitar, electric bass guitar, kit drums, and percussion. The album *Mode Plagal II* (1998) moves from be-bop to jazz-funk to free jazz, while making various other musical stops along the way (including a heavy rock beat one minute and an African guitar riff the next). The album also includes traditional tunes from several Greek regions: a piece metered in a *kalamatianos* dance rhythm (7/8, divided 2–2–3); a carol from Thrace; a song from Epirus featuring, in turn, a chorus of voices, alto sax solos, overdriven and feedback electric guitar with traditional percussion and kit drum accompaniment; another from the western Macedonian region that utilizes multi-tracked saxes, funky sax and fretless bass guitar solos, and wah wah-inflected electric guitar rhythm, and closes with a *La Bamba* (Ritchie Valens/Los Lobos)-style melody; and finally, a Rumelian melody written in memory of Vasilis Soukas, featuring alto sax playing in his clarinet style. A piece called *Ivo* in honor of Bulgarian clarinetist Ivo Papazov features an extended alto sax solo with funky four-piece rhythm accompaniment (chorused guitar, electric bass, kit drums, and congas).

"Accordions and Brass are What You Must Listen For"

Two students attending the University of Leeds in 2003–2004 reminded me of the ways in which traditional music and dance are viewed and even explored (or not) by the younger generations in Greece. Martha Haritoudi from Volos in Thessaly remains an active and long-time member of a local dance troupe. She is well aware of the infrastructure and networks helping to sustain the life of traditional music and dance in her town and throughout her home region. Indeed, she believes that music, dance and community life are still inextricably linked in Greece, from the baptism celebration in Crete to the wedding feast in Thrace, and are also functioning as a part of "modern," "developing" Greece. In her words,

> A whole generation grew up combining *demotic* (folk-popular) song with junta and fascism. It took a long time to mature our inner rhythms of traditional music. The appearance of a new musical style has shown that there has been a "return to the roots," with all the advantages and disadvantages that has created; as a result a totally new generation of artists and audience has appeared.

Martha also commented that many young people are now attracted to dance:

> Many young people start to learn traditional dances as simultaneously they acquaint themselves with the melodic sounds and rhythms. By learning local dances, one develops a deep nostalgia for the homeland, past and present. However, it works like a framework for discovering the special characteristics of our identity against what many young people see as the faceless megalopolis. By being a member of a dancing group there is the opportunity to travel abroad and spread knowledge about our traditional culture. Many young people join dance associations to socialize and also take exercise!

Martha is not so keen on recent blends of traditional music and popular music, calling them *berdema* ["a mix," a Greek slang word]. The recording of a bagpiper from Macedonia with a dance (club) beat behind him (featuring breathtaking instrumental virtuosity) was, she assured me, just the tip of the *berdema* iceberg. So beyond these fusions, what is it that gives the sound of the Balkans in Greek music, I asked? "Accordions and brass are what you must listen for," was her reply. She went on to say,

> Balkan music and singing can sound harsh and strange at first, but high pitches, unfamiliar harmonies and low drones create a unique feeling and sound. A novice musician can appreciate the infectious rhythms; Ottoman, Byzantine influences have resulted in highly danceable and asymmetrical rhythms. Often Balkan music and dance tempos move from slow steps to a dizzying final pace. Another characteristic of Balkan music is the use of emotional contrasts. A melancholic tune can be joyful and lively as the meaning changes. Minor chords, passionate vocal parts, [and] dramatic melodies create a unique Balkan sound.

Martha said that I would find intimations of a Balkan music and dance circuit in the regional Folklore Associations where there was a growing determination amongst many of their members to stress, celebrate, and research connections across the Balkans at every opportunity.

The Balkania Festival

Martha had recently been part of a festival celebrating Balkan music and dance. The June 1999 Balkania Festival in Volos drew on the talents of members of the various local societies for regional "Folk Music and Dance," such as those in which she is a member (Plates 5.1–5.3). These included several directed at helping refugees from other lands—Greeks from the Black Sea area, Asia Minor, and Cyprus being three examples—sustain their customs.[11]

The Festival's keynote address, from which the following excerpt was taken, was delivered on 4 June by Nikos Bazianas, a folklorist trained in philology who was born in Sofrades, Thessaly, in 1930. His remarks promote a vision of diversity within a larger regional unity not unlike that of the music and dance societies in attendance.

> "Music without borders" is the title of my brief proposal . . . . We cannot forget that for centuries the national borders . . . did not exist. The interaction between the people, the cultural exchanges, the loans, the different blendings and syncretisms, the continuous use and process of all this material, create—mainly in bordering places—a united culture, Mediterranean and Balkan with many common points. Besides the great seaports of the Mediterranean were the crossroads of three

continents, the water and the terrestrial contacts, the various merchants who traveled, the emigrants, the varied trade unions of craftsmen, the professional bands of musicians who traveled from place to place . . . all these factors contribute to wide spread of cultural goods—and music, of course—and they had an important role in the partial assimilation of the people. We cannot forget that foreign lands for Greeks were not America or Australia, but the countries of the Balkans bordering on the Danube and in central Europe . . . . The brasses with their rhythmical attendance (trumpets, trombones, saxophones, cornets, cymbals, drums, *daoulia,* and clarinets) are instruments—promiscuously somehow—great in combination producing fantastic rhythms and melodies. We find them in Macedonia and many Balkan countries with many similarities, proof of a common origin and a result of interchanging and interaction.

Clearly, Bazianas's notion of "Balkania" goes beyond a mere showcasing of regional styles. In drawing attention to times when "national borders . . . did not exist" he is not only arguing that regionality should be celebrated and conserved as part of Greece's national historical treasures, but insisting that this "united culture" be once again united, that political obstacles be overcome in a celebration of "common origin." These motivations do not drive all Dance Association officials, nor do they continually surface in media or pop presentations of regional forms. Rather, like the Eurovision Song contest, it appears the Balkans may be "united" for one night as votes are exchanged. Border questions still remain after the show is over.

Beyond the World of "Accordions and Brass"

Dimitris Kyriakidis from Kavala, Macedonia, the other Greek student mentioned above is, on the other hand, more interested in heavy metal than the traditional music of the region of his birth. He says that he has never heard such music and is amazed that I have a recording of a Thracian bagpiper. Nor does he have any interest in combining it with the heavy metal or any other popular music that he plays on his guitar and with his band.

Others, however, hold quite a different view. While artists such as Mode Plagal and Kristi Stassinopoulou appear to be merging the traditional and mainstream Greek musical worlds in their productions, these other artists negotiate between them, moving easily from one to the other as demanded by economic necessity, incentive, and opportunity. Both types of musicians are helping to define the Greek contribution to a new "Balkan sound," one that moves beyond the sound realm of "accordions and brass" and the ideology of a "united culture," and into an industry-driven, transnational world of concert engagements, compilation CDs, and solo albums.

Several coffeehouses in Athens function as meeting places for such musicians, from all over Greece, whose livelihoods depend upon their entrepreneurial skill and ability to shift musical gears. Some teach in the various Academies of Folk Music in the city but continue to do their fair share of traveling. They play at a local village wedding one week, and during the next at a club in Melbourne. Established virtuosi return home to play at intensely local village or club gatherings one night and then start recording sessions or a club season in Athens the next. Perhaps they find work as session musicians on an album by a famous singer or even with a group of musicians from Turkmenistan, India, or one of the Balkan countries elsewhere on the peninsula. Or perhaps they work the Athens recording studios or nightclubs in the winter and then return home to play for the weddings that take place in summer.

Such musicians and producers are entrepreneurs, then, who respond variously to the influences and opportunities offered by emergent *ethniki mousike* and global pop mixes.[12] These responses may be interpreted as symptomatic of general shifts in lifestyle and attitudes as well as revealing of enduring approaches and tendencies, wherever the global is interpreted in Greek terms. This is the nature of *ethniki mousike;* there is, if you will, world music "Greek-style" on the doorstep for musicians and producers, requiring only the most pedestrian of backyard safaris and fieldwork. Yet the *world* of music and dance in Greece can be seen as quite a small world, and thus musicians and producers often look beyond it.

Within the music industry and at festivals, regional voices speak within a national soundscape; they remain locally significant yet at the same time might function as representative of Greece, or as musical exotica in pop mixes—that is, "exotic" even to the Greeks who invented the word.[13] Greece is not the only country in the region embarking on such opportunistic musical experiments. There is a local music circuit that overlaps and intersects with neighboring countries. Yet the similarity of the sounds (melodies, rhythms, instrumentation) coming from both sides of the border encourages producers and musicians to compile, borrow, and fuse. Recent commercially recorded collections such as *Balkans without Borders* (1999), *Balkan Voices* (1999), and *Rough Guide to the Music of the Balkans* (2003) reinforce such a notion, as do collaborations between major recording artists in the region, such as that of Goran Bregović and George Dalaras (see *Thessaloniki-Yannena with Two Canvas Shoes*). Many young people are trying to make sense of the notion of a shared

Balkan cultural heritage, as their parents and folklorists have tried to do for decades. James Pettifer notes at the end of his book *The Greeks* (2000:237):

> To be a Balkan, as much as a European, country in the sense of being part of a potential federal Europe, must be a likely destiny for Greece. In cultural terms, if this means the reaffirmation of many features of traditional Greek life at risk from an increasingly technocratic and conformist culture emanating from the United States and Brussels, it must be a welcome development.

There is as much of a Mediterranean music circuit as a Balkan one flowing through Greece (see Dawe 2002). The Greek singer Glykeria, for instance, mixed traditional and popular sounds in the 1990s and had hits in Bulgaria and Israel. Then there is the musical infrastructure that keeps the record shelves of the Greek diaspora stocked. What do Greek audiences in New York or London expect? Hiotis and Linda? Nana Mouskouri and George Dalaras, yes—but also the *lyra* music of Crete, bagpiping from Thrace, the *rebetiko* of Vamvakaris and Tsitsanis, and now, regional trad-pop, too.[14] The "united culture" of the Greek diaspora dances to a "music without borders" even if in Greece this remains a dream for some and a nightmare for others.

Notes

1. I would like to thank Martha Haritoudi for helpful discussion and procurement of the illustrations in this chapter. Polly Karkula, leader of the Pilion Dance Association in Thessaly, kindly gave me permission to use the poster and photographs.

2. In Athens, for example, one finds general and specialty instrument stores stocked with Turkish *bağlama*, *oud*, *kemence* and Arab percussion as much as Greek *bouzouki*, Cretan *lyres* and electric guitars. One can also hear standard Turkish art music repertory played by the young musicians who try out these instruments, which are imported from Turkey and the Arab Middle East as well as being made in Athens.

3. However, in my interpretation of recordings, liner notes, and academic writings I keep in mind Steven Feld's helpful critique of "celebratory narratives of world music" (2000:179). The Greek music scene, just like any other scene that now intersects with the 'world music' scene, is plugged into an industry where

> global replaces the previous label international as a positive valence term for modern practices and institutions. This has the effect of downplaying hegemonic managerial and capital

relations in the music industry, and bringing to the foreground the ways in which somewhat larger segments of the world of music-making now get somewhat larger returns in financial and cultural capital to match their greater visibility (2000:180).

4. See Cowan, et al. 2001; Danforth 1995; Herzfeld 1982, 1987, and 1997; Pettifer 2000; and Slobin 1996. See also Clogg 2002 for an overview of the different minority groups in Greece.

5. In addition, a series of recent academic writings clearly relate Greek music and dance to the wider world of the Balkan ecumene. These include Cowan 1990 and 2000; and Keil and Keil 2002; which remind us of the importance of Gypsy music in the construction of a Greek soundscape, as well as the focused regional work of The Friends of Music Society (Athens) and their project in the Evros region of Thrace, printed as an edited collection of articles and reports called the *Music of Thrace. An Interdisciplinary Approach: Evros* (see Droulia and Liavis 1999). Compilation albums of Balkan music featuring Greek artists have accompanied this renewed academic interest.

6. As Massey notes: "Moreover, and again as a result of the fact that it is conceptualised as created out of social relations, space is by its very nature full of power and symbolism, a complex web of relations of domination and subordination, of solidarity and co-operation. This aspect of space has been referred to elsewhere as a kind of 'power-geometry'" (Massey 1994:265; see also Dawe 2004b and Massey 1993).

7. The soundpost configuration of the *lyra, gŭdulka*, and Croatian *lijerica* are the same.

8. Greek musical culture has only ever been monolithic when reduced to *bouzouki* bands in the 1960s and early 1970s. Ironically, because this was the music that moved rapidly into films and TV worldwide, it became stuck in the minds of all non-Greeks who thought this was the only way Greeks made popular music (see Dawe 2002). However, the clarinet is widely regarded as the national instrument of Greece, the *bouzouki* being defined as an instrument of urban music culture *per se.*

9. One example is Ishan Ozgen, a multi-instrumentalist from Istanbul known for his *fasıl kemence* playing. The *fasıl kemence* is a bowed lute, similar to the Cretan *lyra* and used in Turkish art music.

10. See Dawe 1996, 1998, 1999, 2001, 2002, 2003, 2004a, 2004b.

11. Such societies are common in large urban centers throughout Greece.

12. In the late 1990s the work of Anna Vissi was often referred to as epitomizing "global pop" in Greece, a mix of Anglo-American pop styles, *ethniki mousike* and Greek popular traditional sounds.

13. See also Charles Stewart (1991) for a study of the deeper meanings of *exotika* in Greece.

14. See Dawe (2001) for a discussion of the stock of a Greek record store in Toronto, Canada.

Part II

BEYOND NATION: REGIONALISMS IN A COSMOPOLITAN FRAME

❖ 6 ❖

Ottoman Echoes,
Byzantine Frescoes,
and
Musical Instruments in the Balkans

Gabriela Ilnitchi

Preamble

The secular musical practices in the Balkan peninsula during the centuries of Ottoman rule have yet to attract the scholarly attention and systematic exploration they rightly merit.[1] For the most part, only a few music historians and folklorists active in the Balkans have engaged in the exploration of the Ottoman musical past, mostly that of their own countries and often in relatively general terms. Even fewer foreign scholars have expressed strong interest in investigating the types of available evidence and addressing the complex web of socio-historical, economic, and cultural issues this evidence may bring to bear. The reluctance to engage this field of research may very well be rooted, at least in part, in the various ethnocentric and ideological stances often espoused by either native or foreign scholars during the last hundred years or so, as well as in the political and socio-economic circumstances that conditioned their choices.

On the one hand, factors such as academic market forces and politically motivated scholarly trends since the Second World War, the powerful (Western-) Eurocentric penchant that has dominated Western musicological studies until fairly recently, and the political situation in the

193

Balkans until a decade or so ago—not to mention the daunting prospect of having to master at least a half dozen languages—discouraged or even outright prevented foreign scholars from systematically exploring the early musical history of either a specific country in the area or of the Ottoman Balkans at large. On the other hand, the circumstances that have shaped dominant musicological attitudes and research methodologies in the Balkans are infinitely more complex. They are contingent upon subtle differences in the kind of nationalistic discourses adopted by these countries during the nineteenth and the early twentieth centuries, upon the different modes in which these discourses adapted to communist ideology after World War II, as well as upon the country-specific ideological solutions designed to solve the conceptual tension between cultural definitions of national specificity and regional commonality. In the context of these variables, the study of music in the Ottoman Balkans has in general been of marginal concern to the dominant Balkan musicological scholarship for several common reasons that, although not easily separable in practice, can be rendered analytically distinct: 1) the increased dominance of Western aesthetic models, 2) the post-war communist ideological ambivalence toward musical practices patronized by social classes that were sometimes selectively, sometimes arbitrarily viewed as dominant, and 3) the emergence of models of musical authenticity derived from nationalist concepts of ethnicity.[2]

Political constraints and ideological constructs aside, even more relevant to the state of both foreign and domestic research on the history of musical life in the Ottoman Balkans is the dearth of available material evidence as well as its fragmentary and eclectic nature. Those primary textual sources that every so often contain references to contemporaneous musical activities, instruments, or performers consist primarily of travel accounts, particularly from the seventeenth century onward, occasional ecclesiastical writings, and documents of various sorts scattered around hundreds of local archives and libraries and written in at least half a dozen languages. Although many of these sources have been published, neither type has been systematically explored by music historians thus far.[3] Even less documented and rarely explored is yet another category of historical evidence: the frescoes of the hundreds of churches built or restored between the fifteenth and eighteenth centuries throughout the Balkan peninsula, from southern Greece to northern Moldavia. Perceived primarily as artistic objects, some of these churches were restored in the twentieth century and converted into museums. Many others, however, are still active centers of monastic, village, or town communal worship. Altogether, they represent different things to different people. At the national level, governmental and ecclesiastical officials often refer to them as embodiments of national artistic expression, as testimony to the country's historic allegiance to the Christian faith, or as centers that helped foster anti-Ottoman sentiments and thus insured the preservation of the nation and the continuity of that faith under the Ottomans. At the local level, villagers still conceive of them as focal points of their shared identity, expressed either in worship or communal celebrations. In addition to the socio-cultural meanings thrust upon these monuments, the frescoes they contain can also be viewed as historical documents of sorts, albeit sometimes problematic and often ambiguous. If carefully interpreted, these frescoes can ultimately provide visual evidence for the dissemination and performance practice of various Ottoman or pre-Ottoman musical instruments in the area, and for the gradual differentiation of courtly, urban, and rural musical traditions. Significantly, their substance also adds a certain historical depth to some current musical practices.

The sheer number of these monuments, the richness of their decoration and, sometimes, their architectural originality is evidence that, counter to historiographic theories still current in some Balkan scholarly circles, artistic life in the peninsula did not come to a standstill under the Ottomans. As Machiel Kiel (1985) convincingly argues, artistic development did not happen in spite of, but was actually facilitated by the administrative system of the Ottomans themselves. As vassals to the Ottomans, the Romanian principalities of Wallachia and Moldavia witnessed bursts of concentrated artistic activity during the long reigns of a few powerful princes; on the other hand, the territories south of the Danube, known as the "core European provinces" of the Ottoman Empire, experienced intense architectural and pictorial activity almost continuously during the sixteenth and the seventeenth centuries. It is precisely the products of these artistic activities, which took place during those times of relative peace and under relatively favorable socio-economic conditions on both shores of the Danube, that provide us with ample iconographic evidence for contemporaneous musical practice. For although painters followed the well established and relatively stable iconographic programs of Byzantine church decoration, they also altered some details in their execution of particular scenes, and depicted a large number of musical instruments and ensembles that often vary from region to region, or even church to church.

Rich and varied as the pictorial evidence is, the socio-historical and cultural factors surrounding its production must be considered integral to the interpretive process, a methodological perspective all too often absent from current writings on Balkan music iconography. On the one hand, the patronage system, long recognized as having an impact on large- and

small-scale pictorial iconographic choices at large, was effectively
conditioned in the Balkans by the Ottoman administrative system. The
social classes responsible for artistic patronage as well as their financial
prowess varied from province to province: primarily the nobility in
Wallachia and Moldavia, regions only tributary to the Ottomans; and the
local village, monastic, or merchant communities in Bulgaria, Serbia, and
Greece—all Ottoman *pashalŭk*-s.[4] On the other hand, periodic population
resettlement by, and under, the Ottomans, as well as the presence of
itinerant painters further complicate the iconographic interpretive process
and the development of a coherent historiographical discourse pertaining
to a specific geographical area.

A perfect example in support of this last point is the village of
Arbanasi. Built on a steep hill near Veliko Tŭrnovo (Bulgaria), Arbanasi,
with its five historic churches and two monasteries, all built and painted
between the sixteenth and the eighteenth centuries, was founded by the
Ottomans at the end of the fifteenth century and populated with "Albanians," hence the name ("Arnavud" in Turkish; "Arbanas" in Bulgarian).
The village held the privileged *vakf-derebend* status, resulting in a much
lower level of Ottoman taxation that insured a flourishing economy and
post-Byzantine culture until their sudden decline around 1800.[5]

The first layer of frescoes in Arbanasi's St. George church dates from
1561 and was executed by Nicholas, the son of one of the most famous
sixteenth-century painters, Onufre of Elbassan (Albania). Nicholas also
painted several churches in southern Albania (Fier, Berat, and Dhermi),
while his father, Onufre himself, is known to have worked in Venice
(Italy), Kastoria (northern Greece), Zrze (Republic of Macedonia),
Shelcan and Balsh (Albania). The group responsible in 1649 for the works
in the porch of Arbanasi's church of the Nativity of Christ consists of the
same masters who in 1647 painted the village church in Tutinje (Novi
Pazar) and in 1654 the narthex of the monastery of Hopovo in Fruska
Gora (both in present-day Serbia) (Kiel 1985:301–2). The frescoes of the
church of St. Athanasius on the other hand, also located in Arbanasi, were
executed in 1724/26 by two Bulgarian painters, while the narthex of Holy
Archangels was painted by Michael of Thessaloniki and George of
Bucharest in the eighteenth century.

How then should one interpret the instruments represented in the
Arbanasi frescoes, such as the long-necked lutes found in the mid-
seventeenth-century representation of Psalm 148 in the church of the
Nativity of Christ (Plate 6.1)? As part of an inherited iconographic
program unrelated to contemporaneous musical practices? Or as instruments familiar to the painters, to other areas where the painters had been
active, or to the Arbanasi community?

Arbanasi is not a unique case; the predilection to hire painters outside the immediate geographical or ethnic community of their patrons is a characteristic shared by many other Balkan townships or villages, such as Kastoria and Vlacho-Klissoura (northern Greece), Voskopoje (Albania), Boboševo (Bulgaria), and Iaşi and Hurezi (Romania). The complex web of socio-historical and cultural processes that were at work in the Balkan peninsula during Ottoman rule ultimately requires a vast array of music-iconographic interpretive strategies, of which strict organological identification is only one. Such strategies would ultimately challenge the common conceptual limitations still current in Balkan historiographies in general and music-iconographic studies in particular, which tend to focus on monocultural, monoethnic, often static or even ahistorical constructs which are largely the result of eighteenth- and nineteenth-century nationalist movements (Pejović 1984; Solcanu 1976 and 1979; Florea 1994 and 1997).

The *Davul* and *Zurna*:
Iconographic Considerations

The present essay cannot even begin to do justice to the whole range of issues I have raised in the rather lengthy and involved preamble above. What it attempts, however, is to offer some food for thought on the manner in which the interpretation of iconographic data, along some of the methodological lines I have sketched above, can expand and diversify our understanding of the introduction, reception, transmission, and performance practice of specific musical instruments in the pre-Ottoman and Ottoman Balkans. In particular, my discussion relies upon iconographic information synthesized in Table 6.1, and focuses on the iconographic representations of two instruments as they appear in various ensembles depicted in the Balkan frescoes between the fourteenth and the end of the seventeenth century: the double-headed drum often known in the Balkans under the name *tapan, tŭpan, lodër, bubanj* or various derivatives of the term *davul* (*daouli, daulle, daulă,* etc.); and the shawm-like instrument known as the *zurna* (*zurla, surla, svirla, curle,* etc.).[6]

Recent scholarship operates on the general assumption that the *davul-zurna* ensemble was brought to the pre-Ottoman Balkans by the Roma in the late thirteenth and early fourteenth centuries (Brandl 1996:15; Picken 1975:103; and Silverman 1996b:70; among others). This hypothesis, first launched and documented by Hoerburger in his *Der Tanz mit der Trommel,* relied to some degree on several iconographic representations

Table 6.1: Iconographic Representations of the *Davul* and *Zurna* in Balkan Frescoes, 14th–17th Century

CHURCH	Date (ca.)	Davul Lacing	Davul Sticks	Zurna	OTHERS Percussion	OTHERS Wind	DANCERS
Bogoroditsa Peribleptos (Ohrid; MA)	1294	W●	A		C	2tr	
Bogoroditsa Levijska (Prizren; Kosovo)[1]	1307	W●	A		C		
Staro Nagoričane (Kumanovo; MA)	1318	W●	A		C	2tr "D"	sl
Nicholaos Orphanos (Salonica; GR)	1315	W	S		C cl	2tr	
Hreljo Tower (Rila; BG)[2]	1335	W left	A				
Lesnovo (Zletovo; MA) – Mocking 1	1349	X	A		C	2trt	
Psalm 150[3]		X●	A				
Mocking 2[4]		X	A				
Sveti Andrej (near Skopje; MA)	1389	?	A		C	2tr	
Sveti Nikita (Banjani; MA)	1485	X? left	B		cl	tr Str	hk
Pătrăuţi (Suceava; RO)	p.1487	——			2xfd	2tr	
Voroneţ (Suceava; RO)	1488	——			C	2tr	
Părhauţi (Suceava; RO)	1497-9	——			fd		
Poganovo (BG)	1499	X? left	B			Str	cl
Bălineşti (N. Moldavia: RO)[5]	1500-11	X	B	1	fd kd cl		hk
Dobrovăţ (Iaşi; RO)	1529	X	B	1	fd kd cl		hk
Humor (Suceava; RO)	1535	X	B	1	kd cl		hk

Continues on next page

Table 6.1—Continued

			B?		fd	tr Str	cl
Prokuplje (Serbia)	1536	X	B?		fd		cl
Moldovița (Suceava; RO)	1537	X	B		fd		
Arbore (N. Moldavia; RO)	1541	X?	B	1	kd cl?		
St. George (Banjani; MA)	1549	X left	B	1		2xStr	cl hk
Bjelo Polje (Serbia)	1570	? left	B	1	kd	2tr	
Morača (Montenegro)	1570s	?	?	1			
Pljevlje (Montenegro)	1595	X?	?	(2?)	kd		
Novo Hopovo (Serbia)	1608	2X left	Bx2			2xStr	
Pustinja (Valjevo, Serbia)	1622	X left	B	2	**SELF STANDING ENSEMBLE**		hk
Stragari (Serbia)	1630s	X? left	?	1	**SELF STANDING ENSEMBLE (?)**	2xStr	
Radijević (Serbia)	1650	X	B	2	**SELF STANDING ENSEMBLE**		
Timiou Prodomou (Serres; Thrace; GR)	17th c.	?	B	1	**SELF STANDING ENSEMBLE**		
'Ai Giannis (Mani; GR)	18th c.	X	B	2?	**SELF STANDING ENSEMBLE**		
Dekoulou (Mani; GR)	1765	X	B	2	**SELF STANDING ENSEMBLE**		

Sigla: C=cymbals; fd=frame-drum; kd=kettle drum; cl=clappers; tr=trumpet; Str=S-trumpet; D="*duduk*"; sl=sleeves; hk=handkerchief

Additional instruments in the scene:
[1] Cymbals; psaltery; harp; *pandura*
[2] Psaltery; *pandura*
[3] Psaltery
[4] Psaltery
[5] Pipe-and-drum; bagpipe

● = snares	S = //
A = ⌈/	B = ⌠/

of the *davul* in numerous fourteenth-century Balkan frescoes from Dečani in Kosovo, and Staro Nagoričano and Lesnovo, both in today's Republic of Macedonia (Hoerburger 1954:20), to which Lawrence Picken (1975: 100) later added Bogoroditsa Ljeviška in Prizren (Kosovo). A careful examination of the frescoes mentioned above as well as of other contemporaneous and later depictions from the Balkan realm does not fully support such a conjecture and reveals a much more complicated historical and cultural reality than previously assumed. As we shall see, the iconographic data synthesized in Table 6.1 suggests that the music-iconographic contexts for the *davul* and *zurna* depictions changed considerably between the fourteenth and the end of the seventeenth century: no early frescoes depict the *davul-zurna* ensemble, but only the *davul*, which iconographically antedates the depiction of the *zurna* by almost two centuries. When painters depict both instruments in the context of the same scene, the *davul* and the *zurna* are at first represented as part of larger musical ensembles and only later as a separate, self-standing group. Artistic penchant notwithstanding, these changes are often contemporaneous with, and to some degree contingent upon, a wide range of pan-Balkan socio-historical factors. In fact, the weight of extant data suggests that these changes reflect in part the cultural and ideological ramifications that the Ottoman political and military presence in the peninsula brought to bear upon artistic production. However, the reader should be aware that due to the limited objectives of the present essay, the less than comprehensive nature of the available photographic documentation of the music-iconographic scenes, and the present state of scholarship, the exact range of permissible interpretation of the evidence is drastically reduced and all the socio-cultural and historical inferences remain limited in scope, preliminary, and possibly subject to later modification.

Davul-s in the "Mocking of Christ" Scene

The double-headed drum appears depicted in a number of Byzantine manuscripts several centuries before it enters the iconographic arena of the Balkan churches. For example, one of the eight musicians featured in the illumination that marks the end of the Psalter section and the beginning of the Odes in the 1059 manuscript Vatican gr. 752 carries a double-headed drum (with snares?) and what appears to be a slightly curved beater.[7] One of the three (female?) musicians depicted in the Constantinopolitan Psalter copied at the Studio monastery in 1066, London, British Museum, add. 19,352, is also playing a double-headed drum, but this time the beater has a solid crook head.[8] Furthermore, the same type of instrument appears in the context of the "birth of Zeus" scene represented in yet another eleventh-century Constantinopolitan codex, Jerusalem Taphou 14, containing the homilies of Gregory Nazianzenus.[9] These relatively early depictions seem to suggest, therefore, that by the middle of the eleventh century Byzantine artists were familiar at least with the iconographic, if not with the actual double-headed drum.

Could Romani migration have played a role in the introduction of the double-headed drum to the Byzantine world during the eleventh century? This is a hypothesis as attractive as it is difficult to prove, for conjectural evidence seems neither to contradict nor strongly support such a possibility. The arrival of the Roma in the Byzantine realm has been commonly connected to the raids of the Seljuks in Armenia, around the middle of the eleventh century. In Byzantine Greek, the Roma were called by the name *atsinganos* (ατσίγγανος), related to, but not necessarily derived from, the name of the heretical sect from Asia Minor known as *athinganos* (αθίγγανος) (Soulis 1961:145–46). It has been generally assumed that the earliest reference to the presence of Roma in the Byzantine Empire comes from a Georgian hagiographical text composed around 1068 at the Monastery of Iberon on Mount Athos. A more recent study contends that the earliest secure Byzantine reference to Roma dates only from the thirteenth century and appears in a letter of the Patriarch of Constantinople, Gregorius II Kyprios (1283–1289), where there is a mention of the taxes that had to be extracted from the so-called "Egyptians and Athinganoi" (*"o toùs kaì Aìgyptíous kaì `Athingánous"*) (Rochow and Matschke 1991:241). Be this as it may, the iconographic evidence mentioned above suggests that Byzantine artists were familiar with the double-headed drum, at least as an iconographic item if not as an actual instrument, at the time or even prior to the Romani migration into the territories of the Empire. While the depictions of the double-headed drum in the Byzantine codices mentioned above all originate from around the middle of the century, and are contemporaneous with the earliest references to *atsinganoi* invoked by the proponents of an eleventh-century migration, they nevertheless seem to follow already well-established iconographic conventions, thus suggesting earlier iconographic models. A definitive chronology for either the beginning of the massive Romani migration into the Byzantine territories or the adoption by the Byzantine iconographic and/or musical traditions of the double-headed drum is for the time being difficult to conjecture. These two phenomena *may* have been relatively contemporaneous and, therefore, possibly historically correlated, but they are not necessarily in a causal relationship.

The earliest depictions of the largest double-headed drum found in the Balkans are characteristic of the Macedonian Paleologan style of painting that survives in several late thirteenth- and early fourteenth-century churches, most of them princely foundations (see Table 6.1). Art historians contend that the Macedonian Paleologan style found one of its earliest realizations in the frescoes of the Bogoroditsa Peribleptos church (Sveti Kliment) in Ohrid, painted in 1294 by the atelier of Michael Astrapas and Eutychios from Thessaloniki. The family Astrapas (John and Michael) together with Eutychios were also responsible for the decoration of some of the churches mentioned by Hoerburger and Picken, such as Bogoroditsa Ljeviška in Prizren (in 1307) and Sveti Djordji in Staro Nagoričano (1318), as well as for the earliest layer of frescoes found at Sveti Nikita near Skopje (1308 or ca. 1321).[10] The double-headed drum depicted at Bogoroditsa Ljeviška appears in the scene representing the Sticheron for the Feast of the Dormition by John of Damascus (Pejović 1985:128). Here, the cylindrical drum appears in the context of a female ensemble that includes a pair of crotales or cymbals, a psaltery, a harp, and a lute. With the exception of the V-shaped snares of the cylindrical drum, both the iconographic detail and the instruments partaking in the musical ensemble emulate much older pictorial models, such as those featured in the miniatures of several eleventh-century Byzantine manuscripts containing the homilies of Gregory Nazianzenus mentioned above. Due to the apparent archaic iconographic features, I suggest that the degree of relevance this fresco carries as evidence in support of, or against Hoerburger's hypothesis is somewhat limited.

The remaining set of examples requires more detailed consideration. In the case of all other monuments considered here, the double-headed drum appears depicted in two programmatic contexts: the representation of the "Mocking of Christ" scene in the iconographic cycle of the Passions—at Bogoroditsa Peribleptos, Staro Nagoričano, Nicholaos Orphanos, and Lesnovo—and that of Psalm 150—at the Hreljio Tower and Lesnovo.

According to Gabriel Millet, the iconographic archetype of the Byzantine representation of the "Mocking of Christ" scene, stemming from the text in Matthew 27.27–30,[11] relates to the illuminations found in the eleventh-century Laurentiana Gospel, where Christ is "mocked" by a jester wearing long sleeves (Millet 1916:612).[12] Nowhere does Matthew refer to musicians or musical instruments in his account of the event; nor does the scene depicted in the Laurentiana Gospel involve any musicians. Whether or not the introduction of musical instruments to the scene's iconography is contingent upon some still unidentified apocryphal writings, later iconographic conventions clearly mandate the depiction of some kind of musicians and jesters as symbolic visual representations of the "mocking" concept. As far as the available evidence seems to suggest, musical instruments enter the "Mocking" scene in great numbers at the time when the scene establishes itself in the program of the Passion cycle, particularly in the Macedonian Paleologan frescoes of the late thirteenth and early fourteenth century. Iconographically, the scene will remain extraordinarily stable. From the late thirteenth century onward, the various depictions relate to each other in respect to the participant characters—Christ-musicians-soldiers-jesters—their spatial arrangement, and their symbolic relationship. However, although the Paleologan iconographic model mandates the inclusion of two large *categories* of musical instruments—wind and percussion—the specific instruments, their numbers, and the composition of the ensemble they form vary significantly.

The "Mocking of Christ" at Bogoroditsa Peribleptos in Ohrid and Staro Nagoričano near Kumanovo, both painted by artists from the Astrapas atelier, feature a common iconographic schema and include among the represented musical instrumentarium a large double-headed drum (Plates 6.2 and 6.3). In both scenes the drum has W-type lacing and parallel snares and is played with two sticks, one larger and slightly curved, and the other a short switch. However, despite their similar iconographic parameters and the fact that they feature identical types of drums, the differences found in the remaining musical details are quite remarkable. Instead of the mocking soldiers at Christ's feet in the Bogoroditsa Peribleptos scene, the Staro Nagoričano scene features two long-sleeved dancers. While the long sleeves of these mockers are most likely reminiscent of the iconographic prototype of the scene (see above, the "Laurentiana archetype") and may thus relate to iconographic representations of jesters at the Byzantine court, they clearly function here as dancers. This brings them in accord with dancers that, as shown in Table 6.1, are often provided with various dance accessories such as handkerchiefs or clappers in other contemporaneous and later frescoes. Moreover, the number, character, and positioning of the instruments in the two scenes differ slightly. Two trumpet-like instruments symmetrically arch over Christ's head in both frescoes, a feature that will remain the most stable element of the iconographic prototype. While the Bogoroditsa Peribleptos scene places the drum and cymbals in a similar symmetrical fashion on the two sides of Christ, the Staro Nagoričano fresco groups them together with a *duduk*-like instrument on one single side of the scene, as though to form an accompanying ensemble of sorts for the dancers.

Products of the same atelier, these two frescoes ultimately embody some of the constants and variables that will characterize the iconographic composition of the scene for the next five hundred years or so. They also feature the only known pictorial examples of the large double-headed drum with W-lacing and parallel snares. Variations of this instrument appear in other contemporaneous frescoes. The double-headed drum with W-lacing but without snares appears at St. Nicholaos Orphanos church in Thessaloniki (Plate 6.4) and at the small chapel in the Hreljio Tower at Rila (Plate 6.5). On the other hand, the double-headed drum found in the 1345 depiction of Psalm 150 in the porch of the Lesnovo church features two parallel snares but its lacing is of the X-type (Plate 6.6). It is worth noting, however, that at the very same church but in the "Mocking of Christ" scene, painted slightly later and by another artist, the drum features the same X-lacing, but has no snares and is played with two curved beaters (rather than only one curved beater and a short switch, which was the standard in most of the other frescoes mentioned here) (Pejović 1984:Pl. 15). Furthermore, in the same scene, we encounter one of the earliest representations of the "dancing mocker" with accoutrements, in this case a pair of clappers.[13]

As discussed above, double-headed drums appear in earlier Byzantine manuscript illuminations, but versions of the W-lacing type with single or double snares and a pair of curved and switch beaters do not. Nor do other known examples of this type appear beyond the middle of the fourteenth century. Its ostensibly short iconographic life suggests that this type of cylindrical drum could have been the mark of the Astrapas atelier, which seemingly pioneered it, and of several other Macedonian Paleologan painters of the first half of the fourteenth century. The iconographic precision and the consistency of some of the organological details, however, suggest that, while maintaining the categories of instruments featured in the inherited iconographic models, the artists depicted an actual contemporaneous instrument. The relatively short life and limited geographical dissemination of what I will call the "Astrapas *davul*" may ultimately indicate that these Thessalonian artists and their followers were in fact assimilating into the established iconographic paradigm of the double-headed drum a set of instrumental properties, such as the type of lacing and the presence of snares, which were either novel or geographically idiosyncratic.

Conjectural evidence suggests that this novel type of cylindrical drum may have indeed been introduced to the area at the time of the massive migration of the Romani people into the Balkan peninsula and particularly the Serbian kingdom in the fourteenth century. All iconographic representations in the frescoes mentioned above are largely contemporaneous with a document that, according to some scholars, contains the earliest evidence for the presence of the Roma in King Dušan's Serbian kingdom: it dates from 1348 and refers to *c'ngar'* craftsmen attached to the monastery of Prizren. Although this interpretation of the term has been rejected by some scholars on the basis of philological criteria (Soulis 1961:161), there are a number of other, less controversial documents from Ragusa, Zagreb, and Wallachia that attest to the presence of Roma in the lands south of the Danube at that time and their migration northward toward Wallachia.[14]

One may reasonably assume that the introduction of the W-laced large-size drum in the iconographic representations discussed above may have been contemporaneous with the arrival of Roma in Thrace early in the century, and their subsequent and relatively rapid westward and northward advance. Based on the available documentary or iconographic evidence, however, one cannot infer that the dissemination of this type of double-headed drum coincided with that of the double-reed instrument known in the Balkans under various derivatives of the term *zurna*, and by extension with that of the *davul-zurna* ensemble. Neither the frescoes discussed above, nor any other fourteenth-century frescoes that have been documented thus far depict anything that can be reliably identified as a *zurna*-like instrument. The debut of the *zurna* on the post-Byzantine iconographic stage takes place later, shortly before 1500 and in a group of frescoes found in churches hundreds of miles away from Thessaloniki, in the principality of Moldavia. However, this does not occur before an important change takes place in the iconography of the *davul*.

A late fifteenth-century group of artists active primarily in geographic Macedonia and known in scholarly circles as the "Last Macedonians" was responsible in 1485 for the younger murals of the monastery church St. Nikita in the village of Čučer (Banjani) in the Black Mountains north of Skopje (Kiel 1985:340). In their depiction of the "Mocking of Christ" scene, the drummer holds a switch between the thumb and little finger of his left hand, and a beater with a solid crook head in his right hand (Plate 6.7). If both the shape and the grip of the switch have by now become a relatively common iconographic feature, the solid crook head of the large beater is somewhat unusual in the frescoes of Balkan churches. Though not unique in Byzantine art at large,[15] this type of drum appears consistently in scenes with military overtones found in Islamic manuscripts from at least the fourteenth century onward, and in Ottoman illuminations as part of the military *mehter*.[16] By the late fifteenth century the Ottomans were firmly established in the Balkans and, as the small but representative sample of frescoes listed in Table 6.1 suggests, it is also from the late fifteenth century onward that the frescoed double-headed drum with a large, solid crook-head beater and a switch begins to emerge as the standard iconographic choice in the "Mocking of Christ" scene. Much as the fourteenth-century Macedonian-Paleologan painters may have reacted to features of the double-headed drum that emerged contemporaneously with the advance of the Roma in the Balkan Peninsula, the "Last Macedonians" may have responded to the pervasive presence of the Ottoman *davul*.[17]

Davul-s and *Zurna*-s in the "Mocking" Scene

To locate early representations of a *zurna*-like instrument in the Balkans we must travel to Moldavia, where more than two dozen or so churches were built and/or painted during the sixteenth century, mostly by local artists. Most relevant to our discussion is the "Mocking of Christ" scene as it appears in the frescoes of two churches: Bălineşti and Dobrovăţ.

The founder of the Bălineşti village church was Ioan Tăutu, elevated to the rank of great logothete by Stephen the Great (1457–1504) in 1475 and who retained that office for almost thirty-five years. One of the few boyars to whom the prince granted the privilege of founding churches in the realm, Ioan Tăutu was also involved in intensive diplomatic activities that took him to Hungary (1494–95) and Poland (1497 and 1506); in 1504 he also journeyed to Istanbul as the head of the Moldavian embassy sent by Bogdan III to Suleyman the Magnificent to pay tribute to and ratify the principality's status as an Ottoman vassal (Popa 1981:9–10). The Bălineşti church, foundation and burial place of the Tăutu family, was built in the last decade of the fifteenth century and probably painted between 1500 and 1511 by Gavril Ieromonachul (1981:35–36). Although it is difficult to hypothesize whether Ioan Tăutu himself had any involvement in the process of iconographic decision-making, it is nevertheless significant that the frescoes of the church he founded were executed during the years of his most intense diplomatic activity, around the time when the political and military vassal status of the Moldavian principality to the Ottoman Porte became a *de facto* reality. This is significant, I believe, because the "Mocking of Christ" scene at Bălineşti is the earliest known iconographic depiction of both the *davul* and the *zurna* together, and as an ensemble that, as we shall see, bears a general resemblance to the Ottoman *mehter*.

The church of the Dobrovăţ monastery, on the other hand, has a slightly different history. Founded by the Moldavian prince Stephen the Great, and a recipient of princely patronage, the church was finished in

1504 but remained unpainted for more than two decades. The pious donation of Petru Rareş, prince of Moldavia and Stephen the Great's natural son, helped finance the frescoing of the church by two anonymous but probably local painters in 1529. The "Mocking of Christ" scene at Dobrovăţ bears a striking iconographic resemblance to its earlier counterpart at Bălineşti. Although there is no evidence to suggest that the Dobrovăţ artists were directly influenced by the Bălineşti frescoes, the similarity between the two scenes is quite remarkable, especially in regard to the number of musical instruments and ensembles they incorporate (Plates 6.8 and 6.9).

In the foreground and flanking Christ in both cases are a *zurna*, a *davul*—with the by now standard large beater with a solid crook head and a switch—a pair of kettledrums, and two handkerchief dancers; in addition, the Bălineşti fresco incorporates a pipe-and-drum player. In the background, in the gallery behind Christ, the Dobrovăţ artist placed three additional characters who play a pair of clappers, a frame drum, and an S-shaped trumpet (from left to right).[18] The Bălineşti painter also depicted a pair of clappers, but at least one of his trumpets is straight, and in addition, to the far right of the scene he inserted a bagpiper.

The Bălineşti fresco is in an advanced stage of deterioration that makes it difficult to infer little more than the general shape and the performing position of the *zurna*-like instrument. The detailed depiction of the *zurna* at Dobrovăţ, however, is picture perfect, so to speak (Plate 6.10). In addition to the conical bore, the flared bell, and several holes, the pirouette and the mouthpiece are clearly visible. Moreover, as in the Bălineşti scene, the Dobrovăţ player directs the bell of the instrument upwards in a playing position that is strikingly similar to that of modern *zurna* players in areas south of the Danube.

Moldavian Fresco Instrumentation and the Ottoman *Mehter*

The depictions of the "Mocking" scene at Bălineşti and Dobrovăţ preserve those families of instruments that Byzantine and post-Byzantine music-iconographic paradigms required—percussion and trumpet (straight or S-shaped). Their individual members here appear to have been updated and diversified in order to conform either to emerging artistic preferences or, more likely, to contemporaneous musical realities, as well as to encapsulate an implicit ideological stance. The organological detail of the depicted instruments, as well as their distribution in what is a relatively well-defined ensemble, suggests that, within the confines of an inherited iconographic program, the Bălineşti and Dobrovăţ painters may have been actually working out a pictorial composite grounded in contemporaneous visual and aural experiences. Artistic imagination aside, the most likely ensemble that might have served as a model for the particular combination of instruments in the two Moldavian frescoes was the Ottoman military *mehter* and/or its generic relative designed for dance and celebratory music, the *mehter-i bîrûn*.[19] Opportunities for direct or indirect exposure to the Ottoman *mehter* did not lack in the early sixteenth century. The military contacts between the Ottomans and the Moldavians, the presence of Moldavian diplomatic envoys at the Porte where they would have experienced the Ottoman courtly customs, as well as the periodic arrival of Ottoman envoys and their entourage at the Moldavian court are well documented. If in the fourteenth century the presumed novelty of the W-type lacing for the double-headed drum caught the iconographic imagination of the Paleologan painters, the might, pomp, and sound of the Ottoman *mehter* could conceivably have had a profound effect on Moldavian sixteenth-century iconographic habits.

Furthermore, the introduction of instruments and ensembles reminiscent of the contemporaneous Ottoman military may very well have had ideological implications that would help bring the symbolism of the "Mocking of Christ" scene in accord with the political and military events of the late fifteenth and early sixteenth centuries. As mentioned above, the frescoes at the Bălineşti church were executed at the height of military and diplomatic contact between Moldavia and the Ottoman Porte, and around the time Moldavia officially accepted the status of Ottoman vassal. Furthermore, the Bălineşti "Mocking" scene is just one of the earliest expressions of a music-iconographic prototype that other Moldavian artists adopted in their production of slightly later frescoes. As shown in Table 6.1, instrumental ensembles similar in their composition to that at Bălineşti appear not only at Dobrovăţ, but in several other Moldavian frescoes executed by local artists during the second reign of Petru Rareş: Humor (1535) and Arbore (1541) (for Humor, see Plate 6.11). This music-iconographic prototype does not seem to have been common in contemporaneous frescoes from the Balkan regions that had long since fallen under Ottoman control, such as the "core provinces" south of the Danube, nor indeed even in Wallachia, the other Romanian principality. In fact, no *zurna*-like instrument appears in *any* surviving frescoes of extant Wallachian churches, and the only non-Moldavian frescoes included in Table 6.1 that feature a mocking ensemble consisting of instruments comprising the core of the Ottoman *mehter*—the *davul, zurna, boru* [S-shaped trumpet], and kettledrums—are found several decades later and hundreds of miles away in Serbia, at Bijelo Polje (1570) and Pljevlje (1595) (Pejović 1984:Plates 46 and 50).[20]

The iconographic formulation of this "Ottomanized" ensemble, as well as the relatively high incidence of the Moldavian depictions, seems to be contingent upon local historical circumstances. Originally embedded in the iconographic paradigm of the "Mocking" scene is the contrast between Christ, unmistakable in his scarlet robe, and who constitutes the axis of compositional symmetry, and his mockers, the "Roman" soldiers of which two usually hold the trumpets that symmetrically arch over Christ's head. The presence of musicians and dancers among the mockers lends negative overtones to the act of music making and to the instruments involved. Grafted onto this earlier paradigmatic symbolism, it is therefore conceivable that the introduction of musical ensembles reminiscent of the Ottoman *mehter* into the Moldavian frescoes, rather than merely reflecting a "cultural novelty," relates to a shift in the symbolism of the "Mocking of Christ" scene itself, a shift that is indicative of contemporaneous Moldavian secular and ecclesiastical politics particularly during the two reigns of Petru Rareş (1527–1538 and 1541–1546).

Scholars have long suggested that contemporaneous ecclesiastical and political views were woven into the iconography of Moldavian frescoes, particularly in the context of the Last Judgment as depicted on the exterior walls of many Moldavian churches during the Rareş regimes (Grabar 1980; Batali 1985). Several groups of people—consistently Jews, Turks and Armenians (monophysites), and sporadically Tartars, Arabs, Catholics (schismatic), and Ethiopians—appear depicted in the upper register of the scene (Plate 6.12). Variously described by scholars as either "ethnic," "national," or "religious" groups, these people line up in the upper register of the scene either already condemned or still in waiting for final judgment (Batali 1985:51–56). The very presence of these groups speaks to the identity of those responsible for the iconographic program, most often high-ranking ecclesiastics or members of the Moldavian aristocracy. The frescoes suggest that, rather than taking root in notions of "national" or "ethnic," the sense of communal identity espoused by these elites was centered on a type of Christian orthodoxism, characteristic of the Moldavian ruling classes, that thus distinguished them from the "other," whether Muslim, Jew, or Christian heretic or schismatic.

Batali (1985) discusses yet another scene whose ideological and political connotations have some bearing upon our interpretation of the instrumental composition of the Moldavian mocking ensembles in the first half of the sixteenth century. The scene appears in the exterior frescoes of several churches and is known as the "Siege of Constantinople." The theme is the Persian siege of the city in 626, yet pictorially, and therefore symbolically, the theme is sometimes historically updated to pertain to the siege of the city by the Ottomans in 1453. Batali remarks that in the fresco at Arbore (1541), by identifying the assailants by their dress as Persians, the artists preserved the historical accuracy of the original siege. At Humor (1535) and Moldoviţa (1537), however, the assailants are dressed as Ottomans who make use of cannons, and as such the scene pertains to the 1453 Ottoman siege of Constantinople. The historical updating of the scene characterizes exclusively those frescoes executed during the first reign of Petru Rareş, when the Moldavian political atmosphere was strongly anti-Ottoman. Arbore, which features the only "historically correct" depiction of the siege by the Persians, was frescoed during his second reign, when Rareş, after having worked out a political compromise with the Ottomans, came to the throne with the support of the Porte. Furthermore, the "Siege" scene is completely absent from the frescoes at Voroneţ. This is probably significant, for the church received its exterior frescoes in 1547, shortly after Rareş' death and during the reign of the turkophile Prince Iliaş (Batali 1985:42–43, n. 7).

The heightened symbolic significance bestowed upon the antagonistic relations already latent in the "Mocking" scene in the first half of the sixteenth century, and particularly during the reigns of Petru Rareş, can be further inferred from the positioning of the scene in the churches' architectural plans. In most of the frescoes executed before and after the first reign of Petru Rareş the "Mocking" scene appears on the narthex absides—Voroneţ (1488), Pătrăuţi (post 1487 or 1497–1499?), Părhăuţi (1495–1497?)—or columns—Suceviţa (1586–1596); even at Bălineşti, although in a more visible position, the scene appears at the western end of the north wall. These various positionings of the scene, while perhaps relevant, are difficult to interpret symbolically. However, at Humor, Moldoviţa, and Arbore, the "Mocking" scene occupies a central and therefore symbolic place. It appears in the middle of the narthex's western wall where the mocked Christ forms the north–south axis of symmetry. In conjunction with its symbolic opposite, the altar's "Communion of the Apostles" scene, it forms the east–west axis of the whole narthex. The increasing symbolism of the scene in some Moldavian frescoes may conceivably extend over its music-iconographic elements as well. One could speculate, therefore, that instruments and ensembles reminiscent of the Ottoman military came to be symbolic of the "Mocking of Christ," an iconographic context that denoted sufferance but promised resurrection, specifically in the highly charged political and ideological environment of late fifteenth- and early sixteenth-century Moldavia.[21]

Pictorial evidence suggests that this symbolism begins to wane shortly after the reigns of Petru Rareş. By the middle of the sixteenth century both the number and the variety of the instruments featured in the "Mocking" scene begin to decrease dramatically, while the rigidity of the iconographic parameters increases proportionally; by the seventeenth century the mocking ensemble becomes nothing but a shadow of its former self. From approximately the middle of the sixteenth century onward, the *zurna*-like instruments completely disappear from the Moldavian frescoes, the kettledrums begin to acquire shapes that conform more to "Western" rather than Ottoman models (at Râşca and Hârlău, for example), and the S-shaped trumpets reminiscent of the Ottoman *boru* often revert to their paradigmatic straight form (Râşca, Hârlău, Suceviţa). This is not symptomatic of a "demusicalization" of Moldavian artistic preferences at large, for while the mocking ensemble gradually loses its music-iconographic richness, ensembles depicted in the symbolically positive context of the Psalms 148–50 and the Wedding of Cana begin to comprise a plethora of instruments, among which are the *davul*, trumpets, and various bowed and plucked string instruments.

Changing artistic practices alone cannot account for these programmatic modifications in the Moldavian music-iconographic spectrum. It is likely that changes in the historical circumstances surrounding the perception of the *mehter* in the Moldavian lands may have had something to do with the new emerging patterns of iconographic choices, as well. Petru Rareş himself, for example, had to accept the presence of Janissaries at his court during his second reign (Sugar 1977:118). This marked the beginning of a diplomatic custom between the principality of Moldavia and the Ottoman Porte that would last for the next several centuries. In the seventeenth century, foreign travelers remarked the presence of "Turkish music" at the court of Moldavian princes. The Moldavian prince Dimitrie Cantemir (1673–1723) wrote in his *Descriptio Moldaviae* (1716) that the Porte traditionally granted a newly confirmed prince like himself a Janissary corps with *mehter* and all, which he called *tabulhanea* (Cantemir 1973:166–69) and described in detail in his later history of the Ottoman Empire (1734–35). It is probably not coincidental, therefore, that the *mehter*'s negative connotations as a mocking ensemble seem to wane shortly after it became an integral part of the Moldavian courtly ceremonial, and gradually lost its exclusive Ottoman referentiality while turning into an emblem of Moldavian princely might.[22]

Autonomous *Davul* and *Zurna* Ensembles

Beginning with the seventeenth century, the music-iconographic details featured in the "Mocking of Christ" scene undergo modifications that are different in nature from those manifest heretofore. No new instruments enter the iconographic instrumentarium of the scene; it seems that the novelty and symbolic value of the Ottoman *mehter* ensemble has run its course. Some of the already familiar instruments, however, begin to coalesce in ensembles not encountered in earlier representations. In several cases, and exclusively in frescoes of churches located south of the Danube, artists chose to bring the *davul* and the *zurna* together in an iconographic self-standing ensemble. Sometimes this instrumental duo is the only music-iconographic component of the "Mocking" scene, such as in the frescoes of the monastic churches at Pustinja near Valjevo and Stragari executed in 1622 and the 1630s, respectively (Pejović 1984:Plates 58 and 62), as well as at the chapel of St. George of the Chilandar monastery painted in 1671 (Pejović 1984:Plate 68). The Pustinja ensemble is particularly noteworthy. It constitutes one of the earliest known depictions of a *davul-zurna* ensemble consisting of TWO *zurna*-s and a *davul*, and it portrays the players holding the instruments in a manner uncannily similar to that of modern practice: the *zurna* is held horizontally at shoulder level and the bell oriented upwards, while the *davul* is suspended on the left shoulder.[23]

From the very beginning of its iconographic existence, however, this ensemble also appears in depictions other than the "Mocking of Christ" scene. In fact, from very early on the *davul-zurna* carries a dual symbolism that is contextually conditioned: in addition to representing a nefarious combination of "mocking music," the *davul-zurna* can also carry celebratory, positive connotations. At times it is an ensemble that participates in the celebrations surrounding the Wedding at Cana, such as in the late sixteenth-century fresco at Morača (Pejović 1984:Plate 42). Often it partakes in the praising of the Lord as witnessed in the representations of the Psalms at Timiou Prodromou in Serres (Anoyanakis 1991:Plate 40) and Dekolou (Plate 6.13), or even in the triumphs of St. George, as in the Radijevič icon (Pejović 1985:132). The connotative ambivalence the *davul-zurna* incurred from the earliest stages of its iconographic inception as either a "mocking" or "celebratory" emblem can be resolved then only in the context of each individual scene; in this regard the ensemble itself is no different from its individual members (see n. 21, above).[24]

Although an adequate assessment of the iconographic dissemination and symbolism of the ensemble would require a sample of seventeenth-century south Balkan frescoes much larger than presently available and than featured in Table 6.1, some provisional hypotheses are in order. Iconographic tradition notwithstanding, the ambivalence of the instrumental symbolism and performative context embedded in the representation of the *davul-zurna* ensemble may ultimately correspond to a gradual transformation of a cultural "other" into a cultural "self" that characterizes the increasing Ottomanization of Balkan urban and, in some cases, village milieus from the seventeenth century onward. It may also correlate to the strengthening of village artistic patronage in the southern Balkans, which may have in turn conditioned the introduction of rural rather than urban musical traditions into fresco iconography. And finally, the emergence of the *davul-zurna* ensemble on the iconographic Balkan stage is contemporaneous with some of the earliest extant mentions of such ensembles by foreign travelers in the area.[25]

There are also some provisional yet interesting parallels that one can draw between the seventeenth-century and modern ensemble. All known iconographic representations, symbolically both positive and negative, come from a region that largely matches that of the modern distribution of the actual musical ensemble: the geographical areas of Serbia and Kosovo, Macedonia, Thrace, and the Peloponnese. Furthermore, in some cases the depicted *davul-zurna* players display characteristic physiognomies that distinguish them from the other participants in the scene (at Pustinja, Dekolou, and Radijević, for example).[26] A possible reading of these iconographic physiognomies, albeit methodologically risky and potentially controversial, is that they *may* be indicative of Romani players. Further research in this direction is badly needed, but if this hypothesis ultimately proves viable, it would bring the iconographic data in line with the modern practice, itself preponderantly associated with Romani musicians.

Concluding Thoughts

Several patterns emerge in respect to the organological details and instrumental composition of the various ensembles depicted in the frescoes that form the sample in Table 6.1. The prototypical ensemble featured in the "Mocking of Christ" scene consists of percussion instruments—the cymbals and a double-headed drum in the earliest representations—wind instruments (the trumpet family), and two soldiers/long-sleeved mockers at Christ's feet. In frescoes later than the fifteenth century one witnesses the emergence of a parallel pictorial tradition, one that relates to the prototype in terms of the families of instruments yet different as far as the instruments proper are concerned. While the survival of the prototypical ensemble is most likely indicative of some artists' adherence to the earlier Byzantine iconographic model, one could speculate that at least some of the changes in its instrumental composition, as carried out by some post-Byzantine artists, may be incumbent upon changes in the music-cultural climate brought about by rising Ottoman political and military power. Many of the alterations to the Byzantine model seem to bring the post-Byzantine composition of the musical ensembles and their organological attributes in closer alignment with Ottoman military musical practices. One can safely assume that Balkan artists became increasingly familiar with these practices especially after the fall of Constantinople in 1453, when the Ottomans strengthened their rule in many of the Balkan provinces, established a number of garrisons, instituted policies concerning population (re)settlement, and initiated military and diplomatic contacts with Romanian principalities. Particularly in the case of the Moldavian frescoes discussed above, grounded in the situational opposition between Christ and the Roman soldiers, the musical component of the "Mocking" scene in post-Byzantine art *may* have become at times symbolic of precisely these historical circumstances. Moreover, when the initial shockwaves of the clash between autochthonous musical traditions and those of the conquerors began to wane, and cultural osmosis was on the rise in certain social quarters, the symbolic ambivalence of the instruments found in iconographic schemata increased proportionally.

The specific modifications that Balkan post-Byzantine artists made to the music-iconographic component of the prototypical "Mocking of Christ" in the first two centuries of the Ottoman rule are manifold: 1) the cymbals—one of the original, "pre-Ottoman" percussion instruments in the iconography of the "Mocking" scene—are gradually replaced by the kettledrum and/or the frame drum; 2) the "updated" S-trumpet is favored, albeit without completely replacing the straight trumpet found in the Byzantine model;[27] 3) the standard mockers become dancers that handle handkerchiefs and/or clappers. Furthermore, as far as the *davul* and *zurna* are concerned, the post-Byzantine tradition positions them in an internally coherent iconographic scenario with strong Ottoman overtones. The available iconographic data indicates that while the double-headed drum is part of the Byzantine model from the late thirteenth century onward, the *zurna*-like instrument is a post-Byzantine addition, for it does not appear in the Balkan frescoes before 1500, and initially not coupled with the double-headed drum in a self-standing duo, but in the context of a *mehter*-like ensemble. It is not until the seventeenth century that the *davul* and *zurna* are iconographically brought together in an independent ensemble, at times in the hands of players who, based on their distinctive clothes or physiognomies, may have been Roma.

This last point corroborates the theory put forth most recently by Rudolf Brandl, who suggests that the *davul-zurna* ensemble entered the Balkan village musical traditions probably sometime in the seventeenth century and through the mediation of the Roma, many of them stationed at the numerous Ottoman garrisons throughout the Balkans (Brandl 1996:16–18). His textual evidence, drawn mainly from travel accounts of the eighteenth and the nineteenth century, in conjunction with the music-iconographic data discussed in the present essay leave little doubt indeed that Ottoman and Romani musical practices historically intersect in the *davul-zurna* domain.

Thus, the critical prerequisite in the dissemination of the ensemble both as representative of the musical life in Balkan villages and as an iconographic motif may well be the presence and distribution patterns of Ottoman garrisons in the Balkans; their presence in a given geographic area would have insured continuous, extended, and more direct contacts between Romani musicians and the Ottoman military, and would have rather quickly become part of the cultural make-up of the painters. The Romani (and to some extent, Turkish) demographic factor is contingent on this Ottoman military presence. The more vigorous dissemination of the actual *davul-zurna* ensemble seems to have historically occurred in the areas that, in addition to Ottoman garrisons, had populations with a significant Romani and Turkish component, which helped bring forth the former as the prevalent performers, and potentially the latter as an initial, amenable audience in sufficient degree to insure the emergence and perpetuation of the tradition outside military confines.

Although this hypothesis requires further study, the iconographic and other types of evidence available thus far seem to provide some support. The *zurna* is not found in any Wallachian frescoes documented thus far—whether alone or in combination with the *davul*, either in the context of a larger group of instruments or as an autonomous ensemble. We have already seen that in Moldavian frescoes the *zurna* appears only in several sixteenth-century scenes, together with the *davul* but always in the context of a larger *mehter*-like instrumental ensemble. In short, there are no known pictorial representations of the independent *davul* and *zurna* ensemble in regions north of the Danube. Moreover, no early travelers through the Romanian principalities mention the ensemble in their writings, and despite a robust Romani presence in the Romanian principalities from late fourteenth century onward both the ensemble and the individual instruments are poorly represented in traditional musical practices in modern Romania, as well (Alexandru 1956:33–35 and 89–91). This music-cultural situation may have been shaped at least in part by the distinctive nature of the political relationship between the principalities and the Ottoman Porte as well as the north Danubian demographic patterns that this relationship engendered.

On the one hand, while military Ottoman music was by the seventeenth century already a component of courtly Moldavian and Wallachian ceremonies, the few extant Ottoman garrisons were situated at the borders of the principalities, and no significant numbers of Turks ever settled on their territories (Sugar 1977:121).[28] On the other hand, as part of the courtly, paid musical retinue, the *mehter* players, by the eighteenth century organized in a *taifa* and led by a *mehter-başa,* were kept separate from the other musical groups at the court such as the Romani slaves, who were string players sometimes trained by Turks.[29] Although a systematic interpretation of the extant documentary evidence has not yet been undertaken, it is conceivable that the stricter regulation of courtly musical activities (manifest, in part, in the clear differentiation existing between *mehter* and "Romani" ensembles, repertoires, and categories of instruments) was not terribly conducive to the formation and proliferation of a *davul-zurna* tradition among Romani musicians in the Romanian principalities. By contrast, their development was perhaps better fostered by the garrison environment of the Ottoman "core European provinces" south of the Danube, where the courts were predominantly Ottoman and there was no local nobility comparable to that in the Romanian principalities. Areas such as Kosovo, Thrace, and geographic Macedonia, which not only benefitted from a large Romani population, but also possessed a large number of Ottoman garrisons and at times, a significant percentage of Turks among the local populace, are precisely where the *davul-zurna* ensemble became a well-established presence both in the traditional musical practices and as an iconographic motif.[30]

Important questions remain: How did differences in the geography of social and demographic composition affect the emergence and dissemination not only of the *davul-zurna*, but also of other instrumental ensembles in the Ottoman Balkans? And to what degree is this embedded in the frescoes? Ultimately, whether and to what extent one can tease out a comprehensive historical narrative, even when more of the pictorial evidence becomes available, remains to be seen. For now, the least that can be asserted is that the frescoes remain by far the richest and visually most pleasing kind of documentation of Balkan bygone musical traditions, and that their careful interpretation affords us a glimpse into the complex web of selective cultural osmoses that took place in the peninsula during the Ottoman era.

Notes

1. This article is part of a larger study of post-Byzantine music iconography in the Balkans; an earlier version was presented at the Annual Meeting of the Society for Ethnomusicology, Toronto, November 2000. Both the early stages of my research and the photographic documentation of a large number of Balkan churches (including some of those discussed in this article) would not have been possible without the generous support of a 1998–1999 American Council of Learned Societies Eastern European Studies Fellowship. I would also like to acknowledge the kind assistance of the following individuals: Ana Bârcă (Directorate of Historical Monuments, Bucharest, Romania), Nada Nováskovska (Zavod i Muzej, Ohrid, FYR of Macedonia), Mirjana Dimovska Colović (Republic Institute for the Protection of the Cultural Monuments, Skopje, FYR of Macedonia), and Vasil Iljov (Zavod za Zashtita na Spomenitsite na Kulturata na Grad Skopje). My warmest thanks to Father Staniša Petrovski for his gracious, jovial, and generous assistance during our trip to Staro Nagoričano and Matejč in the summer of 1998. To all of them, "mulţumesc!" and "благодарам!"

2. After the Second World War, for example, many Romanian musicologists focused their research on those aspects of nineteenth- and twentieth-century musical life and composition that were characteristic of the Romanian upper class and intellectual circles, and that paralleled contemporaneous Western European compositional and aesthetic trends; sweeping histories of "Romanian music" written in the second part of the twentieth century and as of yet not available in any foreign language were very selective in their pre-nineteenth century musical information and relatively cursory in their discussion of the musical practices at the courts of the Romanian principalities during the Ottoman rule (see, for example, Cosma 1973, where the first volume covers the "ancient, old, and medieval" periods up to 1784, while the remaining eight are dedicated to the nineteenth and twentieth centuries). It was mostly scholars of Romanian folklore and ecclesiastical chant such as Tiberiu Alexandru and Gheorghe Ciobanu who explored to any significant extent the predominantly Ottoman courtly and urban musical culture manifest in the Romanian principalities prior to the nineteenth century, primarily insofar as this culture was seen as having informed village or urban musical practices or instruments of the nineteenth and twentieth centuries (see, for example the organological studies of the *nai* [panpipes] and violin in Alexandru 1978:171–196 and 197–238, respectively; see also the collection of essays in Ciobanu 1974b). In part, these scholars were building on a number of nineteenth-century writings by authors such as Burada and Filimon who were historically closer and conceptually more sympathetic to the musical cosmopolitanism characteristic of Romanian cultural life earlier in that century, a cosmopolitanism marked by the coexistence of musical practices strongly affiliated with

either Ottoman or Western European models. For example, the relatively often cited piece of information according to which nineteenth-century *lăutari* used Turkish terms to refer to the strings of the violin (*rast, neva, seba* or *saba*, and again *neva*) was first mentioned by Nicolae Filimon in 1864 (cited among others in Alexandru 1956:130, n. 3; for a plethora of other musical terms associated with Ottoman musical culture and in circulation from the sixteenth century onward in the Romanian principalities, see Ghenea 1965:48–62 and Breazul 1939:53).

3. See, for example, the large collection of accounts by travelers through the Romanian principalities from the fourteenth-century onward published in the monumental *Călători Străini despre Țările Române, 1970–83* (Holban, et al., 1970–83). For an introductory survey of the impressive editorial enterprise undertaken by scholars in various Balkan countries in the twentieth century that resulted in editions, catalogues, and scholarly assessments of an enormous number of historical documents from Ottoman times, see Sugar 1977:289–316.

4. *Pashalŭk*: An Ottoman administrative-territorial unit governed by a pasha. From the perspective of Islamic law, the Romanian principalities were "treaty" territories (*ahd*), occupying an intermediate state between Ottoman borders proper (*dar al-Islam*) and those of its enemies (*dar al-harb*); see Maxim 1998.

5. The status of *vakf* was a category of landed property of a pious foundation (Kiel 1985:61); *derebend* status was granted to villages in dangerous or difficult mountainous areas of the Empire in exchange for their inhabitants guarding the area (1985:93). Kiel's monograph remains one of the most invaluable sources of historical, documentary, and bibliographical information pertaining to the study of art in Bulgarian lands and their limitrophe regions under the Ottomans.

6. The contemporary *davul-zurna* ensemble has been discussed with various degrees of detail and most often from an ethnographic perspective by numerous scholars; see Arbatsky 1953; Cowan 1990:89–133; Hoerburger 1954; Rice 1980, 1982; Silverman 1996b; Trærup 1981; etc. In the present essay I adopt the terms *davul* and *zurna* for convenience.

7. The illumination appears in Rome, Biblioteca Apostolica Vaticana graec. 752, fol. 449v (dated 1059); a color reproduction of the illumination appears as the frontispiece in Seebass 1973 (*Bildband*).

8. London, British Museum, add. 19,354, fol. 191r; a reproduction of the page appears in Der Nersessian 1970:Pl. 107.

9. Patriarchal Library of Jerusalem, Codex Taphou 14, fol. 310v; a color reproduction of the illumination appears in Anoyanakis 1991:40. The double-headed drum appears also in the corresponding scene in other Gregory Nazianzenus manuscripts: Vatican gr. 1947, fol. 146r and Athos, Panteleimon 6, f. 163r; see Braun 1980:318.

10. For a brief, yet informative survey of the monuments frescoed in the Macedonian Paleologan style see Djurić 1995:67–86.

11. "Then the soldiers of the governor took Jesus into the common hall, and gathered unto him the whole band of soldiers/ and they stripped him, and put onto him a scarlet robe / and they spit upon him, and took the reed, and smote him on the head. / And when they had plated a crown of thorns, they put it upon his head,

and a reed in his right hand; and they bowed the knee before him, and mocked him saying, Hail, King of the Jews!"

12. For a detailed study and facsimile reproductions of the illuminations in the Laurentiana Gospel, see Velmans 1971; the "Mocking of Christ" scene appears on fol. 160r (Velmans 1971:Plate 57, fig. 262). The history of the iconography of this scene and the implications of its musical and choreographic details for our understanding of their relations to either Byzantine courtly entertainment or to more archaic, Hellenistic, pictorial models are yet to be fully assessed (see the discussion in Grabar 1928:239–40, esp. n.4). However, in the frescoes of the great majority of Balkan churches, largely predicated upon programs in the Serbo-Macedonian monuments of the fourteenth century, the characters kneeling mockingly in front of Christ—who consistently forms the symmetrical axis of the tableau—belong to two distinct classes: soldiers and/or "jesters" (the latter either long-sleeved characters or dancers, or dancers handling dancing implements). The long-sleeved characters are loosely qualified here as jesters, for although the details of their outfits will be extremely long-lived in the iconography of the scene, their referentiality, precise origin, and function remain to be assessed. Long-sleeved characters appear in sources distant in terms of their geography and chronology. In the fifteenth-century Georgian chronicle of Radzwill (Točkaja and Zajaruznyj 1995:Plate 8), some eleventh-century icons from St. Catherina at Mount Sinai (Weitzmann 1971:Fig. 300), the painted caves–churches at Ivanovo (Bulgaria) (Velmans 1965:Fig. 4 [drawing]), and many examples of the "Mocking of Christ" scene in the frescoes of Balkan churches until late in the seventeenth or even eighteenth century, the characters seem to have a performative function (either dancers or jesters). In an Islamic context, however, dancing Sufi mystics are often depicted with the same clothing detail (see, for example, Denny 1985:Plates 15 and 16).

13. The presence of clappers is not novel in itself; one finds them in the slightly earlier depiction of the "Mocking" scene at Nicholaos Orphanos, for example (see Plate 6.4). In the Lesnovo depiction, however, clappers appear in the hands of a character caught clearly in a dancing pose, and as such they function as dancing accessories rather than just sound-making objects; a dancer provided with clappers appears also in the contemporaneous depiction of Psalm 150 at the Hreljio Tower (Plate 6.5). At Dečani, a church frescoed around the same time as Lesnovo, we find in the "Mocking of Christ" scene yet another type of dancing accessory—a pair of handkerchiefs (Pejović 1984:Plate 11).

14. These include a document from Ragusa (Dubrovnik) issued in 1362 (Petković 1976); the document issued in 1378 by Ivan Shishman (the last Bulgarian tsar) confirming the possessions that Rila monastery had in Kyustendil province (Ilinski 1911, cited in Achim 1998:18); and the Wallachian document issued by Dan I in 1385 (*Documente* B, Vol. 1:19–22).

15. The drummer in the Rome, Vatican gr. 752, fol. 449v, from 1059 (see above) holds in his right hand a beater that appears to have a solid crook head; moreover, the same type of head is quite clearly depicted in the London, British Museum, Add. 19352, fol. 191r (from 1066).

16. See, for example, the W-laced double-headed drum in the often cited 1315 illumination in the Washington, D.C. Freer Gallery of Art, MS 42, fol. 10b, known as "The Clock of the Drummers," from *Kitab fi Marifat al-Hiyal al-Handasiyya* [Book of Knowledge of Ingenious Mechanical Devices], commonly called *Automata* and composed by Badi al-Zaman ibn al-Razzaz al-Jazari (a reproduction appears, for example, in Atil 1981:255, Fig. 1).

17. It is possible that the immediate proximity of the Sveti Nikita church to Skopje may have played a role in music-iconographic choices. Beginning in the 1430s Skopje was rebuilt as a predominantly Muslim city and was populated with a sizeable group of Turkish settlers (Kiel 1985:178–79), facts that would have facilitated an increased familiarity on the part of the local population with Ottoman musical practices (military or otherwise). Moreover, it is worth noting that the name under which the double-headed drum is known in geographic Macedonia, i.e., *tapan* or *tŭpan*, relates to the *derebendjis* founded by the Ottomans in districts with dangerous mountains and woodlands. Muslim in predominantly Muslim areas and Christian in Christian districts, shifts of 30 *derebendjis*, known as *Tapan*, patrolled the passes near their villages equipped with large signal drums and armed with lances and swords (Kiel 1985:83, with further bibliography).

18. By and large, three types of trumpet-like instruments appear in the iconography of the "Mocking of Christ" scene: straight, S-shaped, and looped. The straight shape is the iconographic paradigm. The looped trumpet, called *boru* by the Ottomans and part of the *mehter* ensemble, together with the S-shaped trumpet appears to have entered Balkan iconography only in the sixteenth century.

19. For a description of the instrumental composition of the *mehter* and *mehter-i bîrûn* see Feldman 1996:107–08; and Reinhard and Reinhard 1984:172–76. See also the description of the celebratory ensembles featured in various Ottoman illuminations listed and briefly discussed in Reinhard 1981.

20. The "Mocking" scene at Bijelo Polje clearly represents the *zurna*/*davul*/kettledrum together as a separate, almost self-standing instrumental ensemble.

21. It would be a mistake, however, to consider that the double-headed drum and the *zurna* are at this time consistently invested with negative associations. We should not forget that the double-headed drum had long been featured in Byzantine and post-Byzantine representations of the Psalms, and that it would remain an instrumental component of the "psalm" ensembles well into the eighteenth century. Moreover, although the early depictions of the *zurna* occur in the context of symbolically negative and *mehter*-like ensembles, the instrument is soon introduced in positive contexts, like the scene of the Ark being carried to Jerusalem found at Vaarlam monastery and painted around the mid-sixteenth century by the Cretan artist Frangos Katellanos (for a good reproduction see Anoyanakis 1991:Plate 56).

22. In the context of courtly activities, the *tabulhanea* seems to have had a specific military character, and in addition to being part of the princely suite in celebratory processions, it also performed at sunset for town inhabitants; the term *mehterhanea* seems to have entered the standard vocabulary only by the late

seventeenth century, and usually referred to ensembles performing at noon as well as festivities at the court itself (Ghenea 1965:61). It is still not clear if the later etymological differentiation indicates whether two distinctive ensembles emerged at the Romanian courts only in the late seventeenth century or whether *tabulhanea* was an earlier generic term designating both situations. Nor is it clear that their repertoires were clearly differentiated, although scholars seem to be in relative agreement that the *tabulhanea* pieces were often "songs of the janissaries" while the *mehterhanea* also performed "lyrical pieces" known as *pestrefuri* (or *peşrefuri*), *manele*, *nagmele*, and *taksîmuri* (Ghenea 1965:61; Ciobanu 1974b:108). One has to bear in mind that although scholars tacitly agree that Ottoman musical practices, particularly of a military nature, were an influential factor in shaping the Moldavian and Wallachian courtly musical activities from at least the sixteenth century onward (Ciobanu 1974b:108), most of their studies rely on evidence stemming primarily from the so-called Phanariot rule between 1714 and 1829; the general consensus is that it was during this period that the autochthonous musical and cultural courtly and emergent urban practices were thoroughly "turkified" and "orientalized." (The term Phanariots covers not only the members of powerful Greek families from the Phanar districts in Istanbul that moved to the principalities beginning in the seventeenth century, but also a large number of other Balkan families, by no means all Greek, which made up the retinue and clientele of the leading Phanariots throughout the Empire. It also designates the local, increasingly "turkified" nobility in the Romanian principalities. (For a succinct discussion of the Phanariot period in the Romanian principalities see Sugar 1977:132–41.)

23. For other self-standing ensembles consisting of two *zurna*-s and one *davul*, see Table 6.1. While the iconographic playing position of the *zurna* corresponds to that of modern practice beginning with the earliest known representations of this instrument, that of the double-headed drum varies a great deal. In some depictions (both Byzantine and post-Byzantine), the player uses his left hand rather than a switch—in the present essay I have discussed only those depictions of the double-headed drum played with sticks; customarily, although consistently represented on the left side of the player, the drum hangs on the player's right shoulder and diagonally across his chest. The earliest depiction of the double-headed drum known to me that relates to modern practice, thus positioning the instrument to the player's left and hanging from his left shoulder, is found in the fourteenth-century representation of the Psalms at Hreljio Tower (Rila, Bulgaria); all other similar depictions come from the middle of the sixteenth century, such as the "Mocking" scene at St. George in Banjani near Skopje (Republic of Macedonia), St. Vaarlam monastery at Meteora (Greece), Bijelo Polje (Kosovo), or Novo Hopovo (Serbia).

24. Reinhard (1981:150) describes a similar celebratory function of the autonomous *davul-zurna* ensemble in the context of relatively contemporaneous Ottoman illuminations.

25. In 1658, while in the village of Rača (near Belgrade), the French traveler Quiclet mentions that "they sang songs which are sung in that part of the country and played on bagpipes and oboes beating on drums with a subdued sound. They

played the drum with a kind of curved stick with a carved apple on its end, and a staff which looked like a small mace held in the left hand above the drum" (cited in Djurić-Klajn 1966:139).

26. Even in much later depictions of the "Mocking" scene, one encounters similar physiognomic characteristics; such is the case of the two *zurna* and one *davul* players featured at the church of the monastery St. Naum on the shores of Lake Ohrid, almost on the Albanian border, and painted in 1806 by Terpo, the son of Constantin of Korça (eastern Albania). Machiel Kiel mentions that "the monastery was held in high veneration, not only by the local Christians but also by the Muslim Albanians living in the district around the monastery, members of the dervish order of the Bektashi, who identified Saint Naum as the apostle of their Way of Isalm, Sari Saltik Dede" (Kiel 1985:310, n. 21).

27. Michael Pirker maintains that the oldest evidence of an S-shaped trumpet is from the turn of the fourteenth century and comes from Europe, that there is no Ottoman or Persian iconographic evidence before the middle of the fifteenth century, and that the S-shaped trumpet was imported by the Near East from Europe (Pirker 1993:3–8). Some of the earliest iconographic representations of the S-shaped trumpet in Balkan frescoes date from the sixteenth century.

28. Turks settled in significant numbers only in Dobrogea; it is only in Dobrogea among the Turkish and Tatar population that the *davul-zurna* ensemble, often played by Romani musicians, survives in Romania today; see, for example Alexandru 1956:89.

29. An anonymous German traveler, for example, mentions that at the wedding of the daughter of the Moldavian prince Vasile Lupu in 1652, the groom was received with "military and other musics especially those of the Turks and the Gypsies," and that later in the wedding "the maidens began dancing in the bride's chambers while the Gypsies were strumming their instruments" (". . . la sosirea lui . . . au răsunat muzicile ostăşeşti ca şi celelalte muzici îndeosebi cea a turcilor şi a ţiganilor . . . Fetele au inceput să joace în odaia miresei şi ţiganii zăngăneau din instrumentele lor."); see Holban, et al., *Călători Străini* 1970, Vol. 5:474. Some of these Romani string players may have been conversant in Ottoman (Turkish) musical styles of the time, for at least some of them seem to have been trained by Turks. One of the earliest known documents to mention the musical training of a Romani slave musician by a Turkish *cobuzar* is a donation act from 1578 in which there is mention of "a Gypsy named Opriş with his wife and children who were brought with a lot of effort and expenses by *boyar* Stephen from Turkish lands, from Edirne (Adrianopol) . . . and one of Opriş' sons, namely Stoica, was entrusted to a Turkish *cobuzar* named Curtu who taught him how to play the *cobuz*" (". . .un ţigan anume Opriş cu ţiganca lui şi cu copiii lor, pentru că i-au scos boieriul domniei mele jupîn Ştefan . . .din ţara turcească din cetatea Odriiului cu multă cheltuială . . . , iar pe feciorul lui Opriş ţiganul anume Stoica ei l-au dat la un cobuzar turc anume Curtu de l-au învăţat cu cobuzul . . .") (*Documente* B, Vol. 4:356).

30. I have in mind here the Turks who entered the Balkans as a result of Ottoman-imposed or Ottoman-induced migrations, not the Muslim population resulting from Islamic conversions experienced by various local segments of the

Balkan population. As Maria Todorova observes, population transfers from Anatolia to the Balkans that comprised both nomads and settled groups of peasants and urban dwellers took place primarily during the fifteenth century and stopped by the end of the sixteenth century; in addition to the eastern Balkans, considerable numbers were settled in the Vardar and Maritsa valleys, the two main river routes with strategic importance to the Ottomans, and eastern Thrace. Most of the colonization, therefore, was concentrated in strategic locations around fortified places (Todorova 1996a:63). Whether and to what extent patterns of internal migration within the Empire in general, and the movement of Turks from Anatolia to the Balkans in particular, shaped musical practices of the peninsula are scholarly questions that remain to be addressed.

❖ 7 ❖

Bulgarian Ethnopop along the Old *Via Militaris:* Ottomanism, Orientalism, or Balkan Cosmopolitanism?

Donna A. Buchanan

From antiquity forward the Balkan peoples have been profoundly interconnected economically, politically and culturally.[1] To give but two examples, during the fifth century the Romans established a network of roads linking the major cities of their far-flung empire; this included the *Via Militaris,* which shot across present-day Bulgaria diagonally, joining Constantinople, Edirne, Plovdiv, Sofia, and Belgrade in one continuous sweep. Much later, at various points in the late nineteenth and early to mid twentieth centuries, a Balkan Federation or Balkan Alliance was proposed by Bulgarian leaders, but always without success. Most importantly for this study, recent years have witnessed the cautious establishment of joint regional and international economic, military, and political projects whose inter-alliances may eventually transcend the often polarized ethnic nationalisms that have characterized the region since 1989, if only because most local powers seek NATO and EU membership, which is contingent upon, in part, peaceful relations with one's neighbors. In 1998 alone, some

Table 7.1: Selected Joint Southeast European Initiatives since 1989

Economic Development

◄ *Southeast European Cooperative Initiative (SECI)*, concerned with commerce, enterprise, border crossings, and energy projects

◄ *Central European Free Trade Agreement*, joined by Bulgaria in 1999

Education

◄*Bulgarian-Turkish Education Commission*, est. in 1999 to review the accuracy of history textbooks in both countries

Energy

◄*Trans-Balkan Oil Pipeline*, to range from Burgas (Bulgaria) through Macedonia, Albania (Vlora), and into western Europe, under the direction of **AMBO**, the Albanian-Macedonian-Bulgarian Oil Corporation

◄ *Multiple other energy routes*, to be constructed linking Bulgaria with oil/gas resources in the Caspian basin

Military/Security

◄ *Southeastern European Defense Ministerial*, concerned with regional defense issues

◄ *Multinational Peace Force Southeastern Europe*, deployed under NATO command, a regional defense network (Albania, Bulgaria, Greece, Macedonia, Romania, Slovenia, Turkey) est. in 1998 and based in Plovdiv, Bulgaria

◄ *All-Balkan rapid reaction force*, concerned with regional defense (Albania, Bulgaria, Greece, Macedonia, Romania, Slovenia, Turkey)

◄ *Balkan Stability Pact*, concerned with regional defense (Bulgaria, Romania)

◄ *Signed agreement*, coordinating efforts against smuggling, illegal immigration, money laundering, and financial scams (Bulgaria, Greece, and Romania)

Continued on next page

Table 7.1—Continued

◄ *Action Plan for Southeast Europe*, est. by former President Clinton to battle organized crime and further conflict resolution, economic and political reform, and political, military, and law-enforcement cooperation between the US and Bulgaria, Macedonia, Moldova, Romania, and Slovenia

◄ *NATO's Partnership for Peace program* (inclusive of region, although not Balkan-specific), in association with which Bulgaria hosted international joint military exercises in September 2001

◄ *Organization for Security and Cooperation in Europe* (inclusive of region, although not Balkan-specific)

Transportation

◄ *South Balkan Development Initiative (SBDI)*, directed at upgrading and consolidating regional transportation systems

◄*Trans-Balkan Highway*, to link Durres, Albania with Burgas, Bulgaria

◄ *International highway*, to link Burgas, Bulgaria with Ormenion, Greece

◄ *International highway*, to link Sofia (Bulgaria) and Niš (Serbia)

◄ *Second bridge over Danube River* linking Bulgaria with Romania

---

Sources: Baumgartner 1998a, 1998b, 1998c; Buechsenschuetz 2005; Fuller 1998a, 1998b; Shafir 1998a, 1998b, 1998c, 1998d, 1998e, 1998f, 1998g, 1998h, 1998i, 1998k, 1998l, 1998n; and Vakareliyska 1998.

of the projects under discussion included the South Balkan Development Initiative (SBDI), which seeks to upgrade and consolidate regional transportation systems; the Southeast European Cooperative Initiative (SECI), concerned with commerce and enterprise, border crossings, and energy projects; the Southeastern European Defense Ministerial, which hosts an annual meeting on regional defense issues; and the creation of a multinational regional peace keeping force deployed under NATO command (see Table 7.1 for a more complete list). As my Bulgarian colleague, the ethnomusicologist Tsenka Iordanova, insisted in summer 1996, when Sofia hosted an international conference concerned with regional issues, it was time that the Balkans' citizens be allowed to tender

Balkan solutions for Balkan problems. Only they—not the West—knew what was best for the region.

In this article I assess the extent to which music has further contributed to the construction of Balkan identity from a Bulgarian perspective during the 1990s and first years of the new millennium. As a growing body of recent literature demonstrates, music can tell us something about the making and marking of place.[2] One's sense of emplacement is conceptual; it is cognitively organized in relation to deeply embodied and overlapping multidimensional grids of spatial and temporal orientation. For Edward S. Casey, time and space "come together" in and even "arise from the experience" of place (1996:36–38). They do so through the "gathered" configurations of geographies, historicities, events, and experiences that are a function of any individual's knowledge and that, once imparted, afford place a "cultural character" (1996:24, 34). The perception of place is a dialectical process intricately bound up with senses of self: in Casey's words, "To live is to live locally, and to know is first of all to know the places one is in" (1996:18–19). Or, as the ethnomusicologist Steven Feld poetically remarks, "as place is sensed, senses are placed; as places make sense, senses make place" (Feld 1996:91, quoted in Casey 1996:19). The selection and enactment of particular elements of musical style—choice of a certain percussion pattern, instrument or combination of instruments, scale, ornamentation technique, or performance costume, for example—thus both depends upon and can conjure simultaneously specific moments, sites, events, and experiences that locate, and indeed animate musicians and listeners within matrices of human relations inscribed in memory and evocative of place. Moreover, the act of musical performance can powerfully generate meanings and sentiments that do not just reflect, but reinforce, manipulate, satirize, transform, or transcend the social orders and boundaries borne by the conjured phenomena (Stokes 1994:4).

With this preamble in mind, I wish to examine how the Balkans have been imagined or represented sonically through recent popular culture and how these musical imaginaries have contributed to Bulgarian "senses of place" within Europe, southeastern Europe, and the Balkans themselves, in the post-state socialist era (Feld and Basso 1996). My focus is ultimately transregional or "interlocal" rather than transnational; although the genres I consider draw upon an array of international sources, sometimes in international contexts with global implications, my research suggests that their significance relates largely to domestic and regional issues of place, power, and production.

Bulgarian Ethnopop and the Oriental

The contents of this volume amply illustrate that several contemporary Balkan popular musics display remarkable similarities which, like the regional initiatives noted above, indicate the presence of a growing Balkan geopolity and concomitantly, an emergent popular music circuit extending from southeastern Europe through Greece and Turkey (and perhaps even into the Arab Mediterranean). I see Bulgaria's position within this larger circuit as associated with two discourses: 1) a musical discourse of Arabo-Turkish instrumentation, vocal delivery, melodic constructs, rhythm, and choreography, often filtered through Romani performance practice; and/or 2) a metaphorical discourse of Ottomanism and orientalism exhibited through the imagery of attendant music videos and marketing materials. To demonstrate how these discourses intersect I will examine two Bulgarian music trends popular since about 1990: the amorphous ethnopop category dubbed loosely as *pop-folk*, and within this, the controversial Bulgarian-Romani-Turkish dance music genre called *chalga* with which it was nearly synonymous during the years pertinent to my study; and secondly, recordings by professional women's folk choirs marketed by Elektra/Asylum/Nonesuch and Jaro Records as *Le mystère des voix bulgares*.[3] My analysis will show that these two trends exist in a complex inversional relationship that pivots around orientalist representations of gender and voice. Said differently, in regard to gender and voice, we might regard these two trends as representing flip sides of the same orientalist coin.

Defining Bulgarian Ethnopop

Ethnopop represents only one part of a diverse Bulgarian popular music scene that also includes Euro-American style rock and pop by foreign and domestic bands, some of which contains politically sensitive texts that speak to social issues related to the transition's agonies; and imported ethnopop from Bosnia, Greece, the Republic of Macedonia (hereafter "Macedonia"), Serbia, and Turkey (see Table 7.2). Its contents are quite complex, embracing the jazz-oriented wedding music made famous internationally by Ivo Papazov and his wedding orchestra in the 1980s, and various styles of popular music that incorporate elements of *narodna muzika* [folk, traditional, or "people's" music] to varying degrees.

Table 7.2: The Bulgarian Commercial Music Scene, 1990–2000

- **Classical Music**
    - Bulgarian
    - Euro-American

- **Orthodox Religious Music**

- **Folk Ensemble Repertory**
    - Large professional ensembles
    - "Le mystère des voix bulgares" choirs, derived from professional ensemble personnel
    - Small folk music groups, like Bŭlgari, derived from professional ensemble personnel

- **Popular Music**
    - **Euro-American Rock/Pop/Rap**
        - Foreign bands
        - Bulgarian bands
    - **Imported Ethnopop from Other Balkan Locales**
        - **Greek *laika***
        - **(Yugoslav NCFM; Bulg. *"Yugo-folk"*)**
            - Bosnia
            - Macedonia
            - Serbia
        - **Turkish *arabesk***
    - **Euro/American Pop Music Using Bulgarian Musical Elements**
        - Kate Bush
    - **Bulgarian Ethnopop**
        - **Rock songs with ethnic styling**
            - Use of indigenous instruments, musical gestures, as color
            - Pop/rock rooted in traditional music *gestalt*
        - **Pop, disco, and techno remakes of earlier folk ensemble repertory**
            - Performed almost exclusively by former professional folk ensemble artists
        - **Wedding music (*Svatbarska muzika*)**

Continues next page

- *Pop-folk*
  - *Chalga* (**Bulgarian-Romani-Turkish ethnopop;** *"Kristal," "Folk"*)
  - **"Authored Macedonian songs"** or **"Pirin folk songs"**

Domestic rock bands began utilizing indigenous instruments and vocal polyphony in the late 1980s to imbue their otherwise universal pop sound with a distinctive Bulgarian edge. In their 1994 release *Zhivot sled smŭrtta* [Life after death], for instance, the group Atlas interweaves the *gaida* [bagpipe] playing of Nikola Atanasov, who was employed by the folk orchestra of Bulgarian National Radio for many years, into an otherwise conventional rock ballad (CD 7.1).[4] Other artists, such as Nona Iotova and Ivan Lechev, have produced newly composed pop songs rooted in a *narodna muzika* gestalt and which sometimes also use traditional texts or tunes. *Mitana,* a cut from their mid-1990s album *Omana,* is sung by Iotova in the style of a typical, slow-moving, unpulsed ballad from the Rhodope ethnographic region of southern Bulgaria (CD 7.2). Its heterophonic, multi-track, studio-manipulated electric guitar accompaniment is meant to emulate, according to the cassette's liner notes, the unique ensemble of one hundred large Rhodope bagpipes (*kaba gaidi*) that first performed at the regional folk festival "Rozhen Sings" (*Rozhen Pee*) in 1961.

Pop, disco, and techno remakes of well-known arrangements previously popularized by state-sponsored folk ensembles constitute a third ethnopop category. In some cases, leading pop artists such as Georgi Hristov have adopted favorite songs like *Devoiko, mome hubavo* [Girl, beautiful girl], originally scored by composer Philip Kutev and performed by the folk choir of his National Ensemble for Folk Songs and Dances, to more contemporary accompaniments (see also Buchanan 2006a). On his recent album *Karuzo* [Caruso], Hristov sings this Rhodope song in a traditional manner, decorating the melody with numerous stylistically appropriate ornaments, but substitutes electric organ for the more customary bagpipe (*kaba gaida*) accompaniment. Despite this innovation, the general aesthetic preference for a dense, droning, diaphonic sound indicative of much Bulgarian traditional music is still apparent.

In other cases these covers are performed by artists currently or formerly associated with professional folk ensembles, frequently in a disco folk or techno folk style that lays the often unmodified traditional melody over a synthesized, electronic percussion track. In 1991, Traki, a trio of musicians then employed by the Bulgarian Radio's folk orchestra, produced an instrumental version of *Devoiko, mome hubavo* in disco format (Buchanan 2006a). Numerous other ensemble personnel released similar arrangements in the 1990s, including Yana Minkova, Tanya Velichkova, Daniel Spasov, Vladimir Kuzov, and Snezhana Borisova.[5] This particular fad, which began in the late 1980s among members of the Bulgarian Radio's folk ensemble, originally represented their attempt to win young listeners away from contemporary wedding music, which then enthralled the public (cf. Buchanan 1995, 2006a; Rice 1994). Its continuation and expansion in the 1990s exemplify a similar effort by professional ensemble performers to carve out an ethnopop niche for themselves that might compete with *pop-folk*. In the newly privatized music industry, it is those performers of neo-traditional pop, never formally trained within the state system of folk music education, who have earned public acclaim and financial profit. By contrast, professional folk ensemble personnel are engaged in an expressive form that holds less appeal for the general public and is comparatively poorly funded. These artists have therefore looked for new creative ventures beyond the ensemble sphere to supplement their incomes and professional aspirations.

Within the *pop-folk* category, the newly composed songs of Pirin-Macedonia (southwestern Bulgaria), known formally as "authored Macedonian songs" and more colloquially as "Pirin songs" or "Pirin folk songs," arose in the early 1990s in conjunction with two regional festivals called Pirin Fest and Pirin Folk. The stylistic range of such songs is broad; in general, however, they may be defined as light pop songs about love, family, emigration, and the landscape of the Macedonian region, both in southwestern Bulgaria (Pirin) and the Republic of Macedonia.[6] They are often sung in parallel thirds or sixths to lyrical melodies, some of which make use of scale types, melodic gestures, and meters or rhythmic patterns indicative of the Macedonian region and Turkey, and others which recall the ballroom-dance culture of early twentieth-century urban life. Accompaniments feature symphonic instruments (clarinet, saxophone, trumpet, and sweetly bowed strings), accordion, indigenous Macedonian instruments (*tambura, tarambuka, tŭpan*), synthesizers, electronic drums, electric guitar, and electric bass in a wide variety of combinations. While I discern relationships between each of the genres described thus far, in this article I will address only the historical and stylistic junctions between *chalga*; Balkan Romani musicianship; Yugoslav NCFM, or what some Bulgarians call *Yugo-folk*; its Serbian successor, *turbo folk*; and Turkish *arabesk,* focusing especially on the years 1990–2000.

From *Kristal* to *Chalga*

When it emerged ca. 1992–93, the genre referred to now (2005) as *pop-folk* or *chalga* by the Bulgarian public lacked a single label. A few friends in Sofia initially termed it *kristal* in relation to two popular bands: Orchestra Kristal, from Yambol, and Orchestra Kristali, based in Montana (formerly the city of Mihailovgrad). Orchestra Kristal's director, Krasimir Hristov, produced every aspect of the band's recordings in his own studio, which may also account for how its name came to signify the genre (Dimov 1995:16). These two bands helped inspire the formation of myriad other groups whose recordings, like those of Kristal and Kristali them-selves, incline toward a regionally amalgamated sound, thus defying easy categorization. In the mid 1990s, Bulgarian friends, scholars, musicians, and the press described them according to a range of factors, including performance context ("pub" or "tavern music"), ethnicity ("Romani folklore"), mass-mediated mode of dissemination and commercial popularity ("top folk," "folk hits"), era ("contemporary folklore"), style ("oriental music"), and place ("all-round Balkan music" and "Balkan folklore") (Table 7.3). The large-scale, diffuse nature of these labels, which also subsumed some types of *Pirin folk* song, reveals the emergent nature of Bulgarian ethnopop at this time.

Even at this early stage, when asked to define this emergent ethnopop style, musicians and non-musical friends alike pointed to its relationships with other regional trends. In particular, they insisted that it derived primarily from Serbian ethnopop prototypes, where "Serbian" functioned as a gloss for the larger spectrum of Yugoslav NCFM and later, for its edgier, more electrified, 1990s Serbian derivative, *turbo folk*.[7] They never spoke of Bosnian or Croatian NCFM in this context, although this, too, existed at the time, perhaps because in the 1980s Serbia produced the majority of NCFM recordings, regardless of the music's point of origin (Ceribašić 1995:94). Because most Bulgarians understand Bosnian/Croatian/Serbian language and many consider Serbs their "brothers," to quote one musician, it was hardly surprising that *Yugo-folk*'s star performers became Bulgarian favorites during these years. Although closed in September 1998 on charges of CD piracy, the Sofia-based SMC recording company was licensed exclusively to produce Serbian music (Shafir 1998j). A friend stressed that people preferred Serbian ethnopop because it was simultaneously "more Western" than anything produced locally, and yet, "closer to home." Moreover, the lyrics were better. "They are real," she said; "they can touch you—they aren't false" or "mechani-cally done" like the arrangements performed by folk ensembles. In fact,

Bulgarians embraced Serbian music to such an extent that, according to Ljerka Vidić Rasmussen, Bulgarian bands from Vidin and Sofia began performing *Yugo-folk* for Serbian audiences in Serbia during the early 1990s with good success, as well as in Bulgarian venues (1995:247, p.c., October and December 1998).

Although Bulgarian *pop-folk* performers may not be formally trained in the terminologies and principles of Turkish or Arab music theory, they are adept at employing some of its constructs. Like contemporary *Yugo-folk*, *pop-folk* combines synthesizers and drum machines with a collage of Mediterranean elements: Turkish scale types (*makamlar*; sing. *makam*) and melodic motifs, characteristic rhythmic cycles (*usulleri*; sing. *usûl*) or patterns, and ornamentation. Like many Arab musicians, a few bands simulate the timbres of indigenous Middle Eastern instruments electronically (cf. A. Rasmussen 1996). Wailing, virtuosic, solo instrumental introductions and interludes, usually played by reeds or synthesizer, recall both Middle Eastern improvisations (*taksim*-s) and to a lesser extent, solo moments in Bulgarian wedding music. Interestingly, electric guitar, such an icon of Euro-American pop, does not seem to figure prominently as a

Table 7.3: *Pop-folk* Idioms

Classifier	Bulgarian Description	English Translation
Performance Context	*Krŭchmarska muzika*	Pub/Tavern music
	Kafanska muzika	Café music
Ethnicity	*Rom folklor*	Romani folklore
	Chalga	*Chalga*
Mass-Mediated Dissemination	*Top folk*	Top folk
	Folk hitove	Folk hits
	Pop folk; Pop-folk	Folk pop
Era	*Sŭvremenen folklor*	Contemporary folklore
Musical Style	*Orientalna muzika*	Oriental music
Dance Style	*Kyuchek, Čoček*	*Kyuchek, Čoček*
Place	*Obshta balkanska muzika*	All-round Balkan music
	Balkanski folklor	Balkan folklore
	Orientalna muzika	Oriental music

solo instrument in either *Yugo-folk* or *pop-folk,* although bass lines are common, whether performed on electric bass or synthesizer (L. Rasmussen, p.c., 11 October 1998).[8] Thus while use of Western music technology may signify modernity or the embrace of generic pop culture attributes, in this case they have been given a Balkan stamp. The songs' texts, which principally address romantic relationships, are in Bulgarian or Romani.

Bulgaria's proximity to the Mediterranean and *Yugo-folk*'s popularity may well account for *pop-folk*'s Middle Eastern elements. In addition, Greek pop and *arabesk* have been openly sold in Bulgaria since at least 1992, providing easy access to other Mediterranean styles. The advent of satellite TV in urban centers, at least, in the late 1990s also brought Turkish Radio and Television (TRT) music programs directly into Bulgarian living rooms. Yet as the introduction to this volume details, a strong historical precedent for Ottoman-inspired syncretic urban musics performed with mixed indigenous, Middle Eastern, and West European instrumentation exists in the Balkans. Romani music professionals, who have popularized numerous local styles and tunes—including Turkish-derived repertory—throughout the area since at least the 1800s, whether in restaurant bands or contemporary wedding orchestras, represent another crucial avenue of circulation, leading Bulgarian ethnomusicologist Ventsislav Dimov (1995:14) to consider them the "original intermediary, translator, and integrator between the Balkan's separate musical languages." Likewise, Svanibor Pettan (1996b:35) describes Romani musicians as the primary contributors to the formation of a "Balkan *Musikschatz,*" or music vocabulary resulting from decades of influence and counter-influence amongst the Balkan peoples, which includes an array of similar ensembles and a corpus of shared tunes, albeit performed in regionally specific styles and with locally specific significances.

An advertisement published in the magazine *Folk Panair* (Vol. 4, 1994:43) for a new, annual juried festival called *Trakiya folk* [Thrace folk], held in Dimitrovgrad, 7–10 September 1994, reveals what the label "Balkan folklore" denotes from a Bulgarian perspective. Interested musicians, including foreigners, were invited to contend in either of two categories for prizes ranging from 10,000 to 50,000 *leva* (see Dimov 1994b:6): "Thracian folkore," for those groups whose composed repertory was based on styles from Bulgaria's Thracian ethnographic region; and "Balkan folklore," for those whose repertories derived from "music and songs of the Balkan peoples, including composed repertory built on Greek, Macedonian, Turkish, Serbian, and Gypsy melodies and rhythms." The two categories were deemed mutually exclusive; performers could compete in both, but had to prepare two completely different programs.

Similarly, on its "Folk-Top-Shop" ratings page (a "top ten" forum akin to contemporaneous "Top [Fashion] Model" competitions), *Folk Panair* listed "Balkan Folklore" (*Balkanski folklor*) as a category embracing Serbian, Greek, Macedonian, and Turkish music, including leading *arabesk* artists such as İbrahim Tatlıses, among others.[9]

Like the members of Orchestra Kristali, many performers of *pop-folk*—Bulgaria's contribution to the new "Balkan folklore"—are Roma, while others are of Slavic or Turkish extraction. In fact, *pop-folk*'s popularity accompanied a post-1989 upsurge in the overall visibility of Bulgarian Romani music and culture characterized by formal attention to Romani politics, several Romani music festivals, Romani social affairs such as balls, several audio and video recordings of Romani rap, popular songs, and brass band music, and the return of Romani bear and monkey trainers to city streets (Plate 7.1).[10] At the same time, *pop-folk*'s stylistic compass broadened to embrace songs, instrumentals, and dance tunes associated more and more directly with Romani-Turkish genres such as the *kyuchek* and *çiftetelli* (Bulg. *chiftetelli*), to which I return below. Other European Romani influences, such as the pseudo-*flamenco* style indicative of the Gipsy Kings, as well as occasional Greek flavoring, also became apparent (see also Kurkela, this volume). By the late 1990s, the definitive role played by Romani musicians, genres, and dance styles in shaping Bulgarian ethnopop prompted audiences to dub the genre *"chalga,"* a tangled term whose lengthy history is steeped in associations with Romani-Turkish culture.

Chalga: Bulgaria's Musical Orient

The Bulgarian terms *chalga* and *chalgiya,* which during my fieldwork in the late 1980s and early 1990s were employed more or less as synonyms, derive from the Turkish *çalgı,* meaning musical instrument and instrumental music. Both are related to similar terms used by neighboring populations, such as *çallgi,* found among North Albanians residing in the former Yugoslavia, and *čalgija* (identical to *chalgiya,* but transliterated differently), found among Macedonians and Kosovo Roma (Pettan 1996b; Rice 2000:979; Sugarman 2000:997).[11] Historically, *çallgi* and *čalgija* referred to urban ensembles of mixed Turkish and symphonic (clarinet, violin, accordion) instrumentation that arose in the late Ottoman period and flourished through the WWII era. The instrumentalists in such groups were largely Romani professionals, and their repertories included Ottoman

Turkish folk tunes, performed in the languages of the many ethnic groups found in the surrounding area. These were rendered in a manner that reflected the Romani emphasis on continual innovation: heterophonically, with much individual variation within each melodic phrase and between repetitions of the same phrase, a trait perhaps adopted from the Ottoman Turks or Mediterranean region at large; virtuosically, with the stylistic fluidity and technical fluency born of performing music professionally day in and day out for years on end; and extemporaneously, incorporating metric and non-metric solo improvisations resembling, if not de facto, the *taksim*-s of Turkish musical practice. *Čalgija* musicians embellished melodies extensively with ornaments also derived largely from Turkish idioms, including pitch bending, glissandi, mordents, grace notes, timbral nuances, and turns, among others. Such groups played for family celebrations (weddings, circumcisions) and in the numerous *kafana*-s (cafés) central to town social life. Thus through the performance practice of *čalgija* ensembles, musical notions of Romani-ness, Turkishness, and urbanity became conceptually, and to a large extent, aesthetically fused.

    While it is not clear if Bulgarians used the term *chalgiya* to indicate a similar ensemble, by the late 1800s they did employ the term *chalgadzhiya* (pl. *chalagadzhii*; derived from the Turkish *çalgıcı*, or instrumentalist) to denote a similar class of urban semi-professional musicians who performed village and urban songs or dances of Bulgarian Slavs, local ethnic minorities, neighboring Balkan peoples, and even Western European ballroom dances at all manner of celebrations.[12] As elsewhere, many of these instrumentalists were Roma, whose eclectic repertory was facilitated by their interaction with other small bands of foreign musicians from Serbia, Romania, Turkey, and Macedonia also active in Bulgarian towns during this time. Both types of ensembles were frequently hired to provide nightly entertainment in pubs, taverns, restaurants, cinemas, and other commercial venues between the World Wars, when they became known as salon orchestras—key players in what socialist academics would later call "tavern folklore" or "urban folklore." With the advent of radio in the 1930s such groups gave rise to two other small formations: trios and quartets of indigenous instruments (early "folk orchestras"), and similarly sized groups of Western European instruments, often clarinet, accordion, violin, and bass, called "modern orchestras." Both eventually performed for state-sponsored folkloric productions as well as at local celebrations and restaurants; they were featured frequently on radio broacasts and also appear on numerous early recordings issued by Western European and Bulgarian labels (Brody 1998:1). Under socialism, those modern orchestras that played at taverns and eateries, especially, were dubbed "restaurant bands" and represent a direct extension of the earlier salon orchestras.

Throughout this period of development the term *chalga* remained associated with urban professional instrumentalists of minority extraction, and with the virtuosic, improvisatory, soloistic or heterophonic playing style that often characterized their musicianship. In the 1980s, however, *chalga* gained further significance in the context of a new grassroots tradition called wedding music (*svatbarska muzika*) whose performers—predominantly Roma and ethnic Turks—banded together in small "wedding orchestras" (*svatbarski orkestri*). Such groups, which represent a late twentieth-century transmutation of modern orchestras, restaurant bands, and their *chalgadzhii* predecessors, were initially decried by the socialist government because they operated outside the sanctioned, institutionalized channels of state folklore and blended Bulgarian tunes with aspects of other Balkan musics and Western popular culture in a manner administrators and scholars feared would sully the alleged "purity" of Bulgarian tradition. Nevertheless, by the mid 1980s wedding orchestras had gained tremendous public popularity, eventually winning governmental support with the advance of political transition.

Wedding orchestra instrumentation was, like that of earlier urban groups, eclectic and variable, but typically combined clarinet and/or saxophone, accordion and/or synthesizer, electric bass, electronic drums, and a vocalist. Other bands incorporated violin and even indigenous instruments such as *kaval* or *gŭdulka.* Such orchestras performed lengthy renditions or medleys of Bulgarian, Romani, Serbian, Turkish, and other Balkan songs and dance tunes at weddings (hence their name) and other social gatherings. Importantly, improvisation was a key component of such performances; wedding musicians were technical virtuosos whose jazzy settings of horos, executed at blistering tempos and, in contradistinction to early twentieth-century practices, in a precise rhythmic unison extraordinary in its attention to the smallest ornamentational detail, also featured solo improvisations by all band members rendered in a range of styles, from non-metric, modal *taksim*-s to highly measured, heavily arpeggiated passages cycled through complex progressions of chromatic harmonies.

Because of wedding music's association with minority culture, the transnational nature of its repertory and instrumentation, and the nature of its performance practice, in everyday conversation *chalga* came to signify Romani-Turkish musicianship generally, the wedding music genre specifically, and especially, the latter's improvisational passages. For academics and administrators concerned with wedding music's impact on the remnants of village-style music-making, it was also, in the words of one friend, "a coarse, ugly word" with racial implications connected to the rejection of Muslim, Turkish, and Romani influences in Bulgarian Slavic culture by socialist state institutions. For wedding music fans, the genre represented a home-grown form of Bulgarian popular music that contrasted sharply with state-sponsored traditions in almost every way imaginable. For the State, however, it alluded to a Turkish Orient whose legacy in Bulgarian culture was, at the very least, aesthetically problematic.

Given this historical background, it is not difficult to understand how *chalga* came to signify Bulgarian ethnopop of the 1990s; during this time the genre was often performed by Romani and ethnic Turkish musicians, and even when Bulgarian Slavs were involved, the predominant performance style was Romani-Turkish.[13] As noted above, *chalga*'s stylistic palette encompasses dance rhythms rooted in Romani and/or Turkish precedents. The most prevalent of these is *kyuchek,* with which 1990s *chalga* became nearly synonymous.

Kyuchek

Kyuchek (Serbian, Croatian, and Macedonian *čoček,* among other variants) derives from the Turkish *köçek* (pl. *köçekler),* which referred to a professional male entertainer predominantly of Jewish, Armenian, or Greek, but also of Romani heritage, who danced to accompanying music called *köçekce* for imperial celebrations at the Ottoman court (Feldman 2002:115; Popescu-Judetz 1982:46; Seeman 2002:138). Such dancers, which were one of several classes of entertainers organized into guilds during the Ottoman period, usually performed outside with an "outdoor ensemble" (*mehter-i birûn*) of mixed instrumentation (*zurna, panpipes, santur, daire,* small kettledrums) whose repertory was based in the *makam* system. *Köçekler* were also cross-dressers who adopted "long hair, jewelry, and women's clothes," and occasionally engaged in prostitution (And 1976:136, 139; Feldman 2000:7–21, 2002:116; Öztürkmen 2002: 812).[14]

The female equivalents of the *köçekler* were the *çengîler* (sing. *çengî*), professional dancers who performed at the court as well as inside aristocratic Ottoman homes as early as the 1500s, and who were associated with harems (Feldman 2002:115; Öztürkmen 2002:812). Their name derives from the *çeng,* a harp that originally accompanied their dancing, but which became extinct by the late 1600s (Feldman 2002:115).[15] The ethnicity of those *çengiler* employed by the court prior to the nineteenth century is disputed; they may have included Romani women, but they may also have been largely Circassian or Georgian (Seeman 2002:139–43). Those working outside the court guilds at this time almost certainly included Roma. Although scholars disagree about the exact nature of *çengî* and *köçek* choreography, it is likely that their dances involved artful, delicate undulations of the upper body, extended arms, and hands requiring muscular flexibility and control, self-accompanied with finger cymbals, wooden clappers, or frame drum—a predecessor of the contemporary "bellydance" (cf. And 1976:139–46; Feldman 2002:115; Öztürkmen 2002:812; Sugarman 2003:92).

As a consequence of various social and economic changes, the Ottoman state eventually banned both the *köçekler* and *çengîler* in the mid 1800s, and local Romani musicians soon filled the niche vacated by these entertainers (And 1976:141; Feldman 2002:116). Although Walter Feldman (2002:116) maintains that these Roma created "new, mainly improvisational music and choreography" that became popularized amongst the lower classes of all Ottoman religious communities, in Macedonia it seems that Roma embraced some form of the older dance genres as their own; there *čoček* signified a similar dance, but one performed primarily by Romani women for their own entertainment at gender-segregated community celebrations (weddings, circumcisions, christenings). In fact, according to the ethnochoreologist Elsie Dunin (1971:324, 1973:193, 195), until the 1970s Macedonian Roma considered it poor taste for women to dance *čoček* publicly, or in gender-integrated groups (see also Silverman 2003:122–25). Although young Romani girls locally called *čočeci* were occasionally employed by *kafana*-s to dance for non-Romani, primarily male audiences, this was not the norm.

By the 1990s Romani women danced *čoček* much more publicly and with fewer gender segregation restrictions (2003:128). One reason for this change might be that by the late 1980s, an increasingly erotic and sinuous rendition of *čoček* was becoming a central component of both *Yugo-folk* and Bulgarian wedding music repertories, musically and choreographically. At the national wedding music festival held in Stambolovo in 1988, for example, I saw police caution audience members against dancing *kyuchek* while listening to a concert by Ivo Papazov's band, Trakiya, at that time the leading exponent of the wedding music style. Those attempting to dance were forced to sit down. Importantly, through these two popular music genres *čoček/kyuchek* dancing was embraced, and to some extent practiced, by local Slavic populations, as well as minority groups.

Both in Macedonia and Bulgaria Roma have typically danced
čoček/kyuchek to melodies and *taksim*-like solo improvisations (called
mane in Macedonia) that are rooted in the pitch content and stock motives
of a particular *makam*, over rhythmic ostinati characterized by a variety of
meters or rhythmic modes. Amongst Macedonian Roma, 9/8 (subdivided
2–2–2–3), 7/8 (3–2–2), and 8/8 (3–3–2) prevail, while Bulgarian Roma
typically utilize 8/8 (3–3–2), a pattern they identify as *Turksi kyuchek*
[Turkish *kyuchek*], and 9/8 (2–2–2–3), which they call *Tsiganski kyuchek*
[Gypsy *kyuchek*] (Silverman 2000b:282).[16] In *Yugo-folk* repertory one
encounters songs with a *čoček* groove based in any of the three Macedonian meters, generally enhanced by at least one *taksim*-like improvisation
(an instrumental "break") between verses. Bulgarian *chalga* of the 1990s
features similar dance songs with similar *taksim* breaks, but also lengthy
instrumental improvisations utilizing the meters of "Turkish" and "Gypsy"
kyuchek, performed largely by electronic instruments (CD 7.3).[17]
Moreover, in my experience, Bulgarian *chalga* pieces identified as
kyuchek may use still other Middle Eastern rhythmic cycles, such as the
Arab *iqa' ayyūb*, whose duple-meter framework works well in a pop
music context (Fig. 7.1).[18] In other words, in an ethnopop context *kyuchek*
as musical genre seems as much about the accompanying dance as the
underlying rhythm, although syncopation seems to be a significant feature
of the *kyuchek* groove, whichever rhythmic mode is employed. Bulgarian
ethnomusicologists Lozanka Peicheva and Ventsislav Dimov (2002:136)
summarize this relationship succinctly, observing simply that "*chalga* is
danced as *kyuchek.*"

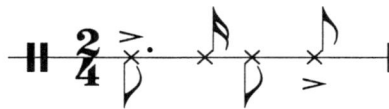

Figure 7.1: The *ayyūb* rhythmic mode

For example, in an additional link with Turkish culture, Bulgarian
chalga artists sometimes employ the rhythmic pattern *çiftetelli* (Fig. 7.2),
whether beneath a *taksim* between verses of a song or as an entire
instrumental composition (CD 7.4). Like *kyuchek*, the *çiftetelli* is a
Turkish dance performed by individuals with arms outstretched at chest
or shoulder height; its choreography may entail spinning slowly in place
with upturned head and eyes partially closed, shifting body weight from
one foot to another, and shaking or gyrating the shoulders, upper body,

and hips (Stokes 1992a:197, 202). Whether in the context of contemporary Turkish *arabesk* or Bulgarian *chalga*, *çiftetelli* performance, like that of *kyuchek,* may take on an erotic character not unrelated to the orientalist stereotypes surrounding bellydance.

Figure 7.2: The *çiftetelli* rhythmic mode

Arabesk *and Other Turkish Influences*

From *makam* to *taksim* to rhythmic modes, to dance styles, Bulgarian *chalga* performers have clearly cultivated relationships with Turkish musical culture, whether resulting from direct contact with Turkish musicians and styles like *arabesk*, or more oblique influence attributable to Romani performance practice, wedding music, or *Yugo-folk.* Yet another connection can be found in song lyrics which, although written in Bulgarian and/or Romani, may incorporate Turkish words. While most address romance or contemporary social issues, a few, like Ivo Barev's *Akh, badzhanak, badzhanak* [Och, brother-in-law, brother-in-law], also treat Turkish topics (Fig. 7.3).

Akh, badzhanak, badzhanak,[19]	Och, brother-in-law, brother-in-law,
vtasakhme ya s tebe pak.	now we're in for it again, you and I.
Za tozh chuden Istanbul,	About this miraculous Istanbul,
po dobre da ne byakh chul.	better that I never heard of it.
Uzh doidokhme na pazar,	We were to go to the market,
a stanakhme darmadar[20]	but became completely ruined instead.
Istanbul—Abanas Sokak,[21]	Istanbul—Ebony Street,
badzhanak, vtasakhme ya pak.	brother-in-law, now we're in for it again.
S pŭlni chanti s bagazh,	With bags filled with luggage,
s doichimarki za kurazh,	with deutschemarks for courage,
Za tozh chuden Istanbul, etc.	About this miraculous Istanbul, etc.

S kadŭnki hubavi,[22]	With beautiful Turkish women,
uzh zhivyakhme dva, tri dni.	we lived two, three days.
Za tozh chuden Istanbul, etc.	About this miraculous Istanbul, etc.
Akh, badzhanak, badzhanak,	Och, brother-in-law, brother-in-law,
kak shte se pribirem pak?	How will we go home again?
Akh, badzhanak, pomisli,	Och, brother-in-law, brother-in-law,
kak shte lŭzhem tez zheni?	How will we lie to these women (wives)?
Za tozh chuden Istanbul, etc.	About this miraculous Istanbul, etc.

Figure 7.3: *Akh, badzhanak, badzhanak.* Composed, sung, and arranged by Ivo Barev. From *Ivo Barev: S Imeto na Bog* [With the name of God]. Unison Stars and Vega-M, n.d.

Other artists perform covers of Turkish, Serbian, Albanian, or Greek songs, adding new Bulgarian or Romani texts. For example, in 1993 the Bulgarian Romani band Dzhipsi Aver [Gypsy Friend] produced a new rendition of the song *Čaje šukarije* (here *Chshae shukarie*; Beautiful girl) on their *Dzhipsi Rap* release. Initially made famous by the Macedonian Romani vocalist Esma Redžepova, the song was also recorded by the Albanian singer Merita Halili.[23] Like the original, Dzhipsi Aver's version is sung in Romani, but interpolates an innovative barrage of rap text against a stylistic backdrop displaying the influences of rock, rap, wedding music, and Romani-Turkish clarinet playing (CD 7.5).

Likewise, in 1994 vocalist Mustafa Chaushev (Plate 7.2) released *S Pesenta v Sŭrtseto* [With song in the heart], an album of pop songs that put new Bulgarian lyrics to melodies derived from Turkish *halk* and *arabesk* pieces. Some, such as the text of *Sam li si* (Are you alone?; Fig. 7.4; CD 7.6), capture the wistful yearning and melancholic sense of fate typical of their *arabesk* counterparts (cf. Dimov 1994a:31, 1995:14; Stokes 1992a:133–62). In addition, this arrangement utilizes synthesizer and violin skillfully to supply dialogue-like interjections reminiscent of the modified string choruses that frequently back *arabesk* hits (see Stokes 1992a:168). The song's underlying rhythmic basis is also Middle Eastern, a variant of the rhythmic mode known as *baladī* among Arab musicians, which becomes especially apparent during the refrain.

Sam li si—pita pogled nyam,	Are you alone—asks a silent glance,
pita i razglezhda me bez sram.	it inquires and regards me without shame.
Sam li si—vzirat se ochi,	Are you alone—eyes stare,
nyakoi plache v men, no az mŭlcha.	something cries in me, but I am silent.
Sam li si—toz vŭpros kŭm men,	Are you alone—was the question [posed] to me
orkestŭrŭt—povtarya v refren.	the orchestra—continues in refrain.
Sam li si—skrit v oblak dim,	Are you alone—hidden in a smoky cloud,
mnogo bikh zhelal da pomŭlchim.	I'd really like us to be silent.
Dori i sam mislya si za neya,	Even though I'm alone I think about her,
vizhdam ya na masata do men.	I see her at the table next to me.
Te chuvstvata ne mogat da iztleyat,	These feelings can't rot away,
makar da sŭm samoten i srazen.	although I'm lonely and crushed.

Chorus

Chorus

Vino mi nalei—i sedni do men,	Pour me some wine—and sit next to me,
da pochuvstvam zhazhda za nastŭpvashtiya den.	so I feel thirst for the coming day.
Vino mi nalei—duma mi kazhi,	Pour me some wine—speak to me,
vsyaka spodelena grizha pomalko tezhi.	every shared care weighs less heavily.

Figure 7.4: *Sam li si* [Are you alone?]. Composed by Ufuk Yildirim; new Bulgarian text by Zhivka Kyuldzhieva. Performed by Mustafa Chaushev. *S Pesenta v Sŭrtseto.* Riva Sound RS0162, 1994.

Chalga's Marketplace

Pop-folk has received considerable press coverage, including regular TV and radio broadcasts, periodical rubrics, and top ten charts (see Dimov 1996a:35). It is supported by a labyrinthine cassette and more recently, videocassette, CD, VCD, and DVD industry so rife with piracy during the

1990s that in 1995, the Recording Industry Association of America, in cooperation with the International Intellectual Property Alliance, named Bulgaria one of the most serious infringers of global copyright stipulations (Anonymous 1990; Holland 1995). Even in November 1998, US trade representatives still considered Bulgaria on their piracy "watch list" (Shafir 1998m), while in May 2000, the International Federation of the Phonographic Industry told Reuters that the country's market was dominated by pirate CDs flooding across the borders from Ukraine, Russia, and Montenegro (Shafir 2000c).[24]

By the late 1990s *chalga* had gained tremendous public support; ethnopop discothèques were established, periodicals featured gossip columns directed at ethnopop stars, and local satellite television promoted ethnopop channels featuring music videos of the sort discussed by Kurkela in chapter four of this volume. Payner Records, one of the chief producers of *pop-folk* as well as other genres, established its own TV channel on which it broadcasts, and hence advertises and popularizes, its latest video recordings. The following vignettes further illustrate *chalga*'s impact. In spring 1998 my colleague Lauren Brody reported that Neshko Neshev, the superb keyboardist who performed with Ivo Papazov's acclaimed wedding band, lost his job as a restaurant musician after just two weeks because "no one wanted to listen to the [more traditionally-oriented wedding] music he was playing" (Brody, p. c., 5 April 1998).[25] Very little older traditional music was being performed in Bulgaria anywhere; rather, people preferred *chalga*. I did not find this surprising, because two years earlier, when I asked *gŭdular* Dimitŭr Lavchev what was then happening with the wedding music scene, he responded that the trend had "already become a classic"—in other words, a bit old-fashioned—replaced by styles like *chalga*. When we spoke again in May 1999 he indicated that the market for *chalga* had grown so large that it eclipsed even Euro-American-style pop music in popularity. "Everyone is recording it," he said, "those who have the ability, and those who don't."

Similarly, Georgi Zhelyazkov, a professional folk musician and my *kaval* teacher, told me that when asked by some European visitors to select some cassettes of traditional music for them at a nearby market during summer 1998, he couldn't find anything performed on indigenous instruments. "I knew exactly what they wanted," he told me. "They wanted authentic material—without clarinet, accordion or other modern instruments." But the only thing available, he emphasized, was *"orientalna muzika."*

Nor has this situation improved recently for consumers seeking older musical styles. When my student Vladka Shikova returned to Champaign-Urbana, Illinois after visiting her parents in Varna, Bulgaria, during January 2000 she reported that stands selling *chalga* could be found "every ten meters" on the city's streets. She searched high and low for a recording of older traditional music to bring me; "I couldn't find folk music (*narodna muzika*) anywhere except the airport souvenir shop!" she exclaimed. This signifies that the indigenous music of Bulgaria's past, rooted in rural musical culture of the late 1800s and transformed, under socialism, into a venerated symbol of the nation through the performances of professional and amateur folk ensembles, was now directed solely at foreign tourists, while marketers considered *chalga* the indigenous music of choice for domestic consumers. For this reason the folk music group Bŭlgari, which toured the US during spring 2001 in conjunction with the fall concert series of New York City's World Music Institute, and whose members are all former or current stars of the professional folk ensemble circuit, has seen absolutely no financial gain within Bulgaria from their two recent CDs (*Bŭlgari: Bulgarian Folk Music* and *Bŭlgari: Bulgarian Rhapsody*), both released in the US. In fact, Bulgarian producers told Bŭlgari that their music did not interest them in the least and that the group should "do something with more market appeal"—in other words, a folk-pop crossover.

Chalga's Orientalist Imagery

This situation represents a complete turn-around from the 1980s, when folk ensemble music was part of the everyday soundscape and when *Yugo-folk* faced strong opposition from Bulgarian authorities, who sought to ban it—like wedding music—for the sullying potential of its inherent links to Turkish and other Balkan musicianship. As Croatian essayist Dubravka Ugrešić (1995:125–26) has observed, *Yugo-folk*'s top performers became gendered, stereotyped idols associated with a commercial, materialistic, romanticized lifestyle: "the gods and goddesses of Yugo-mass culture." In her words, male performers sported "open collars, gold chains round their necks and thick gold signet rings on their fingers," a description that reminded me strongly of the *nouveaux riches* who began frequenting Sofia's many new cafes and pastry shops in the mid 1990s, cell phones in tow (1995:125). Similarly, for her, female vocalists appeared as alluring "Yugo-Barbie-Dolls, with . . . tight skirts, cleavages, and high-heeled shoes."

It was exactly *Yugo-folk*'s erotic and stylistically syncretic qualities that attracted Bulgarian listeners. As my colleague Tsenka Iordanova told me, in sharp contrast to Bulgarian *narodna muzika* [folk music] with its institutionally cultivated connotations of hallowed purity, Serbs freely combined stylistic elements from the cultures around them. They took from everywhere, she explained, including Bulgaria, translating borrowed traits into their own musical language, such that the results sounded "Serbianized." They were not afraid to borrow; culture was a market from which they could select whatever they wished. Therefore, Serbian music sounded freer, more appealing, more innovative, containing "more interesting moves." It was "full of the melismas, orientalisms, and sexual lethargy" indicative of music for the Serbian *kafana*, itself a vestige of the former Ottoman presence. I experienced this for myself in winter 1990, during an evening out at one of the then newly established cooperative restaurants—jointly owned by the government and a private entrepreneur—located in the foothills outside Sofia. Four televisions mounted in the dining room's corners played *Yugo-folk* music videos at high volume, whose performers exhibited exaggerated *čoček*-like dance moves as they sang. Other patrons danced along to these videos on the restaurant's small dance floor throughout the evening.[26]

As the cassette covers on the accompanying CD-ROM illustrate, Bulgarian *chalga* performers emulate the *Yugo-folk* model. For instance, Sashka Vaseva (Plate 7.3), an ethnopop star so popular that her wedding to a German businessman was broadcast on Bulgarian television,[27] has been likened to *Yugo-folk* star Lepa Brena (Delibeev 1994:16–17). Certainly, provocative women's dance and dress have long been central to Western popular culture, from go-go dancers in hot pants to Madonna. But some *chalga* performers have added a revealing Middle Eastern twist to their presentations. With names like Orkestŭr Orient and recording titles such as "The dream of the sheik" (*Mechtata na Sheiha*, by Marin Dzhambazov with Orkestŭr Knezha [Prince]; Plate 7.4), a handful of groups identify themselves directly with Near Eastern stereotypes. More common, however, are the numerous cassettes and videos whose packaging utilizes bellydance erotica or nudity. These include recordings of Romani songs, such as Orkestŭr Kozari's *Yana Bibiyana* (Plate 7.5, Ibro Lolov's "Gypsy varieties" (*Tsiganski Variete*; Plate 7.6), and the first Romani music festival (*Pŭrvi Romski Festival '93: Stara Zagora*; Plate 7.7); Ivo Barev's "With the name of God" (*S Imeto na Bog*; Plate 7.8), the album on which "Och, brother-in-law, brother-in-law" appears; Belite Shisharki's "Forgive me" (*Prosti Mi*; Plate 7.9); and Valentin Valdes's

"Thought of a woman" (*Misŭl za Zhena*; Plate 7.10), "Balkan soul" (*Balkanska Dusha*; see Kurkela 1996, 1997:188), and "Bad company" (*Losha Kompaniya*; Plate 7.11).[28]

In a recent publication (2006a:437), I recount an incident in which my friend Vasilka, anxious that I fully comprehend what, from her perspective, was the kitschy nature of this music, invited me for dinner and to view music videos of Orchestra Kristal. My fieldnotes describe one, in particular, in which a bevy of women wearing garish, revealing bellydance outfits twirled provocatively around a turbaned male singer seated on the floor. In that production, called *Dai mi, dai mi zlaten prŭsten* [Give me, give me, a gold ring], the synthetic fabric, neon colors, and trim of the women's outfits graphically outlined their breasts and pelvic areas, heightening the video's association with an orientalized musical eroticism.

Some months later, Carol Silverman drew my attention to a second song by Orchestra Kristal, *Az sŭm vesela i peya* [I am joyful and sing], recorded on their 1994 album, *Mili Moi* [My dear], which employs similar imagery. The instrumental introduction and refrains are replete with musical allusions to the Middle East, while the lyrics, which comprise a dialogue between a sheik and an unwilling addition to his harem, recall *Dai mi*'s seraglio symbolism (Fig. 7.5; CD 7.7). During the *Dai mi* video, in sharp contrast to the women, whose entire bodies shimmied as they danced, the male musicians stood completely still while they played their synthesizers. Likewise, in "I am joyful" the "sultan's" voice is flat and colorless—devoid of orientalisms—while those of the female leads, who duet largely in parallel thirds (possibly one singer overdubbed), contain characteristic embellishments here and there, and are enhanced with artificial reverberation.

Woman

Az sŭm vesela i peya,
Za edna lyubov kopneya,
I daryavam samo toplina.

Sultan

Imam mila mnogo zlato,
*   zlato i srebro—*
S biseri az shte posipya
*   tvoyeto leglo*

Woman

I'm joyful and sing,
Of a love I'm longing for,
And to bestow only warmth.

Sultan

I have, my dear, lots of gold,
    gold and silver—
I'll strew your bed with pearls.

Woman (Chorus)   **Woman (Chorus)**

Ah, zlato i srebro ne isk-   Ah, I don't want gold and
    am—   silver—
mladostta e tŭi beztsenna.   youth is utterly priceless.
No edva li ti shte razbiresh.   But you'd hardly understand
                              that.

Bikh zhelala da ostana,   I'd like to remain,
vse tŭi mlada i zasmyana,   always young and smiling,
i da nyamam grizhi nikakvi.   and not to have any cares.

Sultan   **Sultan**

V saraiiya ti shte bŭdesh,   In the seraglio you'll be the sun
    slŭntse i luna.   and moon.
Vsichki shte ti bŭdat robi—   Everyone will be your slave—
samo s men ila.   just come with me.

Woman   **Woman**

(Chorus)   (Chorus)

Instrumental break   Instrumental break

Woman   **Woman**

S bogatstvoto nesmetno   With incalculable wealth
lyubovta ne se kupuva—   love isn't bought—
tya e chast ot moyata   it's a part of my soul.
    dusha.

Sultan   **Sultan**

Ti si hubava i mila;   You're attractive and kind;
dai mi lyubovta.   give me love.
Ti si nezhna i krasiva;   You're tender and beautiful;
stani mi zhena.   be my wife (or woman).

Woman   **Woman**

(Chorus)   (Chorus)

Figure 7.5: *Az sŭm vesela i peya,* performed by Orkestŭr Kristal. *Mili Moi,* 1994.

To be sure, not every *chalga* song or music video is so blatantly orientalist. As I have indicated elsewhere (Buchanan 2006a:437), Orchestra *Kristal* may have actually intended "I am joyful and sing" as a parody of such imagery, especially given that Croatian, Bosnian, and Serbian performers produced just such spoofs of *Yugo-folk* culture from time to time (L. Rasmussen, p.c., 11 July 1999). Yet these gendered contrasts point to at least three ways in which the Ottoman past has been interpreted, accommodated, manipulated, and commercially recast by both Balkan musicians and producers and Western recording companies, their promoters, and consumers. First, although by 2000 the phenomenon had become a basic feature of most *pop-folk,* the initial adoption of bellydance by *chalga* artists during the 1990s was particularly apparent in Romani bands, and may be related to general perceptions of things Romani as oriental. According to Carol Silverman (p.c., 1998, 2003:129), Bulgarian Romani music festivals of the 1990s regularly awarded cash prizes to the best bellydancers, but because it is considered improper for Romani women to dance with bared midriffs or for men with whom they are unacquainted, otherwise Romani bands hired Bulgarian Slavic women as dancers. Importantly, Silverman's work documents that this *pop-folk* bellydancing represented a frequently garish, exaggerated, and contorted rendition of in-group Romani *kyuchek,* whose moves, by contrast, are much more subtle, executed from the stomach rather than the hips, and danced fully clothed. Thus by showcasing such bellydancing—even when performed by non-Roma—Silverman suggests that *chalga* groups were presenting (or perhaps selling) a stereotype about who the Roma are, one that they have internalized as representing the non-Romani perception of their identity (2003:130, 139). This may well be true, especially given the lengthy historical association of urban Romani popular culture with Turkish musicianship and dance. My own sense, however, is that the bellydance fad is not just about redefining *Romani* identity through orientalized expressive culture, but that of Bulgarians and even the Balkans generally. While Westerners and Bulgarian Slavs may in fact typecast Roma as more Eastern, exotic, and hence oriental, specific knowledge of Romani-Turkish cultural connections seems more a Balkan than Western phenomenon. In *chalga* performance the erotic dance stereotype has been transferred to and adopted by Slavic women, it has been similarly exploited (through *čoček*) in *Yugo-folk* and *turbo folk* videos (whose performers include both Slavs and Muslims), and in neither Bulgaria nor the former Yugoslav republics was or is the intended audience of these genres Western.

Secondly, the gender differences described earlier (men in Western suits, gold jewelry, not moving, flat voice; the women in bellydance attire, shimmying, singing in embellished voice) have an important historical precedent in the so-called "Turkish" operas of late eighteenth- and nineteenth-century Vienna, which frequently utilized the harem as their paradigmatic setting. In productions such as Mozart's *The Abduction from the Seraglio*, for example, where the two female lead characters were abducted and held prisoner in a harem, the fact that their jailer, the Pasha, never sings, but only speaks, and rarely appears in the drama highlights both his noble bearing and simultaneously, despotic, absolute political power (Hunter 1998:55–58, 63–64). Other operas of this type exhibit similar stereotypes. In both today's Balkan pop and these earlier operas, then, men and women are marked such that orientalism as otherness is bound up with the sensuality of the feminine, on the one hand, and a dominating hypermasculinity, on the other (cf. Todorova 1997:13). This may be, in fact, one overriding Euro-American stereotype of the Mediterranean in general—a stereotype that this video plays into.

Taking this one step further, Finnish ethnomusicologist Vesa Kurkela (1996:46 and this volume) insightfully proposes that the "sexist softporn" and "macho mentality" exhibited by *chalga* point to a "modern exoticism" that is the contemporary analogue of "classic orientalism," where the country's new mafia is, for instance, today's personification of sheiks and sultans. Yet I see little real difference between this "neo-orientalism," as he describes it (1997:187–88), and its precedents elsewhere, particularly in the extent to which it traffics in objectified images of female bodies and conversely (flipping over my theoretical coin), the depersonalized, disembodied female voices of the *Le mystère des voix bulgares* recordings produced by Nonesuch and Jaro Records, to which I turn below.

This antithetical relationship leads me to my third point: the orientalization of Balkan music, from *chalga,* to *Yugo-folk,* to *Le mystère des voix bulgares,* is partially about foregrounding the voice as sensual, a quality also characteristic of Turkish *arabesk,* which may have provided one impetus for this trend. For example, during cadential moments of some *Yugo-folk* and *arabesk* songs, particularly Arab-sounding melismatic vocal passages are set apart from previous material. They may be enhanced with reverb and are either accompanied by a sudden drone or stripped of instrumental accompaniment altogether (cf. L. Rasmussen 1995:247–48, 1996b:107). The resulting sound calls to mind a host of Arabo-Turkish genres, from the call to prayer to *layālī* to *uzun hava* to the *taksim*, further framing these moments—and the voice itself—as orientally marked.

"Le Mystère" and the Oriental

The "Mystery of the Bulgarian Voices" recordings provide another illustration of the voice as sensual, albeit produced differently. As I have demonstrated elsewhere (Buchanan 1996a, 1997, 2006a:360–71), one reason for the choirs' unparalleled success was that their promotional materials drew together the female and the vocal as sensual together in a single package whose wrapper of New Age spiritualism merged the Bulgarian, oriental, mystical, archaic, and exotic as synonymous. It is noteworthy that the earliest "Mystery" recordings left the singers' physical identities to the listener's fancy, for this focused attention on female voices divorced from human shape, thus firing the Western imagination in a manner analogous to the veiled women of some Islamic societies. As Silverman (2004:222) beautifully expresses it:

> The transformation of these socialist singer/workers into ethereal, exotic, "ancient" voices was artfully orchestrated by promoters, who submerged the women themselves and emphasized the female sound aspect of the music, devoid of text and context. Gender surfaced in female voices, not in real people.

In both local and Western orientalized productions of Bulgarian music, then, a configuration of economic and political motivations is at play whose complexity embodies, but also transcends historical links between current and earlier stereotyping of the East (Table 7.4). On the one hand, democracy and market capitalism have meant an explosion of permissive behavior throughout eastern Europe: drinking, drugs, smuggling, business scams, conspicuous consumption, prostitution rings, female sex slavery, and pornography.[29] Many young Bulgarians aspire to a high-life culture of easy money, easy women, flashy clothes, fast food, faster cars, and high-tech gadgets.[30] For instance, the lyrics of one 1996 *chalga* hit applaud the lifestyle of a *"barovets"* (Fig. 7.6). This slang term, which under socialism signified a man with an easy life and many political connections, now essentially means "barfly," but specifically denotes a member of the *nouveaux riches* who subscribes to a lifestyle of flashy materialism and nightclub activities (Karen Peters, p.c., 20 May 1999; cf. Dimov 2001:142).

Diskoteki, i restoranti skitam
    nosht i den,
piyane, pari, i matski, vinagi
    sŭs men.
	I gallivant through discothèques
	    and restaurants night and day,
	drinking, money, and kittens [i.e.,
	    young desirable women],
	    always with me.

Barovets, barovets, barovets
    sŭm az,
barushki shte si zhiveya, vseki
    den i chas.
	A *barovets, barovets, barovets* am
	    I,
	At the bars I'll live every day and
	    hour.

Karam hubava kola, tova e
    moita strast.
Sŭs marki, dolari i zlato, baro-
    vets sŭm az.
	I drive a beautiful car, this is my
	    passion.
	With deutschmarks, dollars and
	    gold, a *barovets* am I.

Barovets, barovets, barovets
    sŭm az,
barushki shte si zhiveya, vseki
    den i chas.
	A *barovets, barovets, barovets* am
	    I,
	at the bars I'll live every day and
	    hour.

Figure 7.6: *Sofiiski barovets* (excerpt), performed by Ts. Nikolich. As heard on Radio Signal Plus, June 1996.

At the same time, political change has meant access to music from other parts of the Balkans, particularly *Yugo-folk*, which as illustrated above, cultivates similarly materialistic imagery. *Chalga*'s sexualized properties are related to both of these factors.

Impending political and economic change also facilitated the western European, North American, and Japanese enchantment with Bulgarian women's voices, which through Nonesuch's skillful marketing became orientalized objects of desire in and of themselves. This latter trend was further commercially exploited by numerous copycat recordings (see Buchanan 1997), whose most convoluted and deliberately easternized representation to date is probably the compact disc *"Fly, Fly My Sadness."*[31] This recording pairs Siberian biphonic throat singers from the Republic of Tuva with a Bulgarian women's choir formerly marketed in association with the mysterious voices fad but known, since 1995, as "The Angels" (Angelite) in arrangements by Mikhail Alperin, a Ukrainan-born Jewish Moldovan piano professor and jazz musician living in Finland. According to the liner notes, Alperin's goal was to reveal, through the metaphoric vision of a bird's flight, the shared meditative structures of these disparate folk musics, which he believes derive from their common origin in the peoples of the East Asian Turkic-Altaic language group, which includes the Tuvans and the Bulgars.[32] The album's final cut, a piece called *Mountain Story* whose composition is credited to Alperin, combines the latter's Hohner accordion; the Tuvan two-stringed horse-head fiddle (*igil*); and several styles of Tuvan throat singing (*khoomei*), a men's tradition characterized by exceedingly low-pitched fundamental drones and whistling overtone melodies; with a Bulgarian women's chorus whose singing phases in and out of the predominantly Tuvan material. The Tuvans sing vocables, as is typical of this tradition, and the Bulgarians two virtually undecipherable repetitive texts. The focus is not the lyrics, but the unpulsed droning of the vocal interplay, whose saturated texture is echoed and intensified by the instruments' reedy quality. The resulting union brilliantly exemplifies the process of "nesting orientalisms," in which a phenomenon already typecast as Eastern or oriental assumes a relatively Western stance in juxtaposition to something else (Bakić-Hayden 1995). Thus here the implied mysticism of the angelic women's voices is further exoticized and easternized by its subordinate association with the physiologically extraordinary ability of the Siberians to produce two pitches simultaneously, a technique largely specific only to Tuvan and Mongolian nomadic herders, some Tibetan Buddhist monks, and the derivative American harmonic choirs of New Age spiritualism. Not surprisingly, Alperin's liner notes indicate that this is a composition "based in meditation." That neither Tuvan nor Bulgarian singing is in reality associated with meditation *per se* seems beside the point.

Table 7.4: Politico-Economic Factors Driving Orientalized Productions of Bulgarian Music

❖Democracy and market capitalism ➡ materialism, corruption, crime, objectification of women's bodies

❖Political transition ➡ Increased access to other Balkan ethno-pop characterized by similarly materialistic and sexualized imagery

❖Western interest in Bulgarian music, fired especially by the Nonesuch and Jaro Records tours of the Le mystère des voix bulgares choirs ➡ further commercial exploitation and objectification of women's voices

To tie all of this together in a single equation, I turn to a key observation by Carol Silverman (2004:231), which I will paraphrase and expand upon here: The former socialist east exported "disembodied females in the form of voices" to the capitalist West. At the same time, as the former socialist east imported Western capitalist principles, they became transfigured, in part, as access to goods previously limited or regulated, including objectified women's bodies, whether in the form of pin-up girl cassette cover images or prostitutes. During the transition era such objectifications, which constitute "female bodies without voices," and Bulgaria's choristers—"female voices without bodies"—were essentially mirror images: both became "gendered commodities for sale." Again, from this perspective, in regard to aspects of gender and voice, these two trends, *chalga* and mysteriously voiced female choirs, constitute flip sides of the same orientalist coin. Moreover, as I will clarify momentarily, the dialectic obtaining between these two traditions—the coin's two faces—springs from the reinterpretation of things Ottoman as emergent markers of Bulgarian modernity.

Transnational Dimensions: The Warrior Princess's Bulgarian Voice

Another gendered popular culture commodity that associated Bulgarian music with an amorphous, remote past and equally nebulous "Eastern" place was the FOX network's television show, *Xena, Warrior Princess,* which played in the mid 1990s. Filmed, in reality, in New Zealand, the show related the exploits of a tough, voluptuous, seductively clad Robin Hood-ess endowed with quick wits, courage, and supernatural powers during the age of Greco-Roman myth in an unspecified Asian locale, which the Universal Studios website describes as "on the distant frontier of known civilization."[33] The program's soundtrack implemented a grab-bag of Mediterranean and Asian musical devices marketed by Western firms in relation to Eastern mysticism or meditation, including Armenian *duduk* melodies, Tibetan Buddhist religious chant, Tuvan biphonic singing, and Chinese temple bells. Bulgarian music figured prominently within this constellation: composer Joseph LoDuca, impressed by one of the "Mystery of the Bulgarian Voices" choirs, employed similar women's singing, Bulgarian texts, traditionally inspired tunes, asymmetrical meters, and indigenous instruments to highlight moments when Xena exercises the esoteric knowledge that she acquired from her

East Asian (probably Mongolian) mentor, a nomadic, yurt-dwelling, female adept.[34] These included her "chakram toss," paralysis tricks, and jumping and fighting feats. In particular, he found that the "warlike, chilling sounds" of *gaida* [bagpipe] and overblown *kaval* [obliquely blown wooden flute], both performed by the California-based Bulgarian emigré Dimitŭr Konstantinov, helped to "create an atmosphere of ancient culture, even though the dialogue is contemporary."[35] The show's main title opened with a brief *gaida* solo. This was followed by a studio-enhanced women's choir—actually a handful of California-based singers boosted by the excellent vocal skills of Konstaninov's wife, Zhivka—singing a Bulgarian text to a tune metered in a seven-beat *rŭchenitsa* dance rhythm (7/16: 2–2–3). The audio dimension accompanied brief video clips from past episodes that presented Xena with her foes in a variety of poses, including that of a veiled *femme fatale*.

According to Suzie North, one of the vocalists who recorded parts of the show's soundtrack, LoDuca regarded Bulgarian women's singing as "an extremely powerful female sound" that he thought most appropriate for a warrior princess (North 1998).[36] His use of Bulgarian vocals was thus to some extent about female empowerment. Certainly, the script's numerous strong female characters and abundant lesbian allusions foregrounded issues of female potentiality and community. But this was an empowerment loaded with orientalist implications, one that only extended prior associations of Bulgarian women's singing with the primeval, ancient, mythical, mystical, sensual, and enigmatic transnationally. In conversation with North I learned that, once again, the actual lyrics to be sung held no real importance. When Konstantinova first read the texts at the studio, she remarked that they made no sense, and altered some of the lyrics to make them "better Bulgarian." Although Konstantinova would often exclaim "What are we singing?!", LoDuca told the women that he just wanted the words to sound "mythic," in keeping with the show's central thrust (North 1998). While this accounts for the downright weird translations of the texts in the liner notes accompanying the first *Xena* CD (see Fig. 7.7), it is also the antithesis of Bulgarian tradition, where a good singer is defined in part by how many song texts she can remember, and a good song is one with a coherent tale. As I will clarify below, one recurring criticism of *chalga* is that its texts are of remarkably poor quality.

Text in Liner Notes	Translation in Liner Notes
Jenata iazi samotna	The Warrior Princess rides alone
Neinoto minalo srazi ia	Her past drives her from shame.
Sreshtu voiskite ot tumen sviat	Against the forces of a dark world
Vouva za dobro tia	She fights for good, not for fame.
Rogovi zvunove idavt	Horns sound her coming, blare her name.
Napraite put na voina!	Make way the Warrior! Cheer!
Tupani biat vuv ritum	Drums beat a rhythm
Princhesata e pak tuka!	Let villains beware!
	The Warrior Princess is here!

Text as Heard on CD	Translation of CD Text
Zhenata yazdi samotna,	The woman rides alone,
Neinoto minalo srazi ya.	Her past crushes her.
Sreshtu voiskite ot tŭmen svyat,	Against the forces of a dark world,
Voiyuvat kato bratya.	They battle like brothers.
Rogovi, zvŭnove idvat.	Horns, bells come.
Napravite pŭt na voina!	Prepare a path for the warrior![37]
Tŭpani biyat vŭv ritŭm,	Drums beat in rhythm,
Printsesata e pak tuka!	The Princess is here again!

Figure 7.7: *Main Title*, composed by Joseph LoDuca, from the Fox Television program *Xena, Warrior Princess*. As heard on *Xena, Warrior Princess: Original Television Soundtrack*, Varese-Sarabande VSD-5750, 1995 [1996].

Conclusions: Balkan Cosmopolitanism?

Bulgarian *chalga*, like *Yugo-folk*, may be viewed productively as a late twentieth-century outgrowth of earlier, Ottoman-Romani-Slavic musical interfaces. Both are, as Jane Sugarman (1998) so aptly describes their Albanian correlates, "Ottoman successor musics" or, more whimsically, "Ottopop." After all, the very concept of the Balkans as a geopolitical construct is, according to the historian Maria Todorova, "the" Ottoman legacy (1997:12). Ironically, while socialist Bulgaria rejected this legacy in favor of state-mandated expressive media, musicians now draw upon its musical and visual stereotypes to create expressive modes that spurn the socialist heritage, in turn. Yet despite their syncretic roots, *chalga* and other ethnopop genres like *Pirin folk* songs are not Serbian, Romani, Turkish, or Greek music. They are Bulgarian musics, produced by local artists for domestic consumption. But they are also Bulgarian musics that reconfigure the nation in a post-1989 *Balkan* context. This was under-scored by some local scholars and early performers of the new ethnopop phenomenon, who viewed it as a resumption of late nineteenth-century trends artificially interrupted in the 1940s by socialist politics. For ethnomusicologist Ventsislav Dimov, for example, these trends, once shared widely across the Balkans, continued to develop freely and as an industry in neighboring states after their evolution in Bulgaria was halted (Dimov 1995:13; cf. Statelova 1995:110). Others perceived these trends as of Bulgarian origin, but then appropriated and popularized by neighbor-ing countries from 1944–89. Speaking specifically about the Serbian factor apropos Bulgarian ethnopop, the celebrated Pirin song artists Sevdalina and Valentin Spasovi, in a published interview with *Folk Panair* magazine editor Petko Delibeev (1994:10), remarked:

> Sevdalina: Here, when it was unthinkable to talk about such music, then our neighbors grabbed up our musical wealth en masse.
>
> Valentin: First they took and popularized all of our Macedonian songs, which I as a child had heard from my grandfather, while by the time I was a grade-school student, in general they weren't performed among us. And when this dawned on us and we began to reconstruct them, they [the neighbors] came out with the authored music [i.e., NCFM and similar trends] and we had to catch up to them once again.

Although riddled with problematic historical assumptions and ethno-nationalist implications, this statement is a profound expression of the extent to which these artists feel the socialist regime cheated them of a local urban popular culture.

Yet Valentin immediately followed his remark with a comment on Bulgarian ethnopop's regionally dispersed origins. "But look," he said to Delibeev, "in Bulgaria many people have come from all over the place and each has brought something. So that now it's [only] natural that we repeat something [i.e., musical styles from elsewhere]." These sentiments were echoed by the Pirin song vocalist Lyubka Rondova in a comparable interview with the *Folk Panair* staff. "It's true," she said, that these songs are heavily influenced by our neighbors, but they are Bulgarian—Bulgarian language, rhythms, [and] motives comprise them. But it's impossible for there not to be influence—we are from a single Balkan singing region. And if we learn from our neighbors now, this is because they began to make this kind of music forty years ago (*Folk Panair* 1994a:6).

In a similar statement, Mustafa Chaushev, defending *pop-folk* against its academic critics, emphasized its Balkan nature as appropriate to Bulgarian modernity:

What is this "kitsch"? In the face of such a boom, such that folklore is making now in Bulgaria . . . it is natural for there to be weak things, because everything is being born now. Yes, there are mediocre songs, there are dreamed-up singers, but the general line [of stylistic development] is correct for our country. Or else what? Everywhere we're distracted by Anglo-American music and I ask myself, are we in Bulgaria? This is disgusting! I travel around the Balkan countries—nowhere else is there such nihilism. And for this they too are guilty, those who impose the ethics [of] 'kitsch' . . . . The people wanted to listen to table songs [i.e., restaurant songs, drinking songs, popular songs to accompany convivial occasions], but they forbid Serbian music—[Was this] for political reasons? Ethical reasons? For songs there are no borders, especially among us, in the Balkans (Dimov 1994a).

Such commentary signifies a conceptual move beyond syncretism to a new cultural position in which the Bulgarian as Balkan (and probably the Balkan as European) is being privileged in musical practice, self-identification, and international alliances (cf. Turino 2000:6). My thesis is that those expressive stereotypes once formerly identified with a despised political hegemony have become a distinctive, yet natural part of the compositional vocabulary of the average Bulgarian ethnopop musician. This is not to say that the links between such features and minority groups, in particular, have been completely defused, but for today's ethnopop artists, they seem to represent the reemergence of a Balkan music *gestalt* with a Bulgarian face—a "Bulgofolk" alternative to *Yugo-folk* that, directly or indirectly, reinterprets the cosmopolitanism of the old Ottoman ecumene in a contemporary Balkan frame (cf. Dimov 1995:15–16; Petkov 1994:21; Sugarman, this volume).

To tease out the complex implications of this thesis I turn to a theory of cosmopolitanism advanced by my colleague Thomas Turino (2000) in relation to his recent work with musicians in Zimbabwe. Turino identifies cosmopolitanism as a process in which aspects of a previously foreign disposition, such as the effects of colonization, become so constitutive of local lifeways that they are no longer thought of as alien or alternative by their actors, but as a natural, even vital part of their sensibilities. This is not a matter of mere influence, or to put this in musical terms, of indigenous artists strategically imitating or incorporating an atypical instrument, chord progression, or rhythmic pattern in order to appeal to those holding the economic or political reins of power. Rather, it is about the internalization of the foreign to the point of self-recognition, self-identification, and self-expression. Cosmopolitanism is therefore inherently international in purview, and here Turino's use of the term jives with its mainstream connotation of being "of the world," sophisticated in one's appreciation and cultivation of translocal phenomena (Turino 2000:7). But the shapes that cosmopolitan forms take are completely local; their international point of origin may be forgotten or discarded as beside the point, and the forms or features themselves invested with new meaning and value *vis-à-vis* contemporary needs and views.

I see this process happening in regard to the ethnopop genres described here. Perhaps we can think of them as illustrations of an emergent Balkan cosmopolitanism, where the Ottoman Empire's musical legacy has become part and parcel of the local grassroots creative lexicon, which in turn coexists with myriad newly established intraregional political and economic ties that recall the Roman trade routes—the *Via Militaris* and its counterparts—interlacing this area in centuries past.[38] As we have seen, even though devices iconic of Western pop, like synthesizers, are utilized by Balkan musicians, they are employed in locally specific ways that impart a sense of identity at once European and Mediterranean, or in a transcendant, cosmopolitan sense, Balkan. *Chalga,* wedding music, *Pirin folk* songs, *Yugo-folk,* Greek *laika,* and Turkish *arabesk* are all manifestations of this emergent cosmopolitanism, but each genre holds a different meaning for the local community in which it is practiced. Moreover, these genres must be interpreted as in an intense dialogue with one another (by virtue of mass mediated intraregional circulation and Romani crosscurrents), and in tension with both older layers of cosmopolitanism resulting from European socialism, and competing visions of modernity.

Importantly, as the rubric *orientalna muzika* indicates, many of my well-educated professional folk musician acquaintances envision these pop music genres as problematically "Eastern" at the same time that they recognize their broad popularity and even consume them themselves (cf. Sugarman, this volume). These professionals represent an older stratum of cosmopolitanism, socialized as they were in the communist aesthetics of a Western European-style staged folkore that monumentalized expressions of the *narod* [people, nation, folk] as culturally and ethnically pure, and thus as symbols of the Bulgarian will to withstand Ottoman oppression (cf. Turino 2000:10). They view the new, amalgamated ethnopop, performed largely by amateurs, as substandard.

Radostina Kŭneva, a professional vocalist who helped me translate some of the lyrics presented in this article, noted that most ethnopop songs contain texts of low quality: unlike the ideal folk song, they lack a coherent narrative, feature thematically unconnected words and lines, employ ungrammatical verb forms and erroneous declensions of personal pronouns and adjectives, or as she put it, are just plain stupid. At the same time, she and her colleagues from Bŭlgari, in the midst of their 1998 tour of the American Midwest—remarked that absolutely everyone listens to this music. The group's *gaidar,* Georgi Doichev, explained this by proposing that in the wake of the hardships presented by the political transition people wanted something lighter to listen to, so as not to have to think about life's difficulties. *Pop-folk* provided one such outlet.

But Georgi Andreev, a *gŭdular* and composer of some of the group's material, speaking to the overwhelming popularity of Serbian *Yugo-folk,* the orientalesque character of *chalga,* and the dearth of support for folk ensembles, added that while it was true that his compatriots found their neighbors' music "fresher and more honest, closer to the soul," this liking actually stemmed from an inferiority complex. Most Bulgarians are ashamed to be Bulgarian, he explained, and are ashamed of things Bulgarian, so they do not want to acknowledge their own folk traditions, let alone listen to them, because they are something which people connect intellectually and emotionally, if not experientially, with archaic village life. Such music may be quintessentially Bulgarian, but it is hardly the height of modernity for the contemporary consumer. Rather, to a certain extent, Bulgarian modernity is about being Balkan.

In creating distinctively Bulgarian types of Balkan ethnopop musicians seem driven by a similar sense of inferiority that compels them to catch up with Greece and Serbia, whose political systems did not derail their urban music scenes to the extent experienced in Bulgaria. Thus in a 1994 magazine interview, Kiril Ivanov, director of the ethnopop band "Roden Kŭt" and composer of some of Sashka Vaseva's repertory, observed,

Personally, it was painful to me that such music was founded there, but
here there were complicated brakes. And in my opinion they [Greece,
Yugoslavia] are far ahead in this development [i.e., the development of
ethnopop], as they have their own [musical] physiognomy—Serbian is
one, Greek is another. And the tragedy is this, that we don't have our
[own] Bulgarian [style] and listen to their songs [instead] (*Folk Panair*
1994b:16–17).

While it may appear from this quotation that *chalga* and related
genres, in answering the need for Bulgarian ethnopop, simply emulate
Serbian, Greek, or Turkish trends, I believe the reality is more complicated. It is not the model's point of origin that is of primary importance,
but the internalization by Bulgarian musicians and consumers of a
particular set of ideas pertaining to the oriental as Balkan. Thus Mustafa
Chaushev, after asserting "For songs there are no borders, especially
among us, in the Balkans," reinforced his point by rhetorically inquiring,
"I mean, what do we really know about Turkish music?" With this he
responded obliquely to those cultural administrators of the socialist past
who had forbidden local musicians from performing neighboring styles or
newer, hybrid Balkan popular musics, for in Zhivkov's Bulgaria, with its
ideology of monoethnism, this was considered inappropriate and even
dangerous. From Chaushev's perspective, however, given that local
musicians possessed only a Bulgarian perspective on anything Turkish,
this hysteria was ridiculous. Their music would always be Bulgarian, no
matter its stylistic mix.

In a similar fashion, Silverman (p.c., 1998) told me that the Bulgarian
Romani bands who employ bellydancers do so because they are aware that
oriental dancing goes on in Turkey, even if they have never actually
witnessed it themselves. Indeed, one acquaintance, a professional folk
instrumentalist, upon returning from a concert tour in Istanbul, expressed
great surprise that throughout his time there, and despite expectations to
the contrary, he saw absolutely no one dancing *kyuchek*, which was in his
mind the quintessential contemporary Turkish dance genre. Here again
cosmopolitanism comes into play. For Bulgarian musicians the actual
nature of Turkish art or indigenous music, how bellydance is really
practiced in Turkey, and whether or not it once served as entertainment at
the sultan's court is irrelevant. Rather, *chalga* and related genres are
Bulgarian spins on orientalism as a central Balkan sensibility. They are
cosmopolitan manifestations of interiorized representations of the Ottoman
Empire and the modern Turkish nation, Bulgarian in form but Balkan in
content.

Here I must digress momentarily to point out that in comparison with other southeast Europeans, Bulgarians have enfolded "Balkan" the most deeply into their psyches. Beyond its application to the region's geography, it is very nearly synonymous with Bulgarian. The term itself is the Ottoman Turkish designation for Bulgaria's magnificent Balkan Mountain range, which the Byzantines and medieval geographers called Haemus, and which effectively bisects the country (see Todorova 1997:26). As Todorova (1997:56) succinctly observes:

> Geography is an important element of the school curriculum, and the 1994 seventh-grade textbook features three parts: Europe, the Balkan Peninsula, and Bulgaria. Bulgaria is a country whose airlines are called "Balkan," whose tourist agencies are "Balkantourist" and "Balkan holidays," whose record-making industry is "Balkanton," whose most fashionable hotel in the center of Sofia is "Sheraton-Balkan," whose third largest bank is "Balkanbank," and which has thousands of citizens with the family name "Balkanski."

Unfortunately, in international forums balkanization denotes not summer vacations, but the militant fracturing of nation-states along ethnic, religious, and linguistic divides. Thus from Todorova's perspective (1997:57), while only Bulgarians seriously consider a Balkan identity, "even among them it is ambiguous and subordinated to their claim of Europeanness."

My sense is that the current ethnopop scene transcends the dichotomies inherent in the name "Balkan" (East vs. West, oriental vs. European, irrational and warring vs. civilized). The anthropologist Michael Herzfeld (1987:7, 1997:158) has long shown convincingly how Greek citizens regularly and strategically invoke one facet or another of an identically polarized continuum in the practice of their everyday lives. I make the same argument here for Bulgaria's ethnopop musicians, whose products aesthetically embrace aspects of both the European and the oriental as positive qualities of being Balkan in a Bulgarian way. In the process, they have created new genres that resonate within the region, but which have a huge domestic listenership that supersedes divisions of class and ethnicity, despite the ethnic identity of their performers or the ethnically eclectic origins of the music. What seems to matter most is that Bulgaria now has its own version of "Ottopop," one which represents Bulgaria's Orient in the social poetics of Balkan cosmopolitanism.

Notes

1. This article originated as a paper, "Ottoman Images and Oriental Imaginings in Bulgarian Popular Culture: Ethnopop, Mysterious Voices, and *Xena, Warrior Princess*," read at the 43rd Annual Meeting of the Society for Ethnomusicology, Bloomington, IN, 1998, and in an expanded version, "Orientalism or Balkan Cosmopolitanism? Bulgarian Ethnopop and the Ottoman Episteme," for the University of Wisconsin at Madison's Center for Russia, East Europe, and Central Asia Colloquium Series. Since I completed the article manuscript in 1999–2000, a wealth of excellent new publications have appeared both in the US and abroad that treat various aspects of Bulgarian and Balkan popular culture. While I have tried to update my article to reflect at least some of the contributions of this burgeoning literature, for further information I direct the interested reader to, in particular, Dimov 2001; Levy 2005; Peicheva and Dimov 2002; Rasmussen 2002; Rice 2002; Silverman 2003, 2004; Sugarman 2003; and van de Port 1998.

2. See, for example, Diehl 2002; Feld 1996; Lee 1999; Qureshi 1997; Rice 2002; Solomon 2000, 2005; and Stokes, ed. 1994, among others.

3. On *chalga,* cf. Kurkela, this volume. The term "ethnopop," by which I mean hybridic styles of popular music combining aspects of local ethnic, folk, or traditional musics with those of Western popular culture, has been incorporated into the local musicological lexicon (Bulg. *etnopop*) by native scholars such as Ventsislav Dimov to refer to this relatively new category of Bulgarian music.

4. See Atlas, *Ne se Predavai!*

5. See recordings listed in the accompanying Discography. Borisova is also one of the Bulgarian vocalists who sang on Sezen Aksu's *Düğün ve Cenaze* album; see Stokes, this volume.

6. For further information on contemporary Pirin songs and their relationship to Macedonian culture see Buchanan 2006a and Peters 2000.

7. On NCFM see esp. L. Rasmussen 2002; on *turbo folk* see Gordy 1999:114n26, 133–64; Kronja 2004; Longinović 2000; and Rasmussen, this volume.

8. However, electric guitar has found a new role in *turbo folk;* see Rasmussen, this volume.

9. By contrast, *Folk Panair*'s other categories include "folklore - singers" (solo artists of the professional ensemble network), "folklore - groups" (wedding orchestras and chamber groups derived from professional ensembles), and "eternal folk songs" (old urban songs, early twentieth-century village music, and classic, well-known folk ensemble arrangements).

10. The first two Romani music festivals were held in Stara Zagora in 1993 and 1994. See, for example, *Pŭrvi Romski Festival '93, Stara Zagora* (Payner Records, 1993). A selection of audio and video recordings featuring Romani music from the early to mid 1990s includes *Dzhipsi Aver: Dzhipsi Rap* (Unison Records, 1993); *Dzhipsi Aver: Imam li Dobŭr Kismet?* (Video Total - OOD), *"Ot*

Kalkuta do Viena": Romski Duhov Orkestŭr YaG (Unison Stars, n.d., but probably 1994); *Ibro Lolov: Tsiganski Hitove, Chast 1* and *Chast 2* (Video Total); and *Ibro Lolov: Tsigansko Variete* (Video Total). On bear and monkey trainers see Silverman 2000b:280–83.

11. Similar ensembles called *saze* (from the Turkish, meaning "instruments") existed in towns throughout Albania (Sugarman 2000:993, 997).

12. Whether or not Bulgarians used *"chalgiya"* to denote a Romani-Turkish style ensemble like those found in Macedonia, Kosovo, and Albania is a question demanding further research. Although like the latter, the Bulgarian groups did usually feature violin, clarinet, and indigenous percussion (*daire, tarambuka,* or *tŭpan*), they more rarely contained the Turkish instruments, such as the *'ud* or *cümbüş,* that were common in the contemporaneous bands of their neighbors. In Bulgaria the *chalgadzhii* also went by numerous other names, including *svirdzhii* (sing. *svirdzhiya,* from the Bulgarian *svirya*; to play music), *bandi* (bands), and *muziki* (musicians, with a Western European connotation). See Buchanan 2006a and especially Vŭlchinova-Chendova 2000 for a lengthier discussion.

13. Cf. Rice 2003:172, who defines *chalga* as "Bulgarianized 'Gypsy' music" and "a kind of pan-Balkan, Rom-influenced popular music, commonly interpreted, both by its proponents and opponents, as a symbol of Bulgaria's areal location in the Balkans."

14. Throughout this discussion, see also Popescu-Judetz 1982, who draws largely upon And 1976 and sources common to both publications; and Sugarman 2003, who provides a marvelous historical overview of *čoček* and its more contemporary corollaries among Albanians.

15. For an excellent discussion of the confusion surrounding the etymological derivation of the term *çengi* and its meaning, see Seeman 2002:138–41.

16. The 8/8 (3–3–2) pattern is closely related to the Arab rhythmic mode *Malfūf* and the underlying swing of the Greek *syrtos/ballos.* It likely represents yet another Turkish influence in Bulgarian and Macedonian culture.

17. Such *taksim* breaks represent an important commonality between Turkish *arabesk,* Bulgarian "authored Macedonian songs," and *chalga.* In all three genres such solos frequently appear roughly midway through a song, between two verses (cf. Stokes 1992a:195–97). Where wedding music is concerned, whether played or sung, the main melodic material frequently frames one or more internal improvisations, some *taksim*-like and others less so, over ostinati.

18. Indeed, Peicheva and Dimov (2002:134) suggest that among professional Romani *zurna* players of southwestern Bulgaria, *kyuchek* as a musical category is broken down into an even more complicated array of types than has been suggested here. Their interlocutors identified Arab, oriental, old, and free *kyuchek* in addition to the Turkish and Romani varieties, and pointed to the locus of bodily movement (head, hands, shoulders, abdomen, bust, pelvis) as well as tempo as being two of the differentiating characteristics.

19. *Badzhanak* – a kin term with no good English equivalent: the husbands of two women who are first cousins.

20. *Darmadar* – dialect; from Bulg. *darmadan* [ruined, down and out; dissolute] and Turk. *darmadan* and *darmadağan*.

21. *Sokak* – dialect; from Turk. *sokaği*.

22. *Kadŭnka* (pl. *kadŭnki*) - from Bulg. *kadŭna*: Turkish woman, lady.

23. Redžepova's version may be heard on *Songs of a Macedonian Gypsy*.

24. The best Western-language discussion of piracy and the Bulgarian recording industry to date is Kurkela 1997.

25. Neshev can be heard on both of Papazov's Hannibal Records releases, *Balkanology* and *Orpheus Ascending*.

26. Rice (2002:32) describes a similar experience. Residents of a village that he often visited in the 1980s, located in the mountains north of Sofia, not far from the Serbian border, set their radios to pick up Serbian broadcasts featuring NCFM, rather than Bulgarian State Radio.

27. One might draw a comparison here with the 1995 wedding of *turbo folk* singing star Svetlana Veličković-Ceca to the Serbian paramilitary leader and mafia boss Željko Ražnatović-Arkan, which was an even more flamboyant public spectacle. See Gordy 1999:136–38.

28. All of these recordings date from the mid 1990s except *Losha Kompaniya*, which appeared in 2002. In recent years the marketing image adopted by *pop-folk* artists has begun to change, but erotic posturing and oriental dance have remained central themes of self-presentation (see Buchanan 2006b and Kurkela, this volume).

29. In 1994, while waiting for Vasilka at a bus stop on Lenin Boulevard near the County Hospital, I counted no less than eight different prominently arrayed pornographic magazines featuring exclusively female full frontal nudity in various poses at a newsstand. The stand's display was a statement on the new Bulgaria and its inherent contradictions: these periodicals were tucked between several publications about guns (another formerly forbidden item), two Harlequin romances translated into Bulgarian, the *Vestnik za Zhenata* [Newspaper for women], an English language text, a computer magazine, sports magazines, and a variety of political newspapers. I also noticed pornographic posters (again, only picturing women) sold in parks, displayed in buses, and on the walls of people's homes. Even the Musicology Institute had a pin-up calendar on the wall, albeit only a woman clad in a wet T-shirt. While I suppose all of this could be interpreted as a celebration of the female physique in a market economy, the concomitant increase in prostitution and female slavery here and elsewhere in eastern Europe leads me to believe that this is not the case. Rather, the new objectification is as restrictive for women as older cultural codes. Silverman (2004:227) writes that some "up-scale secretarial jobs require sexual services." Along the same line, in August 1998 a Bulgarian NGO reported that more than 10,000 local women and girls, many under the age of 18, were "enslaved in the west European sex industry" (Shafir 1998h). Promised marriage to a foreigner, or highly paid employment as dancers, models, personal assistants, or store clerks, they arrived in western Europe only to find themselves forced into prostitution after their passports had been confiscated by their new employers. In April 2000

the International Organization for Migration, which launched a campaign against such practices, added that women were lured into such situations by newspaper ads. In some instances, girls as young as 14 residing in small villages were kidnapped and smuggled across borders (Shafir 2000a, 2000b).

30. See also Rice 2002:34–36 and Dimov 2001; for a *turbo folk* parallel see Gordy 1999:133–35.

31. For further analysis of this recording, whose liner notes abound in the steretypes of orientalism and New Age spiritualism, see Silverman 2004:224–25.

32. The Bulgars were a Turkic group from East Asia who migrated into the Balkan peninsula and merged with the Slavic population already residing there, giving rise to the Bulgarians.

33. See www.universalstudios.com/tv/xena/overview.html.

34. In an interview with LoDuca published at the Universal Studios website (www.universalstudios.com/tv/loduca/interview.html) he credits producer Rob Tapert with initially suggesting Bulgarian women's singing for the show. LoDuca then contacted Timothy Rice, an ethnomusicology professor at UCLA and a leading Bulgarian music specialist, for help in locating appropriate vocalists who could participate in the Los Angeles recording sessions (Rice 2002:34, 2003:171).

35. From "Meet Joseph LoDuca: Composer for Hercules and Xena," at www.universalstudios.com/tv/loduca/interview.html.

36. See also Rice 2002:34. According to North, other vocalists providing music for the *Xena* soundtracks with whom she worked include Dee Ann Hendricks, Trudi Israel, and Janis McGlaze. She identified Zhivka Konstantinova as the real "powerhouse" amongst the vocalists.

37. Depending on the original Cyrillic spelling, which is not available in the liner notes, this line could also translate as "Prepare a path to war!"

38. Cf. Andreas 2004:3, and Hozić (2004), who investigates contemporary cigarette smuggling and other illicit trafficking activities across the Balkans in the historical context of older, Ottoman-era trade routes and practices.

❖ 8 ❖

"The Criminals of Albanian Music": Albanian Commercial Folk Music and Issues of Identity since 1990

Jane C. Sugarman

In the spring of 1999, while researching Albanian commercial music production in Germany and Switzerland, I met in Geneva with a music producer from Macedonia who had begun to underwrite commercial recordings in a variety of styles.[1] When I said that I was interested in speaking with him about the Albanian music industry, he countered me by exclaiming, of himself and his fellow producers, "We are the criminals of Albanian music!" From this, he launched into a long and circuitous apology for the state of one particular music genre: *muzika popullore* or commercial "folk music." By the end of the conversation, even I had been implicated. "And you too are a criminal," he said just before we parted, "because you like [this] music" (Interview in Geneva, May 1999).

Such intensity of sentiment regarding a contemporary cultural form is not unusual within Albanian communities in and from the former Yugoslavia.[2] In the wake of the disintegration of the country, the dismantling of many state institutions, and a period of ethnic polarization that led to devastating warfare in Kosova in 1998–1999, Albanians in these communities have been engaged in protracted debates concerning the directions that they might take as a national group and the types of social, political, and economic institutions that might replace those of the socialist era. Most frequently such debates hinge on the notion of modernity: in what form might a modern Albanian society be reconstituted, and which values and aspirations should be associated with it?

Within this context, a newly constituted private music industry has emerged as a flashpoint of debate both because of its unabashedly capitalist character and because of the wildly divergent genres that musicians of various social classes, based in various regional centers, have been offering up for public consumption. Of the genres that have developed during this period, none has been more popular—or subject to more criticism—than *muzika popullore* ("folk/national/ people's music"), a style of amplified folk-pop music. By merging high technology with musical features from formerly Ottoman regions, commercial folk music sets forth a specific vision of an Albanian countermodernity that challenges many of the modernist aesthetic principles long championed by the Albanian elite. Its status as a lightning rod for debate points both to continuing class and regional tensions within the Albanian populace and to aspects of postsocialist life that many Albanians find unsettling.

Muzika popullore is clearly one of a number of related Middle Eastern-inflected musical styles that have swept through most areas of southeastern Europe since the 1980s, all of which arose within similar political and economic circumstances and have benefitted from specific technological advances in musical production. As such, it is possible to postulate that the kinship among these styles—and the not infrequent borrowing that goes on among them—signal an exploration of commonalities in sensibility and experience that might lead the region's national groups to affirm a common "Balkan" identity. For observers within and outside the region, such a development would be a welcome sign within communities whose relations over the past two decades have often been destructively fractious.

On closer inspection, however, these musics do not all sound alike. Aside from obvious linguistic differences, they are still distinctly and even deliberately national in their stylistic references, and their social role is often to nourish a space for a cultural intimacy that is experienced as ethnically specific. Furthermore, in no country do the exponents of these genres borrow equally from the musics of all their neighbors. In this respect, they may say less about a common feeling of "Balkanness" than about emerging geopolitical realignments within the region. Perhaps these genres, and the debates that swirl around them, are most significant for what they reveal about the ways that members of each national group are reassessing their relationship to Europe, the West, and the modernity that both of these tout themselves as representing, in a period when full capitulation to a "global culture" emanating largely from the historic West threatens to swallow up the individuality of smaller national cultures.[3]

My own involvement with Albanian commercial musics began in 1997 when I embarked on a research project on the transnational Albanian music industry, one that has taken me to Kosova, Macedonia, Germany, Switzerland, and several cities in North America. In my conversations with musicians and other industry personnel, as well as music consumers, among the liveliest exchanges have concerned the value (or lack thereof) of commercial folk music, but I have also engaged in earnest conversations with central figures about their rationales for creating the sounds that they do. Ultimately, an understanding of this music will come not from focusing upon the rhetoric of a single faction but from placing the various discourses in counterpoint. My intention in this essay is thus to listen respectfully to the range of voices in the debate and then to offer my own analysis of the music's significance and success.

Albanian Commercial Folk Music

In the summer of 2002, an announcer on a Kosova radio station began her program with the following humorous verse:

Vjersha e parë nga Turqi,	The first verse is from Turkey,
vjersha e dytë nga Sërbi,	the second verse is from Serbia,
vjersha e tretë magjupi,	the third verse is in Gypsy style,
dhe refreni nga Greqi,	and the refrain is from Greece,
por në vend të buzukit	only instead of a *bouzouki*
futën çifteli.	they've put a *çifteli*.[4]

The verse alludes to two of the more controversial aspects of Albanian commercial folk music: the fact that it draws from the musical styles of other national groups in the region, and the fact that Albanian bands at times perform "covers" of Turkish or Greek hits. The fundamentals of the style, however, lie a good deal closer to home.

One major component is an approach to musicianship that has characterized the Ottoman-derived music performed for Albanian urban celebrations for much of the past century. A second component are features of various Albanian rural musics from throughout the former Yugoslavia. Upon this basis might be added elements both from rock and jazz and neighboring musics, most often Romani *tallava* and tunes for the dance *çoçek*, and Turkish *arabesk*.[5] Basic instrumentation includes a keyboard instrument, a clarinet and/or saxophone, occasionally a violin, guitar and bass, and percussion. Some performances produce some or all of these instrumental parts on one or two synthesizers. Most songs consist of two or three verses and a refrain alternating with instrumental interludes, with both the refrain and the instrumental portion serving as "hooks" that catch the listener's attention. While the majority are in a meter appropriate to local line dances (2/4, 3+2+2/8, 2+2+3/8, 2+2+2+3/8) or to the solo dance *çoçek* (2/4), an important sub-genre consists of slow songs that are not danced to, often performed in a highly melismatic manner. Together they comprise an energetic and emotion-laden musical style whose recordings have topped the Albanian sales charts for the past fifteen years in both homeland and diaspora areas.

Among the first performers to record commercial folk music were the Aliu Brothers (Vëllezërit Aliu) from Skopje, Macedonia, with their band AVI Rinia (The Youth). An excerpt from the song *Mashalla-Mashalla* from their cassette *Këngë Lirike 2* (Lyric Songs 2, 1992) can illustrate many aspects of the genre (Fig. 8.1; CD 8.1):

Ku m'je nis moj bukuri	Where have you set out for, my beautiful one,
zanin tand kur du me ni?	when will I hear your voice?
Kur dëgjoj moj zanin tand	When I hear your voice
gjumi i natës do me m'zan.	I will be overcome by my nighttime dreams.

Refrain	**Refrain**
Ajd' mashalla, mashalla	Oh how wonderful, how wonderful,
t'kalojmë natën me sevda.	let us spend the night together in love.
Hiqe pak moj at' shami	Pull back your headscarf a bit
sa ta shof synin e zi	so that I can see your dark eyes
kur ta shof moj synin tand	when I see your eyes
gjumi i natës do me m'zan.	I will be overcome by my nighttime dreams.

Figure 8.1: *Mashalla-Mashalla.* Music and lyrics by Zyberi. Performed by the Aliu Brothers and AVI Rinia on their album *Këngë Lirike 2*, 1992.[6]

In the song, two young people steeped in Muslim practices (the woman's headscarf, the Arabic expression *"Ma sha'allah"*) contemplate spending an amorous night together, a sentiment that is risqué by community standards. The lyrics provide a succinct portrait of young people whose lives involve an ongoing negotiation between their community's religiosity and moral propriety, for which they still have considerable respect, and a desire to live out a period of courtship based on notions of romantic love, particularly as it has been presented to them by the global media. This mix of the received and the contemporary, the local and the global, is captured also by the musical setting. Backed by accordion, electric guitar and bass, drumset, and clarinet, the two brothers sing in an upbeat duple meter, rendering the chorus of their song in the melody-plus-drone manner characteristic of Albanian rural songs from western Macedonia. During the final fadeout, as the booming bass line jumps around in a syncopated manner, clarinetist Afrim Aliu takes off in a soaring improvisation whose bent notes and intricate, cascading ornaments pay tribute to a regional legacy of virtuoso Romani instrumentalists.

It is scarcely possible to visit any Albanian region within the former Yugoslavia, or spend any significant time in a diaspora community, without encountering performances such as this in either live or recorded form. More so than other Albanian commercial musics, folk music is first and foremost a live genre that from its outset has dominated two distinct performance contexts: weddings and other large family occasions such as circumcision or betrothal ceremonies; and performances in nightclubs known as *kafene* or *lokale* (cf. Serbian and Macedonian *kafana,* Turkish *gazino*). Through its close association with these two contexts, folk music has come to both encapsulate and help to create two distinct types of social atmosphere: the high-spirited, celebratory affect associated with multi-generational occasions that bring large numbers of family members and friends together; and the rapturous, bittersweet affect induced by music, drinking, and camaraderie at late-night gatherings of male friends. In recent years, additional contexts have been created for younger mixed audiences to enjoy live folk music: commemorations of important days such as graduation or patriotic holidays, and late-night venues such as dance clubs in homeland areas and weekly or monthly "youth evenings" (*mbrëmje rinore*) held in many diaspora towns (Plate 8.1). Less frequently, folk music artists may appear in concert or at music festivals, often lip-synching to their top recorded hits.

In a symbiotic relationship to these live contexts exist recorded performances on cassette or compact disc. In homeland areas, these are frequently hawked by music vendors in small kiosks and shops or at tables in the open market (Plate 8.2). Through these practices, pedestrians become intimately aware of the genre's latest prospective hit within hours of its release. Folk music recordings are also the most likely music to be playing in a taxi or on an inter-city bus, some of which are able to screen music videos as well. During the work week, folk music is the preferred fare on some but not all Albanian radio stations. On weekends, however, it dominates the programming, as friends and families dedicate specific songs to individuals in conjunction with an important occasion. Lastly, folk music recordings are played at the less formal portions of family celebrations and for general listening in the home or car. In all these ways, recorded folk music has come to dominate public space in areas where Albanians form a significant part of the population. Since most of these are in fact multiethnic spaces, folk music has also become a major way to mark public space as distinctively Albanian, at times assertively so.

Recorded programs of folk music exist in two forms. It is programs of newly composed or arranged songs that first establish the reputations of singers and define their repertoire of hits. Love songs dominate these programs, whether recounting courtship encounters between two young people, in the manner of many older weddings songs, or tearful accounts of unrequited longing. To these may be added a plaintive song or two about economic emigration (*gurbet*), pitched at families in the diaspora and appropriate to dedication radio shows; and/or songs that are directly about a wedding celebration, also geared to dedication shows as well as actual weddings. For most artists, the majority of songs will be in a dance meter, with one or two slow songs about love or *gurbet* rounding out the program. While the dance songs are appropriate to any live performance context, the slow songs are the most prized repertoire for late-night male carousing in a nightclub. Of the eight to ten songs on a program, one or two will generally become "hits" that enter the core repertoire.

Once singers have sold a couple of successful programs, they may begin to issue recordings labeled *Live* or *Këngë Dasmash* ("wedding songs"), which are long medleys of songs strung together in such a way as to evoke the atmosphere of a live occasion.[7] Here singers alternate their own hits with other older and newer songs that have become part of the current repertoire. With no system of royalties in place to limit one singer's use of another's material, hit songs are re-recorded numerous times by a variety of singers, and the best known quickly attain the status of quasi-traditional songs. While the production values on such programs are generally lower than those that feature original songs, the recordings are highly prized for their spontaneity and their capacity to transport listeners to the emotional pitch associated with live events.

The style and repertoire of contemporary folk music have been shaped most fundamentally by a small number of musicians from Kosova and Macedonia (Plate 8.3). From Kosova, these include the band Besnikët (The Loyal Ones), with its star singer Sinan Vllasaliu; the band Corona, which records with Ramadan Krasniqi ("Dani") and many other singers; and Afrim Muçiqi, who began his career singing with Corona and later formed his own ensemble, Yjët (The Stars). Another influential team has been singer Vera Oruçaj and her husband, violinist and singer Sunaj Saraçi, both of whom now live in New York City. The genre is most closely associated, however, with Macedonian performers such as the Aliu Brothers and singers Zyber Avdiu and Xhezair Elezi ("Xheza"), followed by a host of others. In a field dominated by male performers, Gjyle Çollaku and Dritë Musliu stand out as the most prominent female performers of the genre in Macedonia. In addition to these Albanian artists, a few Romani performers have gained a wide following among audiences, including Sofije Hyseni and Gazmend Rama ("Gazi").[8]

These are the individuals who have come to define the sound of contemporary folk music and have contributed most to its repertoire. But since the early 1990s, the great majority of Albanian singers from all homeland areas who have made their career as any type of folk performer have adopted at least some features of the style of this core group. This applies equally to singers specializing in rural repertoires, such as the Mustafa Sisters from Kosova, and to those known for their execution of the difficult older urban repertoire, such as Kosova's Ismet Peja and Shkëlzen Jetishi and Albania's Merita Halili. All have expanded their repertoire to include new songs in a commercial style, learned at least some of the top hits to sing in live performance, and gradually added more amplification and electronically produced melodic layers to their arrangements, whether live or recorded. As a result, with the exception of a few singers in the "folkloric" style who specialize in a patriotic repertoire, the realm of commercial folk music has come to be almost coterminous with contemporary folk music performance.

Socialist and Postsocialist Music Production

The set of circumstances that propelled commercial folk music to the top of the Albanian hit parade was put in motion by the collapse of Yugoslavia and its socialist system. As a consequence, the central role of the state media in recording and broadcasting most forms of local music was supplanted by new private music industries and networks of private radio and television channels. In this respect, the development of Albanian commercial folk music contrasts strongly with that of its Slavic-language counterpart, newly composed folk music, which arose during the heyday of Yugoslav socialism in the 1960s and 1970s (see Rasmussen 2002). At the same time, its development during the postsocialist period parallels that of styles that have become prevalent in many neighboring countries.

During the socialist period, the center of musical production for all Yugoslav Albanians was Radio-Television Prishtina (RTP), located in Kosova's capital city, which recorded and broadcast virtually all the

Albanian music aired in the country as well as releasing cassettes on its own label. For folk music performance, a second important sphere consisted of the professional folklore ensemble "Shota," also headquartered in Prishtina, as well as many amateur ensembles or SHKA-s located not only throughout Kosova but also in Macedonia and Montenegro.[9] In Kosova, an annual circuit of juried music festivals, from Akordet e Kosovës, which showcased composed songs in both folk and popular styles, to the folklore festival in Gllogovc (now Drenas; Serb. Glogovac), which featured unarranged performances by village ensembles, provided a means of monitoring aesthetic norms and a forum in which the most highly regarded performers of each genre could be "affirmed" (*afirmu*; see Munishi 2001:25–27). The individuals who oversaw these many activities had either been schooled in Western classical music or were folk performers who had worked their way through the system to a position of authority, and they came to represent an important segment of the Albanian cultural elite.

As elsewhere in the country, the media and ensembles were charged with creating styles of music that would not only be entertaining but also support the larger goals of Yugoslav social policy. Styles of music associated with the West, whether classical or popular, were deemed the most "progressive," in that they were seen to embody qualities associated with the type of modern, industrialized, cosmopolitan society that Yugoslavia's leaders wished it to become. These were also the musics that members of the educated elite preferred, or at least were assumed and expected to prefer. But various types of folk music also had crucial roles to play within the Yugoslav system (see also Rasmussen 2002). First, they symbolized the various national groups that comprised the country, and thus became central to presentations that highlighted Yugoslavia's multiethnic principle of "brotherhood and unity." Second, they addressed the concerns of those within each national group who saw folklore as the core of that group's national culture, and who feared that such national identities would eventually be undermined by a larger "Yugoslav" one. In doing so, they helped to maintain and even nourish nationalist sentiments among at least some portion of each national group's elite. Last and perhaps most importantly, they spoke to the musical tastes of the large numbers of Yugoslavs who were less highly educated or whose social orientation was less firmly Western. Among Albanians, the majority of such individuals lived in rural areas or came from families of rural background that had migrated to the towns or emigrated to western Europe and North America; but their ranks also included members of families, often of an artisanal background, who had been urban dwellers for several generations (see Ellis 2003).

For these communities, folk music emerged as a primary site for efforts by the elite not merely to shape their aesthetics but also to encourage in them "modern" values and aspirations. As in neighboring socialist countries, this was done by presenting folk music in a manner that, on the one hand, highlighted those elements considered to be most characteristic of the national group that it represented and, on the other, was "modernized" and "elevated" through recourse to elements of Western classical music. Both rural and urban repertoires were carefully arranged using diatonic scales and modified tonal harmonies, and performed by ensembles dominated by Western orchestral instruments. In Kosova, some early vocalists used a *bel canto* type of vocal production in emulation of singers in Albania. Through these means, utopian sonic images were created that encapsulated Yugoslavia's modernist ideal for each national group: a cultivated people oriented toward the West that nevertheless maintained an identity as culturally distinctive. Needless to say, these were images that mirrored back to elite Yugoslavs their own aspirations and sense of identity.

For Albanians in Yugoslavia, state-sponsored musical activities held special meaning. It was not until the early 1970s, as Kosova was granted increasing autonomy within the republic of Serbia, that Albanians were able to take full charge of the performance of their own folklore within the media and the various ensembles. Many came to regard the degree of professionalism that they achieved as an important testament to their general capacity to run their own affairs. The fact that the Albanian state pursued similar musical policies and engaged in cultural exchanges with Kosova provided a further source of pride. After 1981, when demonstrations for greater political rights for Kosova resulted in massive arrests and renewed suppression of Albanian expression, the conventions of folk music performance allowed Albanians to develop styles of music that spoke to their growing sense of national commitment.

All of this was to change, however, as the socialist system began to collapse. The disintegration of Yugoslavia in the early 1990s brought about a sharp decline in the role of the state media as centers of recording and broadcasting. In the case of Albanians, this situation was complicated by their problematic political status within the new successor states of Macedonia and the rump Yugoslavia (now Montenegro and Serbia). In Kosova, as part of a general rescinding of the region's autonomy by Serbian president Slobodan Milošević, the Albanian employees of Radio-Television Prishtina were removed from their positions in 1990 and replaced by Serbian personnel. Shortly thereafter, ensemble "Shota" was disbanded and state support of amateur folklore ensembles was withdrawn. In neighboring Macedonia, circumstances were only somewhat better. Some Albanian-language programming was included on secondary radio and television channels of the new Macedonian Radio-Television (MRT), and independent radio and television stations gradually opened, but only Macedonian amateur ensembles continued to be funded by the state. The upshot of these many changes was that many musicians and technical personnel found themselves not only unemployed but without any venue in which to continue their activities. Perhaps the single greatest impetus for the development of Albanian commercial folk music was the gradual entry of such musicians into the wedding and nightclub circuits, which had always remained outside state oversight. Already during the 1980s, a number of Albanian musicians from the state media or the ensembles had begun to "moonlight" in the wedding circuit (cf. Pettan 1992a:144; Seeman 1990:30–31). In the early 1990s, with no alternative venues in which to operate and few other employment opportunities to pursue, musicians began to transform such extracurricular activities into a primary profession (cf. Munishi 1997:277–85).

One result of this development was a rapid Albanianization of musical performance in the two spheres, and a consequent sidelining of the musicians that had formerly been associated with them. Throughout the socialist period, wedding and nightclub ensembles had been composed of individuals, primarily Roma, who had honed their skills within those spheres rather than through formal music education (cf. Munishi 1997:280). Pettan (1992a) has described in detail how, as interethnic tensions increased in Kosova during the 1980s, Romani musicians ceased to be hired for many Albanian family celebrations because they also played for Serbs and hence were viewed as potentially untrustworthy. As Albanian bands began to dominate the wedding circuit, they began to mix the repertoire of the Romani bands with music they knew from the ensemble setting. Similarly, before 1990 there were only a limited number of nightclubs that catered to an Albanian clientele. In the early 1990s, however, they became centers of musical performance, both because they represented a new type of business opportunity and because musical activities had been curtailed in many other sectors. Kosova ethno-musicologist Rexhep Munishi described the new personnel in the clubs:

> With regard to age, they are members of several generations: from their teens up to beyond fifty. In terms of their professional orientation, they range from those who have completed elementary or middle school up to those who have finished the faculty of music; and by profession they are similarly varied: teachers, professors of music in the middle school, as well as students and professors at the Faculty of Arts in the music sector. It is really a tragedy of this period when the educated musician,

the professional instrumentalist who could have distinguished himself on another stage, is obliged to become a fixture of the *kafene,* in which music is placed in a completely different context (Munishi 1997:281).

As these transformations were taking place among performers, a new, private recording industry was coalescing around a network of production companies, distributors, and sales outlets. The first private Albanian music firms in Yugoslavia were founded in the late 1980s, when market reforms initiated by prime minister Ante Marković encouraged the increased development of small private businesses. The major impetus for privatization came, however, with the rescinding of Kosova autonomy, and by the mid 1990s several production companies were in place. In addition to firms located in homeland areas, a significant number were located in the diaspora, principally Switzerland and Germany, where large communities of migrant Albanians were keen to purchase recordings from home.

In contrast to the situation with musicians, only a few key personnel within these firms were veterans of Kosova's state cultural institutions. The great majority were men with capital to invest and perhaps some business experience but little training in the arts and, in general, less education than the former media personnel. As one diaspora producer remarked disparagingly, "Ten years ago we were watching the cows, working the land, we were mechanics . . . . We are not businessmen, we are peasants (*katunarë*)!"[10] The industry that they founded also had very different goals than those of the state-run media: it was capitalist to the core, and its aim was to generate profits rather than embody a particular ideology. This meant promoting newly written or arranged songs that could become hits, issuing new albums by top performers in fairly rapid succession, and aiming the majority of the releases at the largest market niches that developed.

From the beginning, the industry produced three categories of recordings, using labels that descend from the socialist period: *muzika popullore* [commercial "folk music"]; *muzika folklorike* [folkloric music], songs in rural style, often patriotic, generally performed with a mix of rural and contemporary instrumentation; and *muzika zbavitëse* [entertainment music], songs modeled on any style of North American or Western European pop music such as techno, rock, hip-hop, or so-called "light" music (*muzika e lehtë*).[11] Although the top artists in each category sold large numbers of recordings, it was programs of commercial folk music by the new lineup of performers that topped the sales charts. The numbers were often staggering: in Kosova, where many programs sold only 3–4,000 copies, and the most successful pop or folkloric recording might sell 20,000 copies, a top folk album could exceed 70,000 copies. The fact that many of its consumers lived in the diaspora, and had more money at their disposal to spend on musical products, further propelled the emphasis on this genre.

As folk music was transformed from a live music into one that was fundamentally connected to a recording industry, a new repertoire needed to be developed to supplement the older favorites that audiences would expect to hear at live events. This necessitated the consolidation of a third new set of music personnel: lyricists, songwriters, arrangers, and studio technicians. From its inception, the issue of studios became the biggest stumbling block in establishing the new industry. In the early 1990s, no one had sufficient capital to invest in professional equipment such as multi-track recorders or mixing boards, nor did anyone have enough room at home to house both a recording booth and a space for performers. This was especially the case in Kosova where, in a political climate in which Albanian-language recordings could be confiscated by the police, any such activities had to be carried on surreptitiously.

The studio dilemma was solved serendipitously by the availability of a new type of recording technology. In 1988, the Korg company intro-duced the M1 synthesizer, which combined several features that allowed it to function as a "workstation," or self-standing production unit. First, it included a library of PCM samples of instruments standard for Western classical or popular musics that were much closer to the sound of their acoustic models than had been the case for earlier synthesizers. Second, it featured a sequencer, which allowed a musician to enter musical lines one by one via the keyboard and then store them, essentially using the synthesizer as a form of multi-track recorder. Additional features were a drum machine with pre-programmed rhythmic patterns and a series of special effects such as delay and reverb. In effect, the M1 was a miniature recording studio that allowed a complete arrangement of a song to be constructed using sampled sounds, with which individual acoustic tracks could be mixed to produce a finished recording.

The Albanian recording industry thus fell into the hands of anyone who could obtain an M1 or a later workstation such as the Korg O1 and the Roland JV-1000. These individuals became the arranger-engineers not just for folk music recordings but for the full range of Albanian commer-cial music genres, and therefore the new industry's most indispensable personnel. Not surprisingly, the majority were keyboard players: either accordionists whose background was in folk music, or individuals with a rock or jazz background. At first, in the early 1990s, a great many albums in all styles featured only a vocalist with a synthesizer, giving them an unmistakably "canned" sound that often contrasted markedly with the performer's live appearances. Gradually, however, arrangers chose to include acoustic instrumental tracks as well.[12]

The "Turkish Essence"

Many of the features that characterize Albanian commercial folk music, including its heavy reliance on synthesized sounds and its emphasis on songs constructed so as to be "hits," are understandable in light of the processes and transformations just outlined. But individual singers and groups have adopted distinct strategies in combining practices associated with state institutions and with the wedding and nightclub circuits, in making use of available technologies, and in recruiting supporting personnel for their projects. While some have chosen to confirm many of the aesthetic principles associated with socialist-era institutions, others have pursued a style that diverges considerably from those principles. One can think of Albanian commercial folk music as existing along a stylistic continuum, with each pole associated with a specific region of the former Yugoslavia.

Of the performers who have chosen to continue most directly the principles of the socialist period, most are from Kosova. For these performers, the productions of that era represent not the legacy of a moribund political system, as they do throughout much of the rest of postsocialist eastern Europe, but rather a precious sphere of Albanian-controlled creativity that was then thwarted by the Serbian state after 1990. Continuing the state aesthetic has meant being careful to foreground musical elements deemed to be characteristically Albanian, and drawing on techniques from Western classical or popular musics in creating arrangements. Many of the lyricists, composers, and arrangers active in Kosova have professional credentials as literary figures or trained musicians, and many were formerly associated with the state media. A number of the musicians come from a popular music or jazz background, and a striking number peopled the Kosova rock bands of the 1980s. Most of them are equally active producing new material for Albanian pop performers. Among such musicians, a style of folk music has developed that leans heavily toward a Western aesthetic, including selections that are sometimes hard to distinguish from pop songs. This style has had a particular appeal for more educated listeners and for those of a more nationalist bent.

O-më beso se një të kam,	Believe me that you are the only one,
ti je mirë, i joti jam,	you are wonderful and I am yours,
vallëzo sonte deri n'agim,	dance tonight until the dawn,
qeshu kënaqu shpirti im.	smile and enjoy yourself, my soul.
O-syt e tua plot shkëlqim	Your eyes full of sparkle
më shikojnë plot gëzim,	look at me full of happiness,
zemra ime për ty ra	my heart has fallen for you
luje belin marshalla!	so move your body, may God be praised!

Refrain

Refrain

Luj me duar luj me krah,	Dance with your hands, dance with your arms,
vallëzo shpirto der në saba,	dance, my soul, until the morning,
kënaqu sonte mos pusho	enjoy yourself tonight and don't let up
vetëm ty zemra të do.	for my heart loves only you.

Figure 8.2: *Kënaqu sonte.* Nexhat Macula, music; Hivzi Krasniqi, text; Valton Beqiri, arr. Performed by Ramadan Krasniqi and Corona on their album *Mi Ke Flokët*, 1997.

One such group is Corona, which has accompanied many of the top Kosova folk performers over the past decade. Corona formed initially within the Prishtina amateur ensemble "Ramiz Sadiku" and had already established itself as a wedding band before 1990. All of its members have had extensive formal music training, and most are currently involved in the classical realm as well.[13] In its recordings, the group's frequent use of acoustic guitar as well as violin links its sound to ensembles formerly associated with the state radio and major ensembles, but the band also performs live in a more standard configuration of clarinet or saxophone, amplified guitar, synthesizer, and drumkit (Plate 8.4).

Corona has frequently collaborated with singer Ramadan Krasniqi, whose clear tenor voice and ornamented vocal style pay homage to older urban practices. His early programs with Corona popularized both older songs long associated with the wedding context and a range of newly written dance songs and slow ballads. His biggest hit of the 1990s both responded to, and fueled, the emerging fad for the dance *çoçek*, in which couples face each other and employ graceful hand, arm, and torso movements (Fig. 8.2; CD 8.2). Like many of Krasniqi's hits, this one was co-authored by lyricist Hivzi Krasniqi, a veteran of the former state media, and composer Nexhat Macula, Kosova's best-known rock guitarist, who also writes songs for his rock band TNT.

At the other pole are performers, largely from Macedonia, whose aesthetic continues much more directly the legacy of the older wedding and nightclub repertoire and of the Romani musicians who played a fundamental role in creating and sustaining it. Rather than being based on media models, their instrumentation represents an updated version of the urban *çalgı* ensemble (see below), with solo clarinet and/or saxophone backed by electric guitar and bass, keyboard, and drumkit. Other features linking these bands to older practices include a modal system derived from Ottoman *makamlar*, rhythmic cycles that arose to accompany urban dance forms such as *çoçek,* and modal improvisations in the style of Turkish instrumental *taksim*-s and vocal *amane*-s. Some recordings continue to employ Romani musicians, particularly as wind players. At the same time, groups from Macedonia also make direct reference to local rural styles. In the early 1990s, for example, the practice of adding a vocal drone to melodies was introduced by performers such as the Aliu Brothers and Xhemil Salihu, and this practice soon spread to Kosova musicians as well. Unlike the premier Kosova groups, most performers from Macedonia have not had formal music training, and only a few were formerly connected to state-supported institutions. Most developed their musical style by absorbing the musical atmosphere of their Muslim-majority neighborhoods in Skopje and other towns. Many performers also write their own songs, or turn to a circle of local musicians that has developed around the new folk music industry.[14]

As early as the late 1980s, Albanian musicians in Macedonia began to purchase synthesizers from Turkey that came equipped with an array of preprogrammed Middle Eastern sounds: rhythmic patterns based on Turkish *usuler* or Arab *iqa'at;* samples of Turkish instruments such as the *saz, ney, kanun, zurna,* and *mey;* synthesized "arrangements" that reproduce the sounds of a large Turkish or Egyptian string orchestra; and above all, the capacity to play in scales with neutral pitches. These instruments endow any recordings on which they are used with a sound that is fundamentally different from any produced on diatonic synthesizers: as perceived by most Albanian listeners, an "oriental" as opposed to a "Western" sound. Some bands such as the Aliu Brothers use these synthesizers primarily as background accompaniment, and have recorded albums that sound very much like their live performances. A number of artists, however, have produced whole albums with such synthesizers as the sole accompaniment. At present, certain synthesized sounds with a vaguely Middle Eastern, reedy timbre are so characteristic of Albanian

folk music recordings from Macedonia that they have become one of the
genre's most defining features.

One of the most successful Macedonian folk performers has been
singer Zyber Avdiu, who began to issue recordings in the early 1990s.
Avdiu has made his career singing simple songs in dance meters with a
couple of verses each and catchy refrains that can instantly be memorized
(Fig. 8.3; CD 8.3):

(Each stanza repeats.)

Sa herë t'shoh me sy	Every time I catch sight of you
shpirtin peshë ma çon.	my soul is lifted,
Unë t'pres n'takim	I wait for a meeting with you
e ti me ardh s'guxon.	but you don't dare to come.

Refrain   **Refrain**

Babën mos dëgjo (mos!)	Don't listen to your father (don't!)
e nanën mos dëgjo (aman!)	and don't listen to your mother (please!).
dëgjo zemrën tënde	Listen to your heart
dhe më dashuro, o-o-o,	and fall in love with me.
dhe më dashuro.	

Sa herë t'shoh me sy	Every time I catch sight of you
sillesh si hyjneshë.	you carry yourself like a goddess.
Me fol nuk guxon	You don't dare to speak,
veç shiqon dhe qesh.	you just look at me and smile.

Figure 8.3: *Dëgjo zemrën tënde.* Rrahman Kryeziu, arr. Performed by Zyber
Avdiu on their album *[N]dëgjo Zemrën Tënde,* 1999.[15]

Avdiu's early recordings were often entirely electronic and in a decidedly
Turkish style, including sampled string interjections in the style of *arabesk*
or the Egyptian music it emulates. On more recent albums, he has
included fiery clarinet and/or saxophone solos on many tracks, played by
what seem to be Romani instrumentalists.

Although most Albanians in Kosova and Macedonia use a local
dialect in everyday speech, the lyrics of songs peformed by Kosova folk
groups are often in something close to the literary language standardized
in Albania, giving them the aura of elevated poetry. Avdiu, however, sings
in unadulterated Skopje dialect and his lyrics, which he himself creates,
are often lambasted by critics as sub-standard doggerel. He responded to
such opinions in an article, "Journey to the Center of Cyberworld," printed

in a Kosova magazine: "I cannot make the song text grammatical (*Nuk muj me gramatizue tekstin*), because then I would have problems selling the cassettes. I sing the way I speak at home. I speak with the language of my mother and father and I am very proud of the way that I speak."[16] Indeed, the everyday quality of his songs' language and themes are a great part of their appeal. Like those of the Aliu Brothers and other Macedonian groups, his lyrics bring to life the world of urban Muslim neighborhoods and the complex negotiations between inherited and emergent aspirations and practices that are unfolding in them (Fig.8.4):

Haj medet na u ba beteri,	Woe is me, a catastrophe has befallen us,
qesh katuni na qesh shehri.	the village is laughing as well as the town.
Për me t'dasht vashat e mira	In order for the desirable girls to fall in love with you
duhet me i mbajt dy mobila.	you have to maintain two cell-phones.
Refrain	**Refrain**
Pa dëgjo moj vajzë e mirë,	Listen to me, my beautiful girl,
thirrëm ti se s'muj me t'thirr.	you call me, because I can't call you.
Cingër, cingër ban mobili,	"Ring, ring" goes the cellphone,
po m'thot vajza unë s'do t'thirri.	but my girl tells me, "I'm not going to call you."
Haj medet o unë i shkreti	Woe is me, poor wretched one,
tuj pagu po m'zbrazet xhepi.	to pay for it empties my pocket.[17]

Figure 8.4: *Mobili.* Performed by Zyber Avdiu on their album *[N]dëgjo Zemrën Tënde,* 1999: B2.

When I have queried musicians and industry personnel about the more Middle Eastern-inflected form of commercial folk music, they have attributed it most often to ties that Albanian families have retained with Turkish culture since the Ottoman period. As they have emphasized, it was once common throughout Kosova and Macedonia for rural Muslim families who migrated to the town to assume a "Turkish" identity, which entailed speaking Turkish as their first language and cultivating Turkish cultural forms such as cuisine, dress, music, and dance. A producer from the Skopje district living in Switzerland explained it in this way:

> In Skopje . . . many of the Albanian families speak Turkish at home.
> This used to be the case for Albanians in towns throughout Macedonia
> and Kosova. When you moved from the *katund* [village] to the *qytet*
> [town], you became a Turk within ten years. If someone asked you what
> you were, you would say, "I'm a Turk" (Interview in Geneva, May
> 1999).

Particularly in Macedonia, a number of urban families have continued to
favor Turkish language and culture to the present day, and refer to
themselves by the Turkish term *shehirli* ("townspeople").[18] During the
1960s and 1970s, as nationalist ideals took root in many communities,
strong pressure arose, particularly in Kosova, to abandon an identification
with Turkish language and culture and to claim instead an Albanian
identity. As a result, in many towns, *shehirli* or "Turkish" families now
coexist with "Albanian" families to whom they are at times related, all
living together in common "Muslim" neighborhoods. Many of the
individuals who identify themselves as Albanian continue to speak
Turkish as a second language.

Commercial folk music in its more Middle Eastern-inflected form has
arisen primarily from the musical tastes of such communities, which
continue to absorb migrants from the countryside. In past decades,
Turkish-style *çalgı* music, performed on *ud, kanon,* violin, clarinet, and
percussion by Romani-dominated ensembles, was played at the weddings
of well-to-do urban families, as well as in local nightclubs descending
from the late Ottoman *café-aman.*[19] Songs in Turkish language, as well as
Albanian-language songs based on similar musical principles, became the
core repertoire both for professional performers and for amateur music
making in the home. Some of the Turkish songs had in fact originated in
the Balkans, and are designated today in Turkish by the term *rumeli.* The
melodies of popular songs from Turkey also became the basis of new
songs in Albanian language, as was the case with virtually every other
language in the Balkans.[20] In contrast to neighboring countries, socialist
Yugoslavia explicitly acknowledged and promoted the region's Turkish
legacy. In both Kosova and Macedonia, the media broadcast local Turkish
music as well as music recorded in Turkey, and the state supported a
number of Turkish folkloric ensembles. Many Muslim families continued
to participate in both Albanian and Turkish musical domains. Commercial
folk musicians are quick to relate their music to this older era. When I
asked Afrim Aliu of the Aliu Brothers why contemporary folk music
sounds so Turkish, he immediately responded that "[Turkish music] is our
music!" and that some older Albanian urban songs "are really Turkish
songs." He and his brother made it a tradition to include one older

Albanian urban song recorded by legendary singer Qamili i Vogël on each of their early albums, an act that asserted their continuity with historic practices (Interview in Skopje, July 1999).[21]

During the 1980s, Turkish musical influences diminished within the repertoire of professional bands. The principal reason was an intensification of nationalist feelings among Albanians, emanating primarily from Kosova, but an additional factor was increased patronage of professional wedding bands by families of rural origin. Especially in those bands dominated by Albanian musicians, the repertoire turned heavily toward Albanian songs of rural origin or new songs created in rural style. The state media of both Yugoslavia and Albania played a major role in the circulation of these songs, as did major folklore ensembles, and many of them functioned as the "hits" of their era.[22] A number of these songs continue to be performed and recorded by commercial folk artists, particularly on "Live" albums. Their influence is also apparent in rural stylistic elements, such as vocal quality and ornamentation, melodic contours, and dance meters, that are incorporated into many recently composed songs.

But this period also saw a new wave of Turkish influence in Yugoslavia. Among Albanians, this was prompted first by the close ties that families there have retained with relatives in Turkey. In the decade after World War II, on the basis of an agreement between Turkey and Yugoslavia, tens of thousands of Muslim families from Kosova and Macedonia, the majority of them of Albanian descent, left Yugoslavia to settle in Turkey (see Ellis 2003; Malcolm 1998:322–23). As a result, it is difficult to find a Muslim Albanian family in the former Yugoslavia, particularly in Macedonia, that does not have close relatives there. Many individuals have told me of hearing recordings of *arabesk* stars such as Orhan Gencebey and İbrahim Tatlıses at their relatives' homes during the 1980s, or of relatives bringing them cassettes from Turkey as gifts. At the same time, *arabesk* began to enter Yugoslav public spaces through Romani performers such as Muharem Serbezovski, who began to record covers of *arabesk* hits in Serbian. By the late 1980s it was common for *arabesk* recordings and videos of films to be sold by vendors in the open markets and aired in inter-city buses as well as teahouses catering to Muslim men (see Pettan 1992a:177–78).

When individuals have discussed with me the appeal of *arabesk* for their communities, it has invariably involved the notion of *dhimbje* [pain, suffering, longing] as expressed through *arabesk* lyrics and vocal style. One man told me that he associated *arabesk*'s sound with Islamic religious genres such as the call to prayer (*ezan*) and recitation of the Koran, as well as with the longing that a young village man might feel for a girl with whom he could not have direct contact. In contrast, several individuals saw the intensely emotional style of slow *arabesk* songs, in which a man expresses his deep suffering over a woman, as having a particular appeal for young women who dream of romantic love. In this respect, *arabesk* can be said both to have spoken to features that have historically defined the life of Albanian Muslim communities and to have encouraged in young people new ways of experiencing gendered relationships.

By the early 1990s, Turkish commercial musics, including both *arabesk* and Turkish pop, became even more influential when several channels of Turkish satellite television began to be directed toward Europe. With its steady fare of music-related programming, and with production values immeasurably higher than those of local stations, Turkish television quickly gained a sizeable audience, particularly in Macedonia. In 1999, when I stayed with an Albanian family in Skopje for a month, they were able to receive 24 Turkish TV channels, which they watched all day to the exclusion of any local programming.[23] Given the growing ubiquity of Turkish musics within Albanian communities, as well as a long history of "covering" popular Turkish tunes, it seems inevitable that Albanian singers would eventually begin both to record covers of *arabesk* hits and to create new songs in their style. Likewise, it seems inevitable that synthesizer players, realizing that a full *arabesk*-style orchestra lay just beneath their fingertips, would begin to turn out arrangements mimicking *arabesk* recordings, even when these were accompanying otherwise Albanian-sounding melodies.

From the perspective of those who make it, the dominant form of Albanian commercial folk music thus arose through a convergence of older urban and rural Albanian repertoires with Turkish *arabesk*. Contemporary performers have taken this rich mix of sounds and updated it through electronic technologies as well as occasional allusions to rock and jazz. Although rural features are most apparent in the present-day dance repertoire, and those from *arabesk* most noticeable in the slow melismatic songs, the genre as a whole has arrived at a distinctive sound that fuses all these elements. For its creators and biggest fans, the Turkish and Romani elements in this music are not experienced as "borrowings" from someone else's music, but rather as quintessential markers of their own heritage. Ultimately, the genre's success lies in the way it crystallizes the complex sense of Islamo-Turko-Albanian identity that many Albanian families continue to cultivate.

The Criminals of Albanian Music

This favorable portrayal of the development of commercial folk music is very much at odds with the most prominent discourses that circulate regarding it. Indeed, perhaps the most striking aspect of the genre is how much Albanians love to say they hate it. Producers, radio programmers, arrangers, musicians, as well as many consumers of the music have been quick to point out to me its many deficient qualities. Even figures at the center of its development have apologized to me for being involved with it rather than another type of music. Those who denounce it tend to fall back upon quite consistent discourses regarding its negative features, ones that have received wide circulation through opinion pieces in newspapers and magazines.[24]

The most common discourse regarding the genre pinpoints what are perceived as its aesthetic shortcomings: it is "kitsch" (*kiç* or *kiq*) or "trash" (*shund*), to which might be added that it is "banal" (*banal*), "simple" (*thjeshtë*), or "without value" (*pa vlerë*). Most commonly these remarks refer to features such as the simplicity of song lyrics and their use of dialect and poetic clichés, the maudlin character of those songs that dwell on longing or nostalgia, and an over-reliance on electronic sounds. The fact that the popularity of even the biggest hits is shortlived, often lasting only until the artist's next release a few months later, is compared negatively to songs from prior eras that have remained popular for decades. All commercial folk music performances, regardless of their style, are subject to such appraisals. But it is the more Middle Eastern-inflected style of performance that is most often castigated, to the extent that singers like Zyber Avdiu have become prime symbols of everything tacky about contemporary Albanian culture. Behind such aesthetic designations is a class judgment: this is a low-class music devoid of the subtlety and sophistication that would come with education and worldliness. In the parlance of some members of the elite, it is the music of *katunarë* or "peasants": a sweeping term that denotes not only present-day rural dwellers or recent migrants to the city, but any Albanian who does not come from an educated, professional-class family of longtime urban residence.

A second discourse focuses on the ethnic basis of the music's stylistic components. This is music that is "orientalized" (*orientalizu*) or "Gypsy-ized" (*magjupsu*), it is a "mixed" music (*e përzier*), it is the product of a "Turkish essence" (*frymë turke*) that has entered Albanian lands. In this regard, the music is viewed as having strayed far from what the designation of "folk music" ought to connote: a genre foregrounding the musical features that distinguish Albanians as a people and help to constitute and symbolize their national identity. Such characterizations shade into harsher ones that add a moralistic dimension: it is a "bastard" music (*bastarde, bastardizu*), it is "degenerate" (*degjeneru*) and "deformed" (*deformu*). Viewed in these terms, commercial folk music is a form of musical miscegenation—the product of an unnatural union between Albanians and neighboring groups. It is "savage" music (*sauvazh*), "wild" (*e egër*; in the sense of "wild" beasts), and "out of control" (*pa kontroll*); it is a music "of the streets" (*e rrugës*). Again, such judgments are aimed primarily at musicians whose productions foreground elements of Turkish or Romani practice, and are contrasted with phrases such as "music of good quality" (*muzika e mirëfilltë*) or "clean/pure Albanian music" (*muzika e pastër shqiptare*), which might be applied to the more "Albanian"-sounding productions.

Anyone who has followed musical developments in the former Yugoslavia over the past few decades will recognize elements of these discourses as central to those that have long surrounded "newly composed folk music" and its successor, *turbo folk*. But strikingly similar discourses have been deployed in neighboring countries as well to criticize genres that are counterparts to the Yugoslav forms: "wedding music" and *chalga* in Bulgaria, *manele* or *muzică orientală* in Romania, and *arabesk* in Turkey.[25] In each case, they have developed among members of the national group's educated elite, most often those directly involved in the production of musical activities but also folklorists, ethnomusicologists, and social scientists. While some might characterize such discourses as elitist, xenophobic, or even racist, a more sympathetic examination of them can highlight the ways that such musics bring into focus the tensions that have emerged in all these countries over the past fifteen years in the face of massive political and economic change.

Throughout the region, such genres have emerged whenever an opening has appeared for some form of market-driven music industry that can cater directly to the tastes of the "masses." Writing of Turkey, Aksoy and Robins (1995, 1997) have referred to the appearance of such cultural forms as a "return of the repressed," in that they have returned to public culture those elements that state policies have deliberately suppressed. In a similar vein, Ditchev has suggested for southeastern Europe in general that "The official high culture is to be understood in dynamic tension with what it represses; norm and transgression form one system and presuppose each other" (Ditchev 2002:245). It could thus be argued that the strictures of state policy throughout the region were a major impetus for the creation of the musical genres that those who set the policies now decry. The elite has resented these genres because they challenge its role as arbiter of culture, and the popularity that these genres have quickly attained has only underscored the failure of state policies to wrest the masses away from long-held musical tastes. In effect, these genres have provided ample evidence that the "people" or "folk," when left to their own devices, can create forms of music based on local features that can achieve broad popular appeal.

While commentators such as myself might thus characterize such musics as arising through "grassroots" efforts, members of the local elite often see them as forced upon the population through the assertive tactics of a capitalist music industry: "Sadly, the Serbian motto of former times has also been accepted in our circles, 'This is what the people want' ('*To voli narod*'). We would say with a deep conviction that the people do not want this; rather, it has been imposed upon the people" (Munishi 1997:268). In this regard, as some musicians pointed out to me, the very term "folk" or "people's" music is problematic. Many cultural officials subscribe to a view of folklore that long ago was transformed from a description of creative processes typical of non-industrialized societies into a list of prescriptive criteria as to how any future folkloric forms should be constituted. Concerns for "authenticity" and "tradition" that arise from such a view often prompt critics to condemn types of innovation that might not be considered problematic within the realm of "entertainment music."

For those members of the elite socialized from childhood to the modernist orientation that is evident in state policies, these genres are experienced as an affront to their whole sense of being. The situation is such that they are virtually compelled not to like these genres, for their qualifications and claims to be cultural arbiters hinge on such aesthetic distinctions. But showing disdain for commercial genres is also widely engaged in by individuals of a more humble background who wish to make a claim for a more elevated status. Hence the consistent association of these genres with "lower" segments of the population, whether these be villagers, migrants, urban workers, residents of marginal regions of the country, or members of ethnic or religious minorities: elite identities need such "others" in order to retain their distinctiveness (cf. Aksoy and Robins 1997).

These are the factors that have prompted critical discourses whenever grassroots musics have arisen in southeastern Europe. But over the past fifteen years these discourses have acquired a new resonance, as well as an acceptance beyond elite circles, because they speak to a new set of troublesome issues that have characterized the postsocialist period. Among Albanians, commercial folk music emerged only in the late 1980s. Its prominence has thus corresponded with a period in which there were no Albanian-controlled state media in either Kosova or Macedonia and in which few other opportunities existed for the performance of non-commercial musics of any sort. In the thinking not only of the elite but also of a broader class of Albanian listeners, commercial folk music was able to develop precisely because there was no state oversight, and is thus symptomatic of what happens when there is no top-down monitoring of cultural production. Indeed, many Albanians expressed to me a strong desire to return to the days of state-supported media and ensembles, even if these were to exist alongside a private music industry.[26]

The media deregulation of the 1990s is but one facet of a fundamental reworking of class structures that began to occur during this period. In a context of rampant unemployment and relative exclusion of Albanians from state jobs, being a singer, instrumentalist, arranger, or producer has become a possible means of livelihood for many individuals who have few other options, but who might also not have the requisite skills or back-ground. Appearances on a recording or in a nightclub have replaced the system of advancement and certification of competence once provided by state institutions. As one producer commented to me derisively of a prominent folk musician, "And where has he been 'affirmed'? In the nightclubs, by the drunks!" (Interview in Geneva, May 1999). Basic stylistic decisions are made by a new class of personnel who were never inculcated into elite aesthetics and their ideological underpinnings (cf. Kurkela 1993). Those individuals who once dominated state institutions have been forced either to put up with this new set of circumstances by compromising some of their ideals, or to cease to gain a livelihood from music, with the result that some are living barely at a subsistence level. Given this situation, elite criticisms of commercial folk music can be seen as attempts to shore up a sense of self-worth in the face of a system that has denied them both social and economic recognition.

Music personnel are not the only ones experiencing such shifts. Indeed, criticism of commerical folk music beyond elite circles speaks more generally to present economic uncertainties and to the way that the introduction of market relations has dismantled everything that provided a reassuring sense of orderliness and predictability to daily life. Many Albanians are disturbed by the blatant capitalism at the core of contempo-rary musical production of whatever sort, and the thorough commodifica-tion and commercialization of musical realms once regarded as national heritage or community expression (cf. Munishi 1997:271). High unem-ployment and growing economic disparities have exacerbated the sense that much current music is produced "simply for money." For many, the music industry and its most financially successful genre have come to symbolize a society in which entrepreneurial savvy and personal connections have replaced orderly forms of advancement, and in which a wealthy minority is emerging from and thrives amidst an impoverished and disenfranchised majority.[27]

Criticism has fallen particularly heavily on Albanian nightclubs, whether in homeland areas or the diaspora. On the one hand, clubs catering to an all-male clientele have become a particular magnet for young women singers, many of them from Albania, who have virtually no musical background but who desperately need an income. Many individuals have complained to me that the audiences at these establishments are not interested in these young women for their singing. As a former club owner from Lucerne, Switzerland explained, "Most men go to Albanian clubs to see girls in short skirts, not to hear music. They think the singer is there just for them. Why don't the singers just go to *Playboy*?" (Interview in Zürich, July 1999). A producer in Switzerland extended such a critique to the lyrics of a common type of commercial folk song that depicts a male customer drinking in a club with a young woman. If his son were to listen to such songs, he told me, he wouldn't grow up to choose a girl who is honorable, but one who goes to clubs and drinks whiskey with men (Interview in Geneva, May 1999). In both these instances, blame is laid at least partially on the women participants, but the situation that they face is demeaning and even treacherous. They may find that they are expected to have sexual relations with the owner or with a musician in return for the opportunity to perform, or that the clientele expects them also to work as prostitutes. Certainly this dynamic existed in former decades as well, but it was not a matter of community concern because the singers were almost never of Albanian ethnicity.[28]

On the other hand, as nightclubs catering to the youth began to proliferate in large towns in the early 1990s, young people gradually forsook multi-generational social events held in their homes for venues in which they could let off steam away from parental supervision. As Munishi describes:

> In several parts of Prishtina small clubs have opened in basements where parties (*zhurka*) are organized for the youth. There all sorts of things go on: people drink beer or Coca Cola and, unavoidably, there is music. And what kind of music? . . . Principally "folk" music with Gypsy elements is in fashion, because only in this manner can the youth be satisfied . . . . the dancing accelerates to the breaking point, and the neighborhood resounds without any sort of consideration for those nearby.
>
> In this manner, the entertainment of the youth can last until two in the morning, and the problem of delinquency is born in our midst. The

neighbors are obliged to put up with terror, with difficulties, with violence against their spirit, forced to listen first of all to what they don't wish to and then don't value, and in the end, to injurious decibel levels (Munishi 1997:287).

In a period in which prostitution, drug use, petty crime, and various black market activities have increased in all homeland areas, the activities surrounding nightclubs have led many to feel that the collapse of state institutions and their replacement by private enterprises, including musical ones, have produced a moral vacuum within their communities.[29]

Aside from its associations with the excesses of capitalism, commercial folk music has also become a flashpoint in debates over how Albanians are to situate themselves within the unfolding post-Cold War geopolitical order. It is hardly surprising that the more ethnically eclectic forms of folk music are highly objectionable to those Albanians for whom nationalism has been an important cause over the past two decades, particularly those who lived through a horrific war to honor those sentiments. The split that has developed between the more "Albanian" productions from Kosova and the more "oriental" style centered in Macedonia has been interpreted by many commentators as indicative of the contrast between the desire of virtually all Kosovarë to have an independent state or to form a larger union with Albania, and the willingness of many Albanians in Macedonia to go along with the multiethnic basis of their new country. In the view of many in Kosova, the Albanians of Macedonia are, quite simply, insufficiently nationalist. The contrast between the two sub-styles reached its peak in the period of the Kosova war, when the Kosova industry shunned commercial folk music releases as inappropriate to wartime while that in Macedonia used the hiatus to promote its own performers. An ironic implication emerges from such thinking: that the cultural policies enforced in Kosova by the pre-Milošević Yugoslav state succeeded in encouraging a proper form of Albanian identity in individuals there that was denied to those in Macedonia.

The particular vision of national identity that developed among Albanians during the 1990s was very much shaped by the need of all groups within southeastern Europe to situate themselves politically and economically within the "New Europe" in the wake of the fall of socialism. In the jostling for position that ensued, each state or national group felt compelled to demonstrate its Europeanness and Westernness so as to be accepted into organizations such as the European Union and NATO. This often entailed scapegoating neighboring groups or resident minorities as less deserving of such recognition, a syndrome that Bakić-

Hayden has dubbed "nesting orientalisms" (Bakić-Hayden 1995). Within Yugoslavia, as both Muslims and non-Slavs, Albanians were particularly stigmatized through such processes, largely by Serbs and Macedonians. As Slavoj Žižek wrote in 1992:

> What is effectively at stake in the present crisis of post-socialist states is the struggle for one's place: who will be admitted—integrated into the developed capitalist order—and who will remain excluded.
>
> Ex-Yugoslavia is perhaps the exemplary case. Every participant in the bloody disintegration tries to legitimise their place "inside" by presenting themselves as the last bastion of European civilisation (the current ideological designation for the capitalist "inside") in the face of oriental barbarism. . . .
>
> For Croats, the crucial frontier, of course, is the one between them and Serbs, between western Catholic civilisation and the eastern Orthodox collective spirit, which cannot grasp the values of western individualism. Serbs see themselves as the last line of defence of Christian Europe against the fundamentalist danger embodied in Muslim Bosnians and Albanians (Žižek 1992:21).[30]

Serb representations of Albanians as potentially linked to both Islamic fundamentalism and international terrorism were deployed widely in this period, both to advance Serbia's cause *vis-à-vis* European institutions and to justify its claims to Albanian-occupied lands. In the words of a Serbian journalist, writing in 1990:

> the truth about Kosovo and Metohi[j]a has not changed much over time, so that even today Muslim fundamentalism, persistently knocking at the door of Kosovo and Metohi[j]a, is trying to approach Europe. It is hard to believe that Europe is not aware of this. Even those in Europe who do not hold Serbia close to their hearts know very well that this old Balkan state represents the last barrier to the ongoing onslaught and aggression of Islam.[31]

Such assertions negatively affected not only Albanians living in homeland areas, but also those living in western Europe, where similar discourses stigmatizing migrants were on the increase, fueled by what Balibar has referred to as a European-wide "collective sense of identity panic" (Balibar 1991:16).

Rhetoric of this sort has virtually required of Albanians, particularly those in Kosova, that they advance an image of themselves internationally that shuns any references to their Muslim and Ottoman heritages in favor of one that emphasizes Western forms of urbanity and cosmopolitanism. One video director in Kosova even implicated the Serbs in this regard: "Albanians are a Western people, but this music had orientalized Albanians a great deal. The Serbs have imposed this music on us so as to associate Albanians with the Orient, fundamentalism, and the like. This isn't our culture" (Interview in Prishtina, July 2002). But in singling out commercial folk music for pointed criticism and associating it with marginal elements of their society, elite commentators both respond to and play into this orientalizing syndrome. Ultimately, the dynamic that compels Albanians and other groups in southeastern Europe to deny periods of their history and disassociate themselves from their region's cultural legacy will continue so long as discourses of the Orient and of East and West remain salient in the "West."

Since the Kosova war, Albanians there and in Macedonia have felt a renewed urgency to demonstrate their European credentials in the face of the NATO peacekeeping forces and myriad international agencies operating in their midst. In Kosova, where new media outlets have been founded with international support, there have been extensive efforts to marginalize broadcasts of productions seen as "oriental" in favor of those seen as "Albanian," as well as to promote styles of music associated with the West such as symphonic music, jazz, and local techno, rock, and hip-hop. As one long-time radio programmer in Kosova exclaimed to me in frustration, speaking of the period immediately following the war, the workers for international agencies "took us for Gypsies" when they heard what sort of music was being played "in the streets."[32] As rationale for such policies, individuals often return to the rhetoric of the socialist period, as encapsulated by the comments of one music producer in Germany: ". . . music is a very great means of spiritually changing people. And when a person listens to rap music or techno or rock, then certainly he has his mind oriented toward somewhere in the West, toward America. If he listens to a song with a Turkish sound, then it is toward the Orient, toward Arabia" (Interview in Stuttgart, May 1999). Nevertheless, the full range of commercial folk music continues to be requested and broadcast on the most highly patronized radio shows.

Toward an Albanian Modernity

When the critical discourses regarding commercial folk music are placed into conversation with the accounts of those who have created it, two points become evident. First is the way that those involved in the production of each type of folk music have erased certain aspects of Albanian history in order to arrive at a notion of what a contemporary Albanian "folk" music should sound like. In the case of the more purely "Albanian" style that elite audiences champion, it is easy to see how elements that once lay at the heart of the music that Albanians both performed and patronized have been labelled as "Turkish" or "Romani" and then excised from the musical mix in order to produce a style that is consistent with nationalist ideologies. Notably, the many Western musical features that are employed are not seen as "foreign" elements parallel to these, but merely as signs of, and claims to, Westernness and modernity. But even the more Middle Eastern-inflected forms of commercial folk music have engaged in forms of erasure. On the one hand, because of Serbian repression during the 1990s, there has been strong pressure within the musical community to avoid vocal techniques, meters, or harmonic progressions that would sound too close to newly composed folk music or *turbo folk,* and performers who have pursued such styles have been excluded from many musical forums. Through these means, Albanian musicians forcefully repudiate a type of music that was popular within Albanian communities in past years, and in the process downplay elements of cultural commonality that their communities share with neighboring Slavic groups. On the other hand, there has been insufficient acknowledgement of the creativity and dedication of generations of Romani musicians—not only those who dominated the wedding and nightclub repertoires in past eras but also those who have continued to contribute to the sound of contemporary folk music.[33] This has been particularly the case since the Kosova war, when most Roma were forcibly expelled from the province by Albanians who accused them of complicity with the Serbian regime. In short, it is not so much that one type of folk music is nationalist and the other not, but that each group of musicians and producers has pursued a particular musical vision of what constitutes musical "Albanianness."

Second, a complex mix of sentiments is evident surrounding each type of commercial folk music that betrays an ambivalence toward Western modernity. On the one hand, although those musicians and listeners who have most closely espoused socialist-era aesthetics have long seen their productions as exemplifying the modern, many of the features of contemporary folk music that most disturb them have resulted precisely from the unfolding of "modern" processes within their society: processes such as the introduction of full-blown market economics and its resulting commodification of culture and cultural democratization. Despite their embrace of the West as an ideal, their prestige has in fact depended on a system that Western countries have been only too eager to help them dismantle, and is now at risk through those very developments. In a sense, they have been betrayed by the modernity for which they were long the vanguard, which is now flaunting the very qualities that they long worked to suppress. Their disillusionment in fact highlights the many contradictions that exist between the political and economic processes associated with Western modernity and the values that it often trumpets.

On the other hand, the more Middle Eastern-flavored form of commercial folk music needs to be viewed not as an exaltation of "anti-modern" qualities, as many elite commentators would have it, but as an alternative imagining of the modern. In musical terms, it signals modernity not through references to elevated Western forms, although those are often present, but rather through amplification, synthesized sounds, and the complexity of its musical arrangements. In this respect, the influence of the Turkish music industry has been crucial. Just as Turkey has promoted itself, in the words of a Rand Corporation study, as "a successful, prosperous, democratic country where Islam, modernization, and westernization have been successfully reconciled" (Henze 1993:7; see also Şahin and Aksoy 1993), so its sophisticated music productions have modeled for Albanians how a Muslim-majority but European national group can create a contemporary music that celebrates global technologies and takes full advantage of capitalist production methods while giving pride of place to a soundworld, social values, and forms of sociability that have long characterized community life.

At the same time, the prominence of Middle Eastern elements can also be read as registering a reluctance to abandon in full the moral codes and religious identity of the genre's constituency so as to blend into an undifferentiated, European Westernness. The fact that this strain of folk music originated, and still thrives, primarily in Macedonia and is especially popular in the diaspora underscores such an interpretation. In both locales, Albanians constitute a minority population, and the wholesale adoption of Western cultural forms could easily be experienced as signalling a willingness to capitulate to majority pressures and thus to risk the loss of both a moral and a national identity. This situation is in marked contrast to that in Kosova, where Albanians form the overwhelming majority and where pressures to Westernize come primarily from the Albanian elite. The more Middle Eastern-inflected folk music may thus be seen as an embodiment, and even celebration, of a firm desire to retain an identity as "different" within multicultural contexts.[34]

From an elite perspective, the world of Albanian commercial folk music could easily be characterized as a socially conservative one. But such an analysis would not give the genre adequate credit for the ways that it is helping many young Albanians to develop a comfortable sense of themselves as modern, even if that modernity is not entirely Western. This role became apparent to me in the summer of 1999, when I attended several evening parties at "Dancing Club Diagonal" in Skopje (Plate 8.5). Located in the basement of a mini-mall in a heavily Muslim residential area, the club was decorated with mirrors and glitter balls, and strobe lights flickered on and off throughout the evening. On most nights, folk music bands performed live, alternating songs for line dancing with çoçek tunes and slow ballads. During the breaks, a DJ played tracks for Western-style club dancing, mixing songs in English, Albanian, and Turkish. Aside from myself, those attending ranged from a twelve-year-old girl who came with her mother to many young couples to large, single-gender groups of friends aged up to forty; and from residents of nearby villages to educated urbanites. In addition to local residents, there were Albanian visitors from both Turkey and western Europe. Most attending seemed more comfortable with the various local dance styles than the Western ones. When the music was at its best, the dancing lasted until five or six o'clock in the morning.

The proprietor, who had operated such a club in Switzerland, ran the evenings in a way that deliberately discouraged male rivalry and encouraged constructive interactions between men and women. In a bid to attract young women, he followed the lead of other clubs in offering all females free admission. Unless they arrived with a male companion, women were seated at their own tables and escorted to a waiting car at the end of the evening. The owner and his brother moved from table to table at regular intervals to monitor alcohol consumption and to catch any unpleasant exchanges before they began. Through these means, he hoped to convince both young people and their families that it was safe for them to congregate late into the night in a public venue with a mixed-gender crowd.

The careful and cautious atmosphere at clubs like the Diagonal is a far cry from that of dance clubs that cater to young elite Albanians in towns like Prishtina, which are more like those found in western Europe, but it is also very distant from the more patriarchal form of nightclub with which folk music is most often associated. In clubs like the Diagonal as well as "youth evenings" in the diaspora, young Albanians are creating an energetic youth culture that draws much of its vibrancy from its basis in local forms of music and dance and the types of socializing that have historically accompanied them. With those local elements nurturing both comfort and intimacy, young people are able to experiment with "modern" ways of being and interacting that do not unduly challenge community legacies. While the atmosphere may seem hopelessly "conservative" to members of the elite, it is likely through such means, rather than a top-down policing of cultural forms, that Albanians will find their way toward a contemporary sense of identity through which they can situate themselves within the new European political order.

A Common "Balkan" Music?

In a conversation in 2002 on the state of the Albanian recording industry, a prominent music arranger in Prishtina offered an unusually dispassionate assessment: "Here is the reality: a common Balkan music is emerging where you can't tell whether it is Serbian, Bulgarian, Greek, Albanian, or Turkish." When I asked if this was a good or bad thing, he said that he couldn't say that it was either one, just that it was happening.[35] During that summer, I noticed that some individuals had begun to label commercial folk music as "Balkan," but in a pejorative manner, as in descriptions of the music as "Balkano-oriental" (*ballkano-orientale*). Indeed, one emerging trend seemed to be an assertion of a "Mediterranean" identity that could counter the "Balkan" one, pursued musically through an interest in the Italianate music and dance of Albanians in Montenegro or of Albanian-speaking communities in Italy. Clearly Ditchev's observation that, within southeastern Europe, "the new identity debate in the 1990s was largely dominated by the question of whether to be or not be Balkan" continues to be true beyond the year 2000 (Ditchev 2002:235; see also Pettan 1996a). The comments of the music arranger in fact referred primarily to Albanian "entertainment music" (*muzika zbavitëse*), which despite its basis in Western pop forms, has in recent years borrowed stylistic elements, if not whole songs and arrangements, from neighboring countries. But the sentiment certainly applies also to Albanian *muzika popullore*. And so the question arises: What relationship does this musical genre, which shares so many elements with similar ones throughout the region, have with the ways that Albanians wish to identify themselves at the dawn of the twenty-first century? And does it imply a desire to participate in a "Balkan" identity?

Despite the similar sounds of these regional genres, the close analyses offered in this collection and elsewhere (Rice 2003; Slobin 1996) suggest that each constructs a quite specific vision of collective identity, and that stylistic eclecticism does not necessarily correspond to an unqualified embrace of regional belonging. In Bulgaria, for example, Rice has argued that the prominent use in *chalga* of Turkish, Romani, and Serbian elements constructs a "new, expanded sense of national identity" (Rice 2003:42) that includes a recognition of the country's largely Muslim minorities and an embrace of domestic multiculturalism. In contrast, the foregrounding in Albanian commercial folk music of Turkish and Romani features and the concomitant shunning of "Serbian" ones reveals the ways that at least some Albanians are aligning themselves culturally with neighboring Muslims while distancing themselves from Christian Slavs. In a sense, Albanians are opting to restore to their sense of collective identity the cosmopolitanism of the Ottoman ecumene (cf. Sugarman 1999) while repudiating that of Yugoslav "brotherhood and unity," which they see as having been discredited by ten years of warfare. In both the Bulgarian and Albanian instances, these constructs seem most of all to be national ones: attempts by a single group to reimagine its internal composition and redefine its particular network of commonalities within its geographic neighborhood. Clearly, the deep divisions existing among member groups of the former Yugoslavia will continue to undermine the development of regionwide feelings of ecumenicism for some time to come.

In arriving at these constructions, musicians throughout the region have pursued similar strategies that do not always imply a sense of political affinity. In some instances, similarities have arisen because of the exigencies of the genre's beginnings: Albanian *muzika popullore* and Bulgarian *svatbarska muzika,* for example, sound similar in part because they were both developed primarily by wedding bands that drew heavily on a shared Romani legacy. The genres continue to interact in interesting ways; clarinetist Afrim Aliu of the Aliu Brothers is an enthusiastic fan of Bulgarian superstar Ivo Papazov, and Papazov's longtime saxophone player Yuri Yunakov frequently plays for Albanian artists in New York. Nevertheless, attitudes toward Roma can undermine such relationships, and Yunakov is often identified on Albanian recordings with an Albanian name. Certain genres such as Turkish *arabesk,* Greek *laika,* and Yugoslav newly composed folk music, as well as commercial Romani music from Yugoslavia, have also achieved particular prominence regionally because their countries of origin developed market-driven music industries earlier in time, thus enabling them to serve as models of musical modernity for groups whose industries privatized later. But whereas Bulgarians and Serbs might be attracted to Greek music out of a feeling of brotherhood with a neighboring Orthodox group, Albanians cover Greek songs while continuing to have extremely strained relations with Greece the country. In short, I read patterns of musical similarity throughout southeastern Europe as evidence for both alliance and cleavage, and as resulting in part from factors that are independent of political resonances.

It is also important to recognize the complicity of Western countries in the particular constructions that these genres advance. Writing of the interest among Serbs in "going to hear the Gypsy musicians," van de Port (1998:154) has proposed that Serbs relate to Romani nightclub music through a form of "projective identification," in which they identify with the Gypsy as Other as an enactment of their own marginal relationship to the West. By foregrounding and celebrating the very elements of their cultural milieu that have caused them to be regarded internationally as insufficiently civilized, Western, or modern, Serbs challenge the power of the West to define them and legislate their future. Alexander Kiossev interprets Bulgarian *chalga* in a similar vein, but relates it also to official state policies:

> It turns the lowermost picture of the Balkans upside down and converts the stigma into a joyful consumption of pleasures forbidden by European norms and taste. Contrary to the traditional dark image [of the Balkans], this popular culture arrogantly celebrates the Balkans as they are: backward and Oriental, corporeal and semi-rural, rude, funny, but intimate. . . . It is a kind of willing regression into a great, scandalous, Balkan "neighborhood," away from both Europe and the annoying official homelands (Kiossev 2002:184).

If such genres embody, as Kiossev argues, a "lack of popular will to be Westernlike" (2002:184), their audiences nevertheless differ in their view of who it is that represents the West and what exactly it stands for.

Although such analyses are salient for national groups and musical genres throughout the region, I see the dynamic that they describe as particularly at work among Christian groups, especially those who are the majority population within their home state. In such communities, a taste for the "oriental" involves a certain form of masquerade as Other that becomes evident in videos and album covers in the use of bellydance imagery or of a Gypsy temptress holding a rose in her mouth.[36] Performances of *çoçek* music and/or dance can take on a kind of mannered, pastiche quality that comes from having to learn anew, through imitation, expressive forms that one's community has not practiced for a few generations. Such distancing can become a way to disavow one's Easternness even as one claims it, or to cast it firmly into one's past. In contrast, Muslim communities in southeastern Europe, from Turks to Roma to Albanians and Bosnians to Pomaks and Torbeši, have been the others of these Christian groups for most of the past century. What their performances often share is a continuity of practice that dates back to an era when a Muslim identity overrode a national one. For most of these groups, the period since 1990 has involved a protracted effort, often a bloody one, to gain political legitimacy or even an acknowledgement of one's existence. I thus see their very similar musical performances as assertions of cultural distinctiveness addressed in large part to neighbors who simultaneously stigmatize them and appropriate their identities. Within this dynamic of musical "nesting orientalisms," Roma are of course in a class by themselves, both as the group which all others have stigmatized and as the musicians who once dominated the spheres in which the majority of the new regional genres arose. If the Ottoman legacy is one factor uniting these genres, then Romani musicianship is certainly another.

One final point of commonality among these genres is the issue of class difference that they raise. In embracing very similar musics, are the "masses" of southeastern Europe proclaiming that, ultimately, they have more in common with their neighbors of similar background than with their elite fellow countrymen? If one were to take the criticisms that surround these genres at face value, one might be led to conclude that deep divisions still persist between the most highly educated class within each country and the much larger segment of the population comprised of rural dwellers, the urban working class, and the bulk of diaspora residents. If this is so, then each new political system will need to address the disaffection of the masses, and policing their expressive forms would hardly seem to be an appropriate response. But I also wonder if, in fact, the differences in perspectives of the two groups are not becoming increasingly small. Perhaps the criticism wielded against these genres is one of the few ways that members of the elite can distinguish themselves within societies that are becoming, if not economically, then socially more homogeneous. If that is the case, then in the years to come such genres may tell us at least as much about how internal tensions within each country are being addressed as about alliances that are being struck across borders.

Notes

1.This essay began as a presentation on a panel on "Balkan Popular Culture and the Ottoman Ecumene" at the 1998 annual meeting of the Society for Ethnomusicology, organized by Donna Buchanan. Field research in Switzerland, Germany, and the former Yugoslavia between January and August 1999 was supported by a grant for East European Studies from the American Council of Learned Societies; research in Switzerland, Germany, and Kosova in 2002 through a summer research grant from the State University of New York at Stony Brook. I want to thank especially my hosts Albana Rexhepi and Toni Bauman in

Zürich, the Shuku family in Skopje, and the Bejtullahu family in Prishtina. For this essay I benefitted particularly from conversations or interviews with, in New York, Albert and Alfred Popaj, Florent Boshnjaku, and as always, Merita Halili and Raif Hyseni; in western Europe, with Zyber and Naser Avdiu, Shenazi Avdiu, Ing. Sutki Hulaj, Fazli Rexha, Sejdi Rexhepi, Fadil Gagica, Ilir Xhemaili, and Skënder and Magribe Hajdari; in Macedonia with Afrim and Beqir Aliu, Fazli Behluli, and the personnel at dance club "Diagonal"; and in Kosova with Valton Beqiri, Rexhep Munishi, Isak Muçolli, Liljana Çavolli, Xhevdet Gashi, Nexhat Macula, Fitnete Tuda, and Alma Bejtullahu; as well as many others too numerous to cite here. I am also particularly grateful to my colleagues Donna Buchanan, Carol Silverman, Svanibor Pettan, Sonia Seeman, and Martin Stokes for ongoing stimulating conversations on our common musical passions.

2. Within the former Yugoslavia, the great majority of Albanians live in Kosova (Serb. Kosovo, presently a United Nations protectorate), Macedonia, Serbia, and Montenegro. This essay focuses on Kosova and Macedonia, the areas where most commercial folk music is produced.

3. The notion of "the West" is an increasingly problematic one. This is particularly true for areas formerly a part of "socialist Eastern Europe," whose populations most often see themselves as inherently part of Europe and yet not fully accepted, either by themselves or by those whom they view as the West, as either "European" or "Western." For individuals in countries such as Albania or Bulgaria, there is an irony to the designation "Western," in that a primary source of European high culture in eras past was the Soviet Union. For Albanians in and from the former Yugoslavia, however, their frame of reference for the West has consistently been western Europe and North America, with which they have close ties through their large diaspora. In this paper, I use the terms "West" and "Western" to indicate the political ideals as well as the cultural forms that have emanated from those two areas.

4. Radio Dukagjini, 13 July 2002. The *çifteli* is the Albanian counterpart of the Greek *bouzouki;* both are strummed lutes.

5. See Stokes 1992a and Ellingsen 1997 for *arabesk;* Pettan 1992a, 1996c, and 2003 for *tallava;* and Silverman 1996b and 2003 and Sugarman 2003 for *çoçek.*

6. AVI is an acronym for Ansambël Vokalo-Instrumental or "Vocal-Instrumental Ensemble."

7. Very few of these albums are "live" in the sense of having been recorded before a live audience. Most are recorded in studio conditions but often with less editing than in other types of recordings.

8. These performers tend to be from Ashkalli communities in Kosova (Romani Arlije), who speak Albanian rather than Romani as their first language (see Pettan 1996b:36).

9. SHKA is an acronym for Shoqëri Kulturo-Artistike or "Cultural-Artistic Society"; cf. Serbian Kulturno-Umetničko Društvo or KUD.

10. Interview in Geneva, Switzerland, May 1999. Major exceptions to this pattern are the Labia and Vizioni companies in Prishtina, founded by professional filmmakers; and EuroLiza in Switzerland, founded by an engineer.

11. "Light music" is patterned most closely after the songs featured in Italy's San Remo Festival or in the Eurovision Song Contest. I discuss major genres of Albanian commercial music in Sugarman 1999, 2004, and in press a.

12. Basic information on the Korg M1 is available at:
    <http://www.korg.com>,
    <http://hem.passagen.se/tkolb/art/synth/m1_e.htm>,
    <http://emusician.com/ar/emusic_korg/>, and
    <http://www.vintagesynth.org/korg/m1.shtml>.
All studios now have far more elaborate setups in larger spaces, and use computer-based arranging programs rather than workstations.

13. Corona is composed of Valton and Valbon Beqiri, sons of the former director of "Ramiz Sadiku," as well as Ylber and Arben Asllanaj. In addition to their activities in Corona, Valton is a professor of composition at the Faculty of Arts in Prishtina, Valbon plays violin in the Kosova Philharmonic, and Ylber conducts a children's chorus. In the early 1990s Corona founded its own studio, and Valton has become a major folk music arranger.

14. Most of these characteristics have also been true for folk music production in the town of Prizren in Kosova, in which a number of Roma have participated. In a conversation in August 2002 with ethnomusicologist Rexhep Munishi, who has conducted research on styles of vocal polyphony in both Kosova and Macedonia, he confirmed my hunch that this style of two-voiced singing had been introduced to Kosova from Macedonia only in recent years. In Macedonia it is practiced by both Albanians and Macedonians, and was used prominently in past decades by Macedonian performers of *izvorna muzika* (lit. "music from the source") on the state radio. It is worth noting that the lead singer of one of the most famous of such groups, the Kumanovsko Trio, was an ethnic Albanian, Ismet Vejseli.

15. *Ndëgjo* is a misspelling of *Dëgjo*. This error was corrected on the album's reissue.

16. From Anonymous 2002b.

17. Many thanks to Kosova ethnomusicology student Jehona Demaku for her help with the texts of the two Zyber Avdiu songs.

18. Ellis 2003 details the history and community life of such urban Muslims. The author points out that, in the past, the words "Turk" and "Albanian" often referred to city-dweller and villager respectively.

19. For information on *çalgı* (Alb. *çallgi*, Slavic *čalgija*) and related derivatives of the Turkish *ince saz* ensemble in the former Yugoslavia, see Ashkari, et al. 1985; Džimrevski 1985; Petrović 1974a; Pettan 1992a and 1996b; and Seeman 1990.

20. A number of Albanian-language urban songs from Kosova and Macedonia are included in Lorenc Antoni's seven-volume collection of Albanian songs (Antoni 1956–1977). Many urban songs from northern and central Albania were also sung in these regions; see Filja 1991 for characteristic examples.

21. Born in the town of Gjakova (Serb. Đakovica) in western Kosova, Qamili i Vogël was the best-known performer of Kosova urban songs during the socialist period. He can be heard on the LP *Vaj Moj Lule* (Jugoton LPY-V-853), and with

Mazllom Mejzini on the cassette and CD *Këndojnë Bilbilat*, produced by the EuroLiza firm in Switzerland in the mid-1990s. The latter includes the song *N'Çanakala u nisa,* an Albanian-language version of the famous Turkish song *Çanakala içinde.*

22. Many of the older rural songs are included in Antoni 1956–1977, which was compiled in part while the author worked for Radio Prishtina (Alma Bejtullahu, p.c.).

23. Private Turkish TV channels actually began broadcasting abroad via satellite before they were permitted to operate within Turkey itself. By 1992, the Turkish government was sending satellite transmissions both to western Europe, for the large Turkish migrant population there, and to Central Asia. In 1993, it launched its own TURKSAT in a conscious attempt to extend Turkey's political and economic influence into both southeastern Europe and the former Soviet Union; see Aksoy and Robins 1997:1944; Şahin and Aksoy 1993:38–39.

24. Among those who wrote frequently about commercial folk music in the Kosova press during the 1990s were ethnomusicologist Rexhep Munishi and music critic Sami Piraj.

25. For examples and/or analyses of these discourses, see Dević 1968; Gordy 1999; Kos 1972; Petrović 1968 and 1974a; Rasmussen 2002; Rihtman-Auguštin 1978; Simić 1978–79; and Ugrešić 1998 for Yugoslavia; Buchanan 1996b; Rice 1994 and 2002; and Silverman 1989 for Bulgaria; and Ellingsen 1997 and Stokes 1992a for Turkey; as well as other articles in this volume.

26. In contrast, the continuing dominance of the state media in Albania is the main reason that a similar type of music did not develop there until recently.

27. To counter these sorts of sentiments, it could be pointed out that a decline in artistic quality is at least as apparent among Western-style Albanian pop singers as it is within the folk music realm; indeed, the great majority of folk vocalists have very solid technique and are compelling performers. And, of course, achieving success through personal connections was also characteristic of the socialist period.

28. The role of the woman nightclub singer descends from that of the *çengi* or *çoçek;* see Sugarman 2003. Before 1990, most of these women were Roma or ethnic Slavs.

29. Despite these concerns, Albanian commercial folk music production has not drawn on either pornographic or criminal imagery, as have those of Serbian *turbo folk* and Bulgarian *chalga.* Clearly the industry has practiced a degree of self-censorship in order to uphold a certain moral standard, but this strategy also allows Albanians to claim a moral high ground with respect to their neighbors.

30. For similar analyses, see Burgess 1996 and Pilbrow 1997. Yugoslav Albanians were in fact subjected to such scapegoating by other Yugoslavs throughout the socialist period.

31. Petar Sarić writing in *Duga,* August 1990, as quoted in Bakić-Hayden 1995:926. In Serbian parlance, "Kosovo" refers to the eastern portion of Kosova and "Metohija" to the western portion.

32. Interview in Prishtina, July 2002, conducted with Alma Bejtullahu.

33. As one example, Pettan (1992a, 1996c, 2003) discusses the genre *tallava* popularized by Romani singers in the late 1980s, which is now an important component of commercial folk performances.

34. Several industry personnel proposed similar interpretations in interviews. One man in Switzerland, for example, offered his analysis that religion has operated as a form of nationalism among Albanians in Macedonia: it has been their form of resistance to assimilation to Macedonian society. In his view, "They have taken Turkish music as a defense against Slavic culture" (Interview in Neuhausen, June 1999).

35. Interview in Prishtina, July 2002, conducted with Alma Bejtullahu.

36. Similar orientalist imagery is now beginning to appear in Albanian commercial musics, but almost exclusively in *muzika zbavitëse*.

❖ 9 ❖

Shedding Light on the Balkans:
Sezen Aksu's Anatolian Pop

Martin Stokes

New forms of cosmopolitan imaginary have been widely noted across the Balkan region in the wake of the Yugoslav wars and the collapse of the East European socialist regimes.[1] Many share a fascination with border regions, an antipathy to state-sponsored national cultural traditions, an embrace of minority cultures erased from these traditions, and a complex re-imagining of (the Ottoman) empire as the grounds for a new civility. Musicians have been quick to respond. The approbation of local middle-class audiences has often been the most immediate issue, with the critical attention of "world music" labels and critics a more distant goal. Ivo Papazov is perhaps the paradigmatic example of a local artist who had flourished outside of the state-sponsored musical tradition in Bulgaria, and was subsequently co-opted by the emerging elites of the free-market system. Papazov was subsequently able to use this new visibility to gain a significant toe-hold in European and American world music/world beat industries (Buchanan 1996b; Rice 1994).

Musical cosmopolitanism in the region might be usefully understood in the terms recently proposed by Thomas Turino (see Turino 2000), which is to say, as deeply and complexly entangled with processes of national imagining (and not simply opposed to it), requiring contextualization in specific locales and histories. Turino's African-derived perspective is valuable in the Balkan context. Balkan musical cosmopolitans gesture insistently to a shared Ottoman past as the basis for a shared musical conversation. These gestures are not unimportant: they endorse and authenticate the cosmopolitanism of self-consciously cosmopolitan

309

music—its main selling point. But what they produce is, nonetheless, music designed for the most part for local consumption (i.e., within the nation-state), and with local, rather than pan-regional, needs, desires, and contexts very much to the fore.

These local cosmopolitanisms interact in complex ways. A characteristic mode of engagement can be seen in collaborative recording and concert projects bringing together, for example, a star from one part of the Balkans with a star from another, or two ensembles, over shared or collaboratively produced repertoire. Such ventures make much of a supposedly shared Balkan culture and stress the symmetrical nature of the relationships involved. Both parties disavow, either explicitly or implicitly, a previous generation's nationalism, and simultaneously confront its taboo topics: its proscribed ethnicities, its sensitive border regions, its disavowed population movements and migrations, and so forth. The interaction of local cosmopolitanisms takes place, however, in a space marked by significant, though complex, disparities of power, forged in the historical *longue durée*. The idiom of sharing, of exchange on common terrain, often conceals rather more particular cultural agendas, the predominance of one party's cosmopolitan mindset over another's, and localized and variegated patterns of reception.

Lux Balcanica est Umbra Orientis

The place of Turkish music and musicians in the cosmopolitan musical imaginaries of the Balkans bears careful consideration in this regard. Though enthusiastic participants and adepts at the language of exchange, at least in recent years, the involvement of Turkish musicians is peculiarly marked. Those elsewhere who would enter into musical dialogue with them confront both the legacy of centuries of Ottoman power and the reviving regional fortunes of the modern Turkish state.[2] They are also obliged to confront processes of disavowal and related forms of repression involved in the construction of national identity in Balkan countries for a century or more.

The reverse is, of course, not the case. As Todorova (1997) notes, the Turkish Balkan imaginary is fairly recent, somewhat self-absorbed, and not much concerned with asking particularly difficult questions about the legacy of the past.[3] She comments: "whenever the concept 'Balkan' is evoked at all, it vacillates between the neutral and the nostalgically positive, maybe because it has never been seriously considered a central category of identity" (1997:51). The very paucity of the Balkanist imagination in Turkey raises a problem for her, though. The Balkan imaginary, in her view, is complex, fractured, and multiply authored, by people both in and outside the region, marked by imperial designs of both its western and eastern neighbors. The very term "Balkan," she notes, is of Ottoman origin. She coins a Latin phrase, *"Lux Balcanica est umbra Orientis"* [Balkan light is oriental shadow], one rich in ambiguities, but registering nonetheless the defining presence of Ottoman Turkey in the Balkan equation (1997:15). It surprises her, then, that modern Turkey has not produced a particularly strong or regionally significant Balkan imaginary.

An approach less firmly wedded to the world of literacy might have produced a slightly different perspective. Popular music in Turkey in the 1990s was very publicly absorbed by the Balkan world, in the context of a fairly explicit process of questioning Turkish national musical identity. Sezen Aksu, a female vocalist and song-writer of enormous public significance and popularity in the mid 1990s, was prominently associated with this move. One collaboration, with Goran Bregović, a Yugoslav musician well-known across the Balkans through the folk-rock group *Bijelo Dugme* and his soundtracks for Emir Kusturica's films, resulted in a CD in 1997, *Düğün ve Cenaze* [Wedding and Funeral], which I will discuss in detail later in this chapter.

Aksu's turn to the Balkans was not unique. In 1996, Candan Erçetin, a music teacher at Istanbul's prestigious Galatasaray Lycée, had released *Hazırım*, whose opening track, *Sevdim, sevilmedim* [I loved, I was not loved in return], tropes a song made popular across the Balkans by Esma Redžepova, *Čaje šukarije*. The Turkish words added to the Redžepova song by Erçetin were hedonistic and extroverted. The sound track added a Romani brass band in the style of those found in south Serbia and the Republic of Macedonia, as well as a heavy *darbuka* drum machine rhythm track and a *zurna* solo to the basic melodic and harmonic framework of the Redžepova original. The driving urban dance rhythms and upbeat lyrics, the folksy *zurna* and the exotic sound of the brass band made for an unusual and striking combination. The CD was a massive hit in Turkey, and could be heard for almost a full year following its release.

The Balkan turn in Turkish popular culture might be usefully understood in relation to a longer standing current of Turkish popular musical "Mediterraneanism" (Özer 2003). *Flamenco* was somewhat in vogue in the early 1990s[4] and collaborations with Greek musicians were becoming increasingly common.[5] The descending Phrygian riff of *Sevdim, sevilmedim/Čaje šukarije* would certainly have suggested *flamenco* to many in Turkey. The Balkan-oriented regional imaginary had, however, a slightly different emphasis, one that was to be significantly underscored by Sezen Aksu, its focus not on Greece and Spain, but on Bulgaria, the former Yugoslavia, and the Republic of Macedonia. This was partly a matter of taking into account the musical culture of near neighbors, interaction with whom had been to a large extent prohibited by the Cold War. But it was also a matter of rethinking and reconfiguring the regional relationships in which the Turkish nation-state was now enmeshed. This rethinking was inextricably bound up with a process of reorganizing national musical culture, previously understood as a diverse but bounded entity supervised by the Turkish state, and now increasingly understood in complex relations with neighboring cultures. Aksu's work in the mid 1990s bore on both processes, and makes the connections between them clear. It is to this that I will now turn.

Sezen Aksu

To understand Sezen Aksu and the Turkish musical fascination with the Balkans in the mid 1990s, one first needs to understand popular and urban Turkish music in a slightly broader historical context. Since the late 1940s (Markoff 2002), the Turkish state invested heavily in constructing and propagating through state-run media (in particular the Turkish Radio and Television corporation, henceforth the TRT) an Anatolian-based folk music as Turkey's national music. "Popular" genres, that one might define simply as those mass-mediated genres which flourished outside of state tutelage (though not necessarily in opposition to it), looked elsewhere for inspiration.

From roughly the early 1960s to the mid 1990s, three distinct currents prevailed. Firstly, Turkish pop (*Türk Popu* or *Türkçe Dili Pop*), the versionizing of popular "Western" song, from tango to rock-and-roll to the cha-cha and chanson (see Stokes 2002). The recording industry of the day did much to promote this music; it could survive without the state's radio and TV network through the patronage of a wealthy, buoyant and cosmopolitan bourgeoisie. Secondly, so-called Anatolian rock (*Anadolu Rock*), from the bourgeois counter-culture of the 1960s, looked explicitly to progressive, guitar-based rock in the US and the UK, and less explicitly to French chanson.[6] Anatolian rockers pitted themselves against the state in the name of a radical nation. They had no solid music industrial base, they were opposed by the TRT, and were dispersed by the generals in 1980. Many of their number have returned to Turkey and enjoyed a nostalgic revival since the early 1990s.[7] Thirdly, *arabesk*, which looked east, built up a strong audience base amongst a rural-urban and transnational migrant proletariat, and was located firmly in an indigenous cassette industry with which the state was not inclined to interfere, despite posing some ideological opposition to it in the 1980s. These are, to a certain extent, ideal typical categories, and musicians wove their way around and between them in interesting ways.[8]

This system, comprising a state-promoted core and a free-market periphery (dominated by *arabesk*), began to break down in the late 1980s. Media deregulation opened the radio and television airwaves to competition and dislodged the TRT corporation from its central place in defining musical tastes and generic hierarchies. Stronger recording companies, now able to use TV and radio to promote their products, enacted legislation against cassette piracy and successfully introduced Turkish middle class consumers to CDs. *Arabesk* lost ground as a consequence, becoming once again, after a brief period of hegemony in the 1980s, the working-class music it was always presumed to be.[9] A burgeoning and liberal middle class, that had grown enormously in wealth and prestige during the Özal years of the previous decade, turned enthusiastically to Turkish pop.[10]

Sezen Aksu was for many the very definition of this moment, one often understood in Turkey, somewhat ahistorically, as a sudden explosion of pent up energies in a climate of liberalism and consumer hedonism.[11] Turkey was consumed by "the fire of the pop age," as Can Kozanoğlu put it (1995). Just as this moment might be seen as the result of more slowly accumulating and even somewhat predictable social forces, repeating similar moments in earlier decades, so too might Aksu's sudden prominence in Turkey in the 1990s. Her national prominence at this time might also be seen as the highly probable outcome of a carefully planned and well-managed career. If the moment was hers, it was hers at least partly because it was one she herself had shaped.

She was born Sezen Yıldırım in Saraköy, Denizli (western Anatolia) on 13 June 1954. Her family moved to Izmir in 1957, where her father pursued his career as a teacher and, subsequently, education administrator. After graduating from high school, Aksu attended Izmir University's Agricultural Faculty. Her heart was clearly not in it, and she dropped out before finishing the course. In the meanwhile, over a six-year period she had been attending classes run by Izmir Radio's arts and culture club (*Izmir Radyosu Sanatçılar Derneği*), where she studied voice, piano, art music, theater, and folklore. The atmosphere was eclectic, creative, predominantly amateur, and evidently not riven by ideological disputes,[12] or run according to tenets of ideological purism, as many in Istanbul or Ankara were during this period. Her parents struggled against, but finally gave in to and subsequently supported her ambitions as a professional musician.[13]

Her first recording, a 45-rpm single called *Haydi şansı/Gel bana*, was released in 1975, under the assumed name of Sezen Seley. By all accounts, this did not do too well. A second followed, *Kursura bakma/Yaşanmış yıllar,* in 1976. Aksu was by then married, and shortly after left for Canada, where her husband was beginning graduate school. She recalls having to all intents and purposes given up on the idea of a recording career, but she returned to Turkey on a visit after the second record was released to discover that it had become a hit and that she had become famous (Interview, 12 July 1996).

Of the early 45-rpms, *Gölge etme/Ask* was perhaps the best known, establishing her as an accomplished singer in a light art music idiom, with a powerful *bel canto* vibrato and a taste for quirky orchestrations. The fact that she had written this song herself was a matter of immediate note in the Turkish press. Her earlier songs were gathered together on her first cassette, *Serçe,* in 1978, as local cassette production took root.[14] By this stage she had moved to Istanbul. There she put her theatrical and compositional skills to use in musical reviews (such as *Sezen Aksu Aile Gazinosu* [Sezen Aksu's Family *Gazino*] in 1981–82 and *Bin Yıl Önce, Bin Yıl Sonra* [A Thousand Years Ago, a Thousand Years Later] in 1985). She wrote for the popular press[15] and represented Turkey (unsuccessfully) in the Eurovision song contests, 1983–85.[16]

At this point, significant changes began to take place in the music she was writing and singing. Perhaps the most visible token of a new current of seriousness and sense of artistic endeavor was the fact that her 1984 CD *Sen Ağlama* was turned down by the TRT's *denetim*. The *denetimi* was at this time a board ostensibly controlling artistic standards, but effectively censoring material that did not clearly fit in with the state's notion of appropriately national musical culture. *Sen Ağlama* was not to be heard on the radio airwaves for another year, though it circulated widely in cassette form beforehand.

An important contributor to this new current of artistic seriousness was her partner and mentor, Onno Tunç.[17] This artistic partnership was cemented by their collaboration over the 1983–85 Eurovision entries. These songs were not particularly successful in the contest, and had a relatively limited impact in Turkey.[18] However, they put Aksu in the national limelight, linking her in many people's minds with semi-official efforts on the part of the state to sculpt a modern and cosmopolitan "Turkish music" for international consumption.

The Aksu-Tunç partnership was as yet in its infancy; their Eurovision efforts gave only the barest hints as to what these artists were to produce. Tunç, born in 1949, began life as an Armenian church musician in Istanbul. He developed a fascination with jazz and American soul music in the late 1960s, whilst the Anatolian rockers were infatuated with the European rock counter-culture. He was in the process of developing a meticulous studio style and a deft hand in matters of arrangement and orchestration. He had a good working knowledge of the *makam* system, which he was interested in integrating with harmonic and voice-leading techniques derived from jazz and soul. For her part, Aksu brought to the partnership a melodic inventiveness which drew on her eclectic background in Western and Turkish music, significant literary talents, and an extraordinary voice, well-trained in the Turkish classical tradition, but inflected by the emotional registers of Western pop and rock. She also had, from the outset, an ability to read Turkish society deftly and subtly, to anticipate the public moods and concerns, and to expand the politically and culturally possible without ever entirely overstepping the limits of the politically and culturally permissible.

From *Sen Ağlama* up to the early 1990s, Aksu and Tunç produced a series of cassettes and later, CDs (*Git*, 1986; *Sezen Aksu '88*, 1988; *Sezen Aksu Söylüyor*, 1989; *Gülümse*, 1991; *Deli Kızın Türküsü*, 1993) that defined a new kind of popular music in Turkey. This was marked by intimate, poetic lyrics with clear literary pedigree and pretensions, by meticulous orchestral arrangements, and by Aksu's expressive and "literary" voice. Though stylistically diverse, this music was recognizably Turkish in its predominantly linear and melodic nature, never stepping too far from the *makam*-based aesthetics of the urban music that prevailed in Turkey from the 1940s onwards.[19] But it was also recognizably Western, associated with an assertively urbane and modern woman,[20] with an up-tempo rhythmic pulse evoking Western rather than Turkish social dancing,[21] with a *bel canto* vibrato, use of the tempered tonal system, with electric keyboards, guitars, drum sets, and so forth.[22] These cassettes clearly sold in numbers that rivaled those of the major *arabesk* singers of the day: İbrahim Tatlıses, Ferdi Tayfur, Orhan Gencebay, and Bülent Ersoy.[23]

In the mid 1990s Aksu's public persona and music began to undergo further changes. As a public figure, her stature and influence grew immeasurably. Her increasingly assertive pronouncement on political issues became the topic of mainstream media commentary. CD releases were media events, early items of report on the state's television news programs. Topics of taboo and more generalized cultural anxiety were identified and broached by Aksu with an almost surgical precision: women's rights, the environment, the legacy of political repression and Turkey's "disappeared," the position of Armenians in Turkish national culture, Kurdish language issues, the war in Iraq.[24] In each case, Aksu was confident and assertive, though non-confrontational, always operating within the law,[25] and in each case a well-judged step ahead of a breaking wave of public opinion.

While Aksu has systematically courted controversy, she has chosen her battles well, and managed to avoid arousing public opprobrium on the issues she espoused. Her recent embrace of minority language issues is a case in point. Turkish official multiculturalism has readily acknowledged Kurds, Armenians, Laz, Georgians and others, whose presence in Turkish national culture is construed as part of the Anatolian "mosaic" under the benign tutelage of the Turkish state. Teaching and broadcasting in minority languages has, however, been emphatically forbidden, despite some cautious efforts, for instance, under President Özal in the 1980s, to liberalize legislation on the issue. Kurdish cassette companies exploited loopholes in existing legislation with varying degrees of success,[26] while politically committed Kurdish musicians, or musicians sympathizing with the Kurdish cause have sung in Kurdish in more or less public manifestations of political determination. A combination of EU pressure and internal debate in recent years has, however, opened the way for further liberalization in minority language broadcasting and education.

Aksu's most recent endeavor, a concert tour of Turkey and the major northwest European capitals, brought together a 174-member orchestra and chorus, comprising the choir of the Feriköy Vatanart Armenian church in Istanbul, the Los Pasaros Shephardic Jewish Music Ensemble, the Oniro Greek Music Ensemble, the Diyarbakır (Kurdish) City Council Children's Choir, together with the Dersaadet Chamber Ensemble and the Izmir State Opera and Ballet. The concert tour, which went simply under the name Türkiye Şarkıları [Songs of Turkey], differed from previous manifestations of state-endorsed "mosaic" ideology in that songs were actually sung in Armenian, Greek, Ladino and Kurdish. Aksu herself sang one song (Buke) in Kurdish, along with the Diyarbakır children's choir. Aksu herself is not Kurdish and does not speak the language. Cynics, unsurprisingly, found plenty to scoff about. Faruk Bildirici, a columnist for Tempo magazine, pointed out that those currently cheering Sezen Aksu's efforts on behalf of the Kurds would probably include people who had, only a few years before, bayed for the blood of Ahmet Kaya, a Kurdish singer who had often insisted on singing in Kurdish.[27] Journalists more commonly praised the concert as an exercise in national integration, and as a showcase of Turkish liberalism and tolerance, likely to reassure European observers concerned about Turkey's EU admissibility.[28] This possibility must have struck the Turkish Ministry of Culture, who generously sponsored the Turkish and European tour of Türkiye Şarkıları.

The cynics, though, may have missed an important point. Aksu's espousal of the issue circulated liberal perspectives on the language debates in ways that would have been quite unimaginable otherwise. Where the surly and bearded Ahmet Kaya's insistence on singing in Kurdish appeared to broad sections of the Turkish public as provocative and aggressive, Aksu's widespread popularity ensured a very different kind of reception and the stirring of broad discussion. This should not be underestimated. *Zaman*, one of the largest liberal daily papers, recently launched a web poll on the subject of Aksu's concert tour.[29] The results have yet to be shared, but the very fact that the issue is being framed as a national debate (alongside issues such as Turkey's involvement in the Iraq war) is interesting and revealing. Respondents were asked to consider whether they considered the concerts "positive and unifying" (*"olumlu ve bütünleş tirici"*), whether they "d[id]n't particularly care" (*"tasvip etmiyorum"*) about them, whether the concerts "promote[d] the cause of destructive elements in society" (*"yıkıcı unsurlarm işine yarar"*), or whether they considered them to be "inappropriate" to the national holiday (30 August) on which the concert series was launched (*"30 Agostos'ta yapılmasıuygun değil"*). The poll provided respondents with a conceptual vocabulary with which to consider the question from a variety of angles, and this, as a broadly shared and public phenomenon, is a striking development in a country in which silence on the issue has generally prevailed.

If Aksu's public status was undergoing a significant transformation, her music also assumed a new prominence in the mid 1990s. Firstly *arabesk* had, as already mentioned, been dislodged from its dominant place in the music market as a result of media deregulation. Aksu played an active part in the process, arguing for more effective state legislation on cassette piracy and fronting a prominent media industry lobby devoted to this task.[30] The Turkish media industry was, at this precise moment, being transformed through partnerships with transnational corporations, notably Warner Bros (as was then), Sony, and PolyGram. Aksu herself signed an agreement with Raks for the production of *Düş Bahçeleri* (1996) and a number of subsequent CDs (including *Düğün ve Cenaze*).[31]

Raks's partnership with PolyGram injected massive and, at that point, entirely unprecedented capital into Turkish popular music production and marketing, and for a period, simply blew the opposition out of the water. CD production replaced cassette; production standards rocketed, with singers now recording either outside of Turkey, or with the assistance of well-known European producers. A great many of the major Turkish singers were contracted to Raks at this moment; the company also attempted to get a grip on the notoriously complex problems of distribution in Istanbul by setting up their own retail outlets (Raksoteks) in many parts of the city. For a moment, popular music in Turkey *was* Raks, and

Aksu appeared to be prominently connected with their efforts to control the industry.

In addition, the city was in the middle of a significant economic boom whose unstable nature became very clear in subsequent years, though at the time many felt that President Özal's confident assertion that Turkey had "leapt through to another age" (*"çağı atladık,"* as he used to say) had at last borne fruit. Middle class young people had money at their disposal as never before, with educational opportunities in new private universities. The twin threats of military service and early marriage that had haunted an entire generation of young middle class men and women in the 1980s were significantly in abeyance.[32] Car ownership (or, at least, car *use*) and foreign travel could be more or less taken for granted by many young people, unimaginable even in relatively wealthy households only five years before. The city was being zoned by its free-marketeering managers not only for business but for pleasure. New road construction linked the emerging suburbs with emerging city center entertainment districts, which flourished in a new wave of bourgeois patronage. The murky *gazino* [casino] culture that had nourished *arabesk* found itself increasingly marginalized in its seedy and dilapidated city-center homeland, Beyoğlu, now undergoing a major facelift. It was replaced by a thriving "rock bar" and club culture, specifically marketed at middle class youth.[33] Turkish pop was now not just about sitting and listening, but urban partying, a celebration of urbane, middle class hedonism. Aksu's music lent itself extremely well to the purpose.

The emergence of a space in which Turkish pop could flourish, both within the music industry and the city itself, involved a major readjustment of Aksu's status *vis-à-vis* her peers in Turkish pop, and elsewhere. This was a moment of major opportunity, and a great many younger singers jumped onto the Turkish pop bandwagon. Aksu's songwriting, mentoring skills and industry savoir-faire were much in demand. Her generous habits in dispensing expertise, compositions, lyrics, patronage, and so forth established her ever more firmly as the dominant force in this rapidly expanding world. Early protéges included Levent Yüksel and Aşkın Nur Yengi; a little later, the new generation of Turkish pop stars, Mirkelam, Tarkan, Rafet el Roman, Mustafa Sandal and others were much indebted to her. Tarkan's most famous hit, for instance, *Şımarık* (now known across much of the world as "Kiss Kiss"),[34] was a Sezen Aksu composition; the examples could be multiplied.

Aksu's songs also circulated widely outside the world of Turkish pop. Given a slight stylistic twist, they were adopted by a number of *arabesk* singers, including Kibariye, Zeki Müren, and others. Turkish pop, for its part, had been adopting many of the musical features associated with *arabesk:* the violin choruses, the Middle Eastern rhythmic patterns, and to a certain extent the fate-absorbed sentimentalism in the lyrics. Recording companies were interested in exploiting the cross-over potential between Turkish pop and *arabesk,* enabling a number of pop singers to consider recording well-known *arabesk* numbers and vice-versa. This was a very new situation: pop listeners would have previously found *arabesk* too tainted by the stigma of its (perceived) Arab musical associations, and insufficiently Western. *Arabesk* listeners, for their part, found Turkish pop lacking in the qualities of vocal emotionality (in particular its "pained" quality, its *"acılık"*) that interested them. The situation was now significantly different, meaning, amongst other things, that Aksu's influence was to be felt in the world of *arabesk,* as well as pop.[35]

Ex Oriente Lux

This was, then, a moment in which Aksu's status in Turkish society grew exponentially, for reasons connected, as I have tried to demonstrate, with political and economic liberalism in the mid 1990s, with the changing structure of the recording industry, and with the changing fabric of the city. It was also a moment in which her musical style underwent significant changes. These can be associated with two particular CDs: *Ex Oriente Lux/Işık Doğudan Yükselir* [Light from the East] of 1995 and *Düğün ve Cenaze* of 1997.

These contained two bold musical moves: one an engagement with the regional diversity of Anatolian music, the other an embrace of Balkan folk styles. They were bold because they positioned Turkish popular music (and, by implication, Turkey) in relational terms. It was not just pop, but "pop in relation to Turkish folk, urban and regional musics," and, by implication, it spoke of Turkey not just as a "Turkey for the Turks," but Turkey in complex relation to its internal others and near neighbors. The promotional material connected with both CDs (the brochures, the CD liner notes, the material released in interviews with the singer)[36] insistently evoked the "Anatolian mosaic," but made little or no mention of Turkey. Reference to the state as the principle according to which Anatolian diversity was to be organized and appropriately shared was conspicuously lacking. An entire representational order, created and controlled by the state, was being quite explicitly challenged.

As she put it to me in an interview the following year, Aksu believed that the TRT's efforts to represent Anatolia's diverse music cultures had failed miserably. She reflected briefly on the iniquities of the TRT *denetim* system (see above), before continuing:

> What they do is really primitive (*çok ilkel*). And what I'm about is producing something new (*yeniden üretim söz konusu*). Something richer, something more colorful, something with a broader perspective, something all the people in the world can get something out of. I mean, our music is monophonic (*tek sesli*); monophonic music contains within it very deep modal resources [lit., "it contains a deep modal treasury"]. But if it were only to slide in the direction of polyphony . . . .[37] There's really no point in perpetuating this primitive approach, there's no meaning in it. It's just folklore . . . . I just want to develop this [i.e., what I am doing] as best I can. Even when I'm old, there'll still be much to do. Those coming after me will continue. But I believe that one day we'll get a sound really appropriate to us, to Anatolia, properly grounded (*"bir gün buraya çok has, çok özel . . . Anadolu'ya çok has bir ses yerleşik bir hale gelecek"*). I mean, it'll develop its own real language, at last. These kinds of efforts [i.e., *Ex Oriente Lux*] are perhaps just the first step; I believe they'll keep on developing, for ever, really, despite Refah and their crowd.[38]

This might well be taken as the subtext informing the publicity material surrounding *Ex Oriente Lux*'s release. The CD duly rang alarm bells amongst the Turkish state media's managers, who scrambled to co-opt it and minimize the damage it might do to the TRT's still privileged role in mediating Turkish culture. *Ex Oriente Lux* was the first item on TRT1's evening news bulletin on the day it was released, 21 June 1995. The report was accompanied by a long interview with Aksu and an impromptu studio performance of a song with Arif Sağ, a well-known *bağlama* player who was featured on one of the CD's tracks. If unprecedented promotion of the CD by the TRT can best be understood as an effort to forestall the criticisms implicit within it, as with all such efforts, this promotion succeeded mainly in drawing attention to the TRT's own inadequacy.

Musically, *Ex Oriente Lux* marked a new current of seriousness in Aksu's work, a moment of self-reflection, a moment of attention to the world around her, and a developing sense of cultural mission. As she put it, in interview, in rather formally intellectual language striking a somewhat odd note in the context of our otherwise very casual and informal discussion:

> Once I had had enough of applause and all that . . . then, well, my period of research began (*o zaman, işte, araştırma dönemin başladı*). I began to look for my own voice, this country's own voice, the voice of

people, of real, living people in the streets, my own inner voice . . . let's
just say, putting all these together, Turkey's own voice, let's say I began
to search for the voice of this country's soil (*bu ülkenin toprağın sesi*).
We can think of *Ex Oriente Lux* and other similar projects [including
Düğün ve Cenaze, which we went on to talk about] as the experimental
products of these research processes. Because it is very difficult to bring
it to any kind of conclusion. It's a serious business bringing it to any
kind of conclusion (*ciddi bir yolculuk, ciddi bir serüven gerekiyor*).

This new current of seriousness is clearly marked by the symphonic-
like orchestral introduction, and by the concept album approach unifying
the individual songs.[39] The introduction is difficult to describe, having no
clear antecedents in Turkish music. Its basis is a rhythmic ostinato over
which a handful of related themes grow, building up to a climax somewhat
in the manner of Ravel's *Bolero*.[40] Aksu provided the thematic material
(one theme, apparently, reworked from a Jan Garbarek piece), which was
subsequently worked together and orchestrated by Tunç.

Ex Oriente Lux turned out to be Tunç's last work. He lost his life in
an airplane accident that year, before the CD actually appeared. Aksu
clearly considered this introduction an appropriate and suitably serious
epitaph to his career when we met in 1996, constantly steering our
interview back to it, seemingly anxious to know my opinion, and for an
opportunity to talk about it.[41] It has very little to do with the music that
follows, which is sparse and intimate. Its main purpose, one might
surmise, is to indicate to the listener from the outset that this is a radically
new point of departure for modern Turkish music, one that entirely merits
symphonic resources, and can appropriately refer to the absolute, the
sublime, the universal, to civilization itself.

If the symphonic introduction stands on its own, the subsequent
pieces are related to one another, their musical and textual connections
working along various different axes. The CD is itself a mosaic (a
metaphor provided by the CD cover) of "Anatolian" styles, very broadly
conceived, identifiable by the melodic and rhythmic patterns and
characteristic instruments. Track 2, *Davet* [Invitation], is Greek and
reminiscent of *rebetika*, featuring a *bouzouki*. Track 3, *Son sardunyalar*
[The last sardines], hints at the Italian presence in Turkish cities with
accordion and mandolin. Track 4, *Alaturka*, features a Turkish urban
classical (*fasıl*) ensemble. Track 5, *Yaktılar halim'ini* [They killed my
Halim]; Track 9, *Ne ağlarsin* [What are you crying at?]; and Track 11,
Var, git, turnam [Come, go, my crane], are Anatolian folk songs, with
bağlama prominent. Track 6, *Rakkas* [Dancer], is an interpretation of
Egyptian dance music. Track 7, *Onu alma, beni al* [Don't take her, take

me] is in Aksu's old pop style, a point of reference for everything that is happening elsewhere in the CD. Tracks 8 and 12, *Yeniliğe doğru* [Towards renewal] and *La ilahe illallah* [There is no God but God] reprise the Mevlevi Sufi tradition, with *ney* featured in the former. Track 10, *Ben annemi isterim* [I want my mother] is a Black Sea piece, whose opening features a *kemençe* and an "ethnographic" recording of a woman singing a lament.[42]

Within each song, the dialogue between Aksu's already established pop style and the regional genres is worked out in different ways. In some cases there is a simple juxtaposition. The verses of *Alaturka* are accompanied by *ud* and guitar, playing in a style somewhat reminiscent of flamenco, while the choruses are accompanied by the *fasıl* ensemble, as if summoned by memory. In the Anatolian folk songs, the *bağlama* predominates, importing, so to speak, its particular tonality into the pop mix. Quarter-tone flattened seconds are not ironed out by the tempered instruments, but are fully observed in Aksu's vocal rendition. This marks a significant departure in her vocal style, as she pointed out in our interview, opening up a rich repertoire of harmonic effects subtly exploited by Tunç.[43] Though perhaps rhythmically over-emphatic, *Rakkas* and *Ben annemi isterim* are, as it were, straight efforts to sing in a traditional style (respectively, urban *Oriyental* dance music and a Black Sea folk song).

These relationships are also configured at a textual level. Each song constitutes a specific engagement between Aksu's lyric style and that associated with the genre in question. *Rakkas*, for instance, contains phrases directed at bellydancers (*"Salla, salla . . ."*), phrases connoting the "Eastern" pleasures of the genre (*"Allah allah,"* *"yallah"* and so forth), and formulaic expressions of fatalism associated with *arabesk* (*"Bu hal dünya halidir . . ."*). The remaining lyric gestures (the arch Ottomanism of *"meclis-i sahane,"* or "the gathered worthies," in line 4; the erotic note struck by *"gül memeler,"* or "rosy nipples," in the chorus) are recognizably Aksu's own. In *Ben annemi isterim*, similarly, the seven-syllable (*heceli*) couplets are, to urban audiences, instantly recognizable as Black Sea folkore, through dialectal details (*uşak* for *çocuk*, or child; lines beginning with *"uy"*) alongside references to landscape (mountains), instruments and dances (the *kemençe* and the *horon*), and the agriculture of the region (hazelnut cultivation). The text of the song dialogues with a metropolitan notion of the rural form, adding Aksu's own specific lyric twists, notably a final couplet which imagines a young girl, already a mother, her youthful dreams already dead, longing for her own mother.[44]

The songs on *Ex Oriente Lux* also constitute an extended narrative, each element of which focuses on moments in the life of women. These move from inadmissable erotic longing (*Davet*), to carefree days remembered (*Son sardunyalar* and *Alaturka*), to youthful love crushed by society (*Yaktılar halim'imi*), to the cruelty of the male gaze (*Rakkas*), to the anxieties of the wedding market (*One alma, beni al'*), to the soul-destroying demands of motherhood in a strange household (*Ben annemi isterim*). The remaining songs, with lyrics by Anatolian folk poets and mystics (Aşık Daimi, Mevlana Celalettin Rumi, and Yunus Emre) imply the cultural resources of patience and forebearance that have enabled women to bear their lot. There is another narrative process, too, in which the individual elements of the Anatolian mosaic are mystically united in the final Yunus Emre song, *La illahe illallah*, whose chorus addresses the individual longing for unity (*"Gel hey kardeş, gel birliğe özen"*), and promises mystical transcendence.

The articulation of these two narratives, the linking of the pieces of the Anatolian mosaic and the story of an Anatolian woman's life, is complex. For Aksu, the feminist angle is paramount, a sharp focus of her own sense of what the CD is about. I suggested that many of the songs, especially the Alevi *deyiş*, *Ne ağlarsin* (Track 9), with its *"bu da gelir, bu da geçer"* [so it comes, so it goes] chorus, might be taken to espouse fatalism, to underline the importance of forbearance, of putting up with the ills of the world. My notes remind me that she "slightly bristled" in her reply:

> But that isn't about passive forbearance (*tevekkul*). *"Bu da gelir"* is about accumulated experience (*bir birikimle ilgili*). I mean, Anatolia was the very last society in which men came to dominate women. Women have struggled against this for centuries. I mean, it's about accumulated experience, that song. I don't think it's about accepting the way things are. I mean, Anatolian women look as though they are dominated by men, but power (*hakimiyet*) in each household is actually held by women. There's a kind of silent agreement. The family unit looks as though it is run by men, but we can actually see the dominant traces (*dominant izleri*) of that older women-run society in each and every Turkish family. Even in my house, if my husband asked for a *börek* [pastry], he'd get a slap real fast (*zıpla zıpla döverim ben*)! [laughs] You can't just ignore that past. Look, we're the granddaughters of those Anatolian mothers who carried ammunition on their backs during the war of independence. I mean, unlikely though it may appear on the surface, the Turkish woman, the Anatolian woman, I mean, has little to be sorry about.

The "accumulated experience" of Anatolian women, the *"birikim"* in question, provides the link between the CD's gendered and ethnic narratives. If the history of Anatolia has been one of wars, conflict and violence, one kind of ethnic cleansing or another, it has also been one of accommodation, reconciliation, of acceptance of difference and getting by with others. Men might have been responsible for the former state of affairs in some respects, and women might have helped them (carrying weaponry for their menfolk, as she suggests, during the war of independence). But women should take full credit, she implies, for their fostering of an indigenous culture of rapprochement. Aksu evokes a common nationalist trope—Anadolu (the Turkish version of the Greek "Anatolia," obviously enough, "the East") as *Ana-dolu*, the land "full of mothers"[45]—but turns it in a new direction. For her, it evokes not the mere nation-state (note that she carefully erased her own "Turkish mothers" in the last sentence above), but civilization (*medeniyet*) itself, made possible through the healing, reconciling and relation-building capacities of Anatolian women. Her use of the term *medeniyet* (one demonized by the early Turkish nationalists) slips between forms of life specific to particular groups ("of the 130 civilizations in the world," she said, "30 originated here in Anatolia"), and a form of life which is capable of embracing and transcending the differences between them. It is this latter, civilization in a broader sense, that constitutes Anatolia's gift of "light" to the world, as the title implies.

Düğün ve Cenaze

The "civilized" capacity to embrace and tolerate difference is located by Aksu in the everyday lives of Anatolian women in *Ex Oriente Lux*, but it also underwrites her own cosmopolitanism. If the accumulated experience of women, the *"birikim"* that they carry with them today, enabled them to reconcile and transcend difference in the classical and early medieval Aegean, it continues to do so in the age of globalization. *Düğün ve Cenaze* [Wedding and funeral], her Bregović collaboration, followed hot on the heels of *Ex Oriente Lux* in December 1997, presenting, in the place of an Anatolian mosaic, a Balkan mosaic, or, more accurately, an Anatolian mosaic with Balkan elements. This, too, identifies a feminized cultural space in which sharing and healing can take place, as we shall see. The cosmopolitanism of this project might be regarded, then, as a natural extension of the feminist/alternative nationalism of *Ex Oriente Lux*.

While there is no opening symphony, the expansive cultural claims of the CD, on behalf of Anatolian women, are underlined by a short introductory essay in the liner notes. This states:

Sezen Aksu is an Aegean vocalist. Music, which has done most to support the unity of the human spirit (*ruh*), was first systematized two thousand five hundred years ago in the Aegean region. The important thing to say about Sezen Aksu's voice and style is that alongside the main feeling [*"duygu,"* i.e., love, sensitivity] supplied by her songs, there is another important feeling: the feeling of Anatolian history, the emotional treasury (*duygu hazinesi*) of a small patch of land possessing the most noble and powerful melodies of love and pain, which reach the people of today, in sobs and plaintive cries, in Ionian Sezen's voice. Only these two dimensions [i.e., love and Anatolian history] cannot be fully separated from one another. In this world of ours, in which even love has been rapidly commodified, we should feel free to luxuriate [literally, wander about] a bit in the depths of Sezen's voice, we should be able to touch the feelings revealed by the historical developments connected with that soil. In the final analysis, with her honesty and goodness-nourishing voice, with a style possessed of a powerful Mediterranean sensibility (*duyarlılığı*), and this time with Balkan colors (*Balkan renkleriyle*) added to our own cultural mosaic, she invites us, all of us, to love.

There are clear connections between the lyrics in the two projects, the latter of which were written either by Pakize Barışta (wife of Üstün Barışta, *Ex Oriente Lux*'s producer), Meral Okay, Sezen Aksu, or some combination of the three. While lacking the explicit overarching narrative of *Ex Oriente Lux*, each song relates episodes in the life of women, often portrayed looking on with dismay at the infantile and violent displays of machismo around them. An underlying narrative can certainly be detected. The first four songs—*O sensin* [You are the one], *Allahım varsa* [If you believe in God], *Kasım yağmurları* [November rain], and *Hıdırellez* [A spring festival]—depict the hopes, frustrations and desires of an as yet unmarried woman. The fifth song, *Düğün* [Wedding], is just that, a "wedding," once again specifically from the point of view of a woman, an indirect plea to a father to recognize her vulnerability at this crucial moment in her life. The sixth bears a strong resemblance, in lyric and musical treatment, to *Rakkas*: it is about the suffocating nature of the male world in which the married woman now finds herself. The lyrics ironize male chit-chat, while the music parodies *arabesk*. The next three songs imagine a woman in a relationship (we assume, from what has gone before, a marital one) falling out of love (*Gül* [Rose], *Helal ettim hakkımı* [I have earned my rights], and *Ayışığı* [Moonlight]). The last up-tempo number, *Kalaşnikof* [Kalashnikov], again parodies male braggadocio, its lyrics alluding to male violence and the confused sexual violence which underpins it.[46]

The music also sounds very similar to Aksu's earlier recording, even though each song is written by Goran Bregović. The CD was put together after Onno Tunç's death, and Aksu does not take credit for any composition or arrangement. Most of the songs come from Bregović's film scores, some of which, particularly *Underground* and *Time of the Gypsies*, would have been well known to art cinema devotees in Turkey. The music from these figures prominently on the CD, with songs from *Underground* bookending the CD as a whole. Though the recording was put together in London, with a large team credited as sound engineers on the CD liner notes,[47] many of the studio techniques deployed by Üstün Barışta are reworked here. A quiet and intimate feel prevails in the early tracks, steadily gathering momentum throughout, with increasingly prominent *darbuka*-driven rhythms. The spare instrumentation of openings, accompanying melancholic, reflective words, is often abruptly interrupted by a full band, playing in a rough, raw, heterophonic style (as in *Davet* and *Alaturka* on *Ex Oriente Lux*).

The full band in question is a Romani brass band of the sort found in Serbia and the Republic of Macedonia. Where Candan Erçetin employed such a band on only one track on *Sevdim, sevilmedim*, Aksu uses it throughout the entire CD, rescoring the Bregović songs to include it even when it was not part of the original conception. One of the great jokes of Kusturica's film *Underground* was evidently borne in mind here. In the film, the brass band follows the two protoganists on their helter-skelter adventure through modern Yugoslav history, ducking for cover with them in combat, running behind them when they are being chased, popping up out of nowhere during the sex scenes, playing all the while. The brass band here, too, constitutes an omnipresent chorus to Aksu's steadily unfolding lyric narrative, whether rudely interrupting, providing a gentle backing, or leading the riotous bacchanal of the last track, *Kalaşnikof*. The brass band is, in many respects, the entire "point" of the CD—its distinguishing feature. This is made clear by the CD cover, showing Aksu and Bregović entwined, with the brass band visible, if somewhat blurred, in the background.

Their physically entwined bodies on the CD cover represents a close cultural kinship between the two star musicians. As Aksu put it, in discussion:

He (Bregović) is after the voice of the person in the street; I, too, am after the voice of the person in the street, like him, with technological intervention when necessary (*teknolojinin gerektiği zaman devreye girecegi*) . . . . We're after the same thing; our life-paths are very close (*çok yakın bir serüven*). Anyway, we met up and talked, we learned a lot from one another. I'm not into this "authentic" stuff. And I've put together this huge archive, which I'm working on now, and it really influences me. I mean, from the Zazas to the Safarads . . . .[48] But the essential thing is to produce new things (*yeniden uretim esas*). I mean, Goran has great songs, and I want to sing them, too. I mean, his too is, basically, *makam*-type music (*yani, o da makamsal müziği içinde zaten*). I wanted to harvest (*harmanlamak*) it *here*, I mean, to do a second, third, fourth *Ex Oriente Lux* [i.e., with new material, "gathered in" from elsewhere]. That's what I was immediately looking for.

Aksu's representation of their relationship stresses the continuity she perceives between *Ex Oriente Lux* and *Düğün ve Cenaze*. But in doing so she also, perhaps unwittingly, underlined a significant tension in the relationship between the two musicians, between a notion of exchange (sitting down, talking, and learning from one another) and a notion of "harvesting," a notion of, however benignly and generously conceived, appropriation. Aksu's representation of this relationship seems to contain a rather frank acknowledgment that while transnational conversation is all well and good, what actually matters, in the final analysis, is the national one. The point of the exercise is, ultimately, to render this Balkan exchange in terms that ultimately support her own cosmopolitan re-working of Turkish national identity.

What, then, of Bregović's involvement in this exchange? Did Bregović "Turkify" as Aksu "Balkanized"? For Aksu's Balkan flirtation has had a significant afterlife. She has, for example, continued to tour extensively with a Macedonian brass band, recycling the songs from *Düğün ve Cenaze*.[49] It was a significant moment in Aksu's career, a defining point in the emergence of a distinct musical personality. It was not so for Bregović. Despite the appeal Aksu makes to a commonly cosmopolitan experience, they are rather different characters, who crossed paths in the course of very different career trajectories. Bregović (born in 1950) worked with the band *Bijelo Dugme* between 1974 and 1988.[50] A Bosnian of mixed Serbian and Croatian parentage with a Muslim spouse, he attracted the opprobrium of many in the region for his adherence to a vision of a nationally intact and multicultural Yugoslavia. This led him to leave the country during the Yugoslav wars, pursuing his career as a composer for a series of remarkable films by Emir Kusturica,[51] and a series of solo recordings.[52] Each of these, a response to isolation and self-imposed exile, perhaps, features a wide range of song-writing and performing collaborations, with David Vison, George Dalaras, Jane Birkin, Neil Harrison, experiments with Irish traditional music, Bulgarian folk polyphony, tango. Aksu figures in one of his most recent CDs, *Songbook*, as one point of contact among many with other musics.

Aksu and Bregović represent significantly different responses to the diffuse currents of Balkan cosmopolitanism of the 1990s. These differences can be understood in terms of the distinctive trajectories of the Yugoslav and the Turkish states during this period, the distinctive positions of the popular wing of the radical intelligentsia in both countries, and the differences between production for a transregional and a national audience. Yugoslavia was in a state of collapse just as Turkish influence and ambitions in the region were growing. The national project in Yugoslavia was co-opted by extremists bent on the destruction or subjugation of minorities, meaning the forcible exclusion of those, like Bregović, committed to some form of democratic national multiculturalism. The national project in Turkey, on the other hand, was at a moment of radical, but for the time being secure democratic experiment making possible the configuration of more multicultural and cosmopolitan visions of Turkish culture than had ever pertained before. Turning back to Bregović, transregional audiences could be found for enterprising cosmopolitan musicians disconnected from their national context, if they could find collaborators of sufficient stature and regional significance with whom to work. The national audience, on the other hand, was still the most significant issue in Turkey (in the case of Aksu). A cosmopolitan link-up with a non-Turkish musician could risk rendering a recording incoherent for nationally based fans. The dialogue had to be subordinated to a clearly comprehensible national project, however radical it might be.

How, then, in conclusion, to evaluate cross-Balkan musical conversations, since they are, undoubtedly, a feature of the contemporary musical landscape in the region? It is difficult at the moment to see cross-Balkan moves by figures such as Sezen Aksu and Goran Bregović (one might also add Theodorakis, Livaneli, Ross Daly, and others) as having wider and more enduring resonance within the region itself, or building towards a common, shared popular musical style. Their various Balkanist and other transregional strategies appear, on the surface, to have a certain amount in common, but this, too, is open to question, as I hope to have shown. They can hardly, yet, be called "shared," in any musical sense. One might, instead, perhaps more optimistically, consider them as local responses to a shared predicament, whose insistence on the possibility of conversations flowing across national boundaries may yet lead to a broader and more dialogical sense of national self.

Addendum
Discography of Recordings by Sezen Aksu

1975   *Haydi Sansi/Gel Bana* (as Sezen Seley)
1976   *Kusura Bakma/Yaşanmış Yıllar*
1976   *Olmaz Olsun/Seni Gidi Vurdumduymaz*
1977   *Allahaısmarladik/Kaç Yıl Geçti Aradan*
1977   *Kaybolan Yıllar/Neye Yarar*
1978   *Gölge Etme/Aşk*
1978   *Serçe*
1979   *Allahaşkına/Sensiz Acime Sinmiyor*
1979   *Iki Gün Gibi*
1980   *Sevgilerimle*
1981   *Ağlamak Güzeldir*
1982   *Firuze*
1984   *Sen Ağlama*
1986   *Git*
1988   *Sezen Aksu 88*
1989   *Sezen Aksu Söylüyor*
1991   *Gülümse*
1993   *Deli Kızın Türküsü*
1995   *Işık Doğudan Yükselir/Ex Oriente Lux*
1996   *Düş Bahçeleri*
1997   *Düğün ve Cenaze*
1998   *Adı Bende Saklı 1998*
2000   *Deliveren*
2002   *Şarkı Söylemek Lazım*

Notes

1. See, for example, Faubion 1993 for a Greece-focused discussion.

2. The fortunes of the Turkish state were indeed reviving, floating on Western loans and aid following the first Gulf war, commercial and political initiatives in Central Asia, and Istanbul's role as a magnet for capital and entrepreneurial energies across the entire region in the wake of the collapse of the Eastern European states and the Yugoslav wars. The fragility of these revived fortunes, the unevenness of the development, and the yawning political contradictions were soon to be exposed. The earthquake of 1998, the collapse of global financial markets in this period, and the so-called "postmodern" coup of 2000,

when the generals invited Necmettin Erbakan's Islamist government to step down, marked the beginning of the current slump in the country's fortunes.

3. Todorova notes that contemporary Turkish interest in the Balkans dates from the Bosnian wars in the mid 1990s. She associates Nedim Gürsel's apology for the pax Ottomana, *Balkanlara Dönüş* (1995), with this particular moment, limiting her discussion to the literary domain.

4. Levent Yüksel's *Med-Cezir* [Ebb and flow] (1993), a recording heavily indebted to Sezen Aksu, contains one *cante jondo*-style *flamenco* number, *Tuana*, a vocal improvisation (in Turkish, with lyrics by Sezen Aksu) with solo guitar accompaniment.

5. Zülfü Livaneli recorded and performed with Mikis Theodorakis on a number of occasions in the early 1980s; Yeni Türkü made a name for themselves singing Turkish versions of Greek *rebetika* numbers in the same period. The extremely strained relations between the Turkish and Greek governments during this time, over continental shelf oil exploration in the Aegean, gave high public prominence to these particular ventures. Aksu has continued this tradition with joint concerts and recordings with Haris Alexiou. (Note her recent recording, *Deliveren*, of 2000.) Alexiou and Aksu performed together in Athens on 3 November 2002, attracting an audience of 3,000, according to an *Anadolu Ajansi* [Anatolian News Agency] bulletin. See www.hri/org/news.Turkey/Anadolu/1999/99-11-24.

6. Gilbert Becaud and Jacques Brel, with their theatrical style and literary pretensions, were the most influential of the French chanson singers in Turkey, particularly for one of the dominant personalities involved in Anatolian rock, Cem Karaca. See Stokes 2002.

7. Notably Moğollar and Cem Karaca.

8. The issue is pursued at length in Stokes 1992a. The main names associated with *arabesk* are Orhan Gencebay, Ferdi Tayfur, Müslüm Gürses, İbrahim Tatlıses and Bülent Ersoy.

9. A cornerstone of the Turkish intelligentia's criticism of *arabesk* was its association with squatter town and rootless urban-rural migrants. This was something of a myth, obscuring its much broader appeal in the 1980s. See Stokes 1992a.

10. Türgüt Özal was the technocrat chosen by the generals to lead the Turkish economic recovery after they stepped down from power in 1983. He emerged as a charismatic prime minister and, subsequently, president, committed to a program of political, economic and cultural liberalism. He died unexpectedly in 1991.

11. For an excellent discussion of this moment, see Kozanoğlu 1995, also a milestone in Turkish cultural studies.

12. Her piano teacher, she told me in an interview (Aksu 1996), quit teaching to run a pastry shop.

13. Her own determined ambitions to perform in some capacity, "in theater, in music, as a dancer (*dansöz*), even" forced her parents to confront and eventually overcome their natural conservatism; from this point on they were highly supportive of her career (Aksu 1996).

14. Esin Engin did a number of the arrangements on *Serçe*. Engin specialized in what was then called *Türkçe sözlü hafif müziği* [Turkish-language light music], by the TRT at least, arranging easy-listening dance-band versions of Anatolian folk music, belly-dancing music and light classical music. "Minik Serçe" [Mini Sparrow] was, incidentally, Aksu's nickname.

15. Her official website contains one of her early writings, from *Laklak Dergisi* 1981. *Laklak Dergisi* was a comic containing the limited kinds of social and cultural satire permitted during the years following the military coup of 12 September 1980. Aksu's talents for wit, verbal dexterity, and social commentary are evident even at this early stage.

16. The word "unsuccessful" should be instantly qualified. The Eurovision song contest was by this stage a minor festival of kitsch, attracting very little attention in western Europe. The Aksu-Tunç songs were serious efforts to prove Turkey's musical modernity, and were thus quite out of step with the general ethos of the competition, at least, from a western European perspective.

17. Onno Tunç, also known as Onno Tunçboyacı and Onno Tunçboyacıyan. His brother is Arto Tunçboyacıyan, a well-known percussionist and composer in Turkey to this day.

18. However, *Hey Dergisi* (a popular music magazine) voted each successive Aksu entry its song of the year. The songs bore the stigma, I would guess, of their repeated failure in what was generally understood in Turkey, but was actually *not*, a serious international songwriting competition (see note 16).

19. This was popularized by Munir Nurettin Selçuk. See O'Connell 2002.

20. I remember reading an article about Sezen Aksu in a village tea shop near Bursa in western Turkey on one of my first ever visits to the country, in either 1981 or 1982. The article was entitled, simply, *"Sezen Aksu pipo içiyor"* [Sezen Aksu smokes a pipe], complete with picture. I remember one villager pointing at the picture and saying, in so many words, look at how our society is changing. The basic sentiment was entirely positive, though the idea of a woman smoking a pipe was clearly outlandish.

21. This was not, as yet, music for social dancing, but music for listening. The connection of Turkish pop with social dance took place with the development of clubs and rock bars in the 1990s. See below.

22. The use of the *tampare sistemi*, the Western tempered system, grew out of her discussions with Tunç, in which they came to consider that some reconciliation between the *yatay* [horizontal] structures of Turkish music and the *dikey* [vertical] imperatives of Western music was possible if the *koma sesleri* of Turkish urban and rural musics were avoided. This was, in other words, about hybridizing the two musics, rather than choosing one over the other, at least as she recollected these discussions in 1996 (Interview 12 July 1996).

23. Facts and figures are more or less impossible to come by, but one can judge the presence in the music market of Sezen Aksu during this period by the prominence of her cassettes in vendors' displays, and by the regularity with which new CDs were reported in the music press (e.g., *Müzik Magazin*, *Hey Dergisi*).

24. Her official website bears a prominent *"Savasa Hayır"* [No to war] logo. In 1996, when we met for an interview, her espousal of the cause of the Cumartesi Anneleri [Saturday Mothers] was particularly public. The Saturday Mothers gathered in silent protest outside a ministry building in Beyoğlu on a weekly basis, bearing pictures of "disappeared" victims of political repression. Towards the end of summer 1996, these gatherings attracted larger and larger crowds, and ultimately, the riot police.

25. Some groups and singers adopted a much more confrontational manner on the Kurdish language issue, notably Grup Yorum and Ahmet Kaya.

26. For example: Promix, Mazlum, Kral, Sevkan, Kaya, Diyar.

27. When Bildirici published this article Kaya had recently died, somewhat unexpectedly. The irony of two singers doing essentially the same thing and eliciting such different public reactions would have struck many strongly at the time. See Bildirici www.tempodergisi.com.tr/kose/faruk_ bildirici/00296.

28. Ozan Ceyhun reports on the Brussel's concert of 3 November 2002 for AB Haber. See www.abhaber.com/ozan/ozan_yorum41.htm.

29. See www.zaman.com.tr/ms/zaman/anket022.php?poll_id=14.

30. In 1996 she was the spokesperson for POPSAV, along with Attila Özdemiroglu.

31. She recently signed a fifteen-year contract with DMC (Doğan Müzik Company), a subsidiary of the multinational BMC (Bertelsmann). See http://www.milliyet.com.tr/2001/10/20/magazin/amag.html.

32. The new private Istanbul universities, Koç and Sabancı, significantly widened the opportunities for high quality English-language University education, providing a springboard for many women, in particular, to extend their education at graduate level outside the country. For men, paying their way out of military service had been an extremely costly option only a few years before, but had now become more affordable, and a less stigmatized route into manhood.

33. For an account of Turkish popular culture in relation to the changing nature of a "globalizing" Istanbul during this period, see Stokes 1999.

34. *Şimarık* has been extensively covered by artists such as Holly Valance. The Latin appropriation of the song has been the most striking; see, for example, covers by *Los Joao* and *Banda Pachuco* (as *Beso Turko* and *La Muchacha Guapa,* respectively).

35. Aksu's views on *arabesk* were, at least in discussion with me, highly accommodating, and interesting. On Müslüm Gürses: "He's got a really special voice, a real sincerity (*müthiş bir samimiyet*) . . . as for the strength (*kapasite*) of his voice, I don't know, but as far as his style of singing is concerned, I'm really interested in what he does. He sticks close to his folk music roots. Every now and again he does great Alevi *deyiş* [mystical songs] kind of stuff (*zaman zaman bu Alevi deyişlerinden falan müthiş bir şeyi var . . .*)." On *arabesk* singers I had heard singing her songs in Gülhane Park: "Even if we travel different routes, there's common emotional ground (*bir temel duygu alanı var*) on which we touch one another . . ." (Interview, 12 July 1996).

36. See the interview with Sezen Aksu in Canbazoglu 1995:14.

37. Implying "we would get something much more interesting."

38. "Refah" refers to Recep Tayyip Erdoğan's Islamist party, currently administering Istanbul's municipality. They were, as we spoke, clearly poised to take over the national government in the forthcoming elections.

39. The last Turkish "concept album" was probably Dervişan's *Safinaz*, of c. 1979. See Stokes 2002.

40. Ravel's *Bolero* was well known enough in Turkey. The harmonic and thematic language hinted at Russian modernism (Shostakovitch, Prokofiev) as well as that of the Turkish "Five" (see Stokes 1992a), which would have been familiar to audiences at the Atatürk Kültür Merkezi in these years.

41. My notes suggest she did not have much to say about it other than recalling Tunç's work in pulling it all together, and her melodic sources of inspiration. She was, rather, looking for me to come up with the insights, and I, finding myself in a somewhat unanticipated situation, was unforthcoming, as I remember.

42. The *ney* is an obliquely blown bamboo flute central to Mevlevi worship The *bağlama* (sometimes known by the generic term, *saz*) is a long necked fretted lute associated with the folk music tradition. The Black Sea fiddle is distinguished from various different regional and urban variants. Its resonator is a small rectangular box, with three strings, a high pitch, and a frenetic and densely polyphonic style, based on the rhythms of *horon* dancing. The "ethnographic recording" was made by an elderly relative of the *kemençe* player on the recording, a friend of mine, Ersin Baykal. She had to accompany him to the studio, for some reason. Ersin told Sezen Aksu she was well known in his home town (Ordu) as a good lament singer. On hearing this, Aksu apparently demanded she sing. The resulting recording begins the track.

43. If one listens to Track 9 carefully one will hear that she had lost the habit of hitting quarter tone flattened seconds in 1995. This is certainly not an issue in more recent recordings.

44. The last couplets are as follows: "You've left me in the cold, father, the stove burns my eyes/*Uy*, cruel world, are you strong enough for us?/I've got a rag doll, my dreams in my knapsack/I'm still half a virgin, and I want my mother."

45. See Delaney 1991 for a full discussion.

46. A translation of the opening lyrics of *Kalaşnikof* to illustrate the point: (Chorus) Bom bom bom bom bom, Allah/the one who is hit to the one doing the shooting, hey ya!/Bom bom bom bom bom, Yallah/the one who is broken to the one doing the breaking! (Verse 1) OK, let's begin the bragging/Man, we understand one another, pasha to pasha/Make those empty threats; shake the mountains and the rocks/Look, like a girl, Kalashnikov (Chorus 2) Bom bom bom bom bom, the sunken ship's treasure/You be the *agha*, me the pasha, let's grab those chances (Spoken section) Neither the work of man nor of djinn, it's a human being, both man and woman, whatever's required.

(followed by Chorus, Verse 2, Chorus, and a concluding Spoken section).

47. Predrag Milanović, Djordje Jaković, and Ender Akay.

48. By "Zazas" she refers to speakers of the westernmost Kurdish dialect in Anatolia. By "Safarads" she refers to the Jewish community that settled in Istanbul after the Spanish reconquista. Many still live around the main synagogue in the Beyoğlu area.

49. See Robin Denselow's *Guardian* review of her Barbican (London) concert, on 19 June 2002. He mentions the Kočani Macedonian orchestra, comprising 8 brass, singer, drummer and accordion accompanying her. See http://www.guardian.co.uk/arts/reviews/story/0,11712,740.391,00.html.

50. See Ljerka Vidić Rasmussen's chapter in this volume for further discussion of *Bijelo Dugme*.

51. Emir Kusturica's films with Bregović's music include *Dom za Vešanje* (1988), *Arizona Dream* (1993), *Underground* (1995), and *Crna Mačka, Beli Mačor* (1998).

52. Bregović's main recordings include *P.S.* (1996), *Ederlezi* (1999), *Songbook* (2000), and *Tales and Songs from Weddings and Funerals* (2002).

❖ 10 ❖

Trafficking in the Exotic with "Gypsy" Music: Balkan Roma, Cosmopolitanism, and "World Music" Festivals

Carol Silverman

In the Balkans and beyond, most people claim that they know who and what "Gypsies" are and what "Gypsy" music is. They repeat stereotypical generalizations with confidence, drawing on a plethora of written, oral, and aural formulations from the last few centuries: "Gypsies" are innately talented, embodying their wildness in their music; they are consummate musical technicians; they magically sense the desires of their patrons; but in the end, they can't be trusted (Port 1998). Indeed, the stereotypical "Gypsy" musician is not only a ubiquitous exotic fantasy figure in classic Western literature, art, and oral tradition (Trumpener 1992), but also a social actor (Herzfeld 1997). When placed in a political economic framework, this historical baggage, which more than ever informs contemporary representations of Roma,[1] reveals a complex political economy of inequality in the realm of representation.

This article explores "Gypsy" music as both a commodity and a discursive symbol in the trafficking of "authenticity" and " exoticism" in recent cosmopolitan contexts such as "world music" festivals.[2] Music, as a participatory, artistic, and processual means of commerce, encodes multiple meanings for performers, as well as for producers, marketers, and audience members. I examine the current marketing and consumption of "Gypsy" music as it charts the relationships among festival producers/managers of Balkan Romani music acts (who provide a saleable item), audience members (who claim to support a liberal, multicultural agenda), the press (eager to create a "catchy" story), and Romani musicians (trying to eke out a living). Significant here is that the former three groups of people are elites with cash to invest while the performers themselves are members of perhaps the most persecuted and marginalized ethnic group in Europe (Barany 2002; Silverman 1995). Paradoxically, Roma are reviled as people and revered as musicians. However, rather than simply viewing Roma as victims of manipulation, I explore how they manage to actively construct and negotiate their own images and representations, albeit within limited options. Sometimes engaging in a type of "self-orientalizing" that sells the product (Ong 1997), Romani musicians, as well as their managers and producers, are all "cultural brokers" with ideological and economic agendas (Kurin 1997).

Rethinking Cosmopolitanism and Modernity

I relate my work to the literature on cosmopolitanism and modernity precisely because Roma have been excluded from these categories and may provide a useful critique of these concepts. I posit that Romani musicians be considered "ironic cosmopolitans." Unlike middle and upper class elites who easily fit the standard definition of cosmopolitanism as embracing mobility, flexibility, diversity, urbanity, and modernity (Robbins 1992; Turino 2000:9–11), Roma are usually presented by non-Romani scholars, music producers, and sometimes, themselves, as "traditional," "pre-modern," bound by kin, custom, and conservatism (Port 1998). On the other hand, Roma may also be viewed as the epitome of global post-modern European citizens—they are a motley, diasporic, urban, transnational group with loyalty to no one state (or to many states), having neither common religion, language, nor territory. Their cultural traits sometimes resemble their non-Romani neighbors more than other Romani groups, and their music is innovative and open to various generic influences. They are always multilingual, multicultural, and multioccupational: in short; they are multisited and cosmopolitan—at home everywhere in a Europe which despises them.

The label "ironic cosmopolitanism" is inspired by Clifford's rubric, "discrepant cosmopolitanism," wherein "cultures of displacement are inseparable from the specific, often violent histories of economic, political, and cultural interaction . . ." (1992:108). Robbins reminds us that we are not dealing with abstractions, but with "actually existing cosmopolitanism" which is not "an ideal of detachment," but rather "a reality of (re)attachment, multiple attachment, or attachment at a distance" (1999:3). Roma precisely engage with multiple attachments, strategically altering their identities not only for survival but also due to an eclectic cultural attitude. Although Paul Rabinow claims that "we are all cosmopolitans" and urges "critical cosmopolitanism" as an oppositional position (1986:258), we must struggle to pry the term from its elite and intellectual moorings. Kelsky, coining the term "emergent cosmopolitanisms" (2001:12), reminds us that it is hard to equate all diasporic subjects (including refugees and migrants) with the progressive cosmopolitan intellectual. We should not assume that the former is

> radical (as the intellectual is radical) by virtue of sheer mobility. One can cross a border in a plane or in a car trunk. Although growing numbers of people may have experiences classifiable as discrepant cosmopolitanisms, these experiences never operate independent of the histories of class, gender, and racial privilege that adhere to the original cosmopolitan category (Kelsky 2001:15).

A recent assessment of the term cosmopolitanism in the pages of *Public Culture* claims that in current times, "a cosmopolitan grounded in the tenebrous moment of transition is distinct from other more triumphalist notions," such as modernity, liberalism, and the Enlightenment; further, such individuals are no longer embodied in the "myth of the nation writ large in the figure of the citizen of the world. Cosmopolitans today are often the victims of modernity, failed by capitalism's upward mobility, and bereft of those comforts and customs of national belonging. Refugees, people of the diaspora, and migrants and exiles represent the spirit of the cosmopolitan community" (Pollock, et al. 2000:581–82).[3] Romani cosmopolitanism, then, may offer a critique of the paradigm of universalizing modernity.

By now it is accepted and even fashionable in anthropology to criticize totalizing definitions of modernity such as those of evolutionary thinkers such as Morgan and Engels, or those of development theorists such as Rostow (Schein 2000:361). As the Comaroffs suggest, classic discourse on modernity is "ideology in the making" (1993:xii), positing itself "as the all encompassing present and future and all alternatives ('the traditional') as an outmoded past" (Turino 2000:6–7). Similarly, Lisa Rofel writes that modernity serves as a sign to mark itself as distinct from the pre-modern or traditional, "a story that people tell themselves in relation to Others" (1992:96). This is particularly relevant for Roma, who are the quintessential "other" for Europeans, being simultaneously South Asian, Eastern, and "oriental." They are pictured as in the West but not of the West, in the modern but not of the modern (Kirshenblatt-Gimblett 1998). One turn in the critique of modernity literature points to alternative modernities that are not derivative of a Western *Ur-* form, but rather are locally sensitive (Ong 1996, 1999).[4] Ong, however, rejects "the simplistic binary opposition of the West and the non-West in accounting for emerging multiple modernities. Alternative visions of modernity may exist within a single country or a single region. Furthermore, there are alternative modernities expressed by subalterns that are marginalized" (1997:172–73). Roma may embrace an "alternative modernity"; consigned to the margins, Balkan Romani musicians have operated in a flexible, mobile, capitalistic mode for centuries, creating and borrowing while simultaneously providing an indispensable commodity.

Romani Music and the Festival Scene

For hundreds of years, some Romani groups in Europe, most notably Eastern Europe, have been professional musicians, playing for non-Roma (as well as Roma) for remuneration in cafés and at life-cycle and calendrical celebrations. This professional niche, primarily male and instrumental, requires Roma to know expertly the regional repertoire and interact with it in a creative manner. Traveling, often enforced upon Roma through harassment and prejudice, gave musicians opportunities to enlarge their repertoires and become multimusical and multilingual.[5] Neither one worldwide nor one pan-European Romani music exists. Roma constitute a rich mosaic of groups that distinguish among themselves musically. For example, contrary to popular conceptions, there is no one "Gypsy scale." Although it is beyond this paper to analyze musical styles per se, I note that popular and scholarly exaggerations run the gamut from the claim that Roma are merely musical sponges to the claim that Roma are the most traditional interpreters of regional musics. The truth is certainly more complicated (Silverman 1996a).

Music is currently one of the few arenas for the positive articulation of a public identity for Roma. Since 1989, numerous festivals and tours of Romani music have been organized all over Europe and more recently in North America, which serve various political and cultural functions and illustrate the paradox that Roma are powerless politically and powerful musically. Gypsy music festivals fall into two broad categories—those that are sponsored by Romani organizations, and those that are sponsored by non-Roma, usually western European or North American impresarios.[6] The materials for this article fall into the latter category, as I am focusing on two tours of the North American "Gypsy Caravan: A Festival of Roma Music and Dance" in 1999 and 2001, with comparative materials from western European Gypsy music festivals.[7] Of course, Romani musicians also perform in general world music festivals where similar marketing tropes are employed. Indeed, music is one of the only bright spots for eastern European Roma in an otherwise bleak picture. Estimates of Romani unemployment hover between 80–90 % in most areas of eastern Europe (Ringold 2000), poverty levels are unprecedented, and skinhead violence and police brutality are escalating.[8] Music, however, is a still in demand in many regions of eastern Europe (both by Romani and non-Romani patrons), and thus the profession is somewhat viable. Out of thousands of Romani musicians, only a few are lucky enough to travel abroad; with international fame, family income dramatically improves.

Why the sudden western European interest in Gypsy music in the 1990s? One reason is that the end of socialism opened up a new vista for enterprising promoters (Gocic 2000). During the socialist period, government regulations in Bulgaria and Romania prohibited Roma from playing their music in public and from traveling abroad. In addition, the French documentary *Latcho Drom* (1993), plus Emir Kusturica's fictional feature films initiated a veritable "craze" for Gypsy music in the European world music scene.[9]

Latcho Drom is a staged documentary which traces the Romani musical diaspora from India to Spain. Stunning musical performances and stark visuals accompanied by few words evocatively show artistry and marginality, but the filmic viewpoint is of an outsider looking into a world of supposed "authenticity." There are no naturally occurring contexts for music-making (all contexts are staged especially for the film), and there is little attention to music as a profession. Made by half-Romani filmmaker Tony Gatlif, the film perpetuates several essentialist notions: all Roma are "natural" musicians; Roma constitute a bounded, unified ethnic group; and finally, that there was a linear path of Romani migration from India to western Europe. Although it is beyond the scope of this paper to analyze *Latcho Drom*, I mention it here because it helped set a model for the presentation of Romani music at world music festivals.[10] In fact, the exact musical groups featured in the film were the first to travel in European world music circuits; in addition, the film in part created the viability of the marketing category "Gypsy music."

After *Latcho Drom* was released, the first western European Gypsy festivals were held in Berlin (Musik and Kultureage der Cinti und Roma) and Paris (Les Tsiganes à l'Opera) in 1992; a number of other spectacles were organized by German impresario Andre Heller under the title Magneten. More recent festivals include Le Vie dei Gitani (Ravenna, 2000), Barbican (London, 2000), The Time of the Gypsies (a tour to several countries, 2001) and the 1995 Lucerne festival, which featured a Gypsy component. North American interest in Gypsy music grew in the mid 1990s when Balkan groups such as Taraf de Haidouks from Romania toured North America and recordings became available. The first North American festival was the Gypsy Caravan tour in Spring 1999, sponsored by the World Music Institute; due to its resounding success, a second tour followed in fall 2001.

Exoticism, Authenticity

From the start, promoters and marketers emphasized the exoticism of Romani performers. Exoticism, indeed, is a theme of much world music marketing (Taylor 1997), and in this case there were hundreds of years of Gypsy imagery and lore on which to draw. Most representations of Gypsies (like other oppressed groups) have been produced by outsiders, due to the historical fact that Roma have had little control over hegemonic discourse and symbol systems (Hancock 1997). Recalling Edward Said's "Orientalism," Roma are pictured as "Gypsies," located on the (eastern) margins of Western civilization. Gypsies (especially women[11]) furnish a "fantasy/escape/danger" figure for the Western imagination; thus scholars such as Trumpener (1992) have focused on the visual spectacle of fictional Gypsies for the West.

The most eastern groups are the most "orientalized." For example, the Rajasthani group Musafir's promotional packet reads:

> classical and mystical musicians, unexpected instruments played by virtuosos, whirling desert drag queens, devotional and frantic folk dances, hypnotizing snake charmers, and dangerous fakirs, including fire eating, balancing acts, sword swallowing, and walking on crushed glass—a fantastic entertainment! Sufi desert trance music by elegant gipsy [sic] wizards . . . . A music of ecstasy, whirlwinded of climaxes punctuated by the gentle gesture of a breathtaking tune. An authentic magical experience (Maharaja, e-mail promotion, 11 July 2001).

The exotic trope extends from India to Europe's margins as groups from southern Spain, eastern Europe, and the Balkans are also "orientalized." The poster for Ft. Worth's Bass Hall concert on the 1999 Gyspy Caravan tour reads: "Get in touch with your inner gypsy. Join in this impassioned celebration of Gypsy traditions . . . . The elders supply soul and experience, the young speed and energy. Come feel the heat of a Gypsy fire" (Plate 10.1). The imagery includes eight photographs, only three of which feature groups in the actual show that the poster advertised. The other five are stereotypical pictures of generic Gypsies: a dark-skinned man with a bare chest playing the violin, three women in seductive poses, and a red rose. Clearly, all Gypsy images are interchangeable, for Gypsies are merely a place holder for the pre-modern, exotic "other." Similarly, Zirbel reports that the campfire and caravan imagery for the 1995 Lucerne festival heightened difference: "such marketing reinforced the belief that the Gypsies were freshly imported, authentic exotics" (1999:38).

Music is an especially fruitful medium for the trafficking in exoticism. In the Balkans exoticism is coded as "oriental" or Eastern (Turkish and Middle Eastern), and marked by scales and rhythmic patterns which are associated with the East, Roma, sex, and passion. These elements of musical style and text have been appropriated by non-Roma and are now widespread in pop and fusion styles such as *chalga* in Bulgaria, *muzică orientală* in Romania, and similar styles in Hungary, Macedonia, Serbia, Greece, and Albania. On the other hand, otherness is sometimes constructed in a manner that ties it to inner truths: "The pattern whereby society's others are recruited from the periphery in order to articulate musically 'the soul' of the more settled members is not an oddity from Serbia" (Port 1999:292). Indeed, African Americans have historically served this role in Anglo-American society. Mattijs van de Port's research shows that devoted Serbian fans of Romani café music in Novi Sad need Gypsy musicians to bring out their souls; the "stranger within" brings out "implicit social knowledge" (1999:292).

Exotic others, however, may conflict with local Roma, who are often less fortunate than touring musicians. The British Gypsy festival Barbican (April–May 2000), for example, had an uneasy relationship with local Roma and Travelers while simultaneously capitalizing on "foreign" Roma from the Balkans. Activist Traveler Jake Bowers pointed out that no British Travelers performed in prominent locations:

> Call me a purist, but surely a Gypsy festival should predominantly feature Gypsies, especially those from the country hosting the event . . . . After receiving a few concessions from the organizers such as extra performances featuring British Travelers and cut-price tickets for Romani refugees, British traveler organizations gave the festival their reluctant stamp of approval. Even crumbs from a table are better than nothing at all in a time of starvation (Patrin Listserve, 25 May 2000).

He continues:

> The trap they fell into was one of exoticism where "real" Gypsies belong to some other place and time. They didn't consult any British Traveler organizations during the planning but used a world music consultant who wouldn't recognize a genuine Traveler if one slapped him with a hedgehog.[12] Musicians in the here and now were turned down in favor of people whose dress and music represented the there and then. Turks in tuxedos and Rajasthanis in turbans are a world apart from the average British Gypsy site or squalid refugee hotel (Patrin Listserve, 27 May 2000).

Bowers' phrase the "time of starvation" refers to the current hostile climate in the United Kingdom (and elsewhere in western Europe) for Roma, related to the fear of incoming waves of Romani refugees from the East.[13] He writes:

> Outside in the streets, Romani women from Romania were causing hysteria . . . by daring to beg for money . . . . Armed with nothing more threatening than children, the women were being vilified by the national press for threatening the shoppers of Chelsea. A housebreaker from a British Romani family had just been shot dead by a racist farmer causing even greater hysteria about Gypsy intimidation (Patrin Listserve, 25 May 2000).

Indeed, we must remember that music festivals take place amidst growing xenophobia and anti-Romani violence. Ian Hancock, a prominent Romani activist, took a stance squarely against Gypsy music festivals, finding them a poor substitute for real activism: "It's not unusual for concerts to be funded for Roma to distract from the real issues. The money could be far better spent" (Patrin Listserve, 24 May 2000). In the United States there is less xenophobia about Romani refugees than in Europe and also less contact with Roma. For these reasons Roma appear more remote to most Americans than Europeans and the festival serves as a window into an inaccessible foreign world.[14]

In addition to displaying the exotic, festivals also cleanse, tame, appropriate, and colonize the exotic (Zirbel 1999:72). The structure of the festival is, in fact, a microcosm of colonialism: the Romani "darkies" wait at the margins of Europe (or in western European ghettos) to be discovered by white promoters; they are then escorted to the West, briefly put on stage, and escorted home.[15] The connection between artistic adoration and colonialism has been noted by Paul Gilroy (1993); in fact, nostalgia for the lost authenticity of the past is often intertwined with domination (Taussig

1987). Rosaldo's phrase "imperialist nostalgia" similarly invokes how colonialists yearn for the very markers of the nonwestern life they have destroyed (1989). Stewart reminds us that nostalgia is a representational practice (1984) and Rofel (1999:137), a strategy of representation; for Roma and their marketers alike, nostalgia for the pre-modern authentic is not only a strategy of marketing but also a strategy of representing identity.

Authenticity is constantly evoked by sponsors and the media to convey that Gyspy music festivals are "the real thing." Statements such as "experience the true arts of the Gypsies," "authentic music," "authentic ensembles," "authentic culture," and "Take a ride on the Gypsy Caravan and discover the power and joy of traditional Gypsy culture" (Kennedy Center Performance Calendar, 1999) pepper Gypsy Caravan advertisements. Similarly, Zirbel reports that for the 1995 Lucerne festival, Gypsies were depicted as "nostalgic throwbacks in the midst of modern Western Europe, persisting embodiments of older values and customs" (1999:38). The structure of the staged performances reinforces the authenticity concept even more than the actual playing of Romani music: the musicians are performing their Gypsy identities on stage. "Live music performance . . . explicitly and publicly encourages and directs audiences to imagine lives and subjectivities of the performers they see before them" (Zirbel 1999:45; Kirshenblatt-Gimblett 1998). Unlike classical music festivals, where the interpretive and technical abilities of the individual artist are paramount, Gypsy music festivals display the amazing fact that Gypsies are on stage! "The 'Gypsiness' of Gypsy music is a construct on the perceivers' part, but which is elaborated and commodified by Gypsy musicians . . . . Gypsy musicians return what is projected onto them" (Port 1999:292).

Western European audiences are especially receptive to the authenticity trope in Gypsy music because they strongly feel that they have lost their own authenticity and traditions. One manager said,

> I think there is a . . . desire to keep something very pure and very traditional because we lost it—most of the Western audience, Western civilization, they lost stuff like this . . . . Music like Fanfare Ciocarlia— a huge brass band—it seems very rootsy, it hasn't been performed in Europe before . . . . For a world music audience, it can't be too electric, too modern; it has to be old time, roots.

This current association of Gypsy music with authenticity is ironic considering the historic East European exclusion of Gypsy music from the category "tradition." In Bulgaria, for example, the socialist government prohibited Romani music from state-sponsored folk festivals, claiming it was not pure and not conservative and thus, could not represent the nation—it was too professional, hybrid, too kitschy, and used too many foreign elements (Silverman 1989).

Paul Sant Cassia's work on Maltese music notes that European "modernity is increasingly pursued through the celebration of traditionalism" (2000:282). Tradition and authenticity, however, are not self-evident categories—rather, they must be defined and narrated in discourse. "'Tradition' thus becomes not just something invented in an identifiable (recent) past (as Hobsbawm's contributors suggest), but a way of talking about the past and the present through the identification of certain practices that require preservation" (2000:289). Like Maltese songs, Romani music becomes a "symbol of marginality . . . not so much power *from* the past, but power that has survived *in spite of* the past, and which is likely to 'disappear' because of the onslaught of the 'modern world'" (2000:293). According to Kirshenblatt-Gimblett, heritage is a mode of cultural production in the present that has discursive recourse to the past (1998). She shows how authenticity oscillates between the concealment and discovery of the marginal or authentic.[16] Oppression, then, may confer authenticity, as the following advertisement narrates: "Whirling wedding dances. Flamboyant fiddle and cymbalom music. Passionate lamentations born of centuries of persecution . . . . The Roma have kept alive their history, tradition and religions solely through oral and musical communication" (Dartmouth University concert advertisement, 1999).

Roma themselves do not usually buy into the dichotomy of tradition vs. modernity. For example, a controversy over authentic instrumentation arose in the last two years when Macedonian singer Esma Redžepova's ensemble toured in western Europe. The ensemble was met with hostile reactions, even booing in Spain because they used a synthesizer, perceived as a non-traditional, modern intrusion. According to one manager, audiences want acoustic Gypsy music:

> The controversy is that many people say, "that is a great band, but it is a shame that the synthesizer is there . . . ." The crowds in Europe have this kind of purist view that it should be authentic; the management in Europe has been trying to talk Esma out of using the synthesizer. It has to do with the image people have of a certain kind of music—they want to see that image on stage. They see something modern and they think it is not the real thing . . . . They might be looking for a certain stereotype of what people think Gypsy music is about.

Another manager claims: "Now it is the fashion to hear real acoustic Gypsy music . . . . If it's amplified, electrified, audiences think it is not authentic . . . . It is quite ironical since Gypsies are very open, very influenced, very open to influences. But it is not accepted if they change something." Yet another manager concurs:

> We can't convince audiences that the Gypsy community in the Balkans uses electric instruments. They want the acoustic way . . . . People want to keep music like it is. They don't see that Gypsies are in flux. They want to keep it so as not to change it . . . . I don't like this kind of purism because it is not so different from colonialism. You like it, it is so sweet, but you don't recognize their reality.

Indeed, labeling the synthesizer as non-authentic is ironic considering the open and eclectic attitude Balkan Romani musicians display toward styles and instrumentation. They have historically adopted and adapted both Western and Eastern elements, including rap, rock, jazz, rumba, and Indian motifs. They were among the first musicians in the region to use amplification, capitalizing on the association of electrification with the West and with modernity (Silverman 1996a). Esma and her band members were adamant in their decision to continue using the synthesizer:

Esma:

> Yes, there was this argument. My manager wanted us to use the contrabass, not the synthesizer—they wanted an older sound. This is stupidity—Romani music has used modern instruments for a long time. I insisted on having my way and we now use the synthesizer.

Simeon Atanasov (Esma's accordionist):

> We had an argument at Womex [European booking conference]. Now there's a new fashion in Europe to do it the old way, to use older instruments. It is stupid. One time (at Womex) we agreed to use the contrabass—it was a total waste. We were very upset; it doesn't go with the music. The synthesizer fills out the sound.

Carol Silverman:

> But the managers told me the audiences themselves didn't like the synthesizer.

SA:

> The audience likes what you give them if you play well. You train an
> audience what to expect.

Zahir Ramadanov, trumpet player, concurring:

> These managers are not musicians. They don't understand music, they
> don't play music. They shouldn't tell us what to play. We are
> musicians—we know what sound we want.

To these performers, the music that they created was more important than
the marketing images which outsiders controlled. Esma not only defied
her managers' directives about the synthesizer, but she fashioned her show
how she pleased. For example, in Berkeley, California in 2001 in front of
over 2000 spectators and in violation of stagehand union rules, she invited
her cousin on stage to dance with her. "What was important here was that
culture was the object of self-conscious display and hence control"
(Schein 2000:380). Performers, then, manage to exert artistic control,
albeit within historical constraints.

Another marketing trope depicts Romani musicians as authentic
peasant villagers. According to one manager,

> European audiences like folklore (but not too staged)—they want
> naturalism—nothing styled up—just how they normally are .... People
> like groups like Fanfare Ciocarlia and Taraf de Haidouks because it
> seems like they just came in from the fields—they just washed their
> hands and picked up their instruments, and then they will go back to the
> fields.

Clothing plays a big role in the audience perception of authentic village
life. For example, both Fanfare Ciocarlia and Taraf de Haidouks perform
in their everyday clothing (Plates 10.2–10.3). According to their manager:
"Fanfare never uses costumes at home in Romania for weddings or
ceremonies. They just dress normally. On tour in western Europe they just
kept this practice, and afterwards we saw this is what audiences like." His
partner concurs: "this creates, ironically, authentic Gypsy culture, because
Europeans like to see a band which can create a really good party and they
came on stage in absolutely normal clothing—not like folklore ensembles." Journalists often write about the appearance of these two Romanian
groups—how everyday it is. As record producer Harold Hagopian
comments, "audiences and promoters want Gypsies to look and act like
Gypsies."

However, Roma are certainly not all villagers, and among themselves there is often disagreement about presentation styles. When the Taraf members showed up at the start of the 1999 Gypsy Caravan tour with suitcases with holes, without cases for their musical instruments, and wearing tattered clothing in which they performed, many of the other Romani performers were horrified. The latter pointed out that this image would reinforce stereotypes of poor, dirty "Gypsies" and do a disservice to Roma all over the world. Bulgarian saxophonist Yuri Yunakov, who is from an urban, clothes-conscious tradition, offered to personally take Taraf members shopping at his expense. Some performers spoke directly to Michel Winter, the Taraf manager, about this "disgrace," but Winter replied that audiences actually like the tattered image—it was good for business.

Yuri's group, by contrast, creates an urban sophisticated image, wearing suits and ties and fashionable styles (Plate 10.4). In his band, performance outfits are discussed and inspected.[17] Yuri's sophisticated attitude is also revealed by his outrage that the Taraf members were busking on the street and collecting money in a hat. To Yuri, this is low-class and crass, while for the Taraf it is another way to make money. It is clear that Yuri sees himself as a modern musician and wants his music to be perceived as modern. By contrast, Winter markets the Taraf as village peasants, part of the past, part of tradition, even though they play contemporary eclectic styles.

Esma Redžepova has yet another attitude toward clothing—her male band members wear identical costumes with Slavic folkloric elements (such as embroidery) while she wears traditional Muslim women's clothing (*šalvari*, wide trousers) with modern touches (Plate 10.5). Her clothing choices reflect the specific musical history of Yugoslavia: in the socialist period, Romani musicians were permitted to form amateur collectives as part of a staged multicultural political display. They appeared in state-sponsored folk festivals where costumes were obligatory. In socialist Bulgaria, by contrast, Romani music was never allowed in state-sponsored festivals—thus it developed in unofficial contexts. It is clear that imagery accomplishes ideological work; it is neither solely dictated by managers nor conceived by Roma in isolation; rather it emerges at the nexus of multiple, and often divergent, representational strategies.

Whereas my stance as a scholar of music questions the concept of authenticity because it conveys a static view of history, the stance of marketers is to promote it. Not surprisingly, some of the Romani performers themselves have begun to use the vocabulary of authenticity and tradition. Not only have they picked up on desirable marketing terminology, but their identities accommodate authenticity as well as modernity, not finding them contradictory. Redžepova, for example, saw the diversity represented in Gypsy festivals as due to all the other Romani groups being assimilated, but not hers. "The Roma from Spain are assimilated to the Spaniards—they play Spanish music. The Indians play Indian music. They have all been assimilated except me. My music is authentic Romani music. We Roma in Macedonia aren't assimilated—we keep our language, we keep our traditions."[18] Remember that this is the same performer who refused to remove the synthesizer from her band even though European audiences found it too modern. Esma's claims are partially based on the fact that Macedonian Roma have retained the use of the Romani language much more than the Gitanos of Spain, but musically, Roma in Macedonia have certainly adopted regional and Western musical styles and instrumentation. Paradoxically, "authenticity" for Balkan Roma may include incorporating new elements into their music; Roma have done this for centuries due to patronage and an eclectic attitude (Pettan 1992b). Esma, however, in her comments above, defines authenticity as purity, a stance which does not hold up to scrutiny. On the other hand, her stance does make sense when we examine her stake in being an "authentic" Gypsy. Under the guidance of her husband/mentor Stevo Teodosievski, she created a performance niche in Yugoslav society that displayed a consciously authentic Gypsy identity in the Yugoslav multicultural patchwork (Silverman 2003).

Politics, Discrimination

While promoters peddle exoticism and authenticity they also appeal to audiences to engage with diversity and multiculturalism. North American and European audiences for Romani concerts tend to be middle or upper class, from 20–60 years of age, well educated, with liberal leanings. Although Roma are familiar to Europeans and North Americans from popular and elite literature and art, and from the current refugee crisis, few Europeans have ever met or socialized with Roma. Suspicion is the main emotion in Europe (Clark and Campbell 2000); according to one manager: "Gypsies are present in European countries—like the begging of refugees at train stations. But Europeans know nothing about the culture—only that it could be dangerous. The concert is a window for people to learn something about this culture." Many Gypsy festivals in Europe (for example, Le Vie dei Gitani in Ravenna and Barbican in London) include educational components in the form of booklets, museum exhibitions, panels, lectures, and film showings with discussions. These events cover history, discrimination, and diversity but in locations and times that are separate from the musical program. During the 1999 North American Gypsy Caravan tour, my role as Education Coordinator included lecturing and writing extensive concert notes. Lectures were always well attended and many audience members appreciated the historical, political, and cultural information in the notes, but in general, only a select portion of the audience was interested in education. On the 2001 tour the Educational Coordinator position was cut due to financial constraints.

World music events in general are sometimes assumed to have a progressive agenda associated with them, according to Zirbel. She writes that Gypsy festival "audiences appeared to believe . . . that participating as audiences in such performances . . . constituted an act of progressive solidarity with whatever historical or current oppressions the performers' people were believed to face" (Zirbel 1999:80). In a xenophobic atmosphere, attending a Gypsy concert or buying a Gypsy CD may indeed be a brave public statement of liberalism, but it can hardly be called activism. It does, however, make audience members feel good about their role. British activist Jake Bowers notes that, "Multiculturalism is fine and dandy when it is at an acceptable distance" (Patrin Listserve, 27 May 2000). Gocic, a commentator on Balkan politics, remarked that

> It is sad that the current fashion for Gypsy music, interest in Gypsy folklore, and dramatic depiction of the Gypsy soul has not translated into some kind of concern for Roma[ni] suffering. Beyond rousing applause for their musicians, Gypsies need substantial support from the West . . . . Of course, "the art of the oppressed" is nothing new. Cultural adoration and political discrimination have often walked hand in hand . . . . Renewed interest in the culture of some ethnic group . . . often means it's in deep trouble (2000).

Gocic further notes that "Gypsies have become a hip accessory for stars such as Johnny Depp who reportedly paid a six-figure sum to Taraf de Haidouks to play at his party in Los Angeles"; these stars, however, never "mention the general plight of the Gypsies. Neither do Roma[ni] artists themselves—attaching oneself to an already lost cause is not exactly a good career move" (Gocic 2000). Roma have learned that they are paid to entertain, not educate.

Producers and promoters feel that education is not a main purpose of performance. One manager said, "It is not my idea to lead lessons with this music—it is entertainment." Another remarked, "I don't think it is very important for the public to be educated." And a third said, "I don't

like the very open educational style. I don't like to play with education .
. . the best way is to take the music and give it to the audience, let them
listen to it. They will like it and for those that are interested, there are
lectures." One promoter expressed the dilemma between entertainment
and education as follows:

> I think it is important to give the political background of the countries
> where the Roma are living. Well, I also understand that people go to a
> concert for experience and they don't care about politics—just to enjoy
> music for a couple of hours and forget about real life. So I wouldn't
> emphasize politics too much in the program—but they could also find
> time to read about what they are going to see . . . . You can't deny
> where these musicians are coming from. You shouldn't separate their
> suffering from their music.

Discrimination became a contested topic when the program notes I
wrote for the 1999 Gypsy Caravan tour were scrutinized by Michel
Winter, the non-Romani manager of the Taraf de Haidouks. I had
courteously asked Winter for feedback on my notes because the organizers
were willing to make changes in the program brochure for the final New
York City concerts. Winter insisted that I remove the following paragraph
which appeared at the end of the Taraf's profile:

> In the 1970's, Ceausescu's policy of homogenization became more
> oppressive and Rom[ani] culture was targeted. Some Roma were
> removed from large government ensembles, where they made up 90%
> of professional musicians. The Rom[ani] ethnicity of musicians was
> frequently covered up and Roma were not allowed to perform in-group
> music, such as songs in Roman[i]. Since the 1989 revolution, life has
> considerably worsened for Romania's approximately 2.5 million Roma.
> While they can now organize their own cultural and political organiza-
> tions, they suffer numerous attacks on their homes, possessions, and
> persons. Groups like Taraf de Haidouks salute the resilience of
> Rom[ani] music under trying conditions.

Winter claimed there was no discrimination against Roma in Romania,
and that Roma could do anything they wanted: "even become president."
Trying to mediate between Winter and me, Robert Browning, director of
the sponsoring organization, the World Music Institute, reduced my entire
paragraph to the last sentence.
The very artists Winter represented, the Taraf members, contradicted
his absurd claim that there is no persecution. In conversations with Taraf
members I learned of systematic abuse, taunting, and discrimination in

schooling, employment, and health care. For me, the most moving moment of the 1999 Gypsy Caravan tour occurred during a panel discussion at Dartmouth University which I organized on music and politics. Nicolae Neacsu, the 85-year old Romanian fiddler in Taraf (now deceased), recounted his life history: how he left school in the fourth grade to work to support his mother and siblings, how he barely survived the Holocaust, how he was neglected during the Socialist period, and how now, only because of western European acclaim, does he have any clout in Romania. Russian musician Sasha Kolpakov and Hungarian musician Gusztav Varga also shared experiences of prejudice and insensitivity. Michel Winter was not present to hear them. In fact, he forbade Ionitsa, an articulate younger member of Taraf, to take part in the panel, even though he was slated to appear. My interpretation of Winter's stance is that he believed that Taraf's reputation would be tarnished by the intrusion of politics, specifically discrimination. Perhaps he felt it would hurt ticket sales.[19]

Besides contesting discrimination, Winter displayed a condescending attitude toward the Taraf members.[20] He implied that the Taraf just didn't know any better about how to dress and act—after all, they were just Romanian villagers. Winter often had a patronizing attitude toward the Taraf; for example, he made decisions for them without consulting them and without informing them. For their part, the Taraf members were not critical of Winter; on the contrary, they were thankful to him as the person who had made them famous in western Europe and North America. Taraf musicians, then, had neither a role in creating their international image nor a desire to modify that image; they perceived themselves as powerless in this arena, dependent on non-Romani mentors and mediators. Winter himself cultivated their dependency by keeping the Taraf ill-informed.

Self-stereotyping

Returning to the point of view of Roma, musicians seem not to resent the use of the exotic/authentic stereotype, but rather they ignore it or engage with it strategically. All of the musicians with whom I spoke, and to whom I showed and translated various media representations seemed neither interested in nor surprised at how they were pictured and narrated.[21] Most agreed that exoticism helps to sell tickets. Several of singer Esma Redžepova's films made for Yugoslav audiences in the 1970s and 1980s, for example, featured campfires and caravans, which are totally foreign to urban sedentary Balkan Roma. Similarly, Bulgarian Romani bands currently feature half-naked bellydancers even though Bulgarian Romani in-group dancing is more subtle and clothed. Likewise, Lemon's research shows how, on a documentary film shoot in a Russian Kelderara Romani neighborhood, the crew insisted on building a campfire in the snow and ordering all the young girls to dance simultaneously, behaviors which were totally foreign to the Roma. Yet she learned that "the Kelderara did not criticize how they had been filmed . . . . In fact . . . Kelderara themselves shared and valued some of the same forms of stereotypic representation valued by the crew" (2000:156–57).

Romani musicians not only do not actively resist stereotyping, but also often employ it fruitfully. Historically, Roma have sometimes believed and transmitted stereotypes (both positive and negative) about themselves, such as their "genetic" gift for music (Peicheva 1999). Fortune-tellers, for example, often presented themselves as exotic and powerful to their clients while Ottoman female dancers capitalized on their perceived sexuality (Silverman 2003). Ong reminds us that "speaking subjects are not unproblematic representers of their own culture" (1997:194). Everyone speaks from a point of view with various motives. "Self-orientalizing" moves should not be taken at face value but should be examined within the webs of power in which they are located. "Self-orientalization" displays the predicaments of marginal "others" in the face of Western hegemony, but also points to their "agency to maneuver and manipulate meanings within different power domains" (Ong 1997:195). Savigliano, writing about tango, coins the term "autoexoticism," defined as "exotic others laboriously cultivat[ing] passionate-ness in order to be desired, and thus recognized" (1995:212). Romani musicians, who have never been in control of their own imagery and reputations, are quite used to being made and making themselves into "exotic others" or "authentic originals." These tropes may be good for business, but more importantly, they are but one of many labels and identities that Roma embrace.

Caravans, Nomadism, and Romani Unity

The most ubiquitous trope of marketing is the caravan concept itself—the theme of linear nomadic migration, starting in India and ending in Spain. The World Music Institute labeled its two tours "The Gypsy Caravan," and their 1999 press packet described the festival as "A musical journey following the Romany trail from Asia to Europe," comparable to Tony Gatlif's film *Latcho Drom*. Sponsors embellished this idea: "The 1000 Year Journey" (Barbican, London); "Take a journey in sound along the winding road followed over the span of centuries by Gypsies" (University Musical Society, Ann Arbor, Michigan); "Roma[ni] ensembles take you on a century-spanning journey of authentic Gypsy culture" (Hopkins Center, Dartmouth College); "thirty-five musicians and dancers will lead you on a nomadic musical journey through the traditions of the Roma[ni] people (gypsies) from their origins in Rajasthan, India to Bulgaria, Romania, Hungary, Russia, and Spain" (Barclay Theater, Irvine CA); "The Gypsy caravan features authentic ensembles representing a sweeping scope of Gypsy migration, beginning with Asian and Indian influences from a thousand years ago and moving westward to contemporary Romanian fiddle music and Andalusian flamenco music and dance" (University Musical Society, Ann Arbor MI). Building on the migration theme, in 1999 the World Music Institute arranged for the sale of the CD *The Gypsy Road: A Musical Migration from India to Spain* at concert venues.

The problem with the theme of linear migration is that it distorts Romani history. Roma were not a unified ethnic group that left northwest India at one time, moving westward together. Rather, recent historical linguistic evidence supports the theory that Roma left India in several waves and probably coalesced as an ethnic and linguistic group outside of India (Hancock 1998). Furthermore, not all Roma are nomadic. Historically, Roma in eastern Europe have tended to be more sedentary than Roma of western Europe due to government policies and economic history (Fraser 1992). In fact, most Romani groups currently in the Gypsy festival circuit have been sedentary since their arrival in Europe.

Drawing upon the structure of the film *Latcho Drom*, all of the European and American festivals employ a schema depicting linear migration from an original Indian homeland. Festivals and concerts begin with Rajasthani music and then travel westward, ending with flamenco music from Spain. This conveys the simplistic linear message that Rajasthani music today represents what Romani music sounded like 1000 years ago. In conversations with Caravan organizer Robert Browning, I tried to problematize the message that might be conveyed by including an Indian group: I was afraid audiences would assume that Rajasthani groups like Musafir/Maharaja perform the music of European Roma from 1000 years ago. My program notes for the Gypsy Caravan tours, therefore, dwell on the symbolic place that a contemporary Rajasthani group has in the tour, the fact that it likely has no direct relationship to European Romani groups, and the fact that its music has changed a great deal during the last 1000 years, as has the music of all the groups. But the market has a life of its own—Musafir/Maharaja's promotional materials label them Indian "Gypsies." This label, however, is not merely a current invention;

the British also mistakenly applied the term to virtually all professional musicians in India. Perhaps the neocolonial mentality of the market has replaced the old colonialism, but with a continuity of labels. For sure, the market dictates that whatever label sells is the correct label to adopt. Zirbel reports a similar ethnic marketing strategy among the promoters of the Egyptian group Musiciens du Nil who also performed in *Latcho Drom*. Although they do not relate to the label at all, they are marketed under the label "Gypsy" (1999:60–64). Indeed, members of both Musafir/Maharaja and the Musiciens du Nil have now begun calling themselves Gypsies.

Related to the idea of a common Indian homeland is the question of the unity of all Romani musics.[22] Reporters and audience members alike continually want to know what it is that unites all these musicians. Cultural features among the performers are extremely varied: any one concert typically embraces several religions and linguistic groups: considering the six groups which participated in the 1999 Gypsy Caravan, for example, the Romanians and Russians were Eastern Orthodox, the Hungarians and Spaniards were Catholic, the Bulgarians and half the Rajasthanis were Muslim, and the other half of the Rajasthanis were Hindu. In terms of language, Romani was spoken by two of the five Hungarians, a few of the Romanians, and all three Russians—none of the Bulgarians, Spaniards or Rajasthanis spoke Romani. I do not wish to give the impression that Romani performers at festivals do not get along with each other. On the contrary, Gusztav Varga, the director of Kalyi Jag, told interviewers in 1999 that all the performers in the Gypsy Caravan seemed like brothers—there was something familiar—perhaps a shared knowledge that they all came from India, or a shared historical sense of discrimination. Indeed, at Gypsy concerts there is definitely a feeling of group camaraderie, but it is derived neither from musical specifics nor from lengthy conversations since few of the performers can communicate with one another. The performers do carefully listen to each other's musics and clearly respect each other's talent.

In regard to music, the media insisted on knowing what the groups had in common and what made Romani music unique and different from other musics. Bulgarian saxophonist Yuri Yunakov was quite honest during interviews in admitting that the groups in the 1999 Gypsy Caravan tour shared nothing musically, except that the Romanian and Bulgarian groups shared some Balkan regional rhythmic patterns. In general, Romani performers do not find the subject of unity one worthy of discussion, and they often remark that their diversity is a strength of the festivals, a point with which I agree wholeheartedly. On the other hand, it seems as if it is intellectually impossible or morally wrong for media writers to accept the concept of diversity. One media review was titled:

"Gypsy Show offers a Lesson in Universality." If the media could not readily find a common musical thread, they groped for one—passion, talent, soul, improvisation which, of course, are not unique to Romani music.

Audience members, too, are caught up in the "detective work" of figuring out what the groups have in common. According to Zirbel's Lucerne research, one audience member suggested, "Gypsies get a certain look in their eyes," while another "suggested they were linked by how they moved" (1999:53).[23] Most remarks about unity, however, centered on music. In 2001, one audience member said:

> One of the people I went with had *just* finished telling me how she could see/hear the commonalities between the Romanian and Macedonian Rom[ani] music but she just *could not* see any connection between those and the Flamenco or Rajasthani music. Then the three singers [Macedonian, Spanish, Rajasthani] did their three little bits [*a cappella* phrases in the finale]—*all* strikingly similar but each done completely within their own styles. They were clearly put together to show *exactly* that connection, and it was a little obvious but educational nonetheless for those who might still not have figured out what these four groups had to do with each other.

After hearing this appraisal, I still am puzzled as to how to evaluate what the three (or four) groups have in common musically; clearly what they have in common is highly ornamented unmetered (*parlando rubato*) singing, but neither the ornamentation nor the unmetered style are unique to Roma—they are shared with regional musics. It is just as plausible to posit that Muslim influence historically caused the similarities!

When Robert Browning suggested the 1999 Gypsy Caravan performers arrange a finale, it was quite a challenge since the groups had no one tune, style, or language in common. There were similarities between the Russian and Hungarian repertoires and between the Bulgarian and Romanian repertoires, but there was nothing everyone shared. Yuri Yunakov suggested performing *Dželem dželem*, a Balkan Romani song which was adopted as the Romani national anthem in 1971 at a Romani International Congress, but the Spaniards and Rajasthanis had never heard of the song and the Romanians hardly knew it. What finally emerged was that the Hungarians began an instrumental tune, the Russians joined, the Romanians joined, and the Bulgarians joined. The Indians then joined, embellishing the rhythm and adding a vocal improvisation, and finally the Spaniards joined, dancing flamenco to the group's rhythm. The Hungarians and the Russians shared the first tune; it was learned on the spot by everyone else. Audiences remarked that the finale worked precisely because it was so unpolished and allowed spontaneous personal interactions between the groups. Indeed, in the finale, Sasha Kolpakov, the elder Russian dancer, would often flirt with Tia Juana, the elder flamenco dancer. Personal connections between performers happened despite lack of a common language and musical style.

The question of unity is further complicated in terms of repertoire. In festivals and concerts, the mandate is to perform Gypsy music, but each group interprets differently what Gypsy music means. For example, before the 1999 Caravan tour, the Bulgarians had prepared a program entirely composed of *kyuchetsi*, a specifically Bulgarian/Macedonian/Turkish Romani dance genre, plus songs in Romani, even though at a typical Bulgarian Romani wedding, the band would also play and sing Bulgarian music. When the Bulgarians heard the Taraf from Romania perform, they realized that Taraf members sang in Romanian only and played Romanian village dance music; the Bulgarians then adjusted their program to include Bulgarian dance music. Ironically, the Romanians originally included an instrumental piece that was very similar to a Bulgarian *kyuchek*, as this has become a very popular genre in Romania in the last ten years (*muzică orientală*), but Browning cut this piece because it didn't sound distinctly Romanian. Similarly, the Hungarians also had a *kyuchek*-like instrumental in their performance, but Browning cut it for similar reasons. Although we may think Browning was too rash or too narrow by cutting these new pan-Balkan Romani-inflected styles, we should also realize that Roma themselves can be very possessive and essentialist about their supposedly "unique styles." The band members in Redžepova's ensemble, for example, were quite upset that Fanfare Ciocarlia performed *muzică orientală* at festivals and concerts. Accordionist Simeon Atanasov said: "I told the Romanians that they shouldn't play *orientală* on stage—they should play their own music—Romanian." Redžepova and Yuri Yunakov both agreed that the Romanians and the Hungarians "stole it from us, from the Balkans." On the other hand, Yuri's and Esma's band members tremendously enjoyed jamming backstage with the younger Romanians precisely because they had this genre in common. This genre is clearly a dynamic means of communication across borders.

These examples illustrate a number of paradoxes. First, Gypsy music means different things to different performers: some groups define Gypsy music as that music which is distinctly Romani while others define it as the entire range of music that Roma perform. Second, while media critics and audience members look for unifying musical factors which might be indexical to older layers, the one genre that is in fact shared by the Bulgarians, Macedonians, Romanians, and Hungarians is not the oldest layer, but rather the newest layer. It is a direct post-1989 import to

Romania and Hungary from the southern Balkans. Indeed, the Romanian performers are all avid listeners of Balkan wedding music and know the names of the famous Bulgarian and Macedonian Romani stars.

Conclusion

Festivals are instructive in investigating the motivations and choices of images and musical styles that are involved in the cultural brokering of Romani music for Western audiences. Economics informs many choices; however, there are varied interpretations as to what sells. Whereas some promoters do not want politics to spoil the entertainment, others believe audiences need to know about persecution and that historical and political information augments the multicultural agenda of world music festivals. Performers themselves have varying artistic and historical interpretations of what Gypsy music is, which they then must negotiate with promoters and managers, who often have discrepant interpretations. Whereas some Romani performers actively take a stake in creating their own images, for example, as urban sophisticates, others collaborate with their promoters to create opposite images, such as backward peasants.

Historically, Romani musicians are used to performing for varied audiences with varying expectations; they are also used to hostility. These skills are useful in the European festival circuit where their exoticism and authenticity are displayed on stage while anti-foreigner sentiments rage outside. Roma negotiate their identities performatively on and off stage, sometimes rejecting, sometimes ignoring, and sometimes embracing stereotypes. Following Appadurai (1996), my approach has emphasized the sphere of the artistic and the imaginary, but always embedded in the political economy of inequality. As Nonini and Ong (1997:26) have written,

> The concept of imaginaries therefore conveys the agency of diaspora subjects, who while being made by state and capitalist regimes of truth, can play with different cultural fragments in a way that allows them to segue from one discourse to another, experiment with alternative forms of identification, shrug in and out of identities, or evade imposed forms of identification.

Romani musicians excel precisely in this fluidity of cultural fragments. Whereas non-Romani audiences seek unity in culture and authenticity in music, Roma play with hybridity, with novel combinations, honing their adaptability. As Lemon remarks, "it is not Roma who find 'hybridity' problematic, but non-Roma who see it as shifty. . ." (2000:212).

Pollock, et al. claim that cosmopolitan practices "come to be seen as mixtures of things believed to have been previously unmixed and on that account . . . all the more authentic"; on the other hand, we must realize that modernity itself is filled with contradictions. It attempts to "separate and purify realms . . . that have never been separate and pure and still are not" (2000:587). Cultures, rather than being individuated, are more profitably seen as "located at the intersection of a range of other cultural objects" (Pollock, et al. 2000:587–88; see also Port 1999:297). Romani music and musical performances are not merely derivative borrowings from other "purer" traditions; they are cosmopolitan cultural constellations that are hallmarks of an alternative modernity. This modernity is located at the margins, receiving its impetus from economic survival, from historical exclusion, and from artistic adaptability. In sum, Roma embrace a surprisingly modern sensibility while dutifully fulfilling their role as Europe's last bastion of tradition.

Notes

1. When using the term Gypsy, I emphasize that it is an outsider term. Along with its cognates *Gitan* (French), *Gitano* (Spanish), *Yiftos* (Greek), and *Gjuptsi* (Macedonian), Gypsy has strong negative connotations and embodies a faulty history, i.e., purported Egyptian origins. Another common outsider term, *tsigan,* comes from the Greek *Atsingani,* a heretical sect in the Byzantine period. I use the term Roma as an ethnonym (singular Rom, adjective Romani) because it has become somewhat of a unifying term in the last decade as political consciousness is mobilized through political parties, conferences, and congresses. In all of these forums, music has played an important role in displaying Romani creativity and in affirming Romani contributions to European culture in the face of growing xenophobia.

2. World music emerged as a marketing category in European and American contexts in the late 1980s; see Timothy Taylor 1997.

3. Kelsky points out that cosmopolitan experiences may "reinforce precisely the relations of power that they appear to be undermining . . . . Cosmopolitanism, then, is not inherently subversive" (2001:15). We need to be suspicious of claims that mobility is inherently liberating, since history shows that many forms of mobility are enforced, unwelcome, or last resorts. As Pheng Cheah writes: "cosmopolitan movements are presented as exemplary instances of active resistance to localism and cultural homogenization under global capitalism . . . . Physical mobility is the basis of emancipatory practice because it generates stasis-disrupting forms of cultural displacement (1998:296–97). Cosmopolitanism, then,

is neither inherently liberating nor inherently constraining, but open to myriad possibilities (see Ong and Nonini 1997:324–25).

4. A number of scholars have investigated what happens when global capitalism encounters local practices (Miller 1994; Rofel 1999). Marilyn Ivy reminds us that although there is no such thing as an "undifferentiated global modernity" (1995:5), nonwestern modernities are always configured with the West as a reference point (1995:4). Indeed, the problematic ways in which the West serves as such a reference point may be one hallmark of modernity (see Dirlik 1997).

5. Music as a profession, however, is not present among many Romani groups. Often, whether Roma are professionals or not, music-making is often the social glue and the context for artistic display in Romani communities. Not only is music an important shared art within Romani communities, but it is also an important commodity in the economic relationship between Roma and non-Roma. See Silverman 1996a.

6. Roma-sponsored festivals such as the Shutka Fest in Skopje and the Stara Zagora festival in Bulgaria serve more overtly political functions, but their cultural displays are often just as stereotypical as non-Roma sponsored events. The issue of self-stereotyping is discussed below.

7. I traveled with the 1999 North American Gypsy Caravan tour and served as the Educational Coordinator, presenting pre-concert lectures and post-concert discussions, and giving numerous media interviews. I was also a vocalist with the Yuri Yunakov Ensemble, one of the featured groups on the tour, and wrote the program notes for the 1999 and 2001 tours. I documented the tours through interviews with producers, managers, performers and audience members, and observation of backstage talk and behavior. For comparative purposes, I examined festivals in Germany, Italy, Spain, Switzerland, and England through festival booklets, media documentation, and through interviews with participants. Many of the key performers, managers, and producers in Europe are the same as in the Gypsy Caravan. Research on "Gypsy" festivals was preceded by a decade of fieldwork with Romani musicians in their communities in Bulgaria, Macedonia, and in the diaspora (New York, Toronto, and Australia). Note that although this article does not directly address the recent plethora of Gypsy music CDs, the main points also apply to the recording industry (see Silverman forthcoming).

8. Linguistic evidence reveals that Roma migrated westward from northwest India and reached the Balkans by the fourteenth century. The Romani language (descended from Sanskrit) exists in many dialects, reflecting the paths of dispersion. Initial curiosity about Roma quickly gave way to hatred and discrimination in virtually every European region, a legacy which has continued until today (Hancock 1987, 1998). Assimilation was attempted in the eighteenth century in the Austro-Hungarian Empire by outlawing Romani language, music, dress, and nomadism, and banning traditional occupations. In the Nazi period, over 600,000 Roma were murdered. Assimilationist legislation was enacted by East European socialist states, although specific policies varied. Today harassment and prejudice continue towards the 10 million Roma of Europe, along with marginalization and low status. In the Balkans, political and human rights

activism among the Roma has increased particularly since the 1989 revolutions and the subsequent rise in pogroms and scapegoating (Barany 2002; Silverman 1995).

9. Kusturica's films include *Time of the Gypsies, Underground*, and *Black Cat, White Cat*. They all prominently feature Romani music; some groups became famous as a result.

10. See my review of the film in *Ethnomusicology* (Silverman 2000a).

11. For a discussion of how female sexuality is marketed in music, see Silverman 2003.

12. Hedgehogs are traditional food for Travelers.

13. There has been some press on this topic; see Clark and Campbell 2000.

14. The penchant Americans have for imitation (or simulation) of the exotic was obvious at a few of the Gypsy Caravan concerts when concertgoers dressed up in their idea of Gypsy clothing. Some men looked like Johnny Depp in the film *Chocolat;* some women had colorful skirts, shawls and gold earrings.

15. Kathryn Zirbel notes that at the Lucerne 1995 festival there was uneasiness among organizers that the Romani performers would overstep their place; indeed when they were simply out on the street as non-performers, they were met with hostility and suspicion (1999:84). "In response to community concerns, it was rumored that the festival organizers had to sign an affidavit promising to reimburse all goods stolen or damaged by the visiting 'Gypsies'" (Zirbel 2000:137). Clearly, racism often lurks beneath artistic adoration.

16. Sant Cassia elaborates on how the category marginal is "confabulated": the marginal is represented as exotic, as a "unique experience" which is discovered; the narrating subject confers authenticity; authenticity is reproduced on a mass scale (2000:293).

17. Yuri's group is composed of several Americans as well as Bulgarians and Roma; whereas one might think that the impetus to wear fashionable Western clothing comes from the Americans, the opposite is true; the Roma insist on formal clothing.

18. At this point, Esma launched into a proud recounting of how tolerant Macedonia is towards Roma: "We are the only country in the world that has Romani representatives and two TV programs .... Macedonia is the only country which recognizes Romani people officially. Roma in Macedonia can learn in their own language. Roma speak the literary Romani language—they aren't assimilated—they have their language and television programs every day" (2001). Most of these claims are only partially true; see "A Pleasant Fiction: The Human Rights Situation of Roma in Macedonia," European Roma Rights Center, 1998. Esma (and other Roma) are often quite patriotic, even in states which have not protected their freedoms (see Lemon 2000).

19. In the liner notes for the 2001 Taraf de Haidouks' CD *Band of Gypsies* (Nonesuch79642-2), this stance has changed. The author of the notes, journalist Marc Hollander, mentions discrimination to illustrate how the Taraf have been ignored in Romania. His narrative strategy here is to market the Taraf as unsung heroes. This relates to my point that discrimination often confers authenticity.

20. Condescension, however, was not typical of the managers I met.

21. Zirbel's research with "Gypsies" from Egypt who perform at European festivals supports this claim: " most groups either did not realize or were just not interested in what they. . . signified for audiences" (1999:86).

22. The question of unity is also an important political issue, for to build a unified human rights movement, Roma have to establish unity based on something tangible. Given the diversity of cultural characteristics, finding unity is problematic (Mirga and Gheorghe 1997).

23. Zirbel's research at the Lucerne festival points out that amidst the different musical cultures that are represented, "there was a sense that such elements formed a thin veneer over a similar underlying, originary identity . . . . In the case of the Gypsies, cultural difference provides a brilliant surface, but part of the curiosity and excitement for audiences and for scholars . . . has been the alleged underlying unity of racial and geographical origins" (1999:52–53). She shows that Swiss audiences were engaged in a kind of safe nation-building (1999:55).

POSTLUDE

❖ 11 ❖

Balkan Boundaries
and
How to Cross Them:
A Postlude

Svanibor Pettan

The Serbian minority should get autonomous status in Montenegro, so
that its members can drink plum brandy, use the Cyrillic alphabet and
sing their Turkish songs.

We listen to Croatian music, and the fact that you, Croatians, listen to
Turkish music is your own problem.

During the weeks prior to the referendum in Montenegro, which on 21
May 2006 enabled the decomposition of the last remaining joint state of
the former Yugoslavia's republics, that of Serbia and Montenegro, readers
of the online versions of area newspapers were widely engaged in
discussing ongoing political issues.[1] The short comments quoted above,
taken from the online version of a major Croatian daily,[2] may be interpreted on several levels. First, they testify that people from different
former Yugoslav republics participate in a public debate offered by a
newspaper in a state other than their own. Second, they largely rely on
unverified stereotypes rather than acquired knowledge and perceive each
other as the Other.[3] Third, they show awareness of current musical
processes and use music to make their points.[4] Fourth, regardless of their
respective states of origin, they share the notion of Turkish—in the

broader sense of oriental and at the same time in the narrower sense of Ottoman—as something foreign and characterized by negative connotations, a perception acquired through formal education, oral tradition, and present political processes.

Views from the Northwest

It is perhaps useful to start this postlude with Croatia, a peripheral state within the broader Balkan context that—just like Greece, Romania, or Turkey—in some sources appears inside and in other sources outside the Balkans' contested boundaries.[5] As with the fluctuating eastern boundary of Europe following the break-up of the Soviet Union, one has to address multiple questions, such as what and where the Balkans are, who decides, and on what basis (cf. Bošković 2005:8).[6] Here I shall consider four categories of arguments—geographical, historical, cultural, and political, all in connection to musics and discourses about musics—to examine the extent to which ethnomusicology can help us first understand and then transcend various boundaries.

Geographers usually describe the Balkan peninsula as an area surrounded by the Sea of Marmara and the Adriatic, Ionian, Aegean, and Black Seas, and the rivers Danube and Sava. There is no consensus in regard to the northwestern boundary that concerns the territory between the Sava River and the Adriatic Sea. Attempts to relate the northwestern Balkan boundary to different rivers often have political rather than geographic connotations: the Drina divides Serbia from Bosnia-Hercegovina,[7] the Una separates Bosnia-Hercegovina and Croatia,[8] the Sutla/Sotla divides Croatia from Slovenia,[9] and the Soča/Isonzo (to an extent) runs between Slovenia and Italy.[10] Until the early 1990s all of these suggested boundaries were encompassed by the former Yugoslavia, which was, as a whole, widely perceived as the westernmost Balkan country.

Geographic factors most directly affect the domain of rural traditional music, which is characterized by regional specifics. The Bosnian ethnomusicologist Ankica Petrović emphasized "the central mountainous regions of Yugoslavia" as a natural barrier between what she called "the Eastern and Western cultural hemispheres" (1994:20). These regions, marked by the shared mountainous Dinaric range encompassing Montenegro, most of Bosnia-Hercegovina and the Dalmatian hinterlands of Croatia, became known as the Dinaric zone (see Dunin, et al. 1998; Gavazzi 1942; Ivančan 1964). Three out of a total of six such distinctive zones were recognized in the territory of Croatia, each pointing to three larger areas: (1) the Pannonian zone (in northwestern Croatia), which points toward Central Europe, (2) the Adriatic zone (in the south), which points toward the Mediterranean, and (3) the Dinaric zone (in the east), which points toward the Balkans.[11] The Dinaric zone continues to be seen as the most archaic and only Dinaric musical soundscapes—in contrast to those of the other zones—are still considered aesthetically unsuitable for regular radio and television broadcasts. Among the features characteristic of rural traditional music and dance within the Dinaric zone, one may point to: use of narrow, untempered intervals; loud two-part *a cappella* singing performed by small groups of singers of the same sex; solo vocal performance of epic songs to single-string bowed lute accompaniment; shepherd music on wooden aerophones; and curving line dances, some of which lack musical accompaniment (more in Dunin, et al. 1998; Pettan 1997).

The majority of historians, according to Maria Todorova, perceive the Balkans as inclusive of Romania, Bulgaria, Greece, Albania, and the territories of the former Yugoslavia (1997:31).[12] Todorova adds the Turks who, for obvious reasons, "dominated the Ottoman experience." She also includes the Croats, since parts of Croatia were under Ottoman rule for considerable lengths of time and because its vassal territories "exerted such an important influence on the Balkan Peninsula that their history cannot be severed from the Balkans." However, Slovenes, "*pace* Cvijić" are excluded (1997:31). The Military Frontier aimed against the Ottomans, which was subject to the Habsburg's military administration, kept the territory of Croatia divided between the sixteenth and late nineteenth centuries.[13] Samuel Huntington's divide between Catholic and Orthodox/Muslim "civilizations," borrowed from Wallace, is situated further to the east, through Bosnia-Hercegovina (Huntington 1996).

Within music scholarship, historical discourse is most often associated with Western urban art music. The centuries-long presence of this music and native composers in the Slovenian and Croatian lands served for decades as an unquestionable indicator of the "Westernness" of the two; by comparison, their eastern neighbors did not produce native composers in the domain of Western art music until as late as the nineteenth century (Andreis, et al. 1962; Cvetko 1981). This evidence, with historical implications pertaining to the Habsburg legacy, led Croatian musicologist Stanislav Tuksar to the following conclusion:

> On the basis of taking into account real historico-political, economic and socio-cultural facts in all pre-Classical musico-stylistical epochs, and especially that of the Baroque, the musical cultures of the Polish, Czech/Moravian, Slovakian, Slovenian and Croatian lands form—in the entirety of their substance and the forms of their products, organizational frames, and consumption—an integral part of West European musical culture (1998:62–63).

Since these five nations fully participated in the development of West European art music, it would be wrong, says Tuksar, to consider them as parts of "an imaginary and unified 'East European musical culture'" that contained only traces of West European musical culture.

The cultural definition of the Balkans is unavoidably linked to the Ottoman legacy. According to Maria Todorova, "it is the Ottoman elements or the ones perceived as such that are mostly invoked in the current stereotype of the Balkans" (1996b:11). Yvonne Lockwood's statement (1983:10), based on her fieldwork in Bosnia-Hercegovina, that "the Ottoman legacy is present in almost every aspect of Balkan culture, both material and non-material, Christian as well as Muslim," could further assist us in determining the Balkans' boundaries.[14] At the same time, one should keep in mind that the territory of Bosnia-Hercegovina was subjected to a rather short but influential Habsburg rule from 1878 until the unification of southern Slavs following World War I into what would become Yugoslavia. This at least to some extent softened the sense of difference surrounding life on opposite sides of the border between the two powerful empires.

The Ottoman legacy can be examined in both rural and urban musical practices. Musicians performing in predominantly rural shawm and drum ensembles, most often Roma, can still be found in many areas that were ruled by the Ottomans, and not in those ruled by the Habsburgs. In regard to the ex-Yugoslav territories, these ensembles were regularly employed to the southeast of Slovenia, Croatia, and Vojvodina (the northeastern corner of Serbia).[15] Recognized as a musical emblem of historical enemies, they were seldom employed in Serbia (except for its southern part) and Montenegro. For example, my research in Kosovo (1989–91) indicated that ethnic Serbian peasants increasingly thought of these ensembles as inappropriate for their feasts due to their alleged ethnically "Albanian" and religiously "Muslim" background (Pettan 1996b:38; Plate 11.1).[16]

The Ottoman legacy is especially apparent in urban musical practices because the Empire's administration was stationed in cities. The urban counterpart of the shawm and drum ensemble was the chamber group, now largely obsolete, known by various local variants of the term *chalgiya* (Plate 11.2).[17] Besides these ensembles, specific urban genres such as the Bosnian *sevdalinka* and Greek *rebetika* emerged that are characterized by so-called oriental musical features: modal melodic and rhythmic organization, elaborate ornamentation, improvisation, and the presence of Turkish-derived words regardless of the language used for singing. The absence of *chalgiya* ensembles and comparable genres in the northwesternmost parts of the former Yugoslavia suggests that this area does not fit in the Balkan musical framework.

There is no doubt that the Balkan issue has a particularly strong political dimension. Once a neutral geographic term, "Balkan" became a root word for dictionary entries such as *balkanization* and *to balkanize*, thus justifying the following question: What country on Earth (which is not unquestionably located within the given territory) would appreciate being characterized by "uncivilized and wild behavior" (Klaić 1972:136), "political-territorial, religious and ethnic fragmentation" (Kovačec 1996:69) and "breaking up into smaller and often hostile units" (Webster's Dictionary 1973)? The Yugoslav author Ivo Andrić (1892–1975), winner of the Nobel Prize for literature, wrote of the "cursedness of homo balcanicus,"[18] while the famous Croatian writer Miroslav Krleža (1893–1981) commented on the horrified cursedness of the Balkans (Rihtman-Auguštin 1997:32).

The first Croatian president Franjo Tuđman expressed the following thoughts in his annual address to the nation for 1996: "Croatia is a Central European and Mediterranean country. The short relationship between Croatia and the Balkans from 1918 to 1990 was just an episode that should happen never again." In the presidential campaign of 1997, one of the official slogans was "Tuđman, not the Balkans." The Croatian situation shows that the (Western-originating) balkanist discourse has been internalized and used within the region to mobilize people, but also that it served as "an effective means of disciplining states like Croatia that aspire to be recognized as European" (Razsa and Lindstrom 2004:634).[19]

How was balkanist discourse reflected in music? The domain of popular culture provides an explanation. In the late 1980s, amid the political tensions that preceded the armed conflict, the Croatian film director Vinko Grubišić and his friends created a humorous music video that parodies the political West–East extremes within Yugoslavia. They used a "neutral" Croatian urban song, *Serbus dragi Zagreb moj* [Greetings to you, my dear Zagreb], which in its first part ridicules Western stereotypes (the "refined" and somewhat ascetic appearance of the singer Željko Pervan in white gloves, singing with smooth voice and pronouncing the Croatian lyrics with a pseudo-French accent), and then—after a sudden change, ridicules Eastern stereotypes. The Eastern features include the macho, shiny dress of the self-confident singer, which emphasizes his hairy chest covered with gold necklaces; loud singing with ornaments typical of NCFM; and several sexual allusions. The video was shown on Croatian national television. What were the audience's reactions? According to Grubišić, some watchers congratulated the editors for finally allowing NCFM to appear on Croatian TV, while others expressed consternation that such "trashy music" was given a chance by the editors in charge. Overtly serious and sharply divided reactions that simply neglected the enormous potential of this music video for amusement became further emphasized during the war years.

According to Ljerka Vidić Rasmussen, "the popular, taste-culture stereotype of Croatians' affinity for pop music and Serbians' affinity for NCFM began to be invoked along with the political effect of cultural schism and overtones of a cultural versus barbarian culture core" during the 1990s (1996b:110). I recall how research-journalist Darko Hudelist shocked many Croatians with his detailed reports on live performances of this genre—repeatedly condemned in public as the very symbol of the Serbian enemy and unacceptable Balkan cultural traits—in several clubs and restaurants even in the capital area of Zagreb (Hudelist 1995).

This short overview has presented discourses, argumentations and musical reflections that address the issue of the Balkans' northwestern boundary. Croatia's location at the crossroads of Central European, Mediterranean, and Balkan spaces, its turbulent history at the meeting point of two powerful empires centuries in duration, the resulting cultural identities and, in particular, political developments over the course of the twentieth century affected musical domains in a variety of ways and granted to the issue of boundaries in general considerable weight. However, both the external and internal factors that contribute to balkanist discourse and its tensions can be addressed in a different way, as suggested by the next section of this essay.

Alaturka–Alafranga: A One Way Trip?

The concepts *alaturka* and *alafranga* are widely known in the Balkans (and also further to the east) and possess the capacity to help us comprehend sociocultural relations within the region in a balanced perspective.[20] Münir Nurettin Beken defines the two broadly as "Turkish and Western socio-cultural practices" (Beken 2003) and John Morgan O'Connell has demonstrated the use of the two by Turks to show cultural (between East and West), historical (between Ottoman and Republican), and gender (between male and female) distinctions (O'Connell 2005). During my fieldwork in Kosovo and elsewhere in the Balkans, I noticed that elderly people employed these concepts to differentiate between everything from food, drink, clothes, furniture, and toilet types to musical features and kinds of ensembles. The former implies connotations of either Turkish or culturally Eastern and old or old-styled, and the latter, culturally Western and new or modern. Did the two imply value judgements, resulting in some sort of hierarchy? Value judgements were often present, but either of the two, depending on the context, could be favored by the given user. The former sometimes invoked nostalgia and the latter anything from technological advantage to a fast lifestyle to bad taste. What was almost always embedded in the use of these concepts was the sense of a seemingly irreversible unidirectional move, regardless of one's wish, from *alaturka* to *alafranga*. The extreme temporal interpretation that "alaturka has ended" (Uğur, quoted in O'Connell 2005:179) may be valid for the center of the former Ottoman Empire, but so long as people in its peripheral parts see both advantages and disadvantages to either concept, they may continue to serve as a useful analytical tool.

The Slovenian ethnologist Božidar Jezernik pointed to characteristic situations in which Balkan countries, after liberation from Ottoman rule, took immediate actions "to wipe out any evidence of Turkish occupation" (1998:217). Belgrade, known for several centuries (until 1867) as Dar al-Djihad, featured one hundred mosques, ten hammams, many hans, two bezestans and a caravanserai in the 1600s (1998:221). Within a few years following the departure of the Turkish garrison, it was almost entirely rebuilt, "rapidly assuming 'a European character' and many of the picturesque Turkish or distinctly Serbian houses gave way to the style of Vienna or Pest" (1998:221). Within twenty years after Bulgaria was freed only one mosque remained in use in the capital (1998:217). In spite of these desperate attempts aimed at "Europeanization," people continued to appreciate customs from Ottoman times, to use Turkish language or at least Turkish expressions to mark their urban status and to differentiate themselves from their ethnic kinsmen from rural areas, and to share regionally based musical expressions.[21] Major political changes in the *alafranga* direction should not mislead us to overlook these cross-ethnically shared cultural features in the spirit of *alaturka*.

It is certainly true that the political discourses in Balkan countries, including those with predominantly Muslim populations, blame the Ottoman legacy for economic and cultural decline in comparison to Western Europe. It is known that Sultan Mahmut II in the first half of the nineteenth century, after abolishing the Janissaries and their indigenous *mehter* military music, brought in European musicians to teach Western military-band instruments in Turkish military schools (Signell 1988). It is also known that the founder of modern Turkey, Mustafa Kemal Atatürk, banned Ottoman classical music and encouraged Western-derived musical forms (Racy 1995; Signell 1988), and that in the late twentieth century the Turkish pop-folk genre *arabesk* was banned, while Western popular music was broadcasted with no restrictions (see Stokes 1992b). According to Immanuel Wallerstein (1990:45),

> The West had emerged into modernity; the others had not. Inevitably, therefore, if one wanted to be "modern" one had in some way to be "Western" culturally. If not Western religions, one had to adopt Western languages. And if not Western languages, one had at the very minimum to accept Western technology, which was said to be based on the universal principles of science.[22]

Negative political rhetoric related to the Ottoman legacy in the Balkans had various, well-documented, harmful consequences within the region. These range from government-supported attempts to re-create pre-Ottoman music at the expense of widely spread Ottoman-influenced local musics,[23] to the officially proclaimed (or at least politically motivated) avoidance of certain musical instruments,[24] to destroying Ottoman cultural monuments, identities, and even living people, namely modern Muslims, whom some politicians in the predominantly Orthodox Christian countries identified with the Ottoman conquerors.[25]

Alaturka as related to Balkan music brings to mind the notion of cross-ethnically shared aesthetic values—soundscapes marked by recognizable melodic molds, rhythmic patterns, use of specific tone colors, and manners of performance, among others. The case of a single tune, *Üsküdara gider iken,* which justifiably attracted the attention of Raina Katsarova, Adela Peeva, and in this volume Donna Buchanan, is one of many such cases. A kind of musical anthem of the Kosovo Romani community in which I worked the most, that of Terzi Mahala in the city of Prizren, was the song *Phuro Hamze.* The community considered it its own due to its Romani lyrics and memorialization of a community member, old Hamze. The close musical proximity of *Phuro Hamze* to the tunes *Telal viče* (Bosnia-Hercegovina), *Dei gidi, ludi-mladi godini* (Bulgaria), *Dimitroula* (Greece) or *Entarisi ala ben ziyor* (Turkey), of course, does not affect its "ownership" by the given community (see Buchanan 2006a; Pettan 2002). The case of another widely known song, that of *Zapevala sojka ptica* [The jay sings], reveals a religious differentiation in the changing of a single letter: Slavic Muslims refer in the lyrics to a female person whose name is Fata (from Fatima), and Slavic Christians to Kata (from Katarina, or Katherine).

Serbian urban songs from Kosovo are generally characterized by *alaturka* features. One of the best known, *Simbil cveće* [Hyacinths], characteristically rests on a melodic structure that employs the interval of an augmented second and a rhythmic structure that is asymmetrical (3–2–2), while its lyrics use the Turkish word *mavi* for blue rather than the Serbian *plavo.* In addition, an insufficiently known study by Ankica Petrović (1986) presents the convincing case from Bosnia-Hercegovina of a shared musical structure that is employed in a Sephardic Shabbat song that is sung in Ladino as well as Hebrew, in Muslim *ilahi* performed in Arabic, and in a secular Bosnian song performed in a language that used to be known as Serbo-Croatian.[26]

Recognized as superior specialists able to serve the needs of a variety of audiences throughout the Balkans, Romani musicians can, of course, be singled out as those who particularly contributed to the merging of "Slavic and Oriental cultures" (R. Petrović 1974b) and more generally in creating the Balkan "Musikbund."[27] Their contribution, which many scholars within nationally defined research traditions were critical of, is the subject of ongoing reinterpretation by several researchers from inside and outside the Balkans (e.g., Keil and Keil 2002; Peicheva and Dimov 2002; Seeman 2002; Silverman, this volume). Roma are carriers of some major soundscapes recognized as Balkan, particularly in regard to the northwestern boundaries of the region. These *alaturka* soundscapes include shawm and drum bands; female singers accompanying themselves on frame drums or by rolling around copper pans; urban ensembles of the *chalgiya* type; a variety of bands formed around violin, accordion, clarinet or saxophone icons or vocalists of either sex; brass bands; and modern, amplified ensembles. At first glance these ensembles symbolize the merging of *alaturka* and *alafranga* domains, but beneath the surface they display many peculiar adjustments and thus possibilities for different interpretations.[28] Such a rich variety of soundscapes reflects the tendency of Romani musicians to be ahead of their customers in terms of instrumentation. The same tendency can be observed in repertoire, which brings together tunes regardless of geographical, ethnic, religious, or other boundaries, and also in the manner of performance, which is expected to be in concordance with the specific occasion and place, virtuosic, and emotionally fulfilling. The combination of all these elements creates a kind of musical excitement encompassed by the term *alaturka* and known specifically as *kefı, kejf, ćef,* and other variants thereof throughout the Balkans.

The attitudes of Romani musicians may point regional scholarship in useful directions, particularly where transcending an interest in one's own or traditional music is concerned, for their musicmaking embraces the traditions of Others as well as that of contemporary and modern musics. Indeed, their musicianship reminds us, in several respects, of music's power, a capacity that should not be underestimated. One would certainly remember the scene from Adela Peeva's film in which Serbian listeners were presented by the filmmaker with the Bosniaks' "jihad" version of *Üsküdara.* Until that moment the film seemed predictable—the tune was recognized in every Balkan country Peeva visited and all performers thought of it as being their own. Suddenly, the Serbs understood the Bosniaks' version as a provocation. The resulting conflict between Peeva and her Serbian listeners gave the film a crucial boost, leading Peeva, via her subsequent experiences in Bulgaria, to conclude, "When I first started searching for the song I had the hope it would unite us. I [would] have never believed that the sparks of hatred [could] be lit so easily."

Peeva's filming trip across the Balkans was preceded by the succession of wars in the Yugsolav territories and it was these wars that set the stage for the conflict episode in her film. The wars also showed how "misuse" of tradition can lead to its "ethnicization" and consequently to its possible disappearance. For example, "In 1992, when Sarajevo was besieged and attacked with mortar shells by the Serbian aggressor, the citizens of some city districts were also assailed by the terrifying sounds of Serbian epic songs and *gusle* accompaniment heard from the loudspeakers and RTV (Radio-Television) programmes emitted from nearby Serbian occupied territory" (A. Petrović 1995:69). Consequently, none of the

Bosnian refugees (predominantly Bosniaks) with whom I worked in Norway in the mid 1990s thought of epic songs with *gusle* accompaniment as a cross-ethnically shared tradition. According to an analysis done by Serbian ethnologist Ivan Čolović for his forthcoming book, even Serbs and Montenegrins have recently expressed a tendency to disassociate themselves from this genre (see Lasić 2006:31). However, a rich body of literature, including Lord (1960), Murko (1951), and Žanić (1998), documents its multi-ethnic basis.

The notion of *alaturka* brings to mind one final, particularly important point—one related to Jeff Todd Titon's concept of "sustainable music."[29] Just as sustainable music is characterized by "a philosophy of balance, of dynamic equilibrium, of local, small-scale, face-to-face musical interactions," so too is *alaturka* compatible with the preservation and renewal of human musical resources. By contrast, both concepts stand counter to the "philosophy of progress, increasing productivity, and unlimited growth" that is embedded in the dominant modernization and westernization paradigms of *alafranga*. Thus *alaturka–alafranga*, as a metaphor of fundamental dilemmas that mark the lives of humankind in the early twenty-first century, reminds us that balanced knowledge and understanding of the past can and should strengthen our sense of responsibility in dealing with various co-existing options and assist us in making decisions about the future.

Selected Issues

The end of the Cold War has opened the Balkans to several challenges and to new opportunities for regional cooperation. The four major political situations—affiliation with the Warsaw alliance (Romania, Bulgaria), affiliation with NATO (Turkey, Greece), self-imposed isolation (Albania), and non-aligned orientation (Yugoslavia)—that for decades and to various extents hindered full-fledged communication have given way to increasing contacts. The tendency toward joining the European Union, which generally continues to function as a shared issue within the region, encourages projects that bring past legacies and current processes together in various creative ways. As examples, one can point to the CD series *Osmanli Mozaiği/Ottoman Mosaic* featuring the works of minority composers from the Ottoman Empire,[30] and the symposium "Urban Music in the Balkans: Drop-out Ethnic Identities or a Historical Case of Tolerance and Global Thinking," which took place in Tirana, Albania in 2006.

It is true that the popularity and influence of musicians crossed political borders even during the Cold War and the wars that marked the break up of Yugoslavia in the 1990s. A crucial factor was what Peter Manuel (1993) has called "cassette culture," with cassettes being smuggled across borders and offered for sale by street vendors on local market days. For example, in Kosovo during the 1970s, this is how some seminal Romani musicians, such as clarinet master Mustafa Kandıralı of Turkey and accordion hero Ibro Lolov of Bulgaria, became widely known.[31] The 1980s in Kosovo were marked by what can subsequently be named "video culture"—the showing of Turkish film videos featuring *arabesk* music and sometimes singers, in public spaces such as tearooms. This was followed by music-centered video spots and related "MTV aesthetics" that in a variety of ways continue to affect the visualization of domestic popular music throughout the Balkans. A comparative study of record industries, in addition to radio and television program policies, counts among the most important and still insufficiently researched realms with substantial potential to reveal transregional notions and mechanisms of music dissemination within recent decades. The recordings of minorities deserve particular attention in this context. A consideration of musics of a) national minorities within a given country, b) those countries in which these minorities comprise majority populations, and c) the same minorities abroad, would reveal variation in specific national minority policies. My own preliminary research indicates a rich minority discography within the former Yugoslavia.[32]

One would imagine that war, with its devastating effects and restrictive cultural policies aimed at forging national unity and entailing the removal of an enemy's music from media and record stores, would create efficient cultural boundaries. To the contrary, the war in the former Yugoslav territories revealed the market potential of musics from both sides of the front lines, which was realized and put to use by street vendors. The elites' promotion of features aimed at supporting the notion of idealized national purities was thus counterbalanced by a blurring of boundaries rooted in elementary market logic. In comparison to legal regulations of the 1980s, which forced street vendors to smuggle demanded items from abroad, the wars in the 1990s encouraged them to turn to piracy—the largely non-sanctioned illegal copying and selling of such sound vehicles. The case of Serbian pop-musician Đorđe Balašević, whose songs from the 1990s adopted a critical distance from the militant politics of Slobodan Milošević and whose popularity across old/new national lines was unquestionable, is self-explanatory. More multifaceted and intriguing perhaps is the case of Serbian NCFM. Croatian newspapers still report from time to time about conflicting situations among the Croats over the dilemma: is it primarily the music of the (former) enemy or music for which a Croat could have an aesthetic preference? While doing research among Bosnian refugees in Norway in the mid 1990s, who were mostly Bosniaks, I noticed that several among them had Serbian NCFM cassettes in their private collections. The fact that the husband of one of the top singers (Svetlana Ražnatović-Ceca) was the leader of the Serbian paramilitary forces and possibly directly responsible for the refugee status of these Bosnians did not prevent them from enjoying her songs.

The NCFM scene's increasing resemblance with that of Western mainstream popular music, as seen in musical style, vocal technique, instrumentation, performance sites, visual images, and media coverage, broadens its appeal among younger generations. A brief overview of a concert by Serbian NCFM star Ceca in Ljubljana, Slovenia, in 2005 may serve as a good example. The event was advertised and media-covered months in advance in the style of major Western pop concerts; it took place in the city's largest sports hall; and the instruments, amplification, stage lights, and audience behavior fully resembled that of major Western pop music productions. The concert started with a techno-like instrumental introduction and light effects reminiscent of a rave party, followed by the performance of an amplified band of classy musicians notably experienced in a variety of Western popular music genres (Plate 11.3).[33]

Throughout this volume, the authors use various general terms to describe related musical phenomena, since the meanings and emphases of constituent words vary across borders. In the former Yugoslav territories, for instance, the adjective *narodna* [folk], which once referred to rural traditional music, now often points to pop-folk or NCFM, while the prefix *etno-* [ethno-] refers to those approaches and projects that intellectual elites see as "more faithful to the roots" and aimed at "more demanding audiences" than is the case with NCFM. It is clear that NCFM and other comparable genres presented in this volume, such as Romanian *muzică orientală,* and Bulgarian *chalga,* exist primarily within their respective national boundaries, have a certain appeal and expanding ambitions within the Balkan realm, and reach other parts of the world exclusively thanks to diaspora communities. In this respect one can talk about a Balkan music circuit, which in turn can be contrasted to "ethno-" performers and their association with what might be called a "world music circuit." Musicians as diverse as Iorgos Mangas and Ross Daly of Greece, Ivo Papazov and Le mystère des voix bulgares of Bulgaria, Fanfare Ciocarlia and Taraf de Haidouks of Romania, Goran Bregović and Mostar Sevdah Reunion of Bosnia-Hercegovina, Esma Redžepova and DD Synthesis of Macedonia, Boban Marković and KAL from Serbia, and Famille Lela and Parashqevi

Simaku of Albania, as well as many others, are recognized as world music artists.

A specific term for a local genre, such as *turbo folk,* somewhat ironically described by its creator, Montenegrin-born pop musician Rambo Amadeus,[34] is not necessarily accepted by the creators, performers, and consumers of that genre.[35] My rather limited research in the city of Banja Luka, Bosnia-Hercegovina, in 2005, indicated a preference for the all-inclusive term *pop* due to what my consultants perceived as the lack of clear categorical boundaries between NCFM and Western pop music. Curiously, *turbo folk* became embraced as far away as Slovenia, where it refers to phenomena as different as Serbian and Bosnian NCFM, domestic *turbo* polka creations and,[36] as described by a colleague—lousy songs poorly performed by media-created "stars." An amusing showcase of playing with *turbo* imagery is the song *Hir aj kam, hir aj go* [Here I come, here I go] by the Slovenian musician Magnifico, which musically, textually, and visually blends Balkan stereotypes with trendy elements from various parts of the world.[37] The extent to which the presence of *turbo folk* is felt can best be illustrated by the fact that the Department of Cultural Studies in Ljubljana's Faculty of Social Sciences celebrated its tenth anniversary in 2005 with a symposium entitled "*Turbofolk* among the Slovenes."

Musical collaborations across political borders have become increasingly common in the past few years. One can legitimately interpret them as efficient marketing strategies, aimed at expanding the saleability of given musics and musicians over national borders and at bringing together differentiated audiences.[38] While these collaborations to some extent reflect fashionable practices within the realm of mediated Western popular music from abroad,[39] they are also—especially following the wars in the former Yugoslav territories in the 1990s—either an apolitical or politically correct statement in crossing boundaries on individual levels. Besides the collaborations already mentioned in this volume, such as between the Bosnian Goran Bregović and Turkish Sezen Aksu (see chapter nine) or Bosnian Dino Merlin and Croatian Ivana Banfić (see chapter two), there are those between the Turk Mustafa Sandal and Greek Natalia, the Croatian Tony Cetinski and Macedonian Toše Proeski, and the Bulgarian Ivana and Serbian Indira (Radić). In some cases the musicians involved represent different genres and their collaborations also imply the wiping out of stylistic boundaries. Ivana sings Bulgarian *chalga* and Indira, Serbian NCFM; Indira's collaboration with the Bosnian Alen Islamović, formerly vocalist for Yugoslavia's leading band Bijelo Dugme, brings together NCFM and rock audiences; while collaboration between the Serbian NCFM star Dragana Mirković and Bosnia's representative at the 2006 Eurosong contest in Athens, Hari Varešanović, speaks to the merger of NCFM and pop.

Conclusion: Is Balkan Beautiful?

In a clear reference to the American civil rights slogan "Black is Beautiful," Maple Razsa and Nicole Lindstrom (2004) entitled a recent article "Balkan is Beautiful." Could such a slogan encourage a rethinking of the Balkans and contribute to raising general awareness about the region as well as self-respect within the region? Or would it make more sense to simply replace "Balkan," heavily burdened by a variety of negative connotations and in many respects deprived of its original spatial and temporal meanings, by the rather neutral term "southeastern Europe"? For a comparable set of reasons, more politically correct names have been introduced for "Negroes" in the United States and "Gypsies" in Europe and elsewhere. Where music is concerned, all three cases are linked by a similar stereotype: musicians related to each are perceived with a high level of appreciation on the one hand but at least some sense of social and/or cultural distancing on the other. This situation should remind us that while terminological change alone can be useful to some extent in changing people's perceptions, dealing with the essence of the problem requires further action.

Committed involvement to the process of "debalkanizing" the Balkans, in other words, to the semantic and factual destigmatization of the region, may serve the purpose. According to the Albanian writer Ismail Kadare, "While naming the Balkans diabolical and underestimating it, Europeans are forgetting that the worst crimes in this [the twentieth] century were not committed in the Balkans but in Europe. They forgot that neither Nazism nor communism were born in the Balkans" (quoted in Brabec 1997:69). Edward Said's deconstruction of orientalism as the complete, Islamic Other (Said 1978) and Maria Todorova's determination of balkanism as the "incomplete Other" or rather, "incomplete Self, the dark side within" associated with Orthodox Christianity (Todorova 1996b:20) are encouraging works and suggest that more in this direction could be done through formal education, media, and other available channels. Milena Dragićević Šešić and Sanjin Dragojević find the notion of countries being "imprisoned by . . . Balkan identity" unusual since "all the countries of Southeastern Europe, apart from their Balkan identity, also have other regional identities" (2004:20). The Balkan peninsula, like the Iberian and the Appenine peninsulas, and like any of the world's other regions, has its own cultural specifics and musics appreciated by many people. Serious and responsible scholarship, as demonstrated by my colleagues in this volume, provides well documented and internalized arguments for rethinking the Balkans.

Desperate attempts at the "Europeanization of the Balkans," internalized in accordance with both imagined and actual advantages signified by the West, resulted in what Božidar Jezernik calls "a curious fact": "While the Balkans are taking great pains to resemble Europe, as it once was, Europe now defines itself on the basis of its difference in relation towards the East, the Balkans included, and claims to be what the Balkans used to be for almost five centuries" (1998:230). This claim of course does not idealize those circumstances that were subject to change over such a long temporal continuum, but while pointing to tolerance for diversity, argues against those "one-sided and biased conclusions" (Moačanin 1991:67) that continue to affect people's lives in the present world. It is my belief that ethnomusicology, aware of the fact that "myth and history intersect and interact . . . , perpetually being interwoven with music and music-making" (Bohlman 1997), is in a position "to make its proper contribution to discourse about culture, now understood less as sets of rules than as relationships" (Slobin 1993:5), and to help improve human relations. The essays in this volume, like the many collaborative projects and musical interrelationships that they analyze, represent, for the Balkans, an important contribution to this effort.

Notes

1. This text grew out of my role as discussant for the Society for Ethnomusicology session that gave rise to this volume. I wish to thank the panel organizer, Donna Buchanan, for her inspiration and meticulous editing. I am also grateful to Sandra Graham for many useful suggestions.

2. See *Večernji list* of 28 April 2006: <http://www.vecernji-list.hr/home/index.do>.

3. For instance, in the first quote given above, the author emphasizes the Cyrillic alphabet as a specifically Serbian feature, while the fact is that Montenegrins use it as well.

4. "Turkish songs" and "Turkish music" in the quotes obviously refer to the "oriental sound" associated with current pop-folk music from Serbia.

5. Kevin Dawe, Margaret Beissinger, and Martin Stokes refer to three other Balkan borderlands in this volume: Greece, Romania, and Turkey, respectively.

6. For instance, *The Garland Encyclopedia of World Music* considers Cyprus a Balkan country and Georgia—but not Armenia and Azerbaijan—as a European country. Various travel brochures sometimes add Morocco to Europe, while Israel

in many respects—judging from its participation in sports competitions and musical events such as the Eurosong contest—seems to have the status of a geographically dislocated European country.

7. This boundary projection reflects the opinion of many Croatian politicians, who preferred to see Bosnia-Hercegovina related to the western side of the river and the region, rather than to the "Serbian," eastern side. The fact that Croatia surrounds Bosnia-Hercegovina from two sides of its triangular shape certainly influenced this projection, considering that the Bosnian territory is essential for an efficient connection between Croatia's northern and southern regions.

8. This was implicitly suggested by anthropologist David A. Kideckel (1996:456).

9. For "a central figure in modern Croatian literature," Miroslav Krleža (1893–1981), there was no doubt about the Balkan boundary on this river (see Rihtman-Auguštin 1997:32).

10. This western Balkan boundary projection was argued by the Serbian anthropogeographer Jovan Cvijić (1865–1927), emphasizing Yugoslavia as a whole and also as part of the larger area populated by the Slavs (Cvijić 1987:17–18).

11. The other three are named the Alpine zone (most of Slovenia), Morava (after river Morava, comprising most of Serbia), and the Vardar zone (after the river Vardar, Macedonia). Depending on the source, the peripheral presence of the Alpine zone was recognized in the westernmost parts of Croatia.

12. Note that Romania is located north of the Danube, thus outside of the northern Balkan boundary suggested by geographers.

13. On musical life along the Military Frontier see Kos 1998.

14. As examples of material culture Lockwood points to food, diet, clothing, crafts, and architecture. However, she notes that "attitudes, values, customs and world view" are "more important" and "long reaching" (Lockwood 1983:10).

15. Cylindrical drums with two membranes are rarely used in Croatia and, if so, they are used in ensembles other than shawm and drum. Unlike in the regions to the east, they are held vertically, only one membrane is struck, and the beaters are of the same kind and size. In fact, along the Ottoman-Habsburg border both "the Eastern" and "the Western" positions and playing techniques were used (Kos 1998), as was still visible in Bosnia-Hercegovina in the late 1990s (ethnomusicologist Vinko Krajtmajer, p.c., Sarajevo, 1997).

16. Importantly, the popularity of shawm and drum ensembles stretches way beyond the historical Ottoman lands into Asia and Africa. Shawms used in the northern Adriatic part of Croatia are of a different kind and origin and are not accompanied by drums (cf. Širola 1932).

17. See Pettan 1996b; Seeman 2002.

18. "Why cannot the Balkan countries enter the circle of enlightened countries, even through their best and most talented representatives? . . . One of the reasons is their lack of appreciation for the full dignity and inner freedom of fellow human beings . . . . We carry this defect all over like a kind of original sin and a signet of an inferiority complex which cannot be concealed . . . . Sometimes it seems that the spirit of most of the Balkan peoples is poisoned forever, making

them capable only of suffering and committing violence" (Andrić, quoted in Đađić 1988:152–53).

19. In 2006, Croatia figures as the westernmost country within what is called, in political jargon, "the Western Balkans," and expects to join the European Union in an undefined future.

20. These two terms come from the Turkish language. *Alaturka* originates in the Italian *alla turca* (in Turkish style), while the closest equivalent to *alafranga* in Italian is *alla francése* (in French style).

21. See also Sugarman, this volume.

22. The irony of this running after the West lies in the fact that, "In the West, the superiority of our science and technology is no longer taken for granted. The majority have little awareness of the knowledges and skills accumulated and transmitted from generation to generation by other cultures. But they know that we are all threatened by nuclear extinction and by the steady destruction of the environment, and that these things have been part and parcel of the development of Western science and industry" (Worsley 1990:93).

23. For instance, Tullia Magrini (1997) shows how Greek folklorists tended to reestablish the "holy" musical practice suitable to the "mythic ancestor of all European culture" that became "polluted by the taint of Turkish culture" (quoted in Herzfeld 1987:7). On a more general level it is worth quoting Greek intellectual Maria Stratigaki:

> If there exists some threat to our identity, it comes from inside the country. It's imposed on you to call the coffee Greek and that you mustn't have anything to do with Turkey. And yet, when you go to Istanbul you think that you are in the capital of your country. Such a policy makes you throw out something which surely exists within your country's history. We are trying to reject these similarities through various modernizing ideas of the West, so that we can appear European. But Europe sees us more or less oriental. Third World, too. More than we think (quoted in Papagaroufali and Georges 1993:246).

24. Shawm and drum ensembles were considered "Turkish" in Bulgaria, whose government in the 1980s was persistent in refusing to recognize the existence of a Turkish minority on its territory (Silverman 1986). For more on their ban in the context of the so called "regeneration process" see Peicheva and Dimov 2002.

25. Vesa Kurkela's claim that negative attitudes towards the Ottoman past expressed by nationalist movements, states, and policies often led to political discrimination of Muslim minorities (Kurkela 1996; see also Peicheva and Dimov 2002:452) was tragically confirmed by all wars of the 1990s in the former Yugoslav territories.

26. The secular song *Kad ja pođoh na Benbašu* may be heard on *Bosnia: Echoes from an Endangered World: Music and Chant of the Bosnian Muslims.*

27. I am grateful to linguist Victor Friedman who in early 1990s called my attention to Kristian Sandfeld's work (1930), which I found applicable to musical processes being studied (Pettan 2002). Friedman himself currently employs the linguistic concept of codeswitching in relating linguistic and musical processes in the Balkans.

28. It was Roma who "updated" the accordion in Kosovo by introducing first its electronic variant and later various other electronic keyboards. A peculiar adjustment can be seen with the drum set, which from a distance fully resembles those used in jazz and rock, while a close look reveals the absence of high-hat and replacement of the snare drum by other drums more suitable to an *alaturka* sound.

29. Titon explored this concept in his address for the University of Illinois at Urbana-Champaign Bruno and Wanda Nettl Distinguished Lecture in Ethnomusicology, 6 March 2006.

30. This series features composers who were sultans, women, or of Armenian, Greek, or Jewish ethnicity and is produced by Sony Music/Columbia (2001).

31. After 1980, ethnomusicological "studies of individual musicians came to play a significant role" (Nettl 2005: 174) and seminal studies on musicians such as Umm Kulthūm (Danielson 1997) or Fela Kuti (Veal 2000) remind us how much in this direction still needs to be done in the Balkans.

32. I am particularly grateful to Victor Friedman and Mozes Heinschink for sharing their private record collections.

33. Online reactions to a series of articles about Ražnatović, published in the major Serbian newspaper *Večernje novosti* in the days prior to her open air concert in Belgrade in June 2006, attended by more than 100,000 people, speak to the fierce, ongoing debate surrounding pop-folk within Serbia itself.

34. "Technical inventions such as synthesizers and rhythm machines fully revolutionized *turbo* culture, in this case newly-composed music [NCFM]. Newly-composed culture sees the essence of civilization in technology, which is just its by-product," claims Rambo Amadeus (www.akordi.co.yu/arhiv/rambo/rambo2 .htm, accessed 4 June 2006).

35. "If somebody could explain to me what *turbo folk* is, then I would be able to say why I am its leading exponent [lit. *perjanica:* plume, tuft of feathers]. *Turbo folk* doesn't exist. Somebody invented this word and everybody accepted it. I sing modern folk, modernized folk music," says Svetlana Ražnatović (quoted in *Večernje novosti*, online issue, 13 June 2006).

36. Ensemble Atomik Harmonik, with its synthesized pan-Alpine polka repertoire, is a characteristic representative.

37. For instance, the synthesized sound of a Balkan brass band and a *taksim* improvisation on saxophone, American scratching and breakdance, Mexican sombrero, references to sex and crime, etc.

38. Financially powerful pop-folk music-based companies such as Bulgaria's Payner Records and Serbia's TV Pink are increasingly involved in processes aimed at enlarging the regional frames of their influences.

39. For instance, the Italian Eros Ramazzotti and American Tina Turner or Italian Andrea Bocelli and English Sarah Brightman performing together.

References

Abu-Lughod, Janet. 1997. "Going Beyond Global Babble." In *Culture, Globalization, and the World-System: Contemporary Conditions for the Representation of Identity,* ed. Anthony D. King, 131–37. Minneapolis: University of Minnesota Press.

Achim, Viorel. 1998. *Ţiganii în Istoria României.* Bucharest: Editura Enciclopedica.

Aksoy, Asu and Kevin Robins. 1995. "Istanbul Rising: Returning the Repressed to Urban Culture." *European Urban and Regional Studies* 2(3):223–35.

———. 1997. "Peripheral Vision: Cultural Industries and Cultural Identities in Turkey." *Environment and Planning A* 29:1937–52.

Aksu, Sezen. 1996. Interview with Sezen Aksu conducted by Martin Stokes and Anne Ellingsen, 12 July.

Alexandru, Tiberiu. 1956. *Instrumentele Muzicale ale Poporului Român.* Bucharest: Editura de Stat Pentru Literatura şi Artă.

———. 1978. *Folcloristică, Organologie, Muzicologie: Studii I.* Bucharest: Editura Muzicală.

———. 1980a. "Dimitrie Cantemir şi muzica orientală." In *Folcloristică, Organologie, Muzicologie: Studii* 2:233–51. Bucharest: Editura Muzicală.

———. 1980b. "Vechi relaţii muzicale între ţările româneşti şi Orientul Apropiat." In *Folcloristică, Organologie, Muzicologie: Studii* 2:252–75. Bucharest: Editura Muzicală.

Alp, Ali Rıza. 1951. "Kâtip Türküsü." *Türk Musikisi Dergisi* 4(39):17, 31.

Alperin, Mikhail. 1996. "From the Altai Mountains to the Balkans and to the Yennisey: Fly, Fly My Sadness." CD jacket notes accompanying *The Bulgarian Voices - Angelite & Huun-Huur-Tu: Fly, Fly My Sadness.* Shanachie 64071.

And, Metin. 1976. *A Pictorial History of Turkish Dancing.* Ankara: Dost Yayınları.

Anderson, Benedict. 1983. *Imagined Communities: Reflections on the Origin and Spread of Nationalism.* London: Verso.

Andreas, Peter. 2004. "Criminalized Legacies of War: The Clandestine Political Economy of the Western Balkans." *Problems of Post-Communism* 51(3):3–9.

Andreé-Zaimović, Vesna. 1998. "Muzički izrazi bosanskohercegovačke dijaspore u Sloveniji." In *Zbornik Radova: Međunarodni Simpozij* "Muzika u Društvu," 186–94. Sarajevo: [n.p.].

Andreis, Josip, et al. 1962. *Historijski Razvoj Muzičke Kulture u Jugoslaviji.* Zagreb: Školska Knjiga.

Anonymous 1990. "Looking East and West." *Billboard* 102(47)[24 November]:68–69.

——. 1997. "Law Enforces Corner Shady Businesses." *Bulgarian Telegraph Agency* (BTA) [3 November]:5. http://www. hri.org/news/balkans/bta/97-03-11.bta.html.

——. 1999. "Music Industry Acts on Ukraine, Europe's New Pirate Haven." http://www.ifpi.org/press/19990721.html.

——. 2002a. "Sezen Aksu pya v Istanbul armenski pesni." *Vakhan* (Plovdiv) [16 October 2002]:11.

——. 2002b. "Udhëtimi në qendër të 'Zyber world'-it." *Eurozëri* (Lucerne) 21–22 [1–14 July]:24.

Anoyanakis, Fivos. 1991. *Greek Popular Musical Instruments.* 2nd ed. Athens: Melissa Publishing House.

Antoni, Lorenc. 1956–77. *Folklori Muzikuer Shqiptar.* 7 volumes. Prishtina, Kosova: Milladin Popoviq; Rilindja.

Appadurai, Arjun. 1996. *Modernity at Large: Cultural Dimensions of Globalization.* Minneapolis: University of Minnesota Press.

Arbatsky, Yuri. 1953. *Beating the Tupan in the Central Balkans.* Chicago: Newberry Library.

Ashkari, Mohammed, Rudolf Brandl and Hans-Jörg Maucksch. 1985. "Das volkstümliche Klarinettenensemble zwischen Orient und Balkan." In *Studia Instrumentorum Musicae Popularis VIII,* ed. Erich Stockmann, 67–85. Stockholm: Musikmuseet.

Ashley, Stephen. 1994. "The Bulgarian Rock Scene Under Communism (1962–1990)." In *Rocking the State: Rock Music and Politics in Eastern Europe and Russia,* ed. Sabrina Petra Ramet, 141–63. Boulder, CO: Westview Press.

Atil, Esin. 1981. *Renaissance of Islam: Art of the Mamluks.* Washington, D.C.: Smithsonian Institution Press.

Bakić-Hayden, Milica. 1995. "Nesting Orientalisms: The Case of Former Yugoslavia." *Slavic Review* 54(4):917–31.

Bakić-Hayden, Milica and Robert Hayden. 1992. "Orientalist Variations on the Theme 'Balkans': Symbolic Geography in Recent Yugoslav Cultural Politics." *Slavic Review* 51(1):1–10.

Balibar, Étienne. 1991. "*Es Gibt Keinen Staat in Europa:* Racism and Politics in Europe Today." *New Left Review* 186:5–19.

Barany, Zoltan. 2002. *The East European Gypsies: Regime Change, Marginality, and Ethnopolitics.* London: Cambridge.

Barthes, Roland. 1985. *Mythologies.* Transl. A. Laves. Aylesbury, Bucks: Paladin.

Batali, Juliana Nina. 1985. "Aspetti dell' iconografia del giudizio finale nella pittura esterna moldava dell' epoca di Pietro Rares (1527–1546)." *Byzantion* 55:39–68.

Baud-Bovy, Samuel. 1935–38. *Tragoudia ton Dodekaneson.* (Ekdoseis Mousikou Laographikou Archeiou 1) Athens: Vivliopoleio I. N. Sidere.

Baumgartner, Pete. 1998a. "Greece, Bulgaria to Develop Infrastructure." *Radio Free Europe/Radio Liberty Newsline, Part II* 2(72)[15 April].

———. 1998b. "Greece Supports Basing Balkan Force in Bulgarian City." *RFE/RL Newsline, Part II* 2(72)[15 April].

———. 1998c. "Balkan Defense Ministers Agree to Form Joint Force." *RFE/RL Newsline, Part II* 2(18)[28 September].

Beissinger, Margaret H. 1991. *The Art of the Lăutar: The Epic Tradition of Romania.* New York: Garland Publishing.

———. 2001. "Occupation and Ethnicity: Constructing Identity among Professional Romani (Gypsy) Musicians in Romania." *Slavic Review* 60(1):24–49.

Beken, Münir Nurettin. 1996. Liner notes to *Masters of Turkish Music, Volume 2.* Produced by Dick Spottswood and Karl Signell. Rounder Records Rounder CD 1111.

———. 2003. "Aesthetics and Artistic Criticism at the Turkish Gazino." *Music & Anthropology* 8 (online journal).

Bilides, Sophia. 1991. Liner notes to *Greek Legacy.* E. Thomas ETD 101.

Bjelić, Dušan I. 2002. "Introduction: Blowing up the 'Bridge.'" In *Balkan as Metaphor: Between Globalization and Fragmentation*, eds. Dušan I. Bjelić and Obrad Savić, 1–22. Cambridge, MA: The MIT Press.

Bjelić, Dušan I. and Obrad Savić, eds. 2002. *Balkan as Metaphor: Between Globalization and Fragmentation.* Cambridge, MA: The MIT Press.

Bodrijar, Žan [Jean Baudrillard]. 1998. *Savršen Zločin* [Le Crime Parfait], transl. E. Ban. Belgrade: Belgrade Circle Journal/*Circulus*.

Bohlman, Philip. 1997. "Music, Myth, and History in the Mediterranean: Diaspora and the Return to Modernity." *Ethnomusicology On Line* 3.

Bošković, Aleksandar. 2005. "Distinguishing 'Self' and 'Other': Anthropology and National Identity in Former Yugoslavia." *Anthropology Today* 21(2):8–13.

Brabec, Mirjana. 1997. "Kadare." *Globus* 332:66–69.

Brandl, Rudolf M. 1996. "The 'Yiftoi' and the Music of Greece: Role and Function." *World of Music* 38(1):7–32.

Braun, Joachim. 1980. "Musical Instruments in Byzantine Illuminated Manuscripts." *Early Music* 8:312–27.

Breazul, George. 1939. "'Patrium carmen': date istorice și filologice." In *Muzica Româneasca de Azi,* ed. P. Nițulescu, 27–56. Bucharest: [n.p.].

Brody, Lauren. 1998. "An Abbreviated History." Liner notes to *Song of the Crooked Dance: Early Bulgarian Traditional Music, 1927–42,* produced by Lauren Brody. Yazoo 7016.

Broms, Henri. 1985 [1984]. *Alkukuvien Jäljillä. Kulttuurin Semiotiikkaa.* Porvoo-Helsinki-Juva: WSOY.

Buchanan, Donna A. 1985. "Musical Change and Ideological Revision: Creation and Concepts of Contemporary Soviet Popular Music." M.M. thesis, University of Texas at Austin.

——. 1995. "Metaphors of Power, Metaphors of Truth: The Politics of Music Professionalism in Bulgarian Folk Orchestras." *Ethnomusicology* 39(3):381–416.

——. 1996a. "Dispelling the Mystery: The Commodification of Women and Musical Tradition in *Le mystère des voix bulgares.*" *Balkanistica* (Special issue on Bulgaria: Bulgaria: Transitions and Turning Points: Papers from the Fifth Joint Meeting of Bulgarian and North American Scholars, edited by Donald L. Dyer) 9 [Summer]:193–210.

——. 1996b. "Wedding Musicians, Political Transition, and National Consciousness in Bulgaria." In *Retuning Culture: Musical Changes in Central and Eastern Europe,* ed. Mark Slobin, 200–30. Durham, NC: Duke University Press.

——. 1997. "Bulgaria's Magical *Mystère* Tour: Postmodernism, World Music Marketing, and Political Change in Eastern Europe. *Ethnomusicology* 41(1):131–58.

——. 2006a. *Performing Democracy: Bulgarian Music and Musicians in Transition.* Chicago: University of Chicago Press.

———. 2006b. "Sounding Postsocialism: Music, Memory, and Marketing in Post-1989 Bulgaria." Paper read at the conference "Post-communist Nostalgia," University of Illinois at Urbana-Champaign, 7–8 April 2006.

Buechsenschuetz, Ulrich. 2005. "End Note: Balkans Divided over Oil-Pipline Projects." *RFE/RL Newsline Part II* 9(38)[28 February].

Burgess, Adam. 1996. "National Minority Rights and the 'Civilizing' of Eastern Europe." *Contention* 5(2):17–36.

Canbazoglu, Cumhur. 1995. "Işık Ikitelli'den Yükseldi." *Cumhuriyet* [29 July]:14.

Cantemir, Dimitrie. 1734–35. *The History of the Growth and Decay of the Ottoman Empire*, transl. N. Tindal. London: J. J. and P. Knapton.

———. 1973. *Descriptio Antiqui et Hodierni Status Moldaviae*, ed. and transl. Gh. Guţu. Bucharest: Editura Academiei Republicii Socialiste România.

Casey, Edward L. 1996. "How to Get from Space to Place in a Fairly Short Stretch of Time: Phenomenological Prolegomena." In *Senses of Place,* eds. Steven Feld and Keith H. Basso, 13–52. Santa Fe, NM: School of American Research Press.

Ceribašić, N. 1995. "Gender Roles During the War: Representations in Croatian and Serbian Popular Music, 1991–1992." *Collegium Antropologicum* 19(1):91–101.

Cheah, Pheng. 1998. "Given Culture: Rethinking Cosmopolitical Freedom in Transnationalism." In *Cosmopolitics: Thinking and Feeling beyond the Nation,* eds. Pheng Cheah and Bruce Robbins, 290–328. Minneapolis: University of Minnesota Press.

Ciobanu, Gheorghe. 1955. *Anton Pann: Cîntece Lume.* Bucharest: Editura de Stat pentru Literatura si Arta.

———. 1974a [1959]. "Despre aşa-numita gamă ţigănească." In *Studii de Etnomuzicologie şi Bizantologie* 1:83–104. Bucharest: Editura Muzicală a Uniunii Compozitorilor.

———. 1974b [1967]. "Folclorul orăşenesc." In *Studii de Etnomuzicologie şi Bizantologie* 1:105–36. Bucharest: Editura Muzicală a Uniunii Compozitorilor.

———. 1974c [1970]. "Legaturi folclorice muzicale ale popoarelor sud-est europene." In *Studii de Etnomuzicologie şi Bizantologie* 1:56–58. Bucharest: Editura Muzicală a Uniunii Compozitorilor.

Clark, Colin, and Elaine Campbell. 2000. "'Gypsy Invasion': A Critical Analysis of Newspaper Reaction to Czech and Slovak Romani Asylum Seekers in Britain, 1997." *Romani Studies* 10(1):23–47.

Clifford, James. 1992. "Traveling Cultures." In *Cultural Studies*, ed. Lawrence Grossberg, 96–116. London: Routledge.

Clogg, Richard, ed. 2002. *Minorities in Greece: Aspects of a Plural Society*. London: Hurst and Company.

Comaroff, John and Jean. 1993. *Modernity and its Malcontents: Ritual and Power in Postcolonial Africa*. Chicago: University of Chicago Press.

Connor, Walker. 1994. *Ethnonationalism: The Quest for Understanding*. Princeton, NJ: Princeton University Press.

Cosma, Octavian Lazar. 1973– . *Hronicul Muzicii Românești*. Bucharest: Editura Muzicală.

Cosma, Viorel. 1996. *Lăutari de Ieri și de Azi*. 2nd ed. Bucharest: Editura du Style.

Cowan, Jane K. 1990. *Dance and the Body Politic in Northern Greece*. Princeton, NJ: Princeton University Press.

———. 2000. "Greece." In *The Garland Encyclopedia of World Music, Volume 8: Europe,* eds. Timothy Rice, James Porter, and Chris Goertzen, 1007–28. New York and London: Garland Publishing, Inc.

Cowan, Jane, Marie-Bénédicte Dembour and Richard A. Wilson, eds. 2001. *Culture and Rights: Anthropological Perspectives*. Cambridge: Cambridge University Press.

Crowe, David M. 1991. "The Gypsy Historical Experience in Romania." In *The Gypsies of Eastern Europe*, eds. David Crowe and John Kolsti, 61–79. Armonk, NY: M.E. Sharpe, Inc.

———. 1996. *A History of the Gypsies of Eastern Europe and Russia*. New York: St. Martin's Griffin.

Cvetko, Dragotin. 1981. *Južni Slovani v Zgodovini Evropske Glasbe*. Maribor: Založba Obzorja.

Cvijić, Jovan. 1987. *Balkansko Poluostrvo. Sabrana Dela, Knjiga 2*. Beograd: Srpska Akademija Nauka i Umetnosti, Književne Novine, Zavod Zaudžbenike i Nastavna Sredstva.

Đađić, Petar, ed. 1988. *Jovan Cvijić/Ivo Andrić: O Balkanskim Psihičkim Tipovima*. Beograd: Prosveta.

Danforth, Loring M. 1995. *The Macedonian Conflict: Ethnic Nationalism in a Transnational World*. Princeton, NJ: Princeton University Press.

Danielson, Virginia. 1997. *The Voice of Egypt: Umm Kulthūm, Arabic Song, and Egyptian Society in the Twentieth Century*. Chicago: University of Chicago Press.

Davis, Ruth. 2002. "Music of the Jews of Djerba, Tunisia." In *The Garland Encyclopedia of World Music, Volume 6: The Middle East,* eds. Virginia Danielson, Scott Marcus, and Dwight Reynolds, 523–31. New York and London: Routledge.

Dawe, Kevin. 1996. "The Engendered Lyra: Music, Poetry and Manhood in Crete." *British Journal of Ethnomusicology* 5:93–112.

———. 1998. "Bandleaders in Crete: Musicians and Entrepreneurs in a Greek Island Economy." *British Journal of Ethnomusicology* 7:23–44.

———. 1999. "Minotaurs or Musonauts? Cretan Music and World Music." *Popular Music* 18(2): 209–25.

———. 2001. "Roots Music in the Global Village: Cretan Ways of Dealing with the World at Large." *The World of Music* 3(2):47–66.

———. 2002. "Between East and West: Contemporary Grooves in Greek Popular Music (c.1990–2000)." In *Mediterranean Mosaic: Popular Music and Global Sounds in the Mediterranean Area*, ed. Goffredo Plastino, 221–40. New York: Routledge/Garland Publishing, Inc.

———. 2003. "Lyres and the Body Politic: Studying Musical Instruments in the Cretan Musical Landscape." *Popular Music and Society* 26(3): 263–83. Bowling Green State University Press.

———. 2004a. "Island Musicians: Making a Living from Music in Crete." In *Island Musics,* ed. Kevin Dawe, 65–75. New York and London: Berg Publishers.

———. 2004b. "'Power-geometry' in Motion: Space, Place, and Gender in the *Lyra* Music of Crete." In *Music, Space and Place: Popular Music and Cultural Identity*, eds. Andy Bennett, Sheila Whiteley and Stan Hawkins, 55–65. Aldershot, Hants, England: Ashgate.

Delaney, Carol. 1991. *The Seed and The Soil: Gender and Cosmology in Turkish Village Society.* Berkeley: University of California Press.

Delibeev, Petko. 1994. "Pesni, koito ni pravyat po-dobri." Interview with Sevdalina and Valentin Spasovi. *Folk Panair* 7–8:9–10.

Denny, Walter. 1985. "Music and Musicians in Islamic Art." *Asian Music* 17(1):37–68.

Der Nersessian, Sirarpie. 1970. *L'Illustration des Psautiers Grecs du Moyen Age II: Londres, Add. 19352.* Bibliothèque des Cahiers Archéologiques V. Paris: Éditions Klincksieck.

Dević, Dragoslav. 1968. "Nove 'narodne' pesme-kompozicije 'zlatne ploce.'" In *Rad 13. Kongresa Saveza Folklorista Jugoslavije u Dojranu 1966. Godine,* 191–214. Skopje.

Diehl, Keila. 2002. *Echoes from Dharamsala: Music in the Life of a Tibetan Refugee Community.* Berkeley and Los Angeles: University of California Press.

Diezi, Daniel and Shaun O'Shea. 2000–2005. "Boney M.: Bobby Farrell" (accessed 22 May 2006). <http://www.diezi.com/boneym/bobby/farrell.html>

Dimov, Ventsislav. 1994a. "Kogato pesnite syadat na masata." *Folk Panair* 2:31.

———. 1994b. "Trakiya Folk '94: Da ti se zavie svyat ot muzika." *Folk Panair* 7–8:4–6.

———. 1995. "Folkbumŭt i popkharakteristikite mu (Kŭm sotsiokulturniya portret na sŭvremennata etnopopmuzika v Bŭlgariya)." *Bŭlgarski Folklor* 21(6):4–19.

———. 1996a. "V presata na presata: Pogled kŭm 'folka' na masmediite i negovata auditoriya." *Bŭlgarski Folklor* 5–6:35–40.

———. 1996b. "Bulgarian muusi etnopop. Perinnebuumi, media ja kulttuuriteollisuus." *Musiikin Suunta* 2:26–35.

———. 2001. *Etnopopbumŭt*. Sofia: Bŭlgarsko Muzikoznanie Izsledvaniya.

Dionysopoulos, Nikos. 2002. "Commentary on the Songs: Musicians and Singers." In the liner notes to *Lesbos Aiolis: Songs and Dances of Lesbos,* 69–122. Supervised by Nikos Dionysopoulos. (Greek Traditional Music 5) Crete University Press C.U.P. 9 and 10.

Dirlik, Arif. 1997. *The Postcolonial Aura: Third World Criticism in the Age of Global Capital.* Boulder, CO: Westview Press.

Ditchev, Ivaylo. 2002. "The Eros of Identity." In *Balkan as Metaphor: Between Globalization and Fragmentation,* eds. Dusan I. Bjelić and Obrad Savić, 235–50. Cambridge, MA: MIT Press.

Djurić, Vojislav J. 1995. "Les étapes stylistiques de la peinture byzantine vers 1300: Constantinople, Thessalonique, Serbie." In *Vyzantine Makedonia, 324–1430 M.Ch: Thessalonike, 29–31 Oktovriou 1992: Diethnes Symposio,* 67–86. Thessaloniki: Hetairea Makedonikon Spoudon.

Djurić-Klajn, Stana. 1966. "Certain aspects de la musique profane serbe de l'époque feodale." In *Musica Antiqua Europeae Orientalis,* ed. Zofia Lissa, 117–39. Warsaw: Panstwowe Wydawnictwo Naukowe.

———. 2006. "Petar Konjović." *Grove Music Online,* ed. L. Macy (accessed 30 May 2006). <http://www.grovemusic.com.proxy2.library.uiuc.edu>

Documente Privind Istoria Românei. B. Ţara Românească, ed. Mihail Roller. Bucharest: Editura Academiei Republicii Populare Române, 1951– .

Dragoumis, Markos. 1991. *85 Demotikes Melodies apo ta Kataloipa tou Nikolaou Fardy.* Athens.

Droulia, Loukia and Lambros Liavis, eds. 1999. *Music of Thrace. An Interdisciplinary Approach: Evros*. Athens: The Friends of Music Society.

Dunin, Elsie. 1971. "Gypsy Wedding: Dance and Customs." *Makedonski Folklor* 4(7–8):317–26.

———. 1973. "Čoček as a Ritual Dance among Gypsy Women." *Makedonski Folklor* 6(12):193–97.

Dunin, Elsie, et al. 1998. "Yugoslavia—Traditional Dance." In *International Encyclopedia of Dance*, Volume 6, ed. Selma Jean Cohen, 426–31. New York: Oxford University Press.

Đurić-Klajn, see Djurić-Klajn.

Dyer, Donald L. 2000. "Romanian Language." In *Encyclopedia of Eastern Europe from the Congress of Vienna to the Fall of Communism*, ed. Richard Frucht, 696. New York: Garland Publishing, Inc.

———. 2002. "The Balkans and Moldova: One Sprachbund or Two?" In *Of All the Slavs My Favorites: In Honor of Howard I. Aronson on the Occasion of His 66th Birthday*, eds. Victor A. Friedman and Donald L. Dyer, 117–38. Bloomington: Slavica (*Indiana Slavic Studies* 12 [2001]).

Džimrevski, Borovoje. 1985. *Čalgiskata Tradicija vo Makedonija*. Skopje: Makedonska Kniga.

Ellingsen, Anne. 1997. "İbrahim Tatlıses and the Popular Music Genre *Arabesk* in Turkey." *Studia Musicologica Norvegica* 23:65–74.

Ellis, Burcu Akan. 2003. *Shadow Genealogies: Memory and Identity among Urban Muslims in Macedonia*. New York: Columbia University Press.

Encylopædia Brittanica Online. 2004. "Üsküdara." *Encyclopædia Brittanica* (accessed 29 October 2004). <http://search.eb.com/eb/article?tocld=9074521>

Erguner, Kudsi. 1991. Liner notes to *Sharki: Love Songs of Istanbul*, performed by Nesrin Sipahi and the Kudsi Erguner Ensemble, ed. by Mitchell Feldman. CMP CD 3009, 1992.

European Roma Rights Center. 1998. *A Pleasant Fiction: The Human Rights Situation of Roma in Macedonia*. Budapest.

Faubion, James. 1993. *Modern Greek Lessons: A Primer in Historical Constructivism*. Princeton, NJ: Princeton University Press.

Feld, Steven. 1996. "Waterfalls of Song: An Acoustemology of Place Resounding in Bosavi, Papua New Guinea." In *Senses of Place*, eds. Steven Feld and Keith H. Basso, 91–135. Santa Fe, NM: School of American Research Press.

——. 2000. "Sound Worlds." In *Sound*, eds. Patricia Kruth and Henry Stobart. Darwin College Lectures. Cambridge: Cambridge University Press.

Feld, Steven and Keith H. Basso, eds. 1996. *Senses of Place*. Santa Fe, NM: School of American Research Press.

Feldman, Walter. 1996. *Music of the Ottoman Court: Makam, Composition and the Early Ottoman Instrumental Repertoire*. Berlin: Verlag für Wissenschaft und Bildung.

——. 2000. "Music of the Dancing Boys." Liner notes to *Lalezar—Music of the Sultans, Sufis & Seraglio, Volume II: Music of the Dancing Boys*. Traditional Crossroads CD 4302.

——. 2001. "Lalezar: Minority Composers." Liner notes to *Lalezar—Music of the Sultans, Sufis & Seraglio, Volume III: Minority Composers*. Traditional Crossroads CD 4303.

——. 2002. "Ottoman Turkish Music: Genre and Form." In *The Garland Encyclopedia of World Music, Volume 6: The Middle East*, eds. Virginia Danielson, Scott Marcus, and Dwight Reynolds, 113–28. New York: Routledge.

Fenster, Mark. 1993. "Genre and Form: The Development of the Country Music Video." In *Sound and Vision: The Music Video Reader*, eds. Simon Frith, et al., 109–28. London and New York: Routledge.

Filja, Hysen. 1991. *Këngë Popullore të Shqipërisë së Mesme* [Folk songs of Central Albania]. Tirana: Instituti i Kulturës Popullore.

Fleming, K. E. 2000. "Review Essays: *Orientalism*, the Balkans, and Balkan Historiography." *American Historical Review* 105(4):1218–33.

Florea, Anca. 1994. "String Instruments in Romanian Mural Paintings between the 14th and 19th Century." *RIdIM/RCMI Newsletter* 19 (Fall):54–65.

——. 1997. "Wind and Percussion Instruments in Romanian Mural Painting." *RIdIM/RCMI Newsletter* 22 (Spring):23–30.

Folk Panair. 1994a. "'Avtorskata folklorna pesen e neizcherpaema.'" *Folk Panair* 5–6:6.

——. 1994b. "Tazi pesen e obshtobŭlgarska." *Folk Panair* 5–6:16–17.

Foster, Robert. 1991. "Making National Cultures in the Global Ecumene." *Annual Review of Anthropology* 20:235–60.

Fraser, Angus. 1992. *The Gypsies*. Oxford: Blackwell.

Frith, Simon. 1988. *Music for Pleasure: Essays in the Sociology of Pop*. Cambridge: Polity Press.

Fuller, Liz. 1998a. "Albania, Turkey Sign Cooperation Agreements." *Radio Free Europe/Radio Liberty Newsline, Part II* 2(30)[13 February].

——. 1998b. "Black Sea States to Discuss Confidence-Building Measures." *RFE/RL Newsline, Part II* 2(40)[27 February].

Garfias, Robert. 1981. "Survivals of Turkish Characteristics in Romanian Musica Lăutărească." *Yearbook for Traditional Music* 13:97–107.

——. 1984. "Dance among the Urban Gypsies of Romania." *Yearbook for Traditional Music* 16:84–96.

Gavazzi, Milovan. 1942. "Etnografijski sustav." In *Zemljopis Hrvatske II*, ed. Zvonimir Dugački, 639–73. Zagreb: Izdanje Matica Hrvatske.

Ghenea, Cristian C. 1965. *Din Trecutul Culturii Muzicale Românești*. Bucharest: Editura Muzicală.

Ghodsee, Kristen. 2000. "Women and Economic Transition: Mobsters and Mail-Order Brides in Bulgaria." *Center for Slavic and East European Studies Newsletter* 17(3):5–13. University of California, Berkeley (see also: <http://socrates.berkeley.edu/~iseees/>).

Gilroy, Paul. 1993. *The Black Atlantic: Modernity and Double Consciousness*. Cambridge, MA: Harvard University Press.

Giurchescu, Anca. 2000. "Gypsy Dance Style as Marker of Ethnic Identity." In *Music, Language and Literature of the Roma and Sinti*, ed. Max Peter Baumann, 321–29. Berlin: Verlag für Wissenschaft und Bildung.

Gocic, Goran. 2000. "Gypsies Sing the Blues." *Institute for War and Peace Reporting: Balkan Crisis Report No. 141.* <http://www.iwpr.net>

Gordy, Eric D. 1999. *The Culture of Power in Serbia: Nationalism and the Destruction of Alternatives*. University Park, PA: The Pennsylvania State University Press.

Grabar, André. 1928. *La Peinture Religieuse en Bulgarie.* (Orient et Byzance, Vol. 1.) Paris: Paul Geuthner.

——. 1980. La représentation des 'peuples' dans les images du Jugement dernier en Europe orientale. *Byzantion* 50:186–97.

Hancock, Ian. 1987. *The Pariah Syndrome*. Ann Arbor, MI: Karoma.

——. 1997. "The Struggle for the Control of Identity." *Transitions* 4(4):36–44.

——. 1998. "Introduction." In *Roads of the Roma*, eds. Ian Hancock, Siobhan Down, and Rajko Djuric, 9–21. University of Hertfordshire Press.

Hannerz, Ulf. 1989a. "Culture between Center and Periphery: Toward a Macroanthropology." *Ethnos* 54(3–4):200–16.

———. 1898b. "Notes on the Global Ecumene." *Public Culture* 1(2):66–75.

Hatzipantazis, Theodoros. 1986. *Tis Asiatithos Mousis Eraste . . . I Akmi tou Athinaikou Kafe Aman Hronia tis Vasilias tou Georgiou tou A.* Athens: Stigmi Editions.

Henze, Paul B. 1993. "Turkey: Toward the Twenty-First Century." In *Turkey's New Geopolitics: From the Balkans to Western China,* by Graham E. Fuller and Ian O. Lesser, et al., 1–35. Boulder, CO: Westview Press.

Herzfeld, Michael. 1982. *Ours Once More: Folklore, Ideology, and the Making of Modern Greece.* Austin: University of Texas Press.

———. 1987. *Anthropology through the Looking-Glass: Critical Ethnography on the Margins of Europe.* Cambridge: Cambridge University Press.

———. 1997. *Cultural Intimacy: Social Poetics in the Nation-State.* New York: Routledge.

Hoerburger, Felix. 1954. *Der Tanz mit der Trommel.* (Quellen und Forschungen zur Musikalische Folklore 2.) Regensburg.

Holban, M., M. Alexandrescu-Dersca Bulgaru, and P. Cernovodeanu, eds. 1970–83. *Călători Străini despre Țările Române, 1970–83.* Bucharest: Editura Științifică.

Holland, Bill. 1995. "RIAA Names 3 Piracy-Infringing Nations." *Billboard* 107(8)[25 February 1995]:10.

Hozić, Aida A. 2004. "Between the Cracks: Balkan Cigarette Smuggling." *Problems of Post-Communism* 51(3):35–44.

Hudelist, Darko. 1995. "Hrvatska estrada 1991–95. U podzemlju hrvatske zabavne glazbe." *Globus* 262 (supplement).

Hunter, Mary. 1998. "The *Alla Turca* Style in the Late Eighteenth Century: Race and Gender in the Symphony and the Seraglio." In *The Exotic in Western Music,* ed. Jonathan Bellman, 43–73. Boston: Northeastern University Press.

Huntington, Samuel. 1996. *The Clash of Civilizations and the Remaking of World Order.* New York: Simon & Schuster.

Huotari, Markku. 1999. "Flamencomusiikin taustaa." In *Flamenco,* ed. Katja Lindroos, 98–129. Jyväskylä: Like Kustannus.

IFPI. 1996. *IFPI Pirate Sales 95.* May.

———. 2000. *IFPI Music Piracy Report 2000.* <http://www.ifpi.org>

Iorga, Nicolae. 1925. *Istoria Literaturii Românești, Vol. 1.* 2nd ed. Bucharest: Pavel Suru.

Ivančan, Ivan. 1964. "Geografska podjela narodnih plesova u Jugoslaviji." *Narodna Umjetnost* 3:165–70.

Ivy, Marilyn. 1995. *Discourses of the Vanishing: Modernity, Phantasm, Japan.* Chicago: University of Chicago Press.

Janjatović, Petar. 1998. *Ilustrovana Yu Rock Enciklopedija, 1960–1997.* Beograd: Geopoetika.

Jezernik, Božidar. 1998. "Western Perceptions of Turkish Towns in the Balkans." *Urban History* 25(2):211–30.

Katsarova, Raina. 1973. "Balkanski varianti na dve turski pesni." *Izvestiya na Instituta za Muzikoznanie* 16:116–33.

Keil, Charles and Angeliki Vellou Keil. 2002. *Bright Balkan Morning: Romani Lives and the Power of Music in Greek Macedonia.* Middletown, CT: Wesleyan University Press.

Kelsky, Karen. 2001. *Women on the Verge: Japanese Women, Western Dreams.* Durham, NC: Duke University Press.

Kessi, Alain. 2001. "Global Mobilizations: What are the Protests in Prague All About? Liquidation of the Economy and New Dependencies: The Example of Bulgaria." *Farce Academy for Applied Applications: Studium Generale* 4. <http://www.copyriot.com/unefarce/no4/prag-en.html>

Kideckel, David. 1996. "Europe, Eastern." In *Encyclopedia of Cultural Anthropology*, eds. David Levinson and Melvin Ember, 456–61. New York: Henry Holt and Co.

Kiel, Machiel. 1985. *Art and Society of Bulgaria in the Turkish Period: A Sketch of the Economic, Juridical and Artistic Preconditions of Bulgarian Post-Byzantine Art and its Place in the Development of the Art of the Christian Balkans, 1360/70–1700: A New Interpretation.* Assen and Maastricht, The Netherlands: Van Gorcum.

Kiossev, Alexander. 2002. "The Dark Intimacy: Maps, Identities, Acts of Identification." In *Balkan as Metaphor: Between Globalization and Fragmentation*, eds. Dusan I. Bjelić and Obrad Savić, 165–90. Cambridge, MA: MIT Press.

Kirshenblatt-Gimblett, Barbara. 1998. *Destination Culture: Tourism, Museums, and Heritage.* Berkeley: University of California Press.

Klaić, Bratoljub. 1972. *Veliki Rječnik Stranih Riječi.* Zagreb: Zora.

Koçu, Reşat Ekrem. 1997. "Reşat Ekrem Koçu ile İstanbul Folkloru Üzerine Sohbet." In *Türk İstanbul,* coll. by Sadi Yaver Ataman, ed. Süleyman Şenel, 445–46. Istanbul: İstanbul Büyükşehir Belediyesi Kültür İşleri Daire Başkanlığı Yayınları No. 39.

Kopytoff, Igor. 1987. "The Internal African Frontier: The Making of African Political Culture." In *The African Frontier: The Reproduction of Traditional African Societies,* ed. Igor Koyptoff. Bloomington: Indiana University Press.

Kos, Koraljka. 1972. "New Dimensions in Folk Music: A Contribution to the Study of Musical Tastes in Contemporary Yugoslav Society." *International Review of the Aesthetics and Sociology of Music* 3(1):61–73.

——. 1998. "East and West in Military Music on the Ottoman-Habsburg Border." In *Music, Politics, and War: Views from Croatia,* ed. Svanibor Pettan, 29–54. Zagreb: Institute of Ethnology and Folklore Research.

Kovačec, August, ed. 1996. *Hrvatski Opći Leksikon.* Zagreb: Leksikografski Zavod Miroslav Krleža.

Kozanoğlu, Can. 1995. *Pop Çağı Ateşi.* Istanbul: Iletişim.

Kronja, Ivana. 2004. "Turbo Folk and Dance Music in 1990s Serbia: Media, Ideology and the Production of Spectacle." *The Anthropology of East Europe Review* 22(1):103–14.

Kurin, Richard. 1997. *Reflections of a Culture Broker: A View from the Smithsonian.* Washington D.C.: Smithsonian Press.

Kurkela, Vesa. 1993. "Deregulation of Popular Music in the European Post-Communist Countries: Business, Identity, and Cultural Collage." *The World of Music* 35(3):80–106.

——. 1995. "Local Music-Making in Post-communist Europe: Mediatization and Deregulation." *East European Meetings in Ethnomusicology* 2:105–15.

——. 1996. "Piraatit, Orientalismi ja Poliittinen Epäkorrektisuus: Näkymiä Itä-Balkanin Musiikkikulttuuriin." *Musiikin Suunta* (Napatanssi ja Turbofolk: Kadonneen Itä-Euroopan Musiikkia) 2:36–51.

——. 1997. "Music Media in the Eastern Balkans: Privatised, Deregulated, and Neo-Traditional." *Cultural Policy* 3(2):177–205.

Lange, Barbara Rose. 1996. "*Lakodalmas* Rock and the Rejection of Popular Culture in Post-Socialist Hungary." In *Retuning Culture: Musical Changes in Central and Eastern Europe,* ed. Mark Slobin, 76–91. Durham, NC: Duke University Press.

Lasić, Igor. 2006. "Gusle su symbol neželjenog bratstva." *Feral Tribune* [April 14]:30–31.

Laušević, Mirjana. 1996. "The *Ilahiya* as a Symbol of Bosnian Muslim National Identity." In *Retuning Culture: Musical Changes in Central and Eastern Europe*, ed. Mark Slobin, 117–35. Durham, NC: Duke University Press.

———. 2000. "Some Aspects of Music and Politics in Bosnia." In *Neighbors at War: Anthropological Perspectives on Yugoslav Ethnicity, Culture, and History*, eds. Joel M. Halpern and David A. Kideckel, 289–301. University Park, PA: The Pennsylvania State University Press.

Lee, Tong Soon. 1999. "Technology and the Production of Islamic Space: The Call to Prayer in Singapore." *Ethnomusicology* 43(1):86–100.

Lemon, Alaina. 2000. *Between Two Fires: Gypsy Performance and Romani Memory from Pushkin to Postsocialism*. Durham, NC: Duke University Press.

Levinson, David and Melvin Ember, eds. 1996. *Encyclopedia of Cultural Anthropology*. New York: Henry Holt and Company.

Levy, Claire. 2005. *Dialogichnata Muzika: Blusŭt, Populyarnata Kultura, Mitovete na Modernostta*. Sofia: Institut za Izkustvoznanie – BAN.

Lloyd, A. L. 1963. "The Music of Rumanian Gypsies." *Proceedings of the Royal Musical Society*, 90th session, 15–26.

Lockwood, Yvonne. 1983. *Text and Context: Folksong in a Bosnian Muslim Village*. Columbus, Ohio: Slavica Publishers.

Longinović, Tomislav. 2000. "Music Wars: Blood and Song at the End of Yugoslavia." In *Music and the Racial Imagination*, eds. Ronald Radano and Philip V. Bohlman, 622–43. Chicago: The University of Chicago Press.

Lord, Albert Bates. 1960. *The Singer of Tales*. Cambridge, MA: Harvard University Press.

Loutzaki, Irene. 1999. "The Association as Milieu for Dance Activity." In *Music of Thrace: An Interdisciplinary Approach: Evros*, eds. Droulia, Loukia, and Lambros Liavis, 193–247. Athens: The Friends of Music Society.

Luković, Petar. 1989. *Bolja Prošlost: Prizori iz Muzičkog Života Jugoslavije 1940–1989*. Beograd: Mladost.

Lupaşcu, Marin. 1994. "Gipsy/Non-Gipsy. A Controversed Music (record chronicle)." *East European Meetings in Ethnomusicology* 1:100–104.

Lyceum Club of Greek Women. 1994. Liner notes to *Songs and Dances of Smyrna and Erythraea, Asia Minor*. LCGW 113.

Maček, Ivana. 1997. "Negotiating Normality in Sarajevo during the 1992–95 War." *Narodna Umjetnost* 34:125–58.

MacKenzie, John M. 1995. *Orientalism: History, Theory and the Arts*. Manchester and New York: Manchester University Press.

Magrini, Tullia. 1997. "Repertoires and Identities of a Musician from Crete." *Ethnomusicology On Line* 3.

Malcolm, Noel. 1998. *Kosovo: A Short History.* New York: New York University Press.

Manuel, Peter. 1993. *Cassette Culture: Popular Music and Technology in North India.* Chicago: The University of Chicago Press.

Marian-Bălaşa, Marin. 2003. "Romani Music and Gypsy Criminality." Unpub. ms.

Markoff, Irene. 2002. "Aspects of Turkish Folk Music Theory." In *The Garland Encylopedia of World Music, Volume 6: The Middle East,* eds. Virginia Danielson, Scott Marcus, and Dwight Reynolds, 77–88. New York: Routledge.

Marković, Mira. 1998. *Izmedu Iztoka i Juga (Dnevnik: Septembar 1994–Oktobar 1994).* Beograd: BMG, Prosveta, VERZAL Press.

Massey, Doreen B. 1993. "Power-geometry and a Progressive Sense of Place." In *Mapping the Futures: Local Cultures, Global Change,* eds. Jon Bird, et al., 59–69. (Futures, New Perspectives for Cultural Analysis) London and New York: Routledge.

———. 1994 [2001]. *Space, Place and Gender.* 3rd edition. Minneapolis: University of Minnesota Press.

Massie, Robert K. 1967. *Nicholas and Alexandra.* Atheneum Publishers.

Massie, Robert K. and Suzanne. 1975. *Journey.* New York: Knopf.

Maxim, Mihai. 1998. "The Romanian Principalities and the Ottoman Empire, 1400–1878." In *Romania: A Historic Perspctive,* eds. G. Dinu and S. Fischer-Galati, 105–32. New York: Columbia University Press.

Michelson, Paul E. 2000. "Romania (History)." In *Encyclopedia of Eastern Europe from the Congress of Vienna to the Fall of Communism,* ed. Richard Frucht, 667–91. New York: Garland Publishing, Inc.

Miller, Daniel. 1994. *Modernity: An Ethnographic Approach: Dualism and Mass Consumption in Trinidad.* Provincetown, RI: Oxford University Press.

Millet, Gabriel. 1916. *Recherches sur l'Iconographie de l'Évangile aux XIVe, XVe et XVIe Siècles.* Paris.

Mirga, Andrzej and Nicolae Gheorghe. 1997. *The Roma in the Twenty-first Century: A Policy Paper.* Princeton, NJ: Project on Ethnic Relations.

Mitrinović, Biljana. 1999. "Ja nisam odavle." *Reporter* [1 September].

Moačanin, Nenad. 1991. "Slavonija pod turskom vlašću." In *Peti Znanstveni Sabor Slavonije i Baranje*, eds. D. Čalić and D. Berber, 67–76. Vinkovci.

Mokranjac, Stevan S. 1957. *Rukoveti: Partiture*, eds. Milenko Živković and Milan Bajšanski. Belgrade: Prosveta.

Morris, Roderick Conway. 1981. "Greek Cafe Music." *Recorded Sound* 80:79–117.

Munishi, Rexhep. 1997. *Probleme Ethnomuzikologjike*. Prishtina: Instituti Albanologjik.

———. 2001. *Identiteti Muzikor*. Prishtina: By the Author.

Murko, Matija. 1951. *Tragom Srpsko-Hrvatske Narodne Epike: Putovanja u Godinama 1930–1932*. Zagreb: JAZU.

Muršič, Rajko. 2000. "The Yugoslav Dark Side of Humanity: A View from a Slovene Blind Spot." In *Neighbors at War: Anthropological Perspectives on Yugoslav Ethnicity, Culture, and History*, eds. Joel M. Halpern and David A. Kideckel, 56–77. University Park, PA: The Pennsylvania State University Press.

Muzykal'no-Etnograficheskaya Komissiya. 1913. *Opyty Khudozhestvennoi Obrabotki Narodnykh Piesen, Tom 1*. (Trudy Etnograficheskogo Otdela, Tom 18; Trudy Muzykal'no-Etnograficheskoi Komissii, Tom 4.) Moskva: Muzykal'no-Etnograficheskaya Komissiya.

Nettl, Bruno. 2005. *The Study of Ethnomusicology: Thirty-One Issues and Concepts*. Urbana and Chicago: University of Illinois Press.

Niculescu-Varone, G. T. and Elena Costache Găinaru-Varone. 1979. *Dicţionarul Jocurilor Populare Româneşti*. Bucharest: Editura Muzicală.

Nikolov, Jovo. 1997. "Crime and Corruption after Communism: Organized Crime in Bulgaria. *East European Constitutional Review* 6(4). <http://www.law.nyu.edu/eecr/vol6num4/feature/organizedcrime.html>

Nonini, Donald, and Aihwa Ong. 1997. "Chinese Modernities: Narratives of Nation and of Capitalism." In *Ungrounded Empires: The Cultural Politics of Modern Chinese Transnationalism*, eds. Aihwa Ong and Donald Nonini, 171–202. London: Routledge.

North, Suzie. 1998. Interview conducted by Donna Buchanan, 27 September.

O'Connell, John Morgan. 2002. "From Empire to Republic: Vocal Style in Twentieth Century Turkey." In *The Garland Encylopedia of World Music, Volume 6: The Middle East*, eds. Virginia Danielson, Scott Marcus, and Dwight Reynolds, 781–88. New York: Routledge.

————. 2005. "In the time of Alaturka: Identifying Difference in Musical Discourse." *Ethnomusicology* 49(2):177–205.

O'Loughlin, Niall. 2006. "Mokranjac, Stevan (Stojanović)." *Grove Music Online*, ed. L. Macy (accessed 25 May 2006). <http://www.grovemusic.com.proxy2.library.uiuc.edu>

Ong, Aihwa. 1996. "Anthropology, China, Modernities: The Geopolitics of Cultural Knowledge." In *The Future of Anthropological Knowledge*, ed. Henrietta Moore, 60–92. London: Routledge.

————. 1997. "Chinese Modernities: Narratives of Nation and of Capitalism." In *Ungrounded Empires: The Cultural Politics of Modern Chinese Transnationalism*, eds. Aihwa Ong and Donald Nonini, 171–202. London: Routledge.

————. 1999. *Flexible Citizenship: The Cultural Logics of Transnationalism*. Durham, NC: Duke University Press.

Ong, Aihwa and Donald Nonini. 1997. "Towards a Cultural Politics of Diaspora and Transnationalism." In *Ungrounded Empires: The Cultural Politics of Modern Chinese Transnationalism*, eds. Aihwa Ong and Donald Nonini, 323–32. London: Routledge.

Otašević, Ana. 2001. "Proslo je njihovo." *NIN* [12 July].

Özer, Yetkin. 2003. "Crossing the Boundaries: The Akdeniz Scene and Mediterraneanness." In *Mediterranean Mosaic: Popular Music and Global Sounds,* ed. Goffredo Plastino, 199–220. New York: Routledge.

Öztürkmen, Arzu. 2002. "Dance and Identity in Turkey." In *The Garland Encyclopedia of World Music, Volume 6: The Middle East,* eds. Virginia Danielson, Scott Marcus, and Dwight Reynolds, 811–18. New York: Routledge.

Papagaroufali, Eleni and Eugenia Georges. 1993. "Greek Women in Europe of 1992: Brokers of European Cargoes and the Logic of the West." In *Perilous States: Conversations on Culture, Politics, and Nation*, ed. George Marcus, 235–54. Chicago: University of Chicago Press.

Pečanin, Senad. 1998. "Polozili u Beogradu, pali u Sarajevu." *BH Dani* [11 May].

Peicheva, Lozanka. 1999. *Dushata Plache, Pesen Izliza*. Sofia: Terart.

Peicheva, Lozanka and Ventsislav Dimov. 2002. *Zurnadzhiiskata Traditsiya v Yugozapadna Bŭlgariya/The Zurna Tradition in Southwest Bulgaria.* Sofia: Bŭlgarsko Muzikoznanie—Izsledvaniya.

Pejović, Roksanda. 1984. *Predstave Muzickih Instrumenata u Srednjovekovnoj Srbiji*. Belgrade: Srpska Akademija Nauka i Umetnosti.

——. 1985. "Folk Musical Instruments in Mediaeval and Renaissance Art of South Slav Peoples." *Studia Instrumentorum Musicae Popularis* 8:126–43. In *Bericht über die 8. Internationale Arbeitstagung der Study Group on Folk Musical Instruments des International Folk Music Council in Piran, Jugoslavien 1983*, ed. Erich Stockmann. (Musikhistoriska Museets Skrifter) Stockholm: Musikhistoriska Museet.

——. 2006. "Petar Krstić." *Grove Music Online*, ed. L. Macy (accessed 30 May 2006). <http://www.grovemusic.com.proxy2.library.uiuc. edu>

Pennanen, Risto Pekka. 1995. "Folk Music Research and the National in the Balkans." *East European Meetings in Ethnomusicology* 2:94–104.

——. 2001. "Folk Music Research and Nationalism in the People's Republic of Bulgaria: A Preliminary Analysis." *Zbornik Radova II. Medunarodni Simpozij "Musika u Drustvu,"* ed. Ivan Cavlovic, 173–83. Sarajevo: Musikolosko Drustvo FbiH.

Peters, Karen A. 2000. "Representations of Macedonia in Contemporary Ethnopop Songs from Southwest Bulgaria. *Balkanistica* 13:131–63.

——. 2002. "Macedonian Folk Song in a Bulgarian Urban Context: Songs and Singing in Blagoevgrad, Southwest Bulgaria." Ph.D. dissertation, University of Wisconsin, Madison.

——. 2003. "Meter as a Marker of Ethnonational Identity? Metric Controversy, Folk Song Variants, and the Representation of Balkan Cultural Identities." *Bŭlgarsko Muzikoznanie* 27(4):56–73.

Petkov, Petko. 1994. "Obrechena sŭm na pesenta." *Folk Panair* 5–6:21.

Petković, Sreten. 1976. "Poreklo ilustratsija u štampanin knjigama Božidar Vukovića." *Zbornik za Likovne Umetnosti* 12:121–35.

Petrović, Ankica. 1986. "Tradition and Compromises in the Musical Expressions of Sephardic Jews in Bosnia." In *Glazbeno Stvaralaštvo Narodnosti (Narodnih Manjina) i Etničkih Grupa/Traditional Music of Ethnic Groups–Minorities*, ed. Jerko Bezić, 213–22. Zagreb: Zavod za Istraživanje Folklora Instituta za Filologiju i Folkloristiku.

——. 1988. "Paradoxes of Muslim Music in Boznia and Herzegovina." *Asian Music* 20(1):128–47.

——. 1993. "Notes on the Music." *Bosnia: Echoes from an Endangered World: Music and Chant of the Bosnian Muslims.* Recorded, compiled, and annotated by Ted Levin and Ankica Petrović. Smithsonian/Folkways SF 40407.

———. 1994. "The Eastern Roots of Ancient Yugoslav Music." In *Music Cultures in Contact: Convergences and Collisions*, eds. Margaret J. Kartomi and Stephen Blum, 13–20. Basel: Gordon and Breach Publishers.

———. 1995. "Perceptions of *Ganga*." *World of Music* 37(2):60–71.

———. 2000. "Bosnia-Hercegovina." In the *Garland Encyclopedia of World Music, Volume 8: Europe,* eds. Timothy Rice, James Porter, and Chris Goertzen, 962–71. New York and London: Garland Publishing, Inc.

Petrović, Radmila. 1968. "The Concept of Yugoslav Folk Music in the Twentieth Century." *Journal of the International Folk Music Council* 20:22–25.

———. 1974a. "Folk Music of Eastern Yugoslavia: A Process of Acculturation: Some Relevant Elements." *International Review of the Aesthetics and Sociology of Music* 5(1):217–25.

———. 1974b. "Narodna muzika istočne Jugoslavije—process akulturacije." *Zvuk* 2:155–60.

Pettan, Svanibor. 1992a. "Gypsy Music in Kosovo: Interaction and Creativity." Ph.D. dissertation, University of Maryland.

———. 1992b. "Lambada in Kosovo: A Case Study in Gypsy Creativity." *Journal of the Gypsy Lore Society*, Series 5 2(2):117–30.

———. 1996a. "Balkan Popular Music? No, Thanks: The View from Croatia." Paper given at the conference "Balkan Popular Music," Ljubljana, Slovenia, November 22–24.

———. 1996b. "Gypsies, Music, and Politics in the Balkans: A Case Study from Kosovo." *World of Music* 38(1):33–61.

———. 1996c. "Selling Music: Rom Musicians and the Music Market in Kosovo." In *Echoes of Diversity: Traditional Music of Ethnic Groups & Minorities*, ed. Ursula Hemetek, 233–45. Vienna and Cologne: Böhlau Verlag.

———. 1997. "The Croats and the Question of their Mediterranean Musical Identity." *Ethnomusicology On Line* 3.

———. 1998. "Music, Politics, and War in Croatia in the 1990s: An Introduction." In *Music, Politics, and War: Views from Croatia*, ed. Svanibor Pettan, 9–27. Zagreb: Institute of Ethnology and Folklore Research.

———. 2002. *Roma Muzsikusok Koszovóban: Kölcsönhatás és Kreativitás/ Rom Musicians in Kosovo: Interaction and Creativity.* Budapest: Magyar Tudományos Akadémia Zenetudományi Intézet/Institute for Musicology of the Hungarian Academy for Sciences.

——. 2003. "Male, Female, and Beyond in the Culture and Music of Roma in Kosovo." In *Music and Gender: Perspectives from the Mediterranean*, ed. Tullia Magrini, 287–305. Chicago: University of Chicago Press.

Pettifer, James. 2000 [1993]. *The Greeks: The Land and People Since the War*. London: Penguin.

Picken, Laurence. 1975. *Folk Musical Instruments of Turkey*. London: Oxford University Press.

Pilbrow, Tim. 1997. "The Nation and Its Margins: Negotiating a National Identity in Post-1989 Bulgaria." *Anthropology of East Europe Review* 15(2):43–50.

Pirker, Michael. 1993. "The Looped Trumpet in the Near East." *RIdIM/RCMI Newsletter* 18(1):3–8.

Pollock, Sheldon, H. Bhabha, C. Breckenridge, and D. Chakrabarty. 2000. "Cosmopolitanisms." *Public Culture* 12(3):577–89.

Popa, Corina. 1981. *Bălineşti*. Bucharest: Editura Meridiane.

Popescu, Diana. 2001. "Cei care se dau anti-manele ne invită să cântăm la petreceri, dar mai pe şest." (Interview with Costi Ioniţă) *Adevărul* 3428 [25 June 2001].

Popescu-Judetz, Eugenia. 1982. "Köcek and Çengi in Turkish Culture." *Dance Studies* 6:46–58.

Port, Mattijs van de. 1998. *Gypsies, Wars, and Other Instances of the Wild: Civilisation and its Discontents in a Serbian Town*. Amsterdam: Amsterdam University Press.

——. 1999. "The Articulation of the Soul: Gypsy Musicians and the Serbian Other." *Popular Music* 18(3): 291–308.

Poulton, Hugh. 1991. *The Balkans: Minorities and States in Conflict*. London: Minority Rights Publications.

Prošić-Dvornić, Mirjana. 1994. "'Druga Srbija': mirovni i ženski pokreti." In *Kulture u Tranziciji,* ed. Mirjana Prošić-Dvornić, 179–99. Beograd: Plato.

Qureshi, Regula. 1997. "The Indian Sarangi: Sound of Affect, Site of Context." *Yearbook for Traditional Music* 29:1–38.

Rabinow, Paul. 1986. "Representations are Social Facts: Modernity and Post-modernity in Anthropology." In *Writing Culture: The Poetics and Politics of Ethnography*, eds. James Clifford and George Marcus, 234–61. Berkeley: University of California Press.

Racy, Ali Jihad. 1995. "Music." In *The Oxford Encyclopedia of the Modern Islamic World*, ed. John L. Esposito, 180–83. New York: Oxford University Press.

Radano, Ronald and Philip V. Bohlman, eds. 2000. *Music and the Racial Imagination*. Chicago: The University of Chicago Press.

Rădulescu, Speranța. 1994. "Consequences of the Political Changes in Romanian Peasant Music." *Revue Roumaine d'Histoire de l'Art* 31:27–30.

———. 1998. "Musique de métissage pan-balkanique en Roumanie." Paper presented at the international colloquium "La diffusion des musiques du monde," L'Institut du Monde Arabe et l'Université de Bourgogne, Paris, 15–17 May 1998.

Rasmussen, Anne. 1992. "'An Evening in the Orient': The Middle Eastern Nightclub in America." *Asian Music* 23(2):63–88.

———. 1996. "Theory and Practice at the 'Arabic Org': Digital Technology in Contemporary Arab Music Performance." *Popular Music* 15(3): 345–65.

———. 1997. Liner notes to *The Music of Arab Americans: A Retrospective Collection.* Rounder Records, Rounder CD 1122.

Rasmussen, Ljerka Vidić. 1991. "Gypsy Music in Yugoslavia: Inside the Popular Culture Tradition." *Journal of the Gypsy Lore Society,* Series 5, 1(2):127–39.

———. 1995. "From Source to Commodity: Newly-Composed Folk Music of Yugoslavia." *Popular Music* 14(2):241–56.

———. 1996a. "Orientalism, Rom Gypsy, and the Culture at Intersection." In *Echoes of Diversity: Traditional Music of Ethnic Groups & Minorities*, ed. Ursula Hemetek, 247–55. Vienna and Cologne: Böhlau Verlag.

———. 1996b. "The Southern Wind of Change: Style and the Politics of Identity in Prewar Yugoslavia." In *Retuning Culture: Musical Changes in Central and Eastern Europe*, ed. Mark Slobin, 99–116. Durham, NC: Duke University Press.

———. 2001. "Cultures in Conflict, Cultures in Exchange: Popular Music at the Post Yugoslav Crossroads. *Muzika* 5(17):67–74.

———. 2002. *Newly Composed Folk Music of Yugoslavia.* New York and London: Routledge.

Razsa, Maple and Nicole Lindstrom. 2004. "Balkan is Beautiful: Balkanism in the Political Discourse of Tuđman's Croatia." *East European Politics and Societies* 18(4):628–50.

Reinhard, Kurt. 1981. "Turkish Miniatures as Sources of Music History." In *Music East and West: Essays in Honor of Walter Kaufmann*, ed. Thomas L. Noblitt, 143–66. New York: Pendragon Press.

Reinhard, Kurt and Ursula. 1984. *Musik der Türkei*. Wilhelmshaven: Heinrichshofen.

Reinhard, Ursula. 2002. "Turkey: An Overview." In *The Garland Encyclopedia of World Music, Volume 6: The Middle East,* eds. Virginia Danielson, Scott Marcus, and Dwight Reynolds, 759–77. New York and London: Routledge.

Revista Ioana. 2001. "Costi Ioniţă: Nopţi şi zile." Bucharest: Nova Music Entertainment.

Riasanovsky, Nicholas V. 1977. *A History of Russia*. Third edition. New York: Oxford University Press.

Rice, Timothy. 1980. "Aspects of Bulgarian Musical Thought." *Yearbook of Traditional Music* 12:43–66.

———. 1982. "The *Surla* and *Tapan* Tradition in Yugoslav Macedonia." *The Galpin Society Journal* 35(3):122–37.

———. 1994. *May it Fill Your Soul: Experiencing Bulgarian Music*. Chicago: University of Chicago Press.

———. 2000. "Macedonia." In *The Garland Encyclopedia of World Music, Volume 8: Europe*, eds. Timothy Rice, James Porter, and Chris Goertzen, 972–85. New York and London: Garland Publishing, Inc.

———. 2002. "Bulgaria or Chalgaria: The Attenuation of Bulgarian Nationalism in a Mass-Mediated Popular Music." *Yearbook for Traditional Music* 34:25–46.

———. 2003. "Time, Place and Metaphor in Musical Experience and Ethnography." *Ethnomusicology* 47(2):151–79.

Rigas, Georgiou. 1958. *Skiathou Laikos Politismos, Vol. I: "Dimodi Asmata," Periodikon Syggramma Eterias Makedonikon Spoudon-Parartima*. Thessaloniki.

Rihtman-Auguštin, Dunja. 1978. "Traditional Culture, Folklore, and Mass Culture in Contemporary Yugoslavia." In *Folklore in the Modern World*, ed. Richard M. Dorson, 163–72. The Hague: Mouton.

———. 1997. "Zašto i otkad se grozimo Balkana?" *Erasmus* 19:27–35.

Ringold, Dena. 2000. *Roma and the Transition in Central and Eastern Europe: Trends and Challenges*. Washington D.C.: World Bank.

Robbins, Bruce. 1992. "Comparative Cosmopolitanism." *Social Text* 31–32:169–86.

———. 1999. *Feeling Global: Internationalism in Distress*. New York: New York University Press.

Rochow, Ilse, and K. P. Matschke. 1991. "Neues zu den Zigeunern im byzantinischen Reich um die Wende vom 13. und 14. Jahrhundert." *Jahrbuch der Österreichischen Byzantinistik* 41:241–54.

Rofel, Lisa. 1992. "Rethinking Modernity: Space and Factory Discipline in China." *Cultural Anthropology* 7(1):93–114.

——. 1999. *Other Modernities: Gendered Yearnings in China after Socialism*. Berkeley: University of California Press.

Rosaldo, Renato. 1989. *Culture and Truth: The Remaking of Social Analysis*. Boston: Beacon Press.

Rubin, Joel. 2003. "The Art of the Klezmer: Improvisation and Ornamentation in the Commercial Recordings of New York Clarinetists Naftule Brandwein and Dave Tarras, 1922–1929." Ph.D. dissertation, City University, London.

Ryback, Timothy W. 1990. *Rock around the Bloc: A History of Rock Music in Eastern Europe and the Soviet Union*. New York: Oxford University Press.

Şahin, Haluk, and Asu Aksoy. 1993. "Global Media and Cultural Identity in Turkey." *Journal of Communication* 43(2):31–41.

Said, Edward W. 1979 [1978]. *Orientalism*. New York: Vintage Books.

——. 1995 [1978]. *Orientalism: Western Conceptions of the Orient*. London: Penguin Books.

Sanfeld, Kristian. 1930. *Linguistique Balkanique*. Paris: E. Champion.

Sant Cassia, Paul. 2000. "Exoticizing Discoveries and Extraordinary Experiences: 'Traditional' Music, Modernity, and Malta and other Mediterranean Societies." *Ethnomusicology* 44(2):281–301.

Sapoznik, Henry. 1987. *The Compleat Klezmer*. With transcriptions and technical introduction by Pete Sokolow. Cedarhurst, NY: Tara Publications.

Savić, Obrad. 1998. "Poslednja adresa: Žan Bodrijar, Srbija." In *Savršen Zločin*, 198–233. Belgrade: Belgrade Circle Journal/*Circulus*.

Savigliano, Marta. 1995. *Tango and the Political Economy of Passion*. Boulder, CO: Westview.

Schein, Louisa. 2000. *Minority Rules: The Miao and the Feminine in China's Cultural Policy*. Durham, NC: Duke University Press.

Scott, Derek B. 1997. "Orientalism and Musical Style." *Critical Musicology Journal: A Virtual Journal on the Internet*; <http://www.leeds.ac.uk/music/Info/CMJ/Articles/1997/02/01.html>

Seebass, Tilman. 1973. *Musikdarstellung und Psalterillustration im früheren Mittelalter*. Bern: Francke Verlag.

Seeman, Sonia Tamar. 1990. "Continuity and Change in the Macedonian Genre of Čalgija: Past Perfect and Present Imperfective." M.A. paper (Ethnomusicology), University of Washington.

———. 2000. Liner notes. *The Road to Keşan: Turkish Rom and Regional Music of Thrace*. New York: Traditional Crossroads CD 6001.

———. 2002. "'You're Roman!' Music and Identity in Turkish Roman Communities." Ph.D. dissertation, University of California at Los Angeles.

Šešić, Milena Dragićević and Sanjin Dragojević. 2004. *Intercultural Mediation in the Balkans*. Sarajevo: Oko.

Shafir, Michael. 1998a. "Clinton Launches 'Action Plan for Southeast Europe.'" *Radio Free Europe/Radio Liberty Newsline, Part II* 2(28)[11 February].

———. 1998b. "Italian Premier in Bulgaria." *RFE/RL Newsline, Part II* 2(38)[25 February].

———. 1998c. "Bulgaria Urges Regional Initiative on Kosovo." *RFE/RL Newsline, Part II* 2(39)[26 February].

———. 1998d. "Bulgaria, Turkey Discuss Kosovo Conflict." *RFE/RL Newsline, Part II* 2(46)[9 March].

———. 1998e. "Balkan States Issue Statement on Kosovo." *RFE/RL Newsline, Part II* 2(48)[11 March].

———. 1998f. "Balkan States Discuss Multinational Peace Keeping Force." *RFE/RL Newsline, Part II* 2(54)[19 March].

———. 1998g. "Bulgarian Pipeline Tender Closes." *RFE/RL Newsline, Part II* 2(96)[21 May].

———. 1998h. "Bulgarian Women Forced into Sex Industry Abroad." *RFE/RL Newsline, Part II* 2(150)[6 August].

———. 1998i. "Bulgaria, Romania, Greece Agree to Combat Crime Together." *RFE/RL Newsline, Part II* 2(174)[9 September].

———. 1998j. "Bulgaria Seals Pirate CD Producer. *RFE/RL Newsline, Part II* 2(178)[15 September].

———. 1998k. "Turkey Backs Plovdiv as Base for Balkan Peacekeeping Force." *RFE/RL Newsline, Part II* 2(212)[3 November].

———. 1998l. "Moldova to be Included in Southeast Europe Action Plan." *RFE/RL Newsline, Part II* 2(223)[18 November].

———. 1998m. "U.S. Hails Bulgarian Progress on Curbing Pirate Compact Discs." *RFE/RL Newsline, Part II* 2(223)[18 November].

———. 1998n. "Multinational Balkan Force to be Located in Bulgaria." *RFE/RL Newsline, Part II* 2(228)[25 November].

———.2000a. "Campaign to End Sex Slavery in Bulgaria." *RFE/RL Newsline, Part II* 4(77)[18 April].

———. 2000b. "IOM Launches Campaign against Women Sex Slavery in Bulgaria." *RFE/RL Newsline, Part II* 4(78)[19 April].

——. 2000c. "Bulgaria Warned over Pirate CD Imports." *RFE/RL Newsline, Part II* 4(10)[25 May].

Signell, Karl. 1988. "Mozart and the Mehter." *Turkish Music Quarterly* 1(1): 9–15.

Silverman, Carol. 1986. "Bulgarian Gypsies: Adaptation in a Socialist Context." *Nomadic Peoples* 21–22:51–61.

——. 1989. "Reconstructing Folklore: Media and Cultural Policy in Eastern Europe." *Communication* 11(2):141–60.

——. 1995. "Persecution and Politicization: Roma (Gypsies) of Eastern Europe." *Cultural Survival* 19(2):43–49.

——. 1996a. "Music and Marginality: The Roma (Gypsies) of Bulgaria and Macedonia." In *Retuning Culture: Musical Change in Eastern Europe*, ed. Mark Slobin, 231–53. Durham, NC: Duke University Press.

——. 1996b. "Music and Power: Gender and Performance among Roma (Gypsies) of Skopje, Macedonia." *The World of Music* 38(1):63–76.

——. 2000a. "Review of *Latcho Drom*." *Ethnomusicology* 44(2):362–64.

——. 2000b. "*Rom* (Gypsy) Music." In the *Garland Encyclopedia of World Music, Volume 8:Europe*, eds. Timothy Rice, James Porter, and Chris Goertzen, 270–93. New York: Garland Publishing, Inc.

——. 2003. "The Gender of the Profession: Music, Dance, and Reputation among Balkan Muslim Rom Women." In *Music and Gender: Perspectives from the Mediterranean*, ed. Tullia Magrini, 119–45. Chicago: University of Chicago Press.

——. 2004. "'Move over Madonna': Gender, Representation, and the 'Mystery' of Bulgarian Voices." In *Over the Wall/After the Fall: Post-Communist Cultures through an East-West Gaze*, eds. Sibelan Forrester, Magdalena J. Zaborowska, and Elena Gapova, 212–37. Bloomington: Indiana University Press.

——. Forthc. *Performing Diaspora: Cultural Politics of Balkan Romani Music.* New York: Oxford University Press.

Simić, Andrei.1978–79. "Commercial Folk Music in Yugoslavia: Idealization and Reality." *Journal of the Association of Graduate Dance Ethnologists, UCLA* 2: 25–37.

——. 1999. "Machismo and Crytomatriarchy: Power, Affect, and Authority in the Traditional Yugoslav Family." In *Gender Politics in the Western Balkans: Women and Society in Yugoslavia and the Yugoslav Successor States*, ed. Sabrina P. Ramet, 11–29. University Park, Penn.: The Pennsylvania State University Press.

Širola, Božidar. 1932. *Sopile i Zurle.* Zagreb: Etnografski Muzej.

Sitheris, Yannis. 2000. *I Istoria tou Neou Ellinikou Theatrou, Tomos A: 1794–1908*. Athens: Kastaniotis Editions.

Slobin, Mark. 1993. *Subcultural Sounds: Micromusics of the West*. Hanover, NH: Wesleyan University Press.

———, ed. 1996. *Retuning Culture: Musical Changes in Central and Eastern Europe*. Durham, NC: Duke University Press.

Solcanu, Ion I. 1976. "Représentations choréographiques de la peinture murale de Moldavie et leur place dans l'iconographie sud-est européene (XVe–XVIIe siècles)." *Revue des Études Sud-est Européenes* 14(1):45–65.

———. 1979. "Les instruments de musique dans la peinture murale des pays roumains (XIVe–XVIIe siècles)." *Revue des Archeologues et Historiens d'Art de Louvain* 12:120–48.

Solomon, Thomas. 2000. "Dueling Landscapes: Singing Places and Identities in Highland Bolivia." *Ethnomusicology* 44(2):257–80.

———. 2005. "'Living Underground is Tough': Authenticity and Locality in the Hip-Hop Community in Istanbul, Turkey." *Popular Music* 24(1):1–20.

Solomonides, Christos S. 1954. *To Theatro sti Smyrni*. Athens.

Soulis, George. 1961. "The Gypsies in the Byzantine Empire and the Balkans in the Late Middle Ages." *Dumbarton Oaks Papers* 1961: 141–65.

Stanković, Borisav. 1966. *Koštana/Gazda Mladen/Uvela Ruzha*. Belgrade: Rad.

Statelova, Rozmari. 1995. *Prezhivyano v Bŭlgariya: Rok, Pop, Folk, 1990–1994*. Sofia.

Stefanova, Julia. n.d. "The Empirical Reader in a Virtualized Reality." In "Conference Abstracts," *Reading in the Age of Media, Computers, and Internet*. <http://www.liternet.revolta.com/iser/iustef1.htm>

Stewart, Charles. 1991. *Demons and the Devil: Modern Imagination in Modern Greek Culture*. Princeton, NJ: Princeton University Press.

Stewart, Susan. 1984. *On Longing: Narratives of the Miniature, the Gigantic, the Souvenir, the Collection*. Baltimore, MD: Johns Hopkins Press.

Stokes, Martin. 1992a. *The Arabesk Debate. Music and Musicians in Modern Turkey*. Oxford: Clarendon Press.

———. 1992b. "Islam, the Turkish State, and Arabesk." *Popular Music* 2:213–27.

412   References

—. 1994. "Introduction." In *Ethnicity, Identity and Music: The Musical Construction of Place*, ed. Martin Stokes, 1–27. Oxford: Berg Publishers.

—. 1999. "Sounding Out: The Culture Industries and the Globalization of Istanbul." In *Istanbul: Between the Local and Global*, ed. Çaglar Keyder, 145–68. Lanham, MD: Rowman and Littlefield.

—. 2002. "Turkish Rock and Pop Music." In *The Garland Encylopedia of World Music, Volume 6: The Middle East*, eds. Virginia Danielson, Scott Marcus, and Dwight Reynolds, 247–54. New York: Routledge.

—. 2003. "The Tearful Public Sphere: Turkey's 'Sun of Art,' Zeki Müren." In *Music and Gender: Perspectives from the Mediterranean*, ed. Tullia Magrini, 307–28. Chicago: University of Chicago Press.

—, ed. 1994. *Ethnicity, Identity and Music: The Musical Construction of Place*. Oxford: Berg Publishers.

Sugar, Peter. 1977. *Southeastern Europe under Ottoman Rule, 1354–1804*. (A History of East Central Europe 5) Seattle and London: University of Washington Press.

Sugarman, Jane C. 1998. "Ottopop: Ottoman Successor Musics and Albanian Identities in the 1990s." Paper presented at the 43rd Annual Meeting of the Society for Ethnomusicology, Bloomington, IN.

—. 1999. "Mediated Albanian Musics and the Imagining of Modernity." In *New Countries, Old Sounds? Cultural Identity and Social Change in Southeastern Europe*, ed. Bruno B. Reuer, 134–54. Munich: Südostdeutsches Kulturwerk.

—. 2000. "Albanian Music." In *The Garland Encyclopedia of World Music, Volume 8: Europe*, eds. Timothy Rice, James Porter, and Chris Goertzen, 986–1006. New York and London: Garland Publishing, Inc.

—. 2003. "Those 'Other Women': Dance and Femininity among Prespa Albanians." In *Music and Gender: Perspectives from the Mediterranean*, ed. Tullia Magrini, 87–118. Chicago: University of Chicago Press.

—. 2004. "Diasporic Dialogues: Mediated Musics and the Albanian Transnation." In *Identity and the Arts in Diaspora Communities*, eds. Thomas Turino and James Lea, 21–38. Warren, MI: Harmonie Park Press.

—. In press a. "Albania." In *The Encyclopedia of Popular Music of the World*, Vol. 7, eds. John Shepherd, David Horn, and David Laing. London: Continuum Books.

———. In press b. "Review of *Whose Song is This? (Chiya e Tazi Pesen?)*," directed by Adela Peeva, 2003. Forthcoming in *Ethnomusicology.*

Suvilehto, Ilkko. 1999. "Bulgaria Balkanen eteläisessä kolmiossa: muutos." In *Balkan 2000: Näkökulmia ja Taustoja Kaakkois-Euroopan Nykytilanteelle*, ed. Vesa Saarikoski, 139–62. Turku: Turun Yliopiston Poliittisen Historian Tutkimuksia 17.

Taussig, Michael. 1987. *Shamanism, Colonialism, and the Wild Man: A Study in Terror and Healing.* Chicago: University of Chicago Press.

Taylor, Timothy. 1997. *Global Pop: World Music, World Markets.* London: Routledge.

Točkaja, I. F., and A. M. Zajaruznyj. 1995. "I musici dell'affresco detto degli Skomorochi mella cattedrale della Santa Sofia a Kiev." In *Arte Profana e Arte Sacra a Bisanzio*, eds. Antonio Iacobini and Enrico Zanini, 281–302. Rome: Argos.

Todorova, Maria. 1996a. "The Ottoman Legacy in the Balkans." In *Imperial Legacy: The Ottoman Imprint on the Balkans and the Middle East*, ed. L. Carl Brown, 45–77. New York: Columbia University Press.

———. 1996b. "The Construction of a Western Discourse of the Balkans." *Etnološka Tribina* 19:7–24.

———. 1997. *Imagining the Balkans.* New York: Oxford University Press.

Trærup, Birthe. 1981. "Wedding Musicians in Prizrenska Gora, Jugoslavia." *Studia Instrumentorum Musicae Popularis* 7:43–52. In *Bericht über die 7. Internationale Arbeitstagung der Study Group on Folk Musical Instruments des International Folk Music Council in Seggau, Österreich 1980*, ed. Erich Stockman. (Musikhistoriska Museets Skrifter) Stockholm: Musikhistoriska Museet.

Troitsky, Artemy. 1987. *Back in the USSR: The True Story of Rock in Russia.* Boston and London: Faber and Faber.

Trumpener, Katie. 1992. "The Time of the Gypsies: A 'People Without History' in the Narratives of the West." *Critical Inquiry* 18: 843–84.

Turino, Thomas. 2000. *Nationalists, Cosmopolitans, and Popular Music in Zimbabwe.* Chicago: University of Chicago Press.

Tuksar, Stanislav. 1998. "The Musical Baroque and Western Slavs." *Music, Politics, and War: Views from Croatia*, ed. Svanibor Pettan, 55–63. Zagreb: Institute of Ethnology and Folklore Research.

Turner, Victor. 1988. *The Anthropology of Performance.* New York: PAJ Publications.

Ugrešić, Dubravka. 1995[1993]. "Folksies." Translated from Serbo-Croatian by Celia Hawkesworth. *Mediterraneans* 7[autumn]:119–31.

———. 1998. "Balkan Blues." In her *The Culture of Lies: Antipolitical Essays,* 129–50. University Park, PA Pennsylvania State University Press.

Vakareliyska, Cynthia, ed. 1998. "Joint Statement: US–Bulgarian Partnership for a New Era (10 February 1998)." Bulgarian Studies Association moderated electronic mailing list, 15 February.

van de Port, Mattijs. See Port.

Veal, Michael E. 2000. *Fela: The Life and Times of an African Musical Icon.* Philadelphia: Temple University Press.

Velmans, Tania. 1965. "Les fresques d'Ivanovo et la peinture byzantine à la fin du moyen age." *Journal des Savants* [January–March]:358–412. Paris: Librairie C. Klincksieck.

———. 1971. *La Tétraévangile de la Laurentienne: Florence, Laur. VI. 23.* Bibliothèque des Cahiers Archéologiques VI. Paris: Éditions Klincksieck.

Verdery, Katherine. 1991. *National Ideology under Socialism: Identity and Cultural Politics in Ceauşescu's Romania.* Berkeley: University of California Press.

———. 1996. *What Was Socialism, and What Comes Next?* Princeton, NJ: Princeton University Press.

Vrdoljak, Dražen. 1984. "Zabavna glazba." In *Diskografija u SR Hrvatskoj* (Studije i Dokumenti X), 24–28. Zagreb: Zavod za kulturu Hrvatske.

Vrelis, Aristotelis. 1985. *Simvoli stin Erevna tis Dimotikis Ipirotikis Mousikis.* Ioannina.

Vŭlchinova-Chendova, Elisaveta. 2000. *Gradskata Traditsionna Instrumentalna Praktika i Orkestrovata Kultura v Bŭlgariya (sredata na XIX–kraya na XX vek).* Sofia: Poni.

Wachtel, Andrew. 1998. "Thoughts on Teaching South Slavic Cultures." *AAASS NewsNet* 38(1):7–8.

Wallerstein, Immanuel. 1990. "Culture as the Ideological Battleground of the Modern World-System." In *Global Culture: Nationalism, Globalization, Modernity,* ed. Mike Featherstone, 31–55. London: Sage.

Webster's New Collegiate Dictionary. 1973. Springfield, MA: G. & C. S. Merriam Company.

Weitzmann, Kurt. 1971. *Studies in Classical and Byzantine Manuscript Illumination,* ed. Herbert L. Kessler. Chicago: University of Chicago Press.

Wheatcroft, Andrew. 1995 [1993]. *The Ottomans. Dissolving Images.* London and New York: Penguin Books.

Wolff, Larry. 1994. *Inventing Eastern Europe: The Map of Civilization on the Mind of the Enlightenment.* Stanford, CA: Stanford University Press.

Wood, Nicholas. 2004. "The Strains of a Balkan Ballad." *International Herald Tribune* [16 November].

Worsley, Peter. 1990. "Models of the Modern World-System." In *Global Culture: Nationalism, Globalization, Modernity*, ed. Mike Featherstone, 83–95. London: Sage.

Yanchuk, N. 1913. "Ot Muzykal'no-Etnograficheskoi Komissii." In *Opyty Khudozhestvennoi Obrabotki Narodnykh Piesen, Tom 1*, iii–v. (Trudy Etnograficheskogo Otdela, Tom 18; Trudy Muzykal'no-Etnograficheskoi Komissii, Tom 4) Moskva: Muzykal'no-Etnograficheskaya Komissiya.

Žanić, Ivo. 1998. *Prevarena Povijest: Guslarska Estrada, Kult Hajduka i Rat u Hrvatskoj i Bosni i Hercegovini 1990–1995. Godine.* Zagreb: Durieux.

Zirbel, Kathryn. 1999. "Musical Discursions: Spectacle, Experience, and Political Economy among Egyptian Performers in Globalizing Markets." Ph. D. Dissertation, University of Michigan.

———. 2000. "Playing It Both Ways: Local Egyptian Performers between Regional Identity and International Markets." In *Mass Mediations: New Approaches to Popular Culture in the Middle East and Beyond*, ed. Walter Armbrust, 120–45. Berkeley: University of California Press.

Žižek, Slavoj. 1992. "Ethnic Dance Macabre." *The Guardian* [28 August 28]: 21.

Websites without Authors

Chapter Seven

"Universal Channel: Xena: Warrior Princess." <http://www. universal studios.com /tv/xena/overview.html>

"Meet Joseph LoDuca: Composer for Hercules and Xena." <http://www. universalstudios.com/tv/loduca/ interview.html>

Chapter Nine

<http://enjoyment.independent.co.uk/music.interviews/story-jsp?story
    =303908> (concert review)
<http://www.abhaber.com/ozan/ozan_yorum41.htm>
<http://www.efes.com/turkiye/sezen/sezen1.html>
<http://www.guardian.co.uk/arts/reviews/story/0,11712,740.391,00.html>
    (concert review)
<http://www.hri/org/news.Turkey/Anadolu/1999/99-11-24>
<http://www.milliyet.com.tr/2001/10/20/magazin/amag.html>
<http://www.sezenaksu.gq.nu/index.html> (Mehmet Ugras Erol's fan site)
<http://www.sezenaksu.net> (Sezen Aksu official website)
<http://www.showtvnet.com/belgesel> (Turkish documentary on Aksu)
<http://www.tempodergisi.com.tr/kose/faruk_bildirici/00296>
<http://www.zaman.com.tr/ms/zaman/anket022.php?poll_id=14>
<http://www.zaman.com/2002/08/23/kultur/h3.htm> (concert review)

Discography

Adrian Copilul Minune. *Prinţesa Mea.* S.C. Studio Recording S.R.L., Timişoara, 1998.

——. *Băieţii de aur, Volume 5.* Amma, 2000.

——. *Of, Viaţa Mea.* Cristian's Studio, Craiova, 2001.

Aksu, Sezen. *Ex Oriente Lux/Işık Doğudan Yükselir.* Foneks 95-34-U 814-023, 1995.

——. *Düğün ve Cenaze.* Karma Müzik/Raks Müzik 97 34U 918, 1997.

——. *Deliveren.* Post Müzik, 2000.

al-Bakkar, Muhammad. *Port Said: Music of the Middle East.* Performed by Muhammad al-Bakkar and his Oriental Ensemble. Audio Fidelity AFSD 5833, AFLP 1833, 1957.

Atlas. *Ne se Predavai!* Unison Stars, 1994.

Balkan Voices. FM Records FM 1051, 1999.

Balkans without Borders. Omnium OMM 2024, 1999 [1989].

Barev, Ivo. *S Imeto na Bog.* Unison Stars and Vega-M, n.d. [ca. 1994].

Belite Shisharki, Gabrovo. *Prosti Mi.* Payner, 1994.

Belite Shisharki s uchastieto na Popa. *Tigre, Tigre.* Payner, 1996.

Bilides, Sophia. *Greek Legacy.* E. Thomas ETD 101, 1991.

Boney M. *The Greatest Hits.* BMG Heritage 65108, 2002.

Bosnia: Echoes from an Endangered World: Music and Chant of the Bosnian Muslims. Recorded, compiled, and annotated by Ted Levin and Ankica Petrović. Smithsonian/Folkways SF 40407, 1993.

Bosno Moja, Jabuko: HELP. Muzički atelje, Tuzla, 1992.

Borisova, Snezhana. *Snejana: Disco Folk, Volume 1.* Produced by Dimitŭr Penev. Superfolk, 1994.

Bregović, Goran. *Dom za Vešanje.* Diskoton DTK-95, 1988.

——. *B.O.F. Le Temps des Gitans & Kuduz.* Philips 842 764-2, 1990.

——. *Music Inspired and Taken from Underground: A Film by Emir Kusturica.* Mercury/Kamarad Productions 528 910 2, 1995.

——. *P.S.* 1996.

——. *Ederlezi.* Polygram 5583502, 1999.

——. *Songbook.* Mercury 564 829-2, 2000.

——. *Tales and Songs from Weddings and Funerals.* Mercury 063079-2, 2002.

Bregović, Goran and George Dalaras. *Thessaloniki–Yannena with Two Canvas Shoes.* EMI 4942632, 1998.

Brandwein, Naftule. *Naftule Brandwein: King of the Klezmer Clarinet.* Rounder Records 1127, 1997. Notes by Henry Sapoznik. Recorded between December 1922 and April 1941.

Bŭlgari. *Bulgarian Folk Music.* Latitudes LT 50613, 1999.

——. *Bulgarian Rhapsody.* Owl's Head Music, 2000.

The Bulgarian Voices-Angelite & Huun-Huur-Tu. *Fly, Fly My Sadness.* Notes by Mikhail Alperin. Shanachie 64071, 1996.

Ceca (& Mili i Marina). *Maskarada.* PGP-RTS 508790, 1997.

Chaushev, Mustafa. *S Pesenta v Sŭrtseto.* Riva Sound RS0162, 1994.

Daly, Ross and Labyrinth. *Mitos.* (World Network Volume 8: Eurasia). Network Medien/Harmonia Mundi, 1992.

Di Grine Kuzine. *Klezmer's Paradise.* Di Grine Kuzine, 1999.

Divahn. *Divahn.* Copyright Galeet Dardashti, Lauren DeAlbert, Michal Raizen, and Emily Pinkerton, 2002.

Djoković, Divna Radić. *Pesme i Igre iz Pozorišnog Komada "Koštana."* RTB LP-1180.

Dorel, Sile. *Romanian Gypsy "Manele" 2004: Sile Dorel Păun and Guests,* Sile Dorel, 2004.

Dragović, Doris. *Marija Magdalena: "Hrvatska Pjesma za Pjesmu Evrope."* Croatia Records HRT & Orfej, CD 525007, 1999.

Duet Apogeasos. *Blyasokot na Rosata.* Payner, 1995.

Dzhipsi Aver. *Dzhipsi Rap.* Unison Records, 1993.

Erçetin, Candan. *Hazırım.* Topkapı Müzik 96103-2 1996.

Folk Magazin 1: Pesni za Dushata. Stars Records, n.d.

Georgi Sergiev, Dimitŭr Kunchev i Orkestŭr Diamant. *Mente, Mente . . .* Grami Ltd., 1995.

The Guardians of Hellenism, Volume 1: Chios, Mytilene, Samos, Ikaria. Performed by the Hellenic Music Archives Ensemble. FM Records FM 801, 1998.

The Gypsy Road: A Musical Migration from India to Spain. Alula 1013, 1999.

Hristov, Georgi. *Karuzo.* ARA Audio-Video ARAMC 019, n.d. [1994].

Iotova, Nona and Ivan Lechev. *Omana.* Unison Stars, n.d. [1994].

Kuzov, Vladimir. *Izlel e Delyu Haidutin: Folklor ot Rodopite.* Subdibula, 1993.

Lazarević, Gordana. *Koštana.* Jugoton LSY 61639, n.d.

Lesbos Aiolis: Songs and Dances of Lesbos. Supervised by Nikos Dionysopoulos. (Greek Traditional Music 5) Crete University Press C.U.P. 9 and 10, 2002.

Levy, Gloria. *Sephardic Folk Songs.* Folkways Records FW 8737, 1958.

Marin Dzhambazov s Orkestŭr Knezha. *Mechtata na Sheiha.* Lazarov Records, 1994.

Masters of Turkish Music, Volume 2. Produced by Dick Spottswood and Karl Signell. Rounder Records CD 1111, 1996.

Merlin, Dino. *Sredinom.* In Takt Records CD-060, 2000.

[Merlin], Dino, & Beatrice. *Putnici/Voyagers/Les Voyagers.* Menart MCD 092, 1999.

Minkova, Yana. *Kosmofolk.* Unison RTM, 1995.

Mode Plagal. *Mode Plagal II.* Lyra ML 0668, 1998.

Mulaomerović, Esad. *Pjesma SDA.* Produced by SDA and RTV Sarajevo.

Music of the Balkans: Songs and Dances, Vol. 1: Albania, Central Balkans, 1920–1940. FM Records FM 706, n.d.

The Music of Arab Americans: A Retrospective Collection. Research and documentation by Anne Rasmussen. Rounder Records Rounder CD 1122, 1997.

Orkestŭr Kozari. *"Yana Bibiyana": Tsiganski Pesni.* Riva Sound, 1994.

Orkestŭr Kristal. *Mili Moi.* n.p., n.d. [1994].

Orkestŭr Melodiya. *Greshen Svyat.* Coproduced by Unison Stars and Milena Records, n.d. [ca. 1994].

——. *Bogat Beden.* Payner, 1996.

Paldum, Hanka. *Čežnja.* Sarajevodisk LP 1111, 1980.

——. *Nek' Je od Srca.* Nirvana Distribution CD, 1999.

Papazov, Ivo. *Ivo Papasov and his Bulgarian Wedding Band: Orpheus Ascending.* Hannibal Records, Ltd. HNCD 1346, 1989.

——. *Ivo Papasov and his Orchestra: Balkanalogy.* Produced by Joe Boyd. Hannibal Records/Rykodisc Hannibal HNCD 1363, 1991.

Parlak, Erol. *Göç Yolları (1): Instrumental Music from Anatolia.* Produced by A. Haydar Gögercin. Güvercin Müzik Üretim 028, ISRC TR-017-05-00300, n.d.

Pesma Nas je Održala (Target). Target Records CD, 1999.

Petrache, Nelu. *Muzică Orientală: Mi-am Cumpărat Celular.* Amma, Bucharest, 1999.

Pŭrvi Romski Festival '93: Stara Zagora. Payner, 1993.

Putumayo Presents A Jewish Odyssey. Putumayo World Music PUT182-2, 2000.

Qamili i Vogël. *Vaj Moj Lule.* Jugoton LPY-V-853.

Qamili i Vogël and Mazllom Mejzini. *Këndojnë Bilbilat.* EuroLiza [mid 1990s].

Ramadan Krasniqi and Corona. *Mi Ke Flokët.* Rozafa 048, 1997.

Rambo Amadeus. *Hoćemo Gusle.* PGP-RTB, 1989 (also on *Zbrana Dela 2,* Vinil: Manija Records, 1998).

RCA Victor Presents Eartha Kitt, RCA Victor LPM 3062, n.d. [ca. 1953].

Redžepova, Esma. *Songs of a Macedonian Gypsy.* Featuring Esma Redžepova and Usnija Jašarova with the Stevo Teodosievski and Nasko Džorlev Ensembles. Monitor MCD 71496, 1994.

Rough Guide to the Music of the Balkans. World Music Network, 2003.

Rumen i Orkestŭr Pautaliya. *Amala/Priyatel.* Unison Stars, n.d. [ca. 1994].

Škorić, Mira. *Kosa Crna.* PGP-RTS 508445, 1997.

———. *Srcekradica.* PGP-RTS 509308, 1998.

Ştefan de la Bărbuleşti. *Mi-e Dor de Tine,* Amma, 2000.

Songs and Dances of Smyrna and Erythraea, Asia Minor. Produced by the Lyceum Club of Greek Women (Athens). LCGW 113, 1994.

Songs of Mytilene and Chios. Produced by the Society for the Dissemination of National Music. SDNM 110, 1974.

Spasov, Daniel. *Byala Mariya: Folk ot Severna Bŭlgariya.* Subdibula, 1993.

Stassinopolou, Kristi. *Echotropia.* Lyra, 1999. (Reissued on Tinder Records 860962, 2001).

Taraf de Haidouks. *Band of Gypsies.* Nonesuch 79642-2, 2001.

Tosko Todorov i Formatsija Enos. *Lek za Moya Zhivot.* 1996.

"Traki" Instrumental Folk Group. *Bulgarian Folk Music.* Balkanton Trading, Ltd. BTThC 3014, n.d. [1991].

Turbo Folk 2000. Razglas Records CD, 1999.

Turkish Folk Songs and Instrumental Music. Produced by Katsuhiko Nishida. King Records Co., Ltd. (World Music Library) KICC 5102, 1988.

Valdes, Valentin. *Misŭl za Zhena.* Payner, 1994.

———. *Balkanska Dusha.* Payner 9602121, 1996.

———. *Valdes: Losha Kompaniya.* Payner Music 2201463, 2002.

Vali, Gus and His Orchestra/Casbah Ensemble. *Dance Bellyrina, Dance!* United Artists Records UAL-3302, 1963.

Vaseva, Sashka. *Sashka s Folk Grupa "Roden Kŭt."* Unison Muzikalna Produktsiya, 1994.

Vatrogasci. *Vatrogasno Zabava Vol. 3: Hit-Parada.* Euroton Recordings (Croatia), EU2194, n.d. [ca. 2001].

Velichkovi, Tanya i Stoyan. *Biseri ot Strandzha.* n.p., n.d.

Vëllezërit Aliu. *Këngë Lirike 2,* BNPP (Skopje) CA-009, 1992.

Xena, Warrior Princess: Original Television Soundtrack. Music composed by Joseph LoDuca. Varese Sarabande VSD-5750, 1995 [1996].

Yüksel, Levent. *Med-Cezir.* Foneks TS 2240, 1993.

YaG. *"Ot Kalkuta do Viena": Romski Duhov Orkestŭr YaG.* Unison Stars, n.d. [ca. 1994].

Zodiak. *"Rok-grupa 'Zodiak.'"* Firma E. Koneva. RIS Record Co., Inc., 206 Jewett Avenue, Jersey City, NJ.

Zyber Avdiu. *[N]dëgjo Zemrën Tënde.* EuroLiza 315 and Cani, 1999. (Reissued on the CD *Turbo Hitet: Best of Zyber Avdiu.* EuroLiza CD-0250 [ca. 2004]).

Filmography and Videography

Chaushev, Mustafa. *Sŭdba: Hitovete na Mustafa Chaushev.* ET Perfekt Video, n.d.

Dj Folk Collection 6 Plus. Payner, 2000.

Duo Juzhen Polŭh i Gosti. *Ah, Zheni.* Folkton, n.d.

Dzhipsi Aver. *Imam li Dobŭr Kismet?* Video Total-OOD.

Gatliff, Tony. *Latcho Drom/Bonne Route.* Montreal, Quebec: France Film Company/ Centre National de la Cinematographie, France, 1993.

——. *Gadjo Dilo/Crazy Stranger.* New York: New Yorker Video NYV 73799, 1999 [1997].

Hitovete na Mustafa Chaushev. Perfekt Video, n.d.

Hitovete na Planeta Payner, Volume 2. Payner Music MK 15698, 2004.

Kuturica, Emil. *Dom za Vešanje/Time of the Gypsies.* RCA/Columbia Pictures Home Video, 1990 [1988].

——. *Arizona Dream.* Warner Bros. Warner Home Video 13236, 1995 [1993].

——. *Underground.* New York, NY: New Yorker Video, 1998 [1995].

——. *Crna Mačka, Beli Mačor/Black Cat, White Cat.* New York: USA Home Entertainment/October Films, 1999 [1998].

Lolov, Ibro. *Tsiganski Hitove, Chast 1* and *2.* Video Total, n.d.

——. *Tsigansko Variete.* Video Total, n.d.

Marin Dzhambasov i Orkestŭr Knezha. *Mechtata na Sheiha.* Lazarov Records, 1994.

Marre, Jeremy. *The Romany Trail: Part Two: Gypsy Music into Europe.* (Beats of the Heart) Shanachie 1211, 1992.

Orkestŭr Kanarite. *Kanarite s Lyubov i Nastroenie.* Payner, 1999.

Orkestŭr Kozari. *Kozari: Kapŭlŭ Charshiya.* Payner, 1995.

Orkestŭr Kristal. *Kristal i Priyateli.* Perfekt Video, n.d.

Orkestŭr Kristali. *Kristali: More ot Lyubov.* Payner, 1995.

Payner Hit Video 1. Video Hit Collection. Payner, 1996.

Payner Hit Video 6. Payner, 1999.

Payner Hit Video 7. Payner, 2000.
Payner Hit Video 8. Payner, 2000.
Peeva, Adela. *Chiya e Tazi Pesen/Whose Song is This?* An Adela Peeva
     film. Adela Media, Ltd., 2003.
Petra. *Hishna Hiena.* Payner, 1999.
Pirin Folk '95. Festival Sandanski. Electroimpex Simex, n.d.
Roman, Sasho. *Bez Upoika.* BMK Kompaniya, n.d.
Vaseva, Sashka. *Prikazka za Vlyubeni.* Multi Video Tsentŭr, 1997.
Zvezdite na Trakiya Folk 1994. Payner, 1995.

Index

West musical imagery, 73–74,
89–90; origins and influences,
57–58, 66, 78; post-war diminished support/attempts to curb
popularity of, 75–76; singers'
links to political power, 72–73.
See also newly composed folk
music (NCFM); *sevdah*-rock
Turbo Folk 2000, 71
turčija. See sevdalinka
turcism/turkism. *See orijental*
Türk Popu or *Türkçe Dili Pop* (Turkish pop). *See* Turkey, popular
music currents in
Turkey, as Balkan Other/orient, 365–
66; as locus of Balkan musi-
cal/cultural influence, xxiv,
235; Balkan presence in popular
music of, 311–12, 327; popular
music currents in, 312–313,
318, 319. *See also* Aksu, Sezen;
arabesk
Turkish Radio and Television corporation (TRT), 312, 313, 319–20;
denetim, 314, 320
Türkiye Şarkıları [Songs of Turkey]
(Sezen Aksu), 316–17
türkü, 4, 47
TV Pink, 72, 74, 75–76

Underground (Emir Kusturica), 326
Uska Dara (Eartha Kitt), 37, 38. *See
also Üsküdara gider iken* [On
the way to Üsküdar]
Üsküdar, 4, and Crimean War,
46–47
Üsküdara gider iken [On the way to
Üsküdar], xxiii–xxiv, 3, 5–6, 7,
373, 374; American orientaliza-
tion of, 36–37; appearance of in
*Opyty Hudozhestvennoi
Obrabotki Narodnykh' Piesen',
Tom 1* [Experiments in artistic
arrangements of folk songs,
Volume 1], 6–8; Arab Middle
Eastern/diasporic dissemination

and performance of, 25–26, 27;
as manifestation of locality and
transnational cosmopolitanism,
48–49; Balkan transnational
ethnopop manifestations of,
39–43; Bosnian Muslim variations, 44–45; Bulgarian variations, 33–35, 45–46;
ethnonationalist sentiments regarding, 44–47; ethnopop variants of in urban Balkans, 26–
36; Greek text/tune variants,
10–21; Indonesian variations,
48; origins as Scottish soldiers'
march, 46–47; performance of
by university Middle/Near East
music ensembles, 26; performance of in Jewish diaspora,
22–25; Turkish/Ottoman provenance and development of,
4–10, 28; Turkish resurgence
of, 48; use of in late Ottoman
operetta, 10–11. *See also Ruse
kose, curo, imaš* [What fair hair
you have, girl]

Valdes, Valentin, 153, 165, 166,
247; *Zhega* [Heat], 153–55
Vali, Gus and his Casbah Ensemble,
38
van de Port, Matjis, 302, 341
Vaseva, Sashka, *Levovete v marki*
[*Leva* into marks], 151–52, 153,
159–60
Vatrogasci, *Raspiči-opiči*, 39–40
Verdery, Katherine, 132, 166
Via Militaris, 225, 260
Vijelie, Vali, 124, 125, 127, 129
Vreteno [Spindle] (Svetlana Raž-
natović-Ceca), 73
Vuco, Siniša, 88
Vuika, Alka, 88

Wachtel, Andrew, xvii, xviii
Wallachia, 100, 101; artistic activity
in, 195, 196, 208, 215

About the Editor and Contributors

Margaret Beissinger teaches and is a research scholar in the Department of Slavic Languages and Literatures at Princeton University. She has published widely on Balkan oral traditions and is presently completing a book on culture and performance among Romani musicians in southern Romania.

Donna A. Buchanan is director of the Russian, East European, and Eurasian Center, associate professor of music, and director of the music ensemble "Balkanalia" at the University of Illinois, Urbana-Champaign, where she teaches ethnomusicology and Balkan studies. She is the author of *Performing Democracy: Bulgarian Music and Musicians in Transition* (University of Chicago Press, 2006).

Kevin Dawe is senior lecturer in the School of Music at the University of Leeds, UK. His published work includes the edited volume *Island Musics* (Berg, 2004) and two co-edited collections: *Guitar Cultures* (Berg, 2001) and *The Mediterranean in Music* (2005). He is currently completing two single-authored books, one focusing on the music and musicians of Crete (Scarecrow Press) and the other comprising a broad ranging study of the guitar. Dawe has carried out fieldwork in Greece, Spain, and Papua New Guinea.

Gabriela Ilnitchi is assistant professor of musicology at the University of Minnesota. Her research interests concern medieval music theory, musical and scientific thought in the early- and pre-modern eras, iconography, and travel accounts of Byzantine, Balkan, and Ottoman musical traditions. She has recently published *The Play of Meanings: Aribo's De musica and the Hermeneutics of Musical Thought* (Scarecrow Press, 2005). Current projects include post-Byzantine music iconography in Balkan churches, and the convergence of late scholastic natural philosophy, mathematics, theories of sound, and musical cosmologies in the works of Nicole Oresme.

Vesa Kurkela is professor of popular music in the Department of Folk Music at the Sibelius Academy in Helsinki, Finland. He is the co-author of a history of Finnish popular music (2003) and has also written several books and articles on folk and popular music in Finland and other European countries. He is currently writing a history of music publishing in Finland.

Svanibor Pettan is associate professor and chair of ethnomusicology at the University of Ljubljana, Slovenia. The editor of *Music, Politics, and War: Views from Croatia*, and the author of the film and CD-ROM *Rom Musicians in Kosovo: Interaction and Creativity* (2002), he is currently working on a DVD project about Kosovo Roma for the Society for Ethnomusicology.

Ljerka Vidić Rasmussen holds a Ph.D. in Ethnomusicology from Wesleyan University and is the author of *Newly-Composed Folk Music of Yugoslavia* (Routledge, 2002). Currently an adjunct professor at Tennessee State University, she has also taught at Middle Tennessee State University and Vanderbilt University, and has worked as the staff musicologist for the Naxos label and its digital music library service.

Carol Silverman, associate professor of anthropology at the University of Oregon, has been involved with Balkan Romani culture, especially that of Bulgaria and Macedonia, for over twenty-five years as a researcher, teacher, activist, and performer. Among her many publications is the forthcoming monograph *Performing Diaspora: Cultural Politics of Balkan Romani Music* (Oxford University Press).

Martin Stokes is associate professor of music at the University of Chicago, where he also serves as director of the Center for Middle Eastern Studies. The author of *The Arabesk Debate: Music and Musicians in Modern Turkey* (Clarendon Press Oxford, 1992) and the editor of *Ethnicity, Identity and Music: The Musical Construction of Place* (Oxford: Berg Publishers, 1994), he is currently completing a second book, provisionally entitled *The Republic of Love: Transformations of Intimacy in Popular Culture in Turkey,* and starting work, with Joel Gordon, on a biography of Abd-Halim Hafiz.

Jane C. Sugarman is associate professor of music at Stony Brook University. She is the author of *Engendering Song: Singing and Subjectivity at Prespa Albanian Weddings* (University of Chicago Press, 1999) and numerous articles relating southeast European music and dance to issues of identity. She is currently writing a book on the transnational Albanian popular music industry.